TSR2

Britain's Lost Bomber

Other titles in the Crowood Aviation Series

TSR2

Britain's Lost Bomber

Damien Burke

The Crowood Press

First published in 2010 by
The Crowood Press Ltd
Ramsbury, Marlborough
Wiltshire SN8 2HR

www.crowood.com

British Library Cataloguing-in-Publication Data
A catalogue record for this book is available from
the British Library.

ISBN 978 1 84797 211 8

Acknowledgements

I have been repeatedly impressed by the time and effort that so many people have spared to assist with my research for this book. My grateful thanks are therefore extended to: BAE Systems' Warton Heritage Group for unprecedented access to its TSR2 archives, including much material that was previously classified, in particular to Dave Ward, Tony Wilson, the late Keith Elmslie, Keith Spong, Peter Hardman, Dave Hutton and the late Bob Fairclough; the Brooklands Museum at Weybridge for similar access to its own TSR2 and Hawker archives, in particular to John Fulton, Julian Temple, Jack Fuller, Albert Kitchener, Chris Farara, Geoff Burchett and Michael Goodall; Barry Guess and Trevor Friend at BAE Systems Farnborough; Guy Revell and Peter Devitt at the Department of Research and Information Services at the RAF Museum, Hendon; the RAF Museum, Cosford for access to XR220, particularly Clare Carr and Keith Woodcock; the Imperial War Museum at Duxford for access to XR222; Barry and Dianne James at the Midland Air Museum; the staff of the National Archives at Kew; and the staff of the Coventry City Council History Centre. Thanks also to Ivan Yates, the late Wing Commander Jimmy Dell OBE, Don Knight, Air Commodore Dennis Reader, Glenn Surtees, Matin Hale, Alan Mansell at Solent Sky and, finally, to Ronnie Olsthoorn for his stunning, and chilling, cover artwork. Any errors are mine; sadly the uneven nature of much surviving TSR2 documentation does not lend itself to firm statements in some areas, but with the valuable assistance of several people who worked on the designing, building and testing of TSR2 I hope I have at least addressed many of the misunderstandings and errors that can be found in other publications on the subject, without introducing too many of my own. Any errors found after publication will be addressed on a dedicated website to be found at www.tsr2.info.

DAMIEN BURKE
March 2010

Websites of organizations that assisted with research for this book:

BAE Systems Heritage – www.baesystems.com/heritage
Brooklands Museum – www.brooklandsmuseum.com
Coventry History Centre – www.theherbert.org/index.php/home/history-centre
Imperial War Museum Duxford – www.duxford.iwm.org.uk
Midland Air Museum – www.midlandairmuseum.co.uk
National Archives – www.nationalarchives.gov.uk
RAF Museum Department of Research and Information Services –
www.rafmuseum.org.uk/research
RAF Museum Cosford – www.rafmuseum.org.uk/cosford

Typefaces used: Goudy (*text*),
Cheltenham (*headings*).

Typeset and designed by
Shane O'Dwyer
Swindon, Wiltshire

Printed and bound in Singapore
by Craft Print International Ltd

Contents

Abbreviations

A&AEE	Aeroplane and Armament Experimental Establishment
AAPP	airborne auxiliary powerplant
AFCS	automatic flight-control system
AFVG	Anglo-French Variable-Geometry (project)
AGC	automatic gain control
AGM	air-to-ground missile
AHB	Air Historical Branch
AI	airborne interception (radar)
APU	auxiliary power unit
ASM	air-to-surface missile
ASP	aircraft servicing platform
ASR	Air Staff Requirement
AST	Air Staff Target
ATE	automatic test equipment
AUW	all-up weight
BAC	British Aircraft Corporation
BEA	British European Airways
BLC	boundary layer control
BSEL	Bristol Siddeley Engines Ltd
CA	Controller Aircraft
CAL	Cornell Aeronautical Laboratories
CAP	combat air patrol
CEP	circular error probable
c.g.	centre of gravity
CCS	central computing system
CPU	central processing unit
CRT	cathode ray tube
CSD	constant-speed drive
CSDS	constant-speed drive starter
CSDE	Central Servicing Development Establishment
CSEU	Confederation of Shipbuilding and Engineering Unions
CWAS	Conventional Weapons Aiming System
CWP	central warning panel
DDOR	Deputy Director of Operational Requirements
DOR	Directorate of Operational Requirements
DRPC	Defence Research Policy Committee
ECM	electronic countermeasures
ECU	engine-change unit
EIT	Electronic Introduction Team
EPR	engine pressure ratio
ETPS	Empire Test Pilots' School
FLR	forward-looking radar
FTB	flying test bed
GOR	General Operational Requirement
GPI	Ground Position Indicator
GTS	Ground Training School
HDU	hose-and-drogue unit
HE	high explosive
HOTAS	hands on throttle and stick
HP	high-pressure
HUD	head-up display
IFF	identification friend or foe
ILS	instrument landing system
INS	inertial navigation system
IR	infra-red
IRD	infra-red decoy
IRBM	intermediate-range ballistic missile
LABS	Low Altitude Bombing System
LCNs	(airfield) load classification numbers
lox	liquid oxygen
LP	low-pressure
MoA	Ministry of Aviation
MoD	Ministry of Defence
MoS	Ministry of Supply
MTI	moving-target indication
MTBF	mean time between failures
NATO	North Atlantic Treaty Organization
NGTE	National Gas Turbine Establishment
OCU	Operational Conversion Unit
ODS	Operational Development Squadron
OR	Operational Requirement(s)
PEP	Project Execution Plan
PERT	Programme Evaluation and Review Technique
PRF	pulse-repetition frequency
psi	pounds per square inch
PSP	pierced steel planking
QRA	Quick Reaction Alert
RAAF	Royal Australian Air Force
RAE	Royal Aircraft Establishment
RAF	Royal Air Force
RAM	radar-absorbing material
R&D	research and development
RBW	rapid-blooming *Window*
RCAF	Royal Canadian Air Force
RCS	radar cross-section
RN	Royal Navy
RPDU	rapid processing and development unit
RPU	rapid processing unit
RRE	Royal Radar Establishment
RWR	radar warning receiver
SAM	surface-to-air missile
SFC	specific fuel consumption
SHAPE	Supreme Headquarters Allied Powers Europe
SLR	sideways-looking radar
SRV	servicing and readiness vehicle
STOL	short take-off and landing
TFR	terrain-following radar
TISC	Tactical Intelligence Steering Committee
TRRV	turn-round and readiness vehicle
TSE	Tactical Strike Establishment
TSR	Tactical Strike Reconnaissance
USAF	United States Air Force
VTOL	vertical take-off and landing

Introduction

In the German city of Hamburg on the night of 27/28 July 1943 over 40,000 people were killed, mostly incinerated or suffocated in their shelters, by a bombing raid that produced a 'firestorm', a conflagration of immense scale, consisting of numerous smaller fires combining to create a hurricane of high winds feeding into the fire. This raid had consisted of 787 aircraft from Royal Air Force (RAF) Bomber Command; forty-one turned back with various problems, and losses en route reduced them further so that a total of 731 bomb loads fell on the city, around 600 of them falling within the space of half an hour over a 2-square-mile (5.2sq km) area on an unusually dry and warm night. In total, 1,127 tons of high explosive and 1,199 tons of incendiaries fell on the city. Bomber Command lost twenty-one aircraft; four over the target itself and the remainder at various points on the journey to and from Hamburg, including four crashed or written off on return to their bases. These losses, over 100 young men dead or missing, were considered 'light'. The raid was one of four of similar scale conducted over the course of a week, but, of the four, only this single raid produced such an immense level of death and destruction.

Around two years later, at 8.15am on the morning of 6 August 1945, a single bomb released from an American Boeing B-29 bomber took slightly less than a minute to fall 30,000ft (9,000m) before detonating around 2,000ft (600m) above central Hiroshima, an industrial city in southern Japan. In the blink of an eye a fireball expanded to a diameter of 1,200ft (370m). Everything flammable within a mile (1.5km) of the centre of the explosion (the hypocentre) burst into flame. Nearest the hypocentre, humans were reduced to shadows burnt into stone and concrete. The blast pulverized buildings, vehicles, people and anything else up to 11,000ft (3,350m) away. Only the strongest buildings, mostly constructed of reinforced concrete to resist earthquakes, survived the initial blast. Fires spread rapidly, consuming shattered build-ings, fed by broken gas pipes and any num-ber of flame sources dislocated by the blast; toppled stoves, lanterns, and so on. The fires merged into a firestorm, and within hours of the release of this single weapon 66,000 people were dead. Nearly 5 square miles (13sq km) of the city and 70 per cent of its buildings had been totally destroyed. The world had entered the age of atomic war-fare. That single bomb was a primitive fis-sion weapon, producing an explosive yield equivalent to somewhere between 13,000 and 15,000 tons (13,200 and 15,250 tonnes) of high explosive. Three days later a second atomic bomb was dropped on Nagasaki, and the Japanese surrendered within a week in the face of threats of further atomic bombings.

Over the next few years Great Britain struggled to recover not only from the direct destruction visited upon the nation by the Luftwaffe during World War Two, but also from the crippling economic costs incurred by fighting the war. Government spending on the armed forces was drastical-ly cut back, the RAF in particular suffering from a lack of investment in new aircraft. There was one notable exception in 1945, when the English Electric company was awarded a contract to design and develop a jet bomber to replace the de Havilland Mosquito. During the war English Electric had impressed the government with its production of Handley Page Hampden and Halifax bombers, and had expanded its aviation activities by buying up the Napier & Son aero-engine company and by pro-ducing Vampire jet fighters for de Havil-land. It was therefore not quite so surprising, perhaps, that English Electric, rather than one of the more established aircraft manu-facturers, was given the job of producing the RAF's first jet bomber, the Canberra.

The RAF's strategic bomber force suf-fered badly, soldiering on with obsolete Avro Lancasters, and Lincolns that were little better. Only in 1947 did work begin on jet-powered replacements, a requirement that would result in the V-bomber trio of Vickers Valiant, Handley Page Victor and Avro Vulcan. Meanwhile, the Communist threat became ever greater, and, by the time the Canberra had flown, the Iron Curtain was firmly in place. Just months after the Canberra's first flight, in August 1949, an atomic explosion bloomed over the Semi-palatinsk test site in what is now northern Kazakhstan. The Russians now had The Bomb too.

Instead of being able to concentrate on recovery, the British nation was forced to prepare for a new war, one that would be fought not with bullets and high explosive but with atomic fire. The run-down of the country's anti-aircraft gun sites that had begun with the end of World War Two was halted, and hundreds of new gun sites were built to protect the major cities and industrial areas. Across the country spread a sophisticated network of radars, anti-aircraft guns and hardened bunkers. Stores of the supplies that would be needed after an atomic attack – food, clothing, and so on – were secreted in various locations. Large numbers of fire fighting vehicles were dis-persed in depots located at safe distances from expected targets. The government put in place plans for running a country torn apart by an atomic attack, devolving responsibility to individual regions in the event of central government being obliter-ated.

The 1950s began with the shock of the Korean War, which kick-started the British aviation industry back into wartime produc-tion, albeit at a much slower rate than dur-ing World War Two. More complex air-craft and engines inevitably took longer to produce, and cost much more than their ancestors. An atomic war was a horrifying prospect but it was not unthinkable, and, more importantly, the government did not believe it was unwinnable. This all changed on 1 November 1952, when the USA det-onated its first full-scale hydrogen bomb. A basic fusion weapon, it was nonetheless around 450 times as powerful as the bomb used against Hiroshima, and when the Rus-sians began tests of similar weapons in 1955 it was horrifyingly clear that the nightmare of an atomic attack upon Great Britain was as nothing compared with an attack with the new 'H-bomb', and the existing defences were laughably inadequate.

A massive construction programme began that would end with nearly 2,000 underground bunkers scattered across Great Britain, most of them being fall-out plotting and monitoring bunkers manned by Royal Observer Corps personnel. They afforded little but basic fall-out protection for the volunteers staffing them; facilities within were primitive, but at the end of the day it was the national will demonstrated by having such a network that was the most important thing. Part of that national will

was also the demonstration that Great Britain had the means to support the North Atlantic Treaty Organization (NATO) in a European conflict. The RAF and Army were far too small to be a viable threat to the Soviets, and the whole of NATO would still be hopelessly outnumbered. NATO doctrine recognized that only tactical nuclear weapons could restore the balance. Thus Great Britain had been placed into a situation where it was operating mostly outmoded aircraft, fielding outmoded weapons, as part of an alliance facing a numerically superior enemy armed with the ability to turn much of Great Britain into a firestorm during just a few hours of unrestricted warfare.

For the RAF's part it was clear that the Canberra, although it was an excellent aircraft, was living on borrowed time. Soviet defences were improving all the time, and improvements in radar and missile technology would soon make the Canberra obsolete. The RAF desperately needed a modern bomber that could survive in the increasingly sophisticated defence environment of a European battlefield and pack a big enough nuclear punch to redress the numerical imbalance that NATO troops faced.

This was the world into which the TSR2 was to be born.

CHAPTER ONE

Beginnings

In September 1951, with the Canberra shortly due to reach RAF squadrons in quantity, the RAF's Directorate of Operational Requirements (DOR) began looking at the prospects for a new light bomber to replace the Canberra in due course. It has traditionally been the case that the RAF has always looked ahead for a replacement type as soon as possible after the existing type has begun to enter service (sometimes even before that milestone was reached). Air Commodore H.V. Satterly at DOR started the ball rolling with a Minute to his staff at the Directorate, asking them start thinking about policy for the Canberra replacement. In it he pointed out that the RAF's Aircraft Research Committee had already begun a study on the pros and cons of a low-altitude bomber, though current policy was that bombers had to be able to evade *or* fight their way through defences, and the low-altitude bomber concept was designed to evade only.

A paper entitled 'An Appreciation on the Requirement for a Future Light Bomber' was produced in July 1952. It laid out the need for a light bomber with a primary role of the delivery of atomic weapons; with the highest performance possible, particularly at low altitude; and the capability to be adapted to secondary roles without compromising its primary role. This was the first real hint of what was to become the TSR2. The paper specifically referred to replacing the Canberra, 'now in Service and already to some extent technically obsolete', with the new aircraft expected to be in service

by 1958 and having a useful front-line life of about four years, until 1962. The RAF mindset at the time was still stuck in the 1940s, when an aircraft type's useful life was sometimes measured in months rather than years; certainly never in decades.

Some of the more interesting aspects of the paper included an appreciation that,

when it came to carrying small atomic bombs, the 'best bomber for any task is broadly the smallest and cheapest that is capable of the required range and accuracy', and that surface-to-surface guided weapons, or 'expendable bombers', could well fulfil the primary role, though accuracy and the attack of fleeting targets would be a

The English Electric Canberra. The RAF expected the type to be obsolete by 1965 and completely worn out by 1970. This is B.2 WK163, which set a world altitude record in August 1957 with the aid of a Napier Double Scorpion rocket engine. This aircraft had a varied trials career, including linescan development work, before being finally retired, still not worn out, in the 1990s. It began a civilian career as G-BVWC in 1994 with Classic Aviation Projects, and is seen here being displayed at Duxford in 2008 just before being grounded by lack of suitable replacement Avon 109 engines. Damien Burke

challenge. Attacking moving targets and targets of opportunity would not be possible for an unmanned system of any kind, and even the best blind bombing system would also be unsuitable for this kind of task, which would demand visual bombing. Visual bombing accuracy depended greatly on going in at low altitude, and as high-altitude operation was also no longer a means of protection from fighter attack, it was clear which way the wind was blowing. As for weapons carriage, guided bombs would demand control surfaces and economy would demand a small fuselage, so external carriage rather than an internal bomb bay was expected to be the result.

By March 1953 a draft Operational Requirement (OR) had begun to be worked on, based on the Future Light Bomber paper, which blithely (and, as it transpired, inaccurately) declared that the Canberra 'is rapidly becoming outdated and has no potentialities for further important development'. Clearly the writer of that requirement did not expect the Canberra to be in RAF service more than fifty years later (albeit purely in the reconnaissance role). The draft requirement called for a new aircraft capable of striking up to 500nm (575 miles; 925km) behind the enemy front line, in all weathers, day or night, with priority given to low-level performance, and relying on speed, routeing and manoeuvrability to protect it from enemy defences, as no defensive armament was to be carried (by this point, evade or fight had become simply evade). A cruising speed of 600kt/690mph/Mach 0.9 was needed, with supersonic bursts of Mach 1.4, and runways of 2,000yd (1,850m) length should be adequate, including pierced steel planking (PSP) or similar improvized surfaces. For 1953 this was all pretty advanced stuff, but the RAF's dated mindset still showed in other aspects of the draft requirement. These included references to the navigator being provided with a crash station should his normal position be unsuitable; the provision of Gee Mark 3 in the radio fit for the marshalling of bomber streams; and armour to protect against cannon attack from below (as per the *Schräge Musik* upward firing nightfighter cannon used by the Luftwaffe in World War Two). Weapons were to include four 30mm cannon and various items fit for particular roles, e.g. *Blue Jay* (Firestreak) missiles for the intruder role, rockets and bombs for interdiction or Pentane torpedoes for anti-shipping strike. Production was to begin in 1958, and the aircraft needing to

be in squadron service by 1959 at the latest, when the Canberra was expected to be on its last legs.

Coincidentally, in January 1953, as part of development work for an improved Gloster Javelin fighter (the 'Developed Javelin') which was being designed to satisfy Specification F.153D, Glosters had submitted a proposal to use a variant of this new 'thin-wing' Javelin as a light strike aircraft, and this attracted a great deal of Air Staff interest. By July 1955 OR.328 had been drafted around Gloster's bomber-Javelin proposals, the broad intention of which was to provide a bomber capable of delivering a tactical nuclear weapon (to OR.1127, the requirement that would result in the atomic bomb later known as *Red Beard*) in the face of modern air defences, at long range (the target was to be up to 1,000nm (1,150 miles, 1850km) away from base, twice as far as the early drafts of the Canberra replacement requirement), in adverse weather by day or by night. Deletion of fighter equipment such as the huge radar and wing guns would enable the carriage of an extra 2,600gal (11,820L) of fuel (for a total of 4,000gal (18,185L) and the fitting of Bristol Siddeley Olympus 6 engines. A single tactical nuclear bomb would be carried externally, slung under one of the wings, with a drop tank balancing it on the other side and further drop tanks under the fuselage. The in-service date was still required to be 1959.

Simultaneously, work was under way to see what, if anything, could be done to upgrade the Canberra, concentrating on the addition of a blind-bombing system so that the type would have much improved tactical capability at night and in bad weather. However, as the RAF fully expected the type to be out of service in less than a decade, it looked like any serious effort to upgrade it would be wasted, as any sufficiently advanced blind-bombing system would take so long to develop that the aircraft would be nearing retirement by the time it was available. Development of the Bomber/Interdictor versions of the Canberra was rushed through as a stopgap measure, the definitive B(I).8 version entering service in RAF Germany with American 'Project E' atomic weapons during 1957.

Unfortunately for Gloster it also soon became clear that the company could not get its thin-wing Javelin bomber into service until 1961. Moreover, a variety of problems, such as dealing with low-level flying and its effect on fatigue life, crew

comfort and equipment reliability, had not been fully addressed in Gloster's proposal. The firm considered that an aircraft with an all-up-weight of 70,000lb (31,750kg) and carrying 4,000gal (18,185L) of fuel would only be able to manage a radius of action of 1,000nm (1,150 miles, 1850km) if most of the flight was to be at high level, and any improvement would entail a complete redesign. As OR.328 required a combat radius of at least 1,000 miles, mostly flown at low level, the bomber version of the thin-wing Javelin did not get far. The Defence Research Policy Committee recommended cancellation of the requirement in late 1955, and when the Chiefs of the Air Staff met in March 1956 they accepted the recommendation. On 11 April 1956 OR.328 was formally cancelled.

The procurement process

The usual process of procuring a military aircraft for the RAF began in the Air Ministry, where the Air Staff (RAF officers) would begin formulating a rough requirement. The result would be an Air Staff Target (AST), which gave a broad outline of what they were after and formed the basis for feasibility studies at industry level, usually submitted in the form of detailed brochures. Assuming these found that the target was a practical and viable proposition, the next step would be to formulate a more detailed Air Staff Requirement (ASR, also often referred to as an Operational Requirement or OR) and award a project study contract to a single firm. The aim of this study was to make an extremely thorough and detailed investigation of the scientific and technical problems involved, and produce a detailed development plan including estimates of cost, timescale and manpower requirements. Assuming this study was approved by all concerned in the Air Ministry (the Air Staff, Operational Requirements department and so on) and Ministry of Supply (MoS, the ministry responsible for the procurement of military aircraft, replaced by the Ministry of Aviation (MoA) from 1960), it would be recommended to the Secretary of State for Defence, who would then ask for Treasury approval to proceed.

The Treasury's job, of course, was to resist spending money, and this would prompt further investigation into the requirement and whether the new project was really needed, including political input. Assuming Treasury authority was finally granted, the next step would be the awarding of a Development Contract to the firm, covering work on a number of prototypes or a development batch of aircraft. While the company was working on these it would be negotiating a Production Contract, approval for this also having to go through the Treasury and thus requiring further investigation and justification from the Air Ministry. At any point in the process continued Treasury co-operation could never be taken for granted, and political decisions could overrule any requirements at any point. Thus it was not uncommon for projects to get as far as the Development Contract stage, with prototypes under construction, and then be cancelled without further ado, sometimes even before the prototype had flown.

All of this took time, and the replacement of the Canberra was becoming an ever more urgent requirement. Within just a handful of years the Canberra would be obsolete and only the V-bomber force would be able to deliver, in *ad hoc* fashion, tactical nuclear weapons. Both the Air Staff and the MoS needed to find some way of shortening the process.

General Operational Requirement No. 339

The DOR now began work on a report defining its future tactical bombardment requirements, and whether they could be fulfilled by an all-new aircraft, a guided weapon or an off-the-shelf aircraft. The Assistant Chief of the Air Staff within the Operational Requirements department was H.V. Satterly (by then promoted Air Vice-Marshal), who had already looked at a new design from Blackburn Aircraft, the NA.39/B.103 low-level strike aircraft being designed to satisfy a naval requirement. Satterly and the Air Staff were unimpressed with the NA.39, considering it 'not much of advance on the Canberra' with high-altitude performance 'handicapped by either lack of span or too early drag rise'. Blackburn had suggested an improved version with redesigned wings and tail, but would not be able to get it into the air until after 1960, again too late. Thoughts turned towards acquiring a suitable aircraft from the USA, preferably as a 'free gift'. The Convair B-58 Hustler was just about to make its first flight and was considered by Satterly to be the only

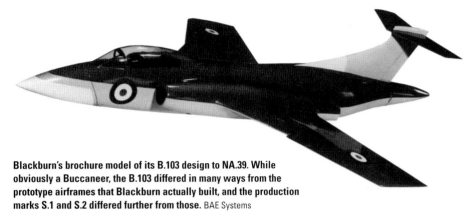

Blackburn's brochure model of its B.103 design to NA.39. While obviously a Buccaneer, the B.103 differed in many ways from the prototype airframes that Blackburn actually built, and the production marks S.1 and S.2 differed further from those. BAE Systems

viable contender, and some quiet efforts were made to find out what sort of performance it was likely to have. However, the B-58's flight-testing turned into a protracted affair, and it had not been designed for conventional strike, nor low-level operation. It was also a big and expensive aircraft, and the RAF soon lost interest. The B-58's impressive high-altitude speed and range was drastically reduced when it was later operated at low level, validating the RAF's loss of interest at the time.

In October 1956 English Electric began discussions of its own with Mr Handel Davies at the MoS about their ideas for a Canberra successor. The talks centred on an aircraft capable of up to Mach 1.3 with a radius of action of more than 350nm (400 miles; 64km) at sea level, carrying conventional or atomic weapons, or reconnaissance equipment (cameras or electronic sensors). Rolls-Royce Conway engines, then in development, were suggested as a powerplant. The target in-service date of the first version would be 1964, a much more realistic prediction than any of the RAF's ideas up to this point, and various versions covering different roles were envisaged. English Electric's initial sketches were of an aircraft with straight, shoulder-mounted wings, podded engines slung under each wing and a high tailplane, though it was also asked to consider a development of its P.1B to do the job.

Within the Air Ministry's Operational Requirements department the discussions prompted the generation of a new 'General' OR, GOR.339, a file on this being first recorded on 28 November 1956, covering the need for a tactical strike and reconnaissance aircraft. A GOR was more of an American concept than the traditional Air Staff Target, but was similarly intended to be the basis upon which various firms

would tender designs, and would be the solution to short-cutting the more usual lengthy procurement process. The most interesting aspects of the firms' submissions would be used to create a more detailed OR to then proceed with. Another bonus would be that, if any of the requirements in the GOR were felt by all the firms to be technically too difficult or expensive, those requirements could be amended or dropped to make sure the project as a whole was feasible.

Feelers were also put out to the various tactical air forces and commands within the RAF, and also to the Army, to gain a better idea of just what type of aircraft was going to be needed. English Electric had another meeting in January 1957 with Gp Capt Wheeler of the Air Staff (Deputy Director of Operational Requirements; DDOR) and Handel Davies, which further firmed up the requirement to cover a two-seat strike aircraft, carrying a single 'Target Marker Bomb'. This was the hilarious euphemism then in use for the atomic weapon to OR.1127 that came to be known as *Red Beard*. (Admittedly, any target hit with such a weapon would certainly be marked in fine style.) A conventional bomb load was also called for, of four or preferably six 1,000lb high-explosive (HE) bombs. Combat radius was to be 600nm (690 miles; 110km) at low level with a speed of Mach 0.9 (with a Mach 1.3 burst) or 1,000nm (1,150 miles; 1,850km) combat radius at higher altitudes and Mach 1.5. Short take-off, or even vertical, would be needed, to operate from strips just 1,000yd (900m) long (for the shorter sortie), and the first mention was made of possibly catering to Royal Navy (RN) needs at the same time.

English Electric had a further meeting with OR and the MoS on 30 January, after a conference on P.1 development. The

English Electric P.1B XA847 in flight near Warton. Compared with the earlier P.1, the P.1B had gained the familiar circular intake with radar bullet centrebody, and is seen here flying 'clean' before the addition of the belly fuel tank. via Warton Heritage Group

importance of the low-level requirement was restated, and English Electric realized that a developed P.1B (the P.18 that it had been working on) would not be up to the job in terms of combat radius or short take-off and landing (STOL) performance. Work on it was discontinued so that the company could concentrate on a far more elaborate design, Project 17. English Electric also pointed out that vertical take-off and landing (VTOL) and any formal preparation of a requirement followed by a prolonged design competition would both rule out any possibility of getting a new aircraft into service by 1964.

By February 1957 the requirement was solidifying into a primarily low-altitude-penetration concept, though Bomber Command wanted to retain high-altitude capability. The Royal Aircraft Establishment (RAE) had been brought in to rough-out a baseline design that could be used to evaluate any submissions from industry. A number of studies had also been carried out of aircraft of interest, such as the Saunders-Roe F.177D (rocket fighter) and Fairey ER103 (the Fairey Delta 3 fighter), both submissions to OR.329 (an all-weather interceptor requirement), to see if they had any possibility of being used in the ground-

attack role, and also of a Short Brothers design for a VTOL low-level strike aircraft.

English Electric also completed project report P/103, entitled 'Possibilities for a multi-purpose Canberra Replacement – Aircraft Project P.17'. This summarized the impressive success of the Canberra, touched briefly on the fact that, despite its many versions, the interceptor version had never been fully developed, addressed the question of whether manned aircraft were still required in the ballistic-missile era and answered that with a firm 'yes'. Missiles were inflexible, and just one part of a deterrent strategy. Being able to reconnoitre and strike accurately at enemy headquarters, missile bases, aerodromes, etc., was all part of the deterrent, and there seemed still to be a requirement for a manned aircraft 'in the tradition of the Canberra'. Keeping development costs reasonable by using Canberra and P.1 experience, and producing an aircraft of maximum flexibility would be the key, ensuring foreign sales and a reduction in the cost to the RAF. The P.17 was then described. At this point the P.17 had obvious P.1/Lightning inheritance, with a similar tailplane and fin and a delta mainplane that was effectively the Lightning mainplane with the area

between the trailing edge of the wingtip and the fuselage filled in. The fuselage, however, bore no such similarities, being much longer, with side-by-side engines and quarter-cone intakes hidden under the wings. Unsurprisingly, given the aircraft's P.1 ancestor, English Electric mentioned the possibilities that it would have as a fighter with long endurance (30min at Mach 1.6 instead of 5min for the P.1). In what would become a common theme, the company also pointed out that keeping a multi-role strike aircraft affordable would require the use of much off-the-shelf equipment, rather than specifying masses of exotic new kit, such as terrain clearance radar. The various strike, interdiction and reconnaissance missions could be carried out by differing equipment packs fitted in a large bomb bay; cameras, cannon, etc.

Interim submissions

In March 1957 the first draft of the GOR was also passed to de Havilland, Vickers, the Hawker-Siddeley Group and Blackburn, though Handel-Davies at the MoS was already concerned that the mix of low-level and high-altitude use, plus huge combat radius, was going to lead to a very large aircraft. Each firm duly submitted proposals to upgrade some of its existing aircraft to provide interim types to satisfy at least some aspects of the GOR. De Havilland offered a developed DH110 (Sea Vixen) and Vickers offered a developed N.113 (Scimitar). Hawker followed up with a proposal of its own based not upon an existing type, but upon one then in early development, the P.1121. The Admiralty had also raised the question of the RN's upcoming new strike aircraft. When this submission arrived in April 1957 it turned out to be, to the RAF's displeasure, Blackburn's B.103 again, though this time Blackburn submitted a brochure containing not only the standard B.103 but also a slightly developed variation of it. English Electric's P.18 was also briefly looked at, but not seriously considered. It is worth describing these four early submissions (plus English Electric's P.18), even if they were only regarded as interim solutions to GOR.339, as they exposed attitudes that would have long-term consequences.

Blackburn and General Aircraft B.103 / B.103A

Blackburn, for the second time in two years, submitted its polished and detailed B.103 brochure, putting forward the standard B.103 as before plus the B.103A, a developed version. The B.103 was destined to satisfy Naval Air Staff Target No. 39, abbreviated as NA.39, which was also the designation the aircraft was widely known by. The NA.39 was a carrier-borne naval strike aircraft primarily designed to deliver a nuclear weapon against a Soviet warship at sea or in inshore waters, or perhaps against a well-defined shore target. It had to be tough and it had to be capable of penetrating the formidable defences of a Soviet warship group. It was no wonder Blackburn thought it a good fit for the RAF's requirement for a tactical bomber.

For the standard B.103 the normal take-off weight would be 40,000lb (18,000kg), though an overload condition with two externally carried 300gal (1,365L) fuel tanks, full internal fuel and a Target Marker

Leading Particulars: Blackburn B.103	
Length	61.5ft (18.75m)
	(51ft (15.5m) folded)
Height	16ft (4.87m)
	(17ft (5.18m) with wings folded)
Wing span	42.5ft (12.95m)
	(20ft (6.09m) folded)
Wing area	500sq ft (46.45sq m)
Wing aspect ratio	3.58
Tailplane span	14.2ft (4.33m)
Tailplane area	75sq ft (6.97sq m)
Tailplane aspect ratio	2.7
Engines	2 × 7,000lb (32,000kg) s.t. Gyron Junior PS43
Max speed	640kt (740mph; 1,185km/h) at sea level, Mach 0.98 at 30,000ft (9,000m)
Empty weight	22,290lb (10,115kg)
Max AUW	46,000lb (20,865kg)

Bomb would bring it up to 45,000lb (20,000kg). The NA.39 had originally been intended to carry a pair of underwing missiles fitted with the *Red Beard* warhead, missiles named *Green Cheese*. Never let it be

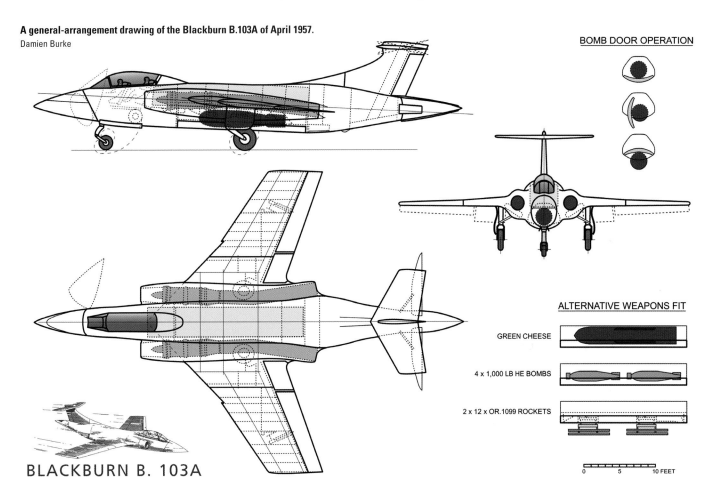

A general-arrangement drawing of the Blackburn B.103A of April 1957.
Damien Burke

BOMB DOOR OPERATION

ALTERNATIVE WEAPONS FIT

GREEN CHEESE

4 x 1,000 LB HE BOMBS

2 x 12 x OR.1099 ROCKETS

BLACKBURN B. 103A

0   5   10 FEET

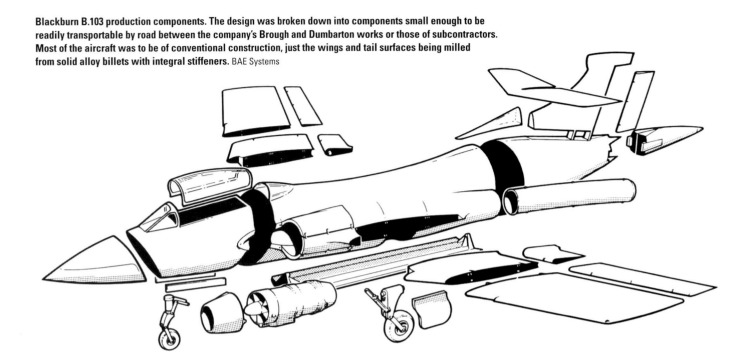

Blackburn B.103 production components. The design was broken down into components small enough to be readily transportable by road between the company's Brough and Dumbarton works or those of subcontractors. Most of the aircraft was to be of conventional construction, just the wings and tail surfaces being milled from solid alloy billets with integral stiffeners. BAE Systems

said that nuclear war is an entirely humourless business!

With a full load of fuel and the means to mark a target to bits, the NA.39's combat radius would be 650 miles (1,050km) (or 725 miles (1,170km) if 400gal (1,820L) external tanks were fitted). The aircraft was basically subsonic, able to cruise at Mach 0.85 with bursts at Mach 0.94, and to just nudge past Mach 1.05 in a dive. Take-off performance on a normal runway rather than an aircraft carrier would be in the order of 1,650yd (1,500m) under standard atmospheric conditions, boundary layer control by blowing forming an essential part of the aircraft's take-off and landing performance. It is noteworthy that this performance, apart from the inability to carry out a supersonic fighter evasion sprint or tool along at high altitude, waiting to be blown apart by a missile, pretty much met all of the needs of the first OR drawn up for a Canberra successor.

A crew of two operated the aircraft, which had a *Blue Parrot* search and ranging radar capable of picking up discrete targets such as ships at sea or large buildings on the shore and a *Yellow Lemon* Doppler navigation system. The accuracy of this system was not good enough on its own, and visual references and map reading would be an essential adjunct to the Doppler. Thus attacking a target at night or in poor weather would be a difficult, if not impossible, task. An internal bomb bay with a rotating door could

accommodate the Target Marker Bomb or four 1,000lb HE bombs, with additional capacity under the wings for further bombs or rockets (though the latter would result in considerable reductions in range). The aircraft would be capable of a reconnaissance role by carrying a battery of five F.95 cameras facing in various directions and having various focal lengths, or a single FX.100 night camera with 200 flash cartridges. Blackburn was predicting a Controller (Aircraft) (CA) release date of 1960 for the NA.39, and expected to be able to begin deliveries to the RAF in 1961. The cost per aircraft would be £0.5 million, and no additional research and development would be necessary as it was already well under way for the RN.

The B.103A was to be a de-navalized version more suited to RAF needs. Wing folding would be deleted, providing an unbroken wing with more room for internal fuel. An extension to the fuselage behind the cockpit would accommodate extra fuel, and the existing rear-fuselage tanks would be enlarged to balance things out (this extension was later incorporated into the standard NA.39). An improved Gyron Junior engine with 10 per cent more static thrust would be fitted. All of these changes gave the aircraft a 300gal (1,365L) increase in internal fuel, bringing take-off weight up to 48,000lb (20,000kg) and combat radius to 850 miles (1,370km), with the ability to carry all the weapons and recon-

naissance kit that the standard B.103 could do, with the addition of a pair of F.96 cameras and eight 8in photo flashes. The all-important take-off run would unfortunately be extended by 50yd (46m) to 1,700yd (1,550m). The additional research and development (R&D) necessary for this version was expected to cost in the order of £5.5 million (including five development batch aircraft at £0.75 million each) and require an additional two years of design effort (to be run in parallel with existing B.103 work, hopefully putting deliveries no later than 1961/1962).

Needless to say, a minor variation to an aircraft the RAF had not wanted two years previously did not go down too well, of which more shortly.

De Havilland Aircraft Company Developed Sea Vixen

De Havilland's existing Sea Vixen was entirely unsuitable, with a ridiculously inadequate 175-mile (280km) combat radius at low level and an expected short fatigue life in these conditions. It was, after all, designed to be a medium- to high-level interceptor, and had relatively low wing loading. However, de Havilland submitted a proposal for a development of the Sea Vixen, termed a 'Tactical Bomber and

Photographic Reconnaissance Aircraft', suitable for both carrier- and land-based operations. Compared with the Sea Vixen this version would have a 6.75ft (2.05m) nose extension (making room for an additional 850gal (3860L) of fuel), a repositioned nose fold (so it could still fit within existing carrier deck lifts), permanent wingtip tanks (with slightly shorter wings so that the overall span remained identical), additional fuel tanks within the wing near the tips, and increased capacity for the existing outboard wing tanks. Measures to improve take-off and landing performance consisted of extra droop on the wing leading edge inboard of the existing wing fence, flap blowing, a larger elevator, a Spectre rocket for take-off assistance and a braking parachute for landing. To deal with the low-level role the structure would be beefed up, using different materials and thicknesses where appropriate (and entailing a complete redesign of the centre fuselage), the navigator/observer would be given a larger window to aid visual navigation, and sprung supports would be introduced for crew seats and instruments. The existing Rolls-Royce RA24 Avon engines could be replaced by the RB133, then under development for the Canberra PR.9, but equally could be left alone. Take-off weight would be 60,000lb (27,000kg) (compared with 40,000lb (18,000kg) for the standard Sea Vixen), with a combat radius of the full 1,000 miles (1,600km) required by GOR.339 if a pair of 250gal (1,140L) drop tanks were carried. Like the B.103, the aircraft would be subsonic at low level, cruising at Mach 0.85 with dashes at Mach 0.95. Above 14,000ft (4,250m), however, it could manage Mach 1.2. The take-off distance would be 1,050yd (960m) with rocket assistance or 1,400yd (1,280m) without, increasing to 1,700yd (1,550m) if the existing RA24 engines were retained. De Havilland expected a fatigue life of up to 1,000 operational hours, more than that of Blackburn's B.103 or B.103A.

As with the B.103, the two-man crew would be retained, but navigation equipment was improved with Decca, a Ground Position Indicator (GPI, a basic moving map) and Doppler. Beyond Decca ground station range, accuracy would be as limited as that of the B.103. Limited fuselage space allowed only a shallow bomb bay, so a Target Marker Bomb would be only semi-recessed in the belly with around half of the weapon exposed to the airstream, introducing possible thermal issues at high

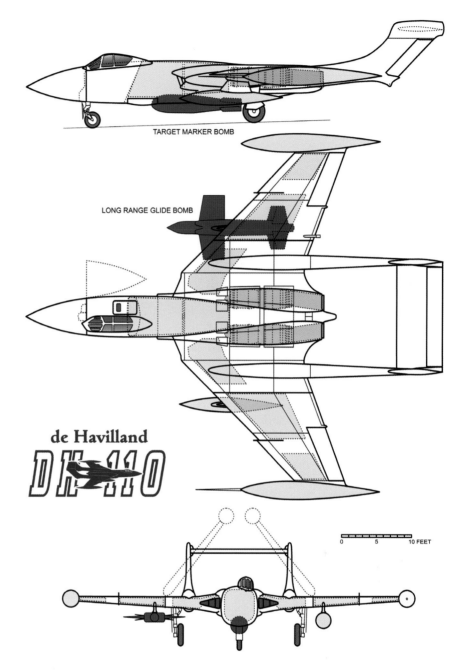

A general-arrangement drawing of the de Havilland DH110 Sea Vixen development of March 1957.
Damien Burke

speed and safety issues during take-off and landing (the Vickers-Supermarine Scimitar would be subject to a ban on carrier landing with a *Red Beard* under the wing because of similarly restricted ground clearance). The small bay could, however, fully accommodate a pair of 1,000lb HE bombs, and two more could be carried on the wing pylons (though with reduced full fuel load).

Leading Particulars: Developed Sea Vixen

Length	59.5ft (18.14m)
Height	11.5ft (3.5m)
Wing span	50ft (15.24m) (including tanks)
Wing area	611sq ft (56.76sq m)
Wing aspect ratio	4.1
Engines	2 × 13,880lb (6,300kg) RB.133
Max speed	Mach 1.2 @ 25,000ft (7,600m)
Empty weight	Not stated
Max AUW	62,080lb (28,180kg)

This photo of a Sea Vixen FAW.1 carrying a *Red Beard* 'shape' gives some idea of the challenges of carrying a bomb of this size on a relatively small strike aircraft. BAE Systems

Alternatives included up to ninety-six 2in rockets underwing or twenty-four OR.1099 rockets. In the reconnaissance role the aircraft was to be fitted with a permanent forward-facing F.95 camera in the nose (the airborne interception (AI) radar would not be fitted), with an optional fit of a pair of either F.95 oblique cameras, F.96 day cameras with 24in lenses or F.97 night cameras with 400 photo-flash cartridges.

Work on the existing Sea Vixen was well under way and aiming at CA release by the end of 1958. De Havilland had already started work on a mock-up of the developed version, and claimed it would be able to get it into service by 1960 at a cost of £0.5 million per aircraft, with R&D costs of around £5.5 million (including five development batch aircraft). This was a particularly attractive concept, as the RN could also operate the uprated version, though it would need to keep maximum weights down by launching aircraft with a restricted fuel load, flight-refuelling them once airborne. However de Havilland's estimates were so optimistic that they raised eyebrows even among a normally sceptical RAF, something no doubt not helped by the RAF knowing of the protracted development period the Sea Vixen had already suffered, albeit due in part to the RAF's own indecision when choosing between the Javelin and DH110 for their own interceptor needs.

English Electric P.18

English Electric's P.18 was a minimal modification of its existing P.1B (and internally was described as 'P.1 LABS version'), given extra fuel capacity (in tip tanks, roughly pencilled in on the only relevant drawing found to date) and carrying a single Target Marker Bomb semi-recessed in the ventral tank. Each tip tank held 100gal (450L) of fuel, extending the basic aircraft's pitiful combat radius. To try and eke out the aircraft's endurance, operation of the P.18 would be rather different from its fighter brethren, and take-off and climb would both be performed without the use of reheat and speed limited to Mach 0.9 with the tip tanks still attached. Once these were empty and jettisoned, speed could rise, but only to Mach 1.3. With the aircraft at an all-up weight (AUW) of 37,500lb (17,000kg) its take-off roll would be a whopping 2,000yd (18,290m). Assuming an entirely low-level and subsonic sortie at Mach 0.9, this would result in a combat radius of a mere 190nm (220 miles; 350km), so it was no wonder that English Electric wasted no further time on this idea. It was not seriously considered by the Air Staff either.

Vickers-Armstrongs Aircraft Developed Scimitar

The RAF must have felt under siege, with the third design submitted being a development of yet another naval type, the N.113 Scimitar. In terms of GOR.339 the standard Scimitar would have been pretty useless owing to a miserly 200nm (230-mile; 370km) combat radius when loaded up with full internal fuel, two 150gal (680L) and one 200gal (910L) wing drop tanks and a single Target Marker Bomb under the port wing.

Vickers, however, had been working on an improved version of the Scimitar for the RN even before the type entered service, and had put together a brochure entitled *N.113 Developments*, covering three major variations. The first was the Type 562, much like the existing Scimitar F.1 but with a new pointed nose radome containing an

Leading Particulars: Vickers Type 565	
Length	62.2ft (18.96m)
Height	15.75ft (4.8m)
Wing span	37.2ft (11.34m)
Wing area	485sq ft (45.06sq m)
Wing aspect ratio	2.84
Engines	2 × RA24 Avon
Max speed	Mach 0.98
Empty weight	Not stated
Max AUW	49,600lb (22,500kg)

**A general-arrangement drawing of the Vickers-Armstrongs
N.113 Scimitar development of March 1957.** Damien Burke

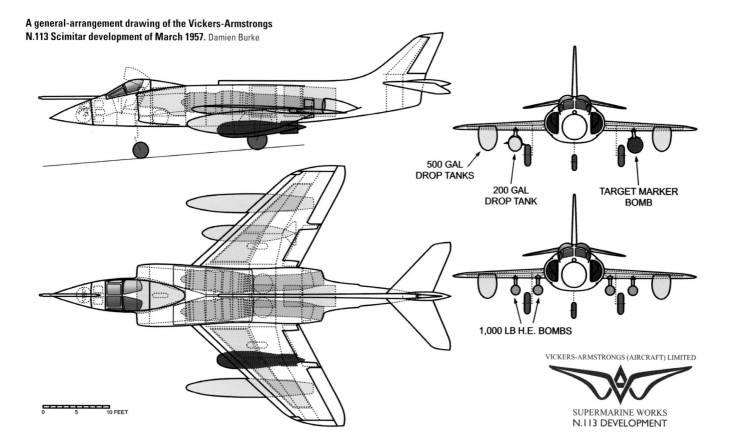

500 GAL
DROP TANKS

200 GAL
DROP TANK

TARGET MARKER
BOMB

1,000 LB H.E. BOMBS

VICKERS-ARMSTRONGS (AIRCRAFT) LIMITED

SUPERMARINE WORKS
N.113 DEVELOPMENT

0   5   10 FEET

AI.23 search radar and huge 500gal (2,270L) slipper tanks under the outer wings. The second was the Type 564, similar to the 562 in most ways, but with *Blue Parrot* radar and Gyron Junior engines instead of RA.24s. The third was the Type 567, a two-seat version of the 564 with side-by-side seating (to keep the length the same and stay within carrier deck lift limits), with optional extra weapons pylons under the wings near the fuselage (thus retaining four pylons for stores use when the slipper tanks were fitted).

While these had all been aimed at the RN, Vickers could see the possibilities in offering such an aircraft to the RAF, so in parallel it had produced another brochure, entitled *N.113 Development, Tactical Bomber for the Royal Air Force*. This described a subtly different development, the Type 565, another two-seat aircraft powered by RA.24 Avons and with the large 500gal (2,270L) slipper tanks and extra pylons. The Scimitar's four cannon would be deleted to make room for extra internal fuel. The canopy was initially sketched as being smoothly curved, unlike the 'double bubble' of the slightly later Type 567, but later drawings of the 565 incorporated the 567's canopy. For navigation,

target identification and attack there would be a moving-map addition to the existing Doppler, a search radar based on the AI.23 being used on the English Electric P.1 and, perhaps most radically, a partly automatic flight control system that could fly the aircraft through an atomic attack release manoeuvre (the Low Altitude Bombing System – LABS). Adding a navigator/observer greatly relieved the pilot's workload, and was considered essential by the RAF in any case. As with the B.103 and DH110, however, final attack was going to be primarily based on a visual search within the vicinity of the target.

Up to 2,000lb (900kg) of weight was saved compared with the 567 by deleting the naval equipment such as folding wings and arrester hook, which gave improved performance all round. Take-off weight would be 48,500lb (22,000kg), with a combat radius of up to 740nm (850 miles; 1,370km) (high-altitude sortie, descending only to attack). Combat radius for a low-level sortie would be between 430 and 560nm (495 miles/795km and 645 miles/1,040km), depending on speed (the higher figure being for a sortie with much of the cruise carried out at 300kt (345mph; 555km/h) with one engine shut down to

save on fuel). Cruising speed would be Mach 0.83, with dashes at Mach 0.93. The take-off distance would be within 1,500yd (1,370m) with rocket assistance, or 1,940yd (1,775m) without.

No specifics on fatigue life were mentioned, as tests were still under way on the existing Scimitar. However, it was built to be a tough beast, and the developed version would no doubt have held up well too. Weapons carriage was basically similar to that of the existing Scimitar, which suffered from the handicap of not having room for a weapons bay of any kind. Thus the wing pylons were the only possible place to put weapons, bringing associated heating and drag problems.

Vickers believed it could get the Type 565 into the air in 1959 and into service by mid-1961, at which time production of the Scimitar F.1 would be ending. Alternatively, the naval features could be retained, cutting back on development time and getting the aircraft into service nine months sooner at a cost of higher weight and reduced performance (8 per cent reduction in combat radius, 50yd (45m) added to take-off distance). Total R&D costs were expected to be £4 million (including £2 million for five development batch aircraft).

Take-off performance fully loaded was a concern, so Vickers took another look at the design. De-navalization and the new nose had moved the centre of gravity (c.g.) forward, and large external stores also tended to lower the c.g. Raising the nose for take-off would therefore take longer, and various means were looked at to improve the situation. These included redistributing weight within the airframe, moving the main undercarriage forward, increasing tailplane size, adding a tailplane flap or even adding an auxiliary system to raise the nose during the take-off roll. Reducing the aircraft's unstick speed was also necessary, and to this end more options were considered, such as tilting the jet pipes downward a further 10 degrees, high-lift devices on the wing, and drooped ailerons with blowing. However, the only serious improvement would be achieved using rocket assistance, so provision was made for a ventrally slung rocket for assisted take-off (initially two Super Sprites but later a single Spectre), the rocket pack being jettisoned and recovered by parachute after use.

A second set of figures was produced for an improved Type 567. This would use integral fuel tanks instead of bag tanks (giving an extra 200gal (910L) of fuel) plus improved RA.24 Avons with 6 per cent better fuel economy and lighter weight. Take-off weight would now be 48,570lb (22,045kg) with a combat radius of up to 950nm (1,090 miles; 1,760km) for the high-altitude sortie and up to 670nm (770 miles; 1,240km) at low level. The take-off distance was much the same, but the actual ground roll was now reduced to as little as 1,070yd (980m) with rocket assistance.

Perhaps the most interesting of the whole slew of developed N.113 proposals was specification No. 566, for an integrated flight control system. Supermarine's work on future aircraft had led it to the firm belief that rising complexity and speeds meant there was a need for a fully integrated flying control system encompassing autopilot, autostabilizer and power controls, with electrical signalling holding it all together. Sperry had created a system that handled much of this requirement, and which would be ideal for installation in an N.113 airframe as it allowed existing mechanical control runs to coexist with the integrated system. Unlike existing simple altitude/heading holding autopilots, this system would effectively have been able to fly complete manoeuvres had it been developed further. In 'Direct' mode

it would act as an orthodox powered control system using existing mechanical linkages; in 'Autostablizer' mode it would use electrical signalling, and control surface movements would be subject to small adjustments superimposed on the pilot's demands. Finally, in 'Little Stick' mode, the aircraft would be controlled by a small side-stick (rather like the General Dynamics F-16, only some years in advance), which would translate pilot demands into co-ordinated use of the control surfaces, the pilot never needing to move the rudder bar unless he wanted to introduce slip deliberately into a manoeuvre. Fully automatic instrument landing system (ILS) approaches could be flown on the system, and the intention was to develop it so that it could fly complex manoeuvres such as programmed climbs, steady turns to a pre-selected radius, automatic attacks coupled to the radar and a complete LABS attack.

Hawker P.1121

Hawker's proposal was contained in a brochure entitled *P.1121 Air Superiority Strike Aircraft*, and referred to an aircraft already unsuccessfully submitted for OR.329. Hawker believed strongly enough in this aircraft to have continued its development using the company's own money, even when it failed to win the tender for OR.329, and claimed that it could easily become a multi-role strike aircraft. As both the Saunders-Roe and Fairey designs to OR.329 had been briefly considered for the light strike role, Hawker certainly deserved to give it a go as well.

The P.1121 was an attractive swept-wing, single-seat multi-role aircraft, and a prototype was under construction, powered by a single reheated de Havilland Gyron engine fed through a chin-mounted intake. Either the Rolls-Royce Conway or Bristol Olympus would have been more suited to the strike role. Hawker was confident that the airframe could be developed into a variety of versions, one of which was a two-seat tactical bomber carrying Doppler, sideways-looking radar (SLR) in underwing pods and forward-looking radar. Relocation of the existing fuselage-mounted tricycle undercarriage to wing nacelles to allow space in the fuselage for extra fuel or bombs was possible. The brochure, however, concentrated on the single-seat P.1121 already under development. Navigation capabilities would be as limited as those of the single-

Leading Particulars: P.1121	
Length	66.5ft (20.27m)
Height	15.33ft (4.67m)
Wing span	37ft (11.28m)
Wing area	474sq ft (44.03sq m)
Wing aspect ratio	2.89
Wing anhedral	2 degrees
Tailplane span	19.25ft (5.87m)
Tailplane area	115sq ft (10.68sq m)
Tailplane aspect ratio	3.23
Tailplane dihedral	10 degrees
Engines	2 × 15,800lb R-R Conway 11R (25,700lb (11,665kg) in reheat)
Max speed	Mach 1.15 at sea level, Mach 2.3 at 36,000ft (11,000m)
Empty weight	27,365lb (12,420kg)
Max all up weight	49,690lb (22,550kg)

seat Scimitar, with equal pilot workload problems.

Carrying 1,500gal (6,800L) of internal fuel, a 2,000lb 'Tactical Strike Weapon' on a pylon under the port wing (balanced, as on the Scimitar, by a drop tank under the starboard wing), up to 600gal (2,700L) of fuel in underwing drop tanks, two nose-mounted cameras, and a pair of retractable rocket packs either side of the fuselage behind the cockpit housing twenty-five 2in rockets each (alternatively, four 30mm cannon in a pack), the Conway-powered P.1121 would have a normal AUW of 43,700lb (19,800kg), rising to 48,200lb (21,900kg) with full weapon load and extra drop tanks. Cruising speed would be Mach 0.85 at altitude and Mach 0.72 at low level with a burst of up to Mach 0.9, all in dry power. With reheat, low-level speed could be Mach 1.05, with an impressive Mach 2.1 at 36,000ft (11,000m). Take-off distance was not so impressive, at 1,950yd (1,780m), and hi-lo combat radius in strike configuration was up to 675nm (775 miles; 1,250km). In reconnaissance fit at high level and high speed, combat radius was reduced to 430nm (500 miles; 800km). With two 300gal (1,360L) and two 150gal (680L) drop tanks, one-way ferry range would be 2,170nm (2,500 miles; 4,000km).

With the Olympus 21R instead of the Conway the aircraft would be 140lb (65kg) lighter overall, capable of up to Mach 2.65 at 36,000ft (11,000m). The maximum combat radius would increase to 800nm (920 miles; 1,480km) and take-off distance would be reduced to 1,790yd (1,640m).

A general-arrangement drawing of the Hawker P.1121 of March 1957.
Damien Burke

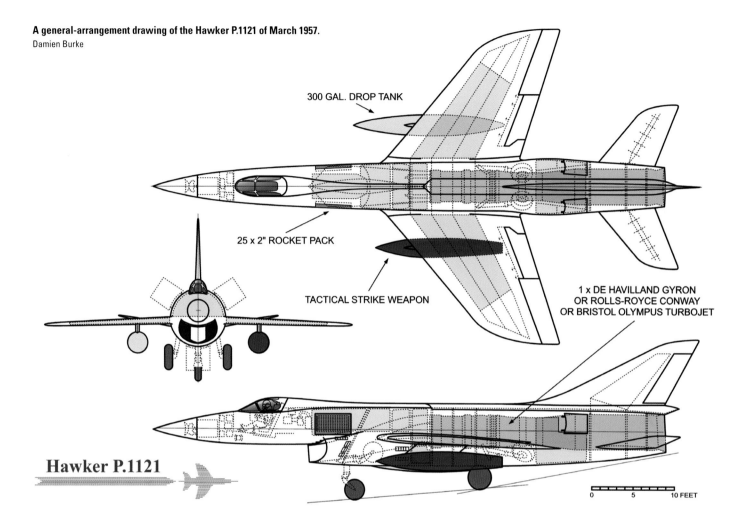

300 GAL. DROP TANK

25 x 2" ROCKET PACK

TACTICAL STRIKE WEAPON

1 x DE HAVILLAND GYRON
OR ROLLS-ROYCE CONWAY
OR BRISTOL OLYMPUS TURBOJET

Hawker P.1121

0   5   10 FEET

Hawker predicted production beginning in 1960, with an in-service date of mid-1961 and an R&D cost of £9 million, which included eight development batch aircraft.

Arguments against the early proposals

The RAF was altogether less than impressed with all of these aircraft, believing they had been foisted upon it under the guise of 'making do' in the grand British tradition of muddling through with whatever was on hand. Contrary to the various companies' promises that these developed types could all be brought into service far faster than a new aircraft, and for much less money, enabling development of a more capable aircraft at a more leisurely pace, the RAF believed it would be stuck with these interim types if it accepted any of them, and never get what it really wanted. The RAF's own updated predictions for a completely new aircraft that did everything

it wanted was for an R&D cost of £15 million and an in-service date of 1964. To save perhaps two or three years off that target and a half to two-thirds of the cost (if the manufacturers' estimates were at all believable), while ending up with an aircraft that simply did not do the job, was not an attractive option. What the RAF did not consider for even one moment was that it could be as woefully optimistic in its estimates as it believed the manufacturers were with theirs.

The major arguments against all four interim aircraft developments comprised a simple numbers game. Only the developed Sea Vixen met the GOR.339 requirement of a 1,000-mile (1,600km) radius of action, a figure the RAF claimed was based on various regional pacts and treaty obligations rather than being 'plucked from thin air', as some would later have it. Fixed targets could not be moved closer to existing bases just because your bombers were unable to go that far (the RN, of course, could often move a carrier closer to a target to begin

with). Take-off and landing distances were generally unsatisfactory except with rocket assistance for take-off, but the two biggest problems were being able to find the target, and to survive while doing so. Finding a target to a high degree of accuracy was the key to attacking it successfully, and none of the naval proposals gave the RAF any confidence that the respective aircraft could reliably manage this. The RN had the luxury of mostly dealing with well-defined targets that showed up well on radar: ships at sea, or coastal installations. The RAF had no such luck, and ground clutter reduced the existing radars of these aircraft to little more than ranging radars. A new and much more sophisticated radar would be necessary at the very least. However, even if that problem was ignored, the fact that most of the aircraft were subsonic doomed them all.

In summary, then, each of these proposals was unacceptable. They could not get to the target area; if they could, they could not find the target; and if they could get there and

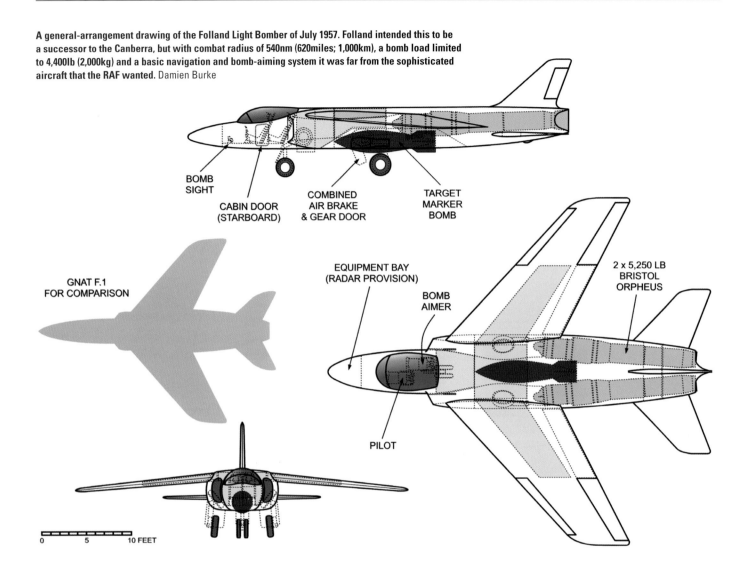

A general-arrangement drawing of the Folland Light Bomber of July 1957. Folland intended this to be a successor to the Canberra, but with combat radius of 540nm (620miles; 1,000km), a bomb load limited to 4,400lb (2,000kg) and a basic navigation and bomb-aiming system it was far from the sophisticated aircraft that the RAF wanted. Damien Burke

BOMB SIGHT

CABIN DOOR (STARBOARD)

COMBINED AIR BRAKE & GEAR DOOR

TARGET MARKER BOMB

GNAT F.1 FOR COMPARISON

EQUIPMENT BAY (RADAR PROVISION)

BOMB AIMER

2 x 5,250 LB BRISTOL ORPHEUS

PILOT

0   5   10 FEET

find it they would probably be unable to bomb it because their external stores would have been cooked by the high-speed flight that all of them could only just manage. If they were delivered late, even by a year or two, enemy defences would have advanced to the point where their slow penetration speed would condemn them to being nothing more than target practice for an alert and well-armed enemy. The last line in the OR department's appraisal of the designs was intended to have an air of finality about it that would bury the proposals for ever: 'Not one of these aircraft could maintain beyond 1965 the viability of the Royal Air Force in tactical strike and reconnaissance.'

Despite that, one chink in the RAF's armour had opened. The Hawker P.1121 was clearly superior to any of the naval aircraft, but still fell far short of meeting GOR.339. However, Hawker's proposed developed two-seat strike version was

viewed with some interest, and the company was asked to work on an improved submission. The possibility of a joint RAF/RN aircraft was also mooted by the MoS, but weight and size limitations precluded all but the smaller Hawker design from being a realistic possibility, and neither was capable of meeting all of the RAF's needs. Another outside contender very briefly looked at was a small aircraft from Folland, but the range and bomb load of such a small aircraft immediately ruled it out of the running for GOR.339. The interest in a joint RAF/RN type was not lost on the Admiralty or Blackburn, and work began on drawing up a further improved version of the NA.39. The one gem among these early proposals was the integrated flight control system put forward by Supermarine/Vickers for the developed Scimitar; such a system would become a vital part of the TSR2.

The 1957 Defence White Paper

Amidst all the work on GOR.339 came the Defence White Paper of 4 April 1957 from Minister of Defence Duncan Sandys, a man smitten with the possibilities of missile and rocket technology since World War Two and the shocking Nazi V2 rocket attacks upon Britain. The White Paper admitted that: 'It must be frankly recognized that there is at present no means of protecting the people of Britain against the catastrophic consequences of an attack with nuclear weapons', and that 'it is unhappily true that the only existing safeguard against nuclear aggression is the power to threaten retaliation in kind'.

As a result almost all of the nation's other defence commitments were to be pushed aside, and the reorganization of the

An artist's impression of the Hawker P.1121. This particular illustration was later amended to cater for political sensitivities, and in a reissue of the brochure a year later the mushroom cloud was conspicuously absent! BAE Systems Heritage via Brooklands Museum

armed forces to present a deterrent posture would override everything else. The size of the armed forces would be reduced by around 50 per cent (although RAF and Army units would be armed with atomic weapons to increase their striking power). Overseas forces would be reduced where possible, and conscription would end by 1960. Only a limited fighter force would be needed, for it would be dedicated to defending the nation's deterrent forces. There was, after all, simply no way a few hundred guns, or the new anti-aircraft missiles then becoming available, could guarantee that some Soviet bombers would not get through to the nation's cities. Most of the gun sites would be abandoned, and their controlling bunkers would become local-authority emergency control centres so that the destruction of central government would not leave the surviving populace entirely ungoverned. The nation's anti-aircraft defences would henceforth be concentrated around the only targets worth defending, the V-force airfields.

Advanced manned aircraft projects were to be cancelled, because missiles would take on their job in the near future. Of the various fighter projects under way, only English Electric's P.1 project (shortly to develop into the highly successful Lightning) would survive, being deemed to have progressed too far to be abandoned, and to be valuable as a short-term high-performance fighter until sophisticated surface-to-air missile systems replaced it. The RAF's future supersonic large bomber project, the Avro 730 to OR.330, did not get such a reprieve and was cancelled. In its place would come the Blue Streak intermediate-range ballistic missile (IRBM), with the American Thor IRBM, somewhat unkindly, if accurately, described by one member of parliament as a 'complete load of rubbish', filling the gap until Blue Streak was available. (Blue Streak itself was later cancelled owing to development difficulties and rising costs.) With Thor itself not expected to be available for at least another year, the V-force would also continue in the deterrent role.

The RAF's OR department, already worried by attempts to foist unsuitable and mostly naval aircraft upon it to meet the future light bomber/tactical strike aircraft requirement, was badly shaken. It was clear to the department, and to most outside observers, that developments in anti-aircraft missiles and radar technology would not be one-sided, and would soon make the V-force's mission nothing more or less than sheer suicide. Moreover, a missile-only offensive air arm was a pipe dream and folly of the worst kind. A missile did not have the flexibility to hit targets such as fast-moving concentrations of troops and vehicles, and a nuclear missile had no use whatsoever in a 'limited' (non-nuclear) conflict. Work continued on getting GOR.339 through the labyrinthine paths of bureaucracy that all aircraft projects had to follow. Luckily the MoS, led by Aubrey Jones, had a rather different vision of future defence needs than Sandys' MoD, otherwise Britain's aviation industry could have vanished practically overnight instead of just being badly mauled. At English Electric the chill wind of the 1957 Defence White Paper had been felt in the weeks leading up to its publication, and the company had been careful to look at the implications for Project 17. The first result was that the company referred to a strategic role only obliquely, in case its brochure ended up at the MoD and got the project killed overnight for daring to suggest a new supersonic strategic nuclear bomber. English Electric would later quietly back-pedal on a possible fighter version, too, for the same reason.

One big change to the GOR at this point was the addition of a much more varied selection of weapons for the aircraft to deliver. With budgets slashed, the RAF now had to put all of its eggs in this single basket, and ask for an aircraft capable of doing more than delivering a single Target Marker Bomb or a handful of dumb bombs. Subsidiary requirements were also generated to cover some of the additional systems that would be needed on board the aircraft; OR.3044 covered a navigation, bombing, reconnaissance and flight control system, for instance.

Reshaping the Aircraft Industry

While the MoD was smugly looking forward to a golden age of shiny pointy missiles and a world in which sideshows such as Korea or Suez did not happen, Aubrey Jones at the MoS realized that Sandys' White Paper had effectively put the aviation industry on notice. With most aircraft projects cancelled, the manufacturers would be desperate to win work on the last major remaining project, GOR.339, and this put the MoS in a uniquely powerful position. It had a golden opportunity to use GOR.339 to reshape an aircraft industry it saw as bloated and inefficient. In this the MoS had a good point. The industry had grown into a mass of independent companies, often duplicating one another's efforts and producing some equipment of frankly questionable utility. However, the increasingly heavy influence of an army of civil servants standing between the armed forces and their equipment suppliers was an example of bloating and inefficiency that dwarfed any in the aviation industry, and the chaotic and sloth-like manner in which aircraft requirements were drawn up and issued and contracts awarded was a good part of the reason behind fiascos such as that of the introduction into RAF service of the utterly useless Supermarine Swift fighter.

Within the Air Ministry, MoD and MoS, discussion on GOR.339 was batted back and forth. The NA.39's case was continuing to be pressed by the Admiralty. This did nothing but harden attitudes within the RAF, which took steps to try to remove the NA.39 from the running in a dramatically permanent manner. The result was that, in April 1957, the MoD sent a letter to the CA at the MoS, suggesting that the NA.39 could be cancelled to save money, and the developed Scimitar put into production as a cheaper alternative for the RN's strike requirement. The MoD also took advantage of the MoS's known plans to reduce the aircraft industry's size by pointing out that killing the NA.39 would make it possible to 'eliminate both the Blackburn Aircraft Company and the de Havilland Engine Company' earlier than would otherwise be possible. Of course, the far less capable Scimitar development would have been of no use at all to satisfy GOR.339, leaving the field clear for the RAF to get exactly what it wanted. The second step in this plan would be to demonstrate that RAF GOR.339s

would be capable of covering all of the RN's strike commitments and enable the removal of the entire RN carrier force. Luckily for the RN, and, as it transpired, the RAF too, this dastardly ploy failed, and in August 1957 the NA.39 project was allowed to continue. The RAF had won no friends in the process, and it was perhaps this episode that turned Admiral Mountbatten into such an implacable enemy of the GOR.339 project.

Meanwhile, the RAF was concerned that, despite its requirements being available in black and white, nothing had been officially communicated to the wider aircraft industry. Its original timetable had included the receipt of detailed design studies from industry by the end of August 1957, and the selection of a design to form a basis for a draft OR by the end of October. August came and went, and the industry had not even received the final GOR yet, let alone managed to respond to it in detail. The reason for this delay was entirely political. The MoS was still trying to decide which aircraft companies deserved to survive, and which groupings they would like to see. By September the MoS finally had some idea of what it wanted the future aircraft industry to look like, and so invited representatives of the major companies to a meeting at the Ministry on 16 September. The Minister himself, Aubrey Jones, was visiting the USA, and left it to his Permanent Secretary, Sir Cyril Musgrave, to preside over what turned out to be a momentous meeting. Attending were Mr (later Sir) Aubrey Burke of de Havilland; Lord Caldecote and Mr H.G. Nelson of English Electric; Captain E.D. Clarke of Saunders-Roe; Sir Roy Dobson and Sir Frank Spriggs of Hawker Siddeley; Sir George Edwards of Vickers-Armstrongs/Supermarine; Sir Frederick Handley Page and Mr R.S. Stafford of Handley Page; Sir Matthew Slattery of Bristol Aircraft and Short Brothers; Mr E. Turner of Blackburn and General Aircraft; and Sir Reginald Verdon Smith and Mr Cyril F. Uwins of Bristol Aircraft.

The message of the meeting was blunt. There are too many of you, and there is too little work. The only significant military contract on the horizon was going to be GOR.339, possibly, and the contract for this aircraft would only be awarded to a group of firms, or perhaps a single firm taking leadership and co-ordinating two or three others. This was a particularly harsh blow to the Hawker Siddeley Group, which was already ahead of the pack in terms of consolidating and tidying up the

industry. Furthermore, while the MoS would prefer the firms to come up with their own groupings, if it proved necessary it would nominate the groupings itself. Were this to be the case, the Ministry would choose them based on the 'long-term structure of the industry'; its own vision being of three or four groups only, covering the entire industry. Regardless, any individual group would need to demonstrate four items to be acceptable: a diverse portfolio of work covering both civil and military projects; optimum design capacity including supersonic work; good productive capacity sufficient to cater for future needs; and, finally, considerable financial strength. It was clear that the Ministry wanted to be shot of the smaller companies altogether.

The meeting also covered future work beyond GOR.339, of which there was very little. There were various small civil projects, including the new British European Airways (BEA) airliner (this became the Trident), a possible supersonic transport (the first whispers of Concorde), and that was that. Beyond GOR.339 there could well be no military work at all, and the industry needed both to amalgamate and broaden its interests to survive in a world that could possibly consist only of civil contracts. Needless to say, this was shocking news to the assembled company directors, and pretty much to a man they pointed out that relying on civil projects only would doom the UK aircraft industry to recession. The USA simply could not be competed against in this sphere, being able to offer much larger production runs and thus lower prices, and with its own military production ramping down, its companies would be gearing up to make even greater inroads into the civil market.

The meeting was summed up by Sir Cyril, who said that they had to take a realistic view of the industry's future prospects, and that 'On this basis the decision had been taken that GOR.339 should be placed with a consortium of firms, or with a firm operating in association with several others.' Furthermore, 'an indication was required with each firm's reply of the other firms it expected to associate with in the event of its being given a share of the contract'. The meeting ended with a procession of dismayed executives trooping out in near silence, resigned to the government's vision of a radically restructured aviation industry. Sir Cyril turned to his Under Secretary (Air), Denis Haviland, and said: 'We've won'.

CHAPTER TWO

Submissions to GOR.339

General Operational Requirement 339 was officially issued to the industry with a deadline of 31 January 1958 for receipt of proposals. (A complete copy of GOR.339 can be found in Appendix I.) While the firms worked on their submissions, the various possibilities of foreign aircraft to meet GOR.339 were also explored, types as diverse as the Convair B-58 Hustler and Republic F-105 Thunderchief being looked at, reduced to sets of numbers and discarded as one number or another failed to match up.

It might be assumed that, having issued the GOR to various firms and asked them to work on a submission to satisfy it, the OR staff would by now have been, at least, pretty clear about what they wanted. However, initial discussions with various firms had proved unsettling for them, most firms describing large and complex aircraft loaded down with various items of equipment to try to satisfy every possible aspect of the GOR, which had itself been gradually amplified by discussions between the firms, the OR staff and the MoS. After publication of the first issue of GOR.339 it was suggested that good supersonic performance at medium altitude would be needed for fighter evasion, and a 600nm (690-mile; 1,100km) combat radius as a basic case was not aiming high enough when the Canberra could manage 1,000nm (1,150 miles; 1,850km). Consequently each firm was sent communications placing greater emphasis on high supersonic speeds at medium to high altitudes, and made the 1,000nm sortie a basic sortie rather than an overload case. With most of the firms already planning for lower performance, this left them struggling to meet the new requirements.

Why the size of most of the aircraft designs under discussion came as a surprise is a mystery, but it prompted a meeting of the OR staff on 6 December to discuss exactly what it was they wanted the aircraft to do after all! The Assistant Chief of the Air Staff (OR) had made it clear that the aircraft was needed to deliver a tactical atomic bomb, with a secondary task of reconnaissance. Additionally, the various military chiefs of staff had recently approved a paper which accepted that the strategic deterrent was all-important and no additional systems should be developed if they were not required for 'shield forces', i.e. part of the NATO shield against Soviet invasion. Clearly GOR.339 had to be able to be considered as part of the shield, or it could not go ahead, and with plans to use it as a Canberra replacement world-wide there were doubts that they could get away with describing it as a shield component. Remarkably, amidst discussions on just about every aspect of the GOR, was the admission that 'it would be an unwarranted penalty to demand a bulky undercarriage arrangement necessary to provide extremely low LCNs [load classification numbers]' (i.e. operation from rough strips), and that it should be planned on the basis of using existing airfields, a complete about-face from what industry had already been asked for. Thus, as late as the middle of December 1957, the firms were receiving communications that were changing the requirements, and their deadline of 31 January 1958 was unchanged.

By the end of January 1958 the firms had submitted their responses. It was an eclectic mix. A few had clearly had many months of detailed work put into them, others were decidedly sketchy, and at least one was little more than a 'back of a fag packet' study from a firm clearly lacking any interest in playing the Ministry's game.

A.V. Roe: Avro Type 739

Fresh from the disappointment of the cancellation of the Avro 730 to OR.330, Avro cannot have had much appetite to begin work on another bomber design, particularly with such a jack-of-all-trades requirement to satisfy. However, the company knuckled down and got on with it. It first addressed the needs for crew comfort by choosing a fairly small, highly loaded wing allied to sprung seating for the crew. A small wing would need lift assistance for landing and take-off, so blowing would be used across deflected leading and trailing edges. Variable sweep and direct-lift engines were considered, but both would have entailed considerable extra development effort and the 1964 deadline would not be met. Lift jets would also result in a much more expensive and difficult to maintain aircraft, conflicting with the dispersed tactical operations concept. Accordingly, neither idea made it into the brochure.

Avro proposed to address the inadequacies of the toss-bombing delivery method by using a winged stand-off bomb. Thus, instead of exposing the aircraft to missile attack during the pull-up to toss a 'dumb' *Red Beard*, and risking the bomb going off-target owing to wind shifts during its long toss, the weapon could be delivered from low level while the aircraft was still some distance from the target; up to 25 miles (40km) away, in fact. The winged bomb would weigh at least 50 per cent more than a standard *Red Beard*, but the increased distance from the delivery aircraft would make it possible to use a fusion rather than fission warhead (for a considerably bigger bang – megatons rather than kilotons). Much of the work going into the *Blue Steel* stand-off missile could be re-used, with a

Leading Particulars: Avro Type 739	
Length	80.8ft (24.63m)
Height	19.4ft (5.91m)
Wing span	41.28ft (12.58m)
Wing area	568sq ft (52.77sq m)
Wing aspect ratio	3
Wing anhedral	5 degrees
Tailplane area	193sq ft (17.92sq m)
Tailplane aspect ratio	3
Fin area	192sq ft (17.84sq m)
Fin aspect ratio	0.86
Engines	2 × 14,600lb (6,630kg) RB.142R
Max speed	Mach 2.2 at 36,000ft (11,000m)
Empty weight	45,870lb (20,820kg)
Max AUW	97,130lb (44,090kg)

A general-arrangement drawing of the Avro Type 739 of January 1958. Damien Burke

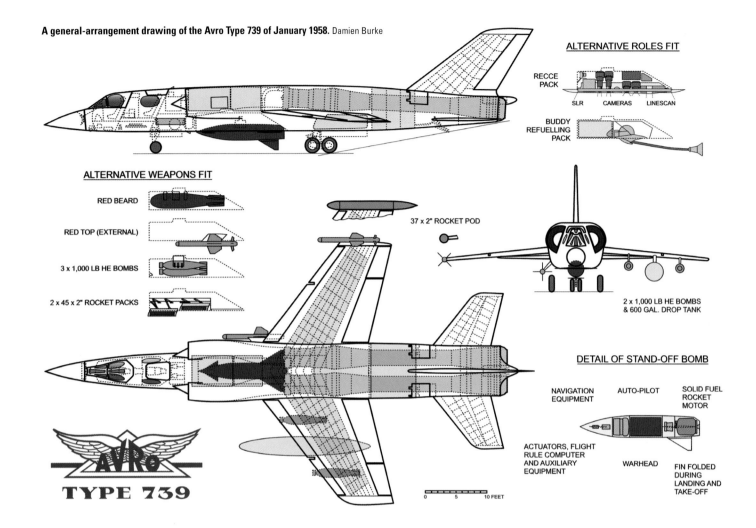

ALTERNATIVE ROLES FIT

RECCE PACK

SLR   CAMERAS   LINESCAN

BUDDY REFUELLING PACK

ALTERNATIVE WEAPONS FIT

RED BEARD

RED TOP (EXTERNAL)

3 x 1,000 LB HE BOMBS

2 x 45 x 2" ROCKET PACKS

37 x 2" ROCKET POD

2 x 1,000 LB HE BOMBS & 600 GAL. DROP TANK

DETAIL OF STAND-OFF BOMB

NAVIGATION EQUIPMENT

AUTO-PILOT

SOLID FUEL ROCKET MOTOR

ACTUATORS, FLIGHT RULE COMPUTER AND AUXILIARY EQUIPMENT

WARHEAD

FIN FOLDED DURING LANDING AND TAKE-OFF

0   5   10 FEET

AVRO

TYPE 739

similar guidance system and the use of a rocket motor based on the principles used in the two-fifths-scale *Blue Steel* test shots. The method of carriage would be similar to that of *Blue Steel* on Avro Vulcans, with the weapons bay doors replaced by a fairing containing a recess into which the bomb would be mounted. With a stand-off bomb reducing the aircraft's vulnerability, other means were also looked at to reduce the risk further. These included the use of radar-absorbing material (RAM), to be applied within aerial cavities, the crew cabin, the intakes and their half-cone centrebodies, and any portions of the exterior skin as necessary. The crew would even have RAM-coated blinds that could be pulled over the transparencies when flying at high altitude. Attack warning would be given by a system similar to the *Blue Saga* (ARI.18105) radar warning receiver (RWR).

When it came to conventional bomb carriage, Avro saw that it could fit three 1,000lb bombs side-by-side by widening the

bay slightly from the dimensions required for *Red Beard*, but fitting four would require extending the bay's length. Accordingly it went with a reduction from the GOR's requirement for four, suggesting external carriage if extra bombs were really needed. Rocket packs would also fit within these dimensions, and would be extended by hydraulic jacks for firing. The weapons bay doors were conventional, being hinged to open at the edges, rather than rotating or sliding. External weapons carriage was provided in the form of six hardpoints on the wings for pylons, two of which would be plumbed for fuel. The wingtips could also carry rocket pods or missiles.

Avro thought terrain clearance was not a realistic prospect and the Type 739's radar suite was to be biased entirely to navigation, coupled with an inertial navigation system (INS). Low-level terrain clearance would therefore be entirely visual, and a head-up display (HUD) for the pilot would be essential. A small radar-ranging

dish would be mounted on the back of the main forward-looking radar (FLR), to be used for rocket attacks. The X-band SLR with a mere 5ft (1.5m) antenna would suffice for position fixes. It did not have sufficient resolution for reconnaissance purposes, so a higher-resolution 14.5ft Q-band SLR was suggested for use in a reconnaissance pack hung from the weapons bay. The pack would also contain four cameras (four 24in and two 6in lenses) and linescan, along with associated recording and transmitting equipment, but Avro provided few details.

While Avro ignored the Ministry's request to consider naval applications, it did point out that the Type 739, with Mach 2-plus performance and a large fuel load, could make a suitable platform for fighter/interception duties, toting *Red Top* or *Blue Jay* Mk 4 missiles. Up to four missiles could be carried, two at the wingtips and two on fuselage-mounted pylons. This version would otherwise be externally identical to the bomber, with only internal changes such as the replacement of the bombing and navigational equipment with AI and missile support equipment. As with other submissions that would mention the possibilities of use as a fighter, this was aimed purely at the bomber destroyer role; it would have been no dogfighter.

The configuration of the airframe was fairly conventional, with engines buried in the upper mid-fuselage both for minimum drag and because this was just about the only place left to put them, the rest of the fuselage being taken up by crew compartment, radars, weapons bay and undercarriage. To keep the wings clear and crew visibility unobscured, the engine intakes were mounted high on the fuselage sides. Fixed half-cone centrebodies were optimized for transonic flight, and spill doors directed excess flow overboard as speed increased, rather than going to the expense and complexity of providing a variable-geometry centrebody. Access to the engines for replacement was provided by a break point in the rear fuselage; the entire rear fuselage would be removed and the engines slid out backwards. The fuselage used area ruling, one consequence of this being that the weapons bay ended up forward of the c.g. The resulting trim changes at weapons release were to be cancelled out by the flight control system. The fairly small mainplane was swept at 40 degrees and mid-mounted, the torsion box extending through the fuselage, between the engines and the weapons bay. A low-mounted tailplane was found to be the best position for stability. The all-moving tailplanes were differentially operated for roll control, backed up by small ailerons on the wing at low speeds. These would be locked in place when the aircraft was supersonic, avoiding the aileron reversal problems experienced on other high-speed aircraft. If the high wing loading proved insufficient to provide crew comfort in low-level turbulence, Avro suggested that an automatic gust-alleviation system could be used. This would deploy the wing flaps and alter tailplane angle as necessary to smooth out the ride. The leading- and trailing-edge flaps were both blown, and a notch in the wing delayed the vortex separation that would otherwise give rise to undesirable pitch-up. All conventional control surfaces were to be moved by duplicated hydraulic rams acting on a rod-lever system to give multiple operating points along the surface's span, based on the units developed for the cancelled Avro 720

supersonic interceptor and 731 (a scale model of the 730 supersonic bomber) projects. The pilot would have a side stick, using mechanical signalling rather than direct mechanical control (i.e. rods and cables) to 'talk' to the control surfaces. Avro thought it likely that a 'manoeuvre demand' system would be needed, whereby the pilot's inputs would not be directly passed to the control surfaces, but instead the automatic flight control system would apply the movements necessary to carry out the manoeuvre demanded by the pilot.

The undercarriage was of orthodox tricycle layout, both the nose and main units retracting rearwards into the fuselage. Avro did not put any serious effort into dealing with the whole question of airfield performance on rough strips and short runways, and as a result the 739 fell short of the requirement when it came to take-off distances, needing rocket assistance to meet the sortie requirements if supersonic bursts were included, and even then being unable to manage the 1,000nm sortie's take-off-distance requirement. Avro felt that keeping the aircraft as small as possible was extremely important, and thus planned to build it large enough to be able to manage only the 600nm sortie on internal fuel. The 1,000nm sortie would require drop tanks, jettisoned before going supersonic, and AUW in this configuration (one *Red Beard* internally, two 600gal (2,730L) drop tanks) would be around 91,000lb (41,300kg) if the lightest of six suggested engines was chosen. A considerable excess was available when it came to ferry range, where the aircraft could manage up to 2,830nm (3,250 miles; 5,240km) with drop tanks. While the GOR specifically mentioned that subsonic cruise was to be no lower than Mach 0.95, Avro chose Mach 0.9 as being near enough. Avro's preferred engine was the Rolls-Royce RB.142R, which would appear in most submissions to GOR.339. It also listed two flavours of Conway and three flavours of Olympus, the Conway needing least development but giving the highest AUW at 97,130lb (44,090kg) for the 1,000nm sortie with supersonic burst.

The construction was to use tried and tested techniques, light alloys being used wherever possible and exotica like titanium being employed only for the flap blowing tubes, reheat pipe heat shields and other areas requiring great heat resistance and strength. In terms of production responsibilities and teaming up with other

firms, Avro's submission was weakened by its wish not only to have overall control of the airframe but also to handle the flight control system itself, and take charge of the radar-navigation-bombing system and any contractors brought on board for this equipment, with vague mentions of using the appropriate design, technical and experimental resources of the rest of the Hawker Siddeley Group. The company predicted that, if a specification was in hand by January 1959, it could have the first of fifteen development-batch aircraft in the air by November 1961, with full CA release by September 1964.

Barnes Wallis–Vickers Type 010 Swallow Momentum Bomber

Barnes Wallis, the inventor of the 'bouncing bomb' of Dambusters fame, had been working on variable-sweep designs since 1948, with partial funding from Vickers as a pure research programme and some desultory contributions from government. He had come up with the 'Swallow', a remarkable tailless design with a variable-sweep wing (from 15 to 75 degrees), an 80-degree swept forebody and eight engines, mounted in paired nacelles mounted above and below the wing, near the tips. These swivelled to retain their fore-and-aft orientation when the wing sweep changed, and tilted up and down to provide flying controls. No conventional control surfaces were to be provided. Wallis claimed that a suitably sized bomber version could cruise at high altitude at Mach 2.5 and deliver a 10,000lb (4,500kg) bomb load to a target up to 2,500 miles (4,000km) away and return, with no hope of fighters being able to reach its altitude, or catch it if they could. Unfortunately he had been unable to convince the government to fund a research

Leading particulars: Swallow to GOR.339	
Length	77ft (23.47m)
Height	9ft (2.74m)
Wing span	37ft (11.27m) swept,
	90ft (27.43m) unswept
Wing area	727sq ft (67.54sq m)
Wing aspect ratio	1.88 swept, 11.14 unswept
Engines	4 × Bristol Olympus 12
Max speed	Mach 2.0 @ 50,000ft
	(15,000m)
Empty weight	22,805lb (10,350kg)
Max AUW	43,935lb (19,940kg)

vehicle, and his Swallow project had never got off the ground. While the Air Staff had shown keen interest in the concept, asking Wallis in late 1956 to submit a brochure for a Swallow variant to satisfy OR.330 (a high-altitude supersonic bomber requirement), Duncan Sandys unilaterally cancelled Wallis's research programme in early 1957, even before publishing his Defence White Paper, in spite of objections from the Air Staff. Wallis, undeterred, went ahead and submitted his brochure on Swallow to OR.330 in February 1957, but OR.330 too was killed by Sandys, and consequently the Swallow was never assessed in that role. The Air Staff continued to show interest in the Swallow throughout 1957, provoking a slap-down from the MoD in August of that year, in which it was stated that the Swallow was not to be proceeded with.

With GOR.339 on the table just weeks later, Wallis made another attempt to convince the government of the viability of his schemes, putting forward a preliminary brochure on a variable-sweep aircraft to meet GOR.339. This was a Swallow variant, the Type 010. Two versions had been schemed, a large one using existing turbojet engines (the Bristol Orpheus BO412), and a smaller aircraft using idealized engines based on project studies from Bristol (the BE36) and Rolls-Royce (the RB.121), better matched to the Swallow design. Both differed from Wallis's original Swallow proposal in having a deeper forebody, a redesigned tandem cockpit (without the rising turret of the original design), and four engines rather than the eight of the original. As an alternative a single Gyron PS.52 engine could be mounted in the fuselage, but this would require conventional control surfaces and additional structural weight to cope with them, and the wings would have had to be stiffened to resist flutter now that the wing-mounted engines were absent.

The larger aircraft with Orpheus engines was to have an AUW of 43,935lb (19,9450kg) and a ferry range of 2,700nm (3,100 miles; 5,000km). The AUW of the smaller aircraft with idealized engines would be just 30,000lb (13,600kg) and it would have an incredible ferry range of no less than 5,000nm (5,750 miles; 9,250km). For the 1,000nm sortie Wallis sketched a hi-lo-hi flight plan in which the aircraft would cruise climb at Mach 0.9 to 36,000ft (11.000m) to begin with, increasing to Mach 2.0 before descending to 1,000ft for a just-subsonic attack run, and then returning to Mach 2 and high altitude for the return home.

Barnes Wallis shows off a magnificent model of his Swallow aircraft, a variation of which was proposed to satisfy GOR.339. BAE Systems

Instead of carrying a 1,650lb (750kg) atomic weapon, the aircraft could carry four 1,000lb HE bombs, seventy-four 2in rockets or thirty OR.1099 rockets. Day, night and radar reconnaissance would also be possible, though no details were provided.

The Orpheus engines had significantly poorer fuel consumption compared with the RB.142 suggested for the Vickers Type 571, but as they had been selected for their ability to be used in a tilting fashion to control the aircraft, replacement with RB.142s would be difficult. Earlier RAE investigations into the Swallow had raised concerns about control loss if an engine failed, but Wallis had argued that this could be countered by a mechanical system to detect thrust loss and angle the remaining engines to compensate automatically, in less time than it would take

for the pilot even to notice that something had gone wrong. In terms of satisfying GOR.339 the Swallow could not meet the take-off roll requirements, and all of Wallis's figures excluded the additional weight of 'assisted take-off units' that would be required to enable it to do so. The RAE's investigations into the characteristics of the design had also found that in the unswept condition the aircraft would also be so stable as to be difficult to manoeuvre, and the addition of a canard, or substantial redesign of the forebody, would be required. If this could be carried out and a realistic 'idealized' powerplant could be developed, however, the design had promise. Several meetings were held in September 1958 to assess the application of the Swallow concept to GOR.339, but it was felt likely that this would put back the entry into service

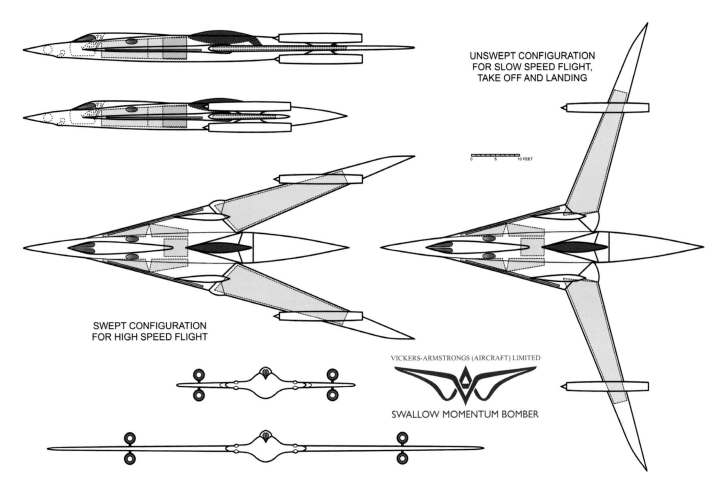

UNSWEPT CONFIGURATION
FOR SLOW SPEED FLIGHT,
TAKE OFF AND LANDING

SWEPT CONFIGURATION
FOR HIGH SPEED FLIGHT

VICKERS-ARMSTRONGS (AIRCRAFT) LIMITED

SWALLOW MOMENTUM BOMBER

A general-arrangement drawing of the Vickers Type 010 of January 1958. The term 'momentum bomber' came about from the winged bomb mounted on the upper rear fuselage. This was designed to carry out its own delivery manoeuvre, using the momentum of the delivery aircraft. The Swallow would fly over the target, whereupon the bomb would be released and then pull into a half-loop and dive back down on to the target. Damien Burke

by four years for dubious benefit. By October the RAF had concluded that there were just too many engineering problems to solve, and that the Swallow concept was better suited to a transport or high-altitude bomber than to GOR.339.

The chances are that, even if the aircraft had been theoretically perfect, politics would have killed it off regardless. Wallis was viewed with distrust by many in power, and a typical government bureaucrat assessment noted that Wallis '... works in an atmosphere of extreme secrecy and as he has got older he has become more and more difficult with the people actually working with him ... ... [He] has shown himself very resentful of any suggestions from the young men working with him, and for this reason has great difficulty keeping together a good team.' As to the Swallow itself: 'It looks extremely impressive but we have not so far found anyone who can understand it ...'.

Blackburn and General Aircraft B.108

Blackburn once again submitted a variation of the NA.39 for consideration, though it had not been in the list of firms specifically selected to be asked for submissions. This time it was designated the B.108, and had moved on somewhat from the B.103 the RAF had originally derided back in 1955. At that time the actual aircraft had not been built, and was only the subject of an order for a development batch. Now, two years down the line, the NA.39 had evolved somewhat in capability as well as appearance. The nose extension of the B.103A had been incorporated; a spine along the fuselage contained control runs and made more room for internal fuel; the selection of a single radar installation for the nose radome had been made, and the

radome and its fold line redesigned to suit. This was basically similar to the aircraft that has since become familiar as the Buccaneer S.1.

The B.108 had other changes too. That fuselage extension was in the area of the cockpit, giving 18in (46cm) more room for radar displays, which would be needed, as the aircraft had SLR in the forward fuselage to provide fix corrections for the new INS. The underwing slipper tanks were enlarged to give 60 per cent more capacity and enable the B.108 to just about manage the 1,000nm sortie. However, with a low-level cruising speed of just Mach 0.89, no realistic supersonic capability, and no improvements in take-off and landing performance, Blackburn had immediately given the RAF just the excuse it needed to discount the B.108 submission.

Support for the NA.39 to meet GOR.339 was strong from all other directions,

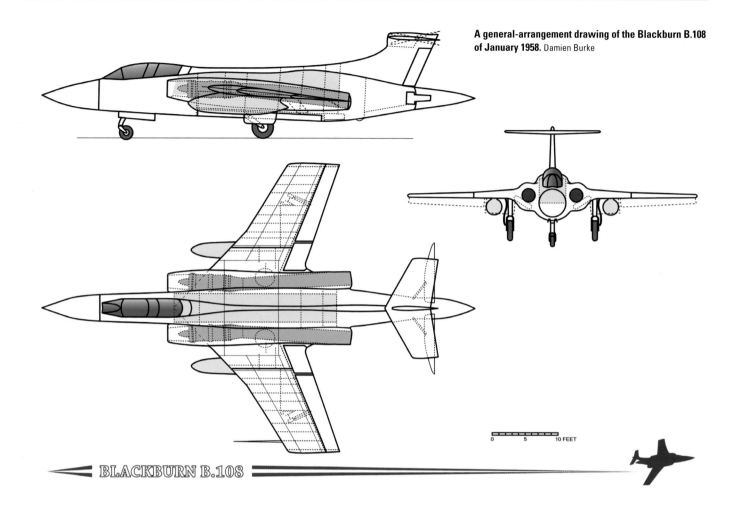

A general-arrangement drawing of the Blackburn B.108 of January 1958. Damien Burke

BLACKBURN B.108

however. Even a former Chief of the Air Staff, Sir John Slessor, wrote to Duncan Sandys in January 1958 to commend the NA.39 to him, albeit as an interim measure. At the time it was thought to be around three years in advance of any other type (including American ones), and it was surely worthwhile to have a stop-gap available right now that would be ahead of the game for three or four years, and could soldier on for eight to ten, by which time a really modern replacement could have been acquired. Blackburn indicated that Fairey would be its partner of choice if either company were to be awarded the contract to build an aircraft to satisfy GOR.339.

Later, in February 1960, Blackburn suggested a further upgraded aircraft, the B.111, re-engined with the new Rolls-Royce RB.168 (Spey) of 19,250lb (8,740kg) thrust (in reheat), with all naval features deleted; an effort owing a lot to the Buccaneer S.2, albeit with reheat. The B.111 would be supersonic, with a top speed of Mach 1.25 at high altitude, normally cruising at Mach 0.85. If it stayed subsonic, combat radius

would be 840nm (970 miles; 1,550km), and the AUW for this sortie would be 46,988lb (21,328kg), with a take-off roll of 1,800yd (1,650m) and landing roll of 1,070yd (980m). Only by carrying drop tanks could the B.111 manage the 1,000nm sortie. Predictably, with the TSR2 by then well under way, the RAF was still not interested.

After that, Blackburn gave up any serious efforts to try and get in on the TSR2 act, though it did come up with another improvement, the B.113, which differed primarily from the B.111 in having a reshaped fuselage and greater fuel capacity, giving it combat radius of 1,290nm (1,480 miles; 2,390km) with external tanks and an AUW of 54,200lb (24,600kg), along with a claimed top speed of Mach 1.85 at altitude. This was aimed at a possible Royal Australian Air Force (RAAF) requirement for a strike and all-weather interceptor aircraft. The RAAF was not interested; and when the proposal was brought up in September 1960 by the MoA, the RAF was quick to point out that it was just a minimal improvement on an already unacceptable design.

Bristol Aircraft Type 204

Undoubtedly the most unusual design submitted to satisfy GOR.339 was Bristol's Type 204. Bristol had put together a truly futuristic aircraft with a beautifully shaped 'Gothic' wing (so named because the curve in planform matches that of the ogival arches of Gothic architecture), above which sat

Leading particulars: Bristol Type 204	
Length	79.5ft (24.23m)
Height	20.75ft 6.32m)
Wing span	32ft (9.75m)
Wing area	820sq ft (76.2sq m)
Wing aspect ratio	1.25
Foreplane span	8.5ft (2.6m)
Foreplane area	55sq ft (5.11sq m)
Foreplane aspect ratio	1.3
Fin area	127sq ft (11.8sq m)
Engines	2 × Bristol Olympus 22SR
Max speed	Mach 2.0 @ 52,000ft (16.000m)
Empty weight	41,000lb (18,600kg)
Max AUW	81,350lb (36,925kg)

a large box containing the engines and intakes, with a long nose extending from below the wing. Finishing off the aircraft's striking appearance was a bizarre canard mounted on a ventral fin below the nose.

Bristol's departure from the more conventional layouts favoured by other companies was its solution to the GOR's demanding mix of subsonic and supersonic flight, low- and high-level performance, good gust response and fatigue strength, and excellent short-field performance. Bristol had already been working on designs for a supersonic transport, and the slender-delta wing (the classic 'paper dart' planform) was clearly the best for high Mach numbers. However, such a wing was far from ideal in the low and slow landing regime, and adding flaps to a delta wing that are big enough to be of any use also introduces such huge trim changes that the aircraft would be impossible to control. Modifying the delta by means of introducing an ogival curve to the leading edge, effectively rounding off

the tips and apex, improved the wing's stability (particularly at high angles of incidence) and was considerably less draggy than a standard delta. When the Gothic wing had first been drawn up, it was intended that an aircraft using it would be 'integrated', with the crew, equipment, fuel and engines all contained within the contour of the wing, which would be of very thick section. The requirements of GOR.339, particularly the sheer amount of fuel needed for the required combat radius, made an integrated design impossible, so Bristol added a long fuselage (almost doubling the aircraft's length in the process), in which was housed the crew compartment, bomb load and electronic equipment. This also enabled Bristol to add a canard flying surface and thus deal with the trim changes caused by flaps, which could now be big enough to be unblown and still effective; they also doubled as ailerons.

The foreplane had a trailing-edge flap of its own, and was mounted underneath the

nose on a ventral fin to give maximum span for the flap and keep the vortices from the foreplane away from the main fin. The foreplane itself was of identical planform to the mainplane, and in normal cruising flight would be all-moving for the limited trim power required in the cruise. The flap would be used only to trim out the large changes introduced by the use of the wing flaps, and Bristol suggested that the foreplane flap might need blowing to be effective enough. Stability was expected to be acceptable through much of the envelope, but an autostabilizer would be necessary for comfortable handling.

The crew were seated in tandem, with large Vitreosil fused-quartz transparencies offering excellent views sideways and downwards. Only the navigator was to be provided with a sprung compartment to improve ride comfort. Behind the crew compartment was a large equipment bay, which also housed the SLR aerials. Aft of this was the 'bomb cell', sized to

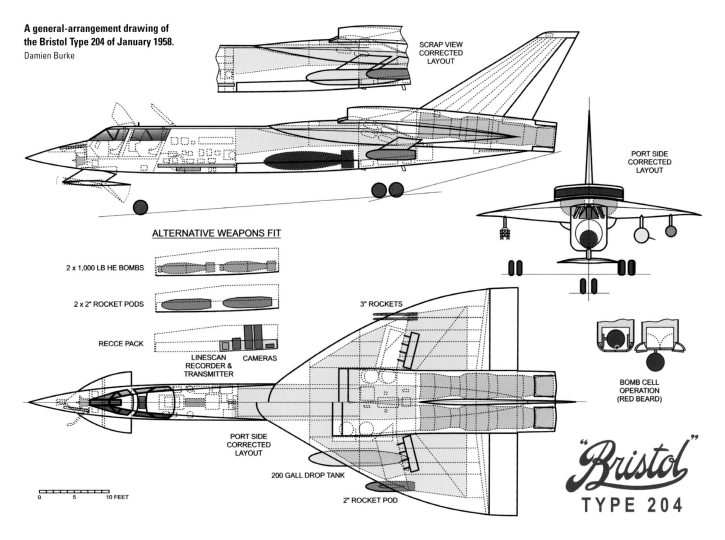

A general-arrangement drawing of the Bristol Type 204 of January 1958.
Damien Burke

accommodate all required stores including the single *Red Beard* store or up to four 1,000lb HE bombs (if six were required, the other two would need to be carried on external pylons). Double doors were used; a single set closed the bay off during flight, with an inner set of doors normally retracted against the cell walls holding the stores. These would fold outwards to lower stores into the air stream before release and also close the cell, eliminating the problem of buffeting experienced with so many bomb bay designs. As with so many other submissions the bomb cell, or weapons bay, could accommodate a dedicated reconnaissance pack including cameras and linescan equipment (though the submission was bereft of any details on this), or a buddy refuelling pack (again, no details were provided). The carriage of rockets was complicated by the foreplane position; they would need to be angled down to clear it when fired (one can only imagine the difficulty of sighting the target). Bristol was the only company to deal with the problem of slow burning or late ignition of rockets. If this happened after retraction the resulting mess could be impressive, so the company proposed a metal grid in front of the pack to stop the rocket leaving the launcher, while the exhaust would be vented through blowout panels in the rear part of the bomb-cell doors.

Fuel tanks occupied much of the space above and behind the bomb cell, with the Doppler radar in the fuselage underneath the rear tank. Further fuel was contained within the thick wings, which also housed the main undercarriage units. The undercarriage used a conventional tricycle layout, with the main gear retracting sideways into the wing (rearward retraction having been investigated originally). Ground clearance gave rise to particularly long main legs, a four-wheel bogie enabling the use of smaller, higher-pressure tyres than would otherwise be the case, giving an overall LCN of 28. The legs were shortened by 20in (50cm) during retraction. The nose gear retracted rearwards and used the same wheels and tyres as the main gear.

The wing's low aspect ratio gave good comfort at low level, inherently high overall stiffness and thus good fatigue life, even with relatively lightweight construction. Conventional skin-stringer construction was to be used, using light aluminium alloy for the most part with limited use of stainless steel and titanium in the hot areas around the engines. Bristol's preferred engine was the Bristol Olympus 22SR (SR standing for simplified reheat); this was the only submission to choose this engine. Other engines considered and rejected for weight and performance reasons were the Olympus 15R and either two or three RB.142Rs. The intakes were simple wedges, well matched to the Olympus 22SR engine, but auxiliary inlet doors were provided on the upper surfaces to provide extra airflow at slow speeds, and small spill doors for higher-speed flight. Bristol's simplified reheat system included a simple convergent-divergent nozzle, the divergent portion sliding forward to reduce the area. While this simplified the mechanics considerably, it led to significant reductions in the amount of thrust available when reheat was not being used. This was a serious issue, but Bristol dismissed it as 'not an embarrassment' owing to the 'operational characteristics of the aircraft'. Clamshell thrust reversers mounted above and below the nozzle considerably reduced landing distances.

On the navigation front, Bristol considered the development of an INS unlikely by 1964 and proposed a simpler gyro system combined with Doppler. The FLR was to be used only for target identification and ranging, with SLR (X or J band) for mapping. Unusually, linescan was to be a permanent fit on the aircraft, with live presentation of the results available to the navigator for navigation purposes, as well as being stored and transmitted to ground stations for intelligence purposes. Only the storage and transmitter equipment would be held within the optional reconnaissance pack. Three permanently fitted cameras would also be carried in the nose. Nighttime photography would require a reconnaissance pack to be carried, as it contained the high-intensity flash equipment. Bristol did not consider a reconnaissance radar necessary.

The all-important performance of the aircraft was a rather mixed bag. Bristol cooked the books somewhat in its sortie profiles, in which the supersonic burst (intended for low-level evasion) was carried out at high altitude on the cruise towards the target (not even within the last 200 miles (320km)); an entirely low-level profile was also to be entirely subsonic, initially at Mach 0.85 and only rising to Mach 0.95 closer to the target. As a result, while the combat-radius requirements were met, the sortie profiles were unrealistic and invalidated the figures. Only in the ferry sortie could it be legitimately claimed that the aircraft met the requirements. To include a supersonic burst where it would actually be useful, Bristol predicted a rise in aircraft weight of more than 10,000lb (4,500kg) (for stronger structure and extra fuel), which would have a deleterious effect on take-off and landing distances. The nuclear LABS attack in high ambient temperatures would result in the aircraft slowing up so much that loss of control was a possibility. To combat

A brochure model of the Bristol Type 204. An attractive but badly flawed design, it displayed some hints of Concorde in its striking lines. BAE Systems via RAF Museum

this it was suggested that water injection be used, to permit higher engine output, or that the aircraft accelerate to Mach 1.2 before the pull-up.

Unfortunately Bristol had made a serious error in its calculations of supersonic wave drag, and did not realize this until it was told so by the RAE in February, after the submission had gone to the Ministry. This was a disaster for the company's chances. The resulting performance impact was massive, resulting in an aircraft incapable of attaining supersonic speeds. Rather than accept this and lose out on the chance to get the GOR.339 contract, Bristol quickly redesigned the wing. The leading edge was straightened slightly and its apex moved forward 15in (38cm) (retaining the same overall area). It became thinner in section, and the undercarriage hinge could no longer be accommodated in the original position. The undercarriage was therefore changed to forward retraction, extra room being made by moving the intakes forward 13in (33cm). The changes lost 780gal (3,545L) of fuel tank space; to regain some of this the engine accessories were relocated below the engine, enabling rearward removal of the engines rather than taking them out through the nacelle floor. Thus part of the rear nacelle could now hold fuel, but only 230gal (1,045L). The forward fuselage tanks were extended by 14in (35cm) to give them another 200gal (910L) capacity, but that still left a deficit of 350gal (1,590L), so to fly the 1,000nm sortie the aircraft now needed to carry a pair of 200gal (910L) drop tanks, to be dropped immediately they were empty. Maximum take-off weight rose by 1,000lb (450kg). With this error added to a succession of vague and hopeful statements scattered through the brochure ('It is believed that...', '...when this [experimental work] becomes available...', '...it should be possible...', and so on), it was clear that Bristol's work on the design was at a very early stage. The company had also failed initially to submit any details of its preferred partner company or companies, though it later indicated that Short Brothers & Harland was the likely partner.

de Havilland Aircraft Company GOR.339

De Havilland did not waste any further effort improving its developed Sea Vixen idea, but came up with an entirely new design to try to satisfy GOR.339. As with just about every other submission, the company was keen to keep the aircraft as small as possible, not only to keep down cost, but for a range of reasons including minimizing maintenance, storage and infrastructure requirements; and also keeping the radar signature low and so reducing vulnerability. Because VTOL by jet deflection, direct jet lift or ducted-fan lift, was too risky, de Havilland discarded such ideas very early in the design process. Its chosen layout was an aircraft of fairly conventional appearance with: a thin fuselage; a shoulder-mounted variable-incidence cranked delta wing, under which were hung the engine pods; and a conventional tail with a mid-mounted tailplane.

The choice of a variable-incidence wing was unusual for a British aircraft company, though it had been briefly considered by some of the other companies submitting to GOR.339. With the wing tilted so that the angle of attack was greater during the take-off run, not only was the aircraft closer to the take-off attitude to start with (with the benefit that the undercarriage legs could be shorter, as the required pitching moment was reduced), but it also enabled the wing-mounted engines to provide a significant vertical thrust component. In addition, the wing was provided with blown flaps and ailerons and a full-span drooped and blown leading edge. The all-moving tailplane's position and span was decided by the requirement to keep it clear of the engine exhausts; de Havilland had not carried out any windtunnel tests to ascertain if this position was actually acceptable, however. The tailplane also had trailing-edge flaps that would come into use at low speeds.

Leading particulars: de Havilland GOR.339	
Length	67.5ft (20.57m)
Height	17ft (5.18m)
Wing span	34ft (10.36m)
Wing area	440sq ft (40.8sq m)
Wing aspect ratio	2.63
Foreplane area	228sq ft (21.18sq m)
Fin area	183sq ft (17sq m)
Engines	2 × 14,000lb (6,350kg) RB.142R (22,400lb (10,170kg) with reheat); optional 1 × DH Spectre 15,000lb (6,800kg) rocket
Max speed	Mach 1.3 @ sea level, Mach 2.0 @ 50,000ft (15,200m)
Empty weight	26,790lb (2,490kg)
Max AUW	60,400lb (5,610kg)

The nose radome was designed to be large enough to accommodate a 30in (76cm) diameter radar dish, but the company said this could be changed easily to cope with alternative equipment. Crew comfort was judged to be good, owing to the high wing loading and hydraulically sprung and damped seats, with a vague prediction that fatigue would be one sixth of that experienced by Gloster Meteor crews. Tandem seating with vertical staggering ensured that both crew members had a good all-round view, though no downward view was provided for the navigator; a periscope was suggested instead. There was also a suggestion that the navigator's task of 'groping' for various switches could be made easier by giving him a master hand-control; an early stab at the hands-on-throttle-and-stick (HOTAS) concept (minus the throttle, naturally!).

The bomb bay would hold the required single Target Marker Bomb, and also accommodate some alternative loads including two 1,000lb HE bombs, a large rocket pack (containing either eighty-five 2in or fourteen 3in rockets), a reconnaissance pack containing radar and photographic equipment or a 200 or 400gal (910 or 1,820L) fuel tank. With a narrow fuselage, the required bomb-bay dimensions resulted in some localized bulging in this area, which also doubled as strong points for the external attachment of bulbous 375gal (1,700L) conformal fuel tanks or small pylons to carry a single 1,000lb HE bomb on each side. Hardpoints under the wings enabled the carriage of 275gal (1,250L) drop tanks (these could be carried while the aircraft was supersonic, whereas the fuselage-mounted drop tanks would be jettisoned while subsonic) or 1,000lb HE bombs. Thus the maximum load of six such bombs would have them evenly distributed between the bomb bay and two external locations, and de Havilland recommended the use of the low-drag Mk 83 weapon being developed for naval use. The proposed large rocket pack was mounted on a trapeze within the bomb bay, and when lowered into the air stream, there was limited clearance to fire the rockets through the gap between the two dive brakes, if these were extended. It was hoped that airflow disturbance from the dive brakes would not affect rocket firing.

Three F.95 cameras were a permanent fit in the nose, with 12in lenses, or 4in if necessary. The reconnaissance pack was to consist of either three 70mm cameras (no such camera existed at the time) with a

A general-arrangement drawing of the de Havilland GOR.339 of January 1958.
Damien Burke

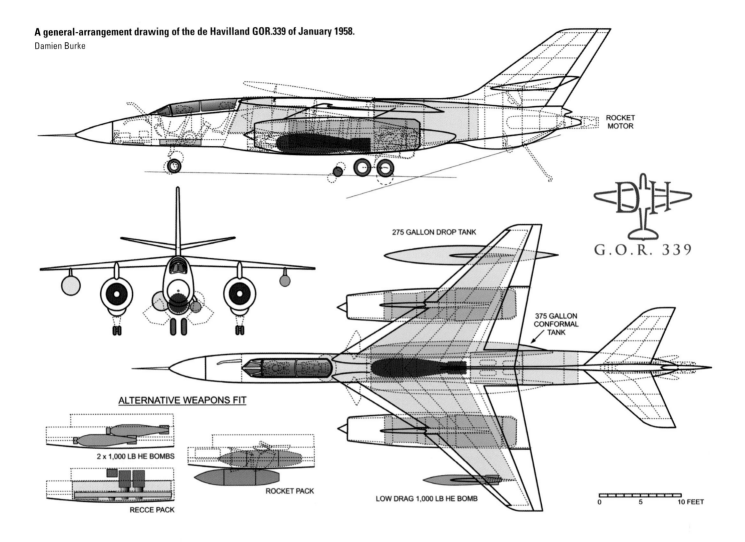

275 GALLON DROP TANK

375 GALLON CONFORMAL TANK

ROCKET MOTOR

G.O.R. 339

ALTERNATIVE WEAPONS FIT

2 x 1,000 LB HE BOMBS

RECCE PACK

ROCKET PACK

LOW DRAG 1,000 LB HE BOMB

0   5   10 FEET

pair of powerful photo flash units rather than a large array of photo flash cartridges, or two F.96 cameras with 24in or 6in lenses, or three F.117 cameras modified with 18in lenses. Also in the pack would be 12ft (3.65m)-long SLR with moving target indication, recording to photographic film for later processing at home base, and linescan (which the company thought could be used to give the navigator a downward view to verify that his photographic coverage was correct; slightly missing the point that linescan was a useful reconnaissance tool in its own right).

For in-flight refuelling, a retractable probe was to be mounted in the nose. De Havilland gave extremely sketchy and vague details of a buddy refuelling system, mentioning only that the bomb bay could accommodate a 200gal (910L) fuel tank, and the drogue would be located in the tail tunnel (which could otherwise accommodate the rocket used for short take-offs), with the hose reel within the rear fuselage.

This would have presumably required the permanent fitting of part of a large portion of the buddy pack equipment. Even assuming this weight penalty was acceptable for the non-buddy-refuelling roles, the company's claim that it would be possible to change to this role in 'minutes' was perhaps overly optimistic.

The ever-popular RB.142R was the engine of choice, mounted in pods under each wing at a distance from the fuselage that would hopefully avoid the need for any strengthening of the fuselage skin and structure to cope with acoustic fatigue. The single-engine-failure case was, remarkably, felt to be no worse than that of a single-engine aircraft, basically involving throttling down the other engine if the aircraft was not at a safe single-engine speed already. De Havilland was not sure of the final form of the intakes, but sketched a simple fixed intake with a conical centre-body and no auxiliary inlets or bypass. A convergent-divergent nozzle was considered

unnecessary, it being believed that the aircraft would spend most of its time at subsonic speeds.

The undercarriage comprised a twin-wheel nose unit, a four-wheel main unit in the central fuselage and small twin-wheel outriggers mounted on the undersides of the engine pods. All units retracted rearwards. A large ventral fairing under the tail housed a small tailwheel and a heavy-duty arrester hook. As with the Sea Vixen, the dive brakes were mounted under the fuselage near the wing leading edge to give minimum trim change on deployment, and doubled as access doors to some of the equipment.

Ferry range was 3,390nm (3,900 miles; 6,270km); however, combat radius was a problem. While the 600nm sortie was possible on internal fuel only, the 1,000nm sortie could be carried out only with external drop tanks. In terms of runway performance the design did rather better. With the aircraft loaded for the 600nm mission, the take-off run to 50ft (15m) would be just 660yd (600m); for the 1,000nm mission it would be 1,090yd (1,000m). For shorter strips the best answer would be the use of a portable catapult and arrester gear, and the company had investigated the use of such a system in co-operation with RAE Bedford. Alternatively, provision was made for a jettisonable liquid-fuel rocket of 15,000lb (6,800kg) thrust, mounted in the tail. Climb to height after take-off would be rapid, to say the least. De Havilland predicted that it would take less than 1.4min to ascend from 1,500ft to 50,000ft (460m to 15,000m), having accelerated to Mach 2 in the process. If the climb was continued the aircraft could be at 80,000ft (24,400m) less than a minute after that, though speed would have dropped, and above 60,000ft (18,000m) the aircraft would basically be ballistic. Such impressive performance was the company's answer to the danger of the nuclear LABS attack. Rather than diving back down to low level, the climb would simply be continued to get away from the nuclear detonation (further suggesting

that, coupled with launch delays, the aircraft could out-accelerate surface-to-air missiles!). De Havilland suggested a landing technique that entailed deploying the braking parachute cluster while on the approach. To overcome this extra drag the engines would need to use higher power settings, which would make available more thrust to be tapped off for flap blowing, and also put the engines into an rpm zone where rapid spooling-up would be easier (when going around after an aborted landing, for instance). The braking parachute's drag would also be available for the entire ground roll. Landing distance, with braking parachute, would be less than 800yd (75m).

While other companies put some real effort into the question of bombing accuracy, de Havilland's treatment was cursory, meriting just a few paragraphs, whereas details of land-based catapult gear occupied several pages. The proposed navigation system was dead reckoning using Doppler radar, with radar identification of a prominent feature near the target to correct the

dead-reckoning position before attack. Targets of opportunity could only be attacked visually, using the over-the-shoulder loft attack. When it came to terrain clearance the company was of the opinion that no suitable radar equipment was available or likely to be developed in time, and the best it could offer was flight 'near' the local safety height (1,000ft (300m) above the highest point in a grid square), based on Doppler radar contour height detection, with the pilot given height steering commands either by a director on a head-up display, or by the navigator talking to him! Radar ranging for rocket attacks was considered unnecessary, as it gave little or no improvement in accuracy compared with a well-practised pilot using a simple fixed sight. Anything other than a basic autopilot and stabilizer was considered unnecessary, and the bombing manoeuvres were to be hand-flown owing to 'safety problems' and the fact that pilots were quite proficient at this sort of flying anyway. The autopilot could handle flying to particular altitudes,

An artist's impression of the de Havilland GOR.339. In this view the aircraft is not burdened by the bulbous conformal fuel tanks it would have needed to meet the combat radius requirements in GOR.339; nor, for that matter, by the *Red Beard* store. BAE Systems via RAF Museum

headings, pitch angles, speeds, etc, and even land the aircraft automatically when linked to the ILS, but this was a world away from the fully automatic flight control systems of other submissions.

De Havilland suggested a couple of additional alternative versions, a naval version and a fighter. The aircraft's wing span was small enough to need no wing folding to fit on the deck lifts of current British carriers, though the nose and a substantial portion of the tail would need to fold. The normal AUW, even with folding mechanisms taken into account, was also within the deck limits. For catapulting at this weight, wind speed over the deck would need to be 24kt (28mph; 45km/h); combat radius would be 645nm (740 miles; 1,190km) with a five-minute combat allowance, and 920nm (1,060 miles; 1,700km) without. This could be increased to 1,205/1,425nm (1,385/1,640 miles; 2,230km/2,640km) if the aircraft was refuelled immediately after take-off. For the fighter role the aircraft's great thrust was its primary selling point. With a reduced fuel load it could go from the end of the runway to Mach 2 at 60,000ft (18,000m) in four minutes; excellent interception performance. A more economical climb and cruising speed could allow a long-range patrol of up to 20min to be undertaken 1,100 miles (1,770km) away from base (including combat time of 7.5min), or a four-hour patrol carried out much closer to home.

In structural terms, de Havilland made a bold claim that at the AUW the aircraft's structure would form just 24 per cent of the total weight. This was said to be due to the extremely simple and efficient structure, with none of the complications introduced by a fuselage engine installation. The wing's large central box would allow bending loads to be distributed evenly, with stiffness benefits from the engine pod arrangement. Aluminium-copper alloys would be the primary material used, with sandwich construction.

Referring to the MoS's requirement for company mergers, de Havilland suggested building the GOR.339 under the banner of the Airco consortium being set up to deal with 'the new BEA aeroplane' (the DH121, or Trident, as it became). This consortium included Hunting and Fairey, and de Havilland believed that the combination of its own Sea Vixen experience and Fairey's supersonic experience from the Fairey Delta project would be perfect for dealing with the RAF's tactical strike

bomber. (In the end Airco never got off the ground, and de Havilland became part of Hawker Siddeley in 1960).

English Electric with Short Brothers & Harland, Project 17

The early discussions on a Canberra replacement enabled English Electric to get a serious head start on meeting the requirement, and its advanced projects office began work on a design labelled Project 17 (or P.17 for short). The P.17 design effort was substantial, and English Electric looked at a large variety of configurations. Several layouts with podded engines had looked promising, giving the ability to readily change the chosen powerplant without having to redesign the fuselage, but there were difficulties in designing a suitably strong pylon/wing joint, and the effects of exhaust on the tailplane and noise fatigue on the rear fuselage were going to be serious. Finally, the control problems of losing an engine killed off these configurations. With a calculated minimum control speed

of 200kt (230mph; 370km/h) on a single engine, loss of an engine clearly meant the loss of the aircraft if it happened during landing or take-off.

Several canard layouts were also drawn up. With a rear-fuselage engine installation a very short intake could be used, the straightening effect of the airflow under the wing being used to advantage, along with the wing's bow wave. The design was easy to balance, but a big problem was introduced by the pitching moment from the large wing flaps; the longitudinal trim problem proved insurmountable, so the canard idea was abandoned. A high T-tail, as used on the new Lockheed F-104 Starfighter was tried, even though English Electric believed the F-104's layout 'looked all wrong'. In windtunnel tests it matched English Electric's predictions, performing poorly, even when the tailplane was mounted on a ridiculously high and impractical fin. A low-set tailplane, as on the P.1, seemed the only possible way to proceed.

The eventual P.17 design chosen bore some passing similarities to the final TSR2, having shoulder-mounted delta wings, a long fuselage with the crew seated in

This early P.17 windtunnel model with 'butterfly' twin tail surfaces looks more like an ancestor of the YF-23 than of TSR2! BAE Systems via Warton Heritage Group

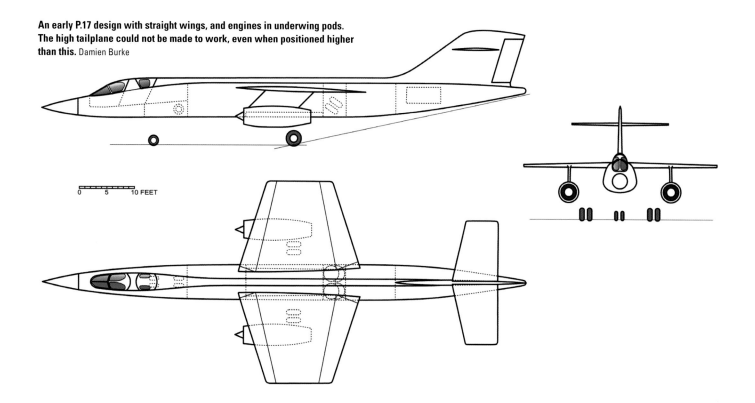

An early P.17 design with straight wings, and engines in underwing pods. The high tailplane could not be made to work, even when positioned higher than this. Damien Burke

0 5 10 FEET

tandem and engines buried side-by-side, a large vertical tail and a low-set tailplane. As previously mentioned, English Electric had issued report P/103, entitled *Possibilities of a multi-purpose Canberra replacement – P.17*, in early 1957. Outlining the company's ideas, it contained an earlier version of this P.17 design, differing mainly in the intake configuration (at that time a quarter circle set well back and underneath the wing). As time had passed and discussions with the Air Ministry and MoS firmed up the RAF's requirements, so English Electric had modified its work to match and hopefully exceed the requirements in some areas.

In December 1957 English Electric and Shorts invited Handel Davies of the MoS to Warton to have a final look at their work on Project 17 before official submission, with the aim of gaining some further insight into what the Ministry really wanted from GOR.339. It was an illuminating meeting, and some unexpected new information was exchanged, affecting English Electric's submission in several areas. Handel Davies had let English Electric know that the requirement to use existing engines was due to Treasury pressure, and that the Rolls-Royce RB.141 now looked very likely to be used for the new BEA airliner, so a military version, the RB.142, could now be considered. (An earlier meeting at the Ministry

had also revealed that the Ministry's definition of 'existing' was considerably more vague than English Electric's, but still excluded the RB.133 development that the company had wanted to use.) It was thought unlikely that the high-resolution SLR would be developed in time, so an existing less-capable unit, *Blue Shadow*, could be used as a stopgap. Davies felt that the P.17 was too heavy at 70,000lb (32,000kg), and asked if English Electric had considered a smaller aircraft. There was still some thought within the Ministry that GOR.339 could fulfil a naval requirement, ironically as a successor to the NA.39 when it became obsolete, and English Electric's suggestion that P.17 could at least use American Forrestal-class carriers as staging posts was welcomed. Other subjects included winged bombs, the STOL requirement and the Shorts 'Flying Base' lifting platform (described below). Finally the meeting moved on to the expected timescale for examination and selection of a winning design.

Davies was clearly a keen supporter of English Electric's work, and led the company to believe that if it won the GOR.339 competition (which Davies and English Electric both saw as pretty much a sure thing, given the amount of work it had put in), and subject to the three Ministries

(MoD, MoS and Air) agreeing, an order would be placed for the aircraft within a month or two, though there would be intense opposition from the Civil Service Administration to this short-cut in procedure. (One wonders why Davies ever suggested such a possible sequence of events in the face of the 'amalgamate or die' requirement introduced by his boss.) Should an OR have to be drawn up first(!), up to three firms would then be approached to build the resulting aircraft, but Davies wondered what would be the meaning of this in the face of the amount of work already done by English Electric. The meaning was, of course, that such co-operation was the whole point of GOR.339 from the MoS's viewpoint.

Having been thoroughly misled as to the purpose of the whole GOR.339 process, English Electric had put a great deal more work into the project than any other firm. In the expectation of the P.17 being ordered in due course, it had advanced well beyond theoretical work into detailed windtunnel testing and assembly of sample structures as part of the preliminary design stage, something a company would not normally do until in receipt of a design contract. The resulting GOR.339 submission was a massive three-volume brochure, explaining in great detail not only what English Electric was offering, but how it had got to that point, along with the various alternative solutions looked at, and mostly discarded, along the way. English Electric's aviation arm was already part of a larger business with varied interests, but, recognizing that this alone would not exempt it from the edict that the contract to build GOR.339 would only be awarded to a co-operative, they had already turned to Short Brothers & Harland, with whom they had already worked on Canberra production. Shorts was working on VTOL, and its SC.1 research aircraft was shortly to fly. It had also come up with an unusual proposal to add a VTOL capability to the P.17 by means of a lifting platform, and was responsible for the P.17's tailplane design, basing it on that of the P.1.

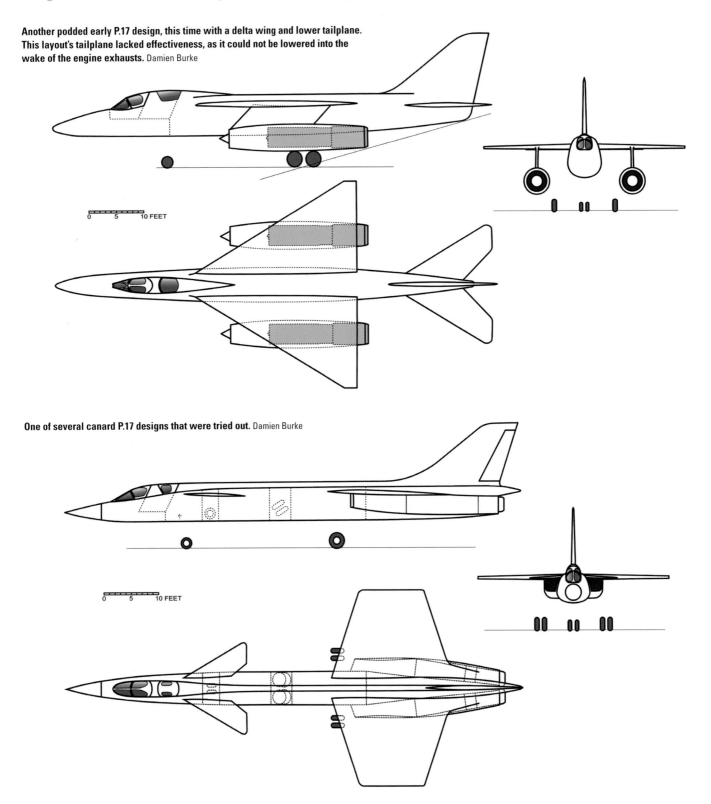

Another podded early P.17 design, this time with a delta wing and lower tailplane. This layout's tailplane lacked effectiveness, as it could not be lowered into the wake of the engine exhausts. Damien Burke

One of several canard P.17 designs that were tried out. Damien Burke

P.17A

This was really what the brochure was all about: English Electric's Canberra replacement, unadulterated by the more exotic wishes of the Air Staff, such as VTOL. The company's succession of possible designs had gradually evolved into a layout with a 60-degree swept delta wing and a low-set P.1B-style tailplane and conventional fin. It was in its fuselage that the design really parted company with the P.1B, this being much longer and having side intakes under the wing, leading to a side-by-side engine installation in the centre fuselage with a reheat installation in the rear fuselage. The long fuselage gave an increased tail-arm compared with the P.1B, which allowed the

A general-arrangement drawing of the English Electric P.17A of January 1958.
Damien Burke

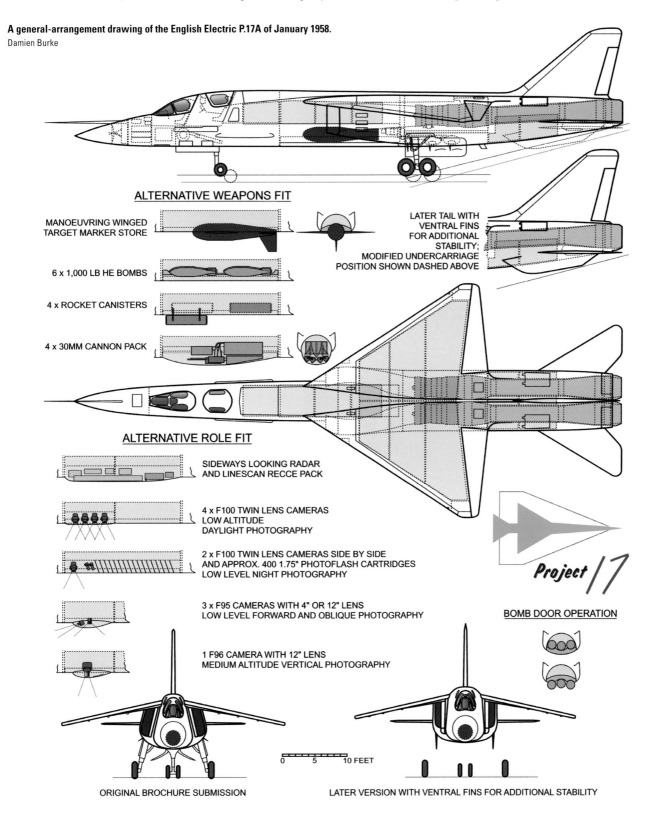

ALTERNATIVE WEAPONS FIT

MANOEUVRING WINGED TARGET MARKER STORE

6 x 1,000 LB HE BOMBS

4 x ROCKET CANISTERS

4 x 30MM CANNON PACK

LATER TAIL WITH VENTRAL FINS FOR ADDITIONAL STABILITY; MODIFIED UNDERCARRIAGE POSITION SHOWN DASHED ABOVE

ALTERNATIVE ROLE FIT

SIDEWAYS LOOKING RADAR AND LINESCAN RECCE PACK

4 x F100 TWIN LENS CAMERAS LOW ALTITUDE DAYLIGHT PHOTOGRAPHY

2 x F100 TWIN LENS CAMERAS SIDE BY SIDE AND APPROX. 400 1.75" PHOTOFLASH CARTRIDGES LOW LEVEL NIGHT PHOTOGRAPHY

3 x F95 CAMERAS WITH 4" OR 12" LENS LOW LEVEL FORWARD AND OBLIQUE PHOTOGRAPHY

1 F96 CAMERA WITH 12" LENS MEDIUM ALTITUDE VERTICAL PHOTOGRAPHY

Project 17

BOMB DOOR OPERATION

0   5   10 FEET

ORIGINAL BROCHURE SUBMISSION

LATER VERSION WITH VENTRAL FINS FOR ADDITIONAL STABILITY

RIGHT: **An artist's impression of the English Electric P.17A.** BAE Systems via Warton Heritage Group

RIGHT: **An artist's impression of the English Electric P.17A.** BAE Systems via
Warton Heritage Group

BELOW: **A breakdown of the P.17A's nose. Note the large equipment bay
with access from below and room enough for groundcrew to stand up
inside it, sheltered from the weather, while working.** BAE Systems via
Warton Heritage Group

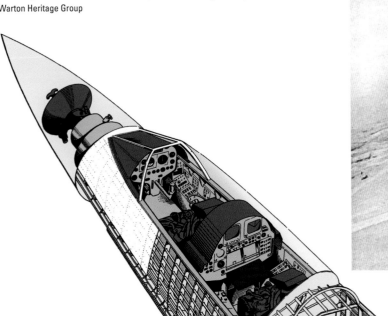

Leading particulars: English Electric P.17A

Length	84.5ft (25.75m)
Height	22ft (6.7m)
Wing span	35ft (10.67m)
Wing area	610sq ft (56.67sq m)
Wing aspect ratio	2
Wing anhedral	10°
Tailplane span	22.7ft (6.91m)
Tailplane area	185.8sq ft (17.26sq m)
Tailplane aspect ratio	2.77
Fin area	187sq ft (17.37sqm)
Fin aspect ratio	0.97
Engines	2 × 14,000lb (6,350kg) RB.142R or 15,460lb (7,020kg) Olympus 15R
Max speed	750kt (860mph; 1,380km/h)/Mach 2.0 at altitude
Empty weight	38,250lb (17,360kg)
AUW	73,400lb (33,300kg)

use of a full delta wing rather than the cut-out version employed on the P.1B. Full-span blown flaps assisted in providing acceptable take-off and landing performance, and roll

control was achieved by differential movement of the tailplane.

Crew comfort at low level was primarily provided by the relatively small, highly-loaded wing of low aspect ratio, attention being paid to structural design so that resonant frequencies did not coincide with human body resonance. The crew sat in tandem, giving a particularly good view for the pilot and a slightly more restricted one for the navigator, who was also supplied with a magnifying periscope that could be tilted and rotated for forward, downward and rearward viewing. Unlike just about

every other firm, English Electric had looked in detail at the requirements of safe escape at high speeds and altitudes. It outlined an ejection seat with automatic leg and arm restraints, and the possibility of using the instrument panel as a deflector plate to protect the occupant from wind blast in the early stages of ejection. Both seats would be mounted on 'vibration insulators' to improve comfort further.

The aircraft would be built of aluminium alloy (L73), which would give satisfactory fatigue characteristics though it would impose limitations on maximum speed (a steel tailplane had been investigated as part of an investigation of the requirements of flight beyond Mach 2). Stiffness was important to overcome aero-elastic problems, and the general concept was that the flying surfaces would have large skin panels unbroken by anything but the smallest of access panels. The fuselage would be a different matter, with so much equipment concentrated within it that access panels needed to be more numerous and larger. The engines, either Rolls-Royce RB.142Rs or Bristol Olympus 15Rs, would be accessed and installed through the roof of the main undercarriage bays. Shear panels would be installed after the engines were in place, completing the bottom skin of a rigid torsion box running throughout the fuselage length above the various cut-outs in the lower fuselage for undercarriage, equipment

Production components for the P.17A. The breakdown was designed for subcontracting, with major items to be manufactured at English Electric's own factories and smaller subassemblies able to be easily transported from elsewhere. BAE Systems via Warton Heritage Group

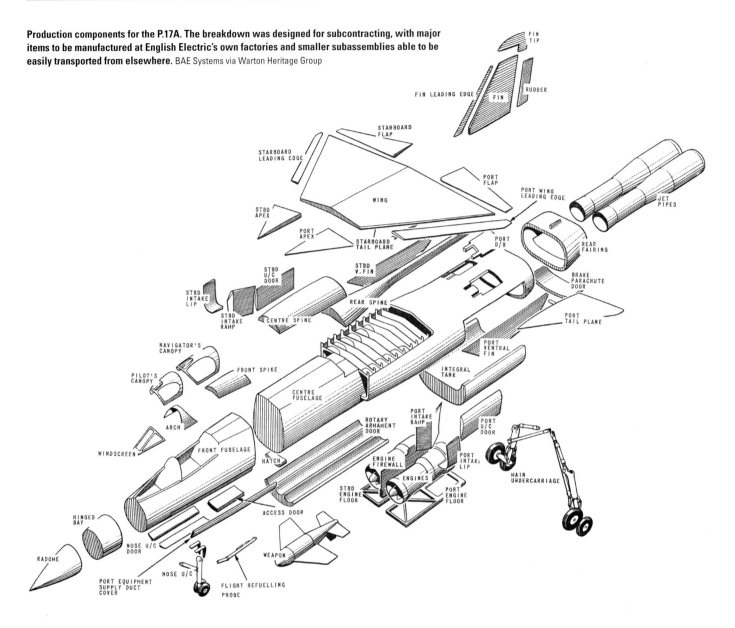

and weapon bays. The quarter-conical intakes originally envisaged gave rise to complicated boundary layer bleeds and were difficult to fair into the fuselage lines, so a simpler fixed vertical ramp intake was used instead, still positioned behind the wing leading edge.

Most of the fuel was contained in the fuselage, in six of eight tanks, with flow proportioning to ensure that each tank was emptied in proportion to its size to keep the c.g. stable. A retractable flight-refuelling probe was mounted in the port side of the nose below the cockpit floor. Unlike the P.1B, where cable ducts had needed to be tacked on to the fuselage exterior, provision was made for cable ducts within the fuselage layout, thus concentrating access to the cables and permitting easier electrical

maintenance. A conventional tricycle undercarriage was mounted on the fuselage, the twin-wheel nose gear retracting forwards and the tandem twin-wheel main units retracting to the rear. A braking parachute was to be fitted, though thrust reversers had also been investigated. The main gear bays doubled as engine access areas, and the nose gear was similarly used for equipment access, along with a large underside door aft of the nose gear bay that allowed ground crew 'stand-up' access to the main equipment bay while sheltering them (and the equipment) from the elements.

The bomb bay was one of the larger ones among the various GOR.339 submissions, able to accommodate the full load of six 1,000lb HE bombs, the Target Marker Bomb, twenty-four 3in Mk 5 rockets in

canisters or 370 2in rockets in canisters. The bomb door was of the rotating type, activated by a jack and lever at each end. Retractable locking pins along the door's length would keep the entire assembly stiff in the open or closed positions. The entire door assembly, to which the weapons would be attached, was to be removable so that arming could be carried out on the door, away from the aircraft. More traditional loading techniques could also be used. English Electric had investigated a more conventional bomb bay with hingeing doors each side, or doors that retracted into the bay, but these would make rearming difficult or make poor use of bomb bay space.

The P.17A could successfully meet the 1,000nm sortie requirement, including a high supersonic dash and the final 200nm

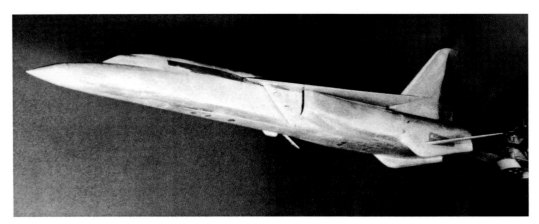

A windtunnel model showing the final P.17A configuration. Much of the P.17 windtunnel research was applied to the eventual TSR2 design.
BAE Systems

to and from the target being flown at sea level, and would weigh in at 73,400lb (33,320kg) for this sortie. Take-off distance would be 1,500yd (1,370m) (communications after the issue of the GOR had made it clear that the longest sortie did not have to be paired with the shortest take-off roll). To stay within the suggested 1,000yd (915m) take-off roll the take-off weight would need to be reduced to 66,000lb (29,930kg), in which case the aircraft still retained enough range to handle the 600nm sortie. Ferry range would be 3,000nm (3,450 miles; 5,550m) clean, or up to twice that with bomb bay and underwing tanks plus buddy flight refuelling en route.

Uniquely, English Electric's brochure actually outlined a complete sortie from start to finish, describing the crew's actions throughout. A typical attack sortie was to be flown almost entirely by the autopilot, only take-off and landing being down to the pilot. In effect, the navigator would be doing more 'flying' than the pilot, by entering fix points on the navigation system to ensure the aircraft was on track and allowing the autopilot to correct its course. Only if the pilot saw something of concern, such as unexpected defences or obvious errors in line-up on the final run-in to the target, would he take control and fly the aircraft manually. Pull-up into the LABS manoeuvre, bomb release and recovery to low level would all be a job for the autopilot. Non-nuclear attacks would need more crew input, with rocket and bomb attacks all requiring visual sighting. Bombing could be accomplished either by blind bombing from medium altitude (very Second World War) or via an over-the-shoulder loft attack (overflying the target, seeing it through the periscope and beginning a programmed climb into a loop to throw the bombs back towards the target).

Directional stability at high speeds and high angles of attack had proved to be a problem with many supersonic designs, and at the time the brochure was submitted English Electric was in the middle of dealing with this on the P.17A. While most of the drawings in the brochure showed a clear rear fuselage, a few showed ventral fins, which contributed to yaw stability at high incidences and Mach numbers. With a low-mounted tailplane similar to that of the P.1, the tailplane root fairing could be usefully combined with the ventral fin mounts, and two small ventral fins were preferable to a single larger ventral fin for ground clearance. As it was, the undercarriage would have to be made a little longer than ideal, to allow sufficient ground clearance if the fins were to be required.

As English Electric had put such a lot of effort into the P.17A already (over 100,000 man-hours) it believed it was virtually at the end of the project stage and could get the first prototype aircraft into the air by the end of 1961, achieving CA release by September 1963.

P.17B STOL variant

The second volume of the brochure moved on to alternative solutions, and as English Electric had been asked to consider a smaller airframe, some work was carried out in this direction. English Electric considered that the only real way to produce a smaller and lighter aircraft would be to go with a single-engine design, but was unwilling to carry out further work on such a type, citing the safety case of engine failure on a supersonic design (not famed for gliding ability). The other alternative was to relax the requirements. Shrinking the airframe was not a straightforward process: the cockpit,

Leading particulars: English Electric P.17B	
Length	86.25ft (26.29m)
Height	23.5ft (7.16m)
Wing span	35ft (10.67m)
Wing area	610sq ft (56.67sq m)
Wing aspect ratio	2
Wing anhedral	10°
Tailplane span	22.7ft (6.91m)
Tailplane area	185.8sq ft (17.26sq m)
Tailplane aspect ratio	2.77
Fin area	187sq ft (17.37sq m)
Fin aspect ratio	0.97
Engines	2 × RB.133R & 3 × 6,300lb (2,860kg) RB.108
Max speed	750kt (860mph; 1,390km/h)/Mach 2.0 at altitude
Empty weight	38,800lb (17,600kg)
AUW	72,130lb (32,740kg)

bomb bay, engines and so on could not be reduced in size. Equipment density was difficult to change also, and a smaller fuselage still had to have enough room for all of these items. Reducing the P.17A to a 50,000lb (23,000kg)-class airframe was impossible, as the only suitable engine would have been the proposed scaled-down version of the Rolls-Royce RB.141, which had been cancelled (though the RB.141 itself was still continuing). Even getting down to 60,000lb (23,000kg) would have needed something like a developed Avon, with fuel consumption reducing combat radius significantly as well as reducing take-off performance. It seemed that the only engine that would be available and suitable would be the Gyron Junior, as used in the NA.39, which would mean a 50 per cent reduction in the combat radius. Correcting the reduced take-off performance in all cases was possible only with the addition of three 6,300lb (2,860kg)-thrust RB.108 lift

A general-arrangement drawing of the English Electric P.17B.
Damien Burke

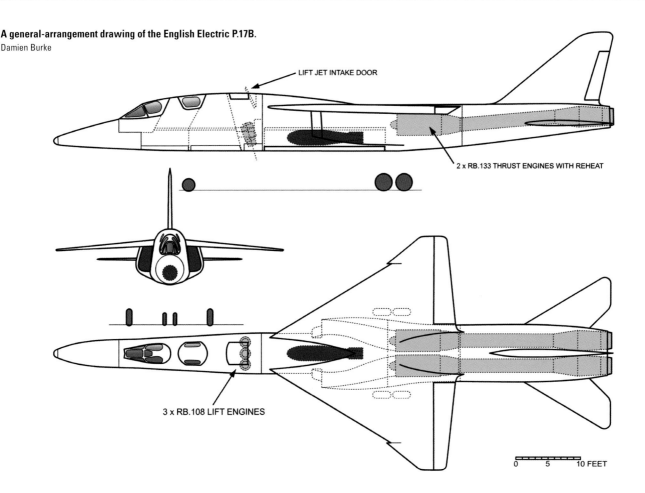

LIFT JET INTAKE DOOR

2 x RB.133 THRUST ENGINES WITH REHEAT

3 x RB.108 LIFT ENGINES

0   5   10 FEET

engines forward of the c.g., and this brought the weight back up to P.17A levels despite the resulting airframe being smaller.

It did, however, raise the interesting possibility of a variant of the P.17 that, while not being reduced in size, could save some time and cost by using an existing less-powerful engine, and use lift-jets to compensate for the losses in take-off performance. This, then, was the P.17B, dimensionally similar to the P.17A but using RB.133R engines along with RB.108 lift jets. Rough calculations showed that it would have a 15 per cent reduction in range, but would benefit from a 25 per cent reduction in take-off roll.

P.17C VTOL variant

English Electric was aware that its P.17A design on its own did not really address the aspect of the GOR that asked for the minimizing of permanent base requirements and operation from dispersed sites, with investigation of unconventional means of improving take-off and landing performance. The most extreme interpretation of

this was VTOL, and the P.17C was the result of incorporating this within an enlarged version of the P.17A airframe, ensuring that no take-off roll would ever exceed 1,650yd (1,500m) while giving complete VTOL capability for lighter loads or shorter sorties. No fewer than twenty-eight RB.108 lift engines were incorporated in two bays within the fuselage, one between the cockpit and wing, and the other between the wing and tailplane. This took up a huge amount of space that was thus no longer available for fuel, so the airframe had to be enlarged to compensate. Unlike the P.17A, the two main thrust engines were mounted ahead of the c.g., with a long jet pipe leading to the reheat units and a shorter pipe leading directly down. A deflector would direct the engine's thrust down either of these pipes (an all-or-nothing affair; not variable) so that the main engines could be used during a vertical take-off. The lift jets would have a small range of tilt so that they could be used to aid transition between vertical and horizontal flight. Bleed air from the engines would power puffer jets at each end of the fuselage and the wingtips, and the

Leading Particulars: English Electric P.17C	
Length	101ft (30.78m)
Height	25.75ft (7.85m)
Wing span	41.3ft (12.59m)
Wing area	850sq ft (78.97sq m)
Wing aspect ratio	2.01
Wing anhedral	10 degrees
Tailplane span	26ft (7.92m)
Tailplane area	158sq ft (14.68sq m)
Tailplane aspect ratio	2.77
Fin area	187sq ft (17.37sq m)
Fin aspect ratio	0.97
Engines	2 × 14,000lb (6,350kg) RB.142R & 28 × 6,300lb (2,860kg) RB.108
Max speed	Mach 1.7 at 30,000ft (9,000m)
Empty weight	Not stated
AUW	112,900lb (51,250kg)

wing would have no control surfaces whatsoever. Roll and pitch control would be exclusively via the tailplane, with the puffer jets coming into use at slow speeds.

The added weight and loss of fuel capacity had a crippling effect. Vertical take-off

A general-arrangement drawing of the English Electric P.17C.
Damien Burke

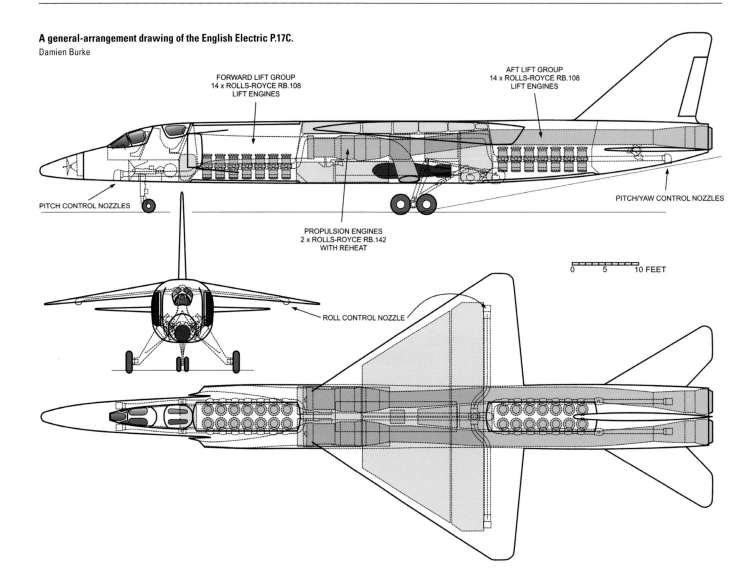

FORWARD LIFT GROUP
14 x ROLLS-ROYCE RB.108
LIFT ENGINES

AFT LIFT GROUP
14 x ROLLS-ROYCE RB.108
LIFT ENGINES

PITCH CONTROL NOZZLES

PITCH/YAW CONTROL NOZZLES

PROPULSION ENGINES
2 x ROLLS-ROYCE RB.142
WITH REHEAT

0 5 10 FEET

ROLL CONTROL NOZZLE

would only be available up to an overall weight of 83,300lb (37,800kg). Subsonic combat radius would be a mere 390nm (450 miles; 720km) in these cases (the brochure neglecting to mention that, in tropical conditions, VTOL would only be possible with no weapons and a nearly zero fuel load). The 600nm sortie could only be carried out with a short take-off roll, rather than a vertical take-off. To manage the 1,000nm sortie the aircraft would have to be overloaded and use a thick concrete runway to perform a normal rolling (albeit fairly short) take-off. With the aircraft weighing in at 112,900lb (51,250kg) for that sortie, it was clear that this would be a self-defeating design even if it did not suffer development problems, being unable to satisfy the most basic range requirements of the GOR and also being unable to operate from a dispersed site for longer missions.

P.17D Lifting Platform

Both the P.17B and P.17C were really a less-than-subtle method of demonstrating that the extreme STOL/VTOL concept would merely produce an aircraft burdened by huge limitations and saddled with developmental problems from birth. They made an alternative solution look a lot more attractive than would otherwise be the case. That alternative was the Shorts 'lifting platform'.

The Shorts PD.17 (P.17D in English Electric parlance) was, to modern eyes at least, a rather bizarre and impractical proposal to provide VTOL performance and operational support at dispersed sites by separating the VTOL component into a separate aircraft. (The idea bore some similarity to the Short-Mayo composite seaplane and flying-boat of 1937.) The concept had been dreamed up by Dr Alan Griffith

Leading particulars: Shorts PD.17	
Length	77ft (23.47m)
Height (normal)	11.6ft (3.53m)
Wing span	47ft (14.32m)
Wing area	1,838sq ft (170.75sq m)
Wing aspect ratio	1.2
Fin area (each)	150sq ft (13.93sq m)
Fin aspect ratio	0.48
Engines	56 × 2,500lb (1,135kg) RB.108
Empty weight (P.17A carrier version)	46,550lb (21,130kg)
AUW (with P.17A at overload weight)	129,300lb (58,690kg)
AUW (freighter version, 21,000kg (9,525kg) load)	110,000lb (49,930kg)

of Rolls-Royce, and Shorts adapted and developed it to propose an operational vehicle for military use. Shorts described

A general-arrangement drawing of the Shorts PD.17 Lifting Platform.
Damien Burke

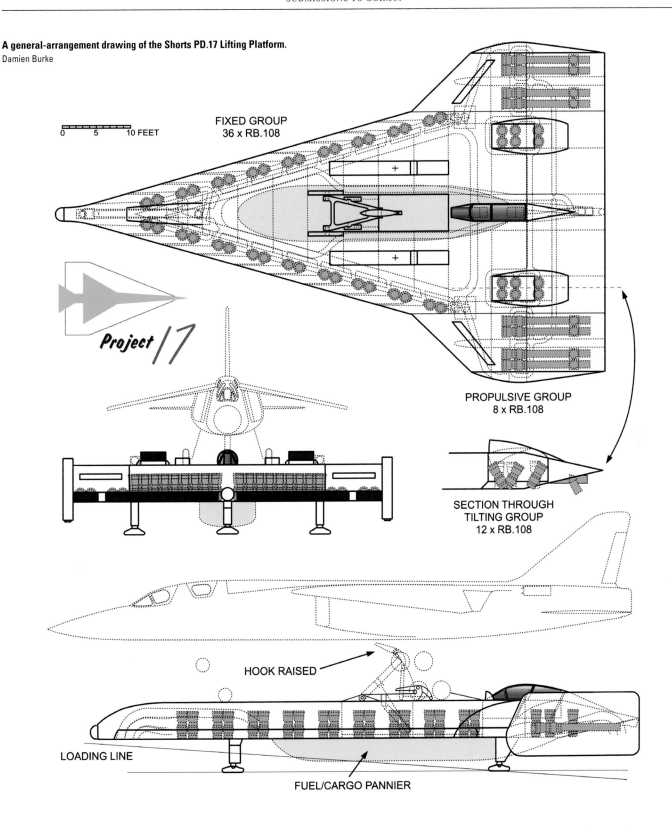

0   5   10 FEET

FIXED GROUP
36 x RB.108

Project 17

PROPULSIVE GROUP
8 x RB.108

SECTION THROUGH
TILTING GROUP
12 x RB.108

HOOK RAISED

LOADING LINE

FUEL/CARGO PANNIER

this as a 'direct extrapolation of SC.1 experience'. The platform itself was a cropped delta flying wing with two endplate fins and a fixed tricycle undercarriage terminating in large flat plates rather than wheels, to enable operation from a variety of surfaces.

The huge array of fifty-six lift jet engines was split into three groups. The fixed group was thirty-six strong and exhausted vertically downwards; the tilting group comprised twelve engines, exhausting downwards but capable of being tilted ±30

degrees, and the final propulsive group consisted of eight engines exhausting aft for forward thrust; these could be tilted down by up to 70 degrees. English Electric/Shorts admitted that such a large number of engines was an unattractive concept, and

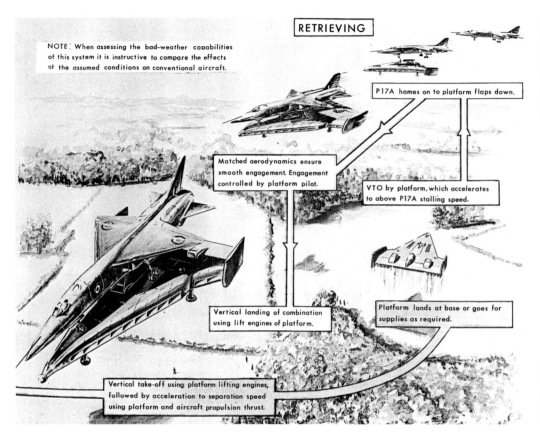

RETRIEVING

NOTE: When assessing the bad-weather capabilities of this system it is instructive to compare the effects of the assumed conditions on conventional aircraft.

P17A homes on to platform flaps down.

Matched aerodynamics ensure smooth engagement. Engagement controlled by platform pilot.

VTO by platform, which accelerates to above P17A stalling speed.

Vertical landing of combination using lift engines of platform.

Platform lands at base or goes for supplies as required.

Vertical take-off using platform lifting engines, followed by acceleration to separation speed using platform and aircraft propulsion thrust.

LEFT: **The retrieval sequence. With IR seekers looking for a bright IR beacon on the underside of the P.17A, the mid-air docking would have been semi-automatic, with manual control only for initial rendezvous and final link-up.** BAE Systems via Warton Heritage Group

BELOW: **With the P.17D, every cargo ship with a sufficiently large area of clear deck could be an aircraft carrier.** BAE Systems via Warton Heritage Group

the brochure also suggested various combinations of much larger and more powerful engines that could be used to reduce the number required drastically. However, there would still need to be a generous number so that an engine failure, or failure of a small number, would not result in loss of control or loss of the ability to land at a safe descent rate.

The P.17A would start each mission parked on top of the P.17D, with a hydraulically powered hook on the P.17D engaging an attachment point on the P.17A. The P.17D would lift off vertically using the fixed engine group, and accelerate to a suitable forward speed using the propulsive group with assistance from the tilting group during the transition from vertical to forward flight, at which point the fixed and tilting groups could be shut down. Once a suitable flying speed was reached the P.17A would be released and fly off on its own to carry out its sortie. The P.17A could then either land in the conventional manner on a normal runway, or rendezvous with the P.17D in mid-air, match speeds and dock back on the platform. The platform would then slow down, the fixed and tilting groups would be restarted, and the combination would transition to the hover and land

vertically. It was claimed that the platform would be relatively cheap and simple to produce, as it had no need of complex navigation systems, no attack system and no weapons.

The leading edge of the P.17D's wing would contain a long slit-type intake. Most of the length of this intake would feed the fixed engine group via a plenum chamber, also fed by spring-loaded doors in the upper surface of the wing. The intake section

nearest the wingtip/fins would direct air to the propulsive group. The tilting group would be fed by spring-loaded doors and retractable ram scoops on the wing's upper surface. Attitude control in the hover would be effected by means of puffer jets using bleed air from the entire engine complement (as on the SC.1), and puffer jets would continue in use during conventional flight, though roll control would be augmented by spoilers on the upper wingtip surfaces.

Operation from dispersed sites introduced huge problems, in that all such sites needed to be supplied with fuel, weapons and support equipment. The lifting platform could double as a freighter and fuel tanker to keep these sites supplied, with an internal cargo bay in a central position and an underslung cargo pannier (which could contain fuel, ground equipment, weapons, etc) able to be delivered to dispersed sites (not just P.17A dispersals; supplies could be delivered to ground forces, too). As a tactical freighter it would able to carry a payload of up to 40,000lb (18,100kg) over a range of 300nm (345 miles; 555km) or up to 20,000lb (9,000kg) over 740nm (850 miles; 1,370km). Carrying a full 8,500gal (38,640L) of fuel, the P.17D could also act as an in-flight refuelling tanker and support P.17As during ferrying operations. One of the major problems of VTOL operation of such a platform was ground erosion. This was barely mentioned in the brochure, which limits remarks on the subject to the prospect of 'messy' ground operations and the need for mesh guards over intakes to stop ingestion of foreign objects.

That tricky rendezvous with the P.17A in mid-air had had some thought devoted to it, too. Ideally, the P.17A would be able to find the P.17D using its own FLR, or by homing on a UHF transmission from the platform, but if both of these were out of action the P.17D could take on the task using a small radar of its own. A rendezvous circuit would be flown at 2,000ft (6,000m) and 250kt (290mph/470km/h) until the two aircraft found each other, and then a recovery course would be flown at 200kt (230mph/370km/h). The P.17D's cockpit housed two crew, who had a good view both up and down (through windows in the floor in the latter case), and infra-red (IR) seeker heads on the wingtips (based on those of the *Blue Jay* missile) would be used to lock on to an IR lamp mounted on the P.17A's rear fuselage underside. Once the P.17A had taken up position ahead and above the platform, with undercarriage down, and an IR lock-on was in place, the platform's pilot would be in charge of the hooking-up procedure. The autopilot, linked to the IR seekers, could control engine thrust to make the platform climb and close the distance between it and the P.17A, with the platform's pilot manually controlling the last few feet of the engagement.

There would, of course, be plenty of occasions when a P.17D platform would need to be loaded with a P.17A on the ground; if

The P.17D lifting off (or perhaps landing) with a P.17A on board. The ground erosion problem from P.17D operations would have been considerable, and in this illustration the groundcrew with their support equipment have clearly retired to a safe distance!
BAE Systems via Warton Heritage Group

the P.17A had landed conventionally, for example. For this purpose there would be a winch to pull the P.17A up ramps on to the platform. The nose leg of the platform could be depressed, allowing the platform to 'kneel', and the ramp sections could be stored in the underslung pannier for transport. Ferry flights of the platform would rely on a basic navigation system similar to that of the P.1B, with a master reference gyro, UHF homer and radio altimeter. While the primary purpose of the platform was to allow tactical operation from dispersed sites on a European battlefield, it also opened up the possibilities of surprise attacks on an enemy unprepared to deal with a sudden attack from close range. On the day of such an attack, P.17As could be fuelled and depart from their normal bases, rendezvousing with P.17Ds which had been pre-positioned closer to the intended target. A final refuelling and rearming here would enable the P.17As to strike at a target much further away from home base

than would otherwise be the case, and either return to a platform rendezvous or go straight home.

The P.17D's real advantage was that it would leave English Electric free to develop the aircraft it really wanted, while being able to offer VTOL as a bolt-on solution at a later date. Shorts had high hopes for the lifting platform and foresaw the possible development of several versions, increasing its own utility and also that of any aircraft linked to it. The most basic development would be the addition of ducted fans to give additional ferry range, but you could then also delete the undercarriage and other items associated with low-speed flight from the strike aircraft, making it entirely dependent on the platform but with a consequent increase in range and performance. A platform developed for higher launching speeds could even act as a booster to launch a ramjet aircraft or missile. (Indeed, a year later Rolls-Royce enquired about just such a use to transport *Blue Streak* missiles to dispersed sites, rather than housing them in underground silos.)

While the P.17D was a simpler aircraft than the P.17A, similar design effort would be needed due to its larger size and the additional investigations required into stability and control in the hover and transition to/from forward flight (which were already under way with the SC.1 programme). By the time of brochure submission there had not been an opportunity to carry out windtunnel tests of a combined P.17A & D model, but these were going to be given high priority. English Electric suggested that an additional year might be necessary compared with P.17A development, leading to a first flight of the platform by the end of 1962, the first composite P.17A/P.17D flight by the end of 1963 and CA release for the combination in mid-1965. If the P.17A was not ready in time, early testing could be carried out using a P.1B as the test vehicle, which would have the bonus of demonstrating if it was feasible to marry the lifting platform to P.1B operations and thereby achieve operational improvements in P.1B range and take-off distance.

P.17E

This was an abortive attempt to design a version of the P.17C fully capable of meeting all of the load and range requirements in GOR.339 while needing no conventional runway at all, operating in a completely VTOL manner. It fell foul of the vicious circle of ever-increasing structure and fuel weight needed. For a combat radius of 400nm (460 miles; 740km) the AUW would be 83,500lb (37,900kg); for 500nm (575 miles; 925km) it jumped to an impractical 182,000lb (82,600kg), and beyond that the figures soon converged on infinity.

P.17F / P.24A

After the initial brochure submission, English Electric and Shorts continued to play with the lifting-platform idea, and the P.17F was the first result, this being a fan version to be used as a military freighter with a higher payload of 35,000–45,000lb (15,875–20,400kg). This could be developed further by the removal of the launching and retrieving roles and associated equipment to create a larger civil VTOL platform, the P.24A. These are beyond the scope of this volume.

P.22

English Electric had also originally proposed a fighter variant of the P.17A, the P.22, on the basis that the P.17A's high thrust-to-weight ratio, large fuel capacity, moderate wing loading and aerodynamic docility made it readily convertible to the long-range interceptor role. The nose had space for a developed AI radar, and the weapons bay was large enough to carry five canisters of unguided 2in rockets (370 rockets in all) or a pair of air-to-air missiles (*Blue Jay*, later known as Firestreak, or the American nuclear-tipped Genie, then under investigation for possible use on the P.1B). All of these weapons would be housed internally, and the rotating bay door would allow the use of a trapeze to lower the missile or rocket canister out of the bay before firing. The aircraft would not have been a great dogfighter, but it could have made a valuable contribution to long-range defence against Soviet bomber formations. The continuing fallout from Sandys' White Paper, however, made sure that English Electric killed off the P.22 itself before it got the company into trouble.

Variable sweep

Volume 3 of the English Electric/Shorts submission included a chapter on the more novel designs that had been studied. The first was a variable-sweep wing. After trials of various planforms a wing that, when fully swept, was similar to that of the P.1, was felt to the most practical. It pivoted on a translating pivot point in the fuselage, thus dealing with the shift in aerodynamic centre as the sweep angle changed. High loads on the centre section in the unswept position would require a complex and weighty mechanism, with a variety of difficult problems to solve for which English Electric could find no existing helpful research material. Carrying stores under the wing and fuel within it was felt to be impractical, and the provision of electrical and hydraulic services to the wings would be difficult. The wing would have to be thicker, too, to provide sufficient lift in the landing configuration, though it could be smaller in area than the existing P.17 delta planform, with resultant higher wing loading; fine for low level, but an embarrassment for high-altitude performance. Overall, English Electric could see only small possible advantages and a slew of disadvantages.

Flexibly mounted wing

As a method of gust alleviation to improve crew comfort, a proposal was made to mount the wing on large dampers within the fuselage, with a pivot point from the front spar to a reinforced frame in the fuselage. This introduced large structural, weight and drag disadvantages, as the wing could no longer carry any fuselage loads and would be mounted higher than normal, and a large variable cowling would be required to fair it in to the fuselage at the rear. The slight advantages of lower airframe and crew fatigue were insufficient to justify proceeding with this idea.

Variable-incidence wing

Raising the wing leading edge by jacks and pivoting by the rear spar was seen as a way to improve the take-off lift coefficient and improve STOL performance. However, with an additional angle of incidence of 10 degrees being needed for a worthwhile improvement, this would have resulted in the front of the wing being raised 4ft (1.2m) above the fuselage. A similar scheme had been used on the Vought F-8 Crusader, but on a much smaller scale, and it was felt that it would be impractical on the P.17. Consquently English Electric, unlike de Havilland, soon abandoned this idea.

P.17Z clipped wing and narrow delta

Assuming the P.17D lifting platform was developed, and the strike aircraft could be acceptable if made entirely reliant on the platform, two P.17 variants were proposed, one a fairly careful and obvious progression and the other a much more extreme example of what could be possible. With the platform taking the aircraft up to 250kt (290mph; 460km/h) before parting company, a smaller wing and lower-thrust engines would be possible. The first suggestion was a variant of the P.17A with a smaller wing (reduced from 610sq ft to 415sq ft (38.5sq m) and span down to 28.8ft (8.78sq m)), the undercarriage deleted and the space used for fuel (thus offsetting the loss of wing fuel space), along with RB.133 engines (whose lower thrust would no longer matter as there was no take-off case to deal with). The second, much more radical suggestion bore no relation to the other P.17 designs

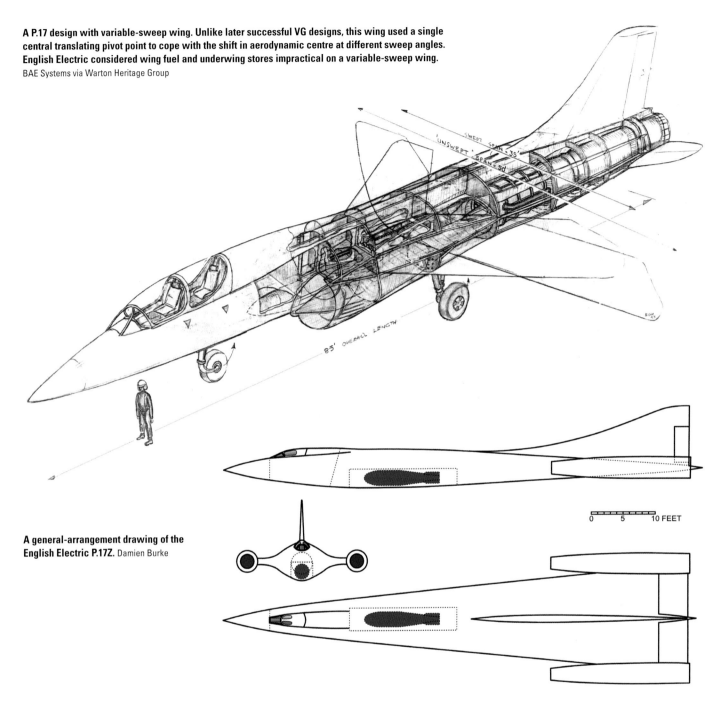

A P.17 design with variable-sweep wing. Unlike later successful VG designs, this wing used a single central translating pivot point to cope with the shift in aerodynamic centre at different sweep angles. English Electric considered wing fuel and underwing stores impractical on a variable-sweep wing.
BAE Systems via Warton Heritage Group

A general-arrangement drawing of the English Electric P.17Z. Damien Burke

whatsoever, and was instead based on a narrow delta shape that had originated from RAE theoretical work, optimized entirely for supersonic cruise at low level. This was very much 'finger in the air' thinking, with very little work on the shape having been carried out and much research still needed.

Other novel layouts

Some idea of the broad scope of English Electric's brochure will now have been gained; yet there was more! A variety of much less conventional overall airframe layouts was combined with various engine configurations to see if the benefits of the P.17B and P.17C could possibly be combined with the performance of the P.17A. These included a canard layout with two podded Olympus engines embedded in the wings and two Orpheus lift engines in the fuselage; another canard with two Olympus 21Rs in the fuselage fed from a 'shark-mouth' ventral intake and two Orpheus lift engines mounted in knife-edge pods under a delta wing; a similar canard delta but with a dorsal intake feeding tilting Olympus 14 engines in the fuselage, and large underwing pods for Orpheus engines with simple aft/downward thrust vectoring; and a twin-boom layout with a modified delta wing, Olympus 21Rs in the booms and Orpheus lifting engines in the central fuselage pod. The least bizarre layout was a fairly minimal variation on the P.17A with twin fins and extra intakes on the fuselage sides behind the wing leading to the Orpheus 12R engines; the forward-mounted intakes led to Orpheus lift engines which had a thrust-vectoring plate to allow them to thrust either to the rear or vertically downwards. Each variation showed some advantages for particular types of operation, if only minimal ones, but the effort and risk involved in developing each of these configurations was felt to be excessive.

English Electric also looked briefly at other possibilities of off-airfield operation, including tail-sitting VTOL and 'zero-length launchers' (i.e. being mounted on a road vehicle and fired into the air by powerful rockets), but concluded that both ideas were impossibly handicapped by the sheer size of the aircraft. Road transport, even with various bits folded or dismantled, would introduce strict route limitations because of the size of the trailer, and that was even before the problems of developing a launcher came into it. A recent mishap involving one of the US Army's huge atomic cannon, which had ended up firmly embedded in a 12ft (3.6m)-deep ditch while being transported from one site to another in West Germany, also illustrated the hazards that could be expected in transporting large and heavy loads over even well-mapped territory (the damage to a TSR2 airframe on delivery to Boscombe Down seven years later would provide an ironic additional demonstration of the risks).

Finally, the possibility of ducted-fan lift was examined. Fans had better lifting efficiency but introduced great structural difficulties. The major problem was the need to pass a large volume of air through an area of the aircraft that had to be fairly structurally dense to cope with the loads experienced, particularly during low-level operations. This would naturally result in a larger aircraft, which would be heavier, and thus ran the risk of cancelling out the lifting gains. The optimum layout that English Electric could come up with was a canard design with RB.142Rs mounted in the fuselage, driving a battery of eight ducted fans exhausting downwards. In normal flight, no penalty (other than the added weight) would be incurred; for STOL operations intake louvres would be opened on the upper fuselage and part of the engine thrust directed to drive the fans. Further louvres underneath would open to allow the relatively low-speed fan exhaust out, with the louvres acting as thrust deflectors to enable transition from high to low speeds and vice versa. In this configuration, the two engines, producing 28,000lb (13,000kg) of thrust, would be augmented

by the eight fans and produce a 70,000lb (32,000kg) vertical thrust component for a weight penalty of around 5,000lb (2,300kg). However, the large volume required by the fan bay would result in an aircraft significantly larger than the P.17A, and, with no quantitative data available on fan efficiency, English Electric left this as an academic exercise.

English Electric followed up its weighty tome on the P.17 and its variants with a summary document that attempted to focus Ministry minds on the urgency of the requirement and the need for minimum delay in making a decision. The company hammered home the point that the P.17 airframe had already entered the detail design stage, was firmly based on their experience with the Canberra and P.1 (much more the latter, of course), and that it was the only aircraft that could meet the 1964 in-service deadline.

Fairey – Project 75 Tactical Strike/Reconnaissance Aircraft

Fairey's submission to GOR.339 was a basically delta-wing aircraft with engines in pods hung under the wings. Unusually, though, it chose a canard layout and side-by-side seating for the crew, very much in the style of the Second World War de Havilland Mosquito. In its brochure Fairey first addressed the whole question of VTOL, and concluded that it would simply result in an excessively heavy aircraft carting around a load of structure and engine weight that would be of no use during the sortie, along with the fuel reserve needed for a VTOL landing. Fairey was striving for the reverse of this; the smallest, lightest aircraft possible for the task. Ideally this

Leading Particulars: Fairey Project 75	
Length	100.75ft (30.71m)
Height	17.75ft (5.41m)
Wing span	34.66ft (10.56m)
Wing area	600sq ft (55.74sq m)
Wing aspect ratio	2
Foreplane area	228sq ft (21.18sq m)
Fin area	183sq ft (17.00sq m)
Engines	2 × RB.142R
Max speed	750kt (860mph; 1,390km/h), Mach 2.2 @ 36,000ft (11,000m)
Empty weight	32,910lb (14,940kg)
Max AUW	65,900lb (29,910kg)

would be a tailless delta, but the problems of meeting the take-off and landing-roll requirements meant that a conventional tail would be required. To make room for the required fuel and bomb load, the fuselage would be unable to hold the engines, so these would be mounted in underwing pods. This then brought up the problem that a low-set tailplane, the only viable location for transonic operation, would be bathed in jet wash. The solution was to choose a canard configuration, though it was acknowledged that this risked some unwanted interaction between the foreplane and the engine intakes.

The navigation system was to vary with the phase of the flight; inertial navigation and Doppler for the high-level part of the sortie, inertial only for the descent to low level, and then switching to X-band 'side viewing radar' at low level. The FLR would be a development of Ferranti's AI.23 set, and would handle terrain clearance and target identification. The resulting large nose radome required a wide fuselage, which as a bonus gave enough room for side-by-side crew seating. The pilot would sit further forward, however, so that his view would not be obscured to one side and the navigator would have more room for his equipment. An offset seating position benefited the pilot, as the high angle of incidence on approach to landing would result in the nose obscuring his view of the runway if he was seated centrally. By being offset to the side by several feet a much-improved view was possible. The navigator's main instrument panel was ahead of him, with a further panel to his left, blocking his direct view in that direction. The view downwards and sideways to aid photographic reconnaissance was through a smaller window inset in the starboard cockpit side. The navigator's seat could be motored down a foot to give him a better angle of view through this window. Contrail detection was by the Mk 1 eyeball, a rear-view mirror enabling the pilot to see the wingtips, the most likely source of contrails.

Below the cockpit were the SLR aerials, and aft of the cockpits and forward of the bomb bay was a large equipment bay. The bomb bay would have a rotating bomb beam, as Fairey believed traditional doors would introduce unacceptable buffet in transonic flight. A side door would open briefly during the rotation period (a clever arrangement of jacks linking both the door and beam to eliminate the use of complex sequencing valves and microswitches),

A general-arrangement drawing of the Fairey Project 75 of January 1958.
Damien Burke

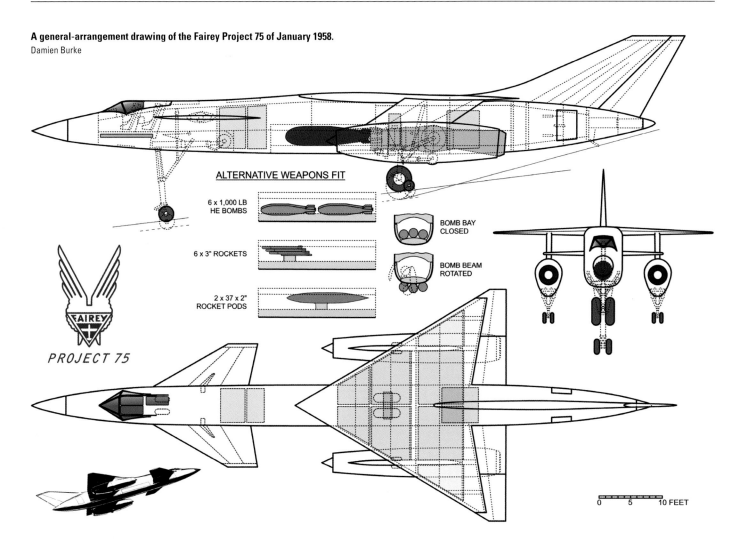

ALTERNATIVE WEAPONS FIT

6 x 1,000 LB
HE BOMBS

6 x 3" ROCKETS

2 x 37 x 2"
ROCKET PODS

BOMB BAY
CLOSED

BOMB BEAM
ROTATED

FAIREY

PROJECT 75

0   5   10 FEET

An artist's impression of Project 75. BAE Systems via RAF Museum

allowing the larger stores to clear the side of the bay, and close again once the beam was fully rotated and the stores were hanging in the air stream. The bay had room enough for all of the stores mentioned in the GOR, including six 1,000lb HE bombs. With the bay located just ahead of the c.g.,

stores release would cause a c.g. shift that would need to be trimmed out by canard movement. To mount a reconnaissance pack in the bay, the bomb beam and both opening and fixed side doors would be removed first. The reconnaissance pack would consist of various cameras, sideways-

looking reconnaissance radar with a moving target indicator, and linescan recording and transmission equipment. A buddy flight-refuelling pack was also an option.

A subsidiary equipment bay was located aft of the bomb bay, with access through the main undercarriage bay roof (similarly, the front equipment bay was reached via the nose undercarriage bay). Dive brakes were mounted on the rear-fuselage sides, extending outwards up to 90 degrees. A braking parachute container was mounted in the extreme tip of the rear fuselage, too, housing three 10ft (3m)-diameter parachutes that would be deployed in a cluster. Flexible bag-type fuel tanks were also distributed about the centre portion of the fuselage, with integral tanks within the wing. For self-protection, RWRs could be mounted in the rear fuselage around the base of the fin. Radar-absorbing material would be used within the cockpit, behind the nose radome and in the intakes; possibly in the jet exhausts as well.

The undercarriage comprised tandem twin-wheel nose and main-gear bogies retracting rearwards into the fuselage, with outrigger wheels extending from the engine pods and also retracting to the rear. The aircraft's 'sit' on the ground was very nose-high to aid unstick on take-off, resulting in a huge and ungainly looking nose gear leg. Nose-wheel steering was aided by differential braking on the outrigger wheels. The outrigger units were not handed, cutting down on the amount of spares backing needed.

For the wing, Fairey stuck with the 60-degree swept delta of the Fairey Delta 2, and chose not to go with any form of leading- or trailing-edge flap blowing, citing expense and maintenance difficulties. The wings had conventional flaps and ailerons, and the canard foreplanes were all-moving. The inner wing housed integral fuel tanks, with outer integral tanks holding water-methanol used to restore engine thrust in hot-and-high conditions. The fuel system itself was fully automatic and self-balancing. In-flight refuelling was catered for via a retractable probe mounted ahead of the pilot on the port side of the nose. The chosen engines were RB.142Rs, in common with many other submissions, though provision was also made to take the Olympus 15R. Access to engine controls was via a removable engine pylon leading edge, and the front and rear fairings of the engine nacelle could be removed to enable withdrawal of the engine or its associated reheat unit.

The Project 75 pilot's cockpit; the offset seating improved the pilot's view during the approach to land. BAE Systems via RAF Museum

The Project 75 navigator's cockpit. The navigator had various blinds he could pull across his outside view to allow a clearer view of his various radar scopes and instruments, and a small window on the right provided some downward view.
BAE Systems via RAF Museum

A Project 75 production breakdown. BAE Systems via RAF Museum

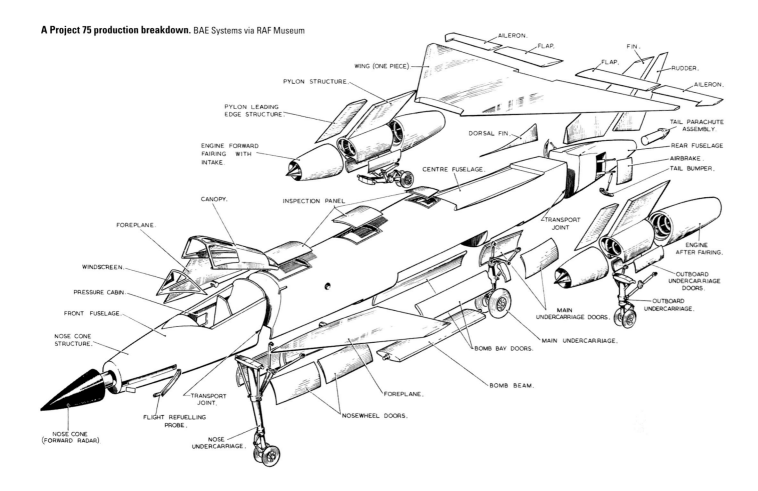

With the aircraft spending most of its flying life below Mach 1, conventional light-alloy construction sufficed, using the structural techniques Fairey had developed for the FD2 of clad sheet, forgings and extrusions. Fairey struck a confident note in its brochure when it came to being able to design and build the aircraft successfully. The company's experience on the FD2 would cut down on the aerodynamic and structural work necessary, and its experience with Gannet production, including envelope jigging, would ensure a smooth production run with good component interchangeability characteristics, enabling assembly of components at dispersed sites. Fairey predicted first flight two years and three months after receipt of the contract, and peak production of sixteen aircraft per month, rising to thirty per month when using the production facilities of an associated company. (No particular company was specified in the brochure, though Blackburn was selected as the preferred associate in the covering letter.)

Ferry range on internal fuel was 2,400nm (2,760 miles, 4,440km), or 2,500nm (2,875 miles; 4,625km) with a bomb bay fuel tank. For the 1,000nm sortie with one *Red Beard* onboard, the take-off weight would be 65,000lb (29,500kg) (or 65,900lb (29,900kg) if a water-methanol load was also carried), and take-off roll to 50ft (15m) would be 1,500yd (1,370m). The landing run in tropical conditions, without braking parachutes would be 900yd (825m), reducing to 570yd (520m) if parachutes were used on a dry runway. However, there was a catch. When it came to meeting the performance requirements of the GOR, Fairey stuck its neck out and expressed some contrary opinions. For instance, supersonic operations at altitude were, it felt, of little value for the primary task of tactical strike. Speed at any significant height was little protection against ground defences, and it would be substantially safer to spend more time at low level, albeit at subsonic speeds. For reconnaissance operations, supersonic speed at medium altitudes would be of more use. Fairey had looked at the use of supersonic bursts at low level, and calculated that for every 10 miles (16km) supersonic at low level, 55nm (63 miles; 100km) would

be lost from the overall combat radius. With any significant time spent supersonic, therefore, the Fairey aircraft would not meet the range requirements, and would run out of fuel on the way home. As a result Fairey decided '... to exclude any supersonic element from the operational profile, and that such supersonic elements would be considered as penalties on the basic missions'.

Navigational and bombing accuracy was another weak area. As a firm believer in the 'near enough is dead enough' principle of atomic attacks, Fairey did not consider high accuracy to be relevant in LABS attacks, and proposed a simple computer that would calculate bomb fall position and enable the pilot to fly the manoeuvre manually following a basic flight director, or hand the task to the autopilot, which would be linked to the bombing computer. With the submission already light on details when it came to the navigational and bombing side of things, this cannot have gone down well at the Ministry, but in the end Fairey's fatal error was effectively in designing a supersonic bomber that could only meet the range requirements if kept subsonic.

Gloster Aircraft design study: P.384 Thin-wing Javelin

Gloster carried out an internal study into resurrecting its thin-wing Javelin bomber concept, which it had originally proposed in the early 1950s. The work resulted in a pair of designs being described. First of all, and by far the least satisfactory, was the P.386, a 'Stage A' development of the thin-wing Javelin originally designed to try and satisfy the F.153D fighter requirement. The 600nm sortie requirement could not be met by the basic design, but with ventral tanks and a bulged fuselage to make room for extra fuel it could just about manage that task. The aircraft would carry the atomic bomb in a similar manner to the Scimitar, under

the port wing, balanced by a drop tank under the starboard wing. Ultimately, no amount of massaging the airframe or figures could get the aircraft anywhere near the 1,000nm sortie requirement, and it could attain a maximum speed of only Mach 1.13 on the way to the target and Mach 1.41 on the way back.

Accordingly, Gloster envisaged an alternative, the P.384, in which the engines were moved to underwing pods, leaving the entire fuselage available for fuel and a weapons bay. The wings were thinned even further, with no room to hold the main undercarriage, which was replaced by a ventral quad-wheel main gear plus outriggers on the outer wings. Carrying all stores in the bomb bay and having a thinner wing reduced drag substantially, and the extra fuel combined with that to make the aircraft capable of the 1,000nm sortie. However, speed was once again lacking, Mach 1.85 being the absolute best that could theoretically be expected, though in reality it would be highly unlikely to be achieved. Gloster considered that the only way to improve on this was with more thrust, and as the design already used the highest-thrust engines then available (the Olympus 21R, though the Conway would be more suitable for a bomber aircraft), that meant more engines. Four Olympus 21Rs would have done the job, but the aircraft would be massive, weighing in at nearly 180,000lb (82,000kg) and having a huge 2,000sq ft (185.8sq m)

wing. Clearly this was not practical. Gloster also considered reducing drag, but expected improvements from area ruling would not have been likely to be anywhere near helpful enough, and it believed the only viable route was to make the aircraft smaller. As this would have resulted in a vicious circle of carrying less fuel and going shorter distances, it was no wonder that Gloster threw in the towel and did not make a formal submission. Its only contribution to the final Hawker Siddeley Group submission, therefore, was to take part in some peer review of the P.1129 proposal before it was sent to the MoS.

Handley Page design study

Sir Frederick Handley Page, a famously strong-willed man, did not think much of the MoS's requirements for mergers and amalgamations within the aviation industry, particularly when they were so crudely tied to carrots such as GOR.339. Given that agreeing to such a merger would only have left the company with a one-in-four chance of being chosen to actually build its submission, and would have involved a great deal of probably fruitless negotiation with prospective partner companies even to get that far, Handley Page declined to submit a formal proposal for an aircraft to satisfy GOR.339. However, it did let its Research Department draw up a preliminary design,

Leading particulars: P.384 Thin-wing Javelin development	
Length	77ft (23.47m)
Height	20ft (6.09m)
Wing span	60.7ft (18.50m)
Wing area	1,240sq ft (115.19sq m)
Wing aspect ratio	2.97
Engines	2 × 17,270lb (7,840kg) Olympus 21R (29,000lb (13,150kg) in reheat)
Max speed	Mach 1.41 @ 30,000ft (9,000m)
Empty weight	57,560lb (26,125kg)
Max AUW	114,500lb (51,970kg)

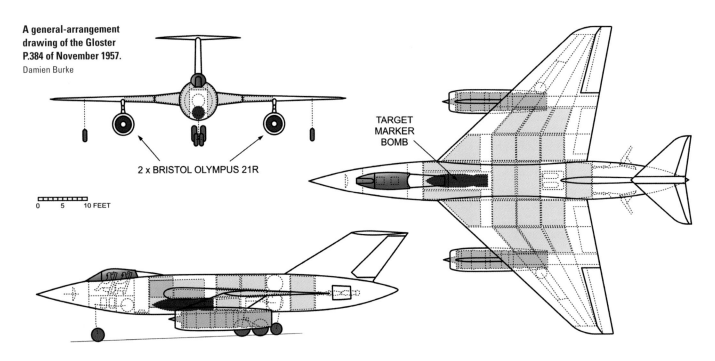

A general-arrangement drawing of the Gloster P.384 of November 1957.
Damien Burke

2 x BRISTOL OLYMPUS 21R

0   5   10 FEET

TARGET MARKER BOMB

Leading particulars: Handley Page GOR.339

Length	75ft (22.86m)
Height	14.8ft (4.51m)
Wing span	48ft (14.63m)
Wing area	924sq ft (85.84sq m)
Wing aspect ratio	2.5
Engines	2 × RB.141R or Conway 11R or Olympus 6R
Max speed	Mach 1.7
Max AUW	60,000lb (27,215kg)

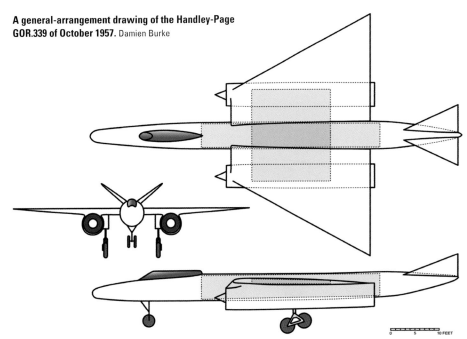

A general-arrangement drawing of the Handley-Page GOR.339 of October 1957. Damien Burke

and submitted this in December 1957, purely for information, along with further notes in January 1958 about a mechanism to smooth the ride at low level.

A large aircraft of 60,000lb (27,000kg) AUW was drawn up, with basically delta-shaped wings and a tiny butterfly tail. The two engines, ideally of bypass type, would be carried in pods under the wings, and the crew would sit in tandem under a bubble canopy. Handley Page recognized that high wing loading was the basic method to resolve the problem of a rough ride at low level, but equally felt that it impinged too much on high-altitude performance and required high-lift devices to achieve sensible take-off and landing performance. Its solution was a mechanical gust response alleviation method using a probe on the nose to measure gusts, linked to equipment to sense the magnitude of the gusts and operate control surfaces on the wing to respond to them as they occurred, thus smoothing the ride. This was an idea somewhat ahead of its time; fly-by-wire would make it a much more practicable proposition some years later.

A rudimentary bomb bay in which bombs could be semi-buried in the fuselage was mentioned, but was secondary to the carriage of bombs under the wings, between the fuselage and engine pods. The positioning of the wing in the middle of the fuselage was chosen so that it did not interfere with the bomb bay or unnecessarily restrict the crew's view to the sides and rear. Interestingly, Handley Page thought a clear field of view much more important than other firms, responding to the requirement that the crews would want to be able to see if they were leaving a contrail and thereby giving their position away. The outer portions of the wings would have 62 degrees of sweepback, but the inner portions would be straight, the company considering any sweepback here to be of little benefit. The

butterfly tail was sized to clear the engine efflux, and was considered a compromise between having no tail at all and having a conventional tailplane arrangement.

The choice of engine dictated performance and fuel consumption, and therefore weight. A bypass-type engine such as the RB.141R would provide best economy and lowest weight. Alternatives such as the Conway and Olympus were mentioned, but carried severe weight penalties owing to their higher fuel consumption and the resultant need to carry much more fuel. In any case, GOR.339's requirement for a supersonic dash across the target area could not be met by the design and the company blithely recommended the removal of this requirement.

In the end Handley Page considered work on the transport variant of the Victor and boundary layer control (BLC) techniques to be more important than jumping through the Ministry's hoops to build an aircraft it did not believe was entirely realistic, so its efforts are just an interesting footnote in the TSR2 story. Thus Handley Page avoided the chaos and heartache of the TSR2 project's cancellation.

Hawker P.1129 & P.1121

Hawker, having had its P.1121 rejected in 1957, began work on some other variations. The P.1123 was the twin-seat tactical bomber mentioned in the original P.1121

brochure, with larger-chord wings with fairings at the mid-point to house four-wheel main undercarriage units, and semi-recessed bomb carriage. The P.1125 was a single-seat strike aircraft with twin RB.133 engines, half-cone intakes on the fuselage sides, a small internal bomb bay and the original P.1121 wings. Finally there was a more impressive type, the P.1129. This bore many similarities to a two-seat P.1121, the most striking difference being that it inherited the twin-engine half-cone intake layout of the P.1125 rather than the ventral intake. After much deliberation it was the P.1129 that Hawker formally submitted to satisfy GOR.339 in January 1958.

In common with some of the other proposals, Hawker proposed a navigation system consisting of Doppler radar (*Yellow Lemon*), Master Reference Gyro, compass, and SLR with 4ft (1.2m) aerials for fix-taking with a Doppler-driven moving-map

Leading particulars: Hawker P.1129

Length	72.75ft (22.17m)
Height	17.25ft (5.26m)
Wing span	48ft (14.63m)
Wing area	630sq ft (58.52sq m)
Wing aspect ratio	3.65
Engines	2 × RR RB.142R or 2 × Olympus 15R
Max speed	Mach 1.3 at sea level, Mach 2.3 at altitude
Empty weight	45,800lb (20,790kg)
Max AUW	79,100lb (35,900kg)

A general-arrangement drawing of the Hawker P.1129 of January 1958.
Damien Burke

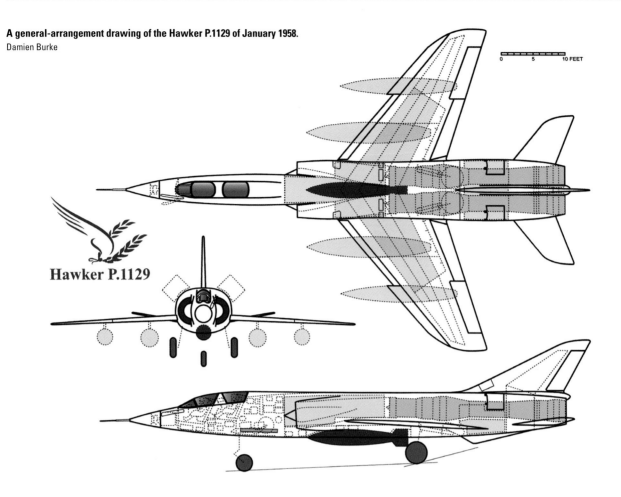

Hawker P.1129

display and SLR display unit. The P.1129's forward-looking radar, *Blue Parrot*, as used on the NA.39, would primarily be used for radar ranging and 'sore thumb' target identification. For the attack phase, sights would be provided for LABS, medium-altitude bombing and rocket attacks, along with a sight-recording camera. Weapon carriage could consist of a single Target Marker Bomb, up to four 1,000lb HE bombs, twenty-four 3in rockets (in two packs of twelve) or seventy-two 2in rockets (in a single large pack). All except the Target Marker Bomb could be carried entirely within the bomb bay; the Target Marker Bomb, however, was too big, and would be carried half-buried and half-exposed with special bomb doors.

The P.1129 would have carried three permanently fitted F.95 cameras in the front fuselage for vertical and oblique coverage, with a downward-looking rotating sight provided for the navigator so he could both verify photographic coverage area and check for the presence of wingtip or tailplane-tip contrails. The reconnaissance pack would have consisted of four more cameras (two

F.100 for vertical photography and two F.96 or F.89 for oblique coverage or vertical coverage from medium altitude), along with flash bombs for use at night as well as SLR with moving target indicator (using an 8 to 10ft (2.4 to3.0m) aerial for low-level use, mounted as far forward in the pack as possible though even so carriage of drop tanks would cause some blanking), plus linescan with UHF data link. For medium-altitude reconnaissance Hawker proposed a different reconnaissance pack which would have had longer SLR aerials (12 to 15ft (3.6 to 4.6m)) tilted down from the horizontal by 10 degrees. Again interference was expected from the drop tanks if carried. The radar recorder would be an item of permanent fit carried on-board the aircraft, and could thus record the sideways-looking navigation radar's output if no reconnaissance pack was carried.

In-flight refuelling and buddy refuelling were also part and parcel of the P.1129 proposal, a retractable probe being mounted in the nose ahead of the cockpit and offset to one side. The buddy refuelling pack, to be mounted in the bomb bay, would include

pump, hose and drum, control unit and a 300gal (1,360L) fuel tank. Fuel jettison would be possible, via a retractable pipe normally hidden within the ventral fin. Standard internal fuel capacity was 2,300gal (700L), in bags in the fuselage and integral tanks in the wing, and to this could be added up to four underwing drop tanks; inners of 500gal (2,270L) capacity and outers of 300gal (1,360L). Only by carrying external fuel would the aircraft be able to meet the 1,000nm sortie requirement. At low level, maximum speed would be Mach 1.05 (without reheat) or Mach 1.3 (with reheat), rising to Mach 2.3 at high altitude.

Hawker predicted a first flight by the middle of 1960 if an intention to proceed was given in July 1958, and CA release during 1964. However, as the company was part of the Hawker Siddeley Group of companies, which also included Avro, Hawker's submission caused some embarrassment, and the Group as a whole soon made it clear to the MoS that Avro's brochure was the one that represented the thinking of the Group, and the Hawker brochure received very little credence as a result. However, some individuals within the Air Staff and Ministry saw great promise in the Hawker design and encouraged Hawker to continue putting forward its ideas, not just the P.1129 but

Leading particulars: Hawker P.1121 Stage B	
Length	70ft (21.34m)
Height	15.3ft (4.66m)
Wing span	39ft (11.89m)
Wing area	509sq ft (47.28sq m)
Wing aspect ratio	2.99
Wing anhedral	2 degrees
Tailplane span	19.25ft (5.87m)
Tailplane area	115sq ft (10.68sq m)
Tailplane dihedral	10°
Fin area	75sq ft (6.96sq m)
Engines	2 × Olympus 22R
Max speed	Mach 2.0 @ 50,000ft (15,000m)
Empty weight	30,970lb (14,060kg)
Max AUW	53,890lb (24,460kg)

also the developed P.1121 variants. This was, no doubt, well-intentioned, but it led to a great deal of wasted effort on Hawker's part over the next nine months or so.

Part of that effort included further work on the P.1121 design. With the P.1129 effectively ignored, Hawker continued to upgrade the P.1121 to meet more of the GOR.339 requirements, and the result was another brochure, on the *P.1121 Two-Seater Development – Supersonic Strike Aircraft*, submitted in July 1958 (just before Hawker submitted a collaborative brochure on a further P.1129 development with Avro). As the introduction to the brochure stated, this was '... with a view to satisfying the broad intentions of GOR.339 without involving the heavy cost of completely meeting all the requirements'. The two-seater was based on the Olympus 21R (no mention of the Conway now), and differed from the original P.1121 in a number of ways besides the provision of a navigator/

radar operator's position. Leading-edge flaps had been added to the wings, with blowing on both these and on the existing trailing-edge flaps. The rocket packs were deleted and the main strike weapon could be installed in a semi-recessed position under the fuselage; alternatively a reconnaissance pack could be mounted there. Three F.95 cameras gave sideways and downward cover; Doppler and FLR assisted with navigation and target identification. The reconnaissance pack would contain an additional two F.100 cameras and SLR. A third role, that of buddy tanker, was catered for with an underwing buddy refuelling pod and extra overload fuel in the form of one 300gal (1,360L) drop tank and two 200gal (910L) drop tanks along with a 200gal belly tank.

Carrying only a single Target Marker Bomb, a subsonic and mostly high-level sortie, descending only to attack the target, would give a combat radius of 600nm (690 miles; 1,110km) at a take-off weight of

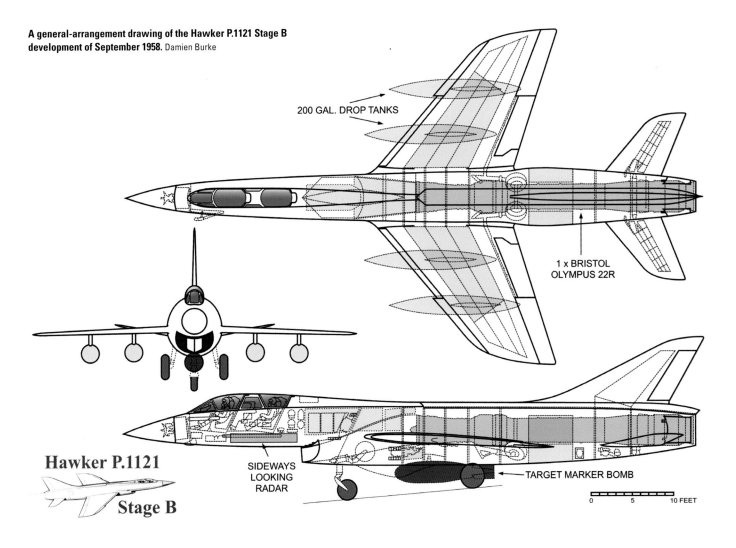

A general-arrangement drawing of the Hawker P.1121 Stage B development of September 1958. Damien Burke

200 GAL. DROP TANKS

1 x BRISTOL OLYMPUS 22R

Hawker P.1121

Stage B

SIDEWAYS LOOKING RADAR

TARGET MARKER BOMB

0   5   10 FEET

45,000lb (20,400kg), and a take-off distance of 1,330yd (1,215m). With a full load of four drop tanks in addition, a combat radius of 500nm (575 miles; 925km) would be available for an entirely low-level sortie with a brief supersonic dash over the target. Alternatively, sticking mostly to high level would give the full 1,000nm combat radius required by the GOR.

Even after submitting a joint brochure with Avro, Hawker continued to work on improving its P.1121 submission, and around October 1958 produced a design for a 'Stage B' version of the P.1121 two-seat strike aircraft. This was to use the new Olympus 22R and had a modified front fuselage, lengthened to accommodate SLR. The rear fuselage was lengthened to keep the aircraft's c.g. in the same place, providing extra room for fuel as a bonus. Rather than bag-style fuel tanks, integral tanks would be used, and this, along with the extra tanks and improved fuel consumption expected from the Olympus 22R, improved combat radius significantly. Wings of greater span improved take-off and cruise performance too. All of these changes meant that the low-level subsonic sortie could now be up to 780nm (900miles; 1,440km) in radius, with up to 1,200nm (1,800 miles; 2,900km) for the high-level sorties. A high speed, Mach 2.0, high-level attack to a target 300nm (345 miles; 555km) away was also now possible. A brochure on the P.1121 Stage B was submitted in a last-ditch attempt to get in on the GOR.339 act, but having confused

the picture with a solo/joint/solo sequence of designs, Hawker never really had a chance.

Hawker Siddeley Aviation Group – P.1129 Development

With the embarrassing situation of both Hawker and Avro having submitted separate brochures in January, the Hawker Siddeley Group had done itself no favours. Hawker and Avro were none-too-gently 'encouraged' to go away and come back with a single proposal from the complete Hawker Siddeley Group. In a strange foretelling of what would happen when the TSR2 was designed, the two companies worked to combine their designs and submitted a joint proposal in July, some five months after the initial deadline for submissions (Hawker having quietly submitted its P.1121 Strike brochure just before, in another defiant attempt to go it alone). The two firms combined the Avro Type 739 and Hawker P.1129 into a single design under the initial banner of the 'P.1129 Development', retaining the small size, low cost and operational flexibility of the original P.1129 while incorporating the best features of the Avro 739. These improvements

consisted of increasing internal fuel capacity by 750gal (3,410L) to a total of 3,000gal (13,640L) by using integral fuselage tanks; using all-moving tailplanes differentially for roll control at supersonic speeds (thus enabling the conventional ailerons on the wing to be reduced in size while increasing the size and power of the flaps); and using lower-pressure tyres for lower pavement loading. Unusual forward-swept intakes, found in neither of the original designs, were also incorporated into P.1129 Development.

The combined design could now better meet the GOR, a 7 per cent increase in range meaning it could manage the 600nm low-level sortie on internal fuel alone, along with a shorter landing roll. Redesigning the structure to accept either of the proposed Rolls-Royce RB.142 or Olympus 22R engines with their higher thrust meant that the aircraft could fully meet the GOR's 1,000nm combat radius requirement on internal fuel plus 1,000lb (450kg) of external fuel, while having a take-off roll a full 15 per cent shorter than required. Adding another 400lb (180kg) of external fuel would bring combat radius up to 1,200nm (1,380 miles; 2,220km), and take-off performance would still have a 5 per cent margin available. Service ceiling would be 70,000ft (21,000m), and top speed Mach

Leading particulars: Hawker Siddeley P.1129 Development	
Length	74.25ft (22.63m)
Height	20.2ft (6.16m)
Wing span	45.83ft (13.97m)
Wing area	600sq ft (55.74sq m)
Wing aspect ratio	3.5
Tailplane span	27.11ft (8.26m)
Tailplane area	210sq ft (19.50sq m)
Tailplane aspect ratio	3.5
Fin area	103sq ft (9.57sq m)
Engines	2 × RR RB142/3 or 2 × Olympus 22R
Max speed	Mach 1.7 @ altitude
Empty weight	45,410lb (20,610kg)
Max AUW	79,360lb (36,020kg)

An artist's impression of the P.1129.
BAE Systems

2.3 with partial reheat at high altitude, or sustained Mach 1.05 in dry power.

Work continued on improving the design so that it better met the requirements of the GOR, which was itself undergoing changes, and to improve combat radius and supersonic performance. A formal brochure was put together several weeks after the submission of the basic July proposal. The major changes were that the engines were now to be either the RB.142 or Olympus 22R; the wing had been reduced in thickness and area, now had leading- and trailing-edge blown flaps; and some attention had been paid to area ruling. The aircraft could now meet the 1,000nm sortie requirement on internal fuel only, weighing in at 75,000lb (34,000kg) and with a take-off distance to 50ft (15m) of 1,650yd (1,510m) (RB.142) or 1,350yd (1,235m) (22R). Landing distance would be 680 to 690yd (620 to 630m).

The weapons bay had been redesigned, and could now accommodate a single *Red Beard*, two Bullpup air-to-ground missiles (AGMs), three 1,000lb HE bombs, ninety 2in rockets, twenty-four OR.1099 rockets, a high- or low-altitude reconnaissance pack or a flight refuelling package. Two reconnaissance packs were proposed, the low-altitude version consisting of two 8ft (2.4m) Q-band SLR aerials with moving target indicator unit, three 70mm cameras with 3in lenses and electronic flash units for night use, two F.96 cameras with 6in lenses for daytime use, linescan plus associated recording and control gear. The medium/high-altitude version had no moving target indicator unit, 24in lenses fitted to the F.96 cameras, and the Q-band SLR aerials would be increased to 14.5ft (4.4m) in length.

An integrated navigation, bombing and flight control system was proposed, based on Avro's work on the *Blue Steel* nuclear missile, with Doppler/inertial navigation mixing with SLR provided for mapping and position fixing, with a 7ft (2.1m) X-band aerial on each side of the nose above the undercarriage bay. An FLR based on the Ferranti *Blue Parrot* as used in the NA.39 was to be used, but with some provision for the additional space and dish elevation requirements that would be required of a terrain-clearance version. Avro's Weapons Research Division had carried out some preliminary work on a simple terrain-clearance system using only a radar altimeter, and believed it could be developed to enable safe flight at 500ft (150m) over most of the terrain the aircraft could be expected to encounter. Unusually steep slopes could be identified in pre-flight planning and avoided accordingly.

For radar camouflage, the intakes would be lined with radar absorbing material and the boundary layer bleeds covered with an inclined metal grid; glassfibre honeycomb panels containing a carbon-based foam would be installed behind the FLR and SLR aerials. Metal film used for demisting the canopy would double as a radar camouflage measure for the cockpit. While no specific electronic countermeasures (ECM)

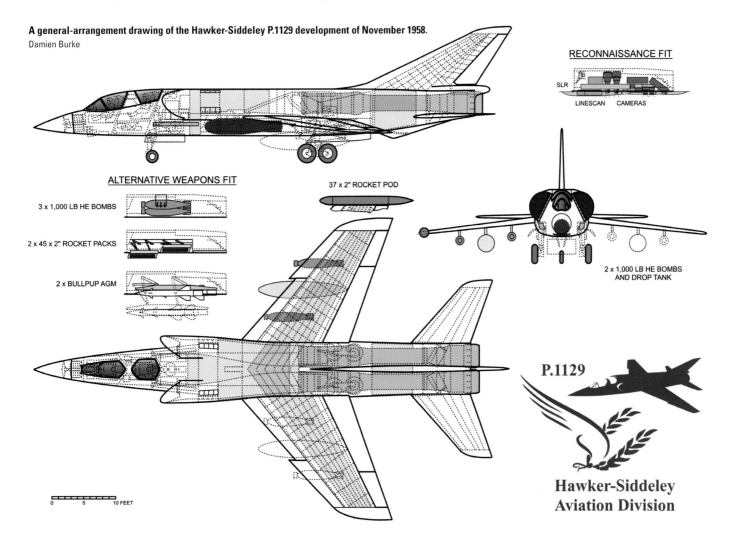

A general-arrangement drawing of the Hawker-Siddeley P.1129 development of November 1958.
Damien Burke

RECONNAISSANCE FIT

SLR

LINESCAN   CAMERAS

ALTERNATIVE WEAPONS FIT

3 x 1,000 LB HE BOMBS

2 x 45 x 2" ROCKET PACKS

2 x BULLPUP AGM

37 x 2" ROCKET POD

2 x 1,000 LB HE BOMBS
AND DROP TANK

0   5   10 FEET

P.1129

**Hawker-Siddeley
Aviation Division**

kit was proposed, space was set aside for up to 300lb (135kg) and 8cu ft (0.23cu m) of such equipment.

Hawker Siddeley had also put together its proposed grouping of companies to deal with production; Hawker plus Avro and Gloster, with some windtunnel staff available from Armstrong Whitworth (the remainder of that firm being too busy on civil work to assist with GOR.339). Assuming an Intention to Proceed in January 1959, the availability of a detailed specification by mid-1959 and the placement of a contract by the end of the year, Hawker predicted it would be able to complete the first airframe by the middle of 1961, with first flight four months after that. A development batch of twelve aircraft, the last three fully equipped, would be required, main assembly taking place at Hawker's Kingston, Surrey, plant and sub-units being built elsewhere (such as wings and tail control units at Manchester; presumably the Avro plant at Woodford). An interim CA release for December 1963 would be followed by full CA release in mid 1964.

Vickers-Armstrongs Type 571

The most interesting of all the submissions apart from English Electric's P.17 was that from Vickers-Armstrongs (Aircraft) Ltd. Design work on an aircraft to satisfy GOR.339 was carried out at the Hursley Park site, a large variety of layouts being sketched out before Vickers settled on an overall configuration with which it was happy. The aircraft's general configuration was fairly conventional, with high-mounted wings with blown flaps and leading-edge slats, tip tanks, an anhedral all-moving tailplane, an all-moving fin and a tricycle undercarriage retracting into the fuselage. Forward-slanting intakes with prominent splitter plates were about the only unusual item. A single large airbrake behind the bomb bay doubled as an access door for the engine accessories bay.

In Vickers's opinion the aircraft was going to have to be a large one to meet all the requirements, so it would be of enormous benefit to engineer all the equipment for the aircraft to minimum size and weight, while splitting separate military tasks into bomb bay packs that could be fitted to the aircraft as necessary. The basic idea was that the aircraft would be designed as a strike aircraft, with the ability to fit alternative equipment packages to carry out the day and night

Leading particulars: Vickers-Armstrongs Type 571		
	Small aircraft	*Large aircraft*
Length	59.4ft (18.10m)	77ft (23.47m)
Height	19.6ft (5.97m)	
Span (including tanks)	32ft (9.75m)	41.5ft (12.65m)
Wing area	200sq ft (18.58sq m)	430sq ft 39.94sq m)
Wing aspect ratio	4	4
Tailplane area	65sq ft (6.04sq m)	
Tailplane aspect ratio	2.76	
Fin area	50sq ft (4.64sq m)	
Engines	1 × 14,000lb (6,350kg) RB.142R (22,700lb (10,300kg) in reheat)	2 × 14,000lb (6,350kg) RB.142R (22,700lb (10,300kg) in reheat)
Max speed	725kt (835mph; 1,340km/h) or Mach 2.1 @ 36,000ft (11,000m)	725kt (835mph; 1,340km/h) or Mach 2.1 @ 36,000ft (11,000m)
Max AUW	45,420lb (20,615kg)	94,075lb (42,700kg)

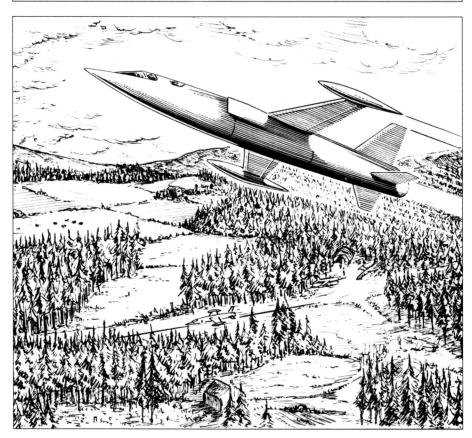

An artist's impression of the Vickers-Armstrongs Type 571.
BAE Systems via Brooklands Museum

reconnaissance roles. This policy of miniaturization was a unique suggestion, and Vickers actually proposed a pair of basic designs, the larger twin-engined aircraft to meet every aspect of GOR.339, and a much lighter and smaller single-engine aircraft relying on the use of miniaturized equipment, which would be particularly viable if the supersonic requirement could be relaxed and a typical strike sortie be carried out entirely at subsonic speeds.

All equipment would be packaged in modules measuring 8in × 8in × 18in deep (20 × 20 × 45cm) and mounted on racks within a single large equipment bay accessible from either side of the fuselage so as to be able to be removed and replaced with ease. There would be twenty-two compartments on either side with cooling air or possibly freon gas circulated through the racking surrounding the modules. Mission packs, such as a reconnaissance pack with

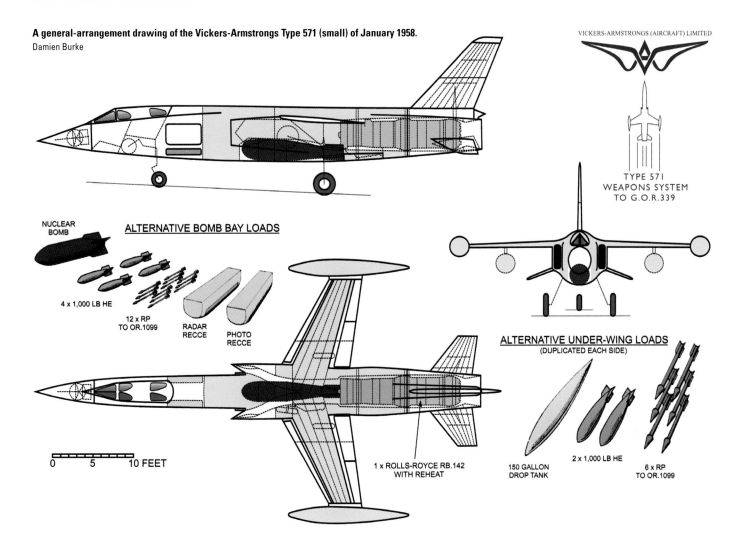

A general-arrangement drawing of the Vickers-Armstrongs Type 571 (small) of January 1958.
Damien Burke

VICKERS-ARMSTRONGS (AIRCRAFT) LIMITED

TYPE 571
WEAPONS SYSTEM
TO G.O.R.339

NUCLEAR BOMB
ALTERNATIVE BOMB BAY LOADS

4 x 1,000 LB HE

12 x RP
TO OR.1099

RADAR RECCE

PHOTO RECCE

0   5   10 FEET

1 x ROLLS-ROYCE RB.142
WITH REHEAT

ALTERNATIVE UNDER-WING LOADS
(DUPLICATED EACH SIDE)

2 x 1,000 LB HE

150 GALLON DROP TANK

6 x RP
TO OR.1099

linescan, would be fitted in the bomb bay, enabling a role change in a matter of hours. Thus the aircraft would not be carrying anything it did not need, with the attendant weight, drag and fuel requirements of dragging around these pieces of equipment. The use of up-to-date techniques, such as transistorization of electronics and printed circuits, would also assist greatly with miniaturization, and Vickers expected to be able to reduce the amount of space taken up by equipment directly related to the military portion of the aircraft's equipment fit by up to 40 per cent. Packaging and modular racking would reduce the space required for equipment from 300cu ft (8.5cu m) down to just 80 (2.26); enough space to hold two-thirds of the internal fuel.

Getting to the target was to be aided by a comprehensive navigation system consisting of SLR using twin 4ft (1.2m) unstabilized aerials, Doppler and an inertial platform (based on a miniaturized *Blue Steel* platform). A roller-map cathode ray tube

(CRT) display would be driven by the Doppler/inertial system, with position fixes maintained by the navigator. Provision would be made for an FLR for terrain clearance, and possibly a navigational/targeting aid, if such a radar could be developed in time. The navigator would have an FLR repeater display, normally hidden, which he could view by stowing the roller-map display to reveal the radar scope. As he would only need the FLR for the attack run it did not need to be visible at all times. No particular FLR was specified, as Vickers expected EMI to develop a new one for the aircraft, but Vickers based its size and weight provision for this equipment on the American APG-53 ranging and terrain search radar with a 22in (55.8cm) dish.

The primary method of attack would be to fly past a target, painting it on the SLR (at a range of up to 30nm (34.5 miles; 55.5km)) and then turning to attack it. Accuracy in the region of 400yd (365m) would be expected. Vickers considered the LABS

technique of 'over-the-shoulder' weapon delivery unacceptably dangerous, as it exposed the aircraft to detection and attack. Its preferred method would be a much shallower 'loft' attack, climbing until weapons release and then turning away to escape at low level once more. Vickers's studies into vulnerability had shown that increasing speed beyond Mach 0.9 at low level did not significantly decrease an aircraft's vulnerability to attack by ground-based weapons, and supersonic dashes at low level would primarily be of use for crossing particularly heavily defended areas or fleeing from a fighter attack. The company acknowledged that supersonic high-level capability would be valuable for reconnaissance, but even above 50,000ft (15,000m) at Mach 2.5 the aircraft had a fifty-fifty chance of surviving a missile attack. The general thrust of the submission was to try and convince the Air Staff that the combined requirements – low-level operation, supersonic speed, and operating from very short strips – were

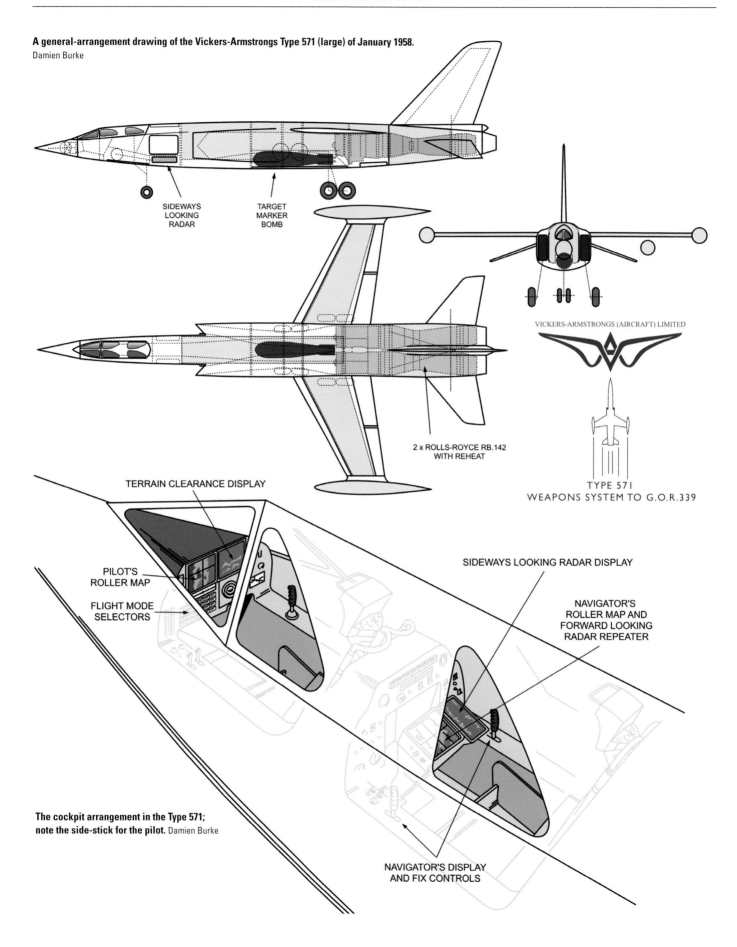

A general-arrangement drawing of the Vickers-Armstrongs Type 571 (large) of January 1958.
Damien Burke

SIDEWAYS
LOOKING
RADAR

TARGET
MARKER
BOMB

2 x ROLLS-ROYCE RB.142
WITH REHEAT

VICKERS-ARMSTRONGS (AIRCRAFT) LIMITED

TYPE 571
WEAPONS SYSTEM TO G.O.R.339

TERRAIN CLEARANCE DISPLAY

PILOT'S
ROLLER MAP

FLIGHT MODE
SELECTORS

SIDEWAYS LOOKING RADAR DISPLAY

NAVIGATOR'S
ROLLER MAP AND
FORWARD LOOKING
RADAR REPEATER

**The cockpit arrangement in the Type 571;
note the side-stick for the pilot.** Damien Burke

NAVIGATOR'S DISPLAY
AND FIX CONTROLS

going to lead to a large and expensive airframe. Compromise would give them something only slightly less capable but much smaller and therefore far more economical both to produce and operate.

The 'new' 1,000nm sortie, including a Mach 2.0 burst at altitude and retaining the 200nm low-level section nearest the target, was not a problem for the lightweight single-engined Type 571. The take-off roll to 50ft (15m) was 1,630yd (1,490m), well within the 1,800yd (1,645m) required. Take-off weight, initially predicted as being 45,400lb (20,600kg), was reduced to 42,200lb (19,150kg) after input from the RAE on improved drag figures. Alternatively, the margin in take-off roll and weight could be traded for longer range, enabling a combat radius of up to 1,150nm (1,320 miles; 2,130km). Ferry range would be 3,300nm (3,795 miles; 6,100km). Fuel load would mostly be contained within fuselage tanks, with additional fuel in the wings and both tip-mounted and underwing drop tanks. In-flight refuelling was also catered for. With internal fuel only, however, the aircraft could not exceed Mach 1.6 and still achieve the required combat radii.

The issue of crew comfort at low level was to be dealt with primarily by the choice of a highly loaded wing (170lb/sq ft; 830kg/sq m), and possibly by having the navigator's cockpit area suspended as an isolated 'crate' within the airframe so that he could carry out his duties with more freedom from the effects of turbulence. Both crew members would sit on hydraulically sprung and damped seats. While the GOR had mentioned good visibility for the navigator as a requirement, Vickers offered only an 'adequate' view, with a lens system for viewing the terrain being overflown (so the navigator could see what was being photographed on a reconnaissance mission), and no means of ascertaining whether a contrail was being formed except possibly via some variation of an icing indicator. Flying controls would be via duplex hydraulically powered controls with electrical signalling, plus a mechanical backup. Autostabilization (damping) on all axes was to be provided, plus auto-stiffening at high Mach numbers to make up for the loss of fin effectiveness at these speeds. A basic autopilot for heading, height and speed holding would be provided, Vickers recommending that a fully automatic control system be looked at, as it would enable the aircraft effectively to fly itself, based on signals from the navigation and bombing equipment.

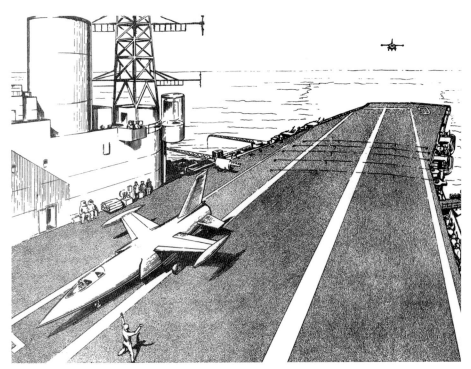

A naval Type 571 is marshalled to its deck spot, while another is on final approach.
BAE Systems via Brooklands Museum

The engine for both the single- and twin-engine designs was to be the Rolls-Royce RB.142, with 10 per cent of the engine's high-pressure (HP) air being bled off to operate full-span BLC and blown flaps for improved take-off and landing performance. For the STOL aspect of the requirement Vickers had investigated the 'Fire Hose' portable catapult and arrester system developed by the US Navy, and believed that airstrips of just 150yd (140m) length would be viable if its Type 571 was fitted with a suitable hook. This also fitted in with Vickers' belief that the smaller aircraft could be a viable joint RAF/RN type, the smaller dimensions allowing it to fit on existing RN aircraft carriers. Designing the aircraft to include built-in STOL capabilities was found to introduce substantial weight and size penalties, nearly doubling the aircraft's size, so Vickers did not proceed beyond basic investigations on this score, mentioning rotating wingtip jets and also a large ducted fan mounted within the wing and blowing downwards, using engine bleed air. Neither scheme was as effective, pound for pound, as simply having a slightly larger wing with blown flaps and relying on a catapult/arrester system. Vickers had spent years trying to get the government to agree to funding of the production of a variable-sweep aircraft, preferably its Swallow bomber, and, no doubt tired of the fight and aware of Barnes Wallis's own plans to submit a variant of the Swallow to GOR.339 himself, made no mention of variable sweep in its brochure.

Construction would be of light copper-based alloys, as they showed the most promise for the environmental conditions in which the aircraft would operate, combined with punishing low-level fatigue. Alternatives such as titanium alloys or stainless steel would be more expensive and would not offer many advantages, as their reduced structural efficiency would result in more material being used, and hence a heavier and larger airframe. Nonetheless, titanium would be used in the engine bays for load-carrying heat shields. The airframe itself would be constructed along conventional lines, with skin stringers and frames for the fuselage and multi-web-plus-post for the wing primary box. Fatigue from engine noise meant that the engines and, more importantly, the exhausts, would be located at the rear of the airframe. Fatigue from turbulent mixing in the boundary layer (effectively wind noise) meant that the equipment bay needed to be located as far forward as possible, just behind the cockpits, which also led to a useful saving in cabling

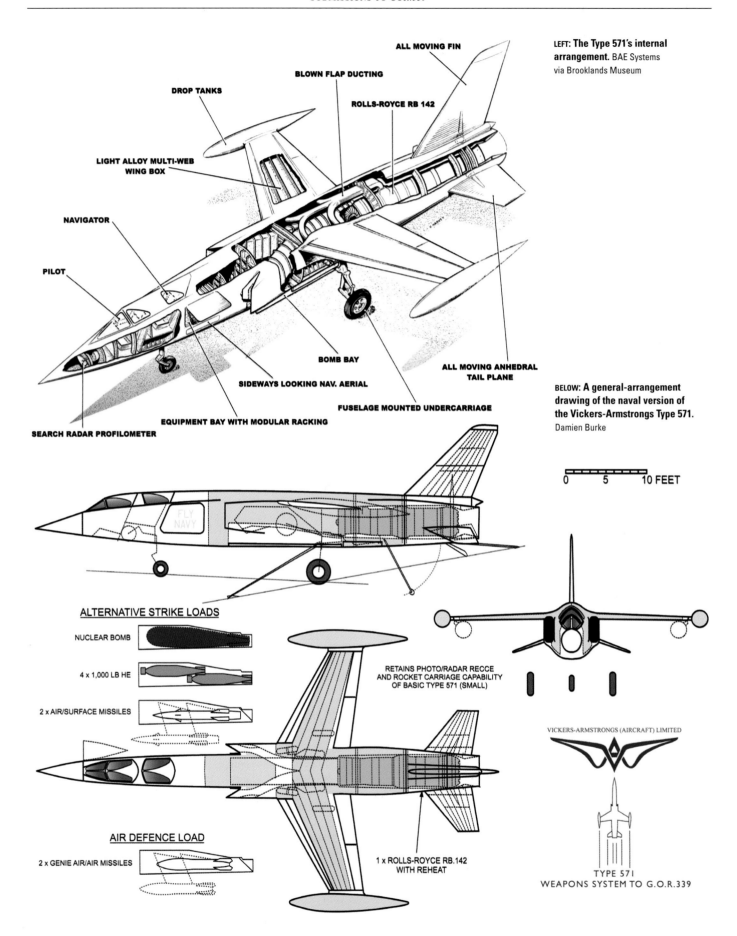

ALL MOVING FIN

BLOWN FLAP DUCTING

DROP TANKS

ROLLS-ROYCE RB 142

LIGHT ALLOY MULTI-WEB
WING BOX

NAVIGATOR

PILOT

BOMB BAY

SIDEWAYS LOOKING NAV. AERIAL

ALL MOVING ANHEDRAL
TAIL PLANE

FUSELAGE MOUNTED UNDERCARRIAGE

EQUIPMENT BAY WITH MODULAR RACKING

SEARCH RADAR PROFILOMETER

LEFT: The Type 571's internal arrangement. BAE Systems via Brooklands Museum

BELOW: A general-arrangement drawing of the naval version of the Vickers-Armstrongs Type 571. Damien Burke

FLY
NAVY

0   5   10 FEET

ALTERNATIVE STRIKE LOADS

NUCLEAR BOMB

4 x 1,000 LB HE

2 x AIR/SURFACE MISSILES

RETAINS PHOTO/RADAR RECCE
AND ROCKET CARRIAGE CAPABILITY
OF BASIC TYPE 571 (SMALL)

VICKERS-ARMSTRONGS (AIRCRAFT) LIMITED

AIR DEFENCE LOAD

2 x GENIE AIR/AIR MISSILES

1 x ROLLS-ROYCE RB.142
WITH REHEAT

TYPE 571
WEAPONS SYSTEM TO G.O.R.339

requirements for all systems that had some cockpit presentation. This bay would have large full-size access doors on both sides of the fuselage, enabling equipment racks to be easily removed for rectification or upgrade.

Production would be undertaken at the South Marston (Supermarine) works, then in use for Scimitar production. Vickers considered its own manufacturing and drawing office capacity to be largely sufficient for a project of GOR.339's expected size, but also pointed out that it subcontracted many of its airframe construction tasks to other companies anyway (e.g. Viscount wings to Saunders-Roe), and additional drawing office capacity could be gained from other companies too, if required. (A none-too-subtle suggestion that, while it was prepared to partner with English Electric, it would much prefer to go it alone.)

Naval version

An addendum to Vickers's submission outlined a version of the smaller aircraft that could be used by the RN. Prepared at the request of the Deputy Director General of the Future Systems department of the MoS, it covered the modifications necessary to turn the single-engine GOR.339 aircraft for the RAF into a naval strike aircraft that remained compatible with the RN's current carriers. To reduce approach speeds the wing was enlarged by 10 per cent, to fit within deck lift dimensions the nose and wingtips would fold, and an arrester hook and catapult attachment points were added.

HMS Eagle's larger 199ft (60.65m) catapult was capable of launching an aircraft of up to 43,600lb (19,790kg) in weight with wind speed over the deck of 25kt (30mph; 48km/h). This permitted the naval Type 571 to operate at maximum weight, and, with a high/low sortie spent half at low level and half at altitude, entirely subsonic, the aircraft could carry a single nuclear store to a target up to 1,100nm (1,265miles; 2,035km) away and return to a deck landing at a weight of 27,000lb (12,250kg). The resulting approach speed and landing weight was not far off Scimitar figures. Throwing in a supersonic burst of up to Mach 2 at high altitude reduced the combat radius to 980nm (1125 miles; 1,800km). By sacrificing some fuel, and therefore range, heavier conventional loads could be carried, such as eight 1,000lb HE bombs, though range could be regained by in-flight refuelling after launch.

Naval fighter

The naval version's high top speed and long range made it equally valuable as an interceptor. The weapons bay could hold a pair of atomic-headed air-to-air missiles, and a combat air patrol (CAP) at 130nm (150 miles; 240km) from the ship could last for nearly two hours from HMS Eagle's shorter catapult, or over three and a half hours from the longer catapult. Both CAPs included allowance for a Mach 2 combat, dealing with targets varying from a Mach 1 low-level bogie to one approaching at Mach 2 and 70,000ft (21,340m).

A miniaturized brochure

The Vickers brochure was a hefty tome, split into several volumes and consisting of 272 pages. Only English Electric's submission was larger, and only these two were of this sort of size and scope, though Blackburn's B.103 brochure was also quite substantial. Vickers soon found out that English Electric's P.17 brochure was, however, considerably more detailed and its work more advanced. If a quick decision was to be made as to which project to go for, the P.17 looked like it was going to win. Vickers, however, had been told during a visit to the RAE that the naval Type 571 it had proposed was of great interest, and believed it was this that was delaying a decision. However, the company did not want to scare the Air Staff off by implying that an RAF version would be penalized by any design for a naval version, and it had heard of the Air Staff's doubts about the feasibility of its miniaturization policy. Consequently Vickers followed up its main submission with a smaller brochure, with an emphasis on easy-to-follow illustrations. This brochure, 'a "miniaturized" brochure describing a "miniaturized" aircraft', addressed the concerns that Vickers felt were important. First of all, it reiterated all the advantages of miniaturization of installed equipment, and the amount of work being done by itself and partners EMI and Elliott Brothers to design suitable equipment. Second, it emphasized in this second brochure that the aeroplane was designed to GOR.339 and 'optimized entirely round the RAF requirement'. Any naval application was a mere bonus brought about by the low size and weight of the design. This smaller brochure was very successful at clearly explaining Vickers's miniaturization concept.

Evaluating the proposals

On 31 January 1958 an Assessment Group began meetings to look at the submissions and begin preparing a report to help in putting together a more definitive draft Air Staff Target, OR.339. The new OR would basically be brewed from the good bits of each of the firms' submissions. Normally this would have been a fairly rapid process, as the number of firms submitting to any particular requirement was always fairly low. Sometimes only a single firm would be interested, and usually no more than five or so. This was not so with GOR.339, with nine official responses and several other possibilities to look at. The RAE's input was extremely important to this process, and it evaluated each proposal against its own thoughts as well as against the other proposals.

No firm had addressed in detail the more unusual aspects of the GOR, such as linescan and terrain-clearance radar, but the Assessment Group as a whole did not seem overly bothered by this, judging linescan to be of questionable use and terrain-clearance radar as being unlikely to be developed in time. The Air Staff representatives in the Group, however, still wanted terrain-clearance radar, and one suggestion was for a separate Air Staff Target to be issued covering such a system, which could then be added to a future development of the aircraft built to satisfy the GOR. Vickers's miniaturization concept aroused a lot of interest, particularly as it could lead to an aircraft small enough to be priced competitively for export and also for use by the RN. However, the concept was greeted with equal amounts of scepticism. The Assessment Group found that Vickers's brochure did not contain sufficient evidence to justify the claims, and the OR assessment was that the design itself was 'extremely superficial'.

On the weapons side, Avro's detailed description of 'powered bombs' to enable stand-off attack was of great interest. Keeping the delivery aircraft some distance from the target had attractions not just because it exposed the aircraft to fewer defences, but also because it would enable nuclear warheads of larger megaton yields to be used. Vickers had also mentioned the use of missiles to avoid the dangerous nuclear bomb delivery manoeuvre, but in nowhere near as much detail as Avro.

Gust response and the quality of ride at low level was difficult to judge for most of the submissions, as the necessary aerodynamic derivative calculations had only been included by Avro, English Electric and Vickers. On the basis of these and statistical work, the Avro design was not expected to be much better than a Meteor (the RAE's baseline for gust-response comparison), the English Electric design was thought to be an improvement and the Vickers best of all. Structural strength and resistance to fatigue were of such high importance that any firm that failed to produce realistic figures instantly had its entire submission teetering on the edge of dismissal. On that basis the de Havilland submission suffered badly, with structural weights that simply could not be tallied with the claims for fatigue strength. De Havilland was also felt by the RAE to have badly underestimated its take-off and landing distances, by up to 30 per cent.

The English Electric and Short proposal for a VTOL version of their aircraft, or a separate VTOL platform to be used in combination with the aircraft itself, were the subject of much discussion. The lifting platform was particularly attractive because it also separated the development tasks, and delays on the VTOL side would therefore not affect the strike aircraft. However, the platform's configuration was of some concern. Its basically delta planform and deep

wing were necessary to provide similar flight characteristics to the strike aircraft and room for the lift engines, but would result in the wing providing little lift itself, and there was inadequate room for sufficiently powerful control surfaces. Gaining enough intake flow for engine starting would also be problematic. The development of a system to enable the strike aircraft to home on the platform and then hook up, no matter what the weather and visibility were like, could take a long time; and it was considered that the strike aircraft would need some downward visibility for docking with the platform, perhaps through a floor window.

Unbeknown to Shorts, however, a chance meeting between Sir Charles Dunphie, chairman of Vickers, and one of English Electric's directors had taken place after the GOR.339 brochure was submitted. The conversation had turned to GOR.339, and Dunphie had mentioned that co-operation between Vickers and English Electric would be a good fit. Vickers had the muscle and a proven track record of production, not only to military but also to commercial standards. English Electric had supersonic experience and a design team second to none. English Electric began quietly looking at the implications of joining up with Vickers; but it had signed up to a binding agreement with Shorts, so any

co-operation with Vickers would need, somehow, to include Shorts as well. English Electric would soon work out a suitable agreement with Vickers and communicate the changes to the MoS, where the English Electric/Shorts/Vickers combination provoked a great deal of interest.

Bristol's design came in for some stiff criticism from the RAE after an initially positive reception based on its expected excellent gust-response characteristics. On further examination the Group considered it to be likely to suffer badly in the areas of stability and control. The RAE had been working on a slender-delta configuration as the basis for the future supersonic transport, and the Type 204 seemed to be close to some of the less-than-ideal variations it had been playing with. On top of that, Bristol's mistakes in its drag calculations soon condemned its proposal to the bin, even though the canard scheme 'had many advantages'. The Fairey design, the only other canard design submitted, would need careful study, particularly in the areas of foreplane/intake interference and lateral stability; it could be that the aircraft would require twin fins. However, Fairey's design was so handicapped by its crippling lack of realistic supersonic capability at low level that it received only the briefest of examinations.

An English Electric P.17A is winched on to a P.17D lifting platform. BAE Systems via Warton Heritage Group

On Hawker Siddeley Group advice the initial Hawker P.1129 submission went unconsidered. Similarly, the Vickers/Wallis Swallow to GOR.339 received no real attention. Handley Page's study was only of brief interest in terms of the gust-alleviation mechanism proposed. Blackburn's NA.39 also received short shrift, being discarded within days owing to its inability to meet the supersonic requirement. Thus the nine formal submissions were very quickly boiled down to three of major interest: the Avro 739, the English Electric P.17A/D combination, and the Vickers Type 571. All of the firms' estimates for a schedule were viewed as overly optimistic, one member of the Assessment Group suggesting that an in-service date of 1966 was more likely than 1964. Even that, as it would turn out, was optimistic.

The economics of GOR.339

The RAF's own internal estimate of total development costs of £15 million now jumped massively to £35 million, a particularly unhappy state of affairs when compared with the much lower costs estimated for the NA.39 variant proposed by Blackburn. A detailed look at savings that could be made on various systems massaged the figures slightly, but the best that could be predicted was £33 million to £34 million for a large twin-engined type, or £32.5 million for a smaller single-engine aircraft. The MoS's estimates were even higher, ranging from £33.5 million to £38.5 million, to include £16.5 million for airframe R&D, £3 million for engines, an additional £5 to £10 million depending on choice of engines and £9 million for weapon system equipment. The cost of the new bomber was already rocketing skywards.

English Electric's submission, while heavy on detail of the P.17, was light on costs. In fact, English Electric had declined to include any predicted costs whatsoever, as it was not its policy to quote costs to anything except a solid specification, which GOR.339 was far from being. This was, in part, due to the cost rises experienced during P.1 development, which had basically doubled between 1955 and 1958. The MoS was outraged by this impertinence and kept returning to the subject time and time again, finally drawing a line in the sand and informing English Electric that its submission could not be considered unless something on costs was added to it. English

Ray Creasey, the Director of Engineering at English Electric and the aerodynamic genius behind the Lightning and P.17 wings. Creasey guided the P.17 project from its beginnings, but was unwilling to produce cost estimates from thin air, to the displeasure of the MoS. BAE Systems

Electric produced a report entitled *The Economics of GOR.339*, in which it continued its policy of quoting no firm costs whatsoever for its own equipment, while trying to teach the Ministry a few things about the economics involved not just in GOR.339, but in all military aircraft. The company pointed out that existing means of estimating cost were laughably crude; for example, quoting a fixed amount per pound of weight to give an overall estimate. When it came to a project involving not just a new airframe but also a new engine and lots of new electronic equipment, this sort of crude estimate would simply be misleading. Furthermore, some types, GOR.339 among them, would make attractive export prospects, and thus end up costing less. Attempts to reduce size to make the airframe cheaper could backfire by putting the aircraft into the same class as foreign competitors, thus losing exports and driving unit costs back up. Trying to share costs with the navy by aiming for a joint RAF/RN type was fraught with danger, as reductions in size and performance to fit the aircraft on current RN carriers would inevitably result in an aircraft less able to carry out its RAF role, and reduce its export attractiveness once again. The lifting platform, however, could give a cheap carrier capability.

On the subject of reducing costs, English Electric pointed out that new equipment was very much more expensive per pound of weight than use of existing equipment; extreme methods of miniaturization as proposed by Vickers could well increase cost even though weight was saved. Statistical analysis of the costs of existing equipment gave them a mean price of £28 per pound, with £92 per pound for new equipment, along with R&D costs as high as several thousand pounds per pound. English Electric did not believe that GOR.339 justified the millions of pounds that would be necessary for R&D of all-new equipment. Only the use of existing kit could keep the equipment bill below £5 million, and it believed it would soar through the £10 million mark otherwise.

With the engines as the single most expensive item, English Electric was later instrumental in getting Bristol Siddeley Engines Ltd (BSEL) to produce a formal brochure on the Olympus 15R that included guarantees as to performance, weight and, most importantly, cost. This was all undone by the later switch to the Olympus 22R, at which point Bristol Siddeley was canny enough to avoid similar guarantees (the result of which would be poor cost control on the engine project in its initial years, and spiralling costs, guarantees and fixed prices not being reintroduced until 1964).

Rethinking some of the more exotic bits of equipment such as linescan, terrain-clearance radar and a complex navigation system, was felt by English Electric to be worthwhile, as these would all result in high costs and, the company believed, would be of questionable value. This was a dangerous game for English Electric to play, flying in the face of the RAF's own requirements and also going up against its chosen partner, Vickers, and its entire ethos of compact new-build equipment. The men at the Ministry already had doubts as to English Electric's management ability, and this was unlikely to have helped reverse that situation. It also meant that the details in English Electric's report showing how it could build the P.17 cheaper than anyone else, but only to an agreed specification, were given less credence than they should have been.

The new bomber goes public

Earlier in the year the RAF's new tactical bomber had been launched by the Press under headlines such as 'MINISTRIES

ROW OVER NEW BOMBER' (*Daily Mail*, 11 March 1958). During a debate in the House of Commons on the latest Air Estimates, the opposition Aviation Spokesman, Geoffrey de Freitas, had pressed Minister of Defence Duncan Sandys, asking several questions about the NA.39 and why he was trying to push the RAF to accept it, when the RAF wanted to order a 'supersonic bomber'. Sandys said that there could be no supersonic replacement for the Canberra for 'economy reasons'. Rumours abounded of various RAF chiefs being on the point of resignation.

In a strangely adversarial move, the Chiefs of the Air Staff put together a publicity exercise in May 1958 called *Exercise Prospect II* (*Exercise Prospect I* was a purely internal RAF conference held the previous month). A remarkable array of people was invited to attend various theatrical presentations on the future shape and role of the RAF; industry figures, MPs, journalists, trades union representatives and so on. The Minister of Defence was also on the invitation list, but although he said he would attend he never turned up. Among the varied topics presented to the audience in a series of mock interviews and presentations was the need for advanced high-performance aircraft in both fighter and bomber form. The result was a storm of controversy, the newspapers reporting an apparent mutiny by the RAF, and the government desperately trying to play down the apparent disagreement between RAF thinking and government defence policy as nothing of the sort (while working behind the scenes to ensure such an exercise was not repeated).

Privately, various members of the government no doubt realized that the 1957 White Paper had badly misjudged the future needs of the nation's defence, but face had been lost. The RAF, and its new bomber, were continuing to lose friends and make enemies. By the end of the year, mention of the words 'supersonic bomber' was anathema, with the Air Staff desperate to point out that their requirement was not for a supersonic bomber, but for a 'strike reconnaissance aircraft' which just happened to be supersonic, naturally. And could drop bombs.

Choosing the winners

Examination of the firms' proposals went hand-in-hand with examination of the firms themselves. Three firms immediately stood out from the rest: Vickers-Armstrongs, Avro and English Electric. The last was considered to be leader of the pack by virtue of the experience gained in the successful development of the supersonic P.1B fighter. De Havilland, which would normally have been considered the equal of these three firms, had the problem that its Hatfield division was busy on civil work, and its Christchurch division was thought to be of significantly lower quality in terms of leadership and production capacity. The top three firms all had adequate staff and windtunnel facilities. For flight-testing, Warton (English Electric), Filton (Bristol) and Woodford (Avro) were all sufficiently large airfields, but Wisley (Vickers) was uncomfortably short at 2,200yd (2,010m). By comparison, Hatfield and Hurn (de Havilland) and Holme-on-Spalding-Moor (Blackburn) had even shorter runways, and Fairey had a comparatively tiny grass runway at White Waltham. All of the companies had adequate manpower for production. Indeed, it was suggested that most were overmanned on their own, never mind grouped together. A blunt assessment of the quality of each firm's design teams by the RAE makes interesting reading: English

George Edwards of Vickers-Armstrongs. Edwards's leadership of Vickers was considered to be of the highest standard by the RAF and the various Ministries, his performance on the Valiant contract having been particularly impressive. BAE Systems

Electric, '... excellent team spirit and from seniors to juniors there is a consistency of strong technical ability...'; Avro, '... thoroughly experienced ...'; Vickers, '... attracts confidence ...'. Things went downhill for the other firms: Bristol, '... strong on theoretical problems but the translation of their solutions into engineered products is often unsatisfactory'; Blackburn and Fairey, '... neither inspires confidence. Each contains one or two competent men but there is no evidence of any well-knit team'; de Havilland Christchurch '... [comparable] with Blackburn and Fairey'.

Of the various groupings proposed, the ones that seemed to offer be the best all-round fit and be the most soundly based in terms of financial muscle and civilian orders were English Electric/Vickers/Shorts and Hawker Siddeley (with Avro as a focal point). Swaying the decision was the technical superiority of English Electric with its supersonics experience, and on 28 March 1958 the recommendation was made that the order for an aircraft to satisfy OR.339 should be placed with a group to be formed by English Electric, Short Brothers & Harland and Vickers-Armstrongs, with design leadership vested in English Electric. Vickers was told to drop its single-engine aircraft and concentrate on the larger, twin-engine type, which could take its 'bonus' higher performance and use it for shorter take-off rolls. The companies had also been informed that their work so far was first-class, and OR.339 was as good as in the bag for them.

The CA produced a note on 8 July 1958, seeking authority to incorporate formally the development of a weapons system to meet OR.339 within the R&D programme, ratify the selection of the firms chosen to undertake the task, and to approach the Treasury for financial approval. Once again the preferred firms were listed: English Electric with Shorts & Vickers, Vickers-Armstrongs with English Electric, or Hawker Siddeley. English Electric was spoken of in glowing terms, but only on the technical side. Confidence in its top-level management was 'exceedingly tenuous', and this led to serious doubt that English Electric should be awarded leadership. This was not helped by its report on the economics of GOR.339 and the complex political situation of including Shorts (who were largely government-owned). In contrast, Vickers's leadership under George Edwards could not be faulted, and they were also technically strong (albeit lacking a little on the aerodynamics and structural sides, where partnership with English Electric would work well). Hawker Siddeley had a high reputation, but Hawker and Avro had muddied the waters by making their own individual submissions, and the proposed structure for the project management raised questions: 'a new design team, led by a highly individualistic designer (in his 64th year)' (Sir Sydney Camm), under the general leadership of 'a strong minded Technical Director' (Avro's Stuart Davies). The inevitable conclusion was that the job should be given to a combination of Vickers and English Electric, with some support from Shorts (notably now downgraded from being an equal partner), and that leadership should be given to Vickers rather than English Electric.

At a meeting on 14 July 1958, the R&D Board of the MoS agreed to recommend the selection of Vickers and English Electric, though by now Short's name was conspicuous by its complete absence. Despite this decision, work continued in an apparently unrestrained and chaotic manner to see if another aircraft could satisfy the requirement. Within NATO, Supreme Headquarters Allied Powers Europe (SHAPE) was considering a similar requirement, and it was suggested that European manufacture of a Republic F-105 Thunderchief variant re-engined with the Conway, Olympus or Gyron engine would be of some interest. Alternatively, the North American A-3J Vigilante had just flown, and its combat radius, take-off performance and equipment were more in line with the RAF's concept of OR.339. Both were examined in some detail before being put aside for work to continue on a wholly British solution.

On 29 July a meeting at the MoS took place, with representatives of English Electric and Vickers in attendance. The Minister made the mistake of saying, in front of these men, that 'we preferred the English Electric design but we also preferred the Vickers management'. The result was unfortunate, in that Vickers was now of the firm belief that it would be in charge, while English Electric believed that the P.17 was actually going to be the aircraft to be built. The CA tried to explain that GOR.339 was not about choosing a design, but about investigating the feasibility of building *any* aircraft to satisfy the requirement, but it was far too late to be saying that. Throughout the project to come, English Electric would be resentful of Vickers taking away 'its aircraft', and negotiations between the two companies to form a joint company would

suffer a setback because of Vickers's attitude that it was to be 'the boss' in any joining.

The late Hawker P.1121 and Hawker Siddeley P.1129 Development submissions complicated matters only a little, in that the men at the Ministry had to deal with letters and meetings with representatives of these companies while knowing full well that their submissions had already been disregarded owing to what they considered was a lack of technical understanding of the sheer scale and complexity of the overall weapons system. Avro's Roy Dobson continued to press his case, however, stating that the company could build two or three prototypes in 'under three years'. When the realism of that estimate was questioned, he memorably stated: 'By God, I'll make the buggers do it'. The Ministry was not impressed by his invective; strong management was obviously only of interest if it did not have a northern accent.

The NA.39 also continued to be a thorn in the RAF's side, pressure to adopt the type (if only as an interim measure until the OR.339 aircraft was fully capable) continuing throughout 1958. The RAF was desperately worried that the limited pot of money available for defence was going to see one of the two projects cancelled in favour of the other, and that it would be OR.339 that suffered, as the NA.39 was already flying. An increasingly bitter battle was going on behind the scenes, but the RAF's efforts to scupper the NA.39 came to naught, and on 10 September 1958 Duncan Sandys wrote to the First Lord of the Admiralty, giving him the good news that he was still satisfied with the requirement for the NA.39 and had informed the Prime Minister and Chancellor of the Exchequer accordingly. Once again NA.39 had survived the RAF's flak, and OR.339's fate apparently remained in the balance.

The choice of a development batch of ten aircraft was made primarily on grounds of economy, but ironically this provoked more Treasury attention than a bigger batch would have done. The NA.39, after all, needed twenty development batch aircraft, and so did the P.1 (in addition to five prototypes). The Treasury was concerned that this was an attempt to sneak an expensive development past it, and that additional development aircraft would have to be paid for out of the production run (precisely what would happen with the so-called 'pre-production' aircraft). The MoS's response was a superb example of the sort of manoeuvring that was going on all the way

through this period. Only ten development batch aircraft would be needed, it said, because '... the in-service date of 1965 limits the design concept for OR.339 to a conventional twin-engined aircraft. It is not as radical a development as either the NA.39 or the P.1', and the various components of the instrument and electronic systems were just 'further developments of existing equipment'. Thus OR.339 was to be a simpler aircraft than the NA.39; but the more sophisticated NA.39 could not meet the requirement because it was too small an advance over the Canberra!

After several tense weeks and flurries of correspondence, the Minister of Defence finally gave the go-ahead to fulfil OR.339 on 13 November 1958, though the Treasury then jumped into the argument, wondering, yet again, why the NA.39 would not do instead, and delaying its own approval for several more weeks in the process while Hawker took the opportunity to make one last desperate attempt to have its P.1121 Stage B considered, to no avail. The choice of Vickers and English Electric, with Vickers in the lead slot, was endorsed and accepted by everybody involved. This was probably the only aspect of the project so far that had not led to sustained arguments (though the Minister of Supply did make it a condition that this grouping could be chosen only if Bristol Aero Engines and Armstrong-Siddeley Motors were given the engine contract).

Shorts gets shafted

Short had realized that the Air Staff's initial enthusiasm for its lifting platform concept had gradually leaked away during 1958. It went away and worked on a smaller and cheaper version that could both carry out a useful task of its own (providing VTOL to lightweight Folland Gnat fighters) and also act as a proof-of-concept vehicle and a preliminary step in the development of the PD.17. This was the PD.34, a ten-engine lifting platform submitted to the Air Staff in September 1958. The PD.34 would weigh 11,960lb (5,430kg), (rising to 21,600lb (9,800kg) with a fully fuelled Gnat on board), and would have a combat radius of 570nm (655 miles; 1,050km) at 275kt (240mph; 390km/h) (minus the Gnat). The ten RB.108 lift jets would be split into three groups; two to be used for lifting and propulsion in forward flight, four for lift only, and four primarily for lift but able to be tilted to provide a horizontal thrust component for acceleration and deceleration. Hovering control would be effected by a 10 per cent bleed from each engine ducted to nozzles around the extremities of the platform, based on the system Short had developed for its SC.1 VTOL research aircraft. The Gnat's own engine would be idling when the platform was static, but throttled up to assist with acceleration during the transition from hover to forward flight.

The initial thoughts of the OR department were that the concept had some legs. It thought it possible that a suitably adapted version of the Gnat combined with the PD.34 might be able to undertake some of the short-range tasks for the Army and thus release its OR.339 aircraft for longer and more demanding operations, and the R&D benefit was obvious. However, further discussions and the revelation of Hawker's work on its P.1127 (which would later be developed into the Kestrel, the basis for the Harrier) soon put an end to any interest in Short's unwieldy lifting-platform concept. By December 1958 the Air Staff's Director of Operational Requirements had replied, saying that he could not see any operational application for the lifting platform, and that R&D money would be better spent on the development of a direct-lift system incorporated within an aircraft, such as the Hawker P.1127. Coupled with the MoS's decision that the OR.339 project should be carried out by a grouping of English Electric and Vickers, with no sign of Shorts, this was extremely disappointing. The lifting-platform concept, it seemed, was dead; and so were Short's chances of being involved in the project to build an aircraft for OR.339.

This was a highly embarrassing situation for English Electric. After all, it had put a lot of work into the joint English Electric/Shorts submission, with the full intention of partnering with Shorts, and now it seemed that both the Air Staff and the MoS had arranged it so that Shorts had nothing useful to do, and was not to be involved at all. Shorts could not simply be dumped by English Electric; it was already a valuable and trusted subcontractor, carrying out some of the design and construction work on both the Canberra and P.1, and the relationship between the two companies could not be thrown away lightly. Efforts were put into hand to try and tactfully wriggle out of the English Electric/Shorts GOR.339 joint arrangement while giving Shorts something else to make up for it.

OR.339 gets the go-ahead, and a name – not a number

The date chosen to announce the start of the programme to build a new strike reconnaissance aircraft for the RAF was 1 January 1959. While initial drafts of the press release included a suggested description of 'B-/58' (i.e. a number using the traditional Air Ministry bomber specification sequence), it was felt that this ran the risk of adverse press publicity. After all, the RAF could not be seen to be getting a supersonic 'bomber' after the Minister of Defence had said there was no money for such an aircraft! An alternative designation was chosen instead; this was 'TSR/2', standing for Tactical Strike Reconnaissance, Mach 2.

An intermediate D. Notice (No. 30.6.55) was issued on the same day, formally preventing any publication of information about the project except for a very brief description that 'this aircraft will be a strike reconnaissance aircraft which will be supersonic and capable of operating from small airfields with rudimentary surfaces'. Vickers-Armstrongs Ltd and English Electric Ltd were listed as the builders. Oddly, the name of the engine manufacturer was omitted, though by this point Bristol-Siddeley Engines had got the job.

Names tended not to be assigned to Service aircraft until a production order had been placed, but with the fuss the Air Ministry had made about not using a traditional bomber sequence number, and its objections to 'TSR/2' as it gave too much away (such was the culture of secrecy at the time), one wag at the MoS, fresh from his New Year's Eve celebrations, wrote a somewhat tongue-in-cheek note on 1 January 1959 suggesting a solution to the problem; simply name the aircraft immediately. His suggestion was 'Velvet', of which he said:

> Apart from the pleasant associations with mailed fist, it of course stands for Vickers English Electric Various Explosives Transporter.
>
> It will annoy the Air Ministry to name the thing at this stage but it is their own fault for being so fussy about the number.

However, his suggestion was not acted upon. If any serious discussions about naming the aircraft ever took place after that point, then no record of them appears to have survived in the archive material consulted at the time of writing. Discussions on naming the General Dynamics F-111

have been recorded; the final two possibilities were 'Richmond' (in keeping with the theme of Commonwealth city names for bombers, and an Australian city in the hope it would convince the Australians to choose the same name) and 'Merlin'. When the Australians decided that 'F-111' was a satisfactory title in itself, 'Richmond' was dropped and the RAF F-111 would have been known as the 'Merlin'. As with the Vickers VC.10 airliner, which ended up simply being called the VC.10 in both commercial and RAF service ('Victoria' having been suggested and discarded), it is likely the TSR2 may simply have soldiered on as 'TSR2' had it entered service. There was, incidentally, no definitive style for the aircraft's designation; TSR/2, TSR-2, T.S.R.2, TSR.2 and TSR2 were all used by the British Aircraft Corporation (BAC) and the various Ministries at one point or another. In this book 'TSR2' is used for consistency and brevity.

Warning bells

The Treasury's concerns with the way the project was going had been mounting steadily. Having examined the most recent draft of the OR, it had seen that there were numerous areas where performance had been upped, and this was bound to have an effect on costs. Rather than a maximum speed of Mach 0.95 at low level, for instance, the requirement now included supersonic speed at low level. High-level speed had risen from Mach 1.7 to Mach 2.0 or even higher. The 1,000nm combat radius was now to be entirely on internal fuel, not as an overload case, and this in particular raised eyebrows. Provision of active RCM now asked for double the weight and nearly treble the cubic capacity. Why did a *tactical* aircraft need such a huge combat radius? If low-level penetration was essential to survival, what was all this monkeying about at Mach 2 at high altitude for? Why did a low-level aircraft designed to sneak in under radar cover need active countermeasures? Almost a year after brochures had been received, it appeared the RAF was now asking for an aircraft of significantly higher capabilities. On that basis, if the requirements were now different, how could the selection of firms stand? These were all good questions, but after nearly a year of discussion and fighting to get the new project approved, the Treasury was not about to be allowed to derail things at this point.

CHAPTER THREE

Designing TSR2

Months before the official announcement of the beginning of work on the new aircraft, English Electric and Vickers-Armstrongs had been hard at work trying to figure out how their differing designs could come together to form a viable aircraft, and how their two organizations could work together. This was a huge challenge, as each company operated in a different manner, with an entirely different culture both on the shop floor and in management. A common feeling at English Electric was that Vickers was home to arrogant Johnny-come-latelies muscling in on English Electric's Canberra replacement and expecting everything to be done their way or not at all. Feelings at Vickers did not run so high, though the company did believe that its long history and recent experience on the Valiant and Scimitar put it in an unassailable position when it came to developing a modern strike aircraft, and that the upstarts at English Electric had some cheek to be trying to go it alone with just the Canberra and as-yet-unproven P.1 under its belt. Emotions ran particularly hot at English Electric because, in the belief that time was short and a head start was necessary if the Ministries were to be kept happy, detail design work on Project 17 had already begun during 1958, and it now appeared that much of the hard work was going to be disregarded by Vickers.

However, English Electric's management, considered its weak point by the MoS, had experienced time and time again the painful, protracted and often fruitless process of translating technical offerings into actual contracts, and introducing Vickers into the mix breathed fresh air into its dealings with the bureaucracy. Vickers's heavyweight management, particularly George Edwards, demonstrated that strong personalities and an illustrious company history went down fairly well with the bureaucrats, and two years down the line Ray Creasey, English Electric's Director of Engineering, would admit to Jeffrey Quill, head of Vickers's Military Aircraft Office, that Vickers 'gave the project a new lease of life towards the end of 1958'.

From the beginning both companies were handicapped by a lack of information received from the Air Ministry and MoA; OR.339 raised a lot of unanswered questions, and getting any response from either Ministry to requests for amplification of the detail of the requirements was a frustrating task. Similarly, reactions or comments were not forthcoming when the companies submitted their own reports on aspects such as predicted bombing accuracy, navigation systems, crew comfort and so on. Vickers in particular knew that the MoS had commissioned lots of reports on similar subjects from RAE and other organizations, but no bibliography of these reports had been made available, so Vickers had no idea whether it was duplicating efforts already under way or completed.

Surprisingly, Vickers's possible layouts for the OR.339 aircraft included an investigation in late 1958 into wingtip and underwing engines, though neither the final Type 571 nor P.17 submissions had included such features. The primary attraction of this idea was that the wing would not need to be as stiff, and could thus be lighter, and more room would be freed within the fuselage for fuel. However, performance would generally be lower, and the result of losing an engine during take-off was a big concern. To improve the adverse-yaw situation with an engine out, the engines would need to be moved further inboard from the tips, introducing further performance penalties and interfering with the tailplane. It was clear that this layout was simply leading them towards a 'pointy Canberra', and thus it again led to a dead end. This sort of work did show that, despite supposedly beginning to co-operate with each other, Vickers and English Electric were still needlessly duplicating effort. In this instance, English Electric had looked at underwing engines and discarded the idea back in 1957. Much of its detailed work and reasoning behind discarding this layout was freely available in the P.17 brochure, yet was not referred to at all in Vickers's work

On 28 October 1958 officials from the MoS had visited Weybridge for a meeting about revising the requirement for take-off performance. Vickers's original plan for a single-engine aircraft with miniaturized, or condensed, equipment had been changed at Ministry request in May 1958 to concentrate on the larger twin-engine aircraft, but retaining the equipment miniaturization; the 'condensed twin'. With an apparent excess of fuel and engine power on this aircraft, this seemed a good opportunity to take advantage of the improved performance available, which Vickers had originally suggested could be taken as 30 per cent increase in range. However, with the tactical desirability of dispersing forces to protect them from a pre-emptive nuclear strike, and many hundreds of relatively short airfields scattered around the world, a reduction in take-off distance was preferable. Additionally, the surfaces of many of these strips would only be adequate for an aircraft using suitable low-pressure tyres. Previous proposals to GOR.339 all had such high-pressure tyres that these airstrips would be unavailable to them. The 'condensed twin' could become a 'STOL twin' if given more wing area and lower tyre pressures, bringing its airfield LCN down to the numbers required by poorer-quality airstrips. The meeting ended with agreement to revise the specification. For the 1,000nm sortie the take-off distance would now be 1,300yd (1,190m); for the 500nm 'Army sortie' (300 miles (480km) at sea level economic cruise, then 200 miles (320km) to the target at Mach 0.9M, carrying a light load of two Bullpup missiles for a short take-off roll of no more than 650yd (595m)), it would be 600yd (550m); tyre pressure would be between 70 and 80psi, giving an LCN of less than 20. The Air Staff had been keen to get the aircraft's maximum speed increased from Mach 1.7 to Mach 2 as well, and Vickers was keen to oblige, successfully getting this added to the OR. 'Mach 2 from a cabbage patch' was born.

When personnel from the Air Ministry visited English Electric in November 1958

The Vickers-Armstrongs Type 571 with tip-mounted engines, October 1958. Damien Burke

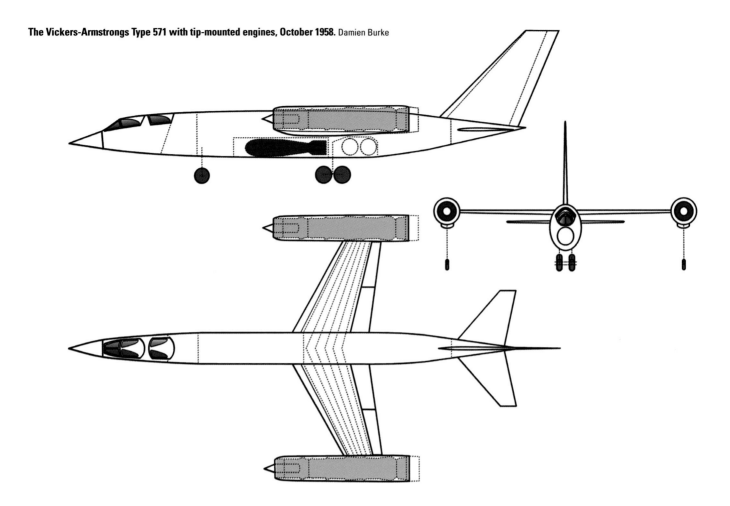

to discuss the P.17 in some detail, they found out just how much effort English Electric had been putting into the project. Some 200 people had been working on the studies since 1956, and windtunnel test results, a mock-up and a simulator were already in place. English Electric was unhappy with how little notice the RAE had taken of its work on gust response, and pointed out that its design was far superior to the Type 571 in this respect and many others; and English Electric was stunned to discover that Vickers had yet to carry out any serious windtunnel work on its design. In fact it soon became clear that English Electric's detailed work on aerodynamics had put it way ahead on this score, though Vickers's work on systems swung the balance back when it came to considering the aircraft as a complete weapons system. Another meeting with the Air Ministry on 26 November prompted revival of the idea of a joint RAF/RN type to OR.339, and further time and effort would be wasted on this non-starter, in which the Admiralty was simply not interested.

On 11 December 1958 Air Chief Marshal Sir Claude Pelly, Controller (Air), visited Weybridge for a presentation of OR.339 work carried out so far. Vickers let him know that agreement with English Electric had been reached in many areas (glossing over the many more where they were at loggerheads), and that the company was prepared to guarantee a timescale for the project, even though it knew at this point that it had insufficient manpower to cover the necessary design work, which would lead to English Electric's burden being somewhat higher than it should have been, based on the work being split fifty-fifty.

Combining the P.17A and Type 571

With the official announcement on 1 January 1959 that Vickers and English Electric were to build the new bomber, no time was wasted. Personnel from Vickers visited English Electric at Warton on the same day to discuss the wing. Given the requirement

for the aircraft to spend so much time at high speed at low level, English Electric had taken care to choose a planform and area that would keep fatigue of both airframe and crew to a minimum, while offering the best compromise between that and the short take-off and landing performance requirements. English Electric had therefore decided upon a low-aspect-ratio delta planform for the P.17's wing by early 1957, after a great many theoretical studies and wind-tunnel tests. It had stuck with this after investigation of many different alternatives and, with its experience of the P.1 wing, firmly believed the choice had produced absolutely the only viable wing design. Vickers's higher-aspect-ratio wing was optimized almost entirely towards the STOL requirement, and English Electric could barely believe that Vickers had paid so little attention to gust alleviation and crew comfort. Vickers considered its wing to give a small but worthwhile improvement in combat radius compared with the P.17 wing, based on aerodynamics alone, and much improved take-off performance. English

The Vickers-Armstrongs Type 571 (large) revised, with anhedral, December 1958.
Damien Burke

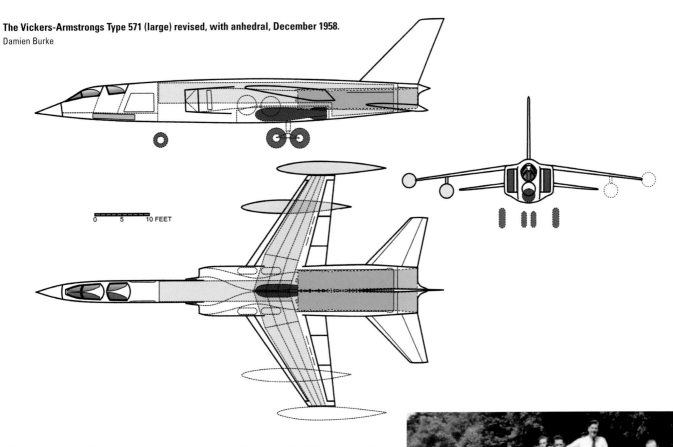

0   5   10 FEET

Members of the TSR2 design team take a break on part of the old racing-track banking at Weybridge.
Brooklands Museum

Electric, naturally, believed the opposite. When English Electric reworked its calculations using Vickers's assumptions and wing drawings, it reluctantly agreed that the Vickers wing did show slight superiority in combat radius. However, the P.17's delta wing could carry so much more fuel, about 4,000lb (1,800kg) worth, that this would contribute to a further superiority of 20 per cent in combat radius, with which the Vickers wing could not compete. Vickers further believed that English Electric had underestimated the weight of its wing by a significant margin, but Vickers based this belief on analysis of B-58 Hustler wing construction data, and the B-58 was famously 'built like a navy destroyer', with high structural density. English Electric was curious to find out on what basis Vickers had calculated the P.17 wing weight. On finding out, and then discovering that Vickers did not believe the same technique applied to calculating the weight of its own wing, English Electric was somewhat unimpressed! Vickers did at least agree that transonic handling would be better with the delta wing. However, despite the P.17 wing's obvious overall superiority, Vickers refused to shift on the subject, as it could not see that the delta was ever going to meet the STOL requirement.

The new STOL requirement had come as an unwelcome addition to English Electric, as the company had thought STOL and VTOL a dead subject ever since Shorts had been unceremoniously shut out of the GOR.339 project. The P.17 simply could not meet the take-off distance requirements. By contrast, Vickers's condensed twin could do so, even if it was forced to use English Electric's wing. Neither company knew it at this stage, but the aircraft's final configuration would effectively mate the P.17 wing with the Type 571 fuselage, though both wing and fuselage would end up looking rather different from those in the initial general-arrangement drawings.

English Electric personnel visited Weybridge on 7/8 January to discuss the fuselage. Both the Type 571 and P.17 fuselages would need to be widened or bulged to accommodate the low-pressure tyres and long-stroke oleos required by the rough-field capability, and the P.17 much more so. It was already quite wide where the undercarriage, wing, engines and bomb bay were all located in the same plane. On the plus side, the P.17's long nose, once extended to make room for a longer nose leg, balanced the delta wing nicely, and the greater fuselage width meant that there was room further aft for fuel. Needless to say, the respective summaries of English Electric and Vickers

Item	Type 571	P-17a
Forward-looking radar	24in scanner based on APG-53, similar to AI.23	32in scanner based on *Blue Parrot*; more space provided
Rear view or rear viewing system for navigator	Nil; contrail detection via air data computer	TV camera in tail; large display in navigator's compartment
OR.946 pilot instrumentation	Limited space; HUD for primary displays, and suggested use of 'futuristic' CRTs	Conventional instrumentation space available
Cockpit space	Similar to that of Scimitar	**Wider and longer after poor reception of P.1 cockpit size**
Nose gear	Low-pressure tyres, forward retracting	High-pressure tyres, rearward retracting
Side-looking radar location	**Lower sides of nose**	Top corners of fuselage
Equipment bay	**90cu ft (2.55cu m); large access doors either side**	225cu ft (6.37cu m); access panel below fuselage
Primary reconnaissance cameras	**Bomb-bay-mounted reconnaissance pack**	Permanent fit in dedicated bay
Fuel system	**Integral tanks, fuel used as heat sink as heat sink**	Bag type preferred but would accept integral; fuel not used
Bomb bay location	c.g.	9ft (2.74m) forward of c.g.
Engine installation	**Inserted/withdrawn horizontally via rear tunnel**	Inserted/withdrawn vertically via undercarriage bays
Intakes	Variable vertical ramp on inboard wall aft of fixed ramp; auxiliary intake doors; forward of wing leading edge	Rectangular wedge style; aft of wing leading edge
Tailplane	**All-moving**	Conventional
Fin	**Large, all-moving**	Small, fixed. Too small, insufficient yaw stability, so ventral fins also required, folding away when on ground
Braking	Wheel brakes	Wheel brakes, air brakes, braking parachute
Thrust reversers	No	Possibly

NOTE: Highlighted items would appear in the final TSR2

showed differences of opinion, but the main differences were as shown in the box above.

Each company had approached the fuselage design from a very different direction. Vickers was working towards a total 'weapons system' concept which, hand-in-hand with its miniaturization philosophy, meant that it was providing limited space for equipment which it expected to be designed as part and parcel of the overall project, and thus fit into the spaces provided, and concentrated more on the type and provision of the various items of equipment, rather than where it would all actually go. Experience with the Scimitar had also showed that view over the nose on landing was an important design consideration, especially in concert with the recently introduced STOL requirement. (The Scimitar's nose was redesigned after early carrier trials found that the view over the nose was hampering the pilot's ability to carry out a safe approach.)

In contrast, English Electric had been burdened by providing limited equipment space in its P.1 fighter project, which had led to access and maintainability problems (these dogged the P.1/Lightning throughout its service career), and the P.17's fuselage was designed with more than ample room for various bits of equipment. Its nose was longer owing to the need to provide more room for the radar, though this made the view on approach to landing noticeably worse. The space allocated for equipment

was far too great in Vickers's opinion, as much of it was going to be left practically empty. (English Electric would later investigate reducing the size of the fuselage by reducing the room set aside for hauling fresh air about, and finally agreed that if the customer was happy to pay for specialized equipment, it could provide restricted equipment space to match.) In return, English Electric criticized Vickers's lack of provision for cable runs and electrical distribution panels, again feeling that detail work on the systems side was lacking. The English Electric equipment bay, size notwithstanding, was the better design for accessibility and weather protection for ground crew and contents. The side doors of the Vickers design meant that the equipment would be vulnerable to inclement weather, and lighting in the area would be visible from some distance; not ideal for dispersed operations.

Placement of fuel within the fuselage was another bone of contention. English Electric recoiled from the idea of fuel in close proximity to the engine (Vickers had drawn a saddle tank above the engines) because of fire risks. English Electric also continued to shy away from too much work to satisfy the STOL requirement, on the basis that the aircraft would spend most of its life operating from normal airfields, never needing the STOL capability (history has certainly proved this point time and time again since then). English Electric had also designed a fin that gave limited yaw

stability, which it proposed to improve initially by means of a pair of small ventral fins, enlarging these by 50 per cent when wind-tunnel tests found even these insufficient. Vickers, naturally, had different ideas when it came to the fin, and wanted an all-moving surface, which it generally considered superior to the conventional fin and rudder for supersonic aircraft owing to reduced vulnerability to aeroelastic effects and larger yaw control power. In combination with an auto-stiffening system (a system sensing side-slip and applying small fin movements to counteract it), such a fin could be smaller than would otherwise be the case, though there were concerns that failure of the auto-stiffener could result in loss of control, and of the aircraft. Additionally, the power controls would need to be beefed up considerably, and the manufacturer slated for that job, Elliotts, had already requested that control surfaces be kept as small as possible. Elliotts was out of luck on that score, and the all-moving fin was pencilled in as part of the design, despite resistance from English Electric.

Combining forces

Vickers and English Electric agreed in January that they needed to work-up a datum aircraft design as soon as possible, from which they could then proceed with detailed design work. English Electric believed it already had such a design, the P.17 as it already stood, but Vickers had so many objections to various features of the P.17 that it was unwilling to start from this point. Vickers insisted that reducing equipment space and striving to attain STOL was the priority, even if meant reducing the margins between the aircraft's predicted superior performance and the requirements laid down in OR.339. These tight margins between expected and required performance would result in the 'Tight Datum' aircraft. English Electric predicted (correctly, as it turned out) that this choice to allow the margins to tighten up would only lead to problems in the future. A joint team began work on 2 February drawing up a datum aircraft design, beginning by using the Vickers fuselage married with the English Electric wings and tailplane.

By the beginning of March 1959 Vickers and English Electric had also thrashed out a formal agreement for how they would work together to undertake the design and development of the airframe. Vickers-Armstrongs (Aircraft) Ltd had been nominated as the prime contractor, and would carry this responsibility throughout the development period. Vickers was led by Sir George Edwards, with Henry Gardner (Vickers's Technical Director) acting as Chief of Staff and co-ordinating all work on the project. A Joint Project Team had already been formed at Vickers's Weybridge plant, consisting of engineers from both companies (though somewhat English Electric-heavy), led by George Henson of Vickers. Creating the aircraft would require a number of stages, starting with the Project or Study Stage. During this stage, lasting approximately six months, joint studies would be carried out in conjunction with the various governmental organizations and subcontractors to put together a firm specification. This would be followed by the Pre-Guarantee Stage, nine months' work on detailed engineering, construction and cost investigations, together with wind-tunnel and rig tests, leading, as Vickers/English Electric hoped, to a contract for the development and delivery of the completed Weapon System with guarantees as to performance, timetable and cost.

The longest stage would then follow: Detail Design and Development, taking 3½ years and covering detail design and development of every component of the aircraft, leading to the first flight of the first aircraft. Once TSR2 was airborne, the Primary Flight Development Stage would

be entered: 1¼ years and 1,200hr of flight development leading to initial CA release in the strike role. A six-month Secondary Flight Development Stage would follow, to clear the reconnaissance equipment, and during this time the aircraft could be introduced into service with the RAF in the strike role, assuming orders for production aircraft had been placed in time.

While work was to be split equally on a fifty-fifty basis, it was recognized that each company had strengths in certain areas. Thus specialists on each side would act as authorities in particular areas, regardless of whether those areas were being built by their own company. For instance, while Vickers was going to build the wings, English Electric was the specialist authority for aero structures, which took in aerodynamics, aeroelasticity, aeroloadings and control. The division of effort in both design and production split the aircraft into a number of components, half assigned to Vickers and half to English Electric. The division was initially as follows:

Vickers – Wings, front fuselage including bomb bay, undercarriage, equipment.
English Electric – Remainder of airframe, powerplant, power supplies.

After a sustained argument between English Electric and Vickers, Vickers had reluctantly agreed that the P.17's delta wing was the one to go for, and it made little sense for Vickers to continue having the wing in its half of the project when it was the English Electric design that was going to be used. Discussions on fuselage design continued, but in the meantime the work division was adjusted, and English Electric now had responsibility for the wing. The first two airframes would be assembled by a joint team at Weybridge, the intention being to split the team into two after that so that both companies would assemble airframes on an alternating basis from airframe No. 3 onwards.

Work on the Joint Datum Aircraft

Meanwhile, the Joint Project Team had been working on the Tight Datum aircraft, soon renamed the Joint Datum aircraft. This became, in effect, a detailed engineering assessment of Vickers's work on the fuselage, something English Electric had been keen to do, as it believed this was impractical in

terms of equipment space and glossed over or omitted many vital items. (There was a commonly held view at English Electric that Vickers had carried out the bare minimum of design-study work.) The complex fuel tank arrangement within the Type 571 fuselage was simplified, and minor changes were made to various other items in the rear fuselage. English Electric was not at all keen on Vickers's forward-retracting main undercarriage, but reluctantly accepted the situation as it was, intending to return to it later.

Adding the P.17 wing to the Type 571 immediately resulted in an unbalanced aircraft, with a shortened tail arm. The obvious solution to this was to extend the fuselage 5ft (1.5m) to the rear, restoring the tail arm, though this also meant that a compensating forward-fuselage extension of 2.25ft (0.7m) was needed. While the aircraft's weight would increase, the additional space could be used for more fuel to restore lost range. The longer rear fuselage necessitated increasing the height of the undercarriage to avoid the fuselage hitting the ground when rotating on take-off. Vickers could not see English Electric's underwing intake ever working, so it stuck with its own intake length, though incorporating English Electric's conventional wedge opening. This first attempt at combining the P.17 and Type 571 weighed in at 81,765lb (37,115kg) fully loaded for the OR's 1,000nm sortie. Freddie Page, head of the Warton design team, had remarked on several occasions that if the aircraft ever got to the 75,000lb (34,000kg) mark it was 'time to rub it out and start again'. That, however, was not about to happen.

The next change was to extend the fuselage again, by 1ft (0.3m) at the nose and 2.5ft (0.76m) at the rear, as the previous extension had not been enough to rebalance the aircraft. This then required that the wing and intake face be moved aft by 2.5ft (0.76m) to retain their relationship with the tailplane. Both tailplane and fin areas were slightly reduced, and provision was made within the fuselage for a water tank, heat shielding around the engines, and various ancillaries such as rain dispersal for the windscreen. With the fuselage looking as though it was going to need to be widened to accommodate the large low-pressure tyres, an attempt was also made to reshape the weapons bay, tapering it towards the forward end to allow the undercarriage to be stowed diagonally rather than vertically.

The engineering penalties of a forward-retracting main undercarriage were now beginning to become obvious, and the joint project team attempted to incorporate rearward-retracting gear. Engines could now be removed vertically via the undercarriage bay roof/engine bay floor, as per the P.17. However, additional heat shielding was necessary, and various weight penalties were incurred. This would further unbalance the aircraft on the ground, and this, combined with some changes in transonic behaviour owing to the larger tailplane, was going to make this change difficult to justify. The idea went on the back-burner.

Vickers now introduced the use of a new aluminium alloy, X2020, which promised much, being lighter and stronger than conventional alloys. As it promised a weight saving of 2,500lb (1,135kg) overall, despite its expense it was just the sort of improvement that Vickers liked, though Henry Gardner was fearful of 'being first to uncover faults', and English Electric was concerned about the cost. The next issue of the datum design drawing had the weapons

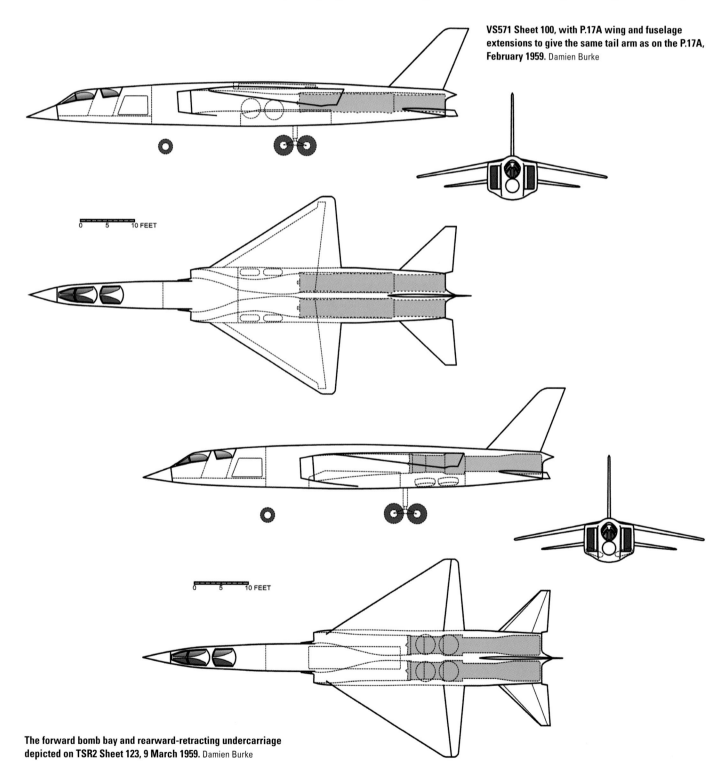

VS571 Sheet 100, with P.17A wing and fuselage extensions to give the same tail arm as on the P.17A, February 1959. Damien Burke

The forward bomb bay and rearward-retracting undercarriage depicted on TSR2 Sheet 123, 9 March 1959. Damien Burke

bay returned to a rectangular shape, and the main undercarriage retracting forward and being stowed nearly vertically alongside. The tailplane area was reduced, and both leading- and trailing-edge flaps were added to the tailplane, allowing a reduction in the amount of tailplane movement and improving ground clearance in the landing attitude. A braking parachute was also added. Because of the weight reduction brought about by the use of X2020 and the improved braking capability, the lighter and less powerful Olympus 15R engine was reverted to (the 22R having been under serious consideration before this point). For the first time in the design process, the upward trend of weight gain was reversed, this version weighing in at 75,004lb (34,044kg), though a re-estimating exercise would soon bring this up to 77,942lb (35,378kg).

Immediately afterwards, another problem confronted the joint project team. The Olympus 15R was proving to have lower thrust and higher fuel consumption than the brochure figures. The 22R was going to be needed after all to meet the OR figures, despite the reduction in airframe weight. The predicted costs of the 22R had tripled since the brochure had been issued, and it was a heavier engine, too. The airframe's weight climbed again. George Edwards's unhappiness with the forced selection of BSEL as the engine provider was one point upon which English Electric and Vickers agreed wholeheartedly. They even went so far as to suggest that the time might soon come when they would have to make it clear that the MoS's decision to go with the Olympus was having a serious effect on the performance of the aircraft, to protect themselves from future criticism. Nevertheless, it was no surprise that the next issue of the design had the Olympus 22R back in place, and the 15R made no further appearance. Dive brakes were also now in place on the fuselage, and the tailplane area was increased once more.

Throughout the work on the drawing up of a datum design, Vickers and English Electric were also keeping abreast of changes being made to the operational requirement. The fourth and final draft of OR.339 had been issued back in December 1958, but it was to be superseded by a new OR, OR.343, the first draft of which was issued in March 1959. Vickers's George Henson attended a meeting at the MoS on 11 March to discuss runway requirements, fighting off an attempt to require tyres of

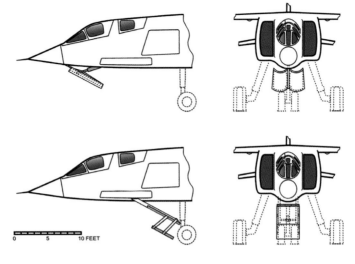

Two variations on nose flaps tested on a wind-tunnel model to see if they could assist with lifting the nose earlier during the take-off run. They were found to give only a small nose-up trim change and were not proceeded with.
Damien Burke

such low pressure (45 to 60psi (3.16 to 4.22kg/sq cm)) that the aircraft would need to be substantially enlarged just to fit the resulting large tyres in the fuselage. About the best Vickers could offer was 80psi (5.62kg/sq cm), with 70psi (4.92kg/sq cm) for the nosewheel, though this would rule out operation from a grass surface. This was agreed, along with an aircraft LCN requirement not to exceed 22. While Vickers had taken the STOL requirement more seriously than English Electric to begin with, it was now English Electric that was becoming concerned about the aircraft's runway performance. High thrust and flap settings on take-off would tend to force the nose down to begin with, delaying the point at which the nose could be lifted, and thus extending the take-off roll. Consideration of a shorter tail arm would make the problem worse. Various methods had been discussed to try to get the nose off earlier in the take-off run, such as using the nose gear doors for lift, auxiliary lifting engines in the forward fuselage, nose flaps, and so on, but no firm decisions had been made other than to investigate an extending nose gear leg.

An Airframe Advisory Design Conference between English Electric and Vickers was held on 22 March 1959, to discuss work so far on the airframe configuration. Discussions also began between Vickers and the MoS in the first week of April as to the terms of a contract covering the design work that by then had already been under way since the start of the year, along with further meetings to discuss individual aspects of the 'new' OR.

OR.339 is dead; long live OR.343

On 19 February 1959 the Air Staff informed the MoS that 'GOR.339 was dead' and the new aircraft would be known as OR.343. The existing description of TSR2 would be retained, however, as 'it was popular with the politicians'. OR.343's final draft was completed on 26 March 1959, and introduced some significant changes to the requirement when compared with OR.339. The first official issue of OR.343, Issue 1, was completed on 8 May 1959 (*see* Appendix II).

One no-doubt-intended side effect of renumbering the requirement was that Short Brothers & Harland was now truly left out in the cold, no longer able to claim any rights in the joint English Electric/Shorts P.17 proposal to GOR.339 because the TSR2 was now supposedly being built to an entirely new OR. There was substantial anger at Shorts, which felt betrayed by both English Electric and their part owner, the government. This boiled over at a meeting on 10 July between the Controller (Aircraft) (Air Chief Marshal Sir Claude Pelly) and representatives of Shorts (Sir Matthew Slattery) and English Electric (Robin Caldecote), at which Shorts forcefully expressed its disappointment at being 'completely excluded from the TSR2 project, despite the fact that much of the aircraft which is emerging from the Vickers/English Electric collaboration bears a close resemblance to the English Electric/Shorts submission to GOR.339'. The mood at Shorts was not improved when, less than two weeks later, English Electric informed Shorts that Vickers was working on a proposal to use RB.108 lift engines on the TSR2 to improve rotation at take-off. Shorts immediately wrote to Sir Claude, claiming design rights on this type of jet lift, pointing out that it was contained within the joint English Electric/Shorts submission. Shorts had already carried out a considerable amount of work on jet lift, and expected to receive some recognition in the form of work under contract or a licence fee. The MoS was unimpressed, considering Shorts claim 'a try-on' and 'preposterous'. It pointed out that the SC.1 research aircraft and the RB.108 were both entirely funded by the Ministry, and that anything deriving from this work would '... fall to the Ministry to exploit for defence purposes as they wished'. Shorts would continue to be excluded from the project.

The jet-lift platform itself, while of no apparent interest to the RAF, was still considered a viable project by Shorts and, to a lesser extent, English Electric, and on that basis English Electric had come up with a way to keep Shorts on side. An agreement had been drawn up between the two regarding collaboration on any future VTO projects, whether they concerned a lift platform or a strike reconnaissance aircraft for a rumoured NATO requirement. This agreement spelled out that work would be shared equally between the two companies, design leadership being vested in either English Electric (if the aircraft using the platform was to be an English Electric design) or with Shorts (if the aircraft using the platform was to be from any other company, e.g. the Gnat). English Electric wrote to the MoS in June 1959, asking for an assurance that any future contract awarded to this English Electric/Shorts partnership would accept that the partnership was valid in and of itself, with no need for a third party; i.e. that there would be no repetition of the Ministry's efforts to shut Shorts out of the English Electric/Shorts/Vickers grouping. The CA wrote back in July, apologising that he felt unable to give such an assurance. It seemed the government was happy for aircraft companies to band together, but only if they did so in a manner entirely approved by the government.

The first Joint Datum Aircraft

At a meeting at Weybridge on 17 April 1959 English Electric and Vickers agreed to accept the then-proposed Joint Datum Aircraft for continued work in all areas. English Electric was still unhappy with many items, believing, for instance, that an intake aft of the wing leading edge (as per the P.17) could be made to work and would provide valuable weight saving and a neater design. (However, its own windtunnel tests did not bode well, and later American experience with a similar intake on the TFX project would run into problems too). The company was also concerned with the emphasis on attaining a high lift coefficient for the wing at all costs (thus reducing approach speed), when weight, drag and parachute delay were all more important to meeting the OR's needs in terms of STOL performance. The undercarriage also seemed too complex, and the coincidence of wheels, intakes and weapon bay in the same area resulted in a large cross-section in a drag-critical area and a weapon bay of limited capacity. Clearance was more than adequate for a single Target Marker Bomb, but very tight for six 1,000lb conventional HE bombs. English Electric would only agree to the joint datum configuration as a basis for further work if work continued on an 'acceptable' forward-retracting undercarriage and a shorter engine installation tunnel (not enclosing the engine itself) was used.

No company relies upon a single customer or a single contract, and TSR2 was

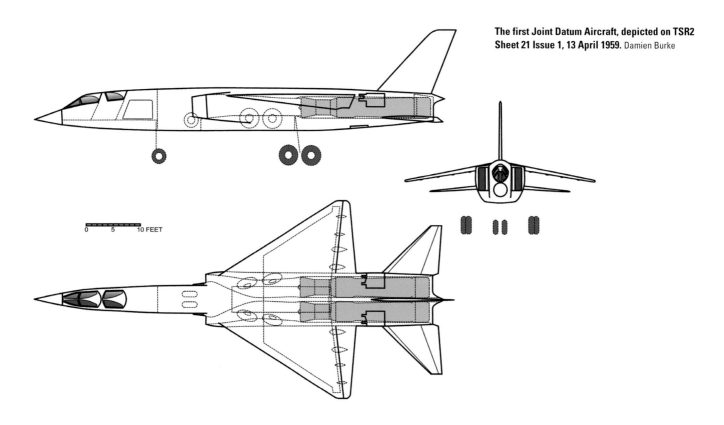

The first Joint Datum Aircraft, depicted on TSR2 Sheet 21 Issue 1, 13 April 1959. Damien Burke

0 5 10 FEET

not being designed in a vacuum. Vickers, flush from apparent success with the Scimitar, Valiant and Viscount airliner, was also busy with the Vanguard turboprop airliner and the VC10 jet airliner. However, it had badly underestimated the development effort required on these two aircraft, and the company's financial position was taking a turn for the worse. Both projects were private ventures, as required by the MoS for all civil developments, and the burden was unexpectedly heavy. Vickers turned to a possible collaboration with de Havilland, which had a guaranteed BEA contract for a new airliner, as a means of pleasing its Ministry masters and convincing them to bail Vickers out with some government funding for the VC10 and a smaller aircraft, the VC11. De Havilland, however, was rightfully wary of an approach from Vickers, correctly judging that it was simply part of a plan to gain aid for the VC10. Moreover, the fact that the VC11 would compete against its own BEA airliner was also a serious problem. The MoS, by now led by Duncan Sandys, was keen to see another aviation industry merger, but less keen to offer government funding. For the time being, Vickers continued to slide into a financial mire. Its efforts on TSR2 suffered as a result, with George Edwards's primary focus elsewhere and English Electric firmly

believing that almost all of the real engineering at this stage was being carried out entirely by its own personnel.

Meanwhile, work continued on the joint datum design, and on the forward fuselage in particular. The nose internal layout underwent substantial revision to move items around and give a more logical arrangement, with room for control runs and air pipes that Vickers had neglected in its original draughting of the Type 571. The centre-fuselage layout also needed careful consideration, as the reconnaissance pack's interaction with this area was an important factor. But the reconnaissance pack was a responsibility of the MoS, not of Vickers or English Electric, which complicated matters greatly. Soon leading-edge flaps were added to the wing to try to gain a bit more lift at the higher angles of attack necessary to meet the shorter-field requirements, and provision was made within the fuselage to house the electronics package necessary to carry and fire Bullpup missiles. With all this and the further addition of a braking parachute rail to improve crosswind braking capability, the weight had now risen to 80,914lb (36,727kg).

Windtunnel work had been under way for months, using models of the original P.17 and P.17 models modified to try to get close to the joint layouts as these became

available, and they were now showing problems with the wing. Downwash from the wing was reducing the effectiveness of the tailplane and moving the aerodynamic centre forward. The aircraft's c.g. was also much too far aft. With flaps down in particular, longitudinal stability was borderline. To add to the problems, BSEL's latest specification for the Olympus 22R was showing increased fuel consumption compared with previous estimates. This would impact on the aircraft's combat radius and its take-off performance. To try to solve these various problems, four layouts were drawn up with different fin, tailplane and wing-area combinations, tailplane root positions, fuselage lengths, undercarriage track and leg lengths, intake and engine positions, and ventral fins. None was entirely acceptable, though the smallest of the enlarged fins was kept.

At a meeting on 11 June it was decided that there was no option but to increase the wing area by 10 per cent to regain the combat radius and take-off performance lost by the new engine figures, correct the c.g. by extending the fuselage, and improve tailplane effectiveness by enlarging it once more. Two versions of this layout were tested, scheme A having the largest tailplane and scheme B having the engines moved forward to try to correct the c.g., along with an enlarged tailplane that was smaller than

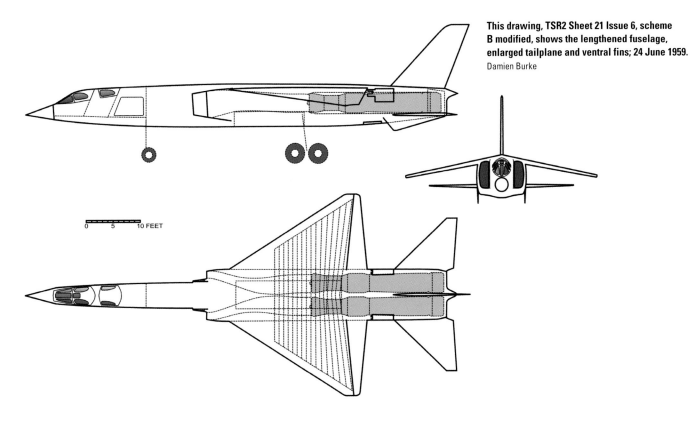

This drawing, TSR2 Sheet 21 Issue 6, scheme B modified, shows the lengthened fuselage, enlarged tailplane and ventral fins; 24 June 1959.
Damien Burke

0   5   10 FEET

that in scheme A. Tailplane effectiveness was still insufficient, and the tailplane would now hit the ground with the aircraft fully flared on landing. The further enlargement of a tailplane that had already seen several increases in size was also bringing it to a critical size at which flutter could be a problem, so work continued on a combination of the two schemes: the tailplane of scheme B, but no engine shift. English Electric had also been pressing for another attempt at bringing the intake back aft of the wing leading edge and including a rearward-retracting undercarriage, and produced a drawing. The disadvantages, however, were just too many, and this configuration was finally buried for good. Along with it went a simplified main undercarriage of four wheels on each side. English Electric had considered Vickers's draft undercarriage design 'impossible', and Vickers had expressed some interest in the simpler four-wheel P.17 arrangement that it claimed not to have seen previously.

By 24 June the next drawing was issued. Ground clearance for the tailplane in the landing flare was regained by reducing its anhedral to zero. Small ventral fins, as on the P.17, were introduced at the tailplane

root. Frustratingly, stability still remained a problem with flaps down. A week later a drastic change had been made to try to break out of the vicious circle of mainplane and tailplane changes. The wing lost its anhedral so that it was flat on the underside, the topside taper giving a little over 1 degree anhedral along the upper surface. This was the most powerful way of reducing wing/tailplane interference, as it allowed an increase in the vertical distance between these surfaces, though it introduced some vulnerability to sideslip-induced rolling. (The Dutch roll phenomenon, an unpleasant rolling/snaking motion that can be exhibited by swept-wing aircraft with low anhedral). The situation was much improved but, frustratingly, some problems with flaps down continued. Tests showed that, with the flaps lowered to 50 degrees, the tailplane could still stall at relatively small pitch angles. To remedy this, two variations of an even larger tailplane with increased sweep were schemed. Additionally, the wing was modified to give a little more lift, the drooped leading edge being extended forward on the outer half of the wing, and notched at its own halfway point. A combination of a 30-degree drooped

mainplane leading-edge extension plus the largest flapped tailplane produced the best results, including the hoped-for increase in lift, and was therefore adopted. (In later windtunnel testing the drooped leading edge would prove to be less effective than predicted, and the sawtooth extension would introduce a kink in the pitching-moment curve; the dreaded 'pitch-up' phenomenon that had dogged so many swept-wing designs). As a bonus, because the wing was now flat, it was found that the tailplane could be moved a little further up the fuselage side, its anhedral reintroduced, and the ventral fins deleted. To improve pilot view on approach to landing, the nose was lowered by reducing the curve along the fuselage underside.

In June 1959 contract negotiations finally resulted in a contract being placed with Vickers to cover the work that both Vickers and English Electric had been carrying out since the start of the year. This would see them through to the end of the year, by which time it was expected that they would produce a detailed technical and administrative plan for completion of the development, complete with cost estimates. Part of the deal was to produce a brochure within a month to show progress so far.

Preliminary Brochure

With the stability problems continuing, the required brochure was put together. It included a general-arrangement of the TSR2 as it now was, with sawtooth extensions on a zero-anhedral wing (though windtunnel work was still going on, to see just how effective the sawtooth extensions were), large tailplanes, a relatively small fin and wedge intakes. The systems work that had been going on in parallel with the basic aerodynamic layout enabled the drawings in the brochure to be finely detailed and recognizably close to the final aircraft. The weight had continued to climb, albeit more slowly, and was now at 85,870lb (38,976kg). A detailed specification could now be put together, and this was issued as RB.192D (D for 'development'; when the time was ripe a new specification, RB.192P, would be worked out to cover production aircraft).

As an aircraft, the brochure TSR2 was far from a practical flying machine, with some problems expected in particular areas aside from the known stability issues, notably in lateral gust response, where the effect on the crew positions of flying

A windtunnel model similar to the aircraft depicted on TSR2 Sheet 21 Issue 6, albeit with no wing anhedral. The ventral fins, a throwback to the P.17 design, did not last long and were soon deleted from the design. BAE Systems via Brooklands Museum

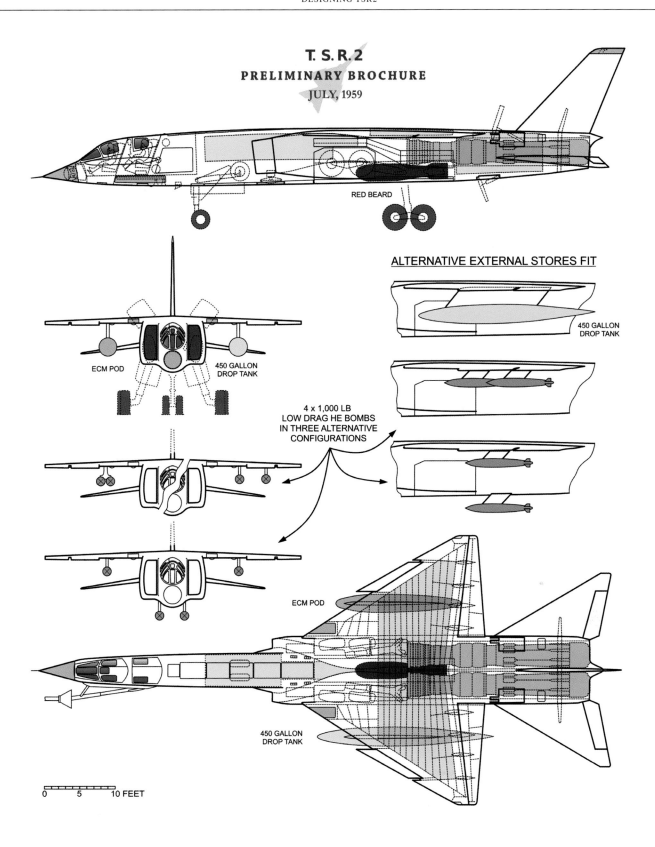

T. S. R. 2
PRELIMINARY BROCHURE
JULY, 1959

RED BEARD

ALTERNATIVE EXTERNAL STORES FIT

450 GALLON DROP TANK

ECM POD

450 GALLON DROP TANK

4 x 1,000 LB LOW DRAG HE BOMBS IN THREE ALTERNATIVE CONFIGURATIONS

ECM POD

450 GALLON DROP TANK

0   5   10 FEET

Drawing TSR2 Sheet 00/1 shows the configuration as published in the Preliminary Brochure of July 1959, with wing anhedral removed and sawtooth leading edges added. The first proposed external stores configurations are also illustrated, though these are based on drawings from October 1959. Damien Burke

79

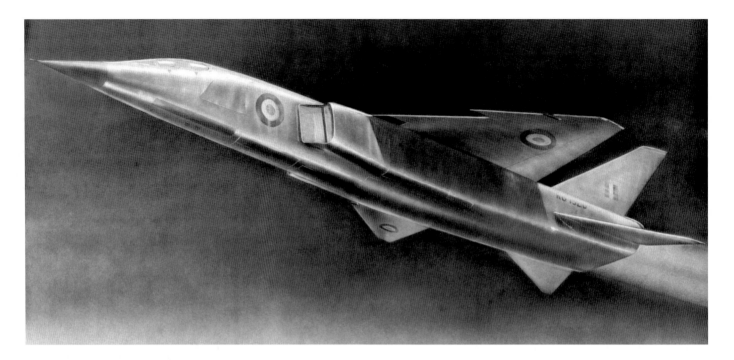

ABOVE: **An artist's impression of TSR2 to RB.192D, July 1959. While becoming recognizably a TSR2, the configuration outlined in the preliminary brochure was far from being a practical design. Changes to the intakes, wings, fin and rear fairing would all be required.** BAE Systems via Warton Heritage Group

LEFT: **A windtunnel model of TSR2 with tufts attached to the starboard wing surface to aid flow visualization. The upper rear fuselage lines seen here were a short-lived variation.** BAE Systems via Brooklands Museum

through continuous low-level turbulence would give a less-than-comfortable ride. However, it was a contractual obligation to produce the brochure, and, had there been any further delay, Vickers/English Electric would not have been popular with the MoS. Naturally the problem areas escaped mention in the brochure. It was also carefully described as a preliminary brochure, as there were various areas covered that neither Vickers nor English Electric wanted to end up being used as guarantee points in the production contract.

Only the most basic of undercarriage layouts had been drawn up to this point (unsurprisingly, given the number of changes the airframe had gone through), and there had been much argument with English Electric over each layout tried. Designing an undercarriage that could cope with poor-quality surfaces, such as Second World War airfields that had seen little use or maintenance since 1945, was going to be a challenge. It was not until August that Vickers was really able to begin detailed work in this area. The conclusions of a meeting on 25 August give some idea of the importance Vickers attached to getting the undercarriage right: 'We are justified in putting our highest grade talent on to this area. If we are relaxed about it we shall get a heavy undercarriage, unsatisfactory performance, lose the contract and deserve it.' Research into surface quality and its effect on existing aircraft was soon begun. Trials using a Scimitar on the grass strip at Wisley and the disused Second World War runway at Turweston were scheduled for later in the year, to give some idea of the stresses to which both airframe and undercarriage were subjected when travelling across rough surfaces.

A programme of research on variable-intake efficiencies had been instigated by English Electric in co-operation with Vickers and BSEL, looking not only at the current wedge intake, but also at a double-wedge intake and a half-cone wedge intake. No design had shown particular theoretical superiority, and the team agreed that the decision on a final choice would be based more on structural and engineering reasons than efficiency calculations.

A Preliminary Brochure windtunnel model, with large blades added to a flattened sawtooth wing leading edge in an attempt to squeeze more lift from the wing without using a cambered sawtooth. Note the simple lines of the underside of the rear fuselage. BAE Systems via Brooklands Museum

Windtunnel tests on models of wedge and conical intakes were carried out, and the results became available in September. While performance was, as predicted, much the same, engineering analysis of the designs showed that the conical intake would be structurally simpler and thus offer a small but useful weight saving, and the rectangular wedge intake had some destabilizing effect in pitch. The wedge intakes were dropped, and cone intakes drawn in. The weight was now down to 85,200lb (38,670kg).

During October, work finished on the comparison of a fixed versus all-moving fin,

and the all-moving fin was confirmed as part of the final configuration. This helps to illustrate part of the problem involved in designing a complete airframe. Decisions on configuration often need to be taken before there is enough information to be sure the decision is correct. In the case of the choice of fin type, the correct decision had been made early on, but in other areas, such as the wing configuration, a continual evolution resulted as more and more configurations turned out to be less than ideal after windtunnel and theoretical work.

By November 1959 Vickers/English Electric had produced some production plans

and estimates, and had submitted them to the MoS. They were an unwelcome shock to the men at the Ministry; it had become clear that the magnitude of the task confronting everyone was far greater than predicted, and the estimated costs of getting the aircraft to CA release had risen from £35 million to £62 million. It was also clear that the complexity of the weapons system was going to create some very tight deadlines if the CA release date of 1965 was to be adhered to; there would be no time for vacillation. English Electric had estimated it would need 44 months from Intention to Proceed to first flight; Vickers

By September 1959 the half-cone intakes had been incorporated within the TSR2 design, and BAC produced this mocked-up scene of the aircraft landing at Warton. (T2-2) BAE Systems via Brooklands Museum

estimated 40 months and, naturally, the lower of the two figures was quoted to the MoS.

Despite the jump in costs and concern on progress, the MoS was still behind the project, and sought Treasury approval to fund development, with a possible additional £15 million to £25 million to cover any unforeseen problems during development and flight testing. It also made it clear that time was short; an extension of the 1959 contract with Vickers would soon be necessary, along with a letter of intent to cover the development batch of aircraft, otherwise there would be an expensive hiatus in the programme.

Vickers's financial troubles had continued to focus the management's minds on ways out of the mess, and English Electric had been brought into discussions on the possible amalgamation of Vickers and de Havilland. English Electric was not keen on this, as it could see itself becoming a junior partner in a much larger enterprise. Various options were considered, including English Electric making a hostile takeover of de Havilland, but Vickers and English Electric could not agree on a course of action that made them both happy. English Electric, realizing Vickers's preoccupation with civil projects, spotted an opportunity to 'take back' P.17 and build TSR2 on its own. Lord Caldecote of English Electric noted in August 1959 that: 'If Vickers are really to undertake these additional responsibilities in the civil field, I think we

should press very strongly indeed for the transfer of the main contract for the TSR-2 to English Electric. This no doubt would be difficult but at the stage when the specification has been agreed during the autumn it would not be impossible.' English Electric then applied to the CA, Aubrey Jones, to take over TSR2 and leave Vickers to get on with its marriage to de Havilland. Jones would have none of it, and TSR2 continued as a joint Vickers/English Electric project. The VC10 would continue to drag Vickers's eye off the TSR2 ball for the immediate future.

Work on the final TSR2 airframe design continued over the next few months, the issuing of general-arrangement drawings slowing down as the airframe came ever closer to the final configuration. Most of the work was related to the internals, and the English Electric members of the Joint Project Team returned home to Warton in October. A tour of the USA and several aerospace companies there had been undertaken by various English Electric/Vickers and government personnel, to study the state of the art there, and this triggered a number of changes to TSR2, such as a switch from mechanical to electrical signalling (with mechanical backup) for the flight control system.

In parallel with airframe design work, there was plenty of research and investigation going on to assist with the detail design of various airframe systems, such as the undercarriage. On this score, trials began at

Vickers's airfield at Wisley, with Scimitar WW134 carrying out three fast taxy runs on the grass at speeds from 65 to 85kt (75 to 98mph; 120 to 157km/h), and then taking off from the grass. The Scimitar's tyres were 100psi (7.0kg/sq cm) mains with a 200psi (14.0kg/sq cm) nosewheel, and the ride was a rough one, though as soon as the nosewheel was lifted all vibration and noise stopped. It was clear that the 100psi main wheels were not doing too badly at all on grass, though braking action was poor and the brakes overheated after sustained use. Trials then moved to Turweston, then used for agriculture and the storage and scrapping of surplus military vehicles. The runway was cleared of farm machinery, rusting tanks and other detritus, leaving just the undulations, potholes, mud and traces of oil common to disused World War Two airfields, and WW134 was flown in to begin trials on 3 December. The arrival was unexpectedly exciting, as the aircraft's brakes disintegrated when full braking was needed, causing a violent swing to one side that the pilot corrected just in time. Having finally stopped after using 1,400yd (1,280m) of runway (800yd (730m) being the usual figure), one tyre was found to be badly cut. No spare part-worn low-pressure tyres were available, so standard 130psi (9kg/sq cm) tyres were fitted and a single taxy run was then carried out, followed by a take-off to return to Wisley. In the process the Scimitar's efflux ripped up huge sections of the runway surface. A rethink on safety delayed further tests until 20 January 1960, when further damage was caused to the runway surface, and the same happened again during two days of testing in March, when lower-pressure tyres were used. The important results, however, were that the aircraft came through the trials well, and relatively small undercarriage oleo displacements were experienced, even going over huge potholes. Braking on grass was going to be more of a problem than operating from rough strips, and it looked as though Vickers's undercarriage design for the TSR2 would fully meet the rough runway requirement.

At about this time the RAF was finalizing the number of TSR2s it wanted. Initial thoughts were of numbers to gladden George Edwards's heart; a front line of 170 aircraft was required. Add to that forty aircraft for the Operational Conversion Unit (OCU), plus ninety aircraft as 'backing' (i.e. replacements for others as they were worn out, crashed or, if the unthinkable

LEFT: **A TSR2 windtunnel fuselage model with half-cone intakes and the in-flight refuelling probe fairing. The latter was later reduced in size slightly so that its aft end would not foul the equipment-bay door.** BAE Systems via Brooklands Museum

BELOW: **Damage to the Second World War runway at Turweston after a single take-off run by Scimitar WW134 in January 1960. Surface erosion of this sort would have been a serious issue when operating the much more powerful TSR2 from rough strips.** BAE Systems via Brooklands Museum

happened, shot down), and you had a total of 300. These numbers would soon tumble downwards as the costs began to rise.

At the end of December the design study contract ran out, but work had to continue regardless if the project was to have any hope of meeting its deadline. On 1 January 1960 the wing thickness taper was made equal on top and bottom, thus losing the flat lower surface and simplifying construction somewhat. The large main undercarriage bay doors were creating a substantial destabilizing effect when open, and various means were tried to ameliorate this, such as smaller bay doors, horizontal strakes on the nose, an extra sawtooth extension on the wing leading edge, and baffles and fairings around and within the undercarriage bays. In windtunnel tests the most impressive results came from an airframe change, lengthening the fuselage by 18in (46cm) to bring it in line with the tailplane trailing edge, and also raising the tailplane position. It was also helpful to ensure that the main doors were closed immediately after the undercarriage had been lowered, and this change, the fuselage extension and the revised tailplane position were incor-

porated. Windtunnel tests had also been carried out in November of a down-turned wingtip designed to combat Dutch roll, and the results were now available and looked promising.

The design was now allegedly frozen so that detailed production drawings could be produced and the work of building the aircraft could begin. However, by late February increases in the weight of the engines, reheat pipes and reheat nozzles had contributed to another rearward shift of the c.g. The sawtooth leading edge with variable leading-edge flap had shifted the aerodynamic centre forward, added weight and further reduced the aft c.g. limit, making the balance problem acute and introducing some undesirable pitch characteristics. Three methods were considered for dealing with this: moving the undercarriage aft by changing the pintle position, along with moving the wing and tail further aft and extending the nose; a similar scheme but with a bodily movement of the undercarriage (entailing centre fuselage redesign); or a similar scheme but using increased rake on the undercarriage oleo to change its position. Transonic stability had suffered in

the most recent windtunnel tests of a fully representative TSR2 layout, the sawtooth leading edge causing an undesirable transonic aerodynamic centre shift. The favoured solution was to delete it and extend the wing chord by moving the trailing edge back.

Windtunnel results on the down-turned wingtip had shown that it introduced no adverse effects and dealt with the Dutch roll issue, and the reduction in the span of the flaps produced no serious change in their performance either. Such wingtips would require a complex joint at the end of the primary wing box, but as there was minimal loss of lift there was a strong case for going ahead with this change. There were, however, some strong disagreements with the analysis produced by the windtunnel section at Warton, one writer describing it as 'the most dishonest windtunnel report I have ever seen'. Discussion bounced back and forth until the matter was eventually brought to a head when the design was placed on Freddie Page's desk for a final decision. He wasted no time; the downturned tips were in, and the sawtooth leading edge was out.

A meeting on 31 March then dealt with the 're-freezing' of the design, and by April 1960 the airframe was very close to the final and now-familiar TSR2 layout. A drawing issued on the 12th showed the fuselage extended by 6in (15cm) and the wing, tailplane and main undercarriage moved aft 3in (7.6cm) to fix the balance problem. As per Freddie Page's decision, the leading-edge sawtooth extension on the wing was deleted, the wing chord had been extended rearward 24in (61cm) at the tip to give a perpendicular trailing edge, and the wing tips extended and angled down at 30 degrees, keeping the overall span the same. The fin had been moved 18in (45.7cm) further aft, and the lines of the rear fuselage had been adjusted. This final shift in the airframe configuration may have dealt with the outstanding issues, but it also dealt a blow to English Electric's production plans, as drawings had to be withdrawn from the production shops, incurring a three-month delay before work could resume.

The rear fuselage had turned out to be another problem area. The July 1959 datum design had included a simple twin reheat nozzle configuration without an ejector nozzle. However, analysis of windtunnel data several months later showed that this area had excessive base drag, and research in Britain and the USA had revealed that afterbody suction was a significant contributor to this. It was a big setback, and leaving the rear-fuselage design unchanged would result in a fuel penalty of up to 6,000lb (2,720kg). Air Ministry staff later misunderstood this, and accused BAC of

'forgetting' base drag in its initial design. To solve the problem, the partial vacuum generated here had to be relieved, and the way to do this was to use a fixed airframe ejector nozzle, opening a small gap between the reheat nozzle and the rear fairing to permit airflow through the gap. Asked to reduce the diameter of the final reheat nozzle by 2in (5cm) to make room for this, BSEL readily agreed. As can be seen, although it was supposedly a frozen design, there was still some work under way on the actual shape of the aircraft, though few further changes would now occur. Windtunnel testing was also finally showing acceptable stability and balance, though underwing stores gave some destabilizing effect. Particularly large underwing stores were proving to be a real worry.

Meanwhile, there had been constant debate within the government's various Ministries as to whether the project was really necessary. The latest NA.39 development and a new foreign contender, the McDonnell F4H Phantom II ('a much more attractive prospect than any Blackburn Beast'), were brought up time and again. The Air Ministry put together a paper clearly laying out the need for the TSR2, and the new Ministry of Aviation (the MoS's successor) finally accepted OR.343. The need for low-level penetration to survive in the modern air defence environment was underlined on 1 May 1960, when a United States Air Force (USAF) Lockheed U-2 reconnaissance aircraft was swatted out of the sky over Sverdlovsk in central Russia by a surface-to-air missile (SAM). Like the October 1959 loss of a Taiwanese Martin RB-57 Canberra over China, this was another victory for the S-75 (SA-2 *Guideline*) missile. The TSR2's low-level capabilities were now, without a doubt, the only way to get to the target.

However, the Treasury remained unconvinced, and the next design contract was not finally signed until mid-June, and only covered the period from the start of the year to September 1960. Work also began around this time on designing test rigs for the powered flying controls, general services hydraulics, fuel system (a sophisticated rig that could tilt to allow testing in various flight attitudes) and flap blowing and gearing. To verify stressing calculations on the wing and fuselage structure, test boxes were drawn up, sample areas of structure that could be put together and strength tested before real production components were put together. Planning also began for the

flight test programme and the instrumentation that would be needed, plus how it could be fitted to the aircraft.

By now, the problem of nosewheel lifting on the take-off run had been rumbling on for many months, Ray Creasey of English Electric being particularly concerned and regarding it as the current design's real Achille's heel. Vickers's solution was to incorporate a nose gear leg extension that would be selectable by the pilot. If both tailplane surfaces were equally used for pitch at their maximum extent, an extension of 2.5ft (0.76m) would suffice to lift the nose early enough to meet the shortest take-off run requirement. However, no roll control would be available, and short take-offs with any significant crosswind would become a serious problem. If 5 degrees of tailplane travel were reserved for roll control, the nosewheel extension would need to be 4ft (1.2m) or more, and that was the absolute limit that could be accommodated in the current design. The tailplane travel could well still be insufficient for full roll control in a strong crosswind, and English Electric even looked at a scheme for fitting small ailerons on the wingtips. Moving the main undercarriage 3in (7.6cm) forward of its current position, however, helped things somewhat. Meeting the take-off requirements would now be possible, although special take-off techniques would be required involving the timed selection of the nose-wheel extension and flap blowing during the take-off run to get the best effect.

The final big airframe problem to be dealt with (or so it was thought) was the fin. The size of fin needed to retain directional stability at supersonic speeds was huge, and weight and drag considerations, along with the massive side loads that would be induced during rapid rolls, meant that this was simply not practical. The way forward seemed to be the smallest possible fin coupled with an auto-stiffener mechanism that detected lateral accelerations and automatically moved the fin by small degrees to compensate, and this relatively small fin, with an area of 87sq ft (8.08sq m), was a feature of almost all of the general-arrangement drawings throughout the design process. However, by September 1960 it was becoming clear that the fin needed some serious work, as its flutter speed had turned out to be unacceptably low, at just half of the design's maximum diving speed. Similar problems with the tailplane had been solved by strengthening the root rib, which avoided the need to improve spigot stiffness; the

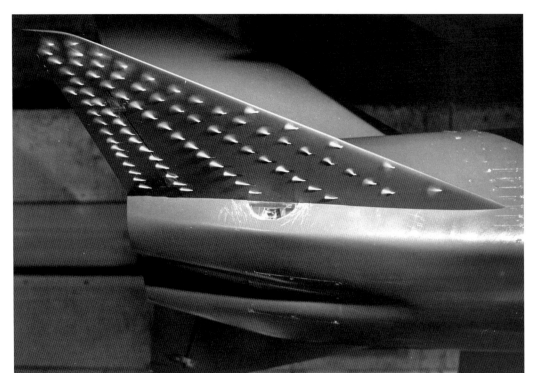

LEFT: **This windtunnel model has a configuration very close to the final layout of tailplane, large fin and contoured rear fairing. Tufts on the underside of the tailplane give an indication of the airflow over the surface.** BAE Systems via Brooklands Museum

BELOW: **TSR2 final layout – with down-turned wingtips, sawtooth deleted and enlarged fin; February 1961. Only minor changes would follow from this date, e.g. to navigation beacon light positions.**

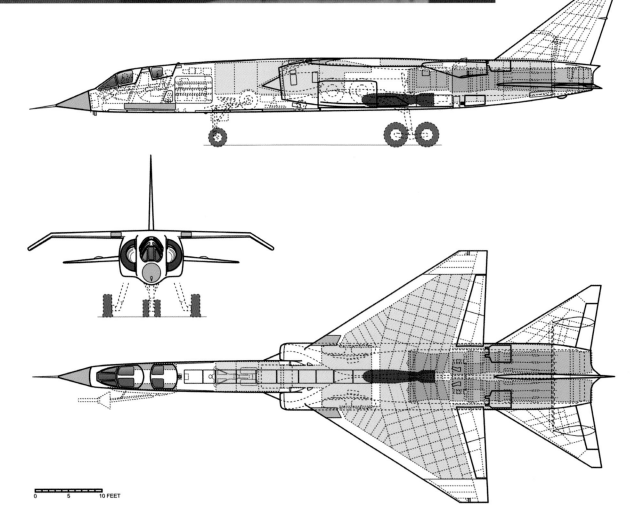

0   5   10 FEET

fin was not so easily fixed. A protracted argument blew up between English Electric and Vickers-Armstrongs over the solution to fin flutter, and to Vickers-Armstrongs' displeasure English Electric presented a much larger 109 sq ft (10.12sq m) fin that went part way to solving the flutter issue, though the necessary root thickness was huge. Vickers-Armstrongs was not at all happy with the resulting serious weight and drag penalty, and while it tinkered with the planform, resulting in the final 105 sq ft (9.75sq m) fin with a small blister at the base to cover the bearing, English Electric discovered that a mass-balance at the base of the leading edge was fairly effective in reducing flutter, and appropriate windtunnel tests were begun. To everybody's horror they showed that flutter was still a problem at high Mach numbers, and increasing the size of the mass-balance was not practical. The eventual solution, born of desperation, was the inclusion of a sprung mass-balance. A pair of spring-linked weights with hydraulic dampers would be installed in

the fin leading edge, by the root, and careful engineering meant no further changes to the planform to accommodate this. Despite the fin's increased size, the auto-stiffener would still be required. This was an interesting early example of the advantages of accepting an unstable configuration that could be compensated for by computer control.

In September the rear-fairing design and construction, which was going to be given to Lucas, came in for some competition when BSEL made a proposal. This was highly attractive on cost grounds alone, apart from the logic of giving the engine maker the job of building the bit that wrapped around the exhausts. The reheat shroud was to be extended, bringing down temperatures in the rear fairing and thereby reducing the use of Nimonic material and enabling more conventional construction to be employed. Moreover, lots of 'free' testing would be available during Olympus 22R test runs. Not surprisingly, BSEL ended up with job, being given an intention to

proceed in December and a contract in January 1961.

Throughout these closing months of the existing design contract the continued need for the aircraft was still being endlessly debated by the bureaucracy. There was brief concern at Vickers when the Americans submitted a brochure on the Republic F-105D to meet OR.343. The Air Staff's OR department gave it short shrift, writing on 29 August: 'This aircraft has no chance of being regarded as a contender for O.R.343'. The TSR2's use in a strategic role was also examined in some detail. The first draft contract covering the production of the actual development-batch aircraft was received by Vickers in August, but the Prime Minister and the Chancellor of the Exchequer both felt that they could not allow the Treasury to approve anything until a full discussion on TSR2 was held in the Defence Committee. On 16 September 1960 a meeting of the Defence Committee finally agreed that TSR2 should continue, and the Treasury could continue to negotiate the

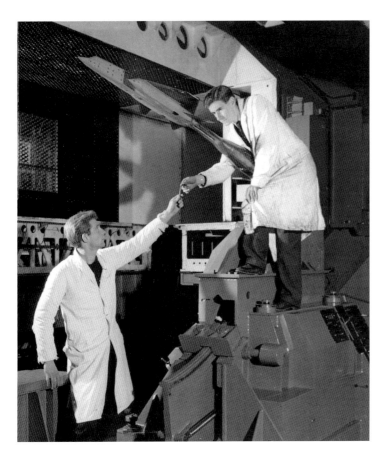

A final-configuration TSR2 model being prepared for windtunnel testing on a rig that permitted various angles of incidence to be set up. Nearly 10,000 individual windtunnel test runs were carried out during the TSR2 project's life. BAE Systems via Warton Heritage Group

A final-configuration TSR2 model positioned at high incidence in a windtunnel; it was in this sort of attitude that most of the stability problems became evident. BAE Systems via Brooklands Museum

terms of the contract covering the development-batch aircraft. The contract was finally signed in October, and it was now time to begin cutting metal.

By the end of 1960 Vickers/English Electric had an aircraft design that was close to 90,000lb (40,825kg) in weight for the 1,000nm sortie, with a promise that, as long as weight was held below 95,000lb (43,100kg), it would be able to meet each performance aspect of the requirement fully. The manufacturers were confident that holding the weight down would not be a problem; the MoA, however, was not.

OR.343 Evolves

Throughout the period of airframe and system design, from 1959 to mid-1961, the Air Staff were refining OR.343 in light of decisions made along the way. Issue 2 of OR.343, completed on 21 February 1961, contained a number of significant changes. High-level cruise, previously to be simply 'supersonic', was now defined as being no less than Mach 1.7. The term 'terrain clearance' was replaced by 'terrain following' (a significant concept change), and in terrain-following mode no single failure was to endanger the aircraft. This simple statement would produce an expensive result. Navigation fixes were relaxed to being taken every 100nm (115 miles; 185km), rather than every 50nm (57miles; 90km). On the armament side the nuclear store was still OR.1127/*Red Beard*, though it was clear that this was now likely to be replaced by a new development. The carriage of 1,000lb bombs changed from 'four or more' to 'six', and the carriage

of at least six 25lb practice bombs was added. The internal carriage of two or more guided missiles to OR.1173 was deleted, along with internal carriage of rockets. External stores were now specified; either two tactical nuclear weapons, four 1,000lb HE bombs, four rocket pods (thirty-seven 2in) or four guided missiles to OR.1173 (Bullpup at the time). All of these were to be carried in combination with internal stores if need be, but no mix of nuclear and conventional stores was required. Various detail changes to the pilot's display, communication equipment, automatic flight-control system (AFCS) and fuel system were also included. Years down the line, all of these changes would be described by the Air Staff and government as 'minor', when in reality almost all of them involved considerable extra development effort and expense.

A general-arrangement drawing of the TSR2 as built.

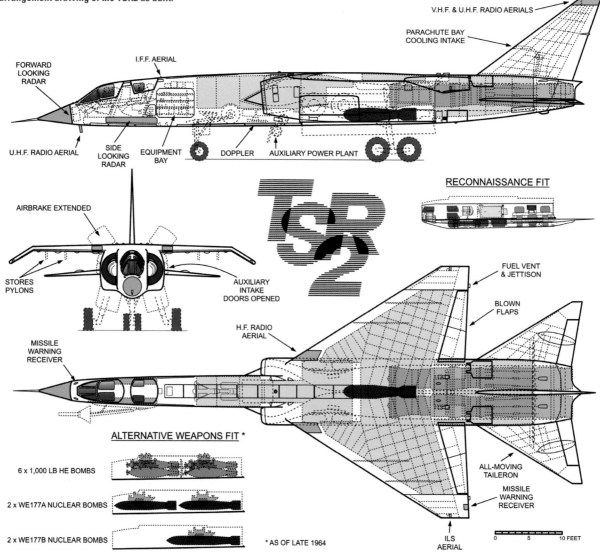

CHAPTER FOUR

Building TSR2

On 1 July 1960 the British Aircraft Corporation was formed, bringing Vickers and English Electric together as subsidiaries of the new firm, along with the Bristol Aero-

Contract KD/2L/02/C.B.42(a) October 1960 Development Batch (Aircraft 1–9)		
Aircraft	*Serial No.*	
1	XR219	
2	XR220	
3	XR221	
4	XR222	
5	XR223	
6	XR224	
7	XR225	
8	XR226	
9	XR227	

plane Company, though for the time being each firm continued on more or less as before, no actual merger taking place. With negotiations under way on the contract to produce the nine development-batch aircraft, BAC was confident enough to begin putting together full-scale mock-ups of the complete aircraft to aid the design of the integrated structure and systems to be built within the real airframes. Various partial mock-ups had already been put together at Warton and Weybridge to aid early design work, but the final mock-ups would be more substantial affairs of wood and metal. Construction of one mock-up at each site began during September 1960, and they were complete by the end of 1961. By this time the major structural components had been designed, so the jigs and tooling needed to

build them could be constructed. From mid 1961 onwards the factory floors had been cleared to take on the task of producing the TSR2 airframes, and jigs were under construction at both sites.

Meanwhile, the Cold War was hotting up. An invasion of communist Cuba had failed in April after President Kennedy lost his nerve and called off supporting USAF and United States Navy air strikes while the US-trained Cuban-exile commandos were still at sea on their way to their target. This set the scene for closer Soviet–Cuban relations, and would eventually lead the world to the very brink of nuclear war. Tensions increased throughout 1961, and on 13 August that year the Soviets closed the border posts in Berlin, and within days began construction of the infamous Berlin Wall.

On 1 September a nuclear explosion bloomed over the Semipalitinsk test site in Kazakhstan, marking the end of Soviet participation in an atmospheric test ban and the beginning of an intensive series of nuclear tests, climaxing with the detonation of the largest nuclear weapon ever produced, the 'Tsar Bomba', with a yield estimated at 57 megatons (the bomb having been dialled down from its maximum yield of 100 megatons). Had such a bomb been dropped on 10 Downing Street, all of London would have ceased to exist. The zone of total destruction would have extended beyond the modern-day M25 motorway and would have included Hatfield, Brentwood, Sevenoaks, Reigate and Woking. Bomber Command's headquarters at RAF High Wycombe in Buckinghamshire would probably have been seriously damaged. The fireball and mushroom cloud would have been visible from anywhere in the British Isles. The Prime Minister, Harold MacMillan, suffered nightmares and wrote in his diary '… the last Russian tests are rather alarming', and '… the one hundred megaton is not just a stunt. It would scorch with fire half France or England if dropped. What then should we do?' It was not, it seemed, a matter of *if* the TSR2 would be needed to carry out is primary task, but of *when*.

Stage 2 assembly jigs under construction at Weybridge in October 1961. These workers are using an optical sighting device to mark the site of the next jig in the sequence precisely. BAE Systems via Brooklands Museum

Multi-layered management

From the outset the TSR2 project was burdened by multiple layers of bureaucracy, all of which helped to introduce further delays. The customer, the RAF, had its own bureaucracy in the form of the Air Ministry, and had written the requirement. Above that was the MoA (the MoS before 1960), which had ultimate say when it came to technical instructions and was also in charge of contracts. When it came to actual funding, however, authority had to be sought from the Treasury.

On the TSR2 project, instead of simply giving the contract for the complete weapons system to a single company, it was decided to divide the project into different categories of equipment. In Category 1 were major systems for which the MoA would be directly responsible in terms of technical direction, the awarding of contracts, and the monitoring and control of costs. Vickers and English Electric would have no control whatsoever over these important items. They included the engines and most associated equipment, almost all of the nav/attack system (including terrain-following radar

TSR2 procurement chain.
Damien Burke

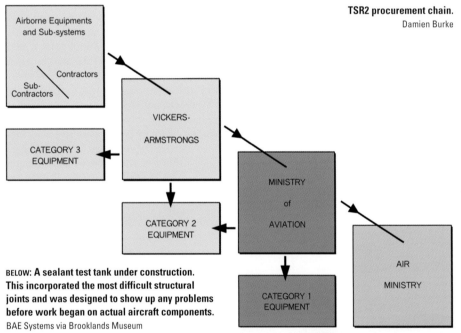

BELOW: **A sealant test tank under construction. This incorporated the most difficult structural joints and was designed to show up any problems before work began on actual aircraft components.**
BAE Systems via Brooklands Museum

(TFR)), the reconnaissance pack, the complete communications and weapons carriage and release subsystems, ground servicing equipment, and the flight simulator. Category 2 contained the crumbs from the MoA's table, for which Vickers would be responsible for technical direction and the award of contracts – albeit subject to Ministry approval of both chosen subcontractor and the contract terms. Category 2 items included the engine gearbox, ejection seats, AFCS, HUD, Doppler radar, SLR (but not its associated display unit) and the Central Computing System. A final category, Category 3, included everything else; basically anything that the Ministry did not consider important enough to exercise any control over, from nuts and bolts to complete airframe components. On this score at least Vickers had control right through from design to contract awards, though of course the Ministry reserved the right to keep an eye on any particular item and jump up and down if it considered Vickers was 'not doing the right thing'.

There was little apparent logic to the distribution of items within the categories, and each individual item was assigned a Director (one of seven, all reporting to an overall Project Director). To ensure that all of the disparate systems talked to each other once installed in the aircraft, an overall Systems Integration Panel was formed, consisting of each of the equipment directors plus representatives from Vickers, English Electric and the Air Staff. Below that were further Sub-panels, for example the Flight Control System Sub-panel. Vickers was held accountable at all times for the performance and cost of anything it subcontracted yet, when it came to anything under Ministry control, not only did Vickers have little say, but it also had no knowledge of the costs involved. It was a weighty and cumbersome management plan, but at least it was put together with the best of intentions.

Production

The British Aircraft Corporation was justifiably proud of the modern methods employed, not only in manufacture of the airframe but also for the jigs. Optical sighting ensured accurate placement (absolutely vital with components being built not only on separate sites, but also at separate companies), and jig borers were controlled by a semi-automatic method based on punched card or tape readers. Along with

RIGHT: **Forming intake tunnel skins over a concrete former. Many of these formers survive to this day at the Brooklands Museum, close to the former Vickers-Armstrongs factory at Weybridge.** BAE Systems via Brooklands Museum

BELOW: **The Weybridge skin milling shop in October 1961, with various TSR2 integrally stiffened panels ready for final polishing.** BAE Systems via Brooklands Museum

the various jigs used in production, a variety of testing jigs were also erected, such as the large and ingenious dynamic fuel test rig built by Napier. Large enough to hold a complete fuselage with wing attached, this had provision to allow the entire assembly to be rotated in both the pitching and rolling planes. Thus the complete installed fuel system could be tested for leaks in various attitudes.

Before starting production of components destined for the first airframes, materials tests were undertaken to assess the suitability of the chosen materials, and build tests were undertaken on example joints and sub-structures to assess the practicalities of putting everything together, and the overall strength of joints. Skin panels were mostly milled from solid billets of aluminium alloy, chemical etching being used on panels that had to be stretched or pressed to shape. Unlike modern-day computer-controlled milling, all such work on the TSR2 was carried out using manually controlled copy routing machines. Wood and rubber patterns were mounted high above or alongside the metal being worked on, and the operator guided the machine along the pattern part while the cutting head mirrored his efforts. Time-consuming polishing followed, initially down to 32 micro inches to remove all evidence of cutting marks, though economy measures were soon introduced to polish down to 60 micro inches, sufficient to remove cutting discontinuities though some cutting marks would remain visible. (These measures, however, did not get communicated to all production facilities, and such waste of effort continued throughout the project's life.) The Skin Milling shop at Vickers Weybridge, the largest in Europe at the time, was simultaneously working on TSR2, VC10 and Vanguard skin sections, while English Electric's workshops at Preston and Accrington produced fuel tank panels, engine-tunnel skins and tailplane spigots among other machined items. Shot-peening machines at Vickers Weybridge and English Electric Samlesbury enabled milled skins to be formed to match templates and, for example, turn flat milled planks into curved engine-tunnel skins.

The first airframe components began to be put together during November 1961, though shortages of particular materials (particularly titanium for bolts) were already delaying progress. The correct grade of steel for the undercarriage legs, which were being built under subcontract by Electro-Hydraulics Ltd, was also proving difficult to obtain, and consequently the first airframe would have its undercarriage built from a lower grade of steel. There were also delays in putting jigs into full production use, because workers had to be trained in their use and the training took longer than expected. Of almost as much concern as the internal delays was the fact that news of external delays at subcontractors was

LEFT: **Machining one of the main fuselage frames from a solid billet of alloy. The guide frame above the work piece enabled the operator to produce identical components time after time, but it was still a time-consuming and skilled task. Note the lack of ear and eye protection.** BAE Systems via Brooklands Museum

BELOW: **The TSR2 construction sequence as drawn up in September 1960. This was carefully designed to cope with the work split between Vickers and English Electric, with the largest chunks of airframe being able to be transported by road without the need for special measures such as removing lamp posts en route. Stages 3 and 4 were eventually carried out in parallel, and the rear fairing became a task for BSEL rather than EE, though BAC was going to take it back in-house for production aircraft.** Damien Burke

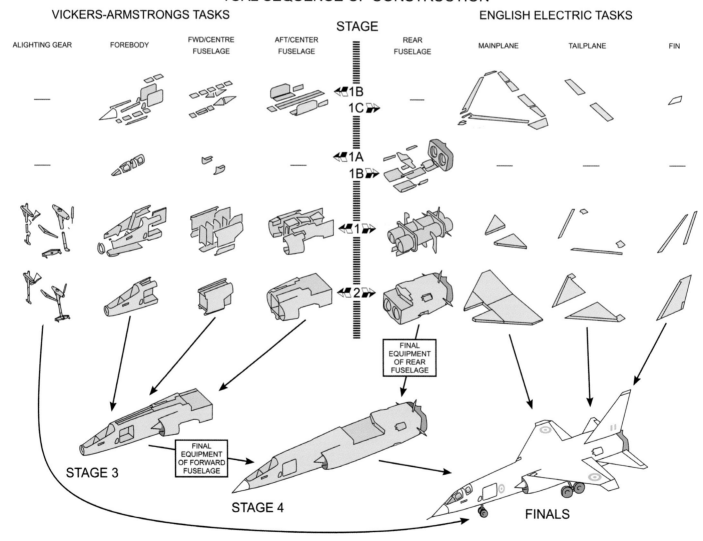

TSR2 SEQUENCE OF CONSTRUCTION

VICKERS-ARMSTRONGS TASKS

ENGLISH ELECTRIC TASKS

ALIGHTING GEAR · FOREBODY · FWD/CENTRE FUSELAGE · AFT/CENTER FUSELAGE · STAGE · REAR FUSELAGE · MAINPLANE · TAILPLANE · FIN

1B
1C
1A
1B
1
2

FINAL EQUIPMENT OF REAR FUSELAGE

STAGE 3

FINAL EQUIPMENT OF FORWARD FUSELAGE

STAGE 4

FINALS

LEFT: **Stage 1 forebody construction at Weybridge. The nose section was initially constructed in two halves, split along the aircraft's centreline.** BAE Systems via Brooklands Museum

BELOW: **Stage 1 centrebody construction at Weybridge, August 1962. These are the intake tunnels, leading aft into the engine tunnels. The aft half of the centrebody was one of the most complex and highly stressed areas of the aircraft, containing the main wing attachment frame, undercarriage, bomb bay and fuel tanks.** BAE Systems via Brooklands Museum

not reaching BAC for weeks or months after the problems had arisen. Because subcontracts were mostly placed by the MoA rather than directly by BAC, there was simply no channel for communications between BAC and most of the subcontractors. As a result, problems inevitably snowballed and gave BAC little or no opportunity to seek or recommend alternatives. This would be a recurring issue throughout the project, and meant that the prediction of a first-flight date in March 1963 was hopelessly optimistic.

Weight was also continuing to rise as more detailed design work 'filled in the gaps' with regard to exactly what was going in the airframe. By November 1961 BAC was predicting a weight of 94,258lb (42,780kg), and the MoA was predicting that this would mean an 'in-service' weight of 97,700lb (44,350kg). If the latter figure was accurate, the aircraft would not meet the requirement in two areas. The take-off run for the 1,000nm sortie would be 1,065yd (975m) rather than 1,000yd (915m), and the landing run would be 625yd (570m) instead of 600yd (550m). This, for the time being, was of no great concern to the RAF's Operational Requirements team, as there was 'nothing that [could] usefully be done about it'.

Problems at BSEL were not limited to engine development (for which see Chapter 8). By mid-1961 English Electric, responsible for the rear fuselage, was becoming concerned about BSEL's lack of progress with rear-fairing design and production. English Electric invited BSEL to send men up to Warton to complete the design and

get things moving, but BSEL did not have the men to spare, and it soon became clear that it was out of its depth when dealing with the stressing and structural design requirements of a chunk of airframe. As engine problems mounted, the rear fairing suffered one delay after another. This was particularly galling to English Electric, which had demonstrated to BSEL the various manufacturing methods used at Preston, because BSEL had ignored them all, choosing more complex and expensive

methods in just about every area in a bid to save weight on the finished item at all costs. The fairing continued to be a problem throughout the project's life.

By March 1962 production of the airframe had also slowed dramatically. So much, in fact, that progress on certain jigs was lagging up to five months behind the original schedule, though other components were a mere two months behind. Much of this was down to the steeper-than-expected learning curve for putting together this most complex of aircraft structures, but BAC was confident that airframes after the first one were going together more quickly, and that it would have regained much of the lost time by the time the fifth aircraft on the line was complete. However, the delays on the first aircraft were unlikely to get any better, and the first-flight prediction was adjusted, first to June 1963 and then to August 1963. As more and more drawings had been produced to fill in the details of various parts of the airframe, the estimated weight of the completed aircraft had also proved to be over-optimistic. By now it had risen to the region of 96,000lb (44,000kg), just past the point of being able to meet the performance specifications fully, and BAC was struggling not to increase it. Almost half of the weight gain was due to changes in the rear fuselage.

The RAE, which had objected to some aspects of English Electric's P.1 design some years earlier (resulting in the creation of the Short SB.5 research aircraft, which thoroughly vindicated English Electric's choices), now set itself up to contribute another expensive mistake to the overall programme. The RAE had convinced Vickers of the need to build some scale models of the TSR2 airframe that could be launched by rocket to high speeds (up to Mach 1.8) to verify and expand on windtunnel results. Much of the TSR2's windtunnel testing had been carried out using modified P.17 models, or using more representative TSR2 models after the design had been frozen, and these had revealed a possibility of some worrying stability characteristics. It was not clear, however, how much the constraints of the windtunnels and the supporting structures on which the models were mounted were affecting the results. The RAE's plan was to verify these results by launching heavily instrumented 1/12th-scale models into the air. Two of the major areas of investigation were yaw stability at high Mach numbers and the effect of incidence at high speeds, using small pulse rockets fitted to the models to try to excite oscillations in these directions and measure the results. The secondary intention was to see what effect a sudden engine loss would have at high speed, to be simulated by a door partly closing off the intake on one side.

Once these expensive models were available, Aberporth became the scene for a farcical series of tests that started in February 1962 and continued until February 1964. During these tests, seven of the eight model launches were either partly or entirely unsuccessful owing to malfunctioning rockets or instrumentation, or to the models settling into spins (their dynamic characteristics did not match those of the real aircraft, particularly in roll, and the tailplanes were set to make each model to fly a gentle barrel roll in order to try and keep the model within the test range area). After launch the rocket would fire for three seconds and then fall away, allowing the model to fly free and decelerate while measurements of pressure and acceleration were recorded, along with Doppler signals from the model. The models were also tracked on ground-based radar. In the end only one test provided really useful results, recording while the model decelerated from Mach 1.48 to Mach 0.78. Every test above Mach 1.5 produced a spin, induced by the model's mismatch to the aircraft's dynamics. Overall, the programme was considered by English Electric's windtunnel team to be little more than the

ABOVE: Royal Aircraft Establishment personnel at a chilly Aberporth load the first TSR2 free-flight model on to a rocket in February 1962. This particular model's configuration was quite unlike that of the final TSR2, exhibiting a small fin and sawtooth leading edge on the wing, and was therefore useful only to prove the launching technique and instrumentation. Rocket and instrumentation malfunctions blighted the free-flight test programme. BAE Systems via Warton Heritage Group

BELOW: One of the RAE's free-flight TSR2 models is launched by rocket booster. Many such launches ended up with the model settling into auto-rotation and providing no useful data. More successful results were achieved with free-fall spinning models that were simply dropped. BAE Systems via Warton Heritage Group

production of some expensive fireworks, and not a good advertisement for the RAE, which hitherto had been redeeming its somewhat tarnished reputation at Warton with some sound theoretical work. Shortly after the tests had begun, further windtunnel work by the Aircraft Research Association at Bedford had pinpointed most of the problem areas anyway, though finding and implementing practical aerodynamic solutions at this late stage was not going to be possible (the AFCS's manoeuvre boost system would end up being modified to compensate).

Meanwhile, progress on the various third-party systems to be fitted to the airframe was as varied as that on individual jigs at Vickers/English Electric. For example, Elliott's AFCS was coming along nicely, with a basic model ready to be incorporated into the integrated testing rig at Weybridge, but the power control actuators from Hobson, a vital part of the AFCS, still showed no sign of arriving a full six months after Hobson had predicted a five-month delay owing to supply problems with high-duty alloys. It did not help that, after initial wrist-slaps about timely communication of delays, subcontractors had now got into the habit of holding on to their own bad news until the last possible minute, in case another system elsewhere within the aircraft fell further behind schedule and thus let them off the hook, if only partly. The lack of firm control over the project as a whole was by now seriously jeopardizing any chance of meeting even the adjusted schedule, never mind the original one.

Further needless delays were introduced by the MoA's love of protracted contractual negotiations. Subcontractors, and even the main contractor, BAC, would often find themselves pressured to complete design studies into particular items of equipment, with a contract arriving weeks or months later to cover this work, but nothing being put in place to cover actual build work after that point. Instead, the design study would remain in limbo, often for months, while the MoA and the contractors argued over the finer points of the sort of contracts that had already been dealt with time and time again. Understandably, companies were reluctant to begin work without written assurance that they would be paid for it (a formal letter of Intention To Proceed at the very least), but, in many cases, had they not done so the overall project would have fallen so far behind as to guarantee its cancellation. This meant that companies

sometimes took huge risks to keep the project on track, if they could afford to do so. Those that could not soon began to wish they had chosen easier customers, and the delivery date of their equipment slipped ever further away through no fault of their own.

TSR2 development batch and pre-production

There were to be no prototypes. Instead, as with the Vickers Vanguard and VC10, and English Electric's own P.1B, all TSR2 airframes were to be assembled on production jigs. Production was to begin with a development batch of nine aircraft plus a structural test specimen, followed by pre-production airframes before full series pro-

duction began. The 'development batch' procedure had been pioneered in the USA and was quickly taken on board by the MoA, though the claimed advantages soon proved to be illusory. Other nations' aerospace companies never fell for the dubious attractions of this method of development, and the Americans, too, would soon back away from it. However, BAC was stuck with it and so, with no prototypes to work out the bugs, it was going to be a matter of getting the airframe right from the start.

The development batch and pre-production airframes were, however, all to be built to a lesser standard than the intended production aircraft. The first two aircraft would be decidedly basic airframes, and by August 1963, the expected date of first flight, they had effectively become prototypes in all but name, with no radars of any

Contract KD/2L/013/C.B.42(a) August 1963 Pre-Production Batch (Aircraft 10–20)		
Aircraft	Serial No.	Delivery to
10	XS660	A&AEE (clearance flying)
11	XS661	A&AEE (clearance flying)
12	XS662	A&AEE (clearance flying)
13	XS663	A&AEE (clearance flying)
14	XS664	A&AEE (clearance flying)
15	XS665	RAF (Operational Development Squadron)
16	XS666	RAF (Operational Development Squadron)
17	XS667	RAF (Operational Development Squadron)
18	XS668	RAF (Operational Development Squadron)
19	XS669	RAF (Operational Development Squadron)
20	XS670	RAF (Operational Development Squadron)

The drawing office at Weybridge, *circa* 1960. The number of drawings necessary for this most complex of aircraft was far beyond initial predictions, and delays in drawing issue were a serious problem to begin with. The production of some components was begun using early drawings, and these components had to be successively modified as new drawings were produced.
Brooklands Museum

A single wing rib with the related full-size drawing behind it. The amount of integral machining necessary to reduce weight and cater for high thermal stresses was much greater than on previous projects, and contributed to additional delays owing to shortage of machines to do the work.
BAE Systems via Brooklands Museum

Vickers type numbers	
No.	Description
571	TSR2 development batch
579	TSR2 pre-production aircraft
594	TSR2 production aircraft
595	TSR2 trainer (proposed)

Production locations		
Location	Firm	Components
Weybridge	Vickers	Forebody and forward fuselage of d.b. a/c, final assembly d.b. a/c
Hurn	Vickers	Forward centre fuselage
Accrington	English Electric	Tailplane & fin
Preston	English Electric	Rear fuselage, forebody & forward fuselage of production aircraft
Samlesbury	English Electric	Wings, final assembly of production aircraft
Warton	English Electric	Final assembly of 2nd static test airframe, flight test centre
Itchen	Vickers	Equipment installation mock-ups
Stevenage	English Electric	Reconnaissance pack

kind (and thus no automatic terrain following), substandard engines, no AFCS, a manual fuel system and basic avionics. Aircraft 3 (XR221, actually the fourth airframe built, the structural test specimen being the third) was to be the first one with AFCS, radar and a nav/attack system. Much later, as the engine accessories bays became a problem, a redesign of the fuselage frames in this area to permit a larger bay meant that many of the development batch and pre-production airframes would be stuck with the smaller bay, and it would probably have been prohibitively expensive to modify them.

Had funding and circumstances permitted, BAC believed that the first fourteen aircraft could eventually have been brought up to something approaching production standard, but the RAF would not have been able to get its hands on them for at least three years after delivery of the first production examples, and some, particularly the first two, could well have proved impossible to upgrade. Even with its best efforts BAC expected that only forty-one of the first fifty aircraft could ever be fully operational.

Production was expected to peak during the period 1968 to 1970, with thirty-five airframes rolling off the production lines each year at their busiest, and the final batch being delivered in 1971/1972, assuming a final RAF order of only 138 aircraft. Had Australia ordered the TSR2, the plan was that the first twenty airframes would have stayed as the development batch and pre-production airframes. The first six production aircraft would have been destined for RAF trials, evaluation and development; the next eight would have gone to the RAF to form its first operational squadron (along with the previous six); the next six produc-

tion aircraft would have been delivered to the RAAF, and then the remainder of production would have been three for the RAF and one for the RAAF until both orders were fulfilled.

Test specimens

Mixed in with the production of components of the development-batch airframes were test specimens of various large assemblies, such as a complete forebody and wing, along with a complete airframe to be used for static strength testing by the RAE at Farnborough. The static-test airframe was produced as the third airframe on the line, and was to be structurally complete but lacking many of the internal systems required on a complete aircraft. Components that did not contribute to the overall strength were unnecessary, so it lacked items such as airbrakes as well. A second test airframe, destined for fatigue tests, was eleventh on the line, but was not completed before the project was cancelled.

The first test-specimen forebody, the sixth of these particular items on the Weybridge line, was destined for escape-system and thermal tests, also with the RAE. The major challenge to crew comfort other than the shaking and vibration produced by low-level flight at high speeds was the heat generated by kinetic heating of the airframe. While much preparatory work had been done at RAE to investigate the most efficient means of cooling the crew compartment (including the use of a modified Bristol T.188 nose section), only a complete TSR2 forebody would enable the RAE to test and finalize the aircraft's air conditioning system layout. The result was a system that worked well. During the limited amount of taxy and flight testing that was eventually carried out, the crew would be complimentary about the distribution of air, with no uncomfortable breezes or whistling noises as experienced with other aircraft. The temperature of this well-distributed air, however, was another matter. The forebody was also used for escape-system tests, entailing canopy jettisoning in front of a blower nozzle and eventually the firing of a complete ejection seat.

Production problems

While work on the airframe was under BAC's direct control and delays were being incurred almost immediately for a variety of reasons, mostly materials shortages, problems with rear-fuselage frame design and manpower issues (particularly in the drawing offices), the situation was much more complex when it came to the various electronic systems to be incorporated in the aircraft. Most of these, as previously mentioned, were not under BAC control, but were Category 1 items ordered and supposedly controlled by the MoA, and the bureaucracy was firing spanners into the works at an impressive rate. By mid-1961, more than two years after the beginning of the project, some items still did not have a contract in place to cover their production. Others were only just beginning to be worked on after months of contractual negotiations whereby the Ministry deluded itself it was saving the taxpayer money, but was actually just introducing needless delays, and therefore increasing final costs. Most of the equipment that would make TSR2 a weapons system was already running up to nine months behind schedule, and this was pretty fairly matched by slippage on the airframe itself (though at the Weybridge end things were slightly better and the slippage was more like six months).

Test specimen	Component	Purpose
T1	Complete airframe minus forebody	Static-strength testing for RAE Farnborough once mated with T7
T2	Complete airframe minus forebody	Fatigue-test airframe for BAC Warton once mated with T4
T3	Equipment bay	Cancelled as handmade specimen created at Vickers Hurn
T4	Forebody	Underwater pressure testing at Weybridge, then fatigue tests at Warton once mated with T2
T5	Forebody	Air-conditioning and blower-tunnel tests at RAE Farnborough
T6	Partial forebody	Escape-system proving for P & EE Pendine high-speed rocket track
T7	Forebody	Static-strength test once mated with T1

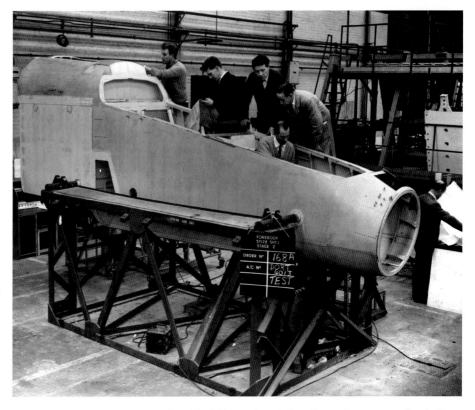

ABOVE: Test forebody T5 in the stage 2 jig at Weybridge, early 1963. One of several test nose sections built on production jigs, this one was used for air-conditioning and escape-system tests. It is currently preserved at the Brooklands Museum, not far from where it was manufactured. BAE Systems via Brooklands Museum

RIGHT: Time-consuming polishing of milled wing-skin planks. Despite instructions issued in 1961 to reduce the amount of polishing and therefore the time and expense involved, this sort of work continued until 1964 in some instances. BAE Systems via Brooklands Museum

In May 1962, as part of an overall progress review, BAC came up with a three-point plan to try to improve matters. First of all, it wanted the first flight to be made from Wisley rather than at the Aeroplane and Armament Experimental Establishment (A&AEE) at Boscombe Down, as it had originally wanted anyway. This would save a month of mucking about dismantling the first aircraft, transporting it to Boscombe, reassembling it and carrying out engine runs. With final assembly at Weybridge, the aircraft could have initial engine runs there just the once, then be transported intact to Wisley and fly from there to Boscombe to begin the initial flight-test programme. Secondly, ground-resonance tests, intended for the first aircraft, could be transferred to the second one, allowing the first to get into the air faster. Finally, prototype procedures could be applied to the first three aircraft. At that time every airframe was being treated in effect as a production airframe, and modifications and strict adherence to interchangeability standards was slowing progress. If the first three aircraft could be allowed to be effective 'one-offs' they could be flying much earlier, albeit to a lower design standard.

A wing under construction at Samlesbury. This is the starboard half, with the apex section on the left of the photo. A new milling machine had to be developed for the large milled skin panels for the wing, as existing machines could not handle large enough planks of alloy. BAE Systems via Brooklands Museum

At Weybridge, Redifon had delivered the five-axis moving cockpit simulator, but when it was installed and first run it had promptly failed to work correctly, and had to be returned to Redifon for major redesign work. Much of the simulated flying was to be carried out on this simulator, so several months of delay on this score was the last thing anybody needed. Happily, many of the effects of this delay could be negated, as the Cornell Aeronautical Laboratories (CAL) in the USA had agreed to let BAC use their Lockheed T-33 variable-stability aircraft for some simulation work, which duly began in late October (during the Cuban Missile Crisis) and proved a very useful exercise. Meanwhile, the world had come terrifyingly close to nuclear war. At the height of the crisis Bomber Command's V-force aircraft were on the very brink of launching to undertake a grand tour of the Soviet Union.

By November 1962 the Americans and the Soviets had stepped back from the abyss, tensions were easing, and TSR2 production was still running well behind schedule. The BAC plan to get back on schedule by the fifth airframe was in tatters. The merger of the two companies within BAC was still not complete in terms of day-to-day working, and it was only in mid-1962 that they had begun to use a unified drawing numbering scheme, for instance. With the scheduled delivery of the first rear fuselage section to Weybridge set for January 1963, BAC suggested that this could go ahead even if the section was incomplete, and it could be completed at Weybridge, with simultaneous marrying-up of the section to the Weybridge half and equipment installation. It was not the most sensible of plans, taking workforce away from Preston and running the risk of fuel tank leaks that could need substantial

The wing of XR219 in the stage 2 jig at Samlesbury, with major structural assembly complete. BAE Systems via Brooklands Museum

rectification work back at Preston, and work continued to get the first airframe's rear fuselage completed before transportation. The structural-test specimen was also running several months behind schedule, and this would mean that the first aircraft would fly before any structural tests had been performed. To try to get back on track, a night and day shift was in operation at both ends of the BAC operation, with work continuing seven days a week. Preston would soon introduce a three-shift system to try and improve matters further.

By early 1963, with the UK covered with snow and in the grip of the coldest winter since 1795, there was no sign of the first aircraft being completed, let alone being within months of its first flight. The Americans had cancelled the Skybolt nuclear stand-off missile intended for the V-force, and it now seemed likely that TSR2 would take on a limited strategic role, delivering larger nuclear bombs to distant Soviet targets to fill the gap until the UK had Polaris submarines. By now the V-force was on its last legs in terms of being able to penetrate Soviet defences successfully, and would have to shift to low-level operations. An RAF study, however, found that low-level operations would reduce the 3,130hr fatigue life of an Avro Vulcan B.1A to a mere 270hr, and wear the aircraft out entirely within just three years if strengthening modifications were not made. Handley Page Victors would fare rather better, but it was clear that the V-force as a whole was not going to last long.

The company's latest cost estimates had also risen again, and George Edwards was about to be hauled over the coals at the MoA. There was concern that the project was being 'gold-plated', that it was over-manned (an inevitable result of extra shifts put on to try to make up some lost time), that financial monitoring efforts were not only totally inadequate but also pointless without associated financial controls, and that nobody was in overall control of the TSR2 project at BAC. While there was a supposed project manager in Henry Gardner, in reality only George Edwards could exercise overall control, and he did so sporadically, when crises arose and when his health permitted. Gardner had little or no control over production issues, and was all too often concentrating his time on design issues. When the MoA tried to pin Edwards down with an incentive contract (guaranteeing a first flight by August 1963 in return for incentive payments, and with penalties

The wing of XR219 in the stage 3 jig at Samlesbury in March 1963, with apex panels and structure being fitted. BAE Systems via Brooklands Museum

'TSR2 In Production', the cover of a BAC brochure of July 1963, produced to illustrate the state of development and production of the aircraft in time for a visit from RAAF personnel. BAE Systems via Brooklands Museum

if this was not managed) he agreed, but only if the break clause was removed (thus making cancellation of the project impossible). Of course the Ministry could never agree to such a deal, and Edwards knew it. There was also, finally, concern that BAC relied far too much on Weybridge experience while ignoring input from the Preston end. At Weybridge over the last few years most experience had been on civil projects (and Gardner himself was more of a guided-

weapons man), whereas Preston had ongoing military experience on the Canberra and Lightning. Neither Ministry had any confidence remaining in the Vickers-originated senior management at BAC, and they had been given the lead position on the project ahead of English Electric precisely because their were expected to perform better than English Electric's management! Needless to say, a certain amount of 'I told you so' was evident at BAC's northern outposts.

An engine tunnel under construction in the stage 1 jig at Preston.
BAE Systems via Brooklands Museum

Edwards did not deny that BAC had substantially failed to keep its promises to improve slippages and keep control of costs, but he blamed it all on the ridiculous enforced amalgamation of two companies with separate cultures, procedures, staff and production locations. Furthermore, the main reasons for BAC's failures to keep to production schedules were delays in construction of the wings and the rear fuselages; the work carried out by English Electric at its factories. In fact, one particular fuselage frame had been giving English Electric severe trouble, and they had to take in-house the work on the tailplane spigots when a subcontractor could not handle the job satisfactorily. The company also had a culture of individual factories working to their own methods, rather than pulling together as part of a single organization. Friction between designers and production departments was all too common, frequent changes in drawings driving the production side up the wall.

Pushed to introduce stronger management, Edwards agreed to several changes in the way BAC was running the project, and also pointed out that they were going to introduce Programme Evaluation and

LEFT: Engine-tunnel skinning at Preston. With hundreds of close-tolerance holes to drill, fasten and seal, this was 'a real watchmaker's job'. Much of the engine tunnels' areas were surrounded by fuel tanks, so the consequences of a hot gas leak (or, in the reverse direction, a fuel leak) would have been extremely serious. Much use of titanium was made in this area, and problems obtaining sufficient quantities of this exotic metal caused significant delays early in the build programme. BAE Systems via Warton Heritage Group

BELOW: A rear fuselage nearly ready to be skinned at Preston. The rearmost frame has yet to have the tailplane and fin spigots installed; these forged items were again subject to initial supply problems. BAE Systems via Brooklands Museum

More or less coinciding with the beginning of airframe production in 1961 was the limited introduction of Programme Evaluation and Review Technique (PERT) project management, initially to cover design work only. Unlike traditional *ad hoc* management techniques, PERT enabled BAC to break up the design work into discrete tasks and show how they depended on each other, if at all, and thus schedule design work in the most efficient manner. Thus, hopefully, no time would be wasted carrying out certain tasks sequentially when they could be carried out in parallel, and the most efficient 'critical path' through the project would be revealed. It follows that PERT's bias was towards time spent rather than cost saving, because lots of parallel tasks would inevitably require greater resources than a linear progression. Allied with PERT was the Project Execution Plan (PEP), which defined plans, procedures and control processes for project implementation and the monitoring and reporting of progress. This covered all sorts of project aspects such as personnel roles and responsibilities, risk analysis, cost management procedures, and quality assurance.

Review Technique (PERT) to the project as a whole in the very near future (as had been requested by the MoA months previously). By May 1963 the scene at Weybridge looked a bit more promising. Construction of the first aircraft was now well advanced, and in terms of structure it lacked only the wingtips, and the engines were about to be test-fitted. The next three airframes were nearly ready to have their front and rear fuselage halves joined together. The 'Stage 3' rig, simulating the aircraft's electrical and electronic systems, was nearly complete as well. By August 1963 further delays had pushed back the first-flight date to January 1964 and an initial release to RAF service was now scheduled for October 1966. An engine for trial installation in the first aircraft had been delivered by BSEL, and a second was due shortly. The electrical distribution system proposed by BAC had come in for stiff criticism from the RAF's Central Servicing Development Establishment (CSDE) and had been redesigned, and this delayed the installation of many systems in the first aircraft. On the second and third aircraft further delays were experienced because pressure transducers and accelerometers that were to be built into the airframe for flutter and load testing were failing at a stupendous rate during bench tests.

January 1964 came and went, with no TSR2 in the air. After a year under supposedly improved management the project had continued to slip. The company's plan

to continue final assembly of all TSR2 airframes at Weybridge, including the main production run, and transport them by road to Wisley for final equipment fit and first flight, had also become a problem. The airfield was only leased to BAC, being owned by the MoA. This lease ran out in 1968, and Surrey County Council was vehemently opposed to any actual use of the airfield for aviation (some things never change). It would be politically difficult to try to overrule Surrey's wishes when there were more suitable alternatives, such as final assembly and first flight at Samlesbury. Consequently BAC was overruled and, from airframe 10 onwards, final assembly and first flight would be from Warton or Samlesbury. It seemed that English Electric, after five years' work, would finally regain almost complete control of 'its' project. By now, however, English Electric and Vickers were no longer separate companies, and both names were increasingly disappearing from BAC paperwork. English Electric was now BAC (Preston), while Vickers was BAC (Weybridge). The loss of TSR2 final assembly and first flight to another division within BAC was no longer the unthinkable insult it would have been just a couple of years before.

With BAC once again being hauled over the coals by a customer who was now

incandescent with rage about the delays and cost overruns, and threatening cancellation, George Edwards took a firm hand and introduced a slew of management changes. They included taking Freddie Page off the Lightning project and putting him in overall day-to-day control of the TSR2, while Ray Creasey took over Page's role on the Lightning. Thenceforth the atmosphere changed radically, and the Ministry began to see results from the 'new head of steam' that had been generated by this and various other new appointments in senior BAC positions. In February 1964 the adoption of Value Engineering within the TSR2 programme indicated that the winds of change really were blowing within the company. This covered the analysis of all engineering solutions on the project to see if they could be reduced in cost while still retaining all of their functionality. For instance, while integral machining of a part produced the lightest and strongest components, traditional die forging and casting could produce a part of the same strength at reduced cost. The trade-off was that the forged or cast part would be heavier. Value Engineering would kick off a series of cost reductions on the TSR2, carefully selected for the largest savings and minimum adverse impacts.

Rear-fuselage production at Preston in full swing. The section nearest the camera has been fully skinned and is undergoing equipment installation.
BAE Systems via Warton Heritage Group

X2020 aluminium-lithium alloy

In the late 1950s/early 1960s the future of aluminium for aerospace use was uncertain, and one of the various developments that took place was the creation of aluminium–lithium alloys. These were less dense, and therefore lighter, than aluminium, and also exhibited greater stiffness. They also cost three times as much as standard aluminium. Early tests showed that the material was reliable under a range of stress conditions including sustained use in a salt-water environment and at high temperatures. Unfortunately the tests did not immediately show up the material's weakness under high impact loads; BAC finally found out late in

1962 that X2020, as well as proving to be much more difficult to form than more traditional alloys, fractured badly when large point stresses were applied. Its much-vaunted stiffness collapsed entirely if a complete penetration of a sheet of the material occurred. The reality, therefore, was that the TSR2 was more likely to suffer critical damage from a missile hit or cannon fire than an aircraft of more conventional construction. In practice, the problem began to show up in production, and even in day-to-day maintenance of the first aircraft. It transpired that the 'large' point stresses BAC had been warned about did not need to be that large. Closing rivets on small panels was sometimes producing cracks radiat-

ing from the rivet location, and dropping a panel could result in cracks at corners. The company's Guided Weapons Division was experiencing so many fabrication problems with X2020 by July 1963 that it wrote to BAC Weybridge, warning of these experiences and saying it had heard that the use of X2020 had been substantially restricted or discontinued on certain aircraft projects in the USA.

This was a massive blow to a project already reeling from cost, weight and schedule overruns. While nothing much could be done about the development batch aircraft, which were already well advanced in production, a crash programme was instigated in early 1964 to investigate where X2020 could be replaced by L71 aluminium alloy on further airframes. This was a large task, as more than 16,000 parts had been designed to use X2020 in the components built by BAC Weybridge alone. Where the stiffness requirements were not so critical this could be done on a like-for-like basis, using L71 of the same gauge as previously specified for X2020. However, in more critical areas, particularly external stressed-skin panels, in-depth studies would be needed to determine what increase in gauge would be required when using L71, or indeed if L71 would do at all. By this time the cost of X2020 as a raw material was more than five times as much as L71, and fabrication costs

Contract KD/2L/16/CB.42(a) April 1964 Production Aircraft (Aircraft 21-50)					
Aircraft	Serial No.	Aircraft	Serial No.	Aircraft	Serial No.
21	XS944	31	XS954	41	XS986
22	XS945	32	XS977	42	XS987
23	XS946	33	XS978	43	XS988
24	XS947	34	XS979	44	XS989
25	XS948	35	XS980	45	XS990
26	XS949	36	XS981	46	XS991
27	XS950	37	XS982	47	XS992
28	XS951	38	XS983	48	XS993
29	XS952	39	XS984	49	XS994
30	XS953	40	XS985	50	XS995

The fuselage of XR219 being transported south on Britain's first stretch of motorway, the Preston Bypass, otherwise known as the M6. This photo was taken from the Cuerdale Lane bridge over the motorway, south of the A59 junction (modern-day junction 31). The view, and traffic level, are somewhat different today! BAE Systems via Brooklands Museum

were 10 per cent higher, so initial estimates suggested that more than £5,000 could be saved on each aircraft for a weight increase of just 40lb (18kg).

This problem of airframe strength manifested itself in a dramatic and wholly unwelcome manner when the wing on the static strength-test specimen suffered an early failure on 28 January 1965, while undergoing heavy static load testing. The wing was constructed of many integrally stiffened panels milled from solid billets of alloy, held together with small titanium bolts or rivets and liberally smeared with PRC sealant, as the wing itself was to be a large fuel tank. The underside of the wing cracked near the line where it met the fuselage, just behind the apex, and the wingtip was also damaged, though this was thought to be induced by mechanical disturbance from the first crack. The first crack began near one of the bolt holes, and a titanium rivet also fractured. The wing had been designed to cope with a maximum loading of up to 10g, with a limit of 6g to be applied in service. The failure occurred at 8.5g, or 85 per cent of the ultimate design strength. This was duly reported to the MoA, and up the line to the Cabinet, and was gleefully pounced upon by the project's many critics. Protests by BAC that the break had occurred at well beyond the loading to be expected in service, and could probably be dealt with by local reinforcement and slightly thicker rivets rather than major changes, were pretty much ignored, and the news was used by many to criticize the project once more.

The BAC investigation into the cause of the early wing failure was never fully completed owing to the cancellation of the project, but BAC's Mechanical Test Department produced a report in June 1965 in which it was admitted that, although results were incomplete, there was 'no definite indication why the wing should have failed'. The investigation had found, however, that X2020's superior strength characteristics could be reduced considerably by 'minor defects such as typical scratches and screwdriver marks which commonly occur in aircraft manufacture'. Stiffeners added to the wingtip, which was skinned with X2020, did not help the strength of the joint of the main wing box to the wingtip, and skinning the tip with L71 did not give satisfactory strength either.

Had the project proceeded, it is certain that the wide-scale replacement of X2020 by L71 would have continued and been

The fin of XR219 nears completion at Accrington in March 1963. The large hole for the spigot is clearly visible. BAE Systems via Brooklands Museum

Skinned, XR219's tailplanes undergo final assembly at Accrington in March 1963. Other tailplane skins are visible in the background. BAE Systems via Brooklands Museum

expanded further, introducing additional delays allied to the redesign plus weight and cost implications (though at least raw material costs would have decreased). In the end X2020 was an expensive mistake, and it is notable that the Concorde airliner project, another Mach 2 design, did not use it.

All change

While most structural parts of the airframe were by now in production, with early examples undergoing strength and fatigue testing, there was one odd one out; the rear fairing. This covered the rear section of the

engine tunnels, surrounding the jetpipes and incorporating the braking parachute housing and door, being manufactured by BSEL. Unfortunately BSEL had proved to be entirely out of its depth when it came to building part of an airframe rather than an engine, and stressing, strength and construction problems had dragged on for months. Eventually, exasperated by the cost and delays, BAC undertook to redesign the rear fairing itself so that it could manufacture it in-house for production aircraft. Having put BSEL's work under the microscope, however, BAC could hardly afford to ignore its own designs for other areas of the aircraft, and the Value Engineering department found that BAC was as guilty of over-engineering as any subcontractor.

For example, most of the wing spars, which were of 'egg box' construction machined from the solid, could be made just as easily from corrugated plate webs, using chemical etching to save weight where needed. Much less material would be wasted, and the result would be just as strong. Fuselage stringers with varying angles over their length were also machined from solid billets at considerable expense, and could be replaced by stretched angles mounted back-to-back. The flap-blowing system varied output with flap angle, yet performance would not be affected if the maximum output was simply used at all times the flaps were down, regardless of angle. Thus an on/off valve could replace a complicated regulator. Airbrakes, intake cones and various other systems were also needlessly complex and could be replaced by simpler, cheaper alternatives. An overall review of possible cost savings resulted in the 'Ewans Report' of June 1964, which detailed all of the major savings that could possibly be made and concluded that the unit cost of each TSR2 could be reduced by 10 per cent, but the weight gain would be in the order of 1,500lb (680kg). For the 1,000nm sortie this would cause a reduction in combat radius of 16.5nm (18.9 miles; 30.5km), and an increase in the dispersed take-off roll of 28.5yd (26m).

Ministry response to this first Value Engineering report was typically shortsighted, concern being expressed that it actually raised development costs over the short term. Saving money on production was apparently of little interest to the bureaucracy if it meant they had to fork out a higher figure for R&D, despite the total cost being lower! The RAF, however, read the report with shock. All along, the MoA had been saying it did not have the resources to keep a close enough eye on the project to keep costs down. Now one man and his tiny team at BAC had come up with umpteen ways of reducing costs and shown that, hitherto, almost no efforts had actually been made to keep them down. The RAF had finally lost almost all faith in BAC's management of the project, and also in the ability of the MoA to do the right thing; it was clear that it was going to obstruct any cost-saving effort that added to the more immediate R&D bill.

First flight

By the beginning of March 1964 the first aircraft, XR219, had finally been completed. There was no formal roll-out; there was no time to waste on that sort of publicity exercise, and no appetite for it, particularly with the security paranoia then endemic in both the government and the RAF. The aircraft was immediately dismantled again for transport to Boscombe Down, and its arrival there on 4 March heralded an even more stressful period for everybody on the project, as reassembly took longer than expected, and the already badly delayed taxying tests were deferred repeatedly owing to problems on the engine development side. The RAF was keen to see the aircraft finally in the air, but also made it clear that it did not want to sacrifice flight safety purely to meet a 'political' date for the first flight. It was concerned that BAC's haste

Early May 1963, and XR219 is now at stage 4 and looking like an aircraft, with its wing test-fitted and equipping well under way in the cockpit and elsewhere. Some idea of the size of the fuselage fuel tanks can be gained from the heads of workers popping out of the top of the centre fuselage. BAE Systems via Brooklands Museum

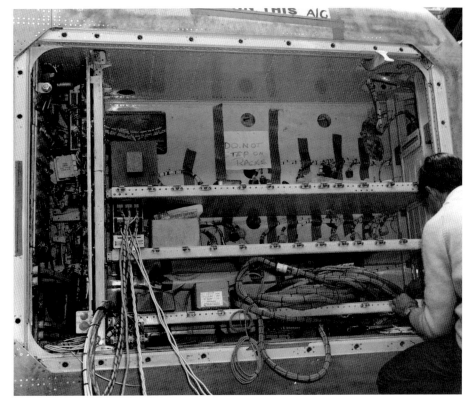

The TSR2's large equipment bay; this is XR219's starboard bay being equipped in May 1963. BAE Systems via Brooklands Museum

The first TSR2, XR219, in the final assembly stage, early July 1963. The forward and centre fuselage sections have been married up to the rear fuselage, and the tailplanes have been fitted. The wing had been test-fitted and then removed to allow equipment to be installed. Following in the background is XR220. BAE Systems via Warton Heritage Group

At the end of August 1963 XR219 was nearing the end of final assembly. It is seen here with the surrounding scaffolding cleared away for the camera. The aircraft is supported by jacks, as the main undercarriage could only be partly extended because the jack height was insufficient for full extension. Cockpit transparencies and the SLR and HF dielectric covers are obvious missing items at this point. BAE Systems via Brooklands Museum

to get the TSR2 airborne could result in a loss of the first aircraft, and mentioned the 'fact' that BAC had now lost a pair of BAC One-Eleven airliners in accidents 'due at least in part to too much haste'.

Meanwhile, at Weybridge, progress on the development batch proceeded fairly well, the second airframe, XR220, coming off the line while XR221 was being equipped. After sustained engine problems and the huge embarrassment of XR220 being damaged on arrival at Boscombe Down, the first flight of the TSR2 finally took place on 27 September 1964, after a summer blighted by negative publicity. It was a brief flight, and was really only made as a political gesture at significant risk (just as the RAF had feared), but was entirely successful in that it did not result in a fireball scattering expensive bits of aircraft over the Wiltshire countryside. To say that the

LEFT: **The publicity department of BAC had been champing at the bit for some months before Ministry clearance was finally given to release some photos to the press. This was one of the handful of shots taken of XR219 in October 1963, released too late to have any possible influence on the attempts to sell the aircraft to the Australians.** BAE Systems via Brooklands Museum

ABOVE: **By April 1964 XR219 had been transported to Boscombe and reassembled in the hangar given over to BAC. The aircraft is seen here on jacks, undergoing functional checks of the undercarriage and other hydraulically powered items such as the bomb bay doors and airbrakes.** BAE Systems via Brooklands Museum

accomplishment of the first flight lifted spirits at BAC would be a huge understatement, and the flurry of congratulatory telegrams and letters that followed further improved the atmosphere. The first flight had been 'copybook stuff' and a 'jolly good show', but, as Freddie Page said, 'Now the hard work really starts'.

In early October, while XR219 was laid up for engine changes and various modifications to bring it up to a standard that would actually enable it to carry out some genuinely useful test flying, thoughts turned to the Ministry's requirement for final assembly of the aircraft to be moved up north as quickly as was feasible. A plan had been worked out by BAC to try to minimize the inevitable disruption caused by moving final assembly responsibilities from Weybridge to Samlesbury. This meant that the first pre-production aircraft, number 10, would have its fuselage components married up at Weybridge and would then be transported to Samlesbury for completion. Numbers 11 and 12 would be completed at Weybridge and 13 at Samlesbury, and thereafter final assembly would alternate between Weybridge and Samlesbury to complete the pre-production batch. Production aircraft (i.e. No. 21 onwards) would all be assembled at Samlesbury. While there

Now structurally complete, XR220 is towed out to the paint shop at Weybridge. The painting of XR219 and XR220 was complicated by widespread surface contamination by DP.47 hydraulic fluid, and for a time it looked like XR219, at least, would fly in primer finish. Additional delays gave enough time for a clean-up job followed by painting. BAE Systems via Brooklands Museum

would be some additional costs because of duplication of some jigs, it was a carefully planned schedule, and this, along with a flight development programme that had received the seal of approval from the

Flight Trials Progress Committee, did a great deal to relieve tension between the Air Ministry, the MoA and BAC. The Air Staff even suggested that they might be able to relax some of their clearance requirements

July 1964, and XR220, freshly painted, is undergoing final equipment installation. Visible in the background are XR221 and XR222. BAE Systems via Brooklands Museum

to assist with an earlier CA release, such as delaying the clearance of the in-flight refuelling system until after CA release. The project, it seemed, was finally showing some real promise.

But it was too little, too late. Delays, poor management (at all levels from subcontractors through to BAC and onward up to the MoA and beyond), development problems and an underestimation of the complexity of the overall weapons system had all conspired to raise the development costs to previously unheard-of levels. While BAC had been desperately trying to get XR219 into the air, the government and the RAF had been quietly realizing that they could no longer afford such an expensive aircraft, and had been looking at alternatives. By the time XR219 was ready for a second flight it was nearly Christmas. A new government was in power; a government that had included in its election manifesto promises to cut back on the excesses of defence spending. The Americans had just flown the first prototype of their new TFX variable-sweep tactical strike aircraft. Bad weather delayed the TSR2's second flight until New Year's Eve, and while XR219 was carrying out a very brief and highly unsatisfactory second flight above a snow-covered Wiltshire landscape, the icy fingers of cancellation were drawing ever tighter around the project's throat.

The final months

Throughout January 1965, as concerns over cancellation became ever more prevalent, assembly of the development-batch aircraft continued fairly smoothly and the flight test programme with XR219 proceeded in halting fashion, dogged by undercarriage problems. The second airframe, XR220, was nearing the end of its repair and reassembly, which had been slowed down by the need to rob it from time to time for spares to use on XR219. Having the aircraft at Boscombe Down inevitably resulted in additional delays, as the most simple of spares had to come from factories a great distance away. Had the aircraft been based at Warton, or even Wisley, the petty day-to-day issues that arose would never have snowballed into larger problems, and BAC was anxious to get the aircraft 'home' to Warton. While the staff at Boscombe were never less than helpful, BAC was also aware of an undercurrent of friction; TSR2 operations were hugely disruptive to the busy Boscombe programme, with all other flying being stopped for a long time either side of any intended TSR2 movement. The staff at BAC was keen to work all hours, in all weathers and over weekends to try and get the project back on track, and there was only so much the Boscombe staff could do to support this.

TSR2 fails to meet the Operational Requirement

At this point BAC was aware that the aircraft had become so heavy that it could not meet two of the most important requirements it had to fulfil: a combat radius of 1,000nm and a short take-off roll of 1,000yd. A confidential BAC summary of problem areas on the aircraft, written in January 1965, paints a depressing picture. In this brief report, various areas of the aircraft are highlighted for the difficulties they were undergoing and those likely to arise. Some of the more worrying of these (such as a concern that fuselage gust response was going to be poor) would evaporate after further flight testing. Others, however, would not. The engine-starting system was complex and troublesome. The undercarriage was unlikely to be able to meet the required full 15ft (4.5m)-per-second descent velocity, and operation on rough fields could be difficult. There was little room to modify the undercarriage, and modifications would only add weight. Poor fatigue characteristics were being exhibited by X2020 and heat-treated steels, and the integral fuel tanks could be expected to leak after sustained flight in turbulence. The windscreen and canopies were compromised by the need for bird-strike protection, and the view was poor. The variable intakes had been troublesome on rigs and on the first aircraft, and it looked as though a redesign would be necessary. The engine installation was too tight, and there was no room for future growth. The fire hazard was higher than it should have been, owing to a lack of conventional zoning and the proximity of fuel and engines. The lack of electrical generation and computer capacity was embarrassing the nav/attack system. Most seriously of all, the aeroplane could no longer meet many of the sortie requirements laid down in OR.343. Combat radius, for instance, was predicted to be 816nm (938 miles; 1,509km), not 1,000nm. Short take-off roll from a dispersed site was 1,403yd (1,283m) rather than the 1,000yd required.

The full extent of this devastating news was not passed on to the customer, in the hope that improvements could be made or the requirements relaxed. In fact the RAF was not entirely ignorant of the implications of weight and engine performance, but its own internal estimates on range and performance shortfalls in the summer of 1964 had predicted a combat radius of 957nm (1,100 miles; 1,770km) and a take-off distance of 1,300yd (1,188m), nowhere near as bad as BAC's better-informed estimates. As part of what was to be a final cost-saving exercise, BAC was asked to come up with fixed prices for the various elements of the TSR2 programme. To make any actual cost reductions a more realistic prospect, it was agreed at a discussion on 27 January that a reduced specification would form the basis for any such offer. This must have come as a relief to BAC management, facing what would have been a protracted and costly struggle to make the aircraft meet the requirements.

There followed an all-day meeting at BAC Weybridge on 11 February, with RAF and MoA representatives thrashing out the details of a relaxed specification for the aircraft. The RAF was prepared to accept quite stunning reductions in performance against a fixed price with guarantee points: the internal-fuel-only 1,000nm sortie was reduced to 750nm (860 miles; 1.380km); the dispersed short take-off roll was up from 1,000yd to 1,250yd (1,140m); the landing roll, similarly, was up from 1,300yd (1,190m) to 1,500yd (1,370m) with a lowered crosswind limit; continuous flight ceiling was down from 56,000ft (17,000m) to 40,000ft (12,000m) (with safe operation up to 50,000ft (15,000m)); and the engine change time was up from 3hr to 12hr. The

After a summer of repeated delays, mostly caused by engine development problems, XR219 lifts off from Boscombe on 27 September 1964. BAE Systems via Brooklands Museum

Guarantee points, TSR2 specification issue 2

Item	Specification	New guarantee point
Continuous speed at sea level	Mach 0.9	Mach 0.9
Maximum speed at 40,000ft (12,000m)	Mach 2.0	Mach 1.75
Combat radius, low-level sortie with 2,000lb (900kg) weapon	1,000nm	750nm
Continuous operation ceiling	56,000ft (17,000m)	40,000ft (12,000m)
Take-off run, dispersed conditions, full fuel and 2,000lb (900kg) weapon, 15°C ISA	600yd (548m)	1,100yd (1,005m)
Landing run, dispersed conditions, wet runway	600yd (548m)	750yd (685m)
Max design speed	The lower of 800kt or Mach 2.25	The lower of 730kt or Mach 1.75
Terrain following	200ft (60m), automatic control	200ft (60m), manual control

dive-toss nuclear attack could be deleted. The TSR2 still could not meet some of these much-relaxed requirements, but the differences were slight and there was a distinct positive margin in some areas, such as combat radius on internal fuel. However, BAC refused to accept Mach 2 as a guarantee point, or even Mach 1.7, though was prepared to accept limited penalties if it did not meet Mach 1.7. There was a distinct fear that a huge amount of flight development would be needed to clear the auto-stiffener system required at speeds above Mach 1.5, and it was was felt that it might be more prudent simply to limit the aircraft to Mach 1.5 instead. In addition, BAC pressed hard for a relaxation of the aircraft's maximum g loading. This was meant to be 6.6g (with a 6g in-service limit), but BAC wanted it reduced to 5.5g (4.8g in-service limit); the static-test wing had failed at 8.5g. On this point, however, the RAF did not want to shift. The company went on to produce its new cost estimates, which included the offer to accept up to £9 million in losses if costs continued to rise beyond the estimates.

Beyond that point, however, any additional funding would have to be borne by the government.

Meanwhile, during the flight of 6 February 1965 XR219's undercarriage retraction problems had been overcome and a new atmosphere of optimism was evident among the BAC team at Boscombe. A date was set for the transit to Warton; 20 February. The day dawned cold and grey. The Press had been invited to Warton to watch the arrival, but all they saw was mist and low cloud. The flight was cancelled, and the result was an inevitable slew of newspaper reports that the RAF's new all-weather bomber could not fly in poor weather. They were not interested in explanations that the aircraft's instrument fit was not really up to blind navigation yet, or that the risks of flying a valuable prototype in known icing conditions were simply unacceptable. After staying at Boscombe for another two days, XR219 finally departed on the 22nd and made a high-speed medium-altitude transit, including use of the Irish Sea supersonic-test-run route. The arrival at Warton was made in typical Roland Beamont fashion, low and noisy (460kt (530mph, 850km/h) at 150ft (4.5m)), and when the aircraft taxied in, followed by the Lightning chase aircraft, the crowd of BAC workers who had been allowed out of the factory to watch broke into cheers and applause.

Thenceforth test flying accelerated, concentrating on meeting various guarantee points that had been agreed, and also dealing with the undercarriage vibration problems being experienced on landing. On the ground, work continued on finishing the third aircraft, XR221, and there was hope for a first flight of XR220 in March, and for XR221 to fly (from Wisley) in late May or June. Once XR222 was complete, much later in the year, it would probably be transported to Wisley for an initial flight and then go straight to Warton. All of this, however, depended on the delivery of flight-cleared engines, and BSEL's problems with the Olympus showed little sign of ending in the immediate future. But XR220 finally had its engines by the end of February, and ground runs began on 1 March.

Meanwhile, early investigations into the static-wing test failure had led to a hurried drawing-up of a strengthened wing and stiffened wingtips, and these were to be introduced on all of the pre-production and production aircraft. As XS660, XS661 and XS662 had already had their wings built, they would be retrofitted with the new strengthened wing when it became available. The various major problems that had arisen were gradually being dealt with and ticked off. There was, however, still no real evidence that costs were being kept under control, or that the delays were going to be reduced. The men at the Ministries had been just as busy as BAC, but they were looking into buying an alternative aircraft. Even the Air Staff had lost interest in TSR2, and BAC men suddenly found it difficult to get hold of people. Telephone calls were not returned, letters were ignored, and senior officers were 'unavailable' for days at a time.

By the start of April 1965 the mood at BAC was one of optimism mixed with fear of cancellation. The first aircraft, XR219, had performed well in the limited test programme, with generally good serviceability and no more scary moments after those of the first handful of flights. Even the weather had been kind. On 2 April, when XR219 had to taxy back to the hangar after suffering an hydraulic leak on the way to the runway for Flight 25, there was no big disappointment, and no hint that the aircraft

A BAC advertisement from 1964.
BAE Systems via Brooklands Museum

had already made its last flight. At BSEL, good news had arrived in the shape of improved fuel consumption figures on the latest standard of engine, and flight-test results had also shown better-than-predicted fuel consumption. The engine's fuel economy was still not up to specification, so the aircraft would still be unable to meet the sortie requirements, but the shortfall was now going to be much less and BSEL was still improving fuel consumption.

However, BAC's fixed-price offer had been examined and rejected, as it still offered no real ceiling to what appeared to be ever-rising costs. At the end of March the most recent progress report from the Department of the Controller (Aircraft) at the MoA included the following confidential policy dates for important milestones in the TSR2 programme (confidential policy dates were generally more pessimistic than BAC estimates, and were never disclosed to BAC lest they were taken as an inducement to relax and meet these dates rather than the company's own promises):

First flight of first pre-production aircraft (No. 11) October 1966
First flight of first aircraft for RAF April 1967
First CA release date (nuclear strike role) January 1968
Full CA release date (all roles in specification) June 1969

The size of the RAF's TSR2 force, once envisaged as a total buy of 300 (170 front-line) aircraft, had dropped to a total buy of 138 (106 front-line) by 1963, and 110 (74 front-line) by January 1965. During those last few months of desperate money-saving studies there had been suggestions that as few as fifty would be purchased, with the balance replaced by Buccaneers – or F-111s. Worse was to come. On 6 April 1965, while BAC factory workers worked on TSR2 assembly and listened to their radios to find out what effect the Budget would have on their pay packets and the cost of their beer and cigarettes, they found out instead that the TSR2 project was cancelled forthwith.

CHAPTER FIVE

Flight Test Development

Flight test programme

BAC's initial flight test programme had the nine development-batch aircraft carrying out an intensive flying programme of around 10hr per aircraft per month, flying by day and being serviced by night, to a total of 2,000hr of flying over 33 months (increased from a very early estimate of 1,200hr). This phase was to be carried out by BAC, with the A&AEE getting some previews to enable it to get a leg-up before its own flying began. This would be undertaken on the first five pre-production aircraft, at around the twenty-four-month point, bringing the aircraft to CA release over 500hr of flying and nine months. The final six pre-production aircraft would then enter service with the RAF for intensive flying trials in the nuclear strike role and the investigation of any problems to be expected in service.

There was some criticism that this plan was unrealistic, and a BAC team visited the USA in October 1962 to study the procedures used in the development and release to service of new aircraft. Contractors associated with the production of the North American A3J Vigilante, Grumman A2F Intruder and F-105 Thunderchief were consulted. Impressed by American methods, the team suggested a complete revision of BAC's own test plan, including closer integration of MoA and RAF personnel with the company testing team, double day shifts to enable flying and servicing to continue simultaneously, and establishment of the first RAF squadron at Boscombe Down, to make early use of BAC and A&AEE flight-test experience. While the average utilization of 10hr per aircraft per month would be kept, the overall flying time to CA release was reduced to 1,500hr, with staged clearances enabling the RAF to begin flying the type earlier. Three fewer aircraft would be needed. Around 50 per cent of the flight testing would be done by BAC, 35 per cent by the A&AEE and 15 per cent by a joint BAC/MoA team. The MoA was naturally upset by this, describing BAC's proposals as 'rambling and difficult to follow'. It believed it was a programme in which BAC would call the tune while the A&AEE and MoA were reduced to playing from the company's music sheet.

Historically, flight testing by manufacturers had created problems, with firms claiming that various targets had been met while withholding precise details of test conditions. Consequently, different results were found when the A&AEE carried out its own trials, and much time and effort was spent duplicating portions of the flight test programme. For that reason it was not unreasonable for the MoA to want a more open and less wasteful programme; but it went further than that. It wanted the flight test programme to be a joint MoA/BAC effort with an entirely integrated flight-testing team consisting of equal measures of BAC staff and A&AEE and RAF personnel, with 'full MoA participation both in the air and in the project office'. Given the MoA's record of introducing delays and confusion throughout the project to date, this was a sure-fire way to turn the flight test programme into a disaster. Furthermore, the anonymous writer of an MoA note on the

The Vickers-Armstrongs plant at Weybridge, bordered by the old Brooklands racing track with the runway at the centre. Vickers flew many newly built aircraft from this relatively short runway, including Valiants and, later, VC10s, but safety precluded flying the first TSR2 from here to nearby Wisley.
BAE Systems

OPPOSITE PAGE:

TOP: Preparing XR219 for an early engine run at Boscombe Down. In this view the bomb bay and engine accessories bay doors are open and several panels have been removed for additional access to various areas of the engine and reheat units. The pristine white finish of the aircraft, nicknamed 'Joe', did not last long. BAE Systems via Brooklands Museum

BOTTOM: Here, XR219 is seen on the 'peardrop' at Boscombe Down, an area on the eastern side of the airfield set aside for TSR2 ground runs and pre-flight preparations, complete with hazard markings painted on the concrete. BAE Systems via Warton Heritage Group

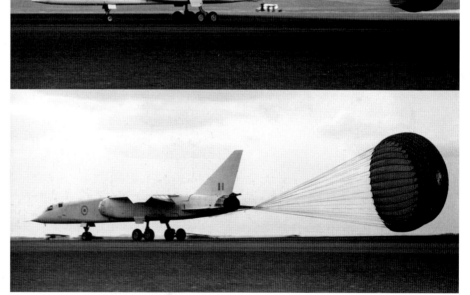

THIS PAGE:

TOP LEFT: The TSR2's braking parachute was stored in a bay above and between the two jetpipes, a 'beak' door springing open when the parachute handle was pulled in the pilot's cockpit. The parachute itself was attached to a railing below the jetpipes, as can be seen here. BAE Systems via Warton Heritage Group

TOP RIGHT: Three photographs of the braking parachute deployment, taken at different points. 1) The drogue is fully open and in the process of pulling the main parachute open; 2) The main parachute is open but reefed and 3) The main parachute de-reefed. BAE Systems

ABOVE LEFT: The auxiliary intake door mechanism soon proved too weak to hold the doors open at the required 25-degree angle at higher power settings, and locks were fitted to hold the doors fully open for the first flight. BAE Systems via Warton Heritage Group

matter stated: '... whilst in no position to question BAC on aerodynamic and engineering competence, I have the strongest misgivings regarding the quality of the flight test organization [allocated to the TSR2] and, in particular, on the suitability of some of the aircrew involved ...'. This was almost certainly a reference to Roland Beamont. While he was a noted Second World War fighter pilot and the test pilot of the Canberra and P.1, he had not been trained at the Empire Test Pilots' School (ETPS), and a strong faction believed that company test pilots with no genuine test-pilot background were 'cowboys' and risk takers.

The RAF was also lukewarm about the new plan, believing it could learn more about the new aircraft by forming the first squadron at an RAF station, away from the sterile flight test environment, and it was concerned that the new plan reduced the number of aircraft on the flight test programme. Statistical analysis of previous aircraft projects was carried out to see how many prototypes could be expected to be lost on a flight test programme, and at a loss rate of one aircraft per 1,000hr or so there appeared a good chance that one or two TSR2s would be lost during testing. With so much riding on the project, BAC would have to be incredibly careful, and lucky.

The development-batch aircraft were all to be extensively instrumented to measure handling, performance and aerodynamic qualities, plus pressure distribution and various parameters to aid with the further development of the auto-stiffening and auto-stabilization systems. The weapons bay would house much of the flight-test instrumentation, wrapped in insulating blankets and provided with air conditioning, and spare space in other bays would be used where possible. On the first two aircraft, for instance, the sideways-looking camera bays below the navigator's position were used, as no cameras were fitted. The second aircraft, XR220, was fitted with various transducers and 'bonkers' to try to excite flutter on the flying surfaces, as well as camera fairings on the intakes to suit it for its reserve role as a backup for XR224, which would be carrying out flight trials with external stores. A MIDAS crash recorder was also installed in each development-batch aircraft, housed in the upper equipment bay behind the navigator's position and fitted with an explosive release unit so that it could be fired clear of the aircraft (through a frangible window in the bay access panel) if needs be. At least that way the conditions leading up to the

loss of an aircraft would be known, and the loss would not be a total one.

The question of the location for the first TSR2 flight and the subsequent flight test programme was, predictably, one on which English Electric and Vickers could not agree. Vickers, in overall charge, wanted to use one of its airfields. Development-batch airframes were undergoing final assembly at Weybridge, which had a relatively short runway (1,500yd; 1,370m) nestling within the old Brooklands motor racing track. This allowed no margin for error whatsoever, so Vickers chose Wisley. A great many Vickers types, such as the Viscount and Valiant, had already flown from there, having been built at Weybridge and either transported by road or flown to Wisley for their construction to be completed. Wisley's runway, at over 2,200yd (2,010m), seemed long enough for TSR2 flying (it was, after all, designed to a STOL requirement), but the local airspace was congested, with London (Heathrow) Airport not very far away, and problems arising during early test flights could require an immediate landing. In that event, Wisley's runway was too short for safety. English Electric assumed that its airfield at Warton, with nearly 2,660yd (2,430m) of runway, was the logical place for the flight-test base, pointing out the proximity to low-level and supersonic training areas, the company's extensive supersonic flight-test experience and that long runway. Vickers resisted. The first flight had to be from Wisley, regardless, though it reluctantly admitted that Wisley's surrounding airspace was perhaps unsuitable for development flying. By early 1961 the creation of BAC had brought the two firms a little closer together, and by May of that year the Vickers component had come round to the use of Warton for test flying. Finally presenting a united front on this important choice, BAC informed the MoA accordingly.

The MoA, naturally, promptly decided that Warton was unsuitable. Only Boscombe Down, with its even larger runway (3,500yd; 3,200m) was suitable, its additional length and width providing the necessary safety factors for early test flights. Any operation of development-batch TSR2s from Warton subsequent to this initial flying would require the aircraft to have arrester hooks installed. This was not a popular decision at either end of the TSR2 project, but, for the time being, that was how it was going to be. A year later Wisley was back on the table, with BAC struggling to get the project back on schedule and

anxious to save the month or so it thought would be lost by dismantling the first aircraft and transporting it to Boscombe for reassembly and first flight. The plan was to regain the lost month by transporting the aircraft intact by road to Wisley, then flying it from there to Boscombe.

Roland Beamont, however, had signed on with English Electric for this final flight-testing job in spite of his wife's ill health, and he was not about to let the change to Wisley go ahead without a fight, particularly as the aircraft's weight had continued to grow and the engine continued to have development problems. In March 1963 Beamont put his objections to the Wisley plan in writing to the MoA. He said that the plan to make a first flight from Wisley, landing at Boscombe was '... made more on the grounds of expediency than of the operational requirements'. There were a number of practical problems. First, if anything went wrong during that first flight and an immediate emergency landing was required, the aircraft's high approach speed meant it would need a very long runway. (As neither braking parachute nor wheelbrakes could be relied upon, a minimum length of 2,500yd (2,290m) was specified for diversion landings.) Only nearby Heathrow was suitable on that score. At that time the first flight was expected to be made in December 1963, and the question of weather was also raised. The chances of good weather all the way between Wisley and Boscombe in the winter months were slim, and the unpredictability of this would make planning impossible.

By August, after further problems had arisen with Olympus development, the MoA was in agreement that Wisley was perhaps not suitable, and the risk of a TSR2 with a problem crashing in the heavily populated surroundings of Heathrow while on approach to an emergency landing did not bear thinking about. Another study was made into the feasibility of dismantling the aircraft and taking it to Boscombe Down for the first flight. Beamont was not exactly happy. Warton was still a more logical choice, but at least Wisley was off the cards. The first-flight date had by now slipped once again, to March 1964, and the need to dismantle the aircraft, transport it to Boscombe and reassemble it would delay the first flight to April 1964.

This would turn out to be yet another optimistic estimate. Once XR219 had been transported to Boscombe its reassembly took longer than expected, and the continuing

The port console in XR219's pilot's cockpit, taken around a month before the first flight, when the cockpit was in the final stages of being equipped. Non-standard items in this view include the instrumentation recorder controls on the block on the windscreen arch. BAE Systems via Warton Heritage Group

The main panel of XR219's pilot's cockpit. The major difference from a production panel is that the moving-map display is replaced by a basic TACAN/VOR/DME navigation display (hiding behind the joystick). BAE Systems via Warton Heritage Group

The starboard console of XR219's pilot's cockpit. The box on the windscreen arch holds a time ident/base display used by flight test crew for accurately recording times of particular events. BAE Systems via Warton Heritage Group

The port console of XR219's navigator's cockpit. This cockpit was considerably denuded compared with the intended production cockpit, and most of the controls visible here relate to fuel management and control of the crash and flight test instrumentation recorders (in the 'role panel' area that would normally be used for weapons/reconnaissance-pack control). The Y-shaped item on the sidewall is part of the air-conditioning system. BAE Systems via Warton Heritage Group

The main panel of XR219's navigator's cockpit. Once again this is considerably different from a production panel, being limited to a selection of flight instrument repeaters, controls for the engine instrumentation recorder, and a basic **TACAN/VOR/DME** navigation display taking up the space intended for the FLR display. BAE Systems via Warton Heritage Group

The starboard console of XR219's navigator's cockpit. At far left the central computing system control panel is replaced by a selection of engine instruments, including warning lights for the troublesome No.7 bearing. The rapid take-off panel on the sidewall to the right of the Y-shaped air conditioning tube shows blanks for many of the missing systems on this aircraft, including stable platform, Doppler, IFF, Computer, HF, ECM and SLR. This was called the rapid-start panel, as pulling any of the obvious bars on this panel upwards would simultaneously turn on all of the systems it controlled. BAE Systems via Warton Heritage Group

Aircraft	Phase	Flight-test role
1 – XR219	–	Handling and performance
2 – XR220	A	Flutter, vibration, structure loads and engines
2 – XR220	B	Backup for XR224 phase A
2 – XR220	C	Handling, roll/yaw coupling
2 – XR220	D	External stores – handling, structure loads, flutter
3 – XR221	A	Nav-attack and terrain following, CWAS (Conventional Weapons Aiming System)
3 – XR221	B	Bombing with navigation
4 – XR222	A	AFCS and handling
4 – XR222	B	Auto terrain following
5 – XR223	A	Preliminary bombing
5 – XR223	B	Conditioning and air system, temperature survey
5 – XR223	C	Strike photography
5 – XR223	D	Tropical trials
6 – XR224	A	Engine handling, engine performance, pressure errors, aircraft performance with and without external stores
6 – XR224	B	Further development
7 – XR225	A	Hydraulics, fuel, electrical, miscellaneous systems
7 – XR225	B	In-flight refuelling
7 – XR225	C	Reconnaissance pack
8 – XR226	A	Nav-attack development with stores
8 – XR226	B	Reserve
9 – XR227	A	Temperature and vibration of internal stores, initial release of internal stores
9 – XR227	B	Additional temperature and vibration of internal stores, subsequent release of internal stores
9 – XR227	C	Temperature and vibration of external stores, release and fusing of external stores (nuclear)
9 – XR227	D	Release of internal and external stores

Flight testing programme – airframe allocation

problems with both the Olympus engine and ejection seat developments meant that engine runs finally began with a single seat installed in the aircraft, and carried on in fits and starts as niggling little problems arose.

Taxying trials

After months of frustrating delays, XR219, nicknamed 'Jim' by the BAC testing team (after a Goon Show character who called everybody Jim), was finally ready to begin taxying trials on 2 September 1964, a hot summer's day. An engine run in the morning was followed by the first taxy runs in the afternoon. Steering via differential braking on the main wheels was initially impossible, as the aircraft came to a standstill each time, and nosewheel steering was used instead. The first taxi run was in dry power to 40kt (46mph; 74km/h), and on the next one reheat was used. Differential braking was tried again and was successful, if jerky, at higher speeds, the run getting up to 60kt (69mph; 111km/h).

Preoccupied with the difficult steering and with the speed building, Beamont inadvertently retarded the throttles past the point at which the fuel cocks were closed. The engines wound down and as a result the aircraft lost electrical power. The liquid-oxygen (lox) system, now without power, began spraying oxygen 'snow' out of the oxygen masks, and, when it was disconnected, lox leaked from the oxygen regulators. This was a serious hazard, as lox can ignite on contact with grease, and it could be pretty well guaranteed that various areas of the cockpit had been smeared with grease during the previous months. Luckily no fire broke out. The next day another morning engine run was followed by a further afternoon taxy run to check differential braking and run up to 60kt once more. This test was terminated owing to an hydraulic leak, and a second attempt later in the day had to be cancelled when the port undercarriage leg warning light lit up, indicating loss of brake pressure.

After a day in the hangar rectifying hydraulic snags and replacing some life-expired reheat fuel inlet pipes, the tests continued on 5 September, a Saturday. The intention was to carry out three faster runs, but in the event there was only time for two, one to 100kt (115mph; 185km/h) and one to 120kt (138mph; 222km/h), both with successful streaming of the braking parachute. Even on a Sunday the taxying tests continued, though a gusting crosswind meant that only one run was possible, in the middle of the day. The No.1 engine on this run exhibited 'hunting' behaviour, and the

auxiliary intake doors were flicking in and out, so an afternoon engine run was carried out to try to diagnose the problem. The next day did not go well either, with a failed braking parachute stream at 140kt (160mph; 260km/h), resulting in heavy use of the wheelbrakes, which then became welded to the wheels and required wheel and brake replacements later. The engines were once again inadvertently stopcocked, and the aircraft had to be towed off the runway. Next morning the throttles were modified to stop a further repeat of the stopcocking, but numerous attempts to start the engines for a run that day were frustrated by various problems culminating in the need to replace the constant-speed drive starter (CSDS).

Wednesday the 9th saw another brake parachute failure on a 140kt run. Heavy braking caused brake temperatures to rise to over 1,000°C, and the starboard forward main gear tyre deflated. The remainder of that day and the next was spent modifying the parachute and beak door, and fitting a crew-operated stopcock on the lox system to prevent further recurrence of the dangerous leak in the cockpit. The auxiliary inlet doors had continued to be problematic, so they were locked open at 40 degrees.

It fell off the back of a lorry, guv! – XR220 arrives

The 9th also saw XR220 delivered to the airfield, with wings on one trailer and the fuselage on another. The driver jack-knifed the latter trailer while turning right to enter B3 hangar shortly before five o'clock, and as the trailer toppled on to its side XR220's 18 tons of fuselage partly parted company with the trailer, the rear end (at the forward end of the trailer) coming to rest on the ground, supported by the port tailplane spigot. This was fortunate, as had it rolled any further it would have smashed into BAC's Lightning chase aircraft, parked just a few feet away. As it was late in the day and the resulting mess appeared stable, it was left overnight. Next morning an inspection was begun to see how much damage had been caused and determine how best to recover it.

Salvage procedures had been created for the type, but they did not cater for a situation in which a wingless fuselage would be lying on its side, partly attached to a trailer. They were designed to cope primarily with aircraft that had suffered landing accidents and were upright on their belly. Some specialized equipment was required, including a fuselage lifting beam, and these were fabricated at Weybridge in a matter of hours, being delivered on the 11th, when the salvage procedure began. After the covers had been removed, the fuselage was lifted with cranes, the trailer was taken away and air bags were placed underneath the aircraft. A ground rig was used to extend the starboard main undercarriage and the fuselage was then lowered until the wheels were on the ground. Then, with careful crane use, the fuselage was rotated until it was upright once more. The port undercarriage was then extended and the fuselage lowered further,

RIGHT: **'Recovery of a crashed aircraft'; unfortunately the recovery procedures did not deal with the problem of a wingless fuselage entangled with a trailer.** BAE Systems via Brooklands Museum

BELOW: **The recovery of XR220 on 11 September 1964. BAC Weybridge came up with a successful recovery technique within hours of the accident, and very little additional damage was caused during the operation.** BAE Systems via Brooklands Museum

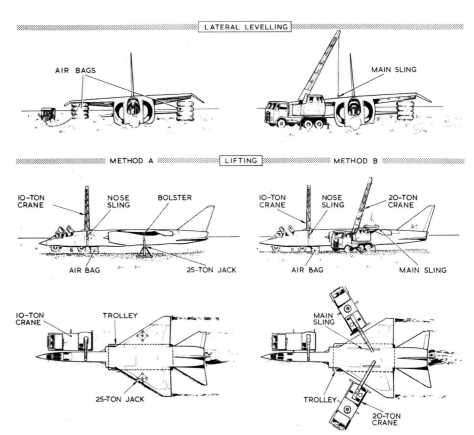

OPPOSITE PAGE:
Refuelling XR219 before an early engine run. At this point the navigator's cockpit lacked a seat, and BSEL personnel manning the navigator's position made do with a wooden crate. BAE Systems via Warton Heritage Group

THIS PAGE:
RIGHT: Roland Beamont boards XR219 for a taxy run. With the cockpits so high above the ground, access ladders were a must, though the specification did call for retractable on-board ladders to be used when necessary. BAE Systems via Warton Heritage Group

BELOW: The Olympus 320 was not a clean-burning turbojet, and an engine run was announced not only by the deafening roar of the engines but also by the cloud of black smoke. BAE Systems via Brooklands Museum

a jack being placed under the nose before the nose leg was finally extended. Everything held together, and the fuselage was towed into the hangar six hours after the salvage operation had begun.

While XR220 was being salvaged, XR219 continued to cause frustration. Fuel pump warning lights illuminated and the aircraft was shut down, whereupon fuel leaks from blown gaskets on the forward fueldraulic pumps were found. The next day it was found that the No.2 booster pump drive had sheared, and a decision was made to stop the taxying tests for several days and replace all the booster and fueldraulic pumps. Beamont had complained of poor visibility through the windscreen, so it was replaced.

Meanwhile, XR220 had been receiving a steady stream of visitors from various BAC departments to assess the damage. Initially this appeared to be nowhere near as bad as it could have been, being mostly limited to minor damage to the port tailplane spigot and main jacking points, and various dents in skin-panels, including the underside of the port intake and by the lower airbrake doors. However, beneath the cracked and dented panels lay a succession of damaged longerons and frames that would require extensive repair.

Late on the afternoon of Thursday 17th another attempt at taxying XR219 was made, but fuel vapour in the cockpit put paid to this. The next day things went from bad to worse. An engine run in the morning produced more fuel leaks, and melted droplets of metal were found on the ground

below the aircraft. Replacing fuel pipes in the accessories bay and tracing the source of the metal droplets occupied the rest of that day and all of the next.

Taxying resumed on Sunday 20th with a 110kt (125mph; 203km/h) run on the shorter cross-runway at Boscombe, as the crosswind on the main runway was out of limits. The brake 'chute streamed successfully, but the parachute beak door hit the base of the fin as it opened. The aircraft was returned to the hangar again for another CSDS change which stretched through into Monday. Another run on Monday afternoon to 125kt (144mph; 232km/h) was again successful, as was a run to 140kt (160mph; 260km/h) on Tuesday, which surprised Beamont when he found he could rotate the nose and lift the nose gear from the runway at just 105kt (120mph; 195km/h) using 10 degrees of tailplane rather than the predicted 130kt (150mph; 240km/h) and 18 degrees. More metal had been found, though, traced to lagging from an oil pipe, and it was decided that filters needed to be installed in the lines between the engine and CSDS to prevent this metal harming the CSDS. Work then concentrated on getting the aircraft ready to fly.

By Friday the 25th further inspection of XR220, including fuel system pressure testing, had found several fairly minor fuel leaks in the rear fuselage and in the forward fuel collector box. On the plus side, a complete alignment check on the fuselage and the port tailplane spigot was passed with flying colours. More engine runs on XR219 had

resulted in more pieces of metal being found, both under the aircraft and also in the newly installed filters. This time the source was finally identified as the starter cart for the Palouste auxiliary power unit (APU), which had internal damage. This was repaired on the 26th, and an engine run in the afternoon cleared the installation, but now the all-important low-pressure (LP) drive shaft strain gauge on the port engine failed, so the first flight could not be made that day.

First flight

As the sun rose on the morning of the 27th, a Sunday, the weather did not look good. Mist blanketed the airfield and it looked as though XR219 would be staying put. An engine run first thing in the morning went well, however, and the intention was then to carry out a final fast taxy with brake-chute stream. However, the mist remained as thick as ever, and it was not until midday that the run could be tried. All went well, but the beak door once again lightly impacted the base of the fin on opening, though no damage was caused to either fin or door. It was decided that a temporary way of avoiding this problem would be to land, keep the nose up for aerodynamic braking and only release the brake 'chute once speed had decayed to below 150kt (172mph; 278km/h). Preparations for a flight later in the afternoon began in earnest. Crewing-in at Boscombe Down at about 14.00hr,

Several taxy runs worked out various bugs in XR219's systems before the first flight, the most serious problems being limited to braking-parachute failures. BAE Systems via Brooklands Museum

Roland Beamont and test navigator Don Bowen carried out their preflight checks and the assembled media on and off the airfield waited expectantly. As the aircraft began to taxy away from the 'pear-drop' area at Boscombe (a circular area at the end of runway 28, near the eastern perimeter), the weather had finally cleared completely and the sun was shining. Two chase aircraft, Canberra WD937 flown by John Carrodus and Lightning T.4 XM968 flown by Jimmy Dell, got airborne first, and then it was the TSR2's turn to line-up on runway 24. A stiff breeze gave a crosswind of 11 to 15kt (12–17mph; 20–27km/h); beyond the 7kt (8mph; 12km/h) limit that had been agreed a month before.

For this first flight XR219 was subject to a host of limitations. The AUW had to be kept below 74,000lb (33,500kg) so that an engine failure at lift-off speed (180kt (205mph; 333km/h)) would not make it impossible to climb away on the remaining engine (although 100 per cent power would be needed, and BSEL could only guarantee safety at up to 98 per cent), or impossible to land on one engine without reheat. This meant a restricted fuel load, and hence a short flight. In view of the short flight time, no attempt would be made to retract the undercarriage, because no time would be available to troubleshoot it if failed to retract or extend cleanly, which was a real possibility, as the required number of successful rig tests had not been completed. The auxiliary intake doors remained locked open, and the airbrakes were kept cracked slightly open, even in what should have been the fully closed position, as fully

Preparation for the first flight, with XR219 joined by Lightning XM968, the chase aircraft. BAE Systems via Brooklands Museum

Take-off for the first flight of the TSR2, Boscombe Down, 27 September 1964. With a change of government on the horizon, BAC gambled everything on a successful first flight of an aircraft that some considered to be far from airworthy. BAE Systems via Brooklands Museum

LEFT: **Beginning the first left-hand turn in the climb, shortly after take-off on the first flight. The Lightning chase aircraft stuck to XR219 like glue for this first flight, allowing the crew to compare instrument readings, and of course enabling BAC's photographer to take a fine sequence of shots.**
BAE Systems via Warton Heritage Group

BELOW: **On the first downwind leg of the first flight, with Boscombe just visible in the haze below the aircraft's undercarriage. No attempt was made to retract the undercarriage on the first flight, as not enough successful cycles had been carried out on the ground. Nor would the limited fuel load have permitted much time to troubleshoot had problems arisen in the air.**
BAE Systems via Warton Heritage Group

closing them could result in one or more of the airbrakes attempting to go past the fully closed point and damaging the mechanism. The short flight time would limit the flight's usefulness to an assessment of the aircraft in flight in its take-off and landing configurations only.

At 15.28hr Beamont released the brakes, and with twin spears of flame from the Olympus engines visible even in the bright sunshine the aircraft rolled forward. The wind was 11kt (12.5mph; 20km/h) at 240

degrees. Flaps were down 20 degrees and flap blowing was on. When the aircraft reached 120kt (140mph; 220km/h) Beamont began a steady rearward stick movement and the nosewheel left the ground three seconds later, by which time speed had risen to 150kt (170mph; 280km/h). Beamont had an impression of reduced acceleration, and ceased rotation for a few moments. However, his perception was in error and just over 23sec from beginning the take-off roll, at 189kt (217mph; 350km/h),

XR219 became airborne, having used a whisker over 1,200yd (1,100m) of runway. By the time the aircraft had reached the magic 50ft (15m) of altitude, 1,688yd (1,543m) of runway had gone by and the aircraft was flying at 206kt (237mph; 380km/h). The aircraft was flying well, and the expected standards of control and stability had been exceeded. Roll damping and fin effectiveness in particular were better than anticipated. Not everything was working well; the cabin air conditioning produced an icy blast of air when selected to 'AUTO COOL'.

Having climbed to 6,000ft (1,800m) with nothing falling off or blowing up, Beamont levelled off and continued with the flight as planned, entering a left-hand turn to proceed back towards the airfield via Salisbury, and flying past to the southeast before turning left abeam Stockbridge to make a pass over the airfield in the same direction as the initial take-off, having descended to 1,700ft (500m) to do so. From this pass he turned left once more to enter the circuit pattern and carry out his landing. No difficulties were experienced with lining-up on the runway and holding the approach path, though the aircraft was a little oversensitive in pitch. Approach speed was 200kt (230mph; 370km/h) with 35 degrees of flap, reducing to 190kt (220mph; 350km/h) at 250ft (75m), 182kt (209mph; 337km/h) at 50ft (15m) and flaring at around 30ft (9m) to give a touchdown speed of 174kt (200mph/322km/h). With just about everything going smoothly up to this point, it

was a rude shock to Beamont when there was a sudden violent vibration from side to side just at the point of touchdown, sufficient to cause him to lose vision almost completely. Continuing to hold the nose-

wheel off for aerodynamic braking, as discussed earlier, Beamont pulled the 'chute just a little too early, at 155kt (178mph; 287km/h), forgivably so given the mayhem he had just experienced, and the beak door

RIGHT: **With Lightning and Canberra chase aircraft in attendance, XR219 leaves a trail of black smoke across the Wiltshire sky halfway through the first flight.** BAE Systems via Warton Heritage Group

BELOW: **Short final to runway 28, with the BAC support crew and vehicles visible on the 'peardrop' area above the aircraft. The tent was the only shelter available to BAC personnel working on this area of the airfield.** BAE Systems via Warton Heritage Group

ABOVE: Safely on the ground, much to the relief of everybody involved. The large braking parachute is seen here at fullest extent; on several occasions later in the flight test programme the parachute split open, and some thought was given to limiting it permanently to the smaller reefed deployment.
BAE Systems via Warton Heritage Group

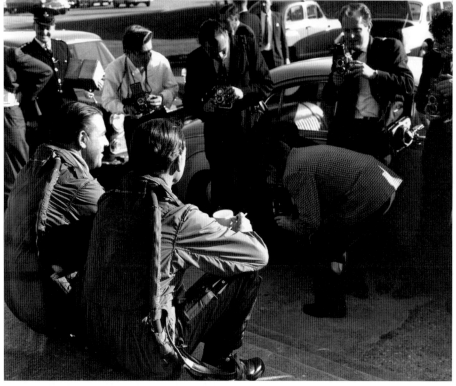

LEFT: Roland Beamont and his navigator, Don Bowen, enjoy a well-earned cup of tea while the assembled press record their reactions to the successful first flight.

once again impacted the base of the fin, denting the door. (A permanent modification using an hydraulic damper was later introduced to cure this problem. Meanwhile, a simple temporary fix was the work of true British genius; a metal strip clamped over the hinge slowed the opening of the door while the strip was being bent out of shape. It was easy to replace the deformed strip for the next use.) Wheel braking came in at 70kt (80mph; 130km/h) and the parachute jettisoned at 40kt (46mph; 74km/h), the aircraft rolling to a stop after using 2,050yd (1,875m) of runway. The aircraft had been airborne for just over 14min, but it was a successful first flight. An extract

from Beamont's report on the flight reads as follows:

Due to virtually complete serviceability this first sortie was carried out in full accordance with Flight Test Schedule No. 1. Stability and response to controls was found to be adequate and safe for flight under the test conditions, and to conform closely to predicted and simulated values. In this 1st flight configuration and under the conditions tested, this aircraft could be flown safely by any moderately experienced pilot qualified on Lightning or similar aircraft, and the flight development programme can therefore be said to be off to a good start.

Such an extract was, of course, just the sort of thing BAC needed to send to the Ministry, but the long list of defects that needed to be dealt with before a second flight (most of which already existed before the maiden flight) was another matter entirely. The amount of instrumentation and data recording being carried out during the flight was unprecedented, and BAC also now faced the task of analyzing over 27 miles (43km) of tape recordings holding over 61 million data points.

Flying XR219 had been a huge gamble (and did not improve the ETPS's opinion of BAC's flight test organization), but it had paid off, relieving some of the pressure for visible progress. The company now had a lot of work ahead to get XR219 to a safer standard for continued flight testing (more than eighty modifications were planned), and to repair XR220. It had been planned to fly the latter aircraft in November, but repair was complicated because much of the damage was to the jacking points. Thus the aircraft could not be jacked up easily, and the repairers would initially have to work round this limitation. The slow delivery of required components to complete the build tasks outstanding on XR220 (which would have been necessary with or without the delivery accident) also frustrated progress,

"Our first snag, Roly—I can hear bells!"

Press reaction to the first flight was generally positive but muted; Raymond Jackson could be relied upon to raise a smile, however. Evening Standard

and on several occasions XR220 was even used as a 'Christmas tree', with parts being removed for use on XR219. The flight date for XR220 slipped back to December and then further, into early 1965.

With XR219's engines replaced by new units, and Beamont's refusal to accept further flights with the 98 per cent thrust limitation, a plan was instigated to allow the use of 100 per cent thrust for brief periods, such as during take-off. Strict conditions were to be put in place; both engines would have to have LP shafts of known history and low usage; both would be strain-gauged and stresses on the shafts recorded at all times; and finally a visual indicator in the cockpit would show when stresses on the shafts exceeded 10 tons/sq in (1,575kg/sq

cm), well below the breaking stress. This plan was put to the MoA at the end of October 1964, and was accepted. Warning lights were soon installed in XR219's cockpit, linked to amplifiers hooked up to the strain gauges on the engines' LP shafts. Beamont was not entirely comfortable with these, being well aware of the unreliable behaviour of amplified low-voltage signals, but accepted that this was the only way forward.

Emergency landings

The second flight of XR219 did not take place until the end of the year, on 31 December (the aircraft was ready on the

23rd, but poor weather intervened), and was cut short owing to intolerable vibrations throughout a large portion of the rpm range on the port engine. At its worst the crew's eyeballs were vibrating so much that vision was lost, and Beamont quickly returned the aircraft to Boscombe, keeping the undercarriage down again while he burned off fuel to a safe landing weight. With a somewhat firm arrival on *terra firma* there was severe undercarriage-induced lateral vibration, sufficient to throw the crew about to the extent of their harnesses.

No immediate cause was found for the engine vibrations, and another taxy run proved inconclusive. Some modifications were made to the undercarriage, with hop-damper pressure reduced and the toe-out of

Flight 2, blighted by intolerable engine vibrations, did not last long. The aircraft's distinctive contrails were a product of the fierce vortices spun off the wingtips at even relatively low angles of incidence.
BAE Systems via Warton Heritage Group

LEFT: **Flight 3 was similarly cut short by engine LP shaft stress warning lights illuminating, and more engine vibrations.** BAE Systems via Warton Heritage Group

BELOW: **The TSR2's large airbrakes were effective, but troubles with the actuating jacks and synchronization mechanism meant that XR219 flew with them cracked open slightly for most flights, and a redesigned mechanism was on the cards for production aircraft. Here, on Flight 4, they are exercised to their full travel for the first time.** BAE Systems via Warton Heritage Group

the bogies slightly reduced. With wary eyes on the all-important engine LP driveshaft warning lights, flight 3 went ahead three days later. At a critical point on the take-off run the warning light for the No.1 engine flickered, but Beamont was now committed to the take-off. In the climb, both engine warning lights came on steadily and the intolerable engine vibration also returned in full force. Carefully keeping the engines away from the range that could result in the LP shafts disintegrating, and trying to stay clear of the range giving the worst vibration, Beamont made an immediate emergency landing. Things were not going well for the flight test programme.

The double LP shaft warning turned out to be a false one, caused by a poorly fitted power supply connector. (Beamont ordered the lamp filaments to be removed from the warning lamps as he considered them a useless distraction; from now on only the navigator's lamps would be operative.) To solve the engine vibration problem, the port engine and jetpipe were replaced, though the cause ultimately turned out to be a faulty fuel pump. Various other minor defects were dealt with, and a camera was mounted on the nose gear leg to film the main undercarriage at touchdown. White stripes were painted on the mainwheel tyres to aid cine film and photographic analysis.

The next flight was made just under a week later. After a frustrating morning in which it was thought the flight would have to be cancelled because the flight test radio frequency was being blanketed by heavy interference (some of the team even thought there was some kind of jamming effort under way by opponents of the project), Boscombe gave permission to use its own tower frequency, as there was expected to be little or no other traffic. The longest flight so far was carried out, a whole 21min in duration, including the use of various flap and airbrake settings. A very gentle landing was made and the undercarriage oscillations experienced on previous flights were much reduced. Beamont was fulsome in his praise of the aircraft's handling qualities in the approach and landing configuration.

Undercarriage retraction problems

Flight 5 saw the first attempt to retract the undercarriage, after ten consecutive successful retractions in the hangar. On this flight the nose gear camera had been removed

and replaced by one on the fuselage, looking down at the port main undercarriage to give another angle on the oscillation problems experienced at touchdown. Unfortunately things did not go well. After a succession of thudding and clunking noises in XR219, the pilot of the chase aircraft reported that the port main gear had stayed down. Inspection through the navigator's periscope revealed that the bogie had failed to rotate fully, thus blocking the retraction sequence. Beamont extended the undercarriage again, but now the starboard bogie failed to rotate to the landing position, and the port bogie had also stayed where it was. None of the emergency drills included the case in which the gear was down but the

bogies were at the wrong angle, so the flight test team on the ground was consulted. They felt sure that a gentle touchdown would result in the bogies rotating to the correct position. Beamont offered his navigator, Don Bowen, the chance to eject, but Don elected to keep him company and the aircraft's remarkably precise controls enabled Beamont to carry out a perfectly judged landing at minimal descent rate. The bogies rotated to the normal angle and the landing was successful; and with far less of the disorienting oscillations previously experienced.

After another undercarriage-down flight to familiarize Jimmy Dell with the aircraft, flight 7 was the next attempt to retract the

TOP: **The first attempt to retract the undercarriage in flight, during Flight 5, resulted in the port main gear leg failing to retract.** BAE Systems via Warton Heritage Group

ABOVE: **When the gear was extended again, neither bogie rotated to the landing position and a careful 'tip-toe' landing had to be made.**
BAE Systems via Warton Heritage Group

ABOVE: Jimmy Dell in the cockpit of XR219 before his first flight in the TSR2. Jimmy soon took over from Roland Beamont as lead pilot on the TSR2 programme, and by the time of cancellation he had the most hours on the aircraft.

BELOW: Jimmy Dell's first flight, on 15 January 1965, was a familiarization sortie with no attempt made to retract the undercarriage. Visible in the background here are Thruxton Airfield (bottom right) and Tidworth (top centre). BAE Systems via Warton Heritage Group

undercarriage. Various changes to the gear had been made by BAC Weybridge to overcome the bogie rotation problem, and twenty-one consecutive successful retractions had been carried out in the hangar. During this flight, after selection of undercarriage up, the port gear successfully retracted. Unfortunately the starboard gear did not. The bogie had rotated to align with the main leg, but had not tilted to match its angle, and once again the sequence came to a halt. This time the selection of undercarriage down was more successful, and the bogies rotated to a nearly level attitude, enabling a normal landing to be made. Jimmy took flight 8, with no attempt to retract the gear, and flight 9 was back to Beamont for assessment of handling with 50 degrees of flap and no gear retraction. Before flight 10 further modifications had been made to the undercarriage, which then finally retracted successfully in the air. Beamont took the opportunity to 'widen the flight envelope', or 'snot the airfield' in RAF parlance, taking the aircraft up to 500kt (575mph; 925km/h) and then making low passes over Boscombe at 450kt (520mph; 835km/h) just 100ft (30m) above the ground. While the chase aircraft were reporting moderate-to-heavy turbulence, the TSR2's cockpit was a smooth and calm environment.

RIGHT: **The second attempt to retract the undercarriage in flight, during Flight 7, resulted in the starboard main gear leg failing to retract.** BAE Systems via Warton Heritage Group

BELOW: **One of a recently rediscovered sequence of superb air-to-air photos taken over a snowy landscape on Flight 7 shows the result of the undercarriage malfunction, leaving the bogies at the wrong angle, though much closer to normal position than on Flight 5.** BAE Systems via Warton Heritage Group

ABOVE: Ironically, the 'wrong' bogie position experienced during Flight 7, on later analysis, was found to assist with reducing vibrations on landing.
BAE Systems via Warton Heritage Group

LEFT: On final approach to a wintry Boscombe Down. The TSR2's stability and controllability in the landing configuration was often praised by the pilots, and was the product of a great deal of hard work at the design stage.
BAE Systems via Warton Heritage Group

A careful landing at the end of Flight 7, though much less stressful than that of Flight 5. An eventful first flight for navigator Peter Moneypenny, nonetheless!
BAE Systems via Warton Heritage Group

ABOVE: Taken during Flight 8, this photo well depicts the large size of the tailplane. Tailplane power was significantly higher than predicted by simulation work. BAE Systems via Warton Heritage Group

BELOW: Jimmy Dell and Peter Moneypenny arrive back on runway 24 at Boscombe after Flight 8. Jimmy remarked in his experimental flight report that '... the overall impression was of a straightforward, uncomplicated aircraft from the handling aspect ...'. BAE Systems via Warton Heritage Group

ABOVE: **Flight 9 was a brief assessment of handling with flaps down at 50 degrees. The results were generally good, though significant buffet at this flap setting warranted further investigation. After landing, Beamont recorded nil defects, a first for the aircraft, but this ignored several defects present during the flight, such as a misreading attitude indicator and, of course, the non-functioning undercarriage.** BAE Systems via Warton Heritage Group

LEFT: **Before any attempt was made to retract the undercarriage in flight, multiple cycles were carried out with the aircraft on jacks in the hangar at Boscombe Down. These tests, however, were unable to simulate the air loading on the assembly, and various modifications were needed to achieve a successful retraction in the air.** BAE Systems via Brooklands Museum

Jimmy Dell and Peter Moneypenny carried out some further low-level, high-speed flying on the next flight, again reporting smooth conditions while other aircraft reported turbulence, and two days later Don Knight got his hands on the aeroplane for the first time. After an uneventful flight, Don had the misfortune to land heavily and the aircraft bounced dramatically. Severe and disorienting oscillations coupled with the bounce made for a close call, and once the aircraft had been stopped it was inspected to see if it was safe to taxy back to the hangar. Some damage was evident, so it

was towed, and repairs meant that the next flight did not take place until six days later.

Flight 13 was the first flight to take the aircraft to medium altitude, 28,000ft (8,500m) and Mach 0.95, and gave the flight-test team the confidence needed to plan the next flight as the departure from Boscombe and delivery to Warton, where the real flight-test programme could get under way. The TSR2's presence at Boscombe had not been a pleasant experience for everybody involved. It was disruptive to the A&AEE's normal schedules, the BAC staff were all working many miles from

home (particularly for those from English Electric), and even minor problems resulted in days of wasted time while parts were sourced and transported from afar. Furthermore, in November 1964 the MoA had informed BAC that the A&AEE would be unable to offer further facilities beyond the third aircraft; apparently under the impression that BAC actually wanted to be there! Needless to say, BAC was delighted to find out that it would soon be able to control its own destiny when it came to flight testing of the TSR2.

Flight 10, and the undercarriage is successfully retracted. By this point in the programme the auxiliary intakes were linked with the undercarriage, and closed when the gear was up. Beamont wasted no time extending the limits of the flight test envelope, taking the aircraft up to a maximum 500kt (575mph) and simulating a low-level attack run over Boscombe Down at 450kt (520mph) and 100ft (30m). BAE Systems via Warton Heritage Group

The undercarriage drop-test rig at Weybridge. Unfortunately such a rig was unable to simulate the actual sequence of events that occurred when the aircraft touched down, and a combination of spin-up drag and interactions between the various components of the undercarriage led to often violent oscillations on touchdown. BAE Systems via Warton Heritage Group

Navigator Peter Moneypenny and pilot Don Knight, the crew for Flight 12. Don found that XR219 performed more like the variable-stability T-33 he had flown in the USA than the fixed-base simulator at Weybridge, though both lacked the 'big aircraft' feel of the TSR2 itself. BAE Systems via Warton Heritage Group

Flight 14 was thus the flight that made everybody happy. Roland Beamont and Peter Moneypenny took XR219 up to 30,000ft (9,000m) for the transit up north, taking the opportunity to carry out a supersonic run along the Irish Sea and reaching Mach 1.12 with 'no fuss' whatsoever. Shortly after reaching Mach 1.0 on dry power only, Beaumont lit a single reheat, initially on the minimum setting, and accelerated away from the Lightning chase aircraft, and its pilot had to use full reheat on both engines to catch up. At Warton just about the entire workforce had gathered by the hangars to greet 'their' aircraft, and after an instrument descent Beamont made a high-speed low-level run across the airfield, 460kt (530mph; 850km/h) at 150ft (46m), followed by another, slower pass before setting up for a landing on runway 08. After this flight Beamont noted that stability and control were of very high quality, transonic handling in particular being superior to that of any other aircraft he had flown. Undercarriage oscillation on landing, however, had been severe once again.

LEFT: **The last of the TSR2 flight crew to get his hands on the aircraft was navigator Brian McCann, seen here at Boscombe in front of XR220.** BAE Systems via Warton Heritage Group

BELOW: **Holding a 40-degree banked turn at Mach 0.9 with 86 per cent power during Flight 13. This flight proved that XR219 was more than up to the transit to Warton, Jimmy Dell and Don Bowen taking it up to 28,000ft (8,500m) and Mach 0.95, and making radio contact with Warton from a distance of 180nm (200miles; 320km). The type's aerodynamic performance was beginning to be appreciated by this point, with power settings 5 per cent less than predicted being necessary to hold any given Mach number.** BAE Systems via Brooklands Museum

LEFT: **Flight 14 saw XR219's departure from Boscombe Down and transit to Warton. On the way the decision was made to use the Irish Sea supersonic Test Run 'A', and with dry power only (95 per cent) XR219 nudged through Mach 1 with no drama whatsoever. When reheat was lit on the port engine only, the aircraft accelerated quickly to Mach 1.12 at 30,000ft (9,000m), the highest speed the type would ever record, leaving the Lightning chase aircraft behind in the process, until it caught up using reheat on both engines.** BAE Systems via Warton Heritage Group

Arrival over Warton at 150ft (45m) and 460kt (530mph; 850km/h), control being 'smooth and precise, and no disturbance was felt from turbulence'. The TSR2's ride quality at low level exceeded all expectations. BAE Systems via Brooklands Museum

RIGHT: **'Home' at Warton, from where all remaining test flights were flown. This was a big event for the workforce, hundreds of employees being allowed to down tools to watch XR219 arrive.** BAE Systems via Warton Heritage Group

One of the most commonly published TSR2 photographs is this one, taken at 12,500ft (3,800m) on Flight 17, with the Esk estuary, Cumbria, in the background. This was the first flight with the airbrakes fully closed. The problems with jack backlash and synchronization were not cured; the airbrakes had simply been locked shut and disabled to permit performance measurements at higher speeds. BAE Systems via Warton Heritage Group

Undercarriage oscillation problems

After the shattering lateral oscillations experienced on landing after the first flight, there was very little hard data available with which to diagnose the problem, despite the mass of instrumentation in the aircraft and

Flight 17 ended with a touchdown on a 300yd (275m) carpet of foam laid on runway 26 by Warton's fire section. With additional strain gauges on the undercarriage, Flights 17 to 20 all ended with landings on foam carpets to see what effect a low-friction surface had on the touchdown oscillations that were being experienced. BAE Systems via Warton Heritage Group

all the recordings generated by that flight. After three further flights and examination of film from the cameras now mounted on the aircraft and pointing at the main undercarriage, BAC was virtually certain that the cause of the oscillation was a torsion-bending vibration of the undercarriage, excited by spin-up drag at the wheels. The rear wheel contacted the ground first, but

did not spin up to speed as fast as expected, tending to 'skip' over the runway in the brief period before the front wheel on the bogie touched down. Rapid spin-up of the pair of wheels then made the bogie yaw sideways, dragging the wheels and bogie to the side and setting off the lateral oscillations. Only when the aircraft's weight was firmly on both sides of the undercarriage did these die down. This was bad enough, imposing severe side-loads on the undercarriage, but the results in the cockpit were another matter. The resonant frequency of the fuselage was similar to that of the undercarriage, and coupling of the fuselage and undercarriage frequencies resulted in the oscillations becoming a violent vibration at the cockpit, lateral accelerations of up to 2.1g being experienced.

As camera footage showed that most of the yawing motion set up in the undercarriage appeared to begin at the torque links, the first attempt to solve the problem was to fit stiffer torque links. Unfortunately, after several further flights the evidence showed that these had no effect. The spin-up rate of the wheels still seemed to be the primary cause, but this was affected by the descent rate at touchdown, and the period between port and starboard main gears touching the

Here is XR219 in flight, probably on Flight 21, with the 'Aylesbury tie' modification. This was a tie-rod connecting the bogie to the fixed portion of the oleo to alter the bogie trail angle so that the front wheels touched down first (similar to the accidental configuration on Flight 7). On the few occasions it was flown, this modification was successful in reducing the violent oscillations experienced on touchdown, but it is likely that some structural changes to reduce fuselage resonance would also have been needed to effect a complete cure. BAE Systems via Warton Heritage Group

runway also had an effect on the severity of the oscillations. Flight 12 had produced a particularly violent sequence of oscillations on landing, owing to a particularly high descent rate.

Examination of film of the main undercarriage during these landings revealed a bewildering variety of movements at touchdown. The bogie was yawing from side to side and pitching up and down as individual wheels contacted the runway. The main leg was spreading outwards and also 'twanging' fore and aft, and it was this fore-and-aft movement that proved to be the key to solving the problem. It was counter-intuitive, but the various lateral motions of parts of the undercarriage were much smaller contributors to the fuselage oscillations than the fore-and-aft movement of the entire assembly. Adding a strut between the oleo leg and the rear of the bogie not only stiffened the whole assembly but also slightly altered the bogie trail angle. It was hoped that this would improve spin-up characteristics as the wheels contacted, and allow far less fore-and-aft movement in the oleo leg. A fixed strut was installed on XR219 for Flight 21. This meant that the undercarriage could not be retracted, but it would serve to demonstrate if the strut worked or not. If it did, a retractable strut could be designed and fitted.

The first flight with the modified undercarriage showed that oscillations were hugely reduced. There was still some lateral movement, but it was no longer a cause of disorientation. Several more flights followed, each with either minimal or no oscillations. It appeared that the new strut was not a 100 per cent cure, but was very close to it. After the aborted Flight 25, XR219 was laid up for a number of modifications, including the installation of the retractable struts, and these were also fitted to XR220. Unfortunately neither aircraft was flown with the retractable strut before

the project was cancelled. The lay-up of XR219 would also have included the fitting of manual controls to allow the intake cones to be moved, strengthened intake lips, an AFCS, a fin mass-balance and the two-stage reheat fuel restrictor system. The last, in particular, would have permitted the aircraft to operate at higher take-off weights and thus carry more fuel, necessary for proving flight up to Mach 2 (though the wing tank system would still have been inhibited, limiting Mach 2 endurance to 15min per sortie).

XR220 and XR221

The accident suffered by XR220 on arrival at Boscombe has often been blamed for losing BAC the opportunity to get more than one aircraft into the air before the nearly inevitable cancellation. While taxy runs did not start until March 1965, this was primarily due to the extremely late delivery of flight-capable engines from BSEL. Even if XR220 had not spent several months being repaired and reassembled, it is not likely that engines would have arrived any sooner, and taxy tests could not, therefore, have begun any earlier than March 1965.

By the end of March XR220 was frustratingly close to flying, and BAC was looking forward to possibly taking it to France for the Paris Air Show in June. The airframe had gone through just about every test programme apart from undercarriage cross-functioning. These tests were scheduled for the 4 April, with the first flight on the 6th. However, a minor foul was found on an undercarriage sequencing valve, and the final tests were expected to have to be delayed until the 7th, with a flight on the 9th. The BAC team at Boscombe worked hard and regained some of the lost time, with the result that XR220 was very nearly ready on the morning of the 6th. A minor hydraulic leak needed to be dealt with, however, and, as it became clear that the aircraft would not be ready until the afternoon, the aircrew knocked off for lunch.

Meanwhile, at Weybridge, XR221 was already 'flying', with a crew aboard and taking it through a complete simulated sortie from Wisley to Land's End and back as a final check of the AFCS installation. Having made a completely successful 'flight', the crew began their debrief and were looking forward to flying the aircraft for real once it had been transported (via road) the short distance to Wisley later in the month.

ABOVE: **Repairs to the damaged areas had been just about completed by the time this picture was taken of XR220 in the hangar at Boscombe Down in late 1965, but final reassembly was delayed by the need to use some components on XR219.** BAE Systems via Warton Heritage Group

LEFT: **Delivery of engines for XR220 was delayed time and time again, and it was not until March 1965 that the aircraft was ready to begin engine runs.** BAE Systems via Warton Heritage Group

That afternoon, in the Budget Speech, the announcement was made that the TSR2 programme had been cancelled. At Boscombe Down the flight crew arrived back at the airfield in a hurry, anxious to fly XR220, only to find that orders had already been given to prevent this. Thus XR220 would never fly, and XR221's one and only 'flight' was made without it leaving the ground.

Initially, XR220's flight-test programme was to permit the aircraft to fly at up to Mach 1 at low altitude, extending the envelope to Mach 1.7 at higher altitudes and then up to maximum altitude during the first 30hr of flying, with the investigation of flutter characteristics as the primary task. A large number of accelerometers were fitted within the airframe to measure vibrations on the various flying surfaces, along

with a number of 'bonkers' (explosive inertia exciters). The housings for the latter are evident on XR220 to this day, as chamfered plates scabbed on to various locations on the aircraft, such as the wingtips, fin and tailplanes. Accelerometers were also fitted to measure loads on the undercarriage. Mounted within the weapons bay instrumentation pack were a pair of more substantial inertia exciters, hydraulic rams that

Details of the 'bonker' layout on XR220. A number of these inertia exciters were mounted on the tail surfaces and wingtips of specific development-batch airframes (not XR219), and have been misidentified as ECM aerials in some publications. BAE Systems via Brooklands Museum

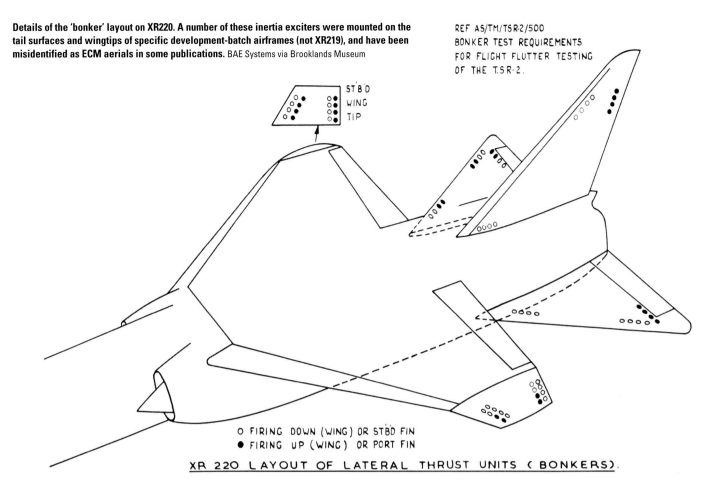

REF AS/TM/TSR-2/500
BONKER TEST REQUIREMENTS
FOR FLIGHT FLUTTER TESTING
OF THE T.S.R-2.

STB'D
WING
TIP

O FIRING DOWN (WING) OR STBD FIN
● FIRING UP (WING) OR PORT FIN

XR 220 LAYOUT OF LATERAL THRUST UNITS (BONKERS).

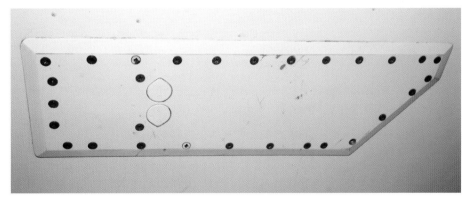

A typical 'bonker' installation on XR220 (this pair is near the leading edge on the underside of the starboard tailplane). Damien Burke

could set up vertical and lateral oscillations within the fuselage. The aircraft's initial flights would primarily be aimed at ensuring that it was in a fit state for the ferry flight to Warton, which was planned for about Flight 5. With gradual modification to bring it to a higher standard, including the fitting of a higher standard of engine (Olympus 320 instead of 320X) and the activation of wing fuel tanks to permit longer sorties at higher

Mach numbers where fuel consumption would be higher, XR220 would gradually widen the envelope. Some problems with AFCS structural coupling meant that a 'frig box' was to be fitted to enable limited auto-stabilization, unlike XR219. Also unlike the first aircraft, XR220 had a sprung mass-balance in the fin to combat flutter, permitting flight at higher Mach numbers than XR219 would be capable of. A fix for the

airbrake closure problems would be embodied in XR220's second phase of flying, along with a production-standard rear fairing.

As well as the primary task of flutter testing, XR220 was also instrumented to measure engine compressor-blade strain, and LP shaft stresses, to verify the effectiveness of the various fixes introduced on the Olympus 320 by BSEL.

TSR2 handling characteristics

After six flights, Roland Beamont wrote a summary for the Air Ministry of his opinions on the qualities of the aircraft:

Briefly the handling assessment of take-off, low-speed flying within the initial landing gear envelope, and approach and landing, has been completed with 100 per cent success. The flying qualities in this configuration are as good or better than predicted in every case, and it is without doubt the easiest high-performance aircraft to land that I have flown. All six landings to date have been, we are told from the visual point of view, perfect; and they have been accomplished

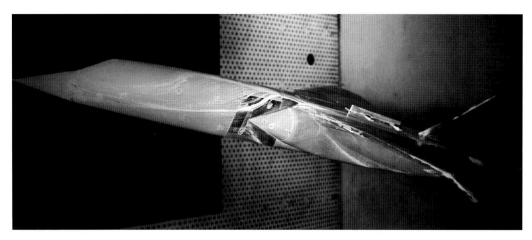

A TSR2 model in the Aircraft Research Association windtunnel at Bedford. The streaks of oil gave an indication of the airflow during the run. This shot shows the results of a Mach 1.2 run with three small vortex generators on the side of the nose in line with the bottom of the windscreen (these were fairly successful in cleaning up the flow on the sides of the nose), and a centreline fence added to the top of the fuselage to try to regain some stability (to no significant effect). Aircraft Research Association

within a recorded scatter of +/− 4kt [4.6mph; 7.4km/h] from the scheduled touchdown speed, and at a measured vertical velocity of 4ft/sec to 1.5ft/sec [1.2m/sec to 0.45m/sec]. Perhaps of more significance than these numbers is the fact that the pilot feels in every case that he can do just this. With this excellent control harmony we feel fairly certain now that there will be no cost growth on the basis of a need to develop basic low-speed stability and control.

Flights 15 to 24 by XR219 were all flown from Warton, and, before the fitting of the additional undercarriage strut, served mostly to expand the flight envelope further and give the crews more experience of various drills and configurations. The aircraft performed well, with serviceability as good as could be expected for the first of any type, and its flying qualities continued to impress the three crews assigned to the flight-test programme. No serious problems other than those already mentioned were experienced, though the view through the canopy transparencies was a constant cause of complaint. Redesigned units were under test when the programme was cancelled.

Sadly, the single example of the TSR2 to fly was never fitted with the AFCS developed for the aircraft, and thus was limited to manual flight control. Regardless of the limitations of flying without automatic assistance, the test pilots who flew the aircraft considered it viceless in the envelope in which test flying took place, and well within the capabilities of the average Lightning pilot. Indeed, test pilots Jimmy Dell and Don Knight both described it as 'just like flying a big Lightning'.

The TSR2 was naturally stable up to about Mach 1.5, when directional stability began to be lost, resulting in negative stability by Mach 1.7. Windtunnel tests at the Aircraft Research Association's facility at Bedford in mid-1962 had determined that this loss of stability resulted from vortices shed from the upper 'shoulders' of the forward fuselage, which interfered with the fin, but no practical aerodynamic solution had been found to cure this. Instead, the hope was the the fin auto-stiffener system, with a lateral accelerometer sensing the amount of sideslip and the auto-stabilization computer calling for a proportional amount of counteracting fin movement, would be able to compensate for the loss of stability. The auto-stiffener was to be active at all times, not just above Mach 1.5, to improve handling. Because an auto-stiffener failure (non-moving fin, or fin runaway) could result in loss of the aircraft, the entire system was triple-redundant, with a voting system taking the majority decision and applying it.

Some handling aspects of the airframe had given rise to concern, based on windtunnel and theoretical work, and in June 1960 English Electric wrote to the CAL in the USA to ask if it could use the laboratory's variable-stability NT-33 research aircraft. This was a highly modified T-33, fitted with a Lockheed F-94 Starfire nose to make room for additional electronic equipment. The front cockpit had its flying controls connected to the control surfaces via an AFCS using servo-mechanisms, the output of which could be varied by the safety pilot in the rear cockpit. Additional servos attached to each control surface could also be controlled by the safety pilot. Each control surface could be tied to a combination of outputs. For example, the rudder could be made to respond not only to a basic rudder input from the pilot but also to a combination of rolling and yawing velocity and acceleration, angle of sideslip and its rate of change, or products of these and various other flight parameters. In this way the aircraft could be set up to simulate the flight dynamics and feel of another type, while the safety pilot had direct and conventional control from the rear cockpit should the simulated flight characteristics prove uncontrollable.

Simulated TSR2 flights using the CAL NT-33 began on 27 October 1962, and twenty-four flights were made, totalling 40hr of flying, the last flight being made on 17 November. The CAL staff were

The Cornell Aeronautical Laboratory's NT-33 variable-stability aircraft provided valuable experience of simulated TSR2 flying characteristics. Don Knight made twenty-four flights in the aircraft, coincidentally the same number of flights made by the TSR2 before cancellation. Calspan Corporation

extremely helpful, holding together a tight flying programme regardless of poor weather conditions, and even managing some extra flights despite strictly limited funding being provided. Don Knight, the evaluation pilot, flew sixty separate TSR2 configurations, forty-three simulating low-speed and seventeen simulating supersonic configurations. The general result was an impression that handling was going to be better than predicted, the ground simulator proving overly pessimistic in many cases. In particular, Don assessed non-autostabilized flight in the approach configuration as 'acceptable and satisfactory', which was a surprise, but it was no surprise at all that the aircraft was nigh on unflyable in Mach 1.8-plus cases. From these flights the required

damping measures for the autostabilizer were verified against the predicted values. In fact, many of the handling problems predicted and simulated were not present on the aircraft when flown.

Handling of the TSR2 itself was described by all of its test pilots as easy and pleasant. Pitch control was responsive and well damped, there was no tendency to pilot-induced pitch oscillations, and the aircraft was exceptionally easy to control on the approach and for touchdown, with good speed stability (the last was particularly surprising to the simulation team, who had predicted somewhat more squirrelly behaviour). The pilots reported resemblances between the ground simulator and the real thing, but said that, in general, the flight

handling was a great deal easier and more pleasant than on the simulator. So XR219 proved to have less drag than predicted, and far superior handling; a stunningly good start. Alas, that was all it ever was.

The members of Warton's windtunnel team were particularly disappointed that they were never able to find out just why all of the windtunnel data analysis had led them to believe that the aircraft would have difficulty in raising its nose during lift-off, yet XR219 exhibited far superior pitch response and there was never any need to use the extending nose-gear leg. The opportunity to take the aircraft to Mach 2 was also denied them, so the aircraft's real stability characteristics beyond Mach 1.2 remained an eternal mystery.

Flight-test Log

Date	Flight	From	To	Take-off	Airborne	Pilot	Navigator	Notes
27/9/64	1	Boscombe	Boscombe	15:30	0:14	Roland Beamont	Don Bowen	1st flight, two circuits, fin damaged by brake parachute door on opening, severe undercarriage vibration on touchdown.
31/12/64	2	Boscombe	Boscombe	15:44	0:13	Roland Beamont	Don Bowen	Intolerable engine vibration causing vision loss at certain rpm range; difficulty with visibility in low sunshine through windscreen; flight aborted owing to engine vibration; violent oscillation on touchdown.
2/1/65	3	Boscombe	Boscombe	12:53	0:08	Roland Beamont	Don Bowen	LP shaft overstress warning lights illuminated after take-off; engine vibration; emergency landing; violent oscillation on touchdown.
8/1/65	4	Boscombe	Boscombe	14:22	0:21	Roland Beamont	Don Bowen	Nearly aborted owing to loud interference on flight-test radio frequency of a 'jamming order'. Camera fitted to nose-gear leg to film main undercarriage. No significant engine vibration; handling checks – flaps at 50 degrees and airbrakes to 65 degrees gave severe buffet; gentle landing with reduced oscillation. Fuel leak in starboard engine tunnel required grounding afterwards for engine removal.
14/1/65	5	Boscombe	Boscombe	15:28	0:22	Roland Beamont	Don Bowen	First attempt at undercarriage retraction; port main gear bogie failed to rotate fully and leg did not retract. On re-extension neither bogie de-rotated. Overshoot to use up fuel followed by landing very gently, on 'tip-toe', bogies de-rotated successfully and very little oscillation felt.
15/1/65	6	Boscombe	Boscombe	11:36	0:24	Jimmy Dell	Don Bowen	Jimmy's 1st flight; familiarization and approach handling. No undercarriage retraction attempted. Violent undercarriage oscillation on touchdown.
22/1/65	7	Boscombe	Boscombe	13:54	0:29	Roland Beamont	Peter Moneypenny	Modified torsion links fitted to undercarriage to try to cure oscillations. Undercarriage retraction: starboard main gear bogie rotated fully but leg did not retract. Extended again, successfully, and normal landing made with little oscillation felt.
23/1/65	8	Boscombe	Boscombe	11:13	0:27	Jimmy Dell	Peter Moneypenny	Low-speed performance and handling; no undercarriage retraction attempted pending fitting of modified hop dampers. Little oscillation felt on landing.
27/1/65	9	Boscombe	Boscombe	13:41	0:22	Roland Beamont	Don Bowen	Handling assessment with 50 degrees flap; no undercarriage retraction attempted pending fitting of modified hop dampers. Heavy buffet again. Landing with little vibration.
6/2/65	10	Boscombe	Boscombe	11:01	0:29	Roland Beamont	Don Bowen	Undercarriage cycling – successful. First high-speed flight – Mach 0.75, 500kt. Low-level runs at 450kt and 100ft in smooth conditions; chase aircraft reported moderate to heavy turbulence. Landing produced heavy oscillation again, but maximum braking attained landing roll of less than 800yd.
8/2/65	11	Boscombe	Boscombe	15:35	0:38	Jimmy Dell	Peter Moneypenny	Performance and handling. Undercarriage retracted, low-level runs at 450kt and 200ft in reported light turbulence but smooth conditions on board. Highest speed recorded 511kt. Gentle touchdown and light oscillations.

(continued overleaf)

Flight-test Log *(continued)*

Date	Flight	From	To	Take-off	Airborne	Pilot	Navigator	Notes
10/2/65	12	Boscombe	Boscombe	11:54	0:36	Don Knight	Peter Moneypenny	Don's 1st flight. Performance and handling and pilot familiarization. Flared slightly late and heavy landing resulted, violent and disorienting oscillations, aircraft bounced and port main gear leg damaged.
16/2/65	13	Boscombe	Boscombe	11:26	0:45	Jimmy Dell	Don Bowen	First medium-altitude flight, to 28,000ft and Mach 0.95. Severe oscillations on landing.
22/2/65	14	Boscombe	Warton	13:13	0:43	Roland Beamont	Peter Moneypenny	Cruise performance, supersonic handling, delivery to BAC Warton. Climb to 30,000ft and supersonic run up the Irish Sea Test Run 'A' at Mach 1.12 with one reheat engaged on 3rd gutter only, leaving Lightning chase aeroplane behind initially. Instrument descent to Warton. Low-level run across airfield at 150ft, 460kt, second run at 320kt, followed by landing runway 08 with usual undercarriage/airframe lateral oscillation. Stability and control of high quality, transonic handling superior to any other aircraft flown by pilot.
25/2/65	15	Warton	Warton	09:03	1:13	Jimmy Dell	Peter Moneypenny	Performance runs and fuel consumption checks at altitude; 24,000 to 30,000ft from Mach 0.86 to 0.95. Moderate clear-air turbulence reported by chase aircraft, barely noticed on board. 480kt run at 200ft across Samlesbury Airfield in slight turbulence. Worst landing oscillation so far, and complaints of poor canopy and windscreen vision quality. Fuel consumption results favourable.
26/2/65	16	Warton	Warton	10:22	0:48	Roland Beamont	Peter Moneypenny	Low-level performance and handling, and fuel consumption checks. Undercarriage oscillations on take-off for the first time. 450–490kt runs at 2,000ft over hilly terrain; high-speed roll-rate measurement and a complete roll flown for the first time. Worst landing oscillation so far, even though touchdown was gentle. Fuel consumption over a 20min leg 1,000lb lower than predicted.
8/3/65	17	Warton	Warton	12:10	0:52	Jimmy Dell	Brian McCann	Flight envelope expansion and single-engine performance, and check of modified undercarriage with reduced oleo pressure and backlash. Also landing on foam carpet to assess effect of reduced spin-up drag on undercarriage oscillations. Airbrakes locked fully closed and disabled from this flight to Flight 20 inclusive. 500kt+ runs at 200ft. Slight vibrations on take-off, none on landing.
8/3/65	18	Warton	Warton	16:21	0:35	Jimmy Dell	Brian McCann	Intended to be flight envelope expansion and single-engine performance. Cut short owing to persistent fuel imbalance indications; caused by faulty fuel transfer valve and massive fuel leak. Slight undercarriage oscillation on landing, on foam again. First time more than one flight made in a day.
11/3/65	19	Warton	Warton	14:33	0:33	Jimmy Dell	Brian McCann	Flight envelope expansion. Measured run at approximately 500kt/Mach 0.7 at 2,000ft through turbulence. More fuel imbalance problems and another fuel leak found. Slight undercarriage oscillation on landing on foam once more.
12/3/65	20	Warton	Warton	17:09	0:46	Jimmy Dell	Peter Moneypenny	Low-level performance. Measured run at approximately 540 to 580kt/Mach 0.9 at around 5,000ft. More fuel imbalance problems and another fuel leak found. Final foam landing, no great improvements evident. Aircraft to be grounded for at least one week for engine X-ray checks and various modifications, including re-enabling airbrakes.
26/3/65	21	Warton	Warton	08:36	0:33	Jimmy Dell	Brian McCann	Single-engine performance and low-speed handling. Undercarriage tie tube fitted to alter bogie trail angle. One roller landing, one normal landing, very mild undercarriage oscillation. 1st flight with nil recorded defects from a pilot.
26/3/65	22	Warton	Warton	11:20	0:35	Jimmy Dell	Brian McCann	Roller landings with fixed undercarriage tie rod. Four roller landings, no vibrations on three, slight vibration on highest-descent-rate landing
27/3/65	23	Warton	Warton	12:22	0:34	Don Knight	Peter Moneypenny	Performance and handling. Flight familiarization for pilot of drills and handling. Four practice approaches and overshoots followed by landing. 1–2 cycles of much-reduced oscillation on landing with mild lifting of port and starboard bogies in turn. Hydraulic services No.1 failure on final approach (artificial-feel unit leak), but accumulators prevented any problems.
31/3/65	24	Warton	Warton	13:27	0:32	Jimmy Dell	Brian McCann	Roll/yaw gearing optimization. Two crosswind roller landings with fixed undercarriage tie rod followed by full-stop landing. No oscillations.
02/04/65	25	Warton	Warton	N/A	N/A	Don Knight	Peter Moneypenny	Aborted owing to hydraulic leak during taxy (fin jack ram fractured).

CHAPTER SIX

The Aircraft

Fuselage structure

The fuselage was built in four sections: forebody, forward and aft centre sections, and the rear section, all of fairly conventional construction with skin stringer panels over bulkheads and frames.

Forebody

The forebody was initially built in two halves, split longitudinally, these being brought together once the basic structure on either side was complete. Sandwiched between the external panels and crew compartment walls was polyurethane foam covered with Melinex, to act as insulation against the high skin temperatures generated at supersonic speeds. Within the forebody were the FLR bay, crew compartment, SLR bays and the main equipment bay (split into port/starboard sides with a web in between). Most of the nose section (crew compartment and main equipment bay) was pressurized, with a secondary pressurized area encompassing the radar bay and radome. (An auxiliary pressure bulkhead also protected the crew compartment in the event of loss of pressurization in the equipment bay.) The radome was a glassfibre/resin-laminate cone fitted on a machined mounting ring, with an inner spherical inner radome that protected the FLR assembly. Unlike those of more-modern aircraft, the radome could not be easily opened and folded to the side for access. Removal required undoing multiple fasteners, and suitable storage equipment for the radome itself once it was removed.

The crew compartment had two sloping bulkheads on which the ejection seats were mounted, with a floor sitting on bracing members linked to the close-pitched frames rising up on either side. The windscreen and quarter panels were glass, with gold film heating and demisting. The pilot's and navigator's canopies were mostly metal framework with metal stressed skin and relatively small transparencies. Unlike the windscreen and quarter panels, these were not glass but a triple laminate of Perspex, once again with gold film heating/demisting.

Systems, control runs, wiring and ducting ran for the most part through the lower fuselage, where access could be had through the undercarriage bays and a plethora of access panels. A spur from the central fuel gallery ran forward through the port side of the forebody to a blanked-off position just under the inter-canopy structure. This was designed to be a mounting point for a retractable in-flight-refuelling-probe pack (similar to that later fitted to the Panavia Tornado). The main equipment bay housed various systems in rack-mounted packages, and a separate upper equipment bay above housed some air-conditioning, lox and fuel-system components.

Leading particulars

Overall dimensions		Powerplant	
Length (including pitot)	89ft (27.13m)	Two Bristol Siddeley Olympus 22R	
Span	37.14ft (11.32m)	Dry thrust	22,000lb (9,980kg)
Height	23.77ft (7.25m)	Reheat thrust	30,610lb (13,895kg)
Wing		Tailplane	
Area	702.9sq ft (65.30sq m)	Area	144sq ft (13.38sq m)
Aspect ratio	1.96	Aspect ratio	2.1
Leading-edge sweepback	58.32 degrees	Leading-edge sweepback	60 degrees
Trailing-edge sweepback	2.5 degrees	Span	17.4ft (5.30m)
Tip chord	4.28ft (1.30m)	Tip chord	1.53ft (0.47m)
Root chord (at fuselage)	27.26ft (8.31m)	Root chord	15.0ft (4.57m)
Thickness/chord ratio	3.6/5 per cent	Range of movement	+10 to −20 degrees
Tip anhedral	30 degrees	Thickness/chord ratio	4 per cent
		Anhedral	4 degrees
Fuselage			
Length (including pitot)	81.21ft (24.75m)	Fin	
Max width	9.75ft (2.97m)	Area	105sq ft (9.75sq m)
Max depth	7.71ft (2.35m)	Aspect ratio	3.0
		Sweep back	35.6 (40) degrees
Flaps		Tip chord	3.0ft (0.91m)
Chord aft of hinge	15 per cent of local chord	Root chord	14.99ft (4.57m)
Inboard limit	23.78 per cent of semi-span	Thickness/chord ratio	5 per cent
Outboard limit	80.61 per cent of semi-span	Range of movement	±15 degrees
Range of movement	Up to 50 degrees		
		Intake cones	
Tailplane flaps		Range of movement	17–25 degrees
Chord aft of hinge	15 per cent inboard of local chord, 31 per cent outboard		
Outboard limit	71 per cent of semi-span	Weights	
Range of movement	±30 degrees	Normal AUW	103,500lb (46,980kg)
		Max. overload AUW	120,970lb (54,910kg)
Radius of Action*		Landing weight	57,200lb (25,960kg)
Hi-lo-lo-hi	750nm (860 miles; 1,390km)		
Lo-lo	600nm (690 miles; 1,110km)		
Hi-hi at Mach 1.7	450nm (515 miles; 835km)		
Ferry range (one-way)	2,500nm (2,875 miles; 4,625km)		

*With 2,000lb (900kg) weapon load, internal fuel only, final specification

---

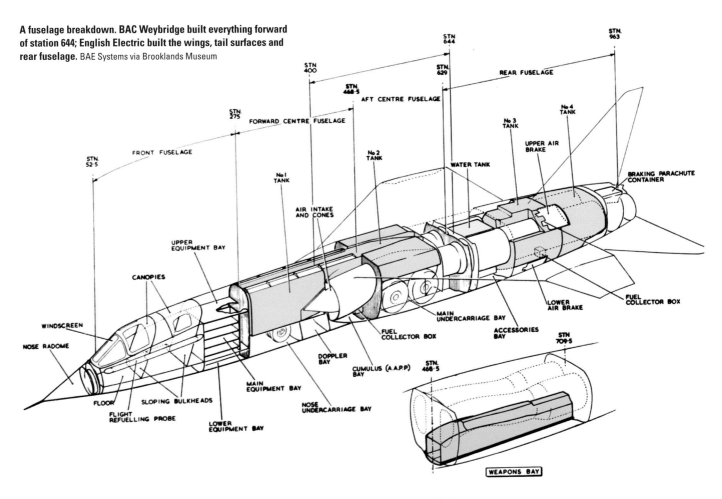

A fuselage breakdown. BAC Weybridge built everything forward of station 644; English Electric built the wings, tail surfaces and rear fuselage. BAE Systems via Brooklands Museum

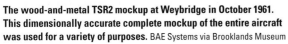

The wood-and-metal TSR2 mockup at Weybridge in October 1961. This dimensionally accurate complete mockup of the entire aircraft was used for a variety of purposes. BAE Systems via Brooklands Museum

Forebody construction in the stage 1 jig at Weybridge. BAE Systems via Brooklands Museum

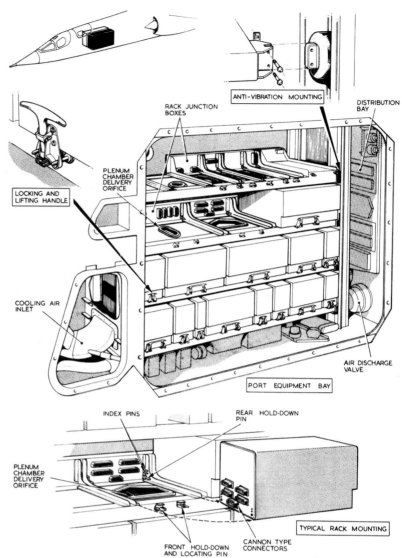

ABOVE: **The port camera bay of XR220. On this aircraft the bay was used to house flight-test instrumentation instead of a camera.** Damien Burke

RIGHT: **The equipment bay and Vickers Electronic Racking.**
BAE Systems via Brooklands Museum

The starboard equipment bay of XR220, restored to a representative fit. The braces between shelving were necessitated by vibration and resonance problems. Damien Burke

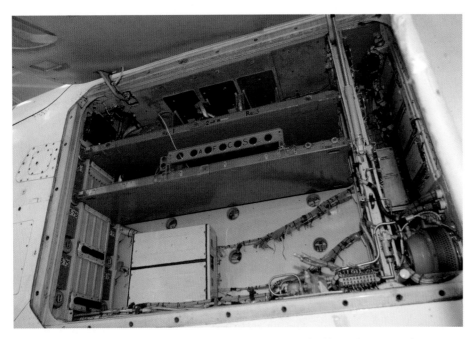

The port equipment bay of XR220 has not been restored, and the severed cables to the missing equipment are evident against its rear wall. Damien Burke

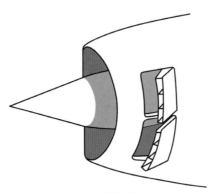

SCHEME 'A'
AS EMBODIED ON D.B. AIRCRAFT BUT
WITH 40° OPENING ANGLE

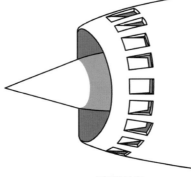

SCHEME 'B'
SPRING-LOADED SUCK-IN DOORS

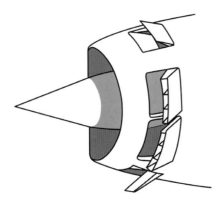

SCHEME 'C'
AS SCHEME 'A' WITH EXTRA DOORS

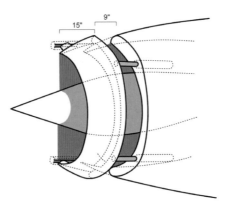

SCHEME 'D'
TRANSLATING INTAKE COWL
PREFERRED SOLUTION FOR
PRODUCTION AIRCRAFT

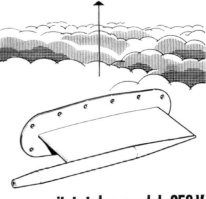
LEFT: **Alternative intake designs for improved auxiliary air supply. The existing twin auxiliary intake doors proved insufficient in both efficiency and actuator strength, limiting take-off performance in the process. The initial 25-degree opening had to be increased to 40 degrees.** Damien Burke

Filling the space between the forward edge of the main equipment bay and the navigator's rear bulkhead was a triangular-shaped compartment in which the side-facing reconnaissance cameras were to be mounted. (The first five development-batch aircraft were not so fitted, this compartment being used for flight-test instrumentation.) Below this, at the bottom of the fuselage, was a bay earmarked to house a down-and-forward-looking camera, though this was later deleted.

Forward centre-section

The forward centre-section comprised the area of the fuselage from the nose undercarriage bay back to the forward part of the intake assemblies. Along the bottom of this section (from forward to aft) ran the nose-gear bay, the Doppler and inertial platform bay and the Cumulus airborne auxiliary powerplant (AAPP) bay. Housed above all of these were the No.1 and No.2 fuel tanks. The No.1 tank was made up of three rectangular units of integral machined stringer skin panels around dividing bulkheads, the tank sides forming the fuselage sides. The No.2 tank was made up of two rectangular units tapering to the rear (situated between the intake tunnels) and two saddle-shaped units (sitting on top of the intake tunnels and extending through into the aft centre-fuselage section). The forward fuel collector box sat below this tank. Access to fuel pipes, collector box and associated pumps was via access panels on top and below the fuselage, and also via the Cumulus AAPP bay roof.

The air intakes extended from a position forward of the wing root, and comprised half frames braced by longitudinal stringers and diaphragms, with internal and external chemi-etched stressed skins broken by auxiliary intake doors to provide additional airflow at low forward speeds and high throttle settings. Intake frontal area was controlled by hinged cones within the intake mouth; a fore-aft pair on each side, with hinges at the points and jacks extending the cone bases outwards when required, varying the cone angle from 17 to 25 degrees. The automatic intake control units were delayed and were never fitted to the only TSR2 to fly, which had the cones locked at the 17-degree mark. Even manual operation was prevented, as clutch slippage was experienced on early tests.

Upper and lower boundary-layer air bleed ducts cut through the intake frames, the

A forward centre fuselage in the stage 1 jig at Weybridge, early 1962. These two open bays formed No.1 fuselage fuel tank, with cut-outs to accommodate the nosewheel tyres visible in the forward bay. BAE Systems via Brooklands Museum

lower bleed also supplying air to a heat exchanger which exhausted below the intakes. Windtunnel tests showed that the intake walls needed to be thickened because of poor subsonic-cruise drag, which reducing efficiency by 10 per cent and imposed a fuel penalty of 300lb (135kg) on the 1,000nm sortie. The RAF was eventually presented with a pair of slightly altered intake designs, one of which would perform slightly better in the supersonic cruise, while the other worked best at subsonic speeds. As the aircraft would spend most of its life subsonic, the latter intake design was chosen for incorporation on production aircraft. The auxiliary intake doors proved highly susceptible to problems in early ground testing, with required jack pressures far in excess of predictions and the surrounding structure unable to deal with the required loading. As a result, on XR219 the doors were locked fully open for the first flight, and then a simplified mechanism was put in place so that they were fully open when the undercarriage was down, and fully closed when it was retracted. In contrast, XR220's auxiliary intakes were locked closed, and a reduction in maximum permissible take-off weight was imposed as a

result. While a temporary modification to incorporate a stronger auxiliary intake door mechanism was in progress at the time of cancellation, several alternative auxiliary intake designs were also suggested at a late stage. The favourite entailed deletion of the auxiliary doors and the introduction of a translating intake lip that would move forward on tracks to give additional airflow at low speeds and bring intake efficiency up to 91 per cent. Work on this was halted by the project's cancellation, as was analysis of windtunnel results on a version of the intake that re-energized the boundary layer and thus dispensed with the drag penalty of having to bleed it away.

The nose gear bay housed the rearward-retracting nose undercarriage, which was attached to a longitudinal beam in the roof of the bay by integrally machined spherical bearings. The fuel tanks forming the roof of the bay were dished to accommodate the nose-gear tyres. Four doors covered the gear bay, the two largest opening only during the extension/retraction sequence and normally remaining closed. They could also be opened for ground servicing access to the various components within the bay.

ABOVE: In this photo the aft centre fuselage has been married to the forward centre fuselage in the stage 3 jig at Weybridge. BAE Systems via Brooklands Museum

BELOW: Rear fuselage construction. This area was as complicated as the rest of the fuselage, with the added difficulties of sealing the engine tunnels against fluid and hot-gas leaks. BAE Systems via Brooklands Museum

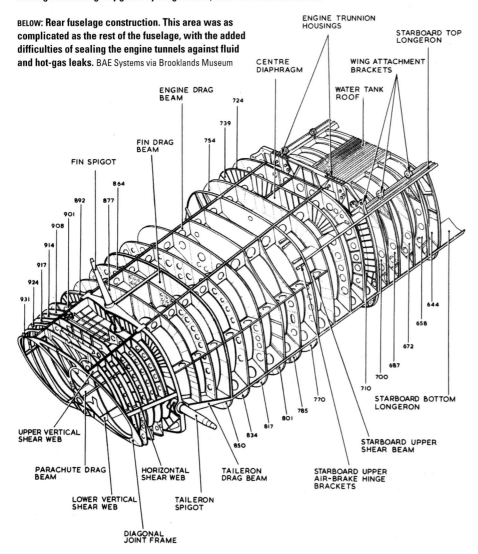

Rear centre section

The fuselage rear centre-section comprised the remainder of the air-intake tunnels, the main undercarriage bays and most of the bomb bay. The air-intake tunnels formed the majority of the structure in this section, composed of frames braced by integrally machined stringer skin planks and inner skins formed by longitudinal stringers and chemi-etched panels. The rear saddle-shaped portion of fuel tank No. 2 sat above the intake tunnels. The bomb bay extended throughout the entire length of this section of fuselage and into the next section, and was constructed in a similar fashion to the intake tunnels, with doors hinged to the bottom longerons. The shape of the bay was dictated by the available space between the intake tunnels; thus the bay narrowed towards its roof, with the lower portion of the tunnels forming the corners of the bay. The sidewalls incorporated several clip-in boxes, used to attach various stores release units or complete role packs, such as the reconnaissance pack.

The internal shape of the main undercarriage bays was decided in part by the intake tunnel arrangement, and in part by the bomb bay walls. The framework within the bay was largely vertical, and the frames bearing the main undercarriage pintle bearings were angled to match the outward and trailing angles of the extended main undercarriage legs. The outer edge of the bay was formed by the bay doors, the smallest rearmost door remaining open whenever the main undercarriage was extended, and the two large forward doors remaining open only during the extension/retraction sequence to avoid the loss of longitudinal stability experienced when these large doors were in the open position. They could, however, be sequenced open on the ground to provide access for ground crew.

The top of this section of fuselage also included cut-outs in the transverse frames to accommodate the wing assembly, with attachments for the wing front spar, drag and vertical links and auxiliary attachments for the wing apex.

Rear fuselage

The final fuselage section, the rear section, primarily comprised ventilated engine and jetpipe tunnels. The fuselage here was constructed of machined and plate-work transverse frames, the engine tunnels being built

RIGHT: **The rear-fuselage mockup at Warton. Different colours were used for particular functional zones, for example, red for fuel.** BAE Systems via Brooklands Museum

BELOW RIGHT: **The rear fuselage of the first pre-production aircraft, XS660, at Preston in early 1965.** BAE Systems via Warton Heritage Group

BOTTOM RIGHT: **The rear fairing, made by BSEL, was blighted by design and production problems, and both tasks were to be taken back in-house by BAC for production aircraft.** BAE Systems via Brooklands Museum

up as the core of the section, formed of stringer skin panels and 'T' booms with a lower vertical shear web and an engine thrust beam running along the top. Rails also ran along the top and bottom of the tunnels to facilitate removal and insertion of the engines and jetpipes. Each engine tunnel had a large cut-out near the forward end, leading to the engine accessories bays, and large doors hinged on the side longerons gave access to the bays and their equipment. Each tunnel was a load-carrying structure in itself, and was surrounded by a heat shield which also acted as a secondary fuel tank wall, designed to contain a fire in the engine tunnel for 5min. The Nos 3 and 4 fuel tanks were located in between and around the engine tunnels, extending rearward to a machined frame forming the rear fuel tank bulkhead, which incorporated integral spigots for the tailplanes and an attachment point for the fin spigot. A fuel collector box was located at the bottom rear of No. 3 tank. A water tank also sat between the engine tunnels, extending down to the roof of the bomb bay.

The rear fuselage section also included a cut-out at the forward edge to accommodate the rear part of the wing assembly, and incorporated attachments for the rear spar, along with drag and vertical links. Aft of the wing trailing edge were two airbrake recesses, the upper airbrake doors being hinged at their forward edges. A further pair of airbrakes was mounted on the underside corners some distance further forward than the upper pair, with a linkage between all four to synchronize their operation. Finally, the rear fairing, a removable aft portion of the rear fuselage (constructed primarily of Waspaloy, a nickel-based superalloy with excellent strength properties at high temperatures), housed the rearmost portion of the jetpipe tunnel and

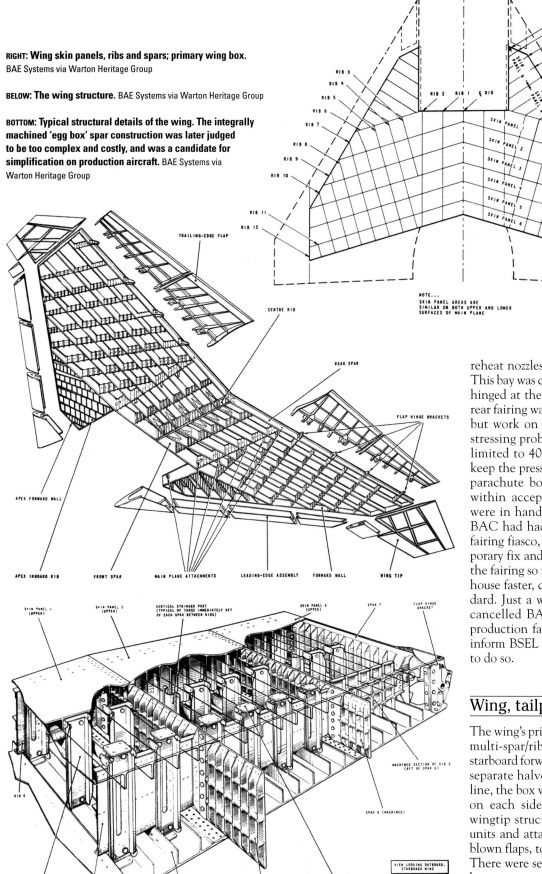

RIGHT: Wing skin panels, ribs and spars; primary wing box.
BAE Systems via Warton Heritage Group

BELOW: The wing structure. BAE Systems via Warton Heritage Group

BOTTOM: Typical structural details of the wing. The integrally machined 'egg box' spar construction was later judged to be too complex and costly, and was a candidate for simplification on production aircraft. BAE Systems via Warton Heritage Group

reheat nozzles plus a brake-parachute bay. This bay was closed off by an aft 'beak' door hinged at the top. The fabrication of this rear fairing was the responsibility of BSEL, but work on it was dogged by costs and stressing problems, and early flights were limited to 400kt (460mph; 740km/h) to keep the pressure differential between the parachute box and engine tunnel walls within acceptable limits. Modifications were in hand in early 1965, but by then BAC had had quite enough of the rear-fairing fiasco, had sorted out its own temporary fix and was determined to redesign the fairing so that it could be produced in-house faster, cheaper and to a better standard. Just a week before the project was cancelled BAC decided to manufacture production fairings at Weybridge, and to inform BSEL the next week; it never had to do so.

Wing, tailplanes and fin

The wing's primary structure consisted of a multi-spar/rib torsion box with port and starboard forward apex extensions. Built in separate halves and joined at the centreline, the box was sealed to form a fuel tank on each side. Leading-edge pieces and wingtip structures were built as separate units and attached, along with two-piece blown flaps, to complete the overall wing. There were seven spars within the torsion box, swept at an angle of 17 degrees and extending from the centreline to the wingtip joint, with the exception of spar 1 (the forward spar), the centre portion of

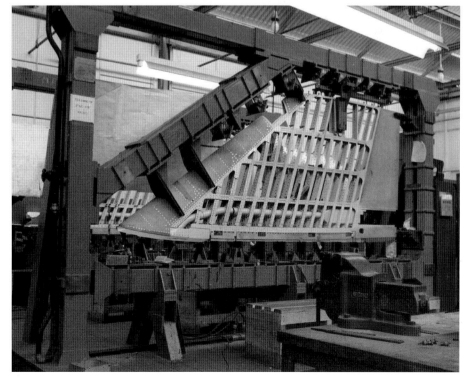

which formed the straight leading edge of the torsion box between the apex extension sections. Each spar was machined from a single light-alloy billet, and formed a solid web with integral vertical and horizontal stiffeners. Interspar ribs, twelve on each side, were either machined from solid billets (in high stress areas) or formed from web-and-post construction. The centreline rib acted as a baffle between the port and starboard fuel tanks. The next two ribs, 1 and 2, ran fore and aft, and rib 2 incorporated the wing-fuselage attachment points on the underside and slinging attachments on the upper surface. The remaining ribs were at right angles to the spars, with the exception of rib 12 at the wingtip joint. The apex extensions were composed of eight open-girder spars.

The flaps on each side were manufactured as two separate subassemblies joined by a spigot, and constructed in a similar manner to the mainplane itself, on a smaller scale. The trailing edges were filled with aluminium honeycomb and covered with chemi-etched light-alloy skins. The leading edges were constructed from titanium to cope with the high-temperature engine bleed air directed through ducts (also titanium) in this part of the flap, which exhausted through slits over the top surface of the flap. The flaps were operated by a powered flying-control unit within the fuselage, connected via a driveshaft to screw jacks on the wing undersurface that were covered by fairings.

The HF radio aerials were mounted within cut-outs in the apex sections of the wing, covered by dielectric panels, though performance in flight testing was poor and a redesign was on the cards for production aircraft. Navigation lights were mounted in cut-outs in the wingtip leading edges, and the wingtips also housed ILS aerials (there was a proposal in being at cancellation to relocate the ILS aerials from the wingtips to the nose radome), the fluxgate compass

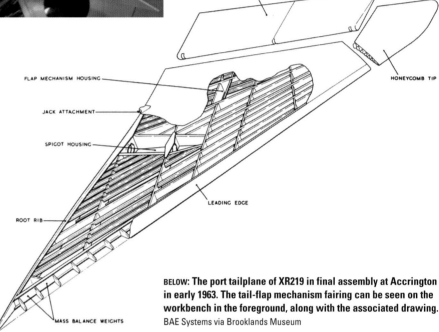

(starboard) and a missile warning receiver (there was originally to be one in each wingtip trailing edge, but interference with the compass meant that this was reduced to a single installation on the port side only). Stores pylons pick-up points were incorporated on the underside of the wing at stations 120 and 155 (120 and 155in (305 and 394cm) outboard of the aircraft's centreline). A fuel venting/jettison gallery passed along the leading edge and was then directed through the wingtip to a vent/jettison outlet in the tip's trailing edge.

Skinning of the torsion box, apexes and wingtips used tapered panels of light alloy (X2020 on the development batch), machined from planks with integral spar booms and spanwise stringers. Each plank was joined to the next by a lap joint and riveted and bolted to attachment brackets on the torsion-box ribs. After the concerns about X2020's strength arose, and the static-test example's wing failed during testing, an alteration to the tips was made so that they would include stiffening patches. Production wings would probably have included redesigned tips skinned with an alternative light alloy.

Tailplanes

The all-moving, cropped-delta tailplanes were operated differentially for roll control (the wing having no ailerons) and in unison for pitch control. Each tailplane comprised a multi-web box with stringer-stabilized skins and chordwise ribs. Both the upper and lower skins were taper-machined from a single piece of X2020 alloy (again likely to be changed on production units to an alternative alloy such as L73). Mass-balances were attached to the root of the forward closing web of the primary box. Each tailplane was mounted on a spigot

BELOW: The fin structure. This illustration predates the addition of a cooling intake in the leading edge, which ducted outside air to the parachute housing in the rear fairing. BAE Systems via Brooklands Museum

DIELECTRIC TIP

HONEYCOMB TRAILING EDGE

LEADING EDGE

SPIGOT BEARING ACCESS PANEL

JACK ATTACHMENT

SPIGOT HOUSING

MASS BALANCE

ROOT RIB

protruding from the rear fuselage section, rotating about it on bearings supported by the root and first outboard ribs. Both of these ribs were made from steel, while the remainder of the tailplane, excluding skins, was of light alloy. Tailplane actuation was via hydraulic jacks within the rear fuselage, acting on a bracket on the root rib close to the rear-fairing/rear-fuselage interface.

For additional pitch authority at low speeds the tailplanes had trailing-edge flaps of light alloy honeycomb construction. The tailplane flaps were operated by mechanical gearings housed within upper-surface fairings, linked to the tailplane angle, but only when the wing flaps were down. For higher-speed flight, when the wing flaps were retracted, the tailplane flap gearing would be disengaged and the tailplane flaps would be locked in the neutral position.

Fin

The fin was an all-moving unit of similar construction to the tailplanes, though it was a slab unit, rather than being fitted with any trailing-edge control surface. It was mounted on an inclined spigot attached to the rear fuselage, access to the outer bearing and securing nut being available through a circular access panel on the port side of the fin. A sprung mass-balance was fitted within the leading edge cover at the root end of the fin, and the leading edge also housed a ram-air intake that directed cooling air to the braking-parachute container. The complete trailing edge of the fin, like the tailplane tips, was a honeycomb unit, and the tip of the fin was a dielectric cover for the UHF aerial.

BELOW: The fin of XR220. A blanking plug is inserted into the cooling intake in the leading edge. Damien Burke

Undercarriage layout. BAE Systems via Brooklands Museum

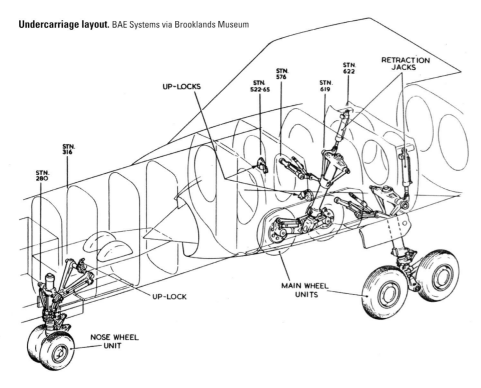

The nose undercarriage.
BAE Systems via Brooklands Museum

Undercarriage, braking parachute and airbrakes

The nose undercarriage consisted of a conventional twin-wheeled steerable oleo strut retracting rearwards into the fuselage. The main oleo incorporated an extension that could be selected by the pilot to give an additional 30in (75cm) of extension to assist with nose lift on short take-offs. This extension was automatically contracted during the retraction process, but was slated to be removed from production aircraft because it proved to be of little assistance in reducing the take-off roll, the tailplane authority proving to be greater than predicted. The leg was powered by the No.2 hydraulic services, emergency operation being provided by the No.1 services. There were four bay doors, split into port/starboard pairs and forward/aft sections. The smaller forward sections remained open with the nose-gear leg dropped, while the larger aft sections sequenced closed when the leg was locked in place. These doors could also be opened on the ground to give access to the nose-gear bay, which included a refuelling control panel.

The main undercarriage was considerably more complex, the design being driven primarily by the rough-field requirements and the limited space available in which to stow it. A main shock-absorber strut, braced at the top, was connected via a swivelling ankle joint to a two-wheel bogie beam with wheels mounted in tandem. Hydraulically operated disc brakes were fitted to each wheel. A hop damper was

OPPOSITE PAGE:
TOP: **XR219 with the nose gear leg in the extended position. Unexpectedly powerful taileron response meant that the extension feature was to be deleted from production airframes.** BAE Systems via Warton Heritage Group

BOTTOM LEFT: **The nose undercarriage of XR220 viewed from behind, looking forward. The bay roof doubles as a fuel tank wall, with dished recesses to accommodate the wheels.** Damien Burke

BOTTOM RIGHT: **Nose undercarriage functioning, also showing the extended strut initially thought necessary to meet the required take-off performance. Unexpectedly powerful tailplanes rendered this unnecessary, nosewheel lifting occurring at speeds 30 to 40kt (34 to 46mph; 55 to 74km/h) lower than predicted, so the extending nose gear strut was to be omitted from later airframes.** BAE Systems via Brooklands Museum

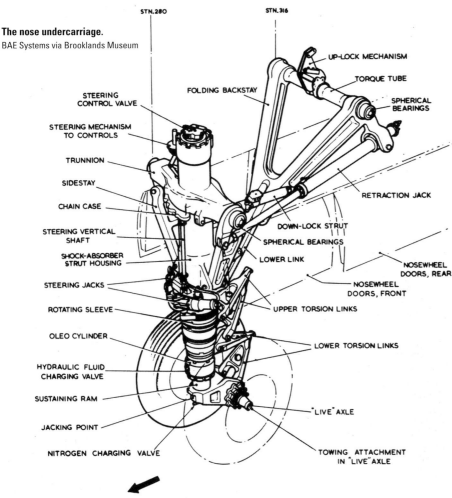

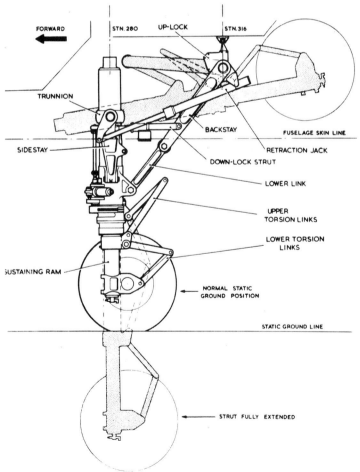

FORWARD

STN.280 UP-LOCK STN.316

TRUNNION

SIDESTAY

BACKSTAY

FUSELAGE SKIN LINE

RETRACTION JACK

DOWN-LOCK STRUT

LOWER LINK

UPPER
TORSION LINKS

LOWER TORSION
LINKS

SUSTAINING RAM

NORMAL STATIC
GROUND POSITION

STATIC GROUND LINE

STRUT FULLY EXTENDED

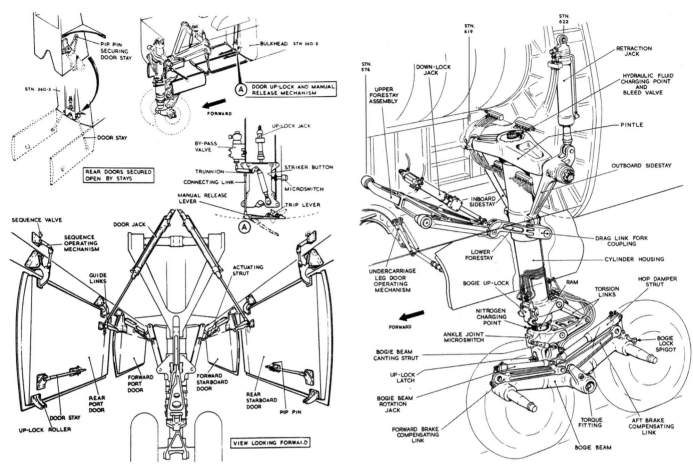

The nose undercarriage doors and operating mechanism.
BAE Systems via Brooklands Museum

The main undercarriage (port side), before the addition of the tie strut to alter the bogie trail angle. BAE Systems via Brooklands Museum

The port main undercarriage of XR220. As can be seen, this aircraft was fitted with the 'Aylesbury tie', as was XR219 for its last few flights. Damien Burke

attached to the rear of the bogie beam in an attempt to eliminate any tendency for the aircraft to bounce from one wheel on the bogie to the other. A retraction jack at the forward end pulled the bogie upwards to the same angle as the shock-absorber strut and then canted the bogie assembly sideways to match the lateral angle before retracting it forwards into the large bay. The three main undercarriage doors on each side consisted of a small aft door, linked to the leg itself and remaining open with the undercarriage down, and two larger underside and side doors that were only open during the retraction or extension cycle. As with the aft nosewheel doors, the main undercarriage doors could also be sequenced open on the ground to give access to the bay. Items requiring immediate groundcrew

Main undercarriage functioning. BAE Systems via Brooklands Museum

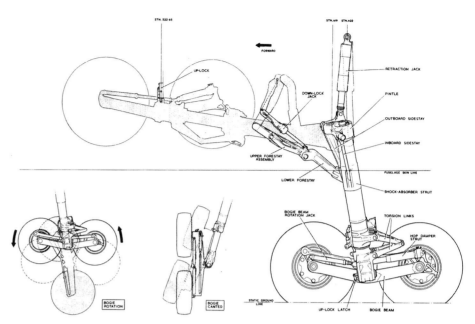

The main undercarriage doors and operating mechanism. BAE Systems via Brooklands Museum

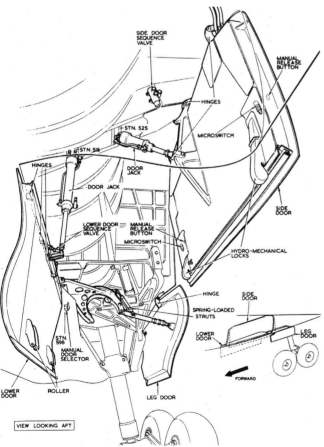

RIGHT: **The starboard main undercarriage bay of XR220, looking aft. The shape of the bay was determined by the walls of the intake tunnels, weapons bay and the fuel tanks above. The three orange cables on the right lead into the weapons bay through holes in the panel here. This was a removable panel designed to provide access for winching items such as bomb suspension units into the weapons bay.** Damien Burke

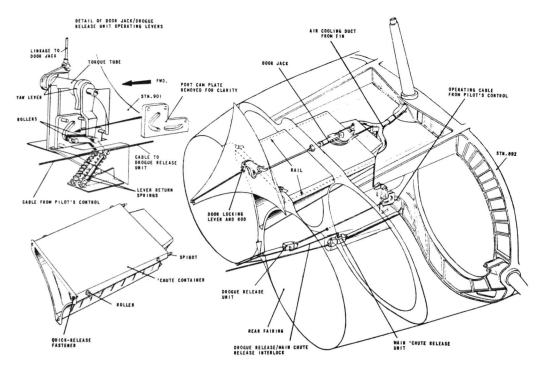

LEFT: **The brake-parachute installation. The parachute container was simply rolled into place, a considerable improvement on the Lightning's lower-fuselage parachute installation, which could require riggers to lie on the ground and push the pack into place with their feet while swearing like navvies.** BAE Systems via Brooklands Museum

BELOW: **The TSR2's brake parachute in fully developed form, seen here at the conclusion of the first flight.** BAE Systems via Warton Heritage Group

access on shut-down, such as the master armament break safety switch, were located in the aft section of the bay, so that access would not be hindered by any possible door problems.

Initial ground-retraction tests of this complex undercarriage threw up several sequencing problems, and as the first flight was to be of very short duration, no attempt was going to be made to retract it initially. (This was also in keeping with traditional Vickers first-flight practice.) One of the most famous of the TSR2's problems originated with this undercarriage design, as on the first landing and almost every subsequent one a shattering lateral oscillation set in at touchdown which was so pronounced at the pilot's position that vision and any semblance of control was lost for the several seconds' duration of the oscillation. A tie strut fitted on the first aircraft to alter the bogie trail angle and detune the whole assembly was found to be very effective in reducing this problem, and was also fitted to the second aircraft. Production aircraft would, at the very least, have incorporated this modification, but it is likely that more substantial redesign of the main undercarriage would have been required to solve the problem completely.

Braking parachute

The TSR2's braking parachute, a two-stage, two-diameter ribbon parachute, was installed in the rear fairing between the engine exhausts. The central part of the aft end of the fairing hinged upwards forming the 'beak door', and the two drogues, primary and emergency (both of 6ft (1.8m) diameter), would stream out, pulling the main parachute out with them. The parachute would deploy initially in a reefed condition, to a diameter of 16ft (4.8m); full deployment created a 28ft (8.5m)-diameter parachute once airspeed had fallen below 135kt (155mph; 250km/h) (assuming there was no crosswind condition).

The choice of a two-stage parachute was dictated by the wide variety of landing speeds the aircraft could experience, from the lightweight landing with full flap at 130kt (150mph; 240km/h), to the much more exciting case of flap and 'blowing' failure at heavy weight; 220kt (250mph; 400km/h). Failure of the reefing mechanism in this case would test the parachute attachment structure to its ultimate design limits; in practice, some damage would no doubt have occurred.

Whereas in the Lightning the brake-parachute attachment was on top of the rear fuselage (an area designed to be strong to cope with rudder loads), on the TSR2 the fin was all-moving and the spigot on which it rotated was much further forward.

Attaching the brake parachute here would have fouled the fin, so the attachment was placed below the fuselage, in line with the fin spigot. To provide clearance for the cable, a small fairing protruded below the valley between the jetpipes. A rail running from this fairing to the rear of the aircraft enabled the first section of the cable to be held straight regardless of the crosswind, spreading the load and easing the stress on the attachment point.

The parachute was activated by pulling the brake-parachute handle in the pilot's cockpit. This was to be a two-pull handle. The first pull would open the parachute beak door and allow the drogue parachute to be ejected by a spring and deploy. The next stage was to be either automatic, in which case switches on the undercarriage would trigger the removal of a pin allowing the secondary drogue and primary parachute to be pulled out by the already-deployed primary drogue; or manual, in which case a momentary release of pressure on the parachute handle, followed by a further pull, would allow the secondary drogue and primary parachute to deploy at pilot command. The first aircraft, XR219, had a lower standard of installation using a single-pull system, both steps being carried out in a single sequence, and no automatic mode.

Airbrakes

Four airbrakes were mounted on the rear-fuselage quarters, each operated by a screwjack that was shaft-driven by a single central unit to ensure symmetrical travel, the shafts running through sealed tunnels in the rear-fuselage fuel tanks. The airbrake control unit was hydraulically powered and electrically controlled, both systems being dual-channel so that a single failure would not disable the airbrake system. An automatic blow-back system was incorporated to protect the airbrake doors and jacks from overload in the event of extension beyond their limiting airspeed. If airspeed increased with the airbrakes out, the increased loading would cause them to retract automatically, and extension commands would be ignored if extension would result in overstress. Unfortunately the choice of screwjacks was not a happy one. On the development-batch aircraft their inherent inaccuracy made it impossible to adjust the airbrakes with sufficient precision to ensure that all four were equally closed without the possibility of one or more overrunning the stops and being damaged, or damaging the

ABOVE: **Brake parachute anchor point and railing. This enabled the first part of the cable to be held straight regardless of crosswind, reducing side loading on the anchor point.** Damien Burke

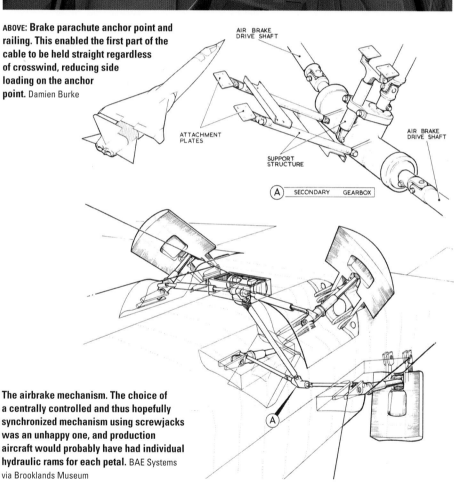

The airbrake mechanism. The choice of a centrally controlled and thus hopefully synchronized mechanism using screwjacks was an unhappy one, and production aircraft would probably have had individual hydraulic rams for each petal. BAE Systems via Brooklands Museum

fuselage structure. An interim solution was to set the 'closed' position so that the airbrakes were actually open by about 1.5in (3.8cm), and XR219 made all but four flights (17 to 20) with the airbrakes cracked slightly open like this.

Slipping-clutch units were to be introduced into the final driveshafts to allow some limited self-adjustment at final closure, but there was also a proposal to

replace the screwjack-and-driveshaft system with hydraulic rams. The existing control unit would have been replaced by a purely electrical one operating push-pull rods connected to hydraulic servo valves positioned near the new airbrake rams. This would have solved the problem of unequal retraction, as the ram's jack-body length could be adjusted to calibrate a particular airbrake door to its recess. As a bonus, time

ABOVE: **The interior of XR220's starboard lower airbrake, showing the large screwjack and the smaller driveshaft linking this brake to the other three.** Damien Burke

BELOW: **Airbrake, flap and taileron flap mechanisms. The inherent inaccuracy of screwjacks was not a problem with the wing flaps or taileron flaps.** BAE Systems via Brooklands Museum

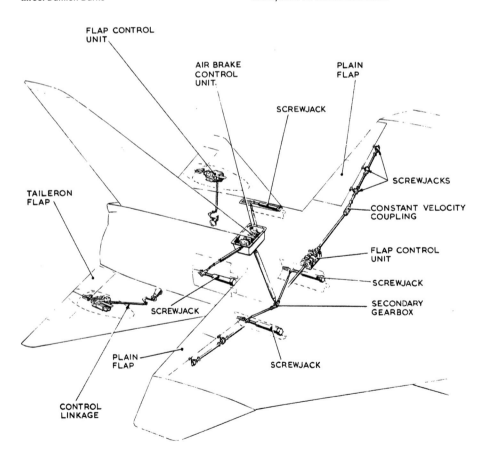

NOTE :-
MAINPLANE FLAP STARBOARD TRANSMISSION BROKEN FOR CLARITY

for full extension of the airbrakes would have been cut by 1.5sec to 4sec, and £12,000 would have been saved on each aircraft. While the airbrakes performed well in flight testing over the first 60 degrees of their extension range, producing no serious trim changes or buffeting, the last 5 degrees of travel produced considerable buffet, and an investigation into the use of perforated airbrakes was due to begin when the project was cancelled.

Arrester hook

A basic design for an arrester hook was drawn up during the overall airframe design stage, but this was not a popular addition as it introduced weight and drag penalties just when the design was having balance problems. Freddy Page said later that he '... had never thought the hook was a sensible suggestion', and it was soon dropped as an easy and early economy measure to take.

As the weight of the aircraft had increased throughout the type's development, so take-off and landing runs had also inevitably increased. The ability of the brakes and brake parachute to stop a loaded TSR2 in emergencies was judged insufficient in all required situations, so the RAF asked BAC to quote some figures on weights, and any possible production implications of adding a simple 'one-shot' arrester hook. The answers arrived just when the engine accessories bay situation began to complicate matters, so work on a design study was not carried out until late 1964, being completed in November and submitted to the MoA for approval. The arrester hook would not have been incorporated in most of the development-batch aircraft, but was expected to be fitted from the pre-production aircraft onwards, had the project not been cancelled. In fact the Ministry never bothered to seek funding from the Treasury for this modification owing to the uncertainty over the project's future, and in February 1965 the Air Staff postponed the implementation of the hook as an interim money-saving measure, intending to reintroduce it later, possibly for full production aircraft only.

Crew space

The pilot's and navigator's compartments together made up the 'crew space', a term coined early in development so that discussion of the two cockpits would always treat them as a single entity, without the acci-

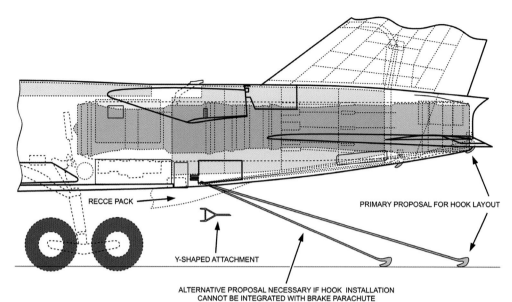

RECCE PACK

Y-SHAPED ATTACHMENT

PRIMARY PROPOSAL FOR HOOK LAYOUT

ALTERNATIVE PROPOSAL NECESSARY IF HOOK INSTALLATION
CANNOT BE INTEGRATED WITH BRAKE PARACHUTE

LEFT: **Early arrester hook design proposal. The hook idea was dropped at an early stage, but the RAF was keen for the aircraft to have one, and production aircraft would probably have been fitted with a simple 'one-shot' hook much like that fitted to later marks of Lightning.** Damien Burke

BELOW: **An early mockup of a proposed pilot's cockpit for the TSR2. Some elements of the final layout can be discerned, such as the warning captions along the coaming edge, the large attitude indicator and moving map display (showing admirable attention to detail, as it is centred on a typical target area, south-eastern Poland, near the Ukrainian border).** BAE Systems via Brooklands Museum

dental overlooking of any aspect. English Electric's mock-up of its P.17 design proved useful in the early stages of deciding crew space layout, along with a Scimitar at Vickers' Wisley plant, as this aircraft had a similarly sized cockpit to that of TSR2.

This was to be an all-weather strike aircraft, and a forward view for the navigator was therefore considered unnecessary. Any visual fixes were to be obtained by the pilot, who would be provided with a colour moving-map display. Roland Beamont did express doubts at an early stage regarding the abilities of a pilot to map-read at high speed and low level, but Vickers thought that some assistance from the navigator (who could not see where he was going), calling out landmarks in advance of their arrival, would suffice.

The choice between a central joystick and a small sidestick was made quite early. Trials carried out on a Gloster Meteor fitted with a sidestick had generally gone well, though one obvious drawback was the use of the stick if the pilot was wounded or injured in the appropriate arm. Beamont considered a sidestick preferable, basing his reasoning on arm fatigue encountered when holding a normal stick for long periods, particularly at low level. However, US experiences with sidesticks on the Convair F-106 had been mixed, and the crews considered central sticks generally preferable. Test pilot Brian Trubshaw suggested that if a central stick was chosen, it should be topped with a W-shaped wheel to decrease the amount of the centre of the instrument panel that was obscured. This, of

course, ended up being used on Concorde. Some months later a U or Y shape was being proposed, and it gives some idea of the amount of time wasted in cockpit meetings that one Minute records a request from the Ministry officials to Vickers to ensure that 'the control column movement was such as to be free from fouls against pilot or aircraft structure'. One can only wonder at the mindset that fears a firm may design a control column that cannot move freely!

Crew vision

A conventional windscreen was chosen, despite the disadvantages of the two struts blocking some of the view forward. At the time the optical qualities of a one-piece curved windscreen were suspect, and a two-piece V-shaped windscreen would have made the required HUD an even trickier proposition.

ABOVE: **The layout of the TSR2 pilot's cockpit as of February 1965. By this point the various warning captions had been moved to a central warning panel, the coaming edge being used for commonly used controls.** BAE Systems via Brooklands Museum

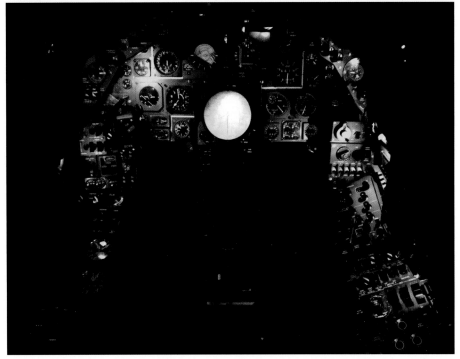

LEFT: **The pilot's cockpit under night lighting conditions.** BAE Systems via Brooklands Museum

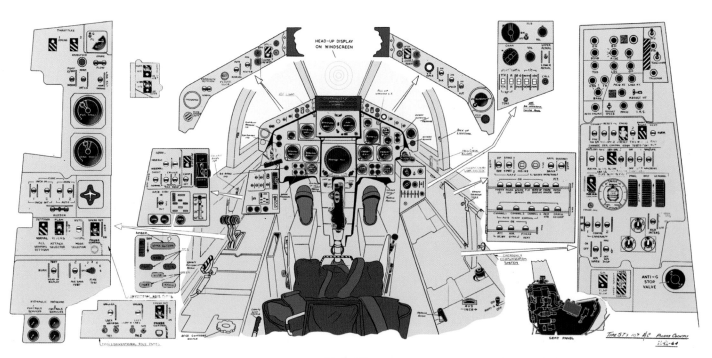

ABOVE: **The pilot's cockpit layout of the Type 579 (pre-production aircraft). The development-batch aircraft differed in having various items omitted; for example, XR219 had no AFCS or role panels.** BAE Systems via Brooklands Museum

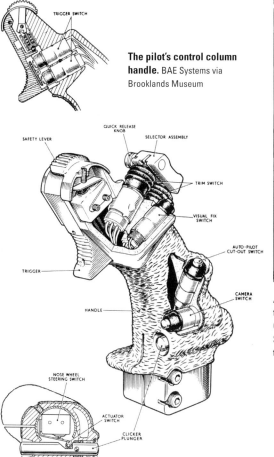

The pilot's control column handle. BAE Systems via Brooklands Museum

ABOVE: **An early mockup of the navigator's cockpit, with TV display on the left (showing Heathrow airport!), moving map (showing southern Czechoslovakia) and fix controls on the right, with a blank area for an SLR display to the left of the moving map. The CRT on the right appears to be for the FLR display.** BAE Systems via Brooklands Museum

The layout of the TSR2 navigator's cockpit as of February 1965. The hooded FLR display sits above the moving-map display, with the SLR display to the left, with magnifying lens overlaid. The binocular-shaped shroud to the left of the SLR display is for the downward sight. BAE Systems via Warton Heritage Group

The navigator's cockpit under night lighting conditions. BAE Systems via Warton Heritage Group

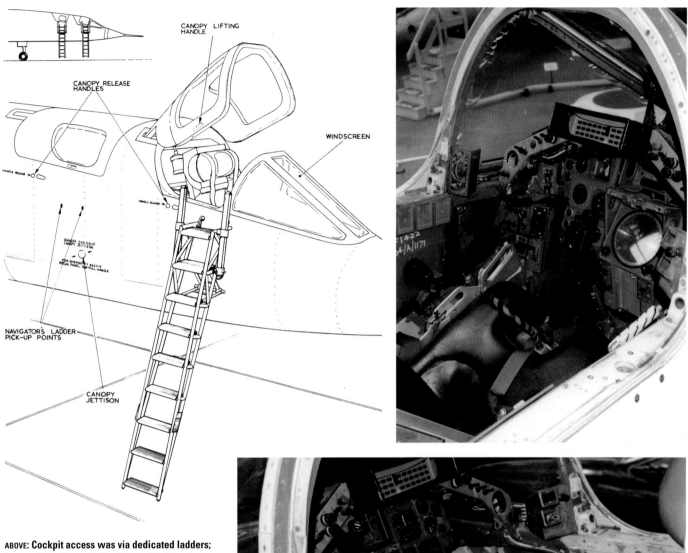

CANOPY LIFTING
HANDLE

CANOPY RELEASE
HANDLES

WINDSCREEN

HANDLE RELEASE

HANDLE RELEASE

DANGER EXPLOSIVE
CANOPY JETTISON

FOR EMERGENCY RESCUE
BREAK PANEL AND PULL HANDLE

NAVIGATOR'S LADDER
PICK-UP POINTS

CANOPY
JETTISON

ABOVE: **Cockpit access was via dedicated ladders; the specification called for integral ladders for use at dispersed sites.** BAE Systems via Brooklands Museum

The front cockpit of XR220 at Cosford in the mid-1990s, showing gaps where various items are missing. BAE Systems

The risk of bird strike at low level and high speed, allied with the heating expected at high speed, meant that special formulations of glass were examined for the windscreen, including formulations that did not expand much with temperature increases, such as alumina-silicate glass. Fused-silica glass was better at dealing with heat but not as strong, so a sandwich of the two was proposed. Given the amount of time the aircraft was to spend at low level and high speed, erosion of the windscreen by impact with rain, sand or insects was going to be a problem. A Hawker Hunter windscreen, for instance, would survive only 6hr of use at low level in sandy environments. The Lightning had an efficient rain-dispersal device at the front edge of the windscreen, which blasted air upwards to shatter or deflect droplets, but this was only thought to be effective at up to 350kt (400mph; 650km/h), not the 750kt (860mph; 1,387km/h) being aimed at with the TSR2.

Experience with types such as the Canberra and de Havilland Sea Vixen had also shown that low-level flight at high speeds through rain or salt spray could result in serious impairment of the view forward in flight, to the detriment of both the mission and flight safety, and salt accumulation could be experienced up to 50 miles (80km) from the coast. Tests were carried out at the RAE with Hunter and Javelin aircraft, both on the ground and in the air, to ascertain the best method of keeping the windscreen clear. These tests simulated not only low-level flight over the sea using salt solutions sprayed on the windscreen, but more exotic contaminants such as dead insects (fruit flies, in particular; smeared on, crushed on, baked on). The results showed that a weak detergent solution flooded over the screen in combination with a hot-air-blast system would keep the windscreen clear of salt and other contaminants, and also provided adequate rain clearance. Consequently such a system was destined to be installed in production TSR2s.

The canopy design came in for some stiff criticism, as American aircraft of similar performance were using clear canopies that were much less restrictive of both view and access. Vickers deflected these objections, arguing that the currently available transparent materials were unable to deal with the heat of Mach 2 flight, and suggested that later in the aircraft's life it might be possible to retrofit clear canopies when appropriate materials became available. Flash screens to block the flash of a nuclear weapon were also proposed; manually erected curtains for the canopy sides, and an automatic screen that would cover the windscreen area, linked to the weapons-release circuit so that it would be erected in time for the detonation. In the end the much simpler (and cheaper) option of smoked helmet visors was chosen.

The windscreen, showing the twin pipes and slots for the windscreen clearance and rain-dispersal system. Damien Burke

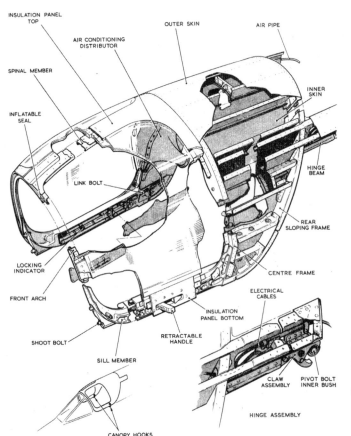

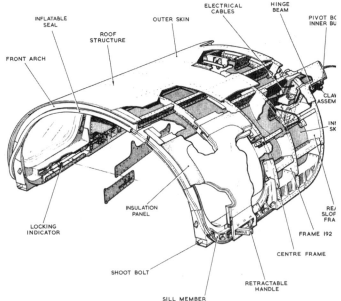

LEFT: The pilot's canopy. Transparency quality was a recurring problem with the first aircraft, and a redesign was under way at the time the project was cancelled. BAE Systems via Brooklands Museum

ABOVE: The navigator's canopy. BAE Systems via Brooklands Museum

Various types of transparencies were experimented with for the TSR2's windscreen and canopies, and a Triplex multi-layer transparency with integral gold film deicing and demisting (with the bonus that it provided some radar signature reduction, though this was not the primary aim) was finally selected. Aircrew remarked that this gold film had an unexpected bonus in that it turned the most dismal of grey days into a cheery golden-hued occasion, until the canopies were raised! Of less use as an anecdote was the fact that the overall experience with both the windscreen and canopy transparencies was by any standards pretty poor. The first windscreen panel on XR219 delaminated and was subject to severe mottling that made the forward view into glare almost totally impossible, and had to be replaced before flight testing could continue. The replacement was little better. Ammonia-based cleaning products were suspected to be the cause, and instructions were issued to use a Lux soap/alcohol/chalk mixture instead, to try to avoid future delamination. The laminated Perspex in the canopies also came in for sustained complaint owing to optical distortions and delamination, but Napier, which was manufacturing the canopies, had already produced a new canopy design using monolithic Perspex by August 1964, and had begun tests on it. These dragged on somewhat, and by the time the project was cancelled the canopy had yet to be fitted to any airframe. The development effort put into the TSR2's transparencies was not wasted, as Concorde ended up using similar material.

Air conditioning

Heat was a major matter of concern from the outset. At high Mach numbers airframe heating would quickly lead to intolerable temperatures within the cockpit, degrading aircrew performance and soon causing unconsciousness and death. Therefore a highly efficient air-conditioning system was going to be a must, along with the provision of air-ventilated suits. The canopies were to have limited glazing to reduce the 'greenhouse effect' from sunshine into the cockpit, and also provide some protection against nuclear flash.

The air-conditioning system proved to be a serious challenge. Research on the provision of air conditioning in aircraft of similar performance included an examination of the system used in the Vigilante, and

of anecdotal evidence of the system in the cancelled Avro Canada CF-105 Arrow interceptor. The latter had similar cockpit cooling needs in a slightly larger cockpit area, and ventilation at a rate of 27.5lb (12.5kg) of air per minute had initially produced 'gales' in the cockpit, only alleviated by modified louvres which then gave rise to a highly unpleasant whistling noise. The TSR2 was going to need 30lb (13.5kg) per minute, so this was an immediate source of concern.

The RAE at Farnborough had an existing air-conditioning test rig that had been put together for the Bristol Type 188 project,

using a fuselage section from the aircraft, and this was modified to simulate the TSR2 pilot's compartment. Electric heaters within the rig would bring the temperature up to the expected limits, while an airflow system pumped cooling air in various configurations to try to bring the temperature down to the levels acceptable to the Institute of Aviation Medicine (33°F on the aircrews' skin). It was found that the optimum performance with an aircraft skin temperature of 125° was attained with air to 0° pumped at 16lb (7.25kg) per minute. As this level of cooling was impractical, air at 6° was tried, and found to provide acceptable cooling,

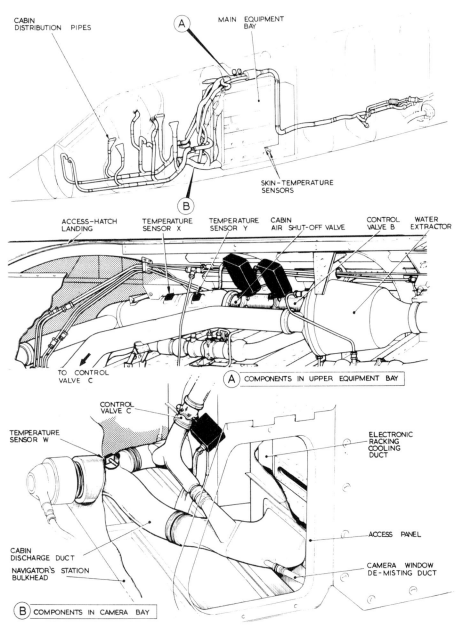

The air-conditioning and cooling system layout. BAE Systems via Brooklands Museum

though with occasional complaints of hot feet! The rig was only of limited use for dealing with heating. Temperatures as low as –20° might be encountered in slow or cruising-speed flight at high altitudes, so tests under these conditions were to be made in a real aircraft.

Once TSR2 construction was under way, a complete TSR2 forebody (nose section) was earmarked for thermal environment tests (along with ejection seat testing and the aforementioned windscreen clearance tests) and delivered to the RAE at Farnborough. There, various configurations of air-conditioning piping based on previous research was tried, in order to come up with a final arrangement that could be built into the airframes then on the production line. In the end the system's performance in the first aircraft, XR219, was only a qualified success, with air distribution considered excellent but the temperature often uncomfortably cold. This was one system that would definitely have benefited from some additional work.

Seating and escape system

Despite efforts in the early stages of the design to alleviate the rough ride at low level, the crew were expected to be subjected to fierce vibration, and a sprung seat was tentatively mentioned as one possible way of dealing with this, along with minimum weight and bulk of personal clothing and, possibly, extra trunk restraints on top of existing harnessing. In September 1960 RAE Bedford performed some experiments with a sprung seat inside Canberra WH975. It was found that that crew comfort could be significantly improved, but no attempt was made to measure crew performance, such as their efficiency in performing tasks. Vickers Research Ltd designed a vibrating seat to try and replicate the conditions crews would experience, and this was programmed to simulate the sort of turbulence experienced at low level in various aircraft types, including the Scimitar, Canberra, P.1B and Hunter, along with predicted values for the TSR2. However, while the sprung seat helped crew comfort it was found that the crew's ability to perform tasks was not significantly improved, so the idea of the sprung seat was eventually dropped, despite opposition from the Institute of Aviation Medicine.

It was recognized early on that existing ejection-seat technology was woefully insufficient to deal with the problems of ejecting at high speed or low altitude. An escape capsule was an attractive prospect, as it eliminated many of the highly complex timing and protection issues involved in ejection seats, but lack of full-scale test facilities in the UK contributed to this possibility being deemed beyond the timescales required.

Ejection seats, therefore, were the only real choice. At the time no data existed on the forces to which the human body could be subjected and survive, but, based on American tests using chimpanzees, these were assumed to be in the order of 30g deceleration and 1,000lb/ft2 (4882kg/m2) loading from wind blast, with tumbling of no more than one revolution per second to start with. No existing British ejection seat could satisfy these conditions beyond speeds of 540kt (620mph; 1,000km/h), and the Americans had already suffered fatalities in unsuccessful high-speed ejections. Added to that was the need to eject at ground level and boost the seat to a height sufficient for safe parachute deployment. Existing 'shotgun'-style seats that used an explosive to fire the seat out of the aircraft had just about reached the limit of their capability, so rocket propulsion would be needed to enable the seat to clear the aircraft's tail at high speeds. This also gave a smoother acceleration out of the aircraft and a smoother deceleration relative to the outside air.

Only English Electric considered the problems of escape at high speeds in detail in its submission, the other firms leaving it up to an independent manufacturer, such as Martin-Baker. English Electric sketched out a design for a seat using the existing gun-style mechanism but with a rocket sustainer, pop-out stabilizing fins, arm and leg restraints, an integrated lox system for high-altitude escapes, wind-blast shields and a head restraint. The parachute was to be fitted into the seat rather than worn by the pilot. The RAE agreed with all of these measures, and recommended development of such a seat. Deadlines for development were to be March 1962 for a basic seat of limited capability, 1963 for more capable seats and 1965 for the completely developed and capable items. It was accepted at an early stage that a fully capable escape system would not be provided in the first aircraft.

At the time Martin-Baker was using a Hunter for high-speed ejection-seat trials, and there was a rocket track at Pendine, but neither were capable of the 750kt (860mph; 1,390km/h) speed being aimed at for the trickiest part of the ejection envelope. (This

The vibrating seat rig at the Vickers Research Laboratories. The lucky subject is performing basic navigation-related tasks while various performance and biological functions are monitored and recorded. BAE Systems via Brooklands Museum

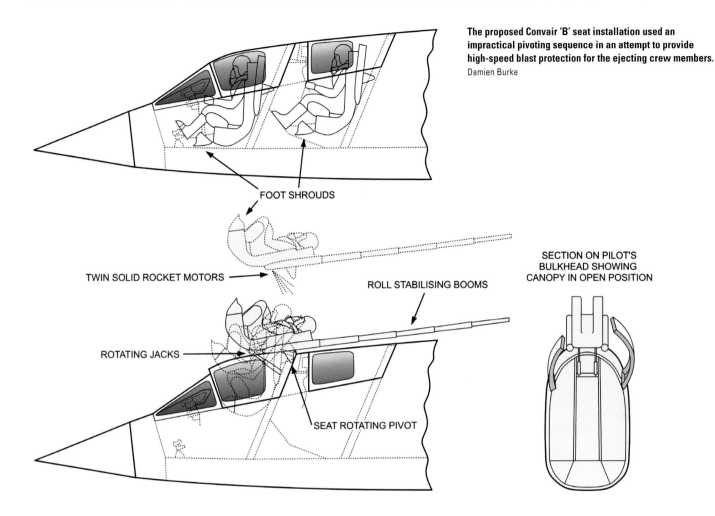

FOOT SHROUDS

TWIN SOLID ROCKET MOTORS

ROTATING JACKS

ROLL STABILISING BOOMS

SECTION ON PILOT'S
BULKHEAD SHOWING
CANOPY IN OPEN POSITION

SEAT ROTATING PIVOT

The proposed Convair 'B' seat installation used an
impractical pivoting sequence in an attempt to provide
high-speed blast protection for the ejecting crew members.
Damien Burke

was soon reduced to 650kt (750mph; 1,200km/h) when it became clear just how challenging the 750kt requirement was.) The Americans had been carrying out some research on high-speed ejection for their 'Century series' fighters, and efforts were made to obtain the resulting data to see if it could help.

It soon became obvious that the seat currently being considered for the American F-106, the Convair 'B', could be a possibility for use in the TSR2, and considerable effort went into investigating this option fully. The Convair 'B' used an unusual method of dealing with the stresses of supersonic ejection. It would only partly leave the aircraft in the initial stage of ejection, before rotating to lie flat along the upper surface. Thus foot pans at the base of the seat were in a position to protect the occupant from the worst of the wind blast. At this point stabilizing booms would pop out, explosive bolts would separate the seat from the aircraft, and rocket motors would fire to push the seat on a trajectory upwards and forwards to reduce the deceleration to

acceptable levels. Simultaneous ejection of pilot and navigator would not be possible, as the navigator's seat would be struck by the pilot's seat on rotation, so a significant delay between ejection of the navigator and pilot was necessary. Thankfully the seat was not chosen, a decision vindicated by several fatalities resulting from unsuccessful F-106 ejections. The F-106 was later modified with a replacement seat that could successfully eject the pilot at low altitudes and speeds as well as high ones. It did not use the rotational method employed by the earlier seat.

The next seat to come up for consideration was the North American HS-1, in use on the new YA3J-1 Vigilante prototype. 'HS' stood for high speed, and the similarity of the Vigilante's crew escape problems to those of the TSR2 were not lost on those tasked with solving them. As with the Convair 'B', new features such as automatic arm and leg restraints were present on the HS-1. A plate underneath the seat added lift to help push it clear of the aircraft's tail, but protection from wind-blast at the

high-speed end of the envelope relied upon the aircrew wearing full pressure suits.

Folland, which had successfully designed its own ejection seat for the Gnat lightweight fighter, was also interested in providing a seat for the TSR2. It proposed a rocket sustainer to give adequate fin clearance, angled to give some forward as well as upward thrust to reduce deceleration forces during ejection. Even so, English Electric felt that the decelerations likely to be experienced on exit and when the rocket burned out were dangerous. Folland also wanted to make use of English Electric's windtunnels during development, which could be tricky with the company's own projects needing them so often.

Martin-Baker, after some initial dragging of feet, put forward its Mk 5 seat, then in development for the F-4 Phantom II, as a possibility for the TSR2, suggesting some modifications to make it better able to deal with the more extreme environment. These basically boiled down to the use of rocket propulsion and a fully automatic body and leg restraint system. Compared with the

HS-1 it had poorer stability, comfort and restraints, and its acceleration profile was likely to be more damaging to the occupant. However, it would be lighter, a quarter of the price, less likely to fall prey to supply problems and also, importantly, more politically acceptable.

Martin-Baker had also supplied details of its patented ejection method using a canopy split along a fore-and-aft line, which would open sideways (as used on the Avro Canada Arrow). Before the advent of miniature detonating cord that shattered Perspex canopies before ejection, this was one way of quickly getting the canopy clear without the problems of jettisoning it (and possibly interfering with the ejection of the crew member behind). This idea was of some interest initially, but the top-opening design and a variation on it, in which the two opening sections were of unequal size, were both tested on a Hunter and the pilots were unimpressed, considering there was a serious risk of mid-air collision because of the poor standard of view. The open-top design was soon ditched, and despite a small penalty in escape time owing to the requirement to jettison the entire assembly, and continued criticism of the amount of view available, more conventional clamshell solid canopies were decided on in April 1960.

The final decision was due to be made in November 1960, but the Martin-Baker submission was still lacking in detail at the time (in fact it was basically a verbal submission from James Martin), so the decision was postponed. James Martin met with the Air Staff in December and pushed his case once more. He was obviously persuasive, because in January 1961 Martin-Baker was given the nod to develop an improved Mk 5 for the TSR2. The HS-1's considerable weight penalty (a total of 390lb (177kg) more compared with two Martin-Baker Mk 5s), discomfort from the parachute (which would be worn on the occupant's back) and larger size were factors that meant the HS-1 fell by the wayside. Most important, though, was the fact that co-operation between Vickers and Martin-Baker in matters of canopy separation and ejection sequencing would be considerably more efficient than any dealings with a US-based manufacturer; as would UK manufacture of the seat, instead of the possible difficulties of licensed production of an American seat. On the Vigilante the HS-1 proved to be an excellent seat and gained a reputation for reliability, saving many lives.

Martin-Baker Mk 8VA ejection seat

Martin-Baker took the opportunity to develop its Mk 5 into an entirely new seat, unrestrained by the need to fit it into a number of existing airframes. By August 1961 the seat for the TSR2 was no longer known as the developed Mk 5, but had been given a new designation: Mk 8VA (for Vickers-Armstrongs). As well as the problems of ejecting at high speeds at both high and low altitudes, Martin-Baker had to deal with the difficulty of ejecting an unprepared occupant, as the pilot was intended to be able to use command ejection, meaning that when he ejected, the navigator would be ejected too. Correct posture is an important part of surviving an ejection without serious injury, so the seat needed to incorporate some means of automatically restraining its occupant very quickly before it was fired. The resulting seat was a revolutionary design embodying several advances that would become part of many future ejection seats.

A single firing handle was located at the front of the seat base; no face blind or side handles were provided. The face-blind

handle in particular was considered too difficult to reach in high-g situations, and the blind itself was deemed unnecessary when TSR2 crews would wear helmets with visors. The helmet itself was attached to the seat by straps that pulled the occupant's head firmly against the headrest before ejection, and leg and arm restraints pulled the limbs into safe positions. After canopy jettison, automatically triggered by pulling the ejection seat handle, or by manual selection, the main ejection gun would fire, and primary and auxiliary explosive charges would boost the seat out of the aircraft, a seat-base rocket array quickly igniting to thrust the seat forward and assist with fin clearance. A duplex drogue system would then fire a small controller drogue, followed by a larger stabilizer drogue parachute, tilting the seat into a horizontal attitude to shield the occupant from further wind-blast and ensure that deceleration forces were approximately in line with the seat axis. The main parachute was housed within the rigid headrest of the seat (which had a large recess to accommodate the head when it was pulled back against the headrest). The drogue chute was held within the left-hand guide beam on the back of the seat. The right-hand beam held the barometric

One of the first mockups of the new Martin-Baker seat for the TSR2. Compared with the final Mk.8VA, the headbox is the most obviously different area. BAE Systems via Warton Heritage Group

release gear for sensing altitude, to open the parachute automatically at a safe height. In the event of a high-altitude ejection, no further action would take place until the seat had descended to a safer altitude (10,000ft (3,000m)) at which seat separation and main-parachute deployment could occur. The occupant would use the emergency oxygen supply on the way down. Otherwise, separation (including guillotining of head, arm and leg restraint straps) would occur after a short delay, just long enough to allow the seat to decelerate to a speed acceptable for deployment of the 28ft (8.5m)-diameter Irvin parachute.

Once the occupant was on the ground (or in the water) the survival pack became his next focus of interest. The seat cushion (much praised by the crews as being far more comfortable than those of other ejection seats on which they had spent time) doubled as a container for a dinghy and survival pack, and separated from the seat assembly at the same time as the occupant, remaining attached to them by a long strap. The dinghy, a simple one-man affair with a canopy and hood for protection against the elements, was inflated by a CO_2 cylinder. Martin-Baker did put forward proposals to include a chaff launcher in the seat so that it could cause a bloom on radar at the point of ejection and pinpoint the site for search-and-rescue efforts, but this was not incorporated in the final seat.

Relations between Vickers and Martin-Baker appear to have been strained from the start, with Martin-Baker repeatedly being blamed for causing hold-ups in the cockpit design owing to lack of a representative seat mock-up. Seat assemblies required for test-track firing trials on various dates in 1962 were not delivered in time, and development dragged on. It has to be said that this was in common with various other systems on the aircraft. BAC Weybridge, however, got on with any escape system tests it could manage without sight of an actual ejection seat, such as canopy jettison tests using windtunnel models. These tended to show that the navigator's canopy would follow a low trajectory and hit the fin when jettisoned at the same time as the pilot's canopy, so a delay between the two was introduced.

By the end of 1963, when the first flight had been originally expected, Martin-Baker had still not managed to test-fire a complete seat, though an earlier mark of seat using the Mk 8's rockets had been test fired from the company's Meteor. Unsurprisingly, the

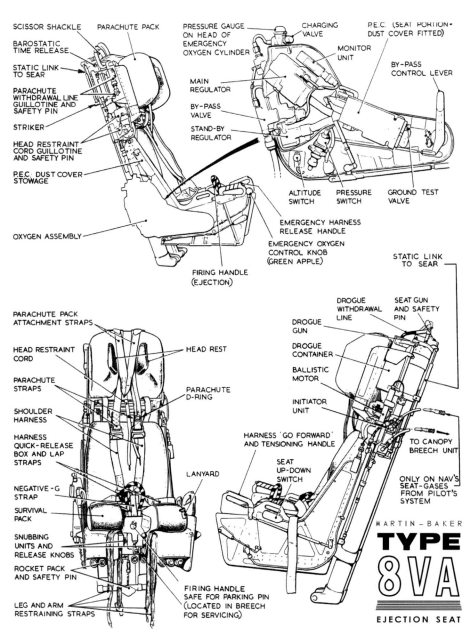

Incorporating several significant advances in ejection seat design, the Martin-Baker Mk 8VA seat was also well-liked by the TSR2 flight-test crews for its unusual level of comfort. Brooklands Museum

company had also been unable to deliver a functional example, and nor had blower-tunnel tests on canopy separation been made. Even the delivery of a structural test specimen seat to the RAE, scheduled for September 1963, was pushed back to February 1964. Two functioning seats were finally delivered to BAC at Boscombe Down on 30 June 1964, by which time the revised first-flight date of mid-May had come and gone, and still no test firings had yet been carried out, so they were not flight-cleared. The Ministry's patience with Martin-Baker was

fast running out, and BAC was similarly exasperated by the lack of visible progress, hoping that the RAF would be able to make more impact and impress upon Martin-Baker the urgency of the situation.

On 17 July Martin-Baker finally managed to fire a seat from one of its Meteors, and BAC and the A&AEE were able to start the initial blower-tunnel tests on various escape-system components on the 23rd, beginning with canopy jettison tests and moving on to a complete automatic ejection sequence including the firing of a seat.

This programme continued throughout the summer, and the resulting report was not actually finished until a month after the first flight. The system was cleared as suitable for use on the development batch aircraft, and had performed well.

Sequencing of ejection was designed to enable the navigator to escape without the risk of being hit by the pilot or his canopy.

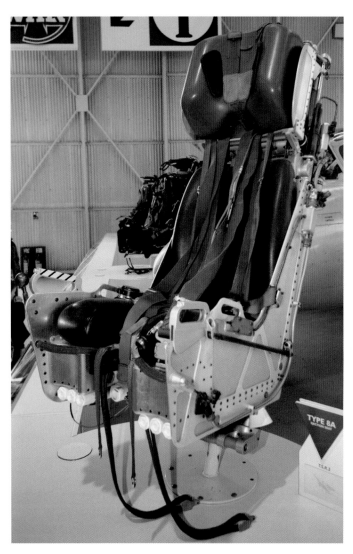

RIGHT: **A TSR2 test forebody mounted in front of the blower tunnel at RAE Farnborough for canopy jettison and ejection sequencing tests. This rig could be mounted at various angles of incidence with differing blower speeds to represent particular configurations, such as slow and nose-up in the approach configuration. This forebody is now preserved at the Brooklands Museum at Weybridge.** BAE Systems via Brooklands Museum

LEFT: **A preserved Mk 8VA ejection seat at the RAF Museum Cosford. Unlike most seats, the 8VA was left in an unpainted alloy finish.** Damien Burke

BELOW: **Canopy jettison tests using a windtunnel model and multiple exposure photography to show the trajectories. These tests were useful to verify roughly the amount of power necessary to boost the canopies high enough to clear the tailplane when they were jettisoned.** BAE Systems via Brooklands Museum

One of many canopy jettison tests carried out with the aid of the blower tunnel and test forebody rig. BAE Systems via Brooklands Museum

Thus a pilot-initiated ejection would result in the navigator's canopy separating, followed by ejection of the navigator's seat, then the pilot's canopy separating and the finally the pilot's seat operating. The navigator could also eject solo, in circumstances where it would perhaps be a safer option than staying with an aircraft the pilot believed he could recover. Each member of the crew could also jettison both canopies without initiating an ejection, this facility being provided to aid escape on the ground, and envisaged as being possible in the air as a precautionary measure preceding a forced landing. In practice, the results of the blower-tunnel tests had found that if both canopies were jettisoned simultaneously they would collide with each other, but would do so behind the crew compartment and thus cause no danger to either occupant. The navigator's canopy would then hit the fin, but as both crew members were on the way out this was not a problem. As a result, the delay between canopies was removed and a fully sequenced ejection would see both canopies fire first, then the navigator's seat, then the pilot's seat, all in quick succession. Below 75kt (85mph; 140km/h) a fully sequenced escape was not possible, and the canopies were to be jettisoned individually before each particular crew member ejected. Above 300kt (345mph; 555km/h) only a fully sequenced escape was permissible.

Larger-scale tests on canopy jettisoning at higher speeds (420kt (485mph; 780km/h)) were carried out at the Proof & Experimental Establishment site at Pendine in early March 1965. One of the RAE's recoverable rocket sleds was modified to accept a TSR2 pilot's canopy, constructed in the same manner as a real canopy but with metal window panels instead of transparencies. The first test, on 2 March, was a failure, as was the second, with the booster unit failing to fire and the canopy staying on the sled as a result. The third attempt worked, and the canopy followed a trajectory that would

have taken it 12ft (3.6m) clear of the fin had the jettison been from a complete aircraft. This was a smaller clearance than predicted by the blower-tunnel results, but was still acceptable.

Testing crew tolerance to any buffeting from 'cabriolet' flying was to be undertaken both in a nose section in a windtunnel and also using a real aircraft. The fifth TSR2 was to undertake some flight trials without canopies, while the first would undertake canopy jettison and (navigator) ejection trials on fast taxy runs. When the programme was cancelled BAC advanced a good case for continuing with escape-system tests, as the problem of high-speed, low-level escape was going to be a recurring one, and blower-tunnel and rocket-sled trials therefore continued as scheduled. A report dated 20 April 1965 summarized the blower-tunnel and static (zero speed, zero height) live seat firing tests carried out so far, which were remarkably successful. In July 1965 a Mk 8VA seat was fired from a rocket sled at Pendine travelling at 247kt (284mph; 457km/h). This was mostly successful, though the correct parachute deployment could not be verified as an additional line attached to the seat for tests fouled the main 'chute before deployment. A successful zero-zero firing was carried out in May 1966.

The Mk 8VA seat was cancelled along with TSR2, but the advances made in its development and production found their way into the Martin-Baker Mk 10. A less capable version of Mk 10 seat, produced for the RAF's Shorts Tucano turboprop trainer, was designated Mk 8LC, but bears no relation to the Mk 8VA. The number 8 was used purely because it was a 'vacant' mark number, the TSR2's Mk 8VA having been long forgotten.

Fuel system

The TSR2's LP fuel system was required to maintain fuel flow to the engines in all flight regimes while also keeping the aircraft's c.g. within strict limits. The fuel tanks were divided into two groups. The forward group comprised two tanks in the forward fuselage plus the port wing, and the aft group comprised two tanks in the rear fuselage plus the starboard wing. Each group fed a 30gal (136L) fuel collector box positioned so that it could be fed by gravity flow, with non-return valves to prevent fuel loss towards a holed compartment in any particular tank. Within the collector boxes were double-ended booster pumps driven by hydraulic pumps, which could be fed from top or bottom ends (thus catering for negative-g conditions) and pumped fuel from each collector into a single two-channel mechanical flow proportioner. Based on the pumps fitted to the Lightning, the booster pumps actually used the fuel tapped from the LP system as their working fluid, and so were known as fueldraulic pumps.

The purpose of the flow proportioner was to ensure that both engines were fed with fuel at the same rate, regardless of differences in supply from the two tank groups, thus also keeping the fuel tanks in balance. Fuel flow rates could vary from as little as 180gal/hr (818L/hr) to a massive 12,100gal/hr (54,934L/hr) in full reheat. However, as it was expected that periods of full flow would be limited and both engines would be running at similar consumption rates during these periods, the proportioner would actually be bypassed whenever the flow rate exceeded 3,500gal/hr (15,890L/hr). The crew could also elect to bypass the proportioner manually. If one fuel group ran dry while the proportioner bypass was

Ejection Sequence	
Time	*Action*
0 seconds	Ejection initiated
0.05 seconds	Navigator's canopy jettisoned
0.05 seconds	Pilot's canopy jettisoned
0.50 seconds	Navigator's seat fires
0.77 seconds	Navigator's seat rocket expended
0.95 seconds	Pilot's seat fires
1.22 seconds	Pilot's seat rocket expended

A rocket sled modified to represent a TSR2 nose section, on the Pendine test track for high-speed canopy jettison tests.
BAE Systems via Brooklands Museum

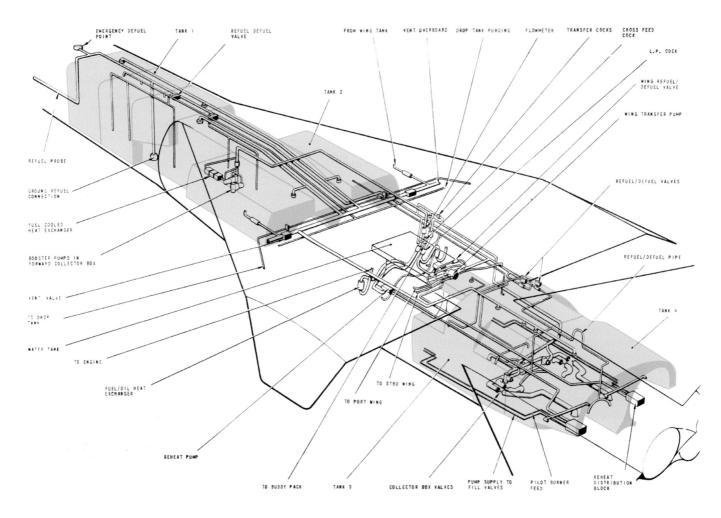

EMERGENCY DEFUEL POINT — TANK 1 — REFUEL DEFUEL VALVE — FROM WING TANK — VENT OVERBOARD — DROP TANK PURGING — FLOWMETER — TRANSFER COCKS — CROSS FEED COCK

L.P. COCK

TANK 2

WING REFUEL/ DEFUEL VALVE

WING TRANSFER PUMP

REFUEL PROBE

GROUND REFUEL CONNECTION

REFUEL/DEFUEL VALVES

FUEL COOLED HEAT EXCHANGER

BOOSTER PUMPS IN FORWARD COLLECTOR BOX

REFUEL/DEFUEL PIPE

VENT VALVE

TANK 4

TO DROP TANK

WATER TANK

TO ENGINE

FUEL/OIL HEAT EXCHANGER

TO STBD WING

TO PORT WING

REHEAT PUMP

REHEAT DISTRIBUTION BLOCK

TO BUDDY PACK — TANK 3 — COLLECTOR BOX VALVES — PUMP SUPPLY TO FILL VALVES — PILOT BURNER FEED

ABOVE: The fuselage fuel tank layout. The fueldraulic system was similar to that of the Lightning, with a complex auto-balancing system to maintain the aircraft's c.g. BAE Systems via Warton Heritage Group

BELOW: The single ground refuelling point was in the aft end of the nose undercarriage bay; it is the blue cylinder at upper centre in this photograph. Damien Burke

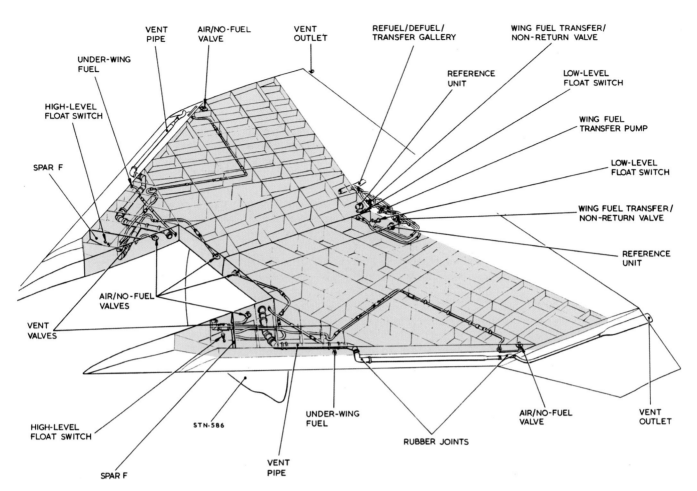

VENT PIPE · AIR/NO-FUEL VALVE · VENT OUTLET · REFUEL/DEFUEL/TRANSFER GALLERY · WING FUEL TRANSFER/NON-RETURN VALVE

UNDER-WING FUEL · REFERENCE UNIT · LOW-LEVEL FLOAT SWITCH

HIGH-LEVEL FLOAT SWITCH · WING FUEL TRANSFER PUMP

LOW-LEVEL FLOAT SWITCH

SPAR F

WING FUEL TRANSFER/NON-RETURN VALVE

REFERENCE UNIT

AIR/NO-FUEL VALVES

VENT VALVES

HIGH-LEVEL FLOAT SWITCH · STN·586 · UNDER-WING FUEL · AIR/NO-FUEL VALVE · VENT OUTLET

RUBBER JOINTS

SPAR F · VENT PIPE

ABOVE: The wing fuel tank layout. Almost the entire wing was an integral fuel tank. BAE Systems via Warton Heritage Group

RIGHT: The fuel system layout as of March 1962, before deletion of the buddy refuelling pack. Several serious fuel leaks occurred during flight testing, with double-walled pipes and junctions failing, mostly owing to over-pressure caused by component failings elsewhere. Luckily the failures occurred late in the flights in question, and no harm was caused. BAE Systems via Warton Heritage Group

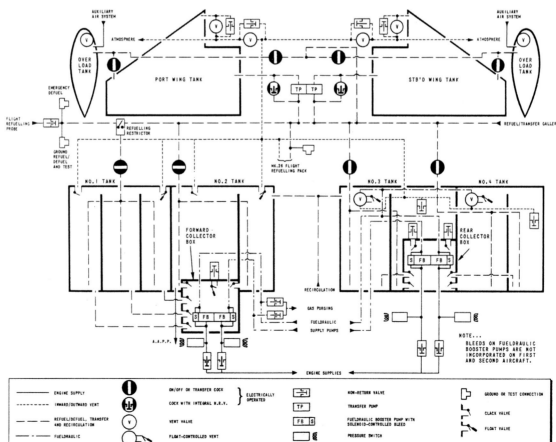

177

in use, this would result in one engine being starved, so when running on low fuel or during landing, the pilot would open a crossfeed between the two engine fuel supply lines and so keep both engines running from the single remaining fuel group. A cavitation warning would also warn the pilot of insufficient fuel pressure at the pumps, with automatic cut-out of reheat in this situation to avoid the engine falling below 100 per cent power, as was found in similar circumstances on Lightnings. A reheat failure during take-off while retaining 100 per cent dry power was far preferable to intermittent reheat with less than 100 per cent dry power – the latter combination could result in serious engine damage.

Fuel was fed from the flow proportioner or bypass to the LP cocks on the engine and reheat systems, each of which were fitted with flowmeters and filters. Fuel destined for the engine was used as a heat sink to cool the hydraulic oil, auxiliary gearbox oil and engine oil, and was therefore fed through three heat exchangers en route. Under certain circumstances this could raise the temperature of the fuel beyond the permissible limits for the engine burners, so a recirculation system could feed fuel back into the fuselage tanks if necessary. Under normal sortie conditions and when using AVTUR fuel, this would introduce no limitations on engine use, but, if AVTAG fuel was used, certain minor limitations in range

and performance would have to be expected due to that fuel's lower boiling point and lower specific gravity. In particular, a period of cruising flight would result in high fuel temperatures and thus introduce speed limits (for example, low speed limit above 27,000ft (8,230m) in the worst case of a Mach 2 cruise at 40,000ft (12,000m) with proportioner bypass in use).

Ground refuelling was via a single fuselage point located at the aft end of the nose gear bay, feeding into a refuelling gallery running along the fuselage with branches running into the wing tanks. Each tank had a top-level switch which would close the tank to further fuel inflow once it was full. The port forward fuselage was plumbed for a retractable in-flight refuelling probe fitted with a standard Mk 8 nozzle, which would be housed in a removable fairing below the port cockpit area. Both ground and in-flight refuelling was specified at a maximum rate of 500gal/hr (2,270L/hr) (later reduced slightly), enabling the aircraft's tanks to be filled in around 12min. Both crew members would have controls to extend or retract the in-flight refuelling probe, but only the navigator could open the refuelling valve, as it was his duty to manage refuelling.

Defuelling was to be carried out via the refuelling point in the rear of the nose gear bay, with low-rate emergency (suction) defuelling or higher-rate defuelling carried out by opening all crossfeeds and non-return

valves and using the fuel booster pumps to drive fuel into the fuel gallery and out of the refuelling point. Fuel jettison in flight was not considered necessary, as the undercarriage was strong enough to handle a landing at maximum AUW. However, as the engine problems arose during development the question of fuel jettison was raised by Roland Beamont, who pointed out that maintaining height on a single engine if one should fail with a full fuel load would require placing the remaining engine into the danger zone of possible LP shaft failure. Accordingly a basic fuel-jettisoning system was incorporated into the development-batch airframes, mounted in the down-turned wingtips and making use of existing fuel vent piping. As BAC had been forced by circumstances into adding this system, the RAF took the opportunity to ask for it to be retained in production aircraft, ideally as a faster jettisoning system than already provided, but had the cost increase been unacceptable the Service would have settled for the basic system already in place.

The weight of remaining fuel within an aircraft naturally has an effect on the aircraft's c.g., and keeping that c.g. within limits is extremely important if the aircraft is to remain controllable. A difference in c.g. position was necessary on the TSR2 for easy take-off, transonic cruise and when carrying underwing stores. Thus the TSR2's fuel system included an automatic balancing

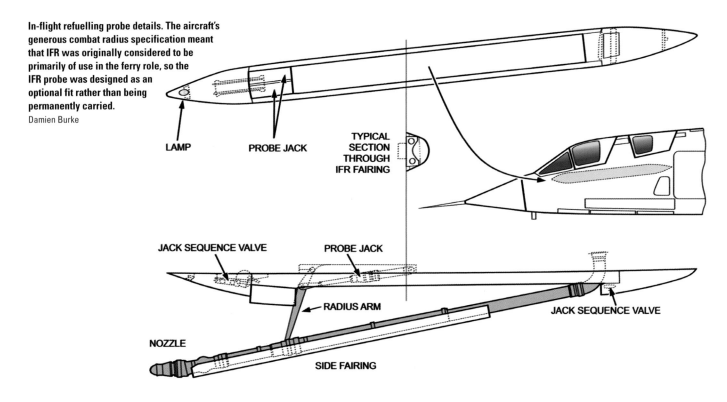

In-flight refuelling probe details. The aircraft's generous combat radius specification meant that IFR was originally considered to be primarily of use in the ferry role, so the IFR probe was designed as an optional fit rather than being permanently carried.
Damien Burke

LAMP   PROBE JACK   TYPICAL SECTION THROUGH IFR FAIRING

JACK SEQUENCE VALVE   PROBE JACK

RADIUS ARM   JACK SEQUENCE VALVE

NOZZLE   SIDE FAIRING

component (an improvement over the manual systems provided in most aircraft), and was designed to feed fuel in such a way as to maintain a slightly forward c.g. Taken to extremes, if the rear fuel group were to be entirely emptied, the forward group would still contain approximately 2,500lb (1,135kg) of fuel. Any imbalance beyond specified limits would result in warning lights illuminating in the cockpit, and the pilot would then be able to rebalance the system manually by transferring fuel from one group to another.

One of the requirements of OR.343 was to provide a 'range remaining' readout for the navigator. To allow for this, not only was fuel contents gauging used, but flow metering was in place too, as both methods had inherent accuracy problems at low fuel levels and the combination could help to eliminate these errors.

Buddy refuelling

Included in the initial requirements was the capability for any TSR2 to act as a buddy refuelling tanker for other aircraft. This would be achieved by fitting a buddy refuelling pack within the weapons bay, with the bay doors removed and a bulbous fairing housing a hose-and-drogue unit (HDU) based on the Mk 20 unit then in common use with Fleet Air Arm Scimitars (the TSR2 unit was to be the Mk 26). Unlike the Mk 20, which generated its own electrical power via a small wind-driven turbine, the Mk 26 was powered by the aircraft's own AC system. An arm would lower from the fairing to give the hose and drogue sufficient clearance away from the hot exhaust gasses from the engines and also the vortices generated by the wings. Work began on this pack at Flight Refuelling Ltd in 1960, and progressed fairly well through 1961. The capacity of the pack itself was not overly impressive, being a mere 400gal (1,818L) (reduced to as little as 325gal (1,475L) when allowance was made for the channel into which the extending arm would retract). With the pack closed, the aircraft's performance was required to be the same as with no pack fitted at all, though lower g limits would apply. With the boom arm deployed, a 450kt (520mph; 834km/h) limit would be in place (the same as for flying with the aircraft's own refuelling probe extended).

In August 1962, after the RAF had carried out a general survey of planned TSR2 operations, it decided that it could do without buddy refuelling, and the requirement was promptly cancelled, saving £0.5 million in the process. The ability to receive fuel from Victor tankers or other types was, however, still a requirement. A study comparing the TSR2's flight envelope with that of the Victor was carried out by BAC, and it appeared that throughout the band in which Victors carried out refuelling, the TSR2 would be able to plug in and keep up in dry power.

Overload tanks

Provision for additional fuel tanks to extend the aircraft's range was written into the requirement and specification from an early date, but actual work on this was very much an on/off affair, with apparent bursts of enthusiasm for the idea punctuated by months of inactivity. Overload tanks to be carried under the wings were expected to

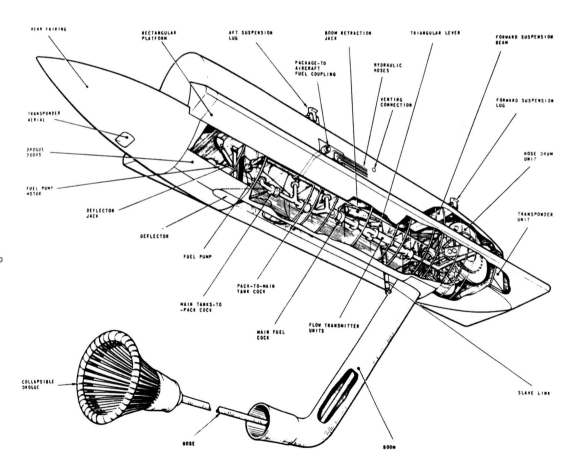

A general arrangement of Flight Refuelling Ltd's Mk 26 buddy refuelling pack. BAE Systems via Warton Heritage Group

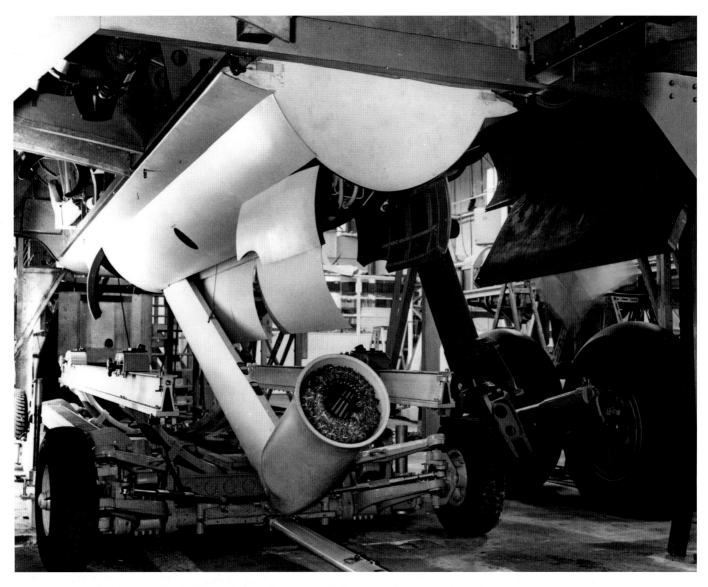

ABOVE: **Flight Refuelling's Mk 26 buddy refuelling pack reached mockup form before the requirement was dropped.** BAE Systems via Brooklands Museum

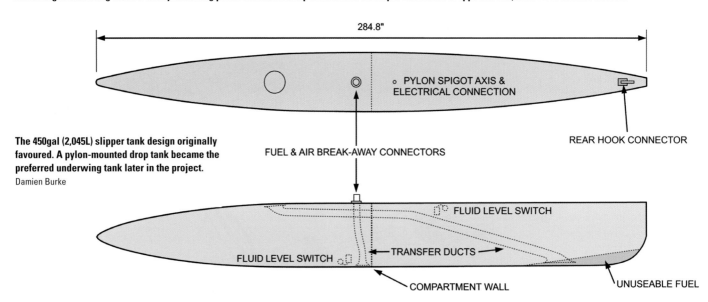

284.8"

PYLON SPIGOT AXIS &
ELECTRICAL CONNECTION

REAR HOOK CONNECTOR

FUEL & AIR BREAK-AWAY CONNECTORS

The 450gal (2,045L) slipper tank design originally
favoured. A pylon-mounted drop tank became the
preferred underwing tank later in the project.
Damien Burke

FLUID LEVEL SWITCH

FLUID LEVEL SWITCH

TRANSFER DUCTS

COMPARTMENT WALL

UNUSEABLE FUEL

be of 450gal (2,045L) capacity each. As the wing was to be designed for external stores carriage on a pair of pylon positions, the first suggestion was to carry drop tanks on one or the other of the proposed pylon locations. However, windtunnel tests with early stores layouts had shown that there were significant destabilizing effects from larger stores and a 450gal fuel tank certainly came under that description. After very brief consideration of an overwing location similar to the overwing tanks on the Lightning, a slipper fuel tank attached directly to the wing was drawn up.

This tank was to be positioned under the wing on a line centred at station 120, the inner pylon mount point. This 450gal tank would afford extra endurance but no actual increase in combat radius unless it was jettisoned when empty (indeed, retaining the tank would actually decrease combat radius); definitely a wartime or emergency-only exercise owing to the expense involved. Jettison would be achieved by an ejector gun pushing the tank downward at its centre point, rotating about the rear attachment until it reached 90 degrees, at which point the rear attachment would disengage and allow the tank to fall free, clear of the tailplane. Windtunnel tests without an ejector gun had found that the tank remained in place or would not drop away cleanly in certain flight attitudes, particularly at slow speeds with the aircraft pitched up (such as during take-off and landing).

The slipper tank later fell out of favour, and pylon-mounted drop tanks re-entered the picture. With a rounded nose similar to the slipper design, the new tanks would not be cleared for supersonic flight, but they were aerodynamically superior to the slipper tanks, and it was estimated that the decreased drag would mean that they would now carry no range penalty if retained when empty, and on the long-range ferry sortie profile a small range increase would result even if the tanks were kept. Jettisoning them when empty was still the only way to gain any appreciable benefit on a combat sortie, however, and in this case an additional 200nm (230 miles; 370km) range (100nm combat radius) would be gained. The fuel cock permitting transfer from the drop tank to the wing tanks was a modification embodied on all TSR2 airframes from XR220 onwards; XR219 would have been unable to carry drop tanks as a result.

A variety of schemes for a fuselage overload tank were also looked at. Initially, in 1961, just two versions were investigated, a 570gal (2,590L) weapons-bay tank (held entirely within the bay and giving 250nm (290 miles; 465km) extra range) and a 900gal (4,090L) tank (which would protrude below the bay to about the same extent as the reconnaissance pack, and require the bay doors to be removed, but give 400nm (460 miles; 740km) more range). In July 1963 a feasibility study into the provision of a jettisonable ventral tank was completed. It outlined a pair of designs, one of 1,000gal (4,545L) capacity and one of a whopping 1,425gal (6,475L). These were rather more attractive than underwing tanks because they would still give a sizeable range increase even if retained when empty. The smaller of the two gave an additional 280nm (322 miles; 520km), and the larger 390nm (450 miles; 725km). Jettisoning the tanks when empty would increase these figures to 400 and 560nm (460 miles; 740km and 645miles; 1,035km) respectively. These tanks would also be supersonic, unlike the wing tanks. Minor structural changes would be necessary on the airframe to cater for the ventral tank attachment points, and the ventral anti-collision beacon would need to be moved, but the ventral ILS aerial would not need to be moved as the rear part of the tank covering this area could be made of glassfibre.

In May 1964, after the arrester hook requirement had been raised, the lines of these tanks were altered so that they could be compatible with the expected hook installation, and the RAF also began to take a long hard look at just what it needed in the way of overload fuel provision. The wing tanks, despite their disadvantages, left the weapons bay free for its intended purpose and would be relatively cheap and fast to develop, so they were in. The internal weapons bay tank was also definitely needed, for ferry purposes. The larger ventral tanks would be more expensive to develop, and introduced possible problems when used in combination with internal weapons. In addition, the engine accessories bay was desperately in need of a redesign, and this could possibly have an impact upon the ventral tank lines, so the big tanks were put on the back burner, to be looked at in the future. The combination tank that sat half in the bay and half out was of no interest, and was dropped.

By the end of 1964 the cautious attitude at the Air Ministry and MoA, where the project's future was already felt to be in serious doubt, meant that no further work on overload tanks was authorized before the cancellation.

A model of the pylon-mounted 450gal (2,045L) drop tank, photographed using a long exposure during a preliminary static-drop test. The pins extending from the pylon were for forcibly separating the tank from the pylon. BAE Systems via Brooklands Museum

Details of the ventral tank fuel system. BAE Systems

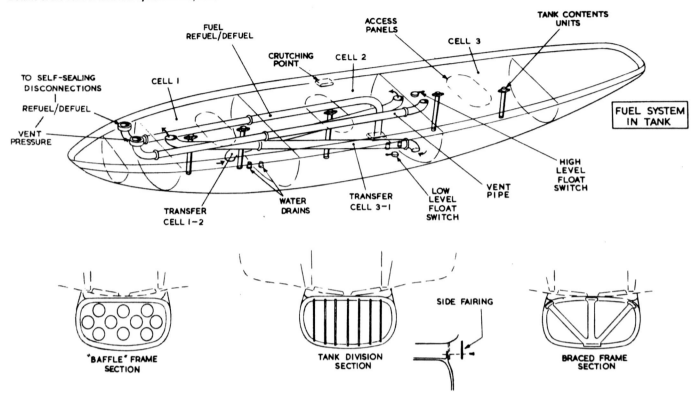

The ventral tank. Primarily intended for the ferry role, this large 1,425gal (6,480L) tank was unlikely to be used on combat missions. BAE Systems

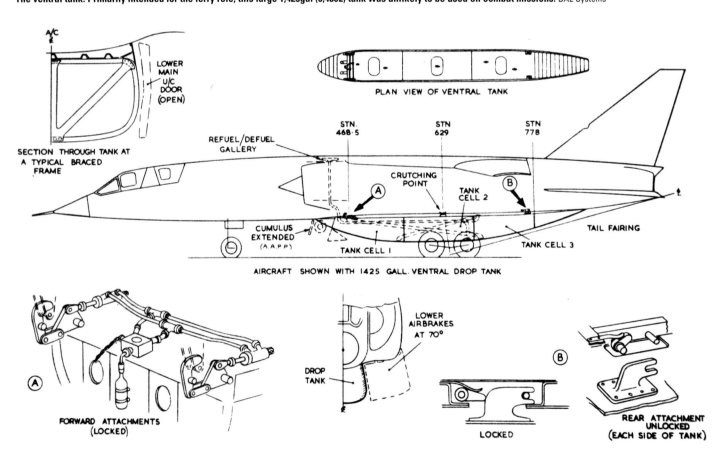

Hydraulic system

Hydraulics were divided into two systems: general services (airbrakes, flaps, weapons bay doors, intake cones, intake auxiliary doors, artificial feel, wheel brakes and steering, flight refuelling probe, etc.), and flying controls (tailerons and flaps, fin, braking parachute release). Each system had a backup, so in total there were four self-contained systems on the aircraft. Each engine drove one controls and one services pump via the accessory drive gearbox, with pressure normally held at 4,000psi (280kg/sq cm). Relief valves would vent excess if it rose above 4,800psi (337kg/sq cm).

The two controls systems included accumulators that acted as boosters during high-rate manoeuvring and also provided limited control surface movement in the event of hydraulic failure (if both engines failed, for example). Windmilling engines would provide enough hydraulic pressure to maintain adequate control power as long as airspeed was kept above 220kt (250mph; 400km/h). Services system No. 1 included two accumulators, one for the artificial-feel

RIGHT: **The layout of the hydraulic system. Two serious hydraulic leaks were experienced during flight testing, one near the end of Flight 23 as an artificial feel unit leaked, emptying the Services 1 system, and the fin-jack-ram fracture that caused Flight 25 to be aborted before take-off.** BAE Systems via Brooklands Museum

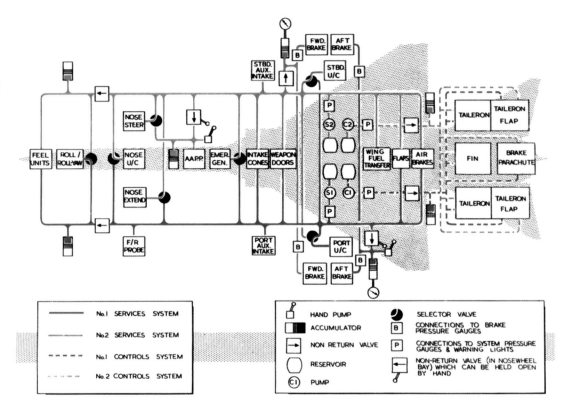

BELOW: **Electrical system components.** BAE Systems via Brooklands Museum

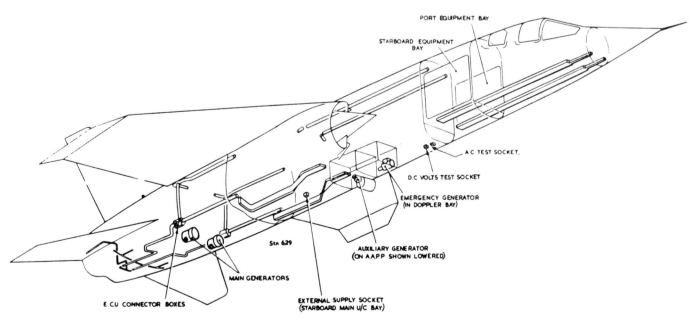

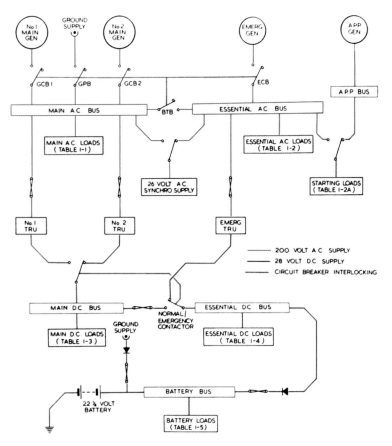

units and yaw/roll gearbox and the other for the aft wheel brakes. Services No. 2 had three accumulators, the first again for artificial feel and yaw/roll gearbox, the second for the forward wheel brakes, and the last for AAPP raising/lowering and emergency nosewheel steering.

The choice of DP47 (Silcodyne H) for the hydraulic fluid was made because of its superior properties at high temperatures and pressures, but gave rise to a succession of problems throughout the project, with filters, seals and couplings all proving inadequate at one point or another. Unlike normal hydraulic fluid, DP47 was colourless, and this led to an unexpected problem in that minor spills were difficult to spot, and the airframes gradually became increasingly contaminated with DP47 throughout production. An expensive clean-up was necessary before any paint could be applied to the first three aircraft, and measures had to be introduced to try to reduce contamination of subsequent airframes.

Electrical system

The aircraft's electrical supply was designed to have safety factors similar to other systems, with duplication and backups. It was a 200V three-phase AC system, driven by two engine-gearbox-mounted 60KVA generators. Ground-running power for the engine starting system and certain other essential services was provided by an auxiliary generator driven by the AAPP, located in the AAPP bay just ahead of the weapons bay. The AAPP could not be run in flight, and before use it would be extended out of its bay. The door hinged at the forward end of the bay and the AAPP exhausted to the starboard side.

There was a further hydraulically driven emergency generator in the Doppler bay, which, in the unlikely event of both generators failing, would provide power to the essential bus-bar and maintain the aircraft's essential services. Transformer-rectifier units in the port and starboard equipment bays provided DC power. A battery in the starboard equipment bay also gave limited DC power for some systems (this was very limited on the first aircraft, the capacity and longevity of the battery coming in for sustained criticism from the crews).

External DC and AC supplies could be plugged in to access points within the nose gear bay. For refuelling operations, only DC would be required.

ABOVE: The layout of the electrical system. BAE Systems via Brooklands Museum

LEFT: A Rotax advert of March 1965. via Brooklands Museum

The Engine

Medway versus Olympus

Both English Electric and Vickers had chosen the same Rolls-Royce engine for their GOR.339 submissions, the RB.142 Medway turbofan. This was to be a military derivative of the RB.141, an engine on which Rolls-Royce was working (and financing itself) for a medium-haul airliner for BEA. (This was the D.H.121, later to be known as the Trident, which ended up using an entirely different engine, the Rolls-Royce Spey.) Turbofans, or bypass engines, direct some of their compressed intake air around the central core of the engine, bypassing the combustion chambers. At the time, dealing with the differing flows of the slower and cooler bypass air and the faster and hotter exhaust air in the reheat jet pipe was thought by some to be a likely cause of development problems, and this, plus lower expected thrust from this type of engine, were factors that did not put it in a favourable position. One big plus point on the Medway's side was its fuel consumption,

which was going to be considerably better than that of turbojet designs.

Among the alternatives was a well-known turbojet, the Bristol Aero Engines Olympus. By mid-1958 the basic Olympus design was already seven years old. It had been in service, powering RAF Vulcans, since 1956, and it was building a reputation for reliability and ruggedness unmatched by any similar engine. The Olympus Mk 101 (B.Ol.1) was a 11,000lb (5,000kg)-thrust engine that powered the Vulcan B.1; the Mk 201 (B.Ol.6) that was being delivered to power the Vulcan B.2 had been uprated to 17,000lb (8,000kg). An even more powerful engine, the Mk 301 (to be fitted to the Vulcan B.2 during the 1960s), was also under development. Bristol had used the 201 as the basis for a research engine, the B.Ol.14R (R for reheat), with turbine and combustion chambers redesigned to operate at lower temperatures and thus improve specific fuel consumption (SFC). By May 1958 the 14R had undergone enough testing to demonstrate 13,620lb (6,180kg) dry

thrust and considerable improvements in fuel economy compared with previous Olympus variants, and the B.Ol.15R (a development of the 14R) was beginning testing. Both the 14R and 15R were proposed by Bristol as possible powerplants for the GOR.339, with reheat units based on work by an American company called Solar. Brochure figures for the 15R predicted a thrust of 16,400lb (7,443kg) (dry, 0.779 SFC) and 24,700lb (11,210kg) (reheat, 1.785 SFC). The Medway's predicted figures were nearly identical in terms of thrust, with better fuel consumption in dry power and worse fuel consumption in reheat, but overall it appeared to be a better choice of engine.

In July 1958 Bristol made a further submission based on a developed 15R, the B.Ol.22R, and withdrew the 14R from the running. This brochure predicted that the 22R would produce a thrust of 16,803lb (7,627kg) (dry, 0.71 SFC) and 30,554lb (13,868kg) (reheat, 1.77 SFC). Purely on brochure figures the Medway now lagged

Olympus B.Ol.22R - Mk.320

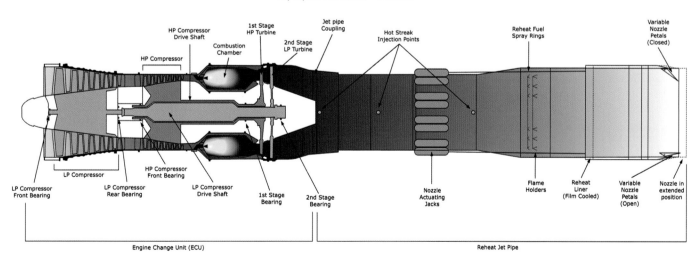

A general-arrangement drawing of the Bristol-Siddeley Olympus B.Ol.22R. Damien Burke

behind, if only slightly, in all but dry power fuel consumption. In September 1958 officials from the MoS and the Treasury made a decision that put Rolls-Royce out of the running, with only cursory attention paid to the actual performance of the competing engines. Rolls-Royce's estimates on development cost for the engine, after appropriately pessimistic adjustments by the Ministry, were seen as much the same as those from Bristol Aero Engines, but unfortunately Rolls-Royce was simply doing too well as an engine company. Both the MoS and the Treasury felt that it was 'desirable to keep some rival to Rolls-Royce' in business. Rolls-Royce products were apparently becoming the engines of choice in both the civil and military fields, and they did not want them to become a monopoly. Bristol Aero Engines went away and came back with revised cost figures that drastically undercut Rolls-Royce. Furthermore, the men from the Ministry also believed that work on the 22R would directly benefit from the Olympus 21 (Mk 301) development and lead to a faster and cheaper result from both engines, despite there being no real commonality in the respective tasks each engine was destined to perform.

Rolls-Royce's proposals were discarded, and the MoS issued an edict in December 1958 that no further proposals for a powerplant would be sought from Rolls-Royce. The arrival of a final brochure from the company merely gave the MoS the opportunity to cite insufficient take-off thrust for the Medway as a reason to go with the Olympus. When the decision was made to go ahead with the GOR.339 (or TSR2 as it was to be known), the choice of engine was also to be announced. There was, technically, 'not much in it', the Ministry admitted privately, but the more important factors were the future size and shape of the aero-engine industry and the shotgun marriage that could be arranged between Bristol Aero Engines and Armstrong Siddeley Motors. This had been pushed into being even before the official announcement of the Olympus decision was made, and the result was Bristol Siddeley Engines, later Bristol Siddeley Engines Ltd.

Unaware of the real reasons for the decision, BAC was not impressed by the choice, and George Edwards stated in a meeting with the Ministry on 1 January 1959 that they needed a further two months to assess the merits of the two engines, and that in any case such a decision should be a choice left to the aircraft designer. The Ministry

was not about to let its decision be overturned, and wanted agreement that very day from BAC. After retiring to discuss it, the meeting reconvened and BAC submitted to the Ministry's choice, on the condition that when the announcement was made it would be made clear that the responsibility for the selection of the engine lay with the Ministry and not with BAC.

Rolls-Royce, unaware of the other factors behind the decision, produced a flurry of communications protesting against the choice of the Olympus, further detailing its belief in the superiority of the Medway, and attempting to enlist help from the RAF and the National Gas Turbine Establishment (NGTE) to press its case. It seemed pretty clear that the Medway was to be a more advanced design (and not 'handicapped' by being a development of an existing engine), would be more economical and had a promise of great development potential. Unfortunately for Rolls-Royce (and arguably, as it transpired, for the project as a whole) all of its protests came to naught.

In February Rolls-Royce received a final brush-off from the MoS that made it clear, based on RAE and NGTE findings, that the Olympus was regarded as being more powerful and more suitable for the TSR2. Contract negotiations and technical discussions with BSEL rumbled on through the first half of 1959. In March the NGTE completed its evaluation of the 15R and found that Bristol's fuel consumption figures had been optimistic to the tune of about 5 per cent, a massive difference which would have serious consequences for the amount of fuel needed and thus the weight of the aircraft. If a reduction in range could be accepted, however, the engine would do the job, especially if take-off thrust could be improved. The NGTE's initial evaluations of the 22R figures indicated that fuel consumption on that engine was also likely to be worse than predicted, but, without an actual engine to run, further evaluation was going to be theoretical.

In April BSEL dropped a bombshell. Exasperated by the snail's pace of contract negotiations with the MoS, and concerned that stretching the 15R to meet the requirement could be a long and expensive process, it warned that the predicted development costs had risen dramatically, from around £4 million to a stunning £15 million. The reaction was not one it expected. The Ministry informed them that it was instigating an immediate investigation into the

circumstances of this increase, and that, if the figures were correct, the competition between engine companies would be reopened. In the meantime the Ministry would not be liable for any costs incurred by BSEL on any TSR2 engine work.

The investigation certainly succeeded in scaring BSEL into producing some lower figures, though the Ministry did not, it appears, have any serious intention of reopening the competition. The Treasury stepped in, objecting to the MoS's edict against further consideration of Rolls-Royce proposals, because if BSEL was being given the opportunity to offer improved figures, then it was unfair not to let Rolls-Royce have another crack at it. The Ministry refused to budge. The RAF also refused to accept a drop in range, and it became clear that the Olympus 15R was not going to be suitable and that the even more expensive 22R was going to be necessary. BSEL offered two versions of the 22R, one containing an extra compressor stage and able to cope with intake air up to temperatures of 146°, and one with two extra compressor stages and able to cope with temperatures up to 180°. Development costs for these would be £8 million and £10.3 million respectively; still much more than BSEL's original estimates, but not as frightening as that £15 million figure.

Further delay ensued while the MoS and the Treasury argued the toss over the selection of an engine supplier, nearly a year after the decision had already been taken. By May BSEL had realized that further work was going to be tricky in the face of uncertainty as to which of its engines was really going to be required, but that work on the reheat unit could at least continue, as the same size of reheat unit would be required regardless of the engine chosen. Not until August 1959 was BSEL in a position to be entirely confident that it had the job of producing the engine, although a signed contract would not be in its hands until nearly the end of the year. The company had agreed to a fixed-cost contract to develop the engine up to initial CA release (predicted at that point to be mid-1965), with provisions for profit reductions and cost penalties if certain targets were not met. The 146° 22R was the choice; and BSEL had been beaten down to a development cost of £8 million, just £1.5 million more than the amount the MoS had privately believed would be necessary.

Engine specification

The final specification for the overall aircraft, RB.192D, laid out a tight requirement for engine performance. Single-engine flight was to enable steady flight at altitudes up to 40,000ft (12,000m) in reheat or 30,000ft (9,000m) without reheat. No surging would be permissible within the aircraft's normal flight envelope, including during weapons release, even when making large throttle movements. Slam accelerations, opening the throttle to 100 per cent as quickly as possible, were to take no more than 1sec below 10,000ft (3,000m) or 3sec above that altitude, with the engine itself responding in a smooth and rapid manner, accelerating to the required speed in a similar timeframe. Repeated slam accelerations or decelerations were to be permitted in a range of flight conditions, and when the aircraft was stationary on the ground, to enable carefree engine handling particularly in the take-off and landing phases. The reheat unit was to be fully variable, and would be required to operate in a stable manner throughout the flight envelope with similarly tight constraints on response time to slam accelerations. Running on either AVTUR or AVTAG fuel, all of the

handling requirements needed to be met throughout the aircraft's flight envelope up to an altitude of 56,000ft (17,000m), with performance to remain satisfactory up to 70,000ft (21,000m). Some limitations would be accepted when running on AVCAT fuel, these to be decided based on flight testing.

Following on from these requirements, the MoA's Directorate of Engine Research and Development issued its own more detailed specification to cover the engines used for bench testing and development-batch aircraft, this specification being issued as D.Eng.RD.2437. The highlights of this specification were that each engine was to weigh 4,290lb (1,950kg) (for the basic unit; including the reheat unit and accessories, the weight would rise to 6,150lb (2,790kg)) and produce thrust of 30,610lb (13,890kg) in full reheat or 16,780lb (7,615kg) in full dry power, with an SFC of 1.87 (reheat) or 0.70 (dry) respectively. The fuel consumption figures in particular would prove difficult targets to meet.

The aircraft's speed and range requirements also complicated matters. Initially, RB.192D had been rather vague about the aircraft's top speed of Mach 2, with no solid requirement for just how long such a speed

should be maintained, though it did mention the ability to cover 1,000nm at Mach 1.7. The 22R could handle the turbine entry temperatures necessary for sustained flight at Mach 2 only at the expense of a short overhaul life. Alternatively, if the turbine entry temperature could be reduced and extra reheat used to restore the lost thrust, sustained Mach 2 flight and a normal overhaul life would be possible, but at the expense of higher fuel consumption and thus a reduction in range.

Engine testing at the NGTE

The major problem facing BSEL was the fact that the existing Olympus variants were all designed for the subsonic role, and sustained supersonic performance introduced a host of challenges regarding intake design and the speed, temperature and pressure of intake air. The addition of a reheat unit was a relatively simple task by comparison, and on this score at least BSEL had already been experimenting with reheat on the Olympus 14R. The Olympus 22R, unlike the 14R, was based upon the Olympus 21 (the Mk 301 for the Vulcan B.2), and its exterior appearance showed some

An Olympus 22R running in reheat in a test cell at Patchway. Without facilities like this and those offered by the NGTE, Olympus development, along with that of most British jet engines, would have been next to impossible for any single manufacturer. Rolls-Royce Heritage Trust via Brooklands Museum

similarities to the 21, the major difference being the large reheat unit. Owing to the higher temperatures and pressures involved, the materials used in constructing the engine were different in some areas, notably the compressors, conventional alloys being used less and being replaced with titanium, steel and nimonic.

While Bristol's own plant at Filton had basic engine-test facilities, the NGTE at Pyestock near Farnborough was to be used for much of the simulated flight-testing engine runs, the Establishment's newly uprated test cells making it possible to test-run engines in a variety of conditions, including high-altitude in the newest test cell. A relatively small establishment, NGTE Pyestock specialized in engine component testing before 1957, but underwent massive expansion from that point onward to enable the testing of complete engines in heavily armoured and instrumented test cells. Complete engines could be lowered by crane into a test cell, connected to an array of instrumentation and run continuously on endurance and power tests. The cells themselves were huge steel-walled cylinders. The first, Cells 1 and 2, designed initially for ramjet testing, were of 12ft (3.6m) diameter and 120ft (36.5m) long. Cell 3, opened in 1962, was designed for altitude testing and had a larger diameter of 20ft (6.0m), though it was shorter, at 80ft (24.4m). Each cell had an adjoining control room (Cells 1 and 2 shared a single room situated between them). Small armoured glass windows looked into the cells, which were supplied with air piped from the huge Air House elsewhere on the site. Exhaust was directed away from the cells into large diffusers, but even so, the thunderous roar from the NGTE could be heard for miles around whenever engines were being run at high power.

Initial tests were made with an Olympus 22DR (a derivative engine, basically an Olympus 201 with an added LP compressor stage), and mostly showed that Cell 2 was not really up to the job of testing such a large engine. Much work was done to improve the cell's capability to handle the amounts of intake and exhaust airflow, and Cell 2 was later used for much of the low-altitude/high-subsonic-speed simulation work, while Cell 3 handled the high-altitude work. The intention was that test results in Cells 2 and 3 would be verified with results obtained from mounting an Olympus on an Avro Vulcan flying test bed (FTB). However, intake temperatures for

sustained supersonic flight were significantly higher than those experienced in subsonic operations, and one of the major tests was to run the engines in a suitable test cell, one with heated intake air. The MoA wanted the engine to be able to deal with intake air at a temperature of 146°, with short periods at 180°. No testing cell existed that was capable of providing intake air of this temperature, so considerable effort went into the creation, and subsequent testing, of a unit to provide heated intake air to the new test Cell 4. On at least one occasion the pre-heater that provided the heated intake air malfunctioned, allowing unburnt heater fuel to be sprayed into the Olympus and causing the engine to overheat as a result.

Engine description

Meeting the sustained 146° intake temperature requirement needed some substantial reworking of the existing Olympus design, some of which would be far-reaching in its implications, notably the relocation of the HP thrust bearing between the LP and HP compressor driveshafts to the intermediate casing, which required lengthening and expansion of the LP shaft. This simplified

the supply of both cooling air and oil to the bearings. The first Olympus 22, the 22DR, initially used a single additional LP compressor stage with aluminium blades, but these proved susceptible to flutter during testing and were replaced by titanium blades that helped alleviate the problem, though did not entirely cure it.

The 22R's LP compressor spool had eight stages (seven for the 22DR and six for previous Olympus variants), and the HP compressor spool, seven. The combustion system had eight fuel injection points as with earlier Olympus marks, but two fewer flame tubes. The reheat system was of conventional design, with a parallel-sided duct linking the engine to the reheat diffuser section, combustion section and the fully variable nozzle. Eight pairs of pneumatic jacks operated rods extending rearwards to the annular shroud, which operated the fully-variable final nozzle area. The nozzle was of convergent shape. Reheat lighting was by the hot streak method, which entailed the injection of fuel upstream of the turbine, producing a streak of flame that was conveyed to the reheat combustion zone via fuel injection points in the jetpipe. Combustion stabilization was again conventional, with three annular spray rings and V-shaped gutters. Thermal blankets

L.P. COMPRESSOR ROTOR

An Olympus 22R LP compressor rotor. The redesigned LP rotor shaft of the 22R suffered several dramatic failures, resulting in expensive delays for the entire TSR2 programme. Rolls-Royce Heritage Trust

wrapped the engine aft of the HP compressor casing, cooling airflow being directed in the space between the engines and the engine mounting tunnel walls.

Control of the engine was to be by a combined electro-hydro-mechanical system, Bristol having successfully used such a system on its Proteus turboprop (used by the Saunders-Roe Princess flying boat and the Bristol Britannia airliner). Rather than have any mechanical link between the pilot's throttle levers and the engines, actuators on the engine would be driven by electrical signals from control units on the levers. In the event of a fault in the 115V 400Hz AC electrical system, the engines would remain in their current running state, and a manually switched backup 28V DC supply would enable emergency throttle control via a DC motor driving the throttle. The engine was fitted with various sensors to protect it against a variety of dangerous conditions, such as a turbine temperature limiter that would progressively close the throttle automatically if preset temperature limits were exceeded. In testing, the control amplifier and associated units that made up the electrical portion of the engine control circuit proved very reliable, and this contributed greatly to the ease of engine handling.

Three initial versions of the 22R were to be developed. The Mk 320X was a limited performance version, given certain concessions to deviate from the required specification, and to be fitted only to the first few airframes (nine engines to be built). The Mk 320 would then attempt to meet all the required targets and be fitted to the remaining development-batch aircraft (eighteen engines to be built). The Mk 321 was the production version of the engine, to be fitted to pre-production aircraft (an initial batch of thity-five engines to be built).

Starting the engine

The original OR had required a rapid engine-starting time of 10sec, similar to that of fighter types required to scramble in a hurry. This was revised downward to 35, to 45sec, and later to 'under one minute' which gave much more scope to consider different starting schemes. Ten different options for an engine starting system were investigated, including external LP air sources and AVPIN starting as used on the Lightning and Javelin, but the final choice was a Palouste carried as a permanent AAPP.

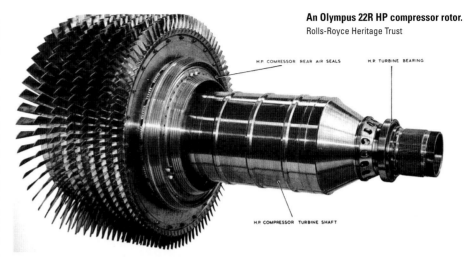

An Olympus 22R HP compressor rotor.
Rolls-Royce Heritage Trust

H.P. COMRESSOR REAR AIR SEALS
H.P. TURBINE BEARING
H.P. COMPRESSOR TURBINE SHAFT

The Cumulus auxiliary power plant was mounted in a small bay forward of the weapons bay and Doppler compartment, though the first two aircraft were not fitted with Cumulus, using the vacant bay for flight test instrumentation.
BAE Systems via Brooklands Museum

Vickers was responsible for this area of the aircraft, and its initial choice of location for the AAPP was on the top of the fuselage behind the wing, within the curved spine present on the early drawings for the aircraft. However, the spine was removed when the wing design was finalized, and the remaining space in the area was reserved for the flap-blowing pipes and flap actuating mechanism. An alternative upper location ahead of the wing was unsuitable, as it encroached upon structural members and fuel tanks, so a significant weight and fuel penalty would be incurred even if the structural issues could be resolved. The third choice therefore became the final location for the AAPP; a small bay just ahead of the weapons bay, where, in retracted position, the AAPP would be on the aircraft centreline.

The lower location also offered distinct advantages in terms of weight and complexity. The unit could be lowered with gravity assistance rather than the hydraulic power needed to raise a unit positioned higher, and could also operate using a gravity fuel feed, needing no additional fuel pump. The AAPP would be attached to the bay door, which hinged at the port edge. When the door was opened for operation the AAPP would hang down, offset to the port side, with the intake forward and exhausting to the rear, inclined 5 degrees downwards. This was quickly found to be an unsuitable orientation, as with the AAPP in operation the hot jet exhaust would preclude any access to the weapons bay or undercarriage bays. Instead, the AAPP's orientation was changed by 90 degrees so that the intake was from the port side with exhaust to the starboard side. Although this would create a substantial danger zone to the starboard side of the aircraft within a narrow cone

starting at the port intake, it was considered to be acceptable. The AAPP would be removable, with the aircraft able to be flown without it. External LP air connectors would be available for ground LP supply if needed.

Blackburn, licensed manufacturer of the Palouste (a Turbomeca product), proposed an improved APU based on the Palouste but of higher power output, smaller dimensions and less weight (though development would see its weight rise). In August 1960 this improved unit was named the Cumulus and accepted as the AAPP for the TSR2. At this time, any thought of being able to extend the AAPP in flight to cater for restart of a flamed-out engine was also discarded, as the characteristics of the Olympus 22R were becoming more apparent and it was realized a windmilling re-start would be possible at speeds down to 200kt (230mph; 370km/h) (a year earlier, 300kt (345mph; 555km/h) had been the expected

figure). A warning light would now indicate if the AAPP was still lowered when the pilot made the switch selection taking the aircraft from Ground to Flight before starting a take-off, and a further warning and automatic retraction would occur if the undercarriage began retracting with the AAPP still extended.

The Cumulus's greater power enabled the addition of an alternator to provide limited AC power to the aircraft to run some systems without engine or external power being provided. Chief among these systems was the Stable Platform, which could then be kept running during a rearming/refuelling turnaround, thus avoiding the 15min warm-up period, though from a flight safety point of view it was preferable that the AAPP was shut down during refuelling in peacetime. The AAPP was initially to be started via a hand-pumped hydraulic accumulator(!) but a more practical cartridge starter was eventually specified.

The auxiliary power plant bay of XR222; the first two aircraft were not fitted with the Cumulus, and the bay housed flight test instrumentation instead.
Damien Burke

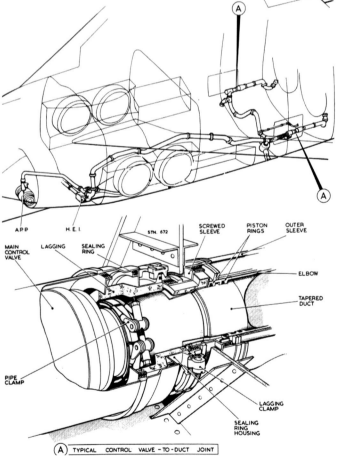

The engine-starting air supply system. BAE Systems via Brooklands Museum

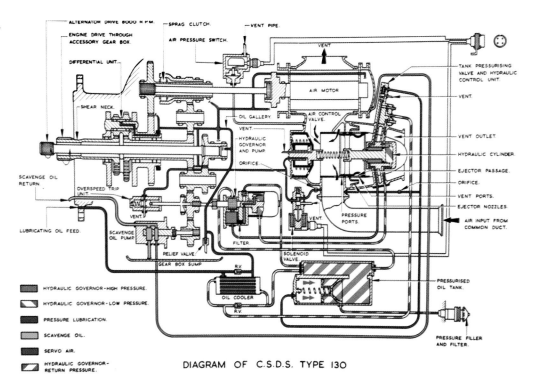

DIAGRAM OF C.S.D.S. TYPE 130

Engine starter motor and electricity generation

Jet engines of the era generated AC power by means of a generator driven by a constant-speed drive (CSD), itself driven from the engine gearbox. Effectively, the CSD was a variable-displacement hydraulic pump driving an hydraulic motor at a constant speed regardless of engine speed, the motor running the generator to provide a steady frequency.

Three CSDs were seriously considered for use on the TSR2, these being from English Electric/Sunstrand, Hobson and an entirely new unit from Plessey. The last had been developed in less than two months to a standard that already met the requirements. It comprised a pneumatic-mechanical drive with an air motor as a constant-speed trimming device, with the added bonus that the air motor could be used for engine starting through the gearbox, when operated by LP air from the AAPP. With the gearbox declutched from the engine, ground checking of gearbox accessories would also be available. Neither of the other two CSD units offered this dual functionality, and both would incur substantial weight penalties and development costs if they were combined with a starter unit. The choice of the Plessey unit was therefore easy to make, and the relatively

few problems found during NGTE's testing were straightforward to fix and resulted in a reliable unit.

Thrustmeter

Monitoring the performance of the TSR2's engines would not be simple. The Olympus engines installed in a Vulcan were easy to meter, as power output was basically decided by one simple variable, the amount of fuel flow. On the TSR2 the calculation would be more involved, with the list of variables including engine fuel flow, reheat fuel flow, intake position, reheat nozzle position (and thus area), the amount of flap-blowing bleed and also water flow. To monitor all these for both engines, along with rpm, turbine temperature and so on, would result in thirty or more gauges and warning lights for the crew to deal with. This was not considered practical for a two-man crew with their high workload at low level. Accordingly, this mass of instruments was reduced to a single thrustmeter, along with centralized warning signals for rpm and turbine temperature.

A joint Naval/Air Staff Target (No. 975) had been issued in 1957 for a gross thrust meter (also known as engine pressure ratio (EPR) indicator because it used aircraft static and jetpipe pressures to produce an indication), but by 1960 little to no work had

been done to meet this requirement, apart from basic research. This was primarily because the various engine firms believed there was no need for such an instrument when rpm and jetpipe temperature indications were adequate for the task in most circumstances. However, in many cases they were talking of multi-crew aircraft with crew members available to deal with the intricacies of calculating or looking up the correct rpm figures to set up the required flight conditions. (For example, a cruise climb at a specific airspeed given a particular outside air pressure and temperature.) In aircraft such as fighters or the TSR2 itself, reduced crew and cockpit room would make this sort of work a tricky proposition. Nor could the pilot rely on a marked throttle position to give a particular power output, as the relatively small amount of throttle movement available to him would cover a much larger variation in engine power, and so there would inevitably be variations between individual aircraft (or, rather, variations between the throttle lever position and any particular engine's response).

In contrast, many American aircraft used EPR indicators successfully, particularly to enable checking of adequate thrust before take-off. A 'gross thrust indicator' was proposed by BSEL for the Olympus 22R/TSR2 project, and as such an instrument was also required for the NA.39 (ascertaining take-off thrust before a catapult launch was a critical requirement), development of a thrustmeter became a Category 1 item. The difficulty of this apparently straightforward task was a good indicator of the unexpected complexity lying in wait for the TSR2's creators around almost every corner.

Elliot Brothers was contracted to develop the thrustmeter, but it was not until August 1961 that a firm development plan was in place. Both BSEL and BAC had put together proposals for how such a meter would measure, calculate and display its readings. Two stages of thrustmeter would be produced. The Stage 1 version, based on BSEL's specifications, was to be fitted to the first five development-batch aircraft, and the

slightly less accurate but more logically presented Stage 2 version as envisaged by BAC was to be fitted from aircraft No. 6 onwards. The Stage 1 meter suffered from a display that did not take into account ambient conditions, so on a cold day in full reheat it would indicate greater than 100 per cent. Similarly, on a hot day, it would indicate less than 100 per cent. In a way this was indeed accurate, as temperature did affect performance, but BAC's Stage 2 proposal would present 100 per cent in full reheat regardless of outside air temperature, and this was a more logical presentation of the measure of available power versus power output.

Fire protection

The TSR2 as built was effectively a flying bomb, with fuel tanks surrounding the hot engines and weapons bay, and no blade containment built into the engines. Normal RAF practice was to compartmentalize engine bays into numerous fire zones, isolating particularly risky areas and adding fire detection and suppression systems where possible. On the TSR2, BAC and BSEL believed that the high temperatures reached by the entire engine and its casing made compartmentalization effectively pointless, and while the engine installation was divided into zones 1, 2 and 3, conventional fire zoning was not practical. The result was that zone 1 enclosed the entire engine and jet-pipe installation, zone 2 was the annular space between the titanium engine heat shields and the engine tunnel walls (the fuel tank walls), and zone 3 was a small area enclosing the bay under the reheat pipe that housed the fuel pipes to the reheat pipe manifold and the nozzle control trim unit. Access to zones 1 and 3 for firefighters' hoses was provided by fire panels with break-in circular panels within them.

The RAF research department dealing with fire disagreed vehemently with the lack of conventional fire zoning, and the result was a number of requirements to reduce the likelihood of an in-flight fire. Firstly, the hydraulic fluid to be used was DP.47, also known as Silcodyne H, a supposedly low-flammability fluid designed for high-temperature areas. Secondly, fuel pipes would be double-walled (later this was extended to oil and hydraulic pipes too), despite strenuous objections from BAC. Double-walled pipes were heavier, took up more room and could actually increase the chances of leakage. The result was just as BAC feared; the double-walled pipes were a total nightmare, and the company ended

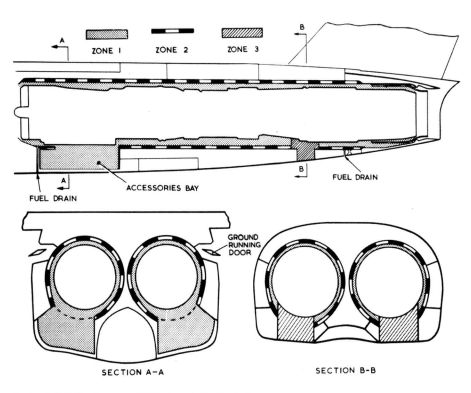

Engine installation fire zones. BAE Systems via Brooklands Museum

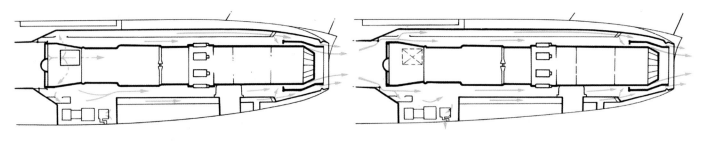

GROUND RUNNING AND LOW FORWARD SPEED CONDITION

HIGH SPEED FLIGHT CONDITION

Engine tunnel cooling arrangement. BAE Systems via Warton Heritage Group up getting a concession to revert to normal pipes later in the programme.

Both zones 1 and 3 would be cooled and ventilated by ram-air bled from the air intakes via the tunnel cooling valve between the intake and engine lip. This airflow would serve several purposes: cooling, removing possible explosive gasses (such as a fine misting fuel leak), and also distributing methyl bromide extinguisher spray throughout the engine tunnels if the fire extinguishers were activated. Methyl

bromide, a toxic chemical widely used as a pesticide, fell out of favour for fire extinguishing purposes in the late 1960s and was finally banned over thirty years later. This airflow would exhaust around the nozzle shroud (relieving some of the afterbody suction in the process and contributing to drag reduction). During ground running or at low speeds there was a danger this flow could reverse, so in these cases the tunnel cooling valve would be closed and ram air directed into zone 1 by ground-running

doors on the fuselage sides below the wing root. As with so many items on the aircraft, these doors had a backup. If the electrical motor that opened them failed, they had inset spring-loaded doors which would be sucked open as the pressure differential rose.

Fire detection was by means of Graviner firewires running throughout the accessories and reheat control bays, and also in rings around the engine. High temperatures would alter the resistance and capacitance of the wires and trigger warnings in the

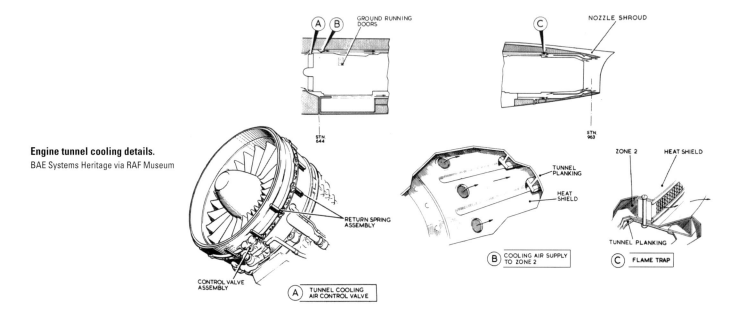

Engine tunnel cooling details.
BAE Systems Heritage via RAF Museum

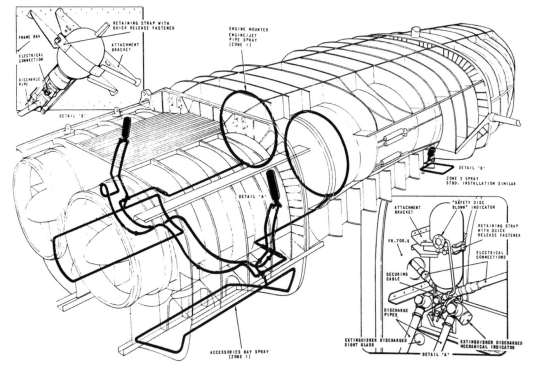

The layout of the fire extinguishing system. BAE Systems via Warton Heritage Group

crew's cockpits on the central warning panel (CWP): ENGINE 1 and 2 lights for zone 1, and REHEAT 1 and 2 lights for zone 3. Pressing the appropriate button would fire the relevant extinguishers; these would also be fired automatically by inertia switches in the event of a crash landing.

Engine test failures and the Vulcan flying test bed

Testing at the NGTE showed up a variety of minor faults with the test engines, and resulted in various design changes (such as the switch to titanium blades mentioned previously). However, of more concern were the catastrophic failures, of which there had been several by December 1962. Two were of particular concern. On 3 November 1961 engine No. 2203 was undergoing an endurance cell test when a flame tube wall broke up owing to fatigue. Consequently the LP driveshaft overheated and fractured, resulting in the overspeed and ejection of an LP compressor disc. Improvements were made, resulting in a single-piece flame wall being introduced. Then, on 16 May 1962, engine No. 2206 suffered a similar failure during another endurance test. An LP compressor disc overheated owing to inadequate cooling and burst, scattering shrapnel through the engine, though on this occasion the disc was contained.

Bristol Siddeley Engines had requested a Vulcan B.2 airframe for use as an FTB, which could then be used for both the 22R and 21 engines. The protracted contractual negotiations on the 22R project, however, soon meant that combining the two projects in a single aircraft was not going to be possible. Making further Vulcan B.2s available would have delayed that much-needed upgrade to the V-force, so the Vulcan provided by the MoS was B.1 XA894. Work began in June 1960 to modify it appropriately. This was complicated by the relatively poor state of the airframe, which required a substantial number of modifications to bring it up to a basic standard even before work began on modifying it for use as a test bed.

The 22R's reheat jetpipe made it considerably larger than the earlier marks, so it could not replace one of the Vulcan's existing engines. Furthermore, the value of the FTB would have been seriously reduced by having to use a specially modified 22R mounted in a completely different manner to the engines destined for the TSR2.

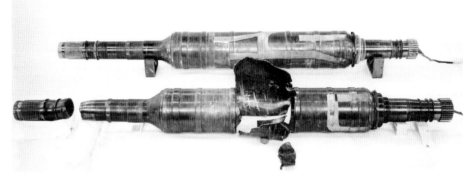

The LP drive shaft from Olympus 320 No. 2203, showing the ruptured area; compare with the undamaged shaft in the background. Rolls-Royce Heritage Trust

Accordingly a ventral installation was chosen, with the engine mounted in a fairing that, internally at least, closely resembled the area of the TSR2 airframe into which the engine would be installed. As the Vulcan airframe was decidedly subsonic there was little value to be had from including a representative TSR2 intake, and there was also the problem of the Vulcan's nose undercarriage leg. This could possibly throw debris into a centrally mounted intake during take-off and landing, so the intake needed to be ahead of the nose gear leg, and to avoid interfering with the leg's operation, a bifurcated intake was necessary.

The complete unit included not just the basic engine but also the TSR2 gearbox, complete with Plessey CSD unit, starter, alternator and two TSR2 fueldraulic pumps. Because of the fuel-flow requirements of the engine when in reheat, two additional 520gal (2,364L) fuel tanks and pumps were installed in the Vulcan's bomb bay. These were, however, still fed by the Vulcan's existing fuel system, and could not be replenished at the same rate as fuel was used by the Olympus 320. This introduced a limit of 10min in reheat within a 30min flight time. A section of lagging protected the underside of the Vulcan in the vicinity of the 320's reheat pipe, and a periscope afforded the crew some view of the entire installation (and was intended to be used for cine camera coverage, though no useful results were ever gained from it). The aircraft was expected to make its first flight with the Olympus 22R fitted at the beginning of August 1961, but delays with both the aircraft fit and the engine test runs put paid to this plan.

During December 1961 a successful 24hr endurance test run of an Olympus 320 was made in one of the Pyestock test cells,

resulting in flight clearance for the FTB installation. After the overheats that had resulted in catastrophic engine failure in the test cell, a temperature gauge for the flight test observer's position on the Vulcan FTB had been introduced so that an eye could be kept on the LP driveshaft temperature and the engine shut down if it began to overheat in this area.

The first ground run of the installed Olympus 320 was made on 31 January 1962, and the first flight followed on 23 February. After 46hr 1min of ground running and in-flight running, the engine and reheat unit were removed and replaced by improved examples, and reheat flights began in June. A further 41hr 45min of running was carried out (including a noisy appearance at that year's Society of British Aircraft Constructors' air show at Farnborough) until 3 December 1962, when events took a dramatic turn for the worse. The vulnerable LP driveshaft was about to demonstrate its destructive power once more.

XA894 had been positioned on the engine detuner stand at BSEL's Filton plant for a full-power ground run with reheat. Observers outside the aircraft saw an orange flash extending from the aircraft's belly to above the fuselage, and the entire airframe visibly lurched forward. In the cockpit the test crew felt a massive shock and saw the flash from the explosion underneath the aircraft lighting up the gloom outside. With all the fire warning lights glowing, the crew immediately abandoned the aircraft while the attending fire crew, in their particularly shiny and new fire tender, responded with commendable speed and began spraying foam over the burning aircraft. However, fuel was by now pouring out of XA894's ruptured fuel tanks, and was running down the gentle incline towards

RIGHT: **Avro Vulcan B.1 XA894, showing the ventral Olympus 320 installation with Y-shaped intake to clear the nose gear leg.** Brooklands Museum

BELOW: **XA894 made a spectacularly noisy appearance at the 1962 Farnborough air show. Nowadays, alas, the gentlemen of the press are not permitted to stand quite so close to the runway.** Brooklands Museum

LEFT: A BSEL advertisement of October 1962. Rolls-Royce Heritage Trust via Brooklands Museum

BELOW: With its Olympus 320 in reheat, XA894 was quite capable of flying along with its own engines at idle. Brooklands Museum

the fire tender. Within minutes the fire crew's position was untenable, and they had to abandon their efforts to fight the air-craft fire and concentrate on saving their own tender. This was to no avail, as the supply of burning fuel was seemingly inex-haustible. Soon they were forced to retire to a safe distance and leave both their tender and XA894 to burn through the night.

The cause of the failure was once again a rupture of the LP compressor driveshaft. The second-stage LP turbine disc was ejected from the engine and exited upwards, carving a path through the bomb-bay fuel tanks that fed the Olympus 22R unit before being directed back at the ground, where the individual blades were torn from the disc and sprayed through the port wing. Here they ruptured the Vulcan's own wing fuel tanks and tore away a section of the wing leading edge. What remained of the disc skipped across the airfield, finally coming to rest just metres away from one of the (also shiny and new) Bristol Type 188 high-speed research aircraft.

Subsequent inspection of what remained of the engine was complicated by the inten-sity of the fire that had taken hold, much of the evidence of the failure having been destroyed. Of the Vulcan itself, nothing was left but the outermost section of the port

ABOVE: Disaster strikes; XA894's Olympus 320 tears itself apart, starting the fierce fire that destroyed the aircraft. Discarded fire hoses litter the foreground of this shot. Rolls-Royce Heritage Trust

RIGHT: Another explosion rocks XA894, its rear fuselage and fin having collapsed by this point. An uncontained engine failure could have had similar results in a TSR2 airframe, in which fuel tanks surrounded the engine installation. Rolls-Royce Heritage Trust

wing and a large collection of melted alloy and ash, with a few more solid parts scattered here and there. Several months of investigation followed, and there was some evidence of fatigue cracking on parts of the LP shaft around the bearing oil drain holes. Vibration was suspected as the root cause, so BSEL's initial response was to strengthen the shaft by making it thicker, and also to try to detune the shaft by adding a pair of damping rings that were shrunk on to it. Engine No. 2203 (repaired after its earlier failure) incorporated the improved LP shaft, and bench tests began once again. Thousands of hours of running would be necessary to get reliable results, so a final verdict on the improvement was not expected until the end of March 1965, well over a year after the TSR2 was expected to have flown! Replacement of the Vulcan FTB also became a sticking point, with the MoA paralyzed by indecision. If it was replaced and another engine blew up, perhaps in the air, it would be a disaster from which the programme would be unlikely to recover. However, if it was not replaced, the overall engine programme could be delayed even further. Finally the engine test facilities at Pyestock came to the rescue, and a replacement Vulcan FTB was never authorized.

The Olympus 320's troubled development continued throughout 1963/64, development costs to CA release now having risen to £46 million, nearly six times the original estimates. Despite numerous improvements, fuel consumption was still 10 per cent above specification, which would have a direct impact on the aircraft's combat radius. The engine was also proving to be overly sensitive to intake airflow distribution conditions. While BSEL was confident it could improve fuel consumption, it was becoming clear that this was going to take a great deal of extra development, and would still be unlikely to meet the requirement, it being suggested that it would end up falling short by 5 per cent.

Performance at altitude was also going to be a problem. It would be fair to say that nobody, not BAC, BSEL or the MoA, had taken the high-altitude requirements very seriously. It had therefore been a shock when the RAF pressed the case in 1961 to require 'continuous operation' at 56,000ft (17,000m). This was a problem, as, based on the engine's current performance figures, the subsonic ceiling would be 36,000ft (11,000m) (42,000ft (12,800m) with reheat), and above this the aircraft would have to be supersonic, requiring constant

use of reheat. But BSEL had been working to a specification that meant the engine need only operate in reheat for 15min periods, and thus the aircraft would only be able to exceed 36,000ft for brief periods. To make matters worse, reheat could only be engaged when the engine was at maximum dry power, and it was limited to 12hr of such use before overhaul was required. At least this limitation could be dealt with fairly easily. The use of reheat was governed by a temperature datum, and an additional datum value could be introduced to permit reheat at less than fully dry power, choosing an appropriate temperature datum to match whatever continuous power setting would be most suitable. The use of reheat in maximum dry power would still be needed for short take-offs and emergencies, however, so a 'double datum' configuration would be needed, with the pilot able to select between them.

On 21 January 1964 Olympus 320X 22213 was into the second of two 24hr tests to clear engine accessories (gear box, fuel pumps, and so on) when the No. 2 bearing failed. This was the intermediate LP shaft bearing situated at the rear of the LP compressor. (Many months later, further investigation would reveal that the No. 3 bearing at the front of the HP compressor had also failed.) On 21 February an Olympus 320X was undergoing flight clearance trials in No. 2 Cell at the NGTE. Reheat had just been engaged when there was a loud bang and the engine spewed a stream of shattered turbine blades from the exhaust. The first-stage turbine blades, cast from G.64, had fallen victim to fatigue caused by flutter (as they had done on three previous occasions). Forged Nimonic blades solved the problem.

In March another engine ingested some bolts from its own casing, which cracked all of the HP turbine rotor blades. The bolts had vibrated loose, so improvements to the casing had to be made, initially with measures to lock the bolts in place. Later, measures were taken to avoid the vibration mode that was causing them to loosen in the first place. On 8 April 1964 engine No. 22220, scheduled to be the fifth flight engine, failed its two-hour pre-delivery test run just one minute short of the test's completion when the No. 7 bearing registered an excessive overheat condition. On strip-down and examination it was found that there had been a bearing oil fire, and that the HP shaft had bent as a result. This engine had already incorporated modifications to deal with previous bearing

fires in the same location, there having been five previous incidents of a similar nature. A further No. 7 bearing fire incident in May was to follow before a successful improvement was made to venting in this area.

By June 1964, with BSEL now suffering from the financial penalties imposed by missing many contractual guarantee points, engines had been installed in the first TSR2 airframe, XR219. After dealing with the multitude of small problems to be expected with a first-time installation of new engines in a new airframe (of which more later), several hours of ground running were carried out. However, an unusual engine note and hammering noises heard on several reheat runs on 5 June 1964, along with overstress indications on the port engine (the only one with a strain gauge fitted to the LP shaft), required further investigation, and both engines were removed and returned to BSEL for examination. The port engine's LP shaft had indeed been overstressed, and was bent. Another disastrous LP shaft failure had been narrowly avoided.

Replacement engines with the strengthened and damped LP shafts, as previously installed on engine 2203 after the Vulcan FTB incident, were delivered and installed into XR219, but BSEL could not clear them for reheat running until the test results from engine No. 2203 were available. To add to the engine's litany of problems, cracks were being found in the turbine entry ducts, so the material used there had to be changed and thickened. All existing engines were given shorter lives in the meantime.

Matching engine to aircraft

Unlike previous Olympus installations, which were effectively underslung units with wrap-around doors as on the Vulcan, the TSR2's engines were to be installed into a pair of fully enclosed tunnels with access only from the rear. The aircraft's installation railing would match up with rollers provided on the engine casing, and the engine had three attachment points: a single trunnion at the top of the casing which held the thrust bearing through which the thrust load of the engine was transmitted to the airframe, and two steadying points in the pitching and rolling planes that could accommodate the inevitable movements and expansions and contractions of the engine in use.

This proved to be a major problem on the development-batch airframes, with the

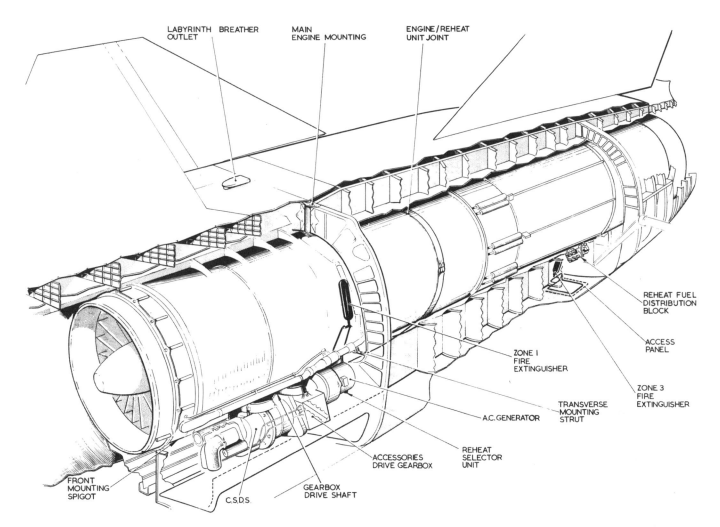

LABYRINTH BREATHER OUTLET

MAIN ENGINE MOUNTING

ENGINE/REHEAT UNIT JOINT

REHEAT FUEL DISTRIBUTION BLOCK

ACCESS PANEL

ZONE 1 FIRE EXTINGUISHER

ZONE 3 FIRE EXTINGUISHER

TRANSVERSE MOUNTING STRUT

A.C. GENERATOR

REHEAT SELECTOR UNIT

ACCESSORIES DRIVE GEARBOX

GEARBOX DRIVE SHAFT

C.S.D.S.

FRONT MOUNTING SPIGOT

ABOVE: **The engine installation. This illustration gives some idea of the tight fit of the engine within the airframe.** BAE Systems via Brooklands Museum

RIGHT: **Trial installation of a mockup engine into a mockup TSR2 at Weybridge. Installation of a real engine in a real aircraft proved to be somewhat trickier.** BAE Systems via Brooklands Museum

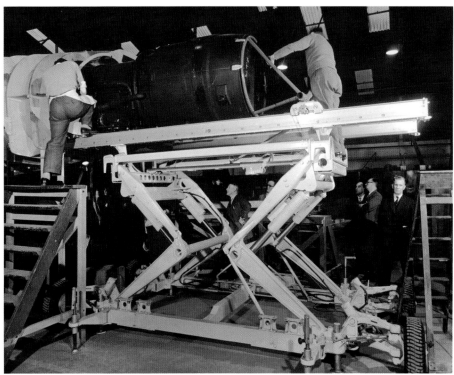

space available in the tunnels being continually reduced as the aircraft's development proceeded. Bristol Siddeley Engines, already running into its own problems and under pressure, was keen to keep its customer happy, and tended to acquiesce to most requests. When BAC asked for the engine to be reduced in diameter, BSEL even said yes to this, though it meant an expensive redesign, with the initial batch of bench-test engines being unrepresentative of production examples. In addition, the space provided in the aircraft for an engine accessories bay had looked just sufficient to begin with, but as development

proceeded the bay became ever more stuffed with components and pipework, to the point where some items that needed to be accessible were now obscured by others. The need for additional instrumentation and associated plumbing on development-batch aircraft exacerbated the situation.

Work to improve the accessories bay layout meant further expensive redesign of existing components, such as reducing the size of the main gearbox, but every improvement was more than matched by a reduction in available space caused by other design changes, especially the switch to double-walled fuel and oil pipes introduced by the MoA and BAC, which enlarged all these pipes and their associated unions. To ease the accessories-bay congestion temporarily for the development-batch aircraft, BAC was working on re-routeing pipes in the bay to give optimum use of space (probably at the expense of accessibility), but the preferred solution was to move the large CSDS unit into a new bay aft of the accessories bay. This would incur a penalty in the form of an 80gal (360L) reduction in fuel capacity, and would also require a change in the configuration of the airbrakes. A further suggestion was to bulge the aircraft in the area of the accessories to give more room, but the RAF did not think much of this idea with its attendant increase in drag and reduction in performance. Nor did it like the frankly bizarre idea of locating the accessory drives in an external pod underneath the bay. On balance, the RAF preferred the solution of adding a ventral 'spine' between the engines to house certain items, as this would create less drag and could also double as a locating point for the emergency arrester hook it wanted.

By February 1964 the situation in the accessories bay had become critical. The RAF declared the current bay unacceptable, and said none of BAC's solutions to improve it were acceptable either. A request was made to revert to single-walled pipes (which the MoA would take until July just to discuss), and even so it was not expected that any improvement to the bay would be available until at least the tenth airframe (the first pre-production aircraft). A meeting at the MoA on 6 March resulted in BAC being instructed to investigate urgently some more feasible layouts than previously suggested. That investigation was completed in the second week of May, and this time the preferred solution was a small enlargement of the bay at its forward end, cutting an arch into an existing fuselage frame and relocating a water pump and LP fuel cock higher in the fuselage. Around 14in (35cm) more room would be available, and the CSDS could be moved to the forward end of the bay.

Furthermore, originally there were twenty-seven connections from the aircraft to the basic engine-change unit (ECU), but by January 1962 there were forty-five (sixty-nine counting the jetpipe and reheat unit). This gives some idea of how many additional pipes and wires needed to be disconnected to enable an engine change. This was a serious safety concern, as many connections had to be made without visual access, and subsequent connections blocking access to previous ones. There would be no way to check many of the connections without running the engines, and even then small air, fuel or hydraulic leaks could go undetected during low-rpm ground-running. The first indication of poor

workmanship during engine installation could be the fire warning lights illuminating in the cockpit during a flight. Many of the electrical connections were also single lines sprouting from apparently random points on the engine, instead of being consolidated into fewer wiring harnesses with connector blocks, as BAC preferred.

Physically getting an engine into the aircraft was also problematic. Installing the first engine in the first airframe took over a week of hard work. Rather than sliding it smoothly into place, days of frustrating and painful work ensued, jockeying the engine into position by fractions of an inch at a time, with frequent minor rotations of the

ABOVE: An Olympus 320 ECU on display at the RAF Museum Cosford; the casing has been replaced by Perspex to reveal the HP and LP compressors. Damien Burke

BELOW: The Olympus 320 reheat unit. At 184in (4.67m) in length, this was longer but far simpler than the ECU. At the far left of the unit can be seen the clamps for attaching it to the ECU. Further right are the jack housings for the reheat nozzle actuators and, at far right, the nozzle area itself. The nozzle was moved back and forth by the jacks, the petals inside being pressed against the nozzle sides by the exhaust flow and thus giving variable nozzle diameter. Damien Burke

The business end of the reheat unit. Running around the inner wall are the rollers for the variable-position petals; deep within the unit are the three concentric rings of the flame holders.
Damien Burke

entire unit to clear obstructions as they impeded further progress. On the first aircraft, XR219, things were further complicated by the port engine tunnel not being perfectly circular; thus a great deal of extra work was necessary to match the port engine jetpipe shroud with the rear fairing.

The overall clearance between engine and engine tunnel had by now dropped to a mere third of an inch, a tolerance that BAC was confident would prove satisfactory in service, but which the RAF thought unacceptable. The 3hr ECU time could not be met even under ideal conditions with trained and experienced personnel, as predicted by the RAF's resident project officer in 1962. Instead BAC initially quoted a figure of 10hr 50min, reducing this to 8hr 15min when pressured to improve. Exasperated by the situation, the RAF wisely decided this probably meant 12hr and accepted this as the best that could be managed without a hugely expensive rethink of the whole question of engine installation. It is noteworthy that most military aircraft that followed the TSR2 have rather more sensible engine installations, such as the SEPECAT Jaguar and the Tornado with their much simpler and far more accessible engine bays.

Flying the engine

In March 1964 the engines were still at such an immature stage of development that multiple limitations were placed on the flight batch of engines. This was particularly serious, as the aircraft's first flight had at that point been expected to take place in May. The limitations included:

Intake Pressure (P1)
A 20psi (1.40kg/sq cm) limit was in place here (expected to be brought up to 27psi (1.89kg/sq cm) for the first flight, but specified at 33psi (2.32kg/sq cm)), which would limit airspeed, particularly at low altitude and in low ambient temperatures (when air is denser).

Intake Temperature (T1)
A 70°C limit (expected to be brought up to 100° for the first flight, but specified at 146° with short periods at 180°) was in place because of insufficient turbine cooling. Bearing fires could be expected at higher temperatures, with resulting LP or HP shaft damage and possible catastrophic turbine disc failure.

Compressor Delivery Pressure (P3)
A 200psi (14.06kg/sq cm) limit (specified at 300psi (21.09kg/sq cm)) was in place because of a weak engine-to-jetpipe joint, which would further limit airspeed; to as low as 320kt (370mph; 590km/h) at low altitude in typical conditions with full power. The joint was made by a single metal strap wrapped around the joint and bolted into place in a single location, something BAC felt was entirely unsound in an area of great heat and vibration. An improved interim design, with four latches added to the strap to keep it in place, had been created, but would not be available on the initial four flight-batch engines. A fully bolted joint would be embodied in production engines.

G
Although 7.3g was specified as the maximum the engine would need to cope with, problems with compressor blades rubbing against the engine casing reduced this to a mere 3.5g. Above this, dependent on altitude, the g loading could result in blades contacting the casing.

Water Injection
Thrust boosting by water injection had not been cleared for flight use.

Turbine Entry Temperature (T4)
Limited to 1180K (specified at 1,240°) to enable 'continuous' use of reheat.

Reheat Temperature
Limited to 1850K (specified at 2,000°) due to cracking the corrugated reheat liner under test; this would reduce available reheat thrust.

Reheat Control
A failure of the aircraft's AC electrical supply, leaving only DC power available, would leave the pilot unable to control reheat, as this was available only on AC power. An engine failure on top of this would leave the aircraft unable to maintain height when heavy with fuel and in the approach configuration. Nor could it climb away with flaps down. An emergency DC reheat control was far in the future, and as a minimum measure BAC's chief test pilot insisted on a fuel jettison system being available so that the aircraft's weight could be reduced in a hurry if needs be, and to also limit fuel loads to keep the AUW below the critical 70,000lb (31,750kg) mark (thus limiting flight duration to below 40min).

Engine Life
Limited to 25hr airborne (8hr in reheat) and 40hr ground running.

All of these limitations combined to reduce the available flight envelope for early flights, and the life limitations also seriously reduced the possible intensity of the test-flying programme. An overall drop in engine performance in the order of 8 per cent could be expected from the limitations,

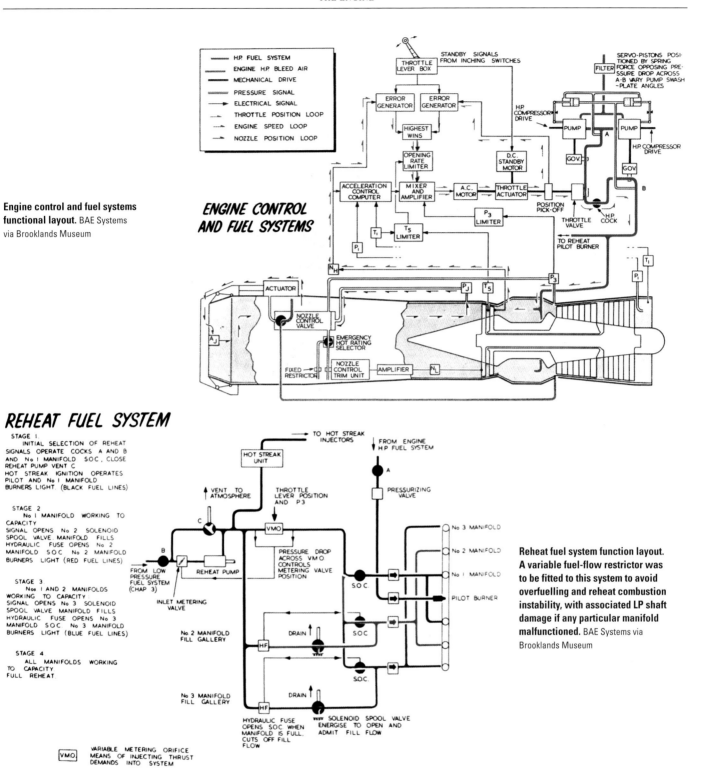

Engine control and fuel systems functional layout. BAE Systems via Brooklands Museum

Reheat fuel system function layout. A variable fuel-flow restrictor was to be fitted to this system to avoid overfuelling and reheat combustion instability, with associated LP shaft damage if any particular manifold malfunctioned. BAE Systems via Brooklands Museum

which BAC was prepared to tolerate for a very few early flights. The major effect would be a lengthened take-off run (in the order of 10 per cent more runway being needed), with the aircraft also restricted to short flights.

The seemingly never-ending stream of often catastrophic problems delayed the clearance to flight of the engine, but it did at least mean that some of the early limitations were able to be reduced, though the first flight was pushed further and further away from the May date. The various catastrophic failures had finally pushed BAC into insisting that some form of blade containment be added to the engine to prevent any further major failures sending blades scything through the surrounding aircraft structure. As that structure included fuel tanks, the consequences of an in-flight failure involving the expulsion of a disc or individual blades would almost certainly guarantee the loss of the aircraft. Although BSEL began working on this, there was no chance that such containment would be available on early test flights.

By July the aircraft still did not have engines cleared for flight, and after 50hr 44min running in a test cell, on 24 July 1964 engine 2203 provided just the results that nobody wanted. The LP driveshaft ruptured once again and the first-stage LP turbine wheel was ejected, causing much excitement in the test cell. The cell's thick steel walls were deeply gouged in many places, and the engine casing and surrounding pipework were wrecked. Clearly, stiffening the LP shaft alone had not been enough to cure the problem, and now the aircraft's first flight was effectively out of the question because the engines simply could not be relied upon.

Intensive investigations at NGTE and BSEL finally found that the LP driveshaft failures were brought on by a bell-mode vibration. Effectively, the shaft was resonating under certain conditions, alternately being squashed into a flattened oval shape

in horizontal and then vertical directions (and ringing like a bell; hence the name). This had not been experienced on previous marks of Olympus, as they had a shorter LP driveshaft with differing resonance characteristics. The conditions under which this vibration occurred had been unclear, but after the 'hammering' incident BSEL had turned to the reheat fuelling system for its next avenue of investigation. The indications were that one of the three reheat fuel manifolds had malfunctioned, forcing extra fuel into the other two. This overfuelling during reheat running was resulting in pressure fluctuations (the hammering noise observers had noted had been a particularly severe manifestation of this), and the torsional frequency of the LP shaft was in resonance with the jetpipe pressure fluctuation. The jet pipe was effectively ringing the LP shaft's bell, to dramatic effect.

The solution was to introduce a fuel flow restrictor to the reheat unit to stop overfuelling from occurring should there be a

manifold malfunction. The first interim fix for this was a fixed fuel-flow restrictor in each manifold that would introduce a number of limitations to the engines, including the loss of any reheat functionality above 13,000ft (3,900m). This was a crude temporary fix, and risked long-term damage to the fuel pumps from back-pressure. Unfortunately it would take until at least September to add the restrictors to the existing engines. The final solution was being worked on by Dowty, and consisted of a fully variable fuel-flow restrictor in each reheat fuel manifold. Thus a malfunction in any particular manifold would not result in overfuelling on the others. However the improved flow-control system was not to be developed and tested until early 1965, and the first flight could not wait that long.

The investigation by BSEL found that it was in the power band in the region of 98 to 100 per cent that LP driveshaft problems were showing up, and even in this region the condition could not be easily replicated.

The initial engine runs of XR219 at Boscombe Down ran into various small problems before a more significant issue with the reheat fuel manifolds became apparent. In this shot the aircraft can be seen to be tied down for early engine runs, with instrumentation cabling and fuel and air supply lines also attached.
BAE Systems

LEFT: **This dramatic shot gives some idea of the sheer power of the Olympus 320. Noise levels exceeded those of all previous engines, and triggered additional research into the health hazards of extremely high noise levels.** BAE Systems via Warton Heritage Group

BELOW: **The take-off on Flight 1, with engines of frankly dubious reliability that were really far from being truly airworthy.** BAE Systems via Warton Heritage Group

If an engine was kept at or below 98 per cent there was a very good chance the problem would not show up at all. Even in the danger zone, up to 3hr of running could be expected on average before damage was apparent. The engines installed in XR219 had not been inspected to ascertain the condition of their LP shafts, but as one had run only 80hr and the other only 120hr, and the one with a strain gauge fitted had shown no detectable stress so far, BSEL was confident that both shafts were in good condition. Thus the first flight now became an option, if a risky one. It was feasible to take off with just 98 per cent power on the engines, but it opened a window of risk during the take-off run, during which there was a period of several seconds when an engine failure allied with a brake-parachute failure would mean the aircraft could not stop before entering the arrester barrier at the end of the runway. The speed region in which the engine failure would be critical would vary with aircraft weight, and Boscombe's barrier had a 66kt (76mph; 122km/h) engagement limit for 'safe' use. To keep below that, the aircraft weight would have to be extremely limited, which meant carrying very little fuel. This was about as far from an ideal situation for a first flight that you could possibly get.

The decision to fly or not was left with BAC, which placed the decision in the

hands of the men at the sharp end, the flight crew. The pressure to fly was immense and the risk was taken. In the event, the first flight proceeded without any engine problems. Henry Gardner of BAC later wrote: 'I must confess to a greater feeling of relief after it had touched down than I have known for many years.' With this flight successfully undertaken, it was thought prudent to not push their luck, and the aircraft was grounded for several months while the engines were changed and the basic fuel restrictor modifications introduced. The port engine of XR219 had had very little life left on it anyway, owing to limitations

imposed by early-design turbine entry ducts, and the starboard reheat fuel pipe had been leaking.

With the LP shaft still considered a weak point, though, the same 98 per cent restriction would only allow a succession of very short flights limited by the tiny fuel load permitted, so the restriction had to be lifted so that 100 per cent power was available (for take-off only). In an attempt to give the crew some warning of impending LP shaft failure, the output from the strain gauges on the LP shaft was linked to an amplifier and the output sent to warning lights installed in the cockpit, with the amplification set

This shot taken during Flight 7 illustrates the other hazard of the Olympus 320: the environmental one. This was a particularly filthy engine, and redesigned combustion chambers would probably have been incorporated in production engines, as happened with the later Olympus 593 for the Concorde airliner. BAE Systems via Brooklands Museum

could take place, as the Warton barrier was rated to 100kt (115mph; 185km/h), permitting heavier fuel loads.

While XR219 initially flew with a single-stage fuel restrictor, a two-stage fuel restrictor (to widen the envelope within which reheat could be engaged) was fitted to the first two aircraft just before the project was cancelled. The fully variable flow restrictor that would not inflict any limitations on reheat operation at all while preventing any overfuelling was never fitted, and its effectiveness on test bench engines was only verified some two weeks after the project's cancellation. The accessories-bay redesign for aircraft 10 to 14 was completed but never embodied in any aircraft. A BAC investigation into any means of improving engine change times was also terminated by the project's cancellation.

Thus the Olympus 320 programme came to an end shortly after TSR2 itself was cancelled, but a lot of the lessons learnt along the way went into the Olympus 593, which powered the Concorde supersonic airliner. That turned out to be another reliable and sturdy version of the Olympus, a reputation that the 320 never achieved.

While most of the Olympus 320 variants produced up to the time of cancellation were scrapped, a handful survived. Several are now on display in museums, notably at the RAF Museum at Cosford, which displays one next to its surviving TSR2 airframe, XR220. The NGTE at Pyestock continued to expand and was the site for Olympus 593 testing in the years after the TSR2 was cancelled, and for many other engines until it was closed in 2000. Sadly, despite the site's history of development and test work of international importance, it has lain mostly derelict since then, and is now scheduled to be entirely demolished.

to trigger the light if the stress on the shaft exceed 10 tons/sq in (1,575kg/sq cm); well below the breaking stress. If these lit up, the crew would know to throttle back immediately and ideally shut the engine down. Unfortunately a single-channel warning system based on amplifying a very-low-voltage signal like the one from the strain

gauge was inherently subject to false indications and could well indicate a problem where none existed. This is exactly what happened on Flight 3, resulting in the flight being aborted and an emergency landing. The warning system was later removed, and once the test flying was based at Warton after Flight 14, even longer-duration flights

Working hours for BSEL and BAC personnel made for a punishing schedule – engine runs for XR219 at Boscombe Down often continued late into the evening. BAE Systems via Warton Heritage Group

CHAPTER EIGHT

Electronic Systems

This chapter describes the various items of equipment fitted to the airframe that enabled it to be not just an aeroplane, but a complete weapons system. Although the aircraft was meant to be procured, designed and developed as a complete system, the realities of the procurement process made a mockery of this idea. Manufacturers of electrical and electronic equipment could not afford to sink large amounts of their own money into development of equipment unless they were sure a contract would result. The end result of this was that, while the project as a whole started on 1 January 1959, work on the various electronic systems was delayed until Vickers-Armstrongs had a firm signed contract, in October 1960. While preliminary work was done on some systems, the delay between the start of the TSR2 project and the first contract meant that much of this work resulted in systems that were nearly obsolete even before their development was completed. The MoA's insistence on controlling many of these items of equipment also injected additional delays into an already over-optimistic schedule.

Navigation

Stable platform

The stable platform was the heart of the INS. A collection of accelerometers – horizontal, vertical and azimuth – detect accelerations and can thus be used to track the acceleration of the overall platform in particular directions. The 'stable' part came in because the platform had to be gyro-stabilized against the rolling, pitching and yawing of the carrying aircraft. With knowledge of the starting position, the stable platform provided the raw data for a navigation system that could fairly accurately track the progress of the aircraft, but only over a theoretically flat Earth with no wind. Correcting for the fact that the Earth is a sphere, and not even close to a perfect sphere at that, along with detecting displacement due to wind (which, displacing

A prototype version of the Ferranti stable platform. BAE Systems via Brooklands Museum

207

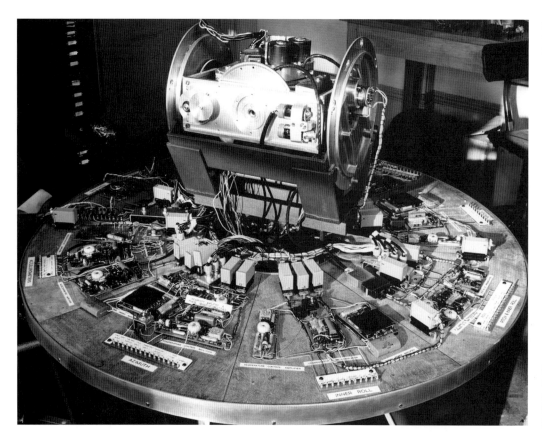

the air mass within which the aircraft is flying, produces no acceleration that can be detected by the accelerometers) was a job for the central computing system. The stable platform was responsible for providing the central computing system (CCS) with outputs of elevation, bank angle, azimuth angle plus horizontal and vertical velocities.

The stable platform was a Category 1 item, selected and controlled by the MoA rather than Vickers. The Ministry overruled Vickers' (and English Electric's) preference for a Honeywell platform incorporating miniature integrating gyros (to be produced under licence by English Electric in the UK), and instead gave the job to Ferranti, using Kearfott gyros and accelerometers despite predicted inferior accuracy, higher costs and the fact that the Honeywell platform was already well-proven and the Ferranti platform was only just beginning development. The decision was primarily a political one, taken by Duncan Sandys, to spread work among the equipment manufacturers. He did not believe that giving further work to English Electric when it already had half the TSR2 work was fair. The RAE's belief that the existing Honeywell system was not up to scratch was just the sort of excuse Sandys needed to force the

issue (ignoring the fact that the RAE actually preferred a Sperry system developed for the North American X-15).

Doppler (ARI.23133)

To deal with the errors introduced to the INS by wind, input was also needed from a

Doppler radar (produced by Decca). With a wind from the side, the aircraft's track over the ground can vary significantly from its heading. Similarly, head- or tailwind components modify the aircraft's velocity over the ground. A Doppler radar fires pulses at the ground both ahead of and behind the aircraft, and measures the Doppler shift in the returns (the same effect as the change in pitch of a train whistle as it approaches and then recedes from you) to ascertain the velocity of the aircraft along its track, rather than its heading. Limited stabilization was provided for the Doppler antenna, which was mounted in a bay within the lower fuselage aft of the nose gear bay, but if the aircraft were manoeuvred too violently, Doppler tracking would be lost and memorized values for drift were used until it was regained. The stable platform had to be capable of withstanding up to two minutes of constant violent manoeuvring without Doppler information. Development proceeded with less drama than with other aspects of the project, and flight tests of the early models began in November 1961 in de Havilland Comet XS235 at the A&AEE. These were encouraging despite the very early standard of the model being used, and progress on this aspect of the aircraft was fairly smooth right up to cancellation.

With the corrected velocities provided by the combination of the stable platform and Doppler inputs, the CCS would be able to calculate where the aircraft was at any given moment. No system is perfect, however, and a variety of errors were constantly being introduced into the overall INS; gyro drift, variations in gravity, and so on. While the computer could correct some errors, such as handling the imperfect sphere that is the Earth, the accumulated hardware errors and small losses in accuracy over repeated computations would inevitably lead to a loss of accuracy in overall position. The longer the flight, the greater the error.

Sideways-looking radar (ARI.23130)

To guarantee that the aircraft, would arrive on the target with acceptable accuracy, some means of correcting the accumulated errors en route was necessary, and this was where the SLR, also known as the navigation fixing radar, came in. The state of the art in FLRs was not up to the job of accurate mapping, and the high power levels and dish sizes were impractical anyway. Consequently SLRs with large aerials were the only viable choice for high-resolution radar mapping. Most of the areas of the world over which the TSR2 was expected to fly were well mapped, so various 'fix points' could be nominated during mission planning, points that would be particularly easy to recognize on radar. On approach to a fix point the navigator would monitor his SLR display (which could be switched to display either

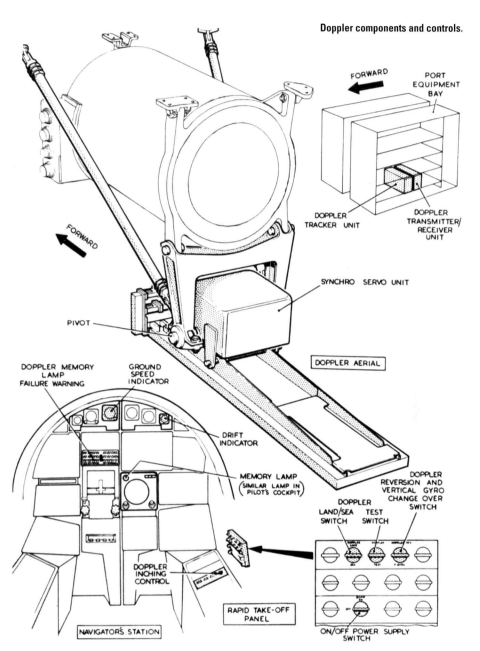

Doppler components and controls.

The waveform generator, transmitter/receiver, modulator and power unit for the SLR.
BAE Systems via Brooklands Museum

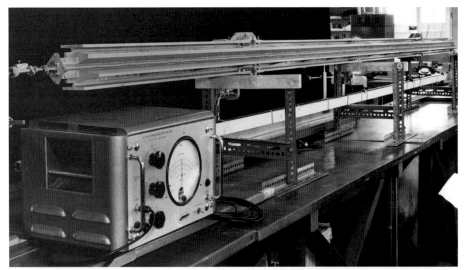

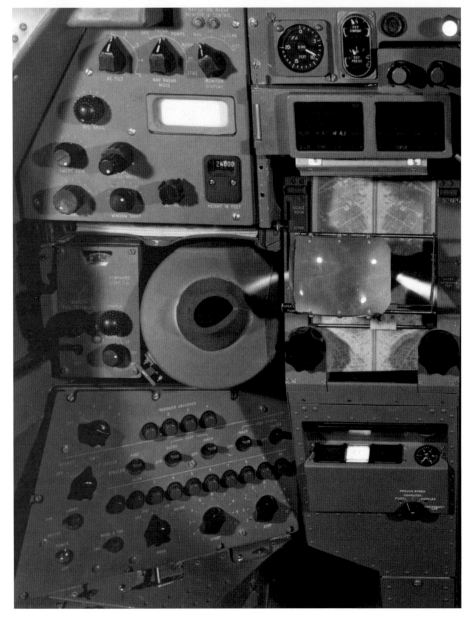

the left or right returns, or both sides at once), and mark it when it was seen. With the SLR able to provide the exact distance and relative bearing to the fix point, the navigation system was then able to reset itself with an accurate position. The frequency of fix points would define just how accurate the navigation could be. Looked at in another way, the accuracy of the inertial/Doppler system decided just how often a fix point would be necessary.

Display of the SLR output also introduced challenges, as the SLR had a secondary task of radar reconnaissance. The output therefore needed to be recorded, and the solution to both recording and displaying this strip of radar data was one that now looks almost Heath Robinson. In basic terms, the SLR on each side displayed its output on a small 45mm-wide CRT buried within the aircraft, out of sight of the crew. A small camera was focused on this and constantly filmed the output, exposing a constantly running roll of 5in (12.7cm)-wide photographic paper that then needed to be processed and fixed so that it could be viewed. A rapid processing unit (RPU) processed the paper, and it was then scrolled along the navigator's SLR display unit. Paper transport and camera exposure (via aperture variation) had to be synchronized with aircraft speed; and processing of the paper had to be incredibly fast (less than two seconds) to provide anything like real-time display of the radar signal. The navigation system would inform the navigator of an approaching fix point within 10 miles (16km) by illuminating a warning lamp. Once the aircraft was within 5 miles (8km) the autopilot would ensure that the wings were kept level to stabilize roll and give a steady SLR display on the final run-up to the fix point. Markers printed on the SLR paper display would lead towards the theoretical location of the fix point, and the navigator would check this display against a pre-prepared folio of fix-point photographs to make sure he had the right position. A cursor overlay, moved by X/Y-axis wheel controls, enabled the navigator to mark both the predicted and real fix points and allow the CCS to get back on track, with cursor movement accurate enough to permit a fix point to be marked within 200yd (183m) of its actual location.

Even with a relatively large 5in-width paper, making out detail from the navigator's seated position in an aircraft subject to low-level turbulence would be a challenge, so a large lens was attached to the cursor bar, giving a magnified view of the paper. This in itself was a compromise, as the large lens found to give the best view was so large that it impeded on the ejection seat's exit path, so a smaller lens had to be used. The RPU was designed such that at low level both left and right SLR returns would be displayed, with scales of either 50,000:1 or 100,000:1. At higher altitudes, either left or right SLR returns would be displayed at scales of 200,000:1 or 500,000:1. Enough paper and developing and fixing solution would be provided for 6hr of coverage. While tests found that radiation doses in excess of 10 rads would fog the photographic paper and introduce navigational difficulties, to incur this sort of dose the aircraft would need to have accidentally flown through at least two mushroom clouds, which was considered unlikely, particularly as the greatest concentration of radioactivity in such a cloud was at high altitude. Therefore no radiation shielding was provided for the RPU.

The navigator also had a moving-map display that displayed map segments on the intended route, rotated so that aircraft track was always 'up' and giving a constant view of what was ahead on track. This further aided recognition of fix points, and a repeater moving-map display was present on the pilot's panel. Of course, were the crew limited to navigating along a preset route using only preset fix points, they would be severely limited in the sort of missions they could undertake, so the navigator was able to miss out or reorder fix points, as well as make *ad hoc* visual and FLR fixes at unplanned points. Thus detours could still be made away from the intended route to avoid unexpected defences or attack targets of opportunity. Preparation of the navigator's fix folio before a mission would have been a significant job, and plans were in hand to carry out a massive survey programme to choose and photograph suitable fix points all over the areas where TSR2 operations could be expected. Naturally provision of fix points deep within

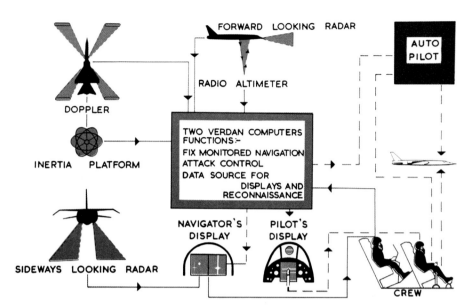

The overall nav/attack system components, showing the basic relationship between them.
BAE Systems via Brooklands Museum

Soviet or other 'enemy' territory would have raised certain difficulties in acquiring the necessary coverage, and navigational accuracy could be expected to decrease gradually in relation to how far into 'Indian territory' the target was.

Development of the SLR went much more smoothly than many other aspects of the project, and EMI delivered the first test model to Weybridge in August 1961, following up just one week later with delivery of a second model to the Royal Radar Establishment (RRE) for airborne test use. The only serious delays experienced were with interfacing to the CCS and provision of suitable display tubes; unsatisfactory electrical connectors caused another minor delay. By July 1963 test models were proving so reliable that an endurance trial at RRE Malvern was terminated because the fault rate was so low that it was not felt worthwhile to continue. The RPU was another story, however, and by late 1964 there were continuing problems with the processing chemicals deteriorating in storage, and clogging the slot through which the paper passed during processing. At one point it seemed likely that the navigator would have to change the slot during longer sorties, which would have brought additional problems of sealing and accessibility. The project was cancelled before the problems were ironed out.

Central computing system

The TSR2's CCS was based on an off-the-shelf Verdan D9D unit (a pair of them in

fact), produced by Autonetics Corporation, a division of North American Aviation, and manufactured under licence in the UK by Elliott Automation. 'Verdan' was a reduction of 'Versatile Digital Analyzer'. It was a solid-state digital computer with two computational centres; an incremental or DA (differential analyzer) integrator section, and a whole-valve or GP (general-purpose) section. The complete memory capacity of a single unit was 1,664 words, equivalent to less than 5Kb, and was held on a rotating magnetic disc (an early forebear of modern hard disks), with an average access time of 5,000 microseconds per location. A single multiplication or division took 2,000 microseconds to be performed; but Verdan could carry out many operations simultaneously. For those more familiar with modern dual- or quad-core central processing units (CPUs) this was a hugely multi-core but very slow CPU!

Electronics and computing have advanced with bewildering speed over the last half-century, and the Verdan seems an incredibly primitive piece of equipment to modern eyes. Comparison with any current-day computer would be embarrassing. Even a 1982-vintage Sinclair Spectrum was hugely more powerful than the Verdan. However, for its time Verdan was a reliable and advanced piece of equipment, and the earlier D9A model was installed in hundreds of American aircraft and warships, primarily driving their navigation systems, and was providing accuracy and reliability unavailable by other means.

The complex calculations that tied together the inputs from the stable platform, Doppler, navigator's fix controls and so on were all handled by the CCS, and outputs of latitude, longitude, distance to go, moving-map display and so on were all displayed in the navigator's cockpit as a result. The CCS also handled all the computation required to fly accurately the manoeuvres involved in any kind of attack, such as the nuclear bombing loft manoeuvre. The results of these would be displayed as cues in the HUD, but were also output to the AFCS, enabling the crew to concentrate on things other than the basic flying task at the time of greatest stress and danger.

As an off-the-shelf buy, you could reasonably expect this to be one part of the TSR2 programme that did not suffer unduly from delays. However, Verdan was on the edge of its capabilities when married to the TSR2's complex nav/attack system, and by late 1961 it was clear that even a pair of Verdan D9Ds together did not have the capacity to run the complete program required by the nav/attack system. In fact the programmers at Elliott Automation privately believed that six D9Ds would barely have coped. By April 1962, all parties involved – BAC, the RAE, the RAF and Elliotts – had agreed that the only way forward was to downgrade the specification. Each of the aircraft's various modes would need to run a separate program, rather than having one program to cater for all modes (this was not a particular limitation as no sortie would involve, for instance, both ferrying and a nuclear-loft attack). The number of navigation check-points was reduced from forty to thirty, the number of bombing modes was reduced from ten to six, and approach tracks to a checkpoint and wind computations were omitted. Similar downgrades had happened already; more would follow. With further development, it was hoped, the programs the system was running could be improved and optimized and enable a more complete system to be brought back into being.

Unfortunately, while further development did indeed result in some optimization, it also showed up just how much was missing from the early system, and flight-testing of prototype units introduced real-world problems that had not been considered. Airborne trials were carried out by the A&AEE from July 1963 to February 1964 using Handley Page Hastings WD496. Programs SO1 (the first development program, intended for TSR2 development-batch use) and SO3 were tested on the standard of Verdans intended for the TSR2, along with a development model of the stable platform. Soon, SO1 was superseded by SO3, which was much more representative but only covered ferry sorties; no bombing calculations were involved. The limited ground testing that had been done on the Stage 2 rig at Weybridge was soon reflected in the airborne trials, with a variety of faults impeding progress. Of 700hr of testing, only 68hr was carried out in the air. The remaining time was made up of installation,

ABOVE: **The Verdan D9D computer. The casing for the memory disk is obvious, as is the large hose providing cooling air.** BAE Systems via Brooklands Museum

LEFT: **The computer control panel and display unit, as fitted at the bottom right of the navigator's instrument panel.** BAE Systems via Brooklands Museum

troubleshooting, on-site repairs, investigation of engineering defects and programme testing and ground simulations. Both the Verdan units and the stable platform suffered repeated failures of one kind or another, caused by a mixture of poor workmanship, faulty components and flawed design. The accuracy shown by the CCS on this trial was unexpectedly poor, and an on-board Decca navigation system performed better. Some flights showed apparently random deviations that could not be explained. Simulated SLR fixes were not processed by the CCS until 7sec had elapsed, enough to introduce small errors at the slow speeds flown by the Hastings, but much more serious for a transonic aircraft. Turns also introduced a variety of issues, the most serious being that the CCS corrected its own integrator drifts every 25sec or so, and in turns there could be large changes in the aircraft's velocity vector that would result in the CCS introducing rather than rectifying errors. On some occasions the CCS erroneously activated the bomb-release signal, something that would have caused great embarrassment to a TSR2 crew, particularly on the ground!

The extra computer capacity needed just to fix the problems and deal with the new items was beyond the remaining capacity available, without including the capacity needed to store navigation checkpoints, etc. There were 256 DA integrators available, and a capacity of 2,048 GP words (1,664 on each D9D, but around five-eighths of the memory disc was reserved for DA use). By September 1964, with estimated increases in program size to cater for all the outstanding problems, one of the bombing-mode programs (low-level nuclear strike) would require 308 DA integrators and 2,777 GP words. So BAC itself had a central computing system that would prevent its aircraft from ever meeting the full OR. The system's speed was also a serious concern, with Elliotts desperately trying to improve matters so that turning points would not be overshot by several miles at supersonic speeds before the computer could catch up. Further airborne trials, this time in Comet XS235 and using programme S04, were begun in November 1964 and continued until February 1965. The results were little better than the Hastings trials. The supplied Doppler unit suffered near-constant unserviceability. Simultaneous Doppler and stable-platform failures resulted in the CCS believing the aircraft was flying at 1,125kt (1,294mph; 2081km/h), and only the

unusual nature of the Comet installation allowed the operators to convince the CCS otherwise. In a TSR2 installation the navigator would have been stuck with the situation. The CCS consistently lost accuracy in turns, the errors piling ever higher as tighter turns were carried out, and the flights that actually resulted in any valid data being collected showed that the system as it stood was up to 3,000yd (2,740m) out of position over a 100nm (115 miles; 185km) leg. Even when the aircraft was taxying on the ground the CCS could suddenly believe it was travelling along with 1,500kt (1,725mph; 2,780km/h) wind drift. Component unreliability would clearly have been a major issue for the complete system, never mind the computer capacity limitations and program errors.

Autonetics did have improved versions of Verdan under development for the Minuteman missile programme, two offering larger GP capacity in the double-unit configuration, and a new single unit with enhanced GP capacity but higher power requirements. The first two were attractive, as the existing D9D could be upgraded to match, retaining existing size, weight and power requirements. However, the DA capacity was still insufficient, so reprogramming to use more GP words would be necessary, and GP calculations were slower. The end result could be a system that would do the job – just about – with no room for future expansion, and it would still be crippled by lack of speed.

Elliotts offered an alternative system, its own MCS 920B, which was a development of the MCS 920 for the airborne environment. This provided 8,192 GP words, no DA section and thus the need to carry out a great deal of reprogramming, but was ten times faster than Verdan. The prediction was that all of the operational requirements could be met within 4,000 to 5,000 GP words. It would fit in the same amount of space as Verdan (actually slightly less, as one supporting piece of equipment could be deleted), cost less, and a trials unit would be available for airborne trials in a Comet by the end of 1964. However, delivery of the first production 920B would not be until June 1967. A miniaturized version, the 920M, would be available 18 months later and give additional weight and space saving. In fact a standard MCS 920 was not available for airborne trials in A&AEE Comet XS235 until March 1965, but a three-week trial was a complete success, the A&AEE being impressed not only by the

reliability, accuracy and speed of the unit, but also by the relative ease with which it could be programmed. The 920 series of computers would all turn out to be similarly reliable (and rugged) units, with capacity for massive expansion. They would go on to be used in the Jaguar's navigation system among others, as well as being used on satellite launcher rockets and warships.

Another competitor was GEC, which was developing, at MoA request, another 8,000 GP word computer, and this one was going to be even faster than the MCS 920B. However, it was even further away and would need to have various supporting equipment created from scratch; cost was an unknown. In the end, the only firm agreement was that a thorough study needed to be made of the alternatives, and an upgraded D9D-1 was fitted for the time being. The study was under way when the TSR2 programme was cancelled. In this area the TSR2 fell victim to nothing more than timing. In 1959 Verdan was the only realistic option, but by 1964 it was clearly obsolete, and the hesitant switch from analogue and hybrid digital-analogue computing to true digital computing was well under way. The miniaturization policy that Vickers-Armstrongs had championed in its Type 571 brochure was ahead of its time, by just a handful of years.

Automatic flight control system

The TSR2 was designed to have adequate handling, even without autostabilization, in the less-exciting portions of the flight envelope, and it was in this state that XR219 flew. The aircraft became increasingly difficult to handle at higher Mach numbers, and the deterioration in lateral stability at speeds above Mach 1.5 precluded flight at these speeds without the fin auto-stiffener being operational. Artificial feel was built into the flying control system, providing suitable feedback to the pilot so that he would not inadvertently overstress the aircraft. Beyond these basic features of the flying controls, all else was the domain of the AFCS.

Produced by Elliott Brothers Ltd, the AFCS provided autostabilization, pitch manoeuvre boost, autopilot and automatic throttle control facilities. Operation of the AFCS was via a control panel on the pilot's starboard console, with selection of the following modes possible:

• Automatic airfield approach using ILS signals

- Terrain-following with altitude and track keeping down to 150ft (50m) between Mach 0.7 and 0.9 using guidance signals from FLR
- Loft bombing and dive-toss attack manoeuvres using guidance signals from CCS

- Three-axis autostabilization under manual control, including auto-stiffening and manoeuvre boost at low indicated speeds
- Three-axis autostabilization under automatic control
- Basic autopilot with individual locks

for altitude (from radar altimeter), barometric height (from pressure altimeter), speed and heading, with the ability to adjust each lock while flying
- Selection of a height or heading target to which the aircraft would then fly without overshooting

Component locations for the AFCS. BAE Systems via Brooklands Museum

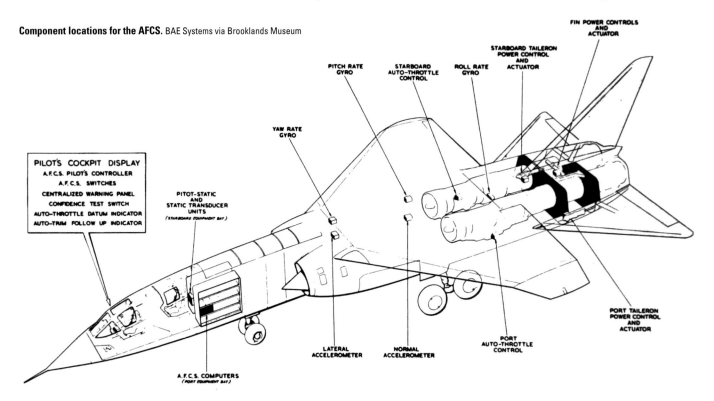

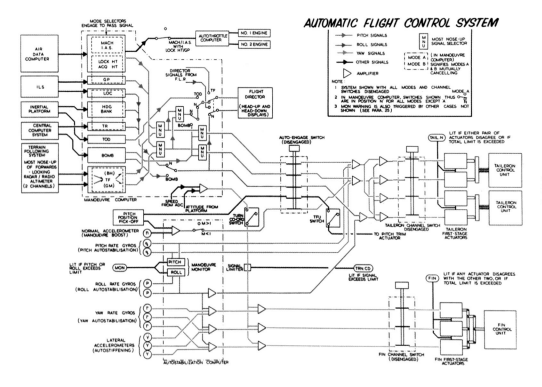

Automatic Flight Control System functional layout. BAE Systems via Brooklands Museum

all the latest British aircraft use Elliott equipment

The Automatic Flight Control System, the Airborne Digital Computing System and the Engine Thrust Measuring System of the British Aircraft Corporation's TSR2 are all supplied by Elliott. The operational capabilities of this remarkable aircraft demand the ultimate in reliable automatic controls for all aspects of its flight, from low level contour-following strike to high level supersonic reconnaisance. Elliott play a vital part in the unique match of aircrew, aircraft and systems which makes the TSR2 the most advanced strike aircraft in the world.

[E LIOTT] ELLIOTT BROTHERS [LONDON] LIMITED/AIRPORT WORKS/ROCHESTER KENT/CHATHAM 44400 *EA* A Member of the Elliott-Automation Group

ABOVE: A mockup of the pilot's AFCS control panel, located on the starboard console. BAE Systems via Brooklands Museum

LEFT: An Elliott Brothers AFCS advert of 1964. BAE Systems via Brooklands Museum

Autostabilization provided three-axis damping of short-period oscillations that would otherwise be experienced, improving handling. The small adjustments to the flying controls made by the autostabilizer would not be reflected by control column movements, unlike larger pitch and roll demands to the flying controls, which would be fed back to the pilot via movements in the control column position. The AFCS also included pitch-manoeuvre boosting, as the combination of low aerodynamic stiffness in pitch and large pitch inertia would otherwise cause a sluggish response to pitch demands. This would be particularly problematic in subsonic dive recoveries, such as during a dive-bombing or rocket attack. Thus during manual (not autopilot) flight at subsonic speeds, the AFCS would apply a large amount of extra taileron pitch angle at the beginning of a pitch demand so that a given aircraft pitch angle would be reached more quickly than would otherwise be the case.

With so much of a sortie being able to be flown entirely automatically, and at high speed and low altitude, safety of the entire system was the number one concern. As a result the taileron control channels were duplicated and the more critical fin control channels were triplicated. A voting system was used for all channels. The AFCS control panel included four emergency cut-out switches enabling the pilot to disconnect the fin and taileron automatic controls as well as the trim follow-up and turn co-ordinator. More immediate means of taking back manual control were also available via the control column. A force cut-out switch would detect if the pilot grabbed the stick and made a control input, to take avoiding action for instance, and would disengage any automatic flight mode (though flight director signals would continue to be displayed on the HUD to enable the pilot to get back on track and follow the directions). Also, an autopilot disengage button was located on the left-hand side of the joystick, easily accessible by the pilot's thumb but away from his fingers if the stick was held normally.

Terrain following – forward-looking radar (ARI.23129)

One of the most important systems on the aircraft, the FLR ended up absorbing 40 per cent of the electronic system development costs on the TSR2 project. Without it there could be no terrain following, and without that, little chance of survival in a hostile environment, because hand-flying an aircraft at high speed and low level would be a tiring job, only possible in daylight. Ferranti was the contractor chosen to develop the FLR, despite the availability of a nearly completed Autoflite system in the USA, and based it on the AI.23B. (*Blue Parrot*, in development for the NA.39, was similarly based on AI.23B.)

Developed to Specification No. RRE X.5647, the FLR was to provide the following facilities for the TSR2:

- Terrain following (both manual and automatic)
- Radar ranging
- Conventional weapon aiming, through a conventional weapon-aiming computer (a related section of the radar assembly, though largely discrete)
- Ground mapping and fixing
- Tanker and airfield homing (through a subsidiary oscillator and receiver interrogating a modified APN 69 beacon)

Design studies began in June 1959, and completion of the first test model was expected by September 1961, with flight

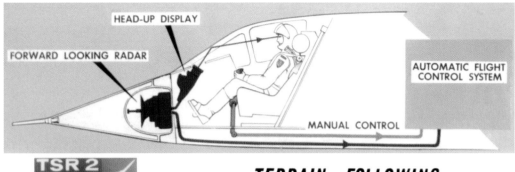

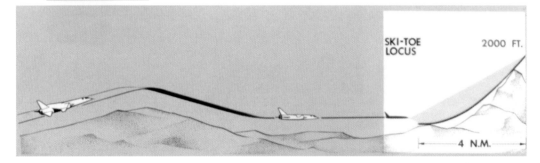

The TFR system components. The initial requirement had been for terrain clearance, a simpler and easier concept than terrain following. BAE Systems via Brooklands Museum

Ferranti's Dakota, TS423, with its AI.23 radar installed in an extended nose. This aircraft carried out some of the early FLR trials using a modified AI.23B set, with little success. BAE Systems via Glenn Surtees

The Ferranti FLR was a relatively compact unit, and is seen here with most of its exterior removed. BAE Systems via Brooklands Museum

trials beginning in March 1962. The basic principle behind terrain following was that the radar continuously mapped the terrain ahead of the aircraft (with the scanner 'leaning into' turns to compensate for curved flightpaths). If the approaching terrain impinged on a virtual 'ski toe' ahead of the aircraft, the TFR would command the AFCS to pull up to avoid it. If there was no terrain conflict the AFCS would be commanded to make the aircraft descend. The quality of the ride for the crew was to be determined by two things: ride height (selectable in steps of 10ft (3m) down to a minimum of 150ft (50m)), and how closely the aircraft would follow the terrain contours. The latter was determined by a rotary switch on the AFCS control panel, simply marked 'RIDE' and graded in five positions from 1 (soft) to 5 (rough). This would vary the length of the imaginary 'ski' on which the aircraft was mounted, the 'rough' ride being the shortest ski and resulting in the harshest pitch demands. The AFCS would not 'trust' the TFR inputs entirely, and would always compare its demands with the signals from the radio altimeter. If a descent was demanded and the radio altimeter indicated this would result in ground impact, the TFR's demand would be ignored.

Early trials with a modified AI.23B mounted in the nose of Douglas Dakota TS423 were a dismal failure, primarily because the trials had been begun prematurely, before the problems of separating terrain from general ground clutter had been solved. One of the Buccaneer development aircraft, XK487, was earmarked as a more suitable testbed for the completed FLR, even though the aircraft was being pushed as an alternative to the TSR2. The Admiralty, unsurprisingly, proved less than co-operative, and negotiations for the use of the aircraft and associated spares backup delayed matters. Blackburn also dragged its heels, stating at one point that it had not expected Ferranti to progress so quickly with the FLR development, and thus had not expected XK487 to be needed so soon.

Progressing quickly was not something of which Ferranti was often accused. Delivery of *Blue Parrot* for the NA.39 programme had already slipped, and progress with the TSR2 FLR was looking so poor in mid-1961 that serious thought was given to cancelling the Ferranti FLR entirely. The Air Staff had its feathers seriously ruffled by the Admiralty also asking Ferranti to conduct a study into fitting a terrain-following version of *Blue Parrot* to the NA.39. The Air Staff had

been told on numerous occasions that Ferranti was 'up to its eyebrows' with work already, hence the lack of progress, and was seriously concerned that any additional loading coming from the Admiralty was going to have a negative impact on the TSR2 programme. The deeper objection was really that the Admiralty appeared to be working on the basis that it could gradually upgrade the NA.39 to the point where it was a serious threat to the TSR2, with RAF officers reduced to squabbling about whether the NA.39 should be allowed to attack inland targets as well as targets ashore!

An MoA delegation then visited the USA to examine an off-the-shelf alternative, the Texas Instruments APN.149. This was J-band radar, already test-flown in a Martin B-26, with proven terrain-following capability, radar ranging and ground mapping and fixing. An RAF pilot had flown in the B-26 down to altitudes as low as 90ft (27m) with the TFR functioning well. The lack of tanker and airfield homing could be dealt with by the installation of an air-to-air tactical air navigation and radio compass (already fitted to the first two aircraft to aid navigation). The lack of weapon-aiming capability was a more serious omission, and

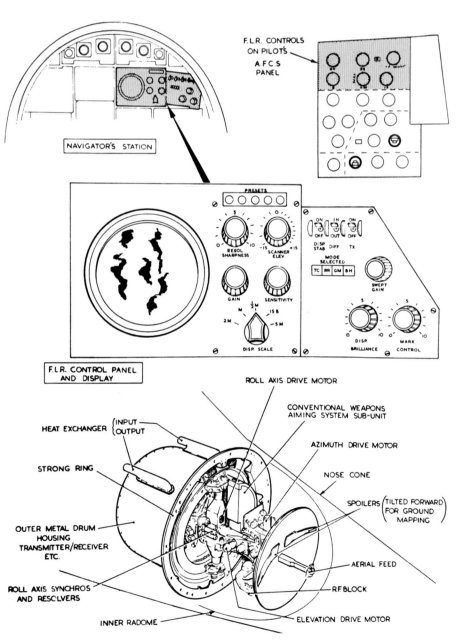

The FLR installation and associated controls. BAE Systems via Brooklands Museum

would require the creation of a weapon-aiming computer to be linked to the APN.149. The ramifications of replacing the expected Ferranti set with the Texas Instruments alternative were studied by BAC, and it was found that while there would be a delay of two months in the flight of the development aircraft, which would cascade down to the in-service date of production aircraft, the guaranteed delivery times from Texas Instruments would enable significantly more testing of the TFR system. Additionally, Texas Instruments was offering a guaranteed mean time between failures (MTBF) of 140hr (compared with a vague promise of 50hr from Ferranti), fixed prices, and discounts if it slipped on the promised production schedule. It was an attractive offer; the saving per production aircraft was expected to be £25,000.

Ferranti was furious. Its FLR was more capable in turning flight (being stabilized to a 45-degree angle of bank compared with the APN.149's 30 degrees), integrated the functions of airfield and tanker homing, and the company believed it had ample room for further development, whereas the APN.149 had none. A new radome would need to be developed for the APN.149, not a minor job, and the TFR capability of the APN.149 was only proven at far lower speeds than specified for the TSR2. The ¼g limit on the APN.149 would result in undershoots at high speeds, or, to put it more bluntly, flight into terrain, though Texas

ABOVE: **The navigator's FLR display and control panel.** BAE Systems via Brooklands Museum

BELOW: **The Buccaneer selected for FLR trials, XK487, at Brough in late 1962 with the newly fitted nose section, awaiting the addition of a TSR2 radome and a new paint job.**
BAE Systems via Brooklands Museum

Instruments claimed this particular limitation would be easy to remove. Trickier to deal with was the frequency at which the APN.149 operated, as J-Band radar could be confused by rain. On one occasion during a B-26 test flight the TFR commanded the aircraft to climb over a rain cloud as if it were an obstruction. The X-Band Ferranti unit had no such weaknesses. The Prime Minister (Harold Macmillan), on finding out about the proposal to use a US radar unit, wrote to the Minister of Defence, Peter Thorneycroft, to express his own unease: 'I must say I find it exceedingly disquieting. The Government is very firmly committed to produce the T.S.R.II as a viable weapons system in the mid-1960s. It would seem very sad if this could only be done at the price of having to purchase American equipment for it'. Elliotts had clearly done well to hide the American origin of the TSR2's central computing system!

By April 1962 Ferranti was offering more guarantees, such as 60hr MBTF, and was becoming much more receptive to the idea of a fixed price and delivery date. Meanwhile, airborne trials on Canberra B(I).8(mod) WT327 had begun on 27 February 1962, with extremely promising results. The modified AI.23B set on this aircraft was linked to an early model of the TSR2's terrain-following computer, and displayed pitch commands to the pilot on a small display unit. The pilots soon trusted the system enough to enter cloud while in terrain-following flight, losing sight of the ground entirely and continuing to follow the pitch commands given by the system. Ferranti won the argument; the Minister of Defence decided on 2 May that there was no alternative but to proceed with the Ferranti FLR, which, despite being the more expensive option, would be more capable. The FLR lived on, and Texas Instruments went away empty-handed.

By 1964 Ferranti had rewarded the faith placed in it, and had regained much of the previous schedule slippage. Several FLR test models were in use, and flight trials on both the Canberra and Buccaneer were generally going well, with some particularly impressive results in the later Buccaneer flights, using a much more representative model of the FLR. Unfortunately, the ground-mapping mode was not quite so impressive, and some serious work was going to be needed to improve this aspect.

In physical terms the TSR2 FLR had a scanner head and transmitter/receiver unit that was basically similar to the existing

Ferranti's Canberra, WT327, flies over Turnhouse Airport. This aircraft carried out much of the early FLR airborne trials before the Buccaneer testbed was available. BAE Systems via Glenn Surtees

AI.23B, but the various ancillary units were different, making extensive use of transistorization. The entire assembly was supported by a surrounding mounting ring. Attached to this ring at the front was the aircraft's radome, and at the rear the FLR canister, shaped rather like a top hat. This meant that the unit was fully enclosed in a pressurized and sealed container to keep the sensitive electronics clean of dust and other contaminants, and the entire thing could be removed from the aircraft, radome and all. The Air Staff objected to this, wanting the ability to remove the radome for servicing or replacement without disturbing the FLR, so an internal dome was introduced to enclose the scanner area. This dome later came up as an item that could possibly be dropped to save costs, the FLR's components having proved to be more reliable and less sensitive to environmental contaminants than expected.

At the time of cancellation, the only flying TSR2, XR219, had never been fitted with the FLR, or indeed AFCS, so the real performance of the TSR2's TFR system was never able to be demonstrated. However, the most recent flight trials at the time had suffered from several spurious pitch-up demands, and clearance height over peaks

had been dangerously low on several occasions, so it was clear that some months of further work were needed before a fully automatic system could be safely demonstrated.

Head-up display

The TSR2 was to be one of the first aircraft to incorporate a HUD, that is, a display superimposing various flight data and flight director cues over the pilot's view of the outside world. This was to use a CRT display (the Precision Display Unit) buried within the cockpit coaming, focused at infinity via a 6.5in lens and reflecting off the aircraft's windscreen. Information to be presented was to include a flight director to lead the pilot through manoeuvres as required (including terrain following and bombing) plus readouts of airspeed, altitude and heading.

Early work on such a display had taken place at the RAE, which had also come up with suitable symbology to use, and after early tests of very basic HUDs on Meteor WL375 and Javelin XA831 the RAE commissioned Hawker to produce a one-off Hunter airframe to use in HUD development trials. This was XE531, the one and only Hunter T.12, which as well as provision

Derek Whitehead, Blackburn's Chief Test Pilot, hands over XK487 to John Field, chief pilot of the Ferrranti Flying Unit. After months of delay, more demanding airborne trials could finally begin. BAE Systems via Glenn Surtees

The RAE's Hunter T.12, XE531, was used for HUD trials. BAE Systems via Brooklands Museum

for a HUD also included a nose bulge to house a new camera (the FX.126, also destined for TSR2 use). Among other changes, XE531 had been given a master reference gyro, an air data computer and an ILS (all to be linked to the HUD), along with a small joystick to be used by the second pilot to control the Flight Director. Thus the second pilot could 'fly' the aircraft in simulated terrain-following by using his side-stick to control the demanded flight path displayed on the HUD, hoping that the other pilot was following the director symbology correctly. This demonstrator aircraft was flying regularly throughout 1964 and proved quickly that the whole HUD concept was excellent.

The contract for TSR2 HUD development went to Rank-Cintel, and by 1963 an early model was ready for testing at Weybridge. While it worked well given a suitable reflecting surface, the TSR2's windscreen was anything but that. With multiple layers and an overall thickness decided by the birdstrike resistance requirement, it gave multiple ghost images, and early models also suffered from highly distracting cyclic variations in brightness owing to tiny voltage variations. A demonstration of a supposedly improved unit in August 1963 received a slew of complaints about the ghosting, and resulted in an attempt to improve matters by the addition of a slightly reflective layer on the windscreen's inner face. A portable cockpit mock-up was built to include an elliptical reflective patch on the windscreen, and this was positioned on a hill overlooking the Weybridge site so that typical viewing angles at low level with varied lighting levels could be experienced. The result was a significant improvement, but pilots who tried the mock-up complained that the obviously different elliptical area was distracting, and the reduction in light transmission through the windscreen might cause target identification problems. An alternative application, covering the entire windscreen, was also demonstrated, but this introduced additional distractions from reflections of other cockpit objects. The Air Staff decision was to apply the reflective coating on a band across the middle covering the required area, and to fade it out top and bottom to reduce the distraction factor. This, naturally, would be the most expensive option.

By late 1964 the latest laboratory models were performing rather better than earlier models, and reliability of components was being improved with soak testing. However, there were constant complaints about

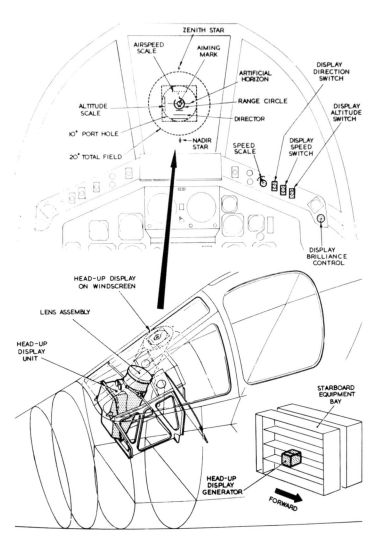

TSR2 HUD symbology.
BAE Systems via
Brooklands Museum

windscreen quality from the pilots carrying out TSR2 taxy runs and test flights, so there was a very good chance that the final HUD would have needed to use a separate reflector plate, as used in all practical installations after the TSR2.

Reconnaissance pack

The TSR2 was designed to carry out reconnaissance as a dedicated role and also in addition to its more usual strike role. In dedicated reconnaissance fit the aircraft was to obtain information for tactical purposes, including target mapping at low altitudes and in all weather conditions, by day or by night using radar and/or photographic methods. In strike fit the aircraft would still be required to carry out the maximum photographic and/or radar reconnaissance without this adversely affecting its strike capabilities. The primary purpose of the TSR2's reconnaissance information was to support both the counter-air battle and the land battle. For the latter task in particular

ABOVE: Head-Up Display installation details.
BAE Systems via
Brooklands Museum

RIGHT: The HUD installation in the mockup cockpit at Weybridge. Restricted viewing angles and the poor reflective qualities of the TSR2 windscreen was a continual problem, and the final HUD would probably have needed substantial redesign.
BAE Systems

it was essential that information could be got back to interpreters as soon as possible, so that it could be studied and effective use made of it before the information became stale. The defences to be expected on the European battlefield further complicated

the task, as extreme low-level flying and transonic speeds would be necessary to allow anti-air units as little time to respond as possible. For coverage of wider areas, medium-level sorties would be required, and here supersonic speeds would be necessary.

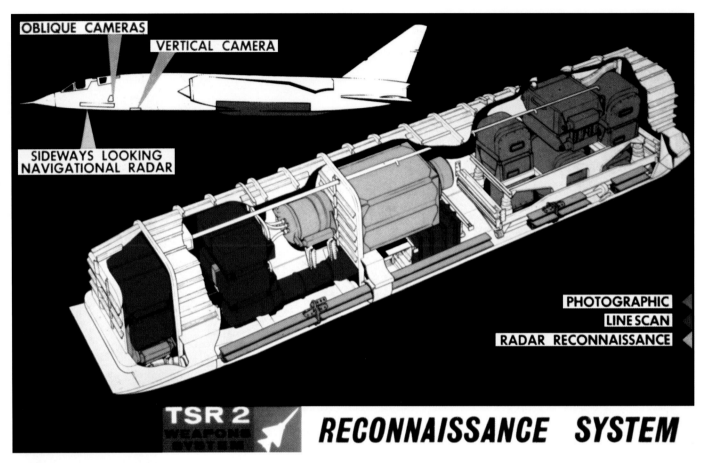

OBLIQUE CAMERAS

VERTICAL CAMERA

SIDEWAYS LOOKING
NAVIGATIONAL RADAR

PHOTOGRAPHIC

LINE SCAN

RADAR RECONNAISSANCE

TSR 2 WEAPONS SYSTEM

RECONNAISSANCE SYSTEM

The TSR2's reconnaissance system was made up from permanently fitted items, such as the strike cameras and SLR, and a dedicated reconnaissance pack.
BAE Systems via Brooklands Museum

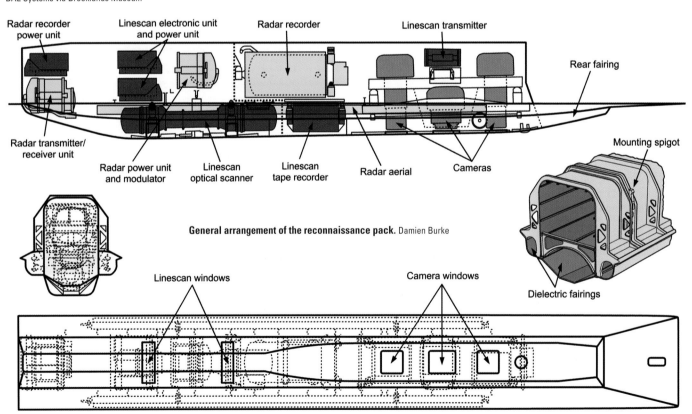

Radar recorder power unit

Linescan electronic unit and power unit

Radar recorder

Linescan transmitter

Rear fairing

Radar transmitter/ receiver unit

Radar power unit and modulator

Linescan optical scanner

Linescan tape recorder

Radar aerial

Cameras

Mounting spigot

Dielectric fairings

General arrangement of the reconnaissance pack. Damien Burke

Linescan windows

Camera windows

In dedicated reconnaissance fit the aircraft would have the navigator's bombing control panel replaced by a reconnaissance control panel, and a large reconnaissance pack would be mounted in semi-conformal style below the fuselage. The bomb-bay doors would be removed and fairings fitted to the forward and aft ends of the reconnaissance pack, which would hang from the bomb-bay roof racks. The pack was self-contained apart from relying on the aircraft for control, power and air conditioning supplies. Early windtunnel tests showed that the pack added no detectable drag, and therefore performance was expected to be unaffected. There was some consideration given to flight testing the pack by fitting it to a Canberra B(I).8 bomb bay – the fit was a surprisingly good match once the forward fairing was removed, though the aircraft would have needed an enlarged tail bumper to ensure ground clearance was sufficient with the tail down. However, the position of the Canberra's engine nacelles was expected to interfere with the SLR, so this was not proceeded with. A mock-up pack was fitted to XR225 at Weybridge in February 1965, and some minor fouls were experienced in matching the pack to the airframe which necessitated both pack and airframe modifications. These were to be incorporated on airframes from XS665 onwards.

The reconnaissance pack embodied three separate systems: optical linescan, SLR and standard photographic cameras.

Optical linescan (ARI.23132)

The linescan fit was from EMI, and consisted of a high-speed rotating scanner that picked up variations in brightness as it swept the ground at right angles to the aircraft's track. Unlike traditional cameras, linescan was not limited to the field of view of a fixed lens, as the scanner would rotate and thus the field of view was theoretically a full 360 degrees. In practice, from horizon to horizon was the area of interest, and the physical make-up of the reconnaissance pack meant that the actual scan area was limited to a 144-degree sweep.

Passive linescan was to be used in daylight, and active (illuminated) linescan would be used at night. Optimized for best performance while flying at 500ft (150m) above ground level, in active mode an extremely narrow beam of light would be projected in concert with the rotation of the scanner unit. The beam's narrow width, 5 milli-radians, and the high-speed rotation of the scanner (12,000rpm)

An experimental linescan unit on its servicing trolley. The TSR2's linescan worked in purely visual wavelengths, as opposed to the IR linescan units that became more popular later. BAE Systems

would combine to make the illumination practically invisible to the naked eye, and thus would not endanger the aircraft, unlike the traditional means of illuminating the ground for photography, which entailed the ejection of parachute flares and the attraction of lots of undesirable attention. While daylight linescan coverage would not match the quality of traditional photographic results, in low light, before dawn and during twilight, the light-sensitivity of the photocells at the heart of the unit would be superior to the exposure characteristics of photographic film and thus produce more usable results.

The scanner unit consisted of a motor rotating a pair of mirror drums. In active mode one of these mirror prisms would reflect a powerful Philips CS200 arc light source at the ground. The other mirror was the receiving mirror, collecting light entering the unit and directing it to the scanner for amplification and processing. The scanner unit itself was sealed (with a window to let light in and out, of course), and the drums operated in a vacuum environment

A linescan image of Tewkesbury, Gloucestershire, with the River Severn on the left, crossed by the A38 and the long-since-vanished railway line. The resolution of the original image is sufficient to distinguish cars from lorries, though distortion towards the horizons renders the edges of the image of far less use. BAE Systems via Brooklands Museum

to ease the load on the motor. The belly of the reconnaissance pack itself had a sliding shutter covering another window, through which the scanner operated. When the scanner was not being used, the shutter would be closed to protect the window glass from erosion or foreign-object damage.

Originally it was intended that the output be recorded on photographic film with rapid onboard processing and enough film for 50nm (57 miles; 90km) of coverage (passive) or 150nm (170 miles; 270km) (active), but this was changed so that the varying electrical signals from the linescan sensor were recorded on magnetic tape instead. This enabled the linescan record to be buffered onboard the aircraft, so that delayed transmission of linescan data could be made in circumstances in which live transmission was not possible. Coverage width would vary from 0.2nm at 200ft (60m) to 1nm at 1,000ft (300m), increasing above this height, but with resolution increasingly suffering to the point that it would no longer be able to identify a three-ton truck, as required by the specification. Signal processing included automatic contrast adjustment to deal with hazy conditions and automatic gain control (AGC) to deal with extreme variations in brightness on what was a rather low level of signal produced by the scanner. The processed signal was then combined with digital data of the aircraft's flight parameters before being recorded on the videotape recorder unit. The data track on the tape could briefly be replaced by an event marker under the control of the aircraft's navigator, so any particularly noteworthy location could be highlighted for the interpreters looking through the tape afterwards.

In practice, one drawback of AGC was that it rendered the scanner incapable of imaging sudden changes in the terrain, in particular the change from over-water imaging to coastal areas. The AGC took several seconds to cope with the change, valuable seconds in which the imagery would not be of acceptable quality. Thus reconnaissance of coastal targets would have been extremely problematic. Early testing of the active linescan system also found that contrast was much lower than expected, challenging the haze filters, and only after a fruitless investigation into the characteristics of the light source being used was it realized that the main problem was simply the lack of any shadows, the light source always pointing directly at any one point on the scanned line. Thus the RAF's preference for the

'more natural' illuminated scene actually resulted in an entirely unnatural image. It is noteworthy that other linescan systems produced after the TSR2 project was cancelled went with IR imaging, rather than natural light or active illumination.

Linescan airborne radio link (ARI.23135)

With one of the TSR2's primary purposes for reconnaissance being tactical support of the army on the battlefield, timely reception and processing of reconnaissance information was essential. Accordingly the linescan system needed to be able to transmit its data in real time if at all possible, or, at the very least, shortly after scanning and before the aircraft returned to base. The transmitter would use one of five frequencies in the C-band (around 4,600Mhz), pre-selected on the ground before the sortie.

Linescan radio-link ground stations

Requirement ASR.2153 covered the requirement for mobile, air-transportable installations capable of receiving and processing signals from the linescan radio link called for in OR.343. Each station was to receive linescan pictures transmitted via HF from TSR2 aircraft, process the data into photographic imagery suitable for first-stage interpretation, in real time, and to provide display facilities for this imagery. A range of up to 110nm (125 miles; 200km) to the transmitting aircraft was specified, with acquisition of the aircraft at 120nm (140 miles; 220km). All of the information received was to be recorded for later re-use and processing to a permanent negative or positive image on 5in film as fast as possible (no more than a two-minute delay being allowed).

High-frequency communications for the receipt of linescan information would be supplemented by UHF facilities and telephone/telex links along with display units, tables and seating for operators/interpreters. Air-conditioning and filtration and, of course, power supplies and lighting, would also be required. All of this was to fit within a standard Signals Container Body Mk 6, with all external mountings able to be stored inside for air transportation in an Armstrong Whitworth Argosy or similar aircraft. Rough estimates on the number required gave a total of twelve at a cost of £50,000 each, four of which were to be located in Germany. Each station would only be able to work with a single aircraft at any one time, and the aircraft would need to remain

within range throughout its transmission. This would require some careful traffic control within a busy battlefield environment. Ground stations would also need to be able to deal with downloaded information provided from landed aircraft that had been unable to transmit while airborne.

In the early months of 1965, as part of the desperate cost-cutting exercises being undertaken to try to stop the project from being cancelled entirely, the requirement for live linescan data transmission was unceremoniously dropped, and all work on the transmitter and ground station came to a sudden halt.

Sideways-looking reconnaissance radar (ARI.23136)

The reconnaissance pack also contained a high-resolution Q-band SLR for reconnaissance, with 15ft (4.6m)-long aerials on the port and starboard sides. Each aerial could be shortened to an effective length of 8ft (2.4m) via a mechanical shutter, and each could be tilted in the roll axis between 10 and −20 degrees from the horizontal, the navigator being able to select one of five positions throughout this range (both aerials would tilt to the same setting). At low altitude the lateral coverage for each aerial was between 2 and 5nm (2.3 and 5.75 miles; 3.7 and 9.25km), rising to around 10nm (11.5 miles; 18.5km) at medium altitude. The dead zone directly beneath the aircraft, in between the port and starboard radar coverage zones, could be filled by use of the linescan (at low level), or by overlapping passes to get 100 per cent radar coverage.

Two modes of operation were provided for; firstly, moving-target indication (MTI), primarily at low level, using the 8ft aerial length and comparing successive pulses to ascertain whether contacts had moved, and, secondly, medium-altitude reconnaissance without MTI, using the full aerial length. MTI recording would be available up to 10,000ft (3,000m) and 800kt (920mph; 1,480km/h) ground speed, with the non-MTI role being available from 5,000ft (1,500m) upwards through the aircraft's full speed range. The radar transmitter/receiver, modulator and power units were developed from the *Red Neck* radar system that had been intended for use on the Handley Page Victor, but which never entered service. Several modifications had been made, most notably to the pulse-repetition frequency (PRF), to enable better detection of moving targets travelling at speeds characteristic of military vehicles.

Beam configuration and coverage of SLR.
Damien Burke

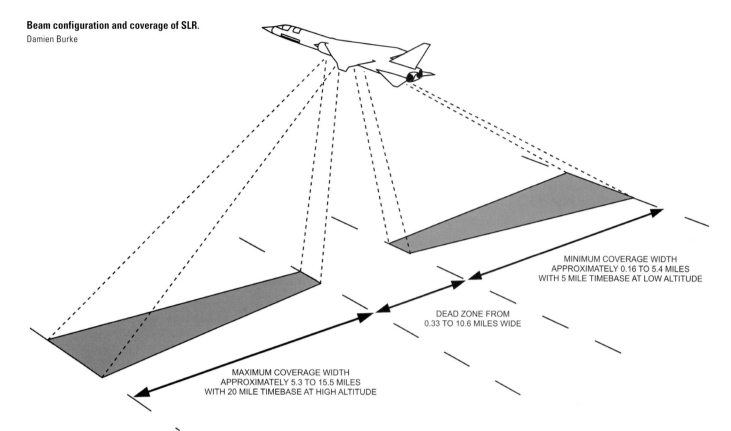

MINIMUM COVERAGE WIDTH
APPROXIMATELY 0.16 TO 5.4 MILES
WITH 5 MILE TIMEBASE AT LOW ALTITUDE

DEAD ZONE FROM
0.33 TO 10.6 MILES WIDE

MAXIMUM COVERAGE WIDTH
APPROXIMATELY 5.3 TO 15.5 MILES
WITH 20 MILE TIMEBASE AT HIGH ALTITUDE

Continuous recording of the radar returns would be carried out along with data from the aircraft's navigation system: altitude, heading, pitch angle, timebase delay, latitude and longitude. The actual recording was carried out using a similar 'Heath Robinson' means to that of the navigation SLR display, radar returns being displayed on a pair of 3in (7.6cm) CRT monitors, and the output being recorded on photographic film running at a speed varying with the aircraft's ground speed. Three separate 80mm f/4 lenses would record the CRT traces, the central one recording non-radar data from a smaller 2in (5cm) CRT, while the outer lenses recorded the radar returns (left and right radar returns only in non-MTI mode, or half-width tracks showing radar returns and MTI traces if MTI was in use). Exposure would automatically vary with the speed at which the 5in-wide film strip was transported past the lenses. Unlike the linescan unit, radio transmission of radar data was not considered practical or necessary, and post-flight processing and interpretation of radar reconnaissance data would be the only means of getting at this data. Unlike the aircraft's on-board navigation SLR, there was no rapid processing unit to enable

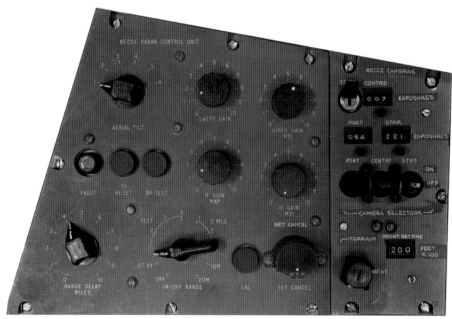

The reconnaissance pack control panel in the navigator's cockpit. This panel would have occupied the 'role panel' slot at bottom left of the navigator's instrument panel.
BAE Systems via Warton Heritage Group

near-real-time display of the reconnaissance radar. Instead, a rapid processing and development unit (RPDU) would be part of the ground station supporting TSR2 reconnaissance operations.

The amount of coverage possible from the SLR was limited by two things. First of all, the length of the film strip dictated the distance that could be covered on the track (25ft (7.6m) of film gave 1,500nm (1,725 miles; 2,775km) of cover at 5nm per inch), and secondly the altitude flown at and angle of the SLR aerials dictated the lateral depth of the coverage. The aerials could be set at five angles ranging between 10 degrees above the horizon to 20 degrees below, with the angle chosen not just to vary lateral coverage width, but also to make best use of available radar power. With 5, 10 and 20-mile (8, 16 and 32km) time bases, the lateral coverage could vary between 866 and 28,580ft (264 and 8,710m) with a 5-mile time base, and from 28,020 to 82,040ft (8,540 to 25,000m) with a 20-mile time base. The gap of no coverage below the aircraft would therefore vary from 1,732 to 56,040ft (530 to 17,080m). The film scale would vary between 5 and 9 miles per inch.

The MTI feature could only detect objects with a perpendicular movement component of at least 3.5 mph (5.6km/h). A moving vehicle could theoretically go entirely undetected if it was heading along a track parallel to that of the aircraft. In practice this was unlikely to have been a major problem, as reconnaissance sorties would have been planned to avoid flying parallel to the track of any roads or rail lines of interest, and targets moving over open country would be unlikely to stick to a straight line for long, minimizing the already small chance that their track would coincide with that of the aircraft.

The SLR requirements were particularly demanding in terms of reliability; up to 6hr continuous airborne use, and 200hr between maintenance checks, without any loss in accuracy.

Photographic reconnaissance

While OR.343 initially specified a front-facing camera mounted in the aircraft, this was changed when it was pointed out that the average time between the pilot spotting a target and needing to get the camera pointing at it would be around 1/10th of a second, which was simply not possible in most circumstances. The results from forward-facing cameras on existing reconnaissance types were proving to be extremely limited as a result. A downward-facing camera was substituted instead, along with two side-facing cameras giving oblique coverage. These were all Vinten F.95 Mk 7s, the downward-facing one being fitted with a 1.5in (38mm) lens and the obliques with 4in f/1.8 lenses tilted down at 15 degrees from the horizontal. Shutter speed was 1/1500 at six frames per second, or 1/3000 at twelve frames per second, with image

movement compensation. The film magazine on each camera could accommodate 100ft (30m) of film, enough for 40sec continuous coverage at the highest frame rate.

Three FX.126 cameras were intended to be fitted within the rear half of the reconnaissance pack, with a variety of lens sizes to enable a mixture of imagery resolutions from various altitudes: one with a 6in f5.6 lens, and the others with either 24in f5.6 or 36in f6.3 lenses. Shutter speeds could be 1/250, 1/500 or 1/1000, and film capacity for this 9 × 9in (23 × 23cm)-format film was 250ft (76m) of film or 320 exposures. Latitude and longitude would be recorded on each frame, and markers recorded on the SLR traces to show where each photographic frame was taken (if the SLR was operating). One drawback of traditional photographic film was its susceptibility to radiation, and given the nuclear environment in which the aircraft could expect to be operating in a full-scale European war, provision was made for filtration of the air entering the reconnaissance pack camera bay to stop radioactive contaminants accumulating on or around the film cassettes. In peacetime the filters would be bypassed owing to the expense and maintenance hassle of fitting and removing them all the time.

Mobile photographic-interpretation units were intended to be located with TSR2 units at forward airfields, enabling all air-reconnaissance imagery to be passed through human interpretation before being communicated to the Army. There would, however, never be enough of these to go round, so the idea was they would be located at a handful of 'master' airfields rather than attempting to provide facilities at every dispersed site.

Self-protection: passive electronic countermeasures

While TSR2's primary defence against detection was low-level flight, there would still be plenty of opportunity for the aircraft to be blown out of the sky by sufficiently advanced missiles, and the loft attack in particular exposed the aircraft to radar detection and lock-on. The Guided Weapons Department at Vickers produced a report at the end of January 1959 which concluded that active jammers should not be carried by the TSR2 except in exceptional circumstances, that a warning receiver would be essential, that the natural radar echoing area of the aircraft should be kept

An FX.126 camera with 12in lens. Development of the camera lagged behind that of the TSR2 but continued after the aircraft's cancellation, airborne trials starting in 1967. With automatic focus, exposure and image stabilization, plus the ability to record navigational information alongside the images, this was an advanced piece of equipment. A&AEE

as low as possible, and passive measures such as applying radar camouflage material to the airframe and carriage of *Window* (chaff) would be useful. A Sub-Committee on Electronic Countermeasures was formed and examined this area in detail.

Missile warning system (ARI.18203)

To give the aircrew some indication that they were the subject of a radar-guided-missile attack, a passive RWR fit was to be integrated within the airframe. An outline requirement for this was drawn up in May 1960, and detailed a system that was to weigh no more than 50lb (23kg), nor exceed one cubic foot (0.03cu m) of space. The system was to indicate the presence of lock-on radars of all polarizations, whether airborne or ground; indicate and discriminate between S-, X-, J- and Q-band signals; discriminate between continuous-wave and pulse signals; give all-round cover; give aural and visual indications of a lock-on, and be ready by June 1963. Competitive study contracts were placed with Marconi and Ferranti in August 1960. Tenders were submitted in November and the job was given to Ferranti at the end of December. Incredibly, it then took the MoA a full year to negotiate a contract with Ferranti, a ridiculous length of time, beating even its own normally slothful standards. Consequently the development of the system did not begin until late in 1961, nearly two years after the TSR2 project as a whole had begun.

The passive warning receiver was initially to consist of two forward-facing missile-warning heads on the nose just in front of the windscreen, projecting at about 45 degrees on either side, and a rearward-facing pair of heads within the trailing edge of each of the down-turned wingtips. Each pair of heads could thus detect radar energy in both horizontal and vertical polarizations, and included three aerials to cover the microwave bands S, C/X and J. Detection of a missile lock would sound a tone in the aircrew headsets; an RWR display to show threat direction was not provided, though a simple left/right indicator was originally mentioned as being of use. However, difficulties were experienced with this equipment during development. First, reception of pulse signals caused overloading of a test unit, requiring considerable amplifier redesign, and then Ferranti's aural signal, a relatively simple amplification of the received radar signal, was judged inappropriate, and a steady aural tone was required instead. This instantly meant the unit could not recognize a track-while-scan radar, as Ferranti had relied upon the distinct aural tones of such a radar to give the crew warning. Addition of a new circuit to cope with recognizing a TWS pattern and translating it to the standard aural warning tone was necessary.

Then it was found that the proposed wingtip locations would interfere with the aircraft's fluxgate compass, also mounted in the wingtip. As a result, the installation was

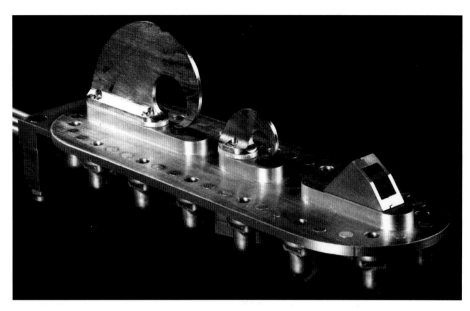

The forward (nose) aerial of the missile warning receiver. Two of these would have been enclosed within a dielectric fairing on the nose, ahead and on either side of the windscreen, on production airframes. BAE Systems via Brooklands Museum

downgraded to a single wingtip receiver, leaving a small gap in the rearward coverage which the Air Staff initially accepted but later objected to, forcing a rethink to see if a four-station unit could be made to work. The problem was insuperable, and a three-station system had to be accepted. By June 1963 the system was nowhere near

ready. Flight trials were initially scheduled to take place on the ninth development-batch aircraft during late 1964, but the delays in development of both the RWR and the aircraft itself caused a decision to be made to transfer trials to the eleventh aircraft (these being scheduled for the spring of 1966). By April 1965, problems with the casings for the wingtip receiver had prevented the installation of a complete system in any TSR2 airframe; the project's cancellation came days later.

Chaff and flares

On the active countermeasures front there were no systems installed within the airframe, but various investigations were also carried out into the carriage of what was then called 'rapid-blooming *Window*' (RBW, now commonly called 'chaff'). *Window* was the codename used by the RAF in the Second World War for foil strips used to confuse enemy radars. Rather than being thrown out in handfuls by aircrew, as was done during the war, modern jets needed the ability to eject RBW as and when required, preferably automatically. The main thrust of the investigation regarding use of RBW by the TSR2 was into masking the airframe during the loft attack, for which a forward-firing rocket was felt to be the best idea. The rocket would burst well in front of the aircraft and produce a cloud of *Window* that would hopefully either stop a radar lock-on from occurring, or break an existing lock.

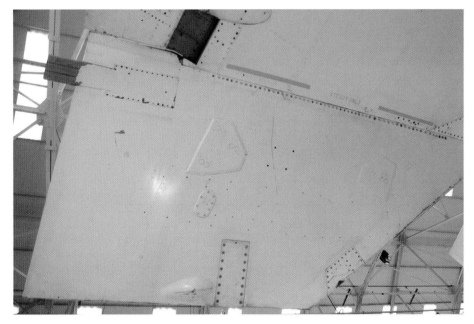

The port wingtip trailing edge would have housed the third missile warning receiver aerial, in the area below the fuel vent/jettison pipe. Also evident here are the ILS aerial (bottom centre), fluxgate compass (bulged) and two 'bonker' plates (fitted only to some development-batch aircraft). Damien Burke

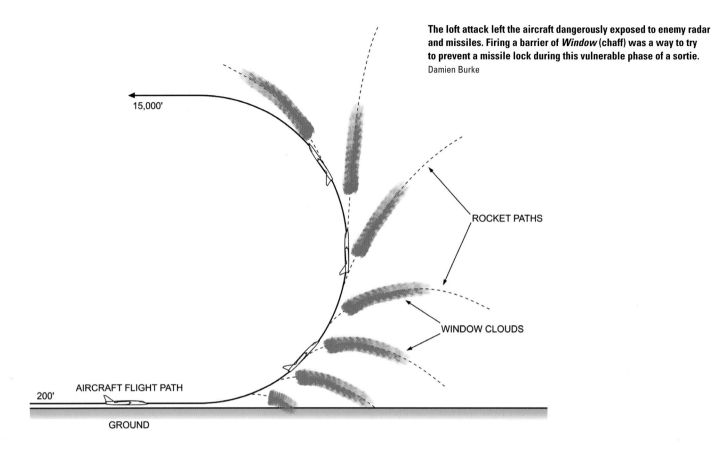

The loft attack left the aircraft dangerously exposed to enemy radar and missiles. Firing a barrier of *Window* (chaff) was a way to try to prevent a missile lock during this vulnerable phase of a sortie.
Damien Burke

ROCKET PATHS

WINDOW CLOUDS

15,000'

AIRCRAFT FLIGHT PATH

200'

GROUND

Because BAC was initially frustrated on this front by lack of available data and existing equipment, it was agreed with the MoA that provision of firing circuits and pylons suitable to take a variety of rocket pods would be enough to fulfil the requirement. It did not take long for the MoA to come back to the subject and ask BAC for a detailed study. Early suggestions for RBW dispensers concentrated on the underwing carriage of dispensers on each side, whether by pylon, slipper pod or wingtip pod, all of which carried penalties in terms of loss of weapons carriage space, drag or excessive weight gain owing to a redesigned wingtip structure. Holding to the concept of projecting *Window* as far forward as possible, BAC also suggested a dorsal pack mounted above the fuselage, just ahead of the wing. However, the Air Staff were not keen on this addition, with its attendant ground-support requirements. (Loading the pack sections so high above the ground would require some sort of crane, and this went against the whole dispersed airfield and minimum-ground-support philosophy.) Despite the drawbacks of the loss of pylons for weapons carriage, and drag, the pylon-mounted dispensers were felt by the Air Staff to be the best option, and in July 1960

it was decided that pylon-mounted dispensers would be the way forward.

In November 1960 the Air Staff had drawn attention to an American RBW rocket then under development, and in October 1961, nothing further having been done in the interim, they asked the RAE to investigate this further. It was not until March 1962 that an RAE team visited the USA to assess the suitability of Revere Copper & Brass Inc's RCU-2B *Window*-sowing rocket to contract QRC-142(T). This was designed to be fired at altitudes of around 50,000ft (15,000m) from Boeing B-52s travelling in a straight line, using twenty 2.5in folding-fin rockets carried in a pod under each wing. Each rocket would pull ahead of the launch vehicle and descend gently, exploding a sequence of *Window* units and thus laying a cloud that would begin ahead and below the launching vehicle and grow with further rockets, to try to seduce the enemy radar's range gate into following the larger target of the *Window* cloud rather than the aircraft. Test carriage and rocket firing had also been trialled on Boeing B-47, North American F-100 and Lockheed F-104 aircraft, using an existing high-speed ALE9 pod, which alleviated most of the RAE's worries of the

susceptibility of the rocket to high-speed carriage and firing during manoeuvres, though some components would need to be replaced to cope with the sustained high temperatures of supersonic flight.

Meanwhile, BAC had continued working on the dorsal idea, and by November 1962 had come up with a dorsal 'fin', much smaller than the previously suggested installation, which would fire window cartridges sideways and upwards. The Air Staff were still not impressed, and in December, having looked at the RAE's study on the American rocket, pushed once again for a complete design study into suitable RBW/infrared decoy (IRD) dispensers, including carriage of a suitable rocket. Accordingly, a contract was awarded to Microcell to carry out a design study for a suitable counter-measures launcher to be pylon-mounted. Completed in June 1963, Microcell's design study proposed an impressive variety of dispensers, with and without forward-firing *Window* rockets in addition to the launch of both RBW and IRD cartridges. Standardized RBW and IRD cartridges were already under development to RRE specifications, of 2.25in diameter and 5.3in long. The operational requirement for these dispensers was that they should be suitable for

The various RBW dispenser proposals made by Microcell in April 1962. Eventually the pylon-mounted pod became be the favoured solution.
Damien Burke

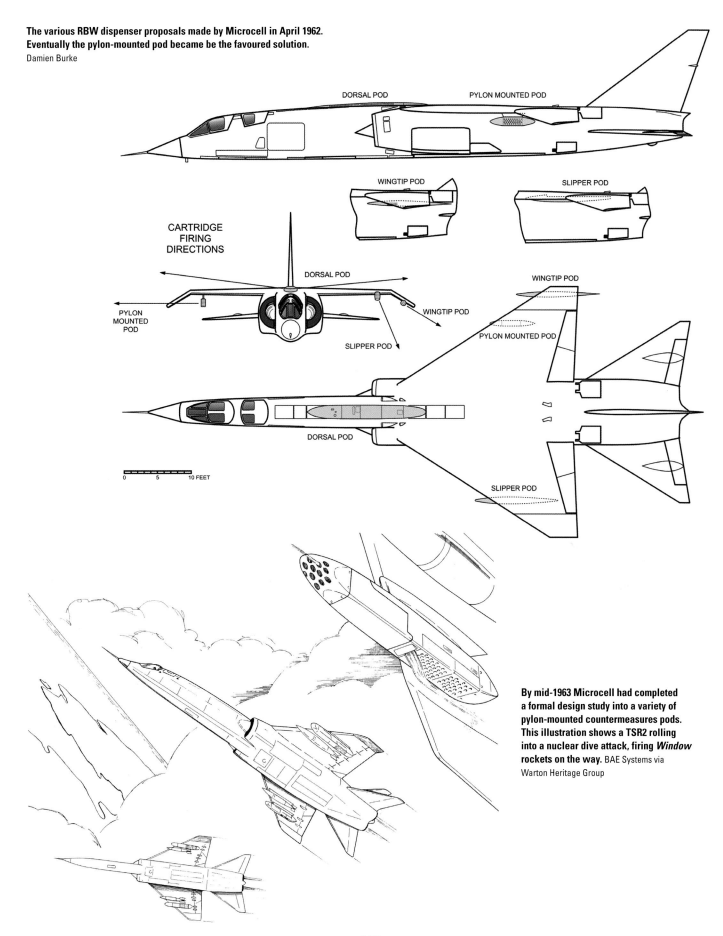

DORSAL POD

PYLON MOUNTED POD

WINGTIP POD

SLIPPER POD

CARTRIDGE
FIRING
DIRECTIONS

DORSAL POD

PYLON
MOUNTED
POD

WINGTIP POD

SLIPPER POD

WINGTIP POD

PYLON MOUNTED POD

DORSAL POD

0   5   10 FEET

SLIPPER POD

By mid-1963 Microcell had completed a formal design study into a variety of pylon-mounted countermeasures pods. This illustration shows a TSR2 rolling into a nuclear dive attack, firing *Window* rockets on the way. BAE Systems via Warton Heritage Group

carriage on both port and starboard outer stores pylons over the aircraft's full flight and temperature envelopes, capable of jettison, and carry as many cartridges as possible; a minimum of 100 for an RBW/IRD-only dispenser. Spent cartridge cases were to be retained within the dispenser after ejection of their payload. A variety of firing combinations was to be provided, and counters in the cockpits provided to show the

remaining capacity of each type of cartridge. *Window* rockets, if chosen, would be fired singly at crew command, but RBW/IRD cartridges were to be capable of both manual and automatic firing in conjunction with the aircraft's missile warning system.

Microcell's first proposal was for a slab-sided dispenser, pylon-mounted of course, firing RBW/IRD either to the side (and slightly downward to avoid the down-

turned wingtips), or an alternative version that fired downwards. The latter would ease the positioning of different cartridge types within the dispenser, as side loads on the pylon were a limiting factor, and simultaneous ejection of the heavier IR decoys would require that IRD cartridges were concentrated near the pylon centre for a sideways-firing dispenser. The obvious problem with the downward-firing version was

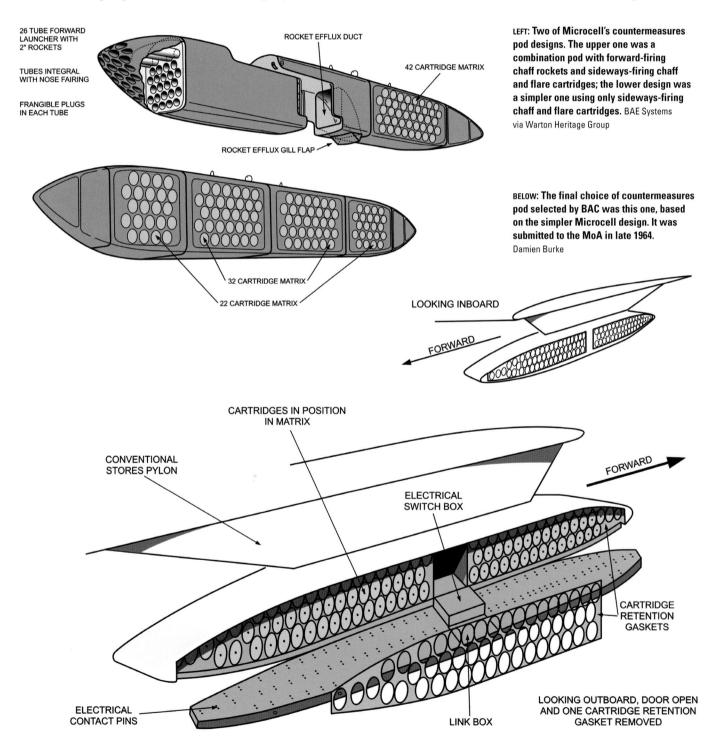

26 TUBE FORWARD LAUNCHER WITH 2" ROCKETS

TUBES INTEGRAL WITH NOSE FAIRING

FRANGIBLE PLUGS IN EACH TUBE

ROCKET EFFLUX DUCT

42 CARTRIDGE MATRIX

ROCKET EFFLUX GILL FLAP

LEFT: Two of Microcell's countermeasures pod designs. The upper one was a combination pod with forward-firing chaff rockets and sideways-firing chaff and flare cartridges; the lower design was a simpler one using only sideways-firing chaff and flare cartridges. BAE Systems via Warton Heritage Group

32 CARTRIDGE MATRIX

22 CARTRIDGE MATRIX

BELOW: The final choice of countermeasures pod selected by BAC was this one, based on the simpler Microcell design. It was submitted to the MoA in late 1964. Damien Burke

LOOKING INBOARD

FORWARD

CARTRIDGES IN POSITION IN MATRIX

CONVENTIONAL STORES PYLON

FORWARD

ELECTRICAL SWITCH BOX

CARTRIDGE RETENTION GASKETS

ELECTRICAL CONTACT PINS

LINK BOX

LOOKING OUTBOARD, DOOR OPEN AND ONE CARTRIDGE RETENTION GASKET REMOVED

that at low level any cartridge contents would hit the ground in very short order, after less than half a second if the aircraft was flying at 50ft (15m). To avoid this, Microcell suggested an overwing fit, but this would need the addition of overwing hardpoints, and perhaps the addition of rear fins to the dispenser to aid clean separation if jettisoned.

The second proposal was for a dispenser that included forward-firing *Window* rockets. No suitable British rocket was then available, and one suggestion was to use the QRC-142 rocket that the RAE had been studying. The length of these rockets, and others suggested, would mean that the cartridge capacity of the dispenser would need to be reduced to a total of forty-two cartridges, and the low frontal area required for the dispenser would limit the number of forward-firing rockets, to just sixteen of the 2.75in-diameter QRC-142 rockets, or up to twenty-six if a suitable 2in-diameter rocket could be developed. With the rear of the dispenser taken up by the cartridges, rocket exhaust would be directed via a downward curving duct to a spring-loaded flap on the underside, or possibly through exhaust stacks directed to the sides, though this would require a longer dispenser.

While the American QRC-142 system went on to be developed successfully into the ADR-8 rocket fired from AN/ALE25 pods fitted to all B-52G/H models from 1964 onwards, interest in its use for the TSR2 evaporated, and BAC Warton went on to produce a design study of its own, based on the Microcell proposal for a side-wards-firing RBW/IRD dispenser. BAC's pylon-mounted RBW/IRD dispensers were a minor variation on the Microcell design, similarly accepting existing 2.25in-diameter and 5.3in-long cartridges in an internal matrix. Each dispenser had room for 108 cartridges (72 RBW, 36 IRD, or all RBW if preferred), slightly more than the Microcell version. As the dispensers would be around 10ft (3m) off the ground when loaded on the pylon, the loading of cartridges would be carried out before hoisting the dispenser up to the pylon, and no special hoisting equipment would be required over and above the equipment already accepted as being required for TSR2 use. Existing pylon connections needed only a small modification to accept a seven-pin electrical connection rather than the existing three-pin connection, and the dispenser pod would be canted 7.5 degrees downwards to ensure that the fired cartridges cleared the wingtip.

TSR2 is capable of modern reconnaissance or of the pin point delivery of any kind of weapon. It is designed to operate at very high speed under the radar screen in all weathers, and has a high degree of invulnerability against any known defence. Its STOL capability frees it from large prepared bases and its long range gives it a flexibility hitherto unattained by any other aircraft. TSR2, which is now on the production line, will augment the operational power of the Royal Air Force in a wide range of roles.

UNDER THE RADAR SCREEN

TSR2

TACTICAL · STRIKE · RECONNAISSANCE

Powered by Bristol Siddeley **Olympus** *Turbo-jets*

BRITISH AIRCRAFT CORPORATION ONE HUNDRED PALL MALL LONDON SW1

A BAC advertisement of 1963. BAE Systems via Brooklands Museum

Control of dispenser firing would be the navigator's job, and he would be able to fire cartridges in various permutations and intervals. Counters showing the remaining content of each dispenser would be present on the navigator's panel, along with firing and sequencing controls. In terms of aircraft performance the RBW/IRD dispensers would have a slight negative effect on transonic longitudinal stability and introduce a fuel penalty of approximately 1,870lb (850kg) on the standard 1,000nm sortie. Trials using a Scimitar with a basic RBW dispenser in late summer 1964 were less

than encouraging, and by January 1965 the requirement for such a dispenser had been suspended and work ceased 'for the time being'. It was not restarted before the project was cancelled.

Active decoys and jammers
As well as RBW and IRD, OR.343 had required the carriage of an active decoy system. The idea here was that some kind of rocket would be fired with a radar reflection area similar to that of the aircraft, and perhaps carrying a noise jammer. Fairey Aviation had looked at using its Fireflash missile

as the basis for such a decoy missile, to be used on the NA.39 on the final approach to a naval target. Such a decoy could conceivably have a large enough frontal radar cross-section (RCS) at least to cause confusion to the enemy radars tracking the incoming aircraft, but the TSR2's overland role was entirely different. Radars could be anywhere alongside the aircraft's path, not just at the end, so a decoy's RCS needed to be large enough to duplicate the aircraft's RCS from any aspect. Such a decoy would be so large as to introduce weight and carriage problems of its own, and in the end the NA.39 never used such a system either. One finding from the NA.39 studies was that Plessey had an experimental jammer that could run for about 10min on battery power, and this was felt to be more likely to be useful than a simple radar reflector decoy. Such jammers could be carried within the bomb bay, occupying space forward of the nuclear store, or in wingtip pods. Firing would be automatic during the loft manoeuvre, or when a radar acquisition turned into a radar lock. The biggest problem with this was that the aircraft presented its largest echoing area to any ground-based defence systems during the loft manoeuvre, so any decoy or jammer would have to be excessively large and powerful to be of any use. The problems mounted up rapidly, and

as a result the requirement for the carriage of decoys and/or jammers was deleted from OR343 in August 1961.

Little information on other possible active ECM equipment for the TSR2 has come to light. Studies to Naval/Air Staff Targets 830 (jammer), 836 (towed decoy), 837 (combined pod to include jammer, towed decoy, chaff and flares) and 841 (draft for a passive-warning IR detector) were all under way at the time of cancellation, and these are mentioned in the context of TSR2 subsystems being still required after cancellation. However, these were all general requirements applicable to all tactical aircraft, very much theoretical studies rather than real projects, and no particular work appears to have taken place to link these to the TSR2 specifically, certainly not at the BAC end of things at least. Given that active ECM had been deleted from the requirement, this is unsurprising. None of the studies resulted in real hardware, and some years later the RAF would buy American ALQ-101 ECM pods instead.

Radar camouflage

The airframe had been designed to give minimum possible radar echoing area in the head-on aspect, particularly in the X-band, and as a result flat, forward-facing bulkheads were kept to a minimum and the engine

compressor faces were partly hidden from direct forward view by long, twisted intake tunnels. The intake tunnels, while hiding the engines nicely, were a source of considerable reflection themselves, and the thermal and structural loads to which they were subject precluded the application of radar-absorbing material (RAM) to them. Thus the intakes provided approximately 60 per cent of the total frontal RCS of 20m². In 1960 RAM was in its very early days, and the most crucial areas requiring camouflage were also those to which it would be most challenging to apply any such materials: the intake ducts and lips. The temperatures and structural distortions experienced in the intakes were sufficient to break off any currently available material, whether it was used as an additional application to the basic structure or formed the structure itself, and send it flying into the engines with possibly catastrophic results. No solution was found to this problem, and in March 1960 the Air Staff agreed that no radar absorbing material should be applied to the intakes. It was suggested that research should begin on the creation of a suitable high-temperature and high-strength RAM for future use on other aircraft, and for application to the TSR2 as an in-service upgrade.

The cockpit area's radar reflectivity was one area that *could* be dealt with. Metallized glass in cockpit transparencies was a known method of reducing radar echoes from the cockpit area, and this dovetailed nicely with the gold film heating/demisting system created by Triplex. No additional work was necessary. No figures have yet come to light on the resulting RCS reduction. By February 1963 RAM technology had moved on, and research had found that very thin metallic films, such as copper oxide paint mixed with resin, gave promising results in radar-absorbency trials. Vickers wrote to the Air Staff requesting views on this, and whether it could result in a reversal of the decision not to use radar camouflage on the intakes. If so, however, additional budgetary cover would be required. By late 1964 the subject was still coming up occasionally, but no firm decisions appear to have been made before the project was cancelled.

Gold film inlaid in the cockpit transparencies for heating and demisting purposes had the bonus of reducing the radar cross-section of the cockpit area. Damien Burke

CHAPTER NINE

Weapons

Weapons delivery and accuracy

The aircraft's primary mission, that of delivering a tactical nuclear weapon, was, using existing tactics, also its most dangerous. The then-current means of attack, for which *Red Beard*'s fuzing system had been designed, was to use LABS, which described a selection of manoeuvres, all variations on a common theme known as 'loft bombing' or 'toss bombing'. Rather than the classic bomb runs of the Second World War, in which the aircraft flew in a straight line over the target, releasing its bombs when the target was centred in the bombsight (level bombing), loft bombing entailed the aircraft effectively throwing a bomb in the manner of an underhand bowl. This was accomplished by pulling up into a hard climb (commonly 3 to 4g) and releasing the bomb at a preset angle (typically 45 degrees) that would give the best 'throw' distance). The aircraft would continue the pull-up, describing half a loop before rolling wings-level and escaping in the direction from which it came. The bomb would initially continue upwards too, but would describe a parabola back to earth, hopefully arriving on the target or at least very close by. The advantages of this delivery method were that the aircraft did not need to enter the immediate area of the target at any time, and thus kept considerable distance between itself and the atomic explosion. However, this manoeuvre also threw away the low-level interdictor's primary means of protection, staying at low altitude. A typical loft-bombing attack could result in the aircraft gaining as much as 12,000ft (3,600m) in altitude during the manoeuvre, which left it extremely vulnerable to SAMs or fighter attack.

The RAE suggested a variation on this attack, in which the release angle was restricted to just 10 degrees and the aircraft terminated the climb immediately after release, rolling left or right to pull hard away from the target. The height gain would be

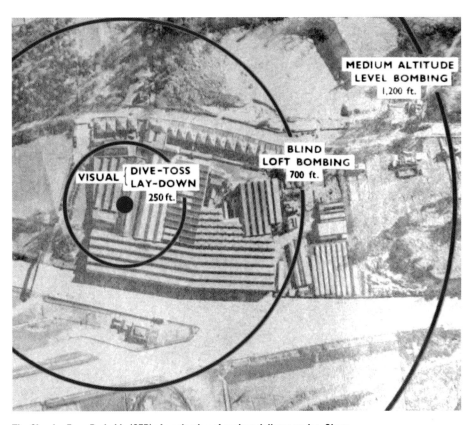

The Circular Error Probable (CEP) of a selection of nuclear delivery modes. Given a big enough bomb, of course, CEPs measured in hundreds of yards were effectively irrelevant. BAE Systems via Brooklands Museum

much less, perhaps just 1,500ft (460m), and the aircraft would retain more speed and energy. However, the bomb would arrive on the target much quicker and would therefore need a delay mechanism to allow the aircraft to escape to a safe distance before the explosion. This also meant the bomb itself had to be tough enough to survive the initial impact without destroying the fusing system and disrupting the structure of the 'physics package' that made up the warhead.

An alternative means of attack was the dive toss, in which the aircraft approached the target at a higher altitude and then started a dive, releasing the weapon in the dive and then pulling out to escape. This, however, was even more dangerous than

loft bombing, because the aircraft was exposed to detection for a much longer period. By late 1962 the requirement for a blind dive-toss attack was removed. However, a lay-down attack was now introduced, for both low-level and medium-level delivery.

Releasing bombs at low level also presented problems. The classic 'lay-down' attack, if performed at 200ft (60m), would result in the aircraft being damaged or destroyed by the explosion (certainly destroyed if the bomb was a nuclear one). Release would need to be from 400ft (120m) for conventional weapons, exposing the aircraft to defences, or a new type of bomb would have to be designed. Retarded bombs, using pop-out fins or parachutes to slow their descent, were being worked on elsewhere, but the Air Staff had already decided to save money on TSR2 by not requiring the design of any new conventional weapons, so their applicability was doubtful at the beginning of the project.

The answer to both sets of problems was the adoption of a stand-off weapon, a missile, that could be released some distance from the target and make its own way over the remaining distance. An Air Staff Target (AST.1168) was already in existence calling for an air-to-surface missile (ASM) that could be launched in blind conditions from low level, along with an Operational Requirement, OR.1173, for a nuclear-armed, visually aimed ASM, based on the characteristics of the American Bullpup missile. Although AST.1168 eventually resulted in the Martel missile, OR.1173 ended up being cancelled.

Visual sighting was always going to be a problem for TSR2 crews. The thick windscreen and surrounding metalwork provided poor view quality in the most important directions, and trials with a Hawker P.1109 (Hunter variant) with a mocked-up TSR2 windscreen had found that vision angles were inadequate for visual identification of targets of opportunity. The use of visually guided missiles such as the Bullpup or AS.30

would have been severely limited by their minimum launch ranges being some distance away from the point at which the TSR2's crew would actually be able to identify the targets.

Reversionary bombing capability

With a complex nav/attack system there was always going to be a chance that one or two items within the system could fail during the sortie. Part of the requirement for the aircraft was that no single failure could prevent it attacking its target, so a great deal of effort went into ensuring that the overall system could cope with failures and still permit the crew to carry out an attack, even if it had to be manually flown. For instance, the CCS was responsible for commanding the AFCS to pull up into the loft attack. If the AFCS had failed or degraded and was not responding to CCS commands, the manoeuvre would not be flown. However, a 'pull up' light would be energized at the same time, so the pilot could manually pull up, using the g-meter in the cockpit and azimuth lines on the HUD to monitor the manoeuvre. Loss of the SLR for navigation fixes would entail use of the FLR or visual fixes; accuracy would be degraded but

should remain within limits for a successful attack. Similar replacements for just about every element of the nav/attack system were available; all would result in loss of accuracy and a higher workload for the crew.

Attack profiles

Loft attack

A typical attack profile for a TSR2 carrying an atomic bomb would be to approach the target at low level at between Mach 0.75 and 0.9 in the terrain-following mode at 200ft (60m), and take a navigational fix when within 30 miles (50km) of the target. This last fix, normally taken using the SLR but possibly taken visually, would enable the attack to be accurate enough to destroy the target with the selected weapon. The Verdan computer was programmed with bombing calculations that would use target position, aircraft fix position, approach speed and preset approach speed to decide when the aircraft should begin the pull-up into the loft manoeuvre. Verdan was programmed with two loft-attack modes, low and high. For each type of loft a constant pitch-up of 5 degrees per second would be flown until a preset angle was reached, with the bomb doors opening shortly beforehand. With the preset angle (30 degrees for low

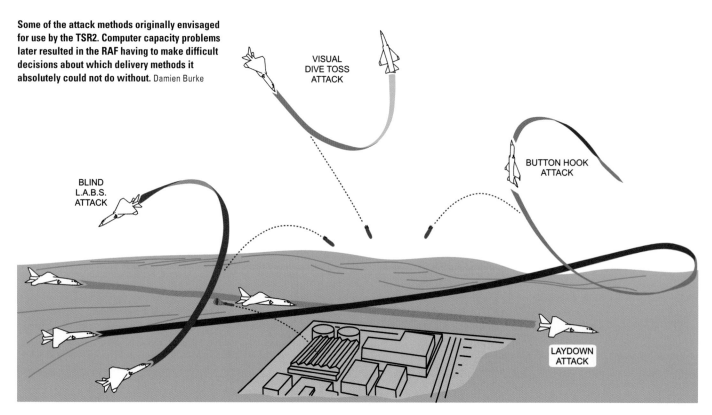

Some of the attack methods originally envisaged for use by the TSR2. Computer capacity problems later resulted in the RAF having to make difficult decisions about which delivery methods it absolutely could not do without. Damien Burke

loft, 65 degrees for high loft) reached, the bomb would be released and the bomb doors cycled closed immediately afterwards, while the aircraft continued to pitch at a constant rate for a total of 190 degrees, leaving it inverted and pointing 10 degrees below the horizon. The aircraft would then roll wings-level and continue the dive to escape the explosion. Whether low loft or high loft was used depended upon the yield of the bomb. Higher yields used the high-loft attack, as this gave the bomb a longer trajectory and therefore extended the escape time. Most bombs would be air-bursts, designed to explode at 2,000ft (600m), and accuracy would be in the region of 1,200ft (365m) circular error probable (CEP).

Loft attack with chandelle escape
A variation on this attack, the loft attack with chandelle breakaway, modified the procedure. The pitching manoeuvre was terminated at weapons release and the aircraft rolled to 140 degrees bank angle, the pilot holding the bank until the aircraft was headed radially away from the target and then diving to escape.

Button-hook attack
For targets of opportunity, or where no fix was possible within 30 miles (50km) and thus accuracy would be unacceptably degraded, the 'button-hook attack' was a further option. This involved taking a direct fix on the target itself, either by flying past it and using the SLR to paint the target, or by flying directly over it and taking a visual fix. Continuing to fly away from the target for several miles, the aircraft would then begin a 2g turn to bring it back on course towards the target and begin a low- or high-loft attack. With the last fix being precisely on the target, this was the most accurate type of attack, with a CEP of less than 600ft (185m) expected to be met.

Over-the-shoulder attack
A further low-level attack mode was the over-the-shoulder attack. The aircraft would fly directly over the target for a visual fix and then pulled into a climb, pitching at a constant rate until the computed bomb throw matched the distance travelled from the target. This was programmed to be at the 110-degree pitch point, thus throwing the bomb back towards the target. Escape would be made by rolling wings-level and diving, as in the loft attacks. Again a 600ft CEP was the aim, and this was expected to be just about met by this type of attack.

Laydown
The aircraft would approach the target at 500ft (150m) and between Mach 0.75 and 0.9, and the target would be fixed when within 30 miles (48km) and overflown, the bomb being released just beforehand. By necessity, all such attacks would be ground-bursts.

Medium-level attack profiles

Level attack
The first medium-level attack was a simple Second World War-style bomb run. Approach at 25,000ft (7,600m) and Mach 1.7, take a fix within 30 miles (50km), fly straight over the target, releasing the bomb when its throw is computed to match the distance to the target, and continue straight and level to escape. Although 1,200ft (365m) CEP was the requirement here, BAC believed it an unlikely possibility, given the limitations in SLR fix accuracy and the distance the bomb had to fall.

Dive toss attack
Far more likely to hit the target was the medium dive toss attack. In this case, the approach was the same as for the level attack, but at a computed distance from

the target the aircraft would bunt at ½g into a 17.5-degree dive to point at the target. Visual means would be used to take another fix on the target during the dive. At a predetermined slant range from the target (25,000ft (7,600m)) the aircraft would pull out of the dive and effectively begin the later stages of a loft attack, pitching up at a constant rate until the computed bomb throw matched up with the target and the bomb was released. Escape would be identical to the loft attack, with or without chandelle. The blind dive toss attack was later deleted, though visual dive toss was retained.

Nuclear strike

The UK's first tactical nuclear bomb was developed to OR.1127, the weapon itself being named *Red Beard* and often referred to as a 'Target Marker Bomb' in an amusing attempt to hide its true nature while allowing discussion of its dimensions and approximate weight. The carriage of just one of these weapons, to be held within the aircraft's bomb bay, was initially required by OR.343. Of nominal 2,000lb (900kg) weight (the bomb actually weighed around 1,700lb (770kg)), both versions of *Red Beard* were just over 12ft (3.6m) long and had a diameter of 28in (71cm). The Mk 1 version had an explosive yield of 10 kilotons, and the Mk 2 a yield of 25 kilotons. The RAE's Working Party on Weapons for the Aircraft to OR.343 had found that most 'hard' targets (reinforced structures) would require a yield of 32 kilotons, and that only softer targets could therefore be destroyed by *Red Beard*. The weapon's fuzing system also introduced limitations to its use. *Red Beard* was designed to be released in a loft attack, with the aircraft pulling into a climb before release. The bomb would be ejected and also continue to climb, with the fuzing

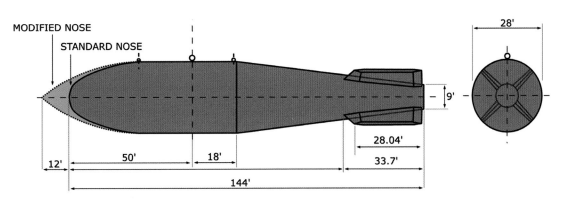

Red Beard, or the nominally 2,000lb 'Target Marker Bomb', was not designed for supersonic carriage, and a redesigned casing was initially proposed for external carriage by TSR2, though not proceeded with. Damien Burke

mechanism activating once a pre-set altitude was reached. Thus a laydown attack, releasing the weapon from low-level flight without climbing, or a shallower loft attack was not possible. (In the former the weapon would never be fuzed, and in the latter the releasing aircraft would not be able to escape before the weapon exploded.) These limitations, plus the single yield setting for each mark of the weapon, led, in November 1959, to the Air Staff deciding against the carriage of this weapon on the OR.343 aircraft, and they decided to begin work on a new requirement for a more modern and flexible bomb; this would be ASR.1177. For the time being, however, development had to continue as if *Red Beard* would still be used, there being no readily available alternative.

In mid-1960 the Air Staff raised the stakes on OR.343 with a request to upgrade the requirement, changing to the carriage of a pair of nuclear bombs. (While the TSR2 was then scheduled to replace Canberras on a one-for-two basis, the number of targets with which the force was committed to deal was not going to reduce.) *Red Beard*, a big and heavy bomb, could only have been carried in pairs externally, and would have seriously reduced the aircraft's range as a result of the increased weight and drag. The tail unit was also suspected to be only viable if the bomb was released at speeds below 750kt (860mph; 1,390km/h), though the

bomb was capable of surviving the expected levels of temperature and vibration to which it would be subjected when carried externally. All of this certainly supported the Air Staff's decision in November 1959 to move on from *Red Beard* to something better. The American Mk 28 weapon was looked at instead, as it had already been considered for use with the Canberra interdictor force and was small enough to be carried as a pair internally. In October 1960 OR.343 was modified to include provision for the carriage of either one weapon (internally), a pair of the right size internally or a pair externally, the paired weapons being Mk 28s or a possible British future weapon (ASR.1177), and *Red Beard* if there was no other option.

Air Staff Requirement 1177 called for an improved tactical nuclear bomb for low-level deployment. This would eventually result in the WE177 bomb, of significantly smaller size and weight than *Red Beard*. By January 1961 it was also clear that all existing stocks of *Red Beard* would be past their 'use by' dates, and the weapon out of service by the time the first TSR2 strike squadron was formed, but once again there was no alternative but to continue to develop the aircraft to carry *Red Beard* as well as the American Mk 28. After the first WE177 warhead was successfully detonated at a test site in Nevada in March 1962, TSR2 weapons planning began to firm up, and

references to *Red Beard*/1127 weapons progressively disappeared and were replaced by references to ASR.1177, and later specifically WE177A. This was to be a bomb of similar destructive power to *Red Beard* Mk 1, with a yield of 10 kilotons. Owing to its significantly reduced size compared with *Red Beard*, it was hoped it could be carried as an internal pair (in tandem), and the 'insurance' requirement of carrying *Red Beard* was reverted to the original idea of carrying a single weapon internally, then dropped entirely in December 1962 (though it continued to appear in some RAF correspondence, prompting a final formal cancellation of the requirement to carry it as late as September 1963).

As well as the American Mk 28, the American Mk 43 was considered for TSR2s assigned to NATO. The bomb bay was neither wide enough nor long enough to accommodate a pair of Mk 43 No. 2s, the preferred weapon because of its higher yield. The Mk 43 was also subject to environmental limitations in terms of temperature, release speed and vibration, all of which would preclude external carriage. The Mk 43 No. 1 was a lower-yield weapon, 14.5in (37cm) shorter and thus able to be carried in pairs internally. Similarly, Mk 57s could be carried as pairs within the bomb bay. As costs rose and economy measures were sought, this variety of possible armament came under fire and gradually the options

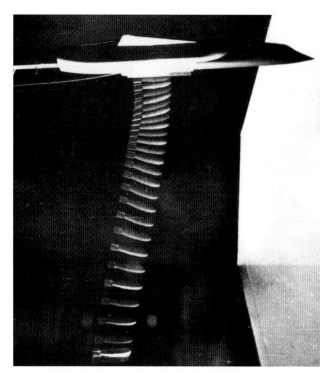

THIS PAGE:
A *Red Beard* windtunnel model drop in simulated release conditions of level flight at 25,000ft (7,600m) and Mach 0.88. BAE Systems via Brooklands Museum

OPPOSITE PAGE:
TOP LEFT: A mockup of the American Mk 43 nuclear bomb mounted on the mockup TSR2. These weapons were too large to allow more than one to be carried internally, so if two were carried they would have had to be mounted externally. BAE Systems via Warton Heritage Group

TOP RIGHT: A Mk 43 mockup, single internal carriage. It was for this sort of configuration that the TSR2 was originally required, albeit carrying *Red Beard* rather than an American weapon. Note the baffle plates with circular holes that surround the forward section of the bomb to reduce turbulence within the bay with the doors open. BAE Systems via Warton Heritage Group

BOTTOM LEFT: Internal carriage of twin WE177s, tandem configuration. The more powerful variants of WE177 were too long to be carried in this manner. BAE Systems via Warton Heritage Group

BOTTOM RIGHT: Internal carriage of twin WE177s, side-by-side configuration. With the bay and doors originally designed to accommodate *Red Beard*, the doors had to be dished to accommodate other stores, and side-by-side carriage of WE177 required further indentationss to make room for the fins, as seen on the extreme edges of this photo. BAE Systems via Warton Heritage Group

were narrowed down. An approach was made to the Americans via the US National Military Representative at SHAPE on 20 November 1962, to ask about availability of Mk 43 bombs for the TSR2 force. The response did not arrive until December, and it was not positive. As the question had been asked just weeks after Skybolt's cancellation, it was no surprise that it had become mixed up in the less-than-friendly negotiations between the Prime Minister and the US President about the future of the UK's nuclear deterrent. In late 1960, after examination of the strategic possibilities

of TSR2, this 'bonus' capability had been considered to be a possible insurance against the failure of Skybolt. The aircraft was now in precisely the position feared in 1960.

By July 1963 plans centred almost entirely around the use of WE177, the scheme being for the world-wide TSR2 force to be assigned a stockpile of seventy-six of these weapons, plus a further eight to be held in reserve. The low yield (10 kilotons) of WE177A, the first version planned, was a product of the Prime Minister's edict in July 1962 that tactical nuclear weapons should be low-yield in order to try to stop

limited tactical nuclear use escalating into a full-scale nuclear war. Many of the RAF's assigned targets in the event of nuclear conflict could not be effectively destroyed by a single such weapon, and this prompted some discussion on the use of multiple weapons on a single target; in effect, stick bombing using nuclear weapons. This meant that the requirement to carry just a pair of WE177s now had to be rethought, and the obvious solution was to double this and carry a pair internally plus one under each wing. The incorporation of a suitable timed-release device into the nuclear bomb release panel to enable stick bombing was another addition to costs, but in the end this facility was not required, as by August 1963 it had become clear that fifty-three of the weapons assigned to the TSR2 force would in fact be higher-yield (300-kiloton) WE177Bs. Accordingly the requirement to carry up to four weapons simultaneously was dropped, to BAC's relief. A pair of WE177Bs could be carried internally, side-by-side.

The carriage of US nuclear weapons had been attractive when WE177 was still in doubt, but now that it was nearly a sure thing, the disadvantages of carrying US weapons became overwhelming. The USA had strict controls and procedures to deal with when it came to carrying (and indeed using) its weapons. Dispersal of the TSR2 force would be very difficult, as it would need prior arrangement and the co-operation of the US guard forces. In exercises, Vickers Valiants equipped with US weapons had been so held up by this issue that it had been calculated that they would have been destroyed on the ground before a dispersal operation could have been started. On the other hand, TSR2s with British weapons could disperse at a moment's notice; and strike any target the UK wanted to hit without the need for prior US approval.

After TSR2's cancellation, WE177 development changed tack, and WE177B became a larger and much more powerful version, with a yield of 450 kilotons. This was the first to enter service, being carried by RAF Vulcans and later by Tornadoes. The WE177A had a dual role as a low-level tactical weapon and also a nuclear depth charge (with yield limited to 0.5 kilotons for situations where 10 kilotons would endanger non-combatant or friendly shipping), and ended up being mainly used by the RN's anti-submarine helicopter force. A third version, WE177C, of approximately 200 kilotons yield, was deployed by RAF

Another view of the side-by-side WE177 configuration. The forward end of the bay was left clear for a weapons bay fuel tank. BAE Systems via Warton Heritage Group

ABOVE: **A WE177C training round. This would probably have been the version of WE177 most often carried by the TSR2 force, had the project not been cancelled.** Damien Burke

RIGHT: **A windtunnel model with Matra rocket pods mounted on light stores pylons.** BAE Systems via Warton Heritage Group

Germany's Jaguars and Tornados. Had the TSR2 continued, it would probably have been this version that it would have ended up carrying, though its increased size would have precluded the carriage of more than one internally.

Conventional strike

Conventional strike was regarded by the Air Staff as very much a tertiary role, and they resisted any attempts to develop dedicated weapons for the type, instead preferring to use existing bombs and rockets, despite the obvious shortcomings of relying upon weapons that were not designed to be carried in the temperature and vibration conditions expected to be experienced by the TSR2. They also neglected to specify any kind of conventional weapon sighting for the aircraft other than the visual dive attack.

Rockets

The 'battleship broadside' effect of a well-executed rocket attack was particularly effective against soft and medium targets, such as troops, vehicles, aircraft on the ground and lightly constructed buildings. However, an aircraft firing rockets is burdened by a number of limitations in speed, approach angle and visibility, so rocket

attacks would only have been possible on relatively lightly defended targets, which OR.343 recognized.

Early studies by the Air Staff into rocket effectiveness resulted in them requesting that OR.343 would include a requirement for 2in rockets in pods of thirty-seven rockets each, which could be mounted both on underwing pylons and also within the bomb bay, from where they would be lowered before firing, and also for 3in rockets mounted on standard underwing rails (as used by Hunter fighter/ground-attack variants). The RAE and the MoA objected to the plan to carry standard pods within the bomb bay and the associated cost and complexity of a lowering mechanism, and suggested that a dedicated rocket pack housed in the bomb bay would be a cheaper solution (quite how they came to this conclusion is

unclear). It did not take long for the rocket situation to be simplified. By November 1959 the requirement to carry 3in rockets was under consideration for removal (and was indeed deleted by October 1960), and for 2in rockets the use of standard underwing rocket pods was being considered (these soon became preferred to the development of any special-to-type weapons-bay rocket pack). With the acceptance that standard existing pods would be used, no particular extra development was needed, and it was not until August 1964 that windtunnel tests began, using scale models of the underwing pylons and standard Matra rocket pods. These showed that the pylons needed to be stiffer, and that the pods themselves would benefit from the fitting of small fins, but no further work was carried out before the project was cancelled.

High-explosive bombs

In 1959 the 'dumb iron bomb' was not considered to be a weapon of any accuracy or particular tactical value, and the OR acknowledged that 'normal HE bombs can never provide an effective method of attacking targets unless saturation tactics can be adopted .... The main use of these weapons will be for morale or political purposes and therefore a much degraded accuracy can be accepted.' As with rockets, attacks with bombs would be limited to lightly defended targets, and targets with significant defences or requiring any serious accuracy would need to be hit with a missile instead.

While the original GOR had asked for carriage of first four, then later six 1,000lb HE bombs, the TSR2 was going to be capable of carrying many more. The weapons bay would hold two triple-ejector launcher units, thus holding the basic requirement of six bombs internally. Underwing carriage of HE bombs was more fluid, the situation changing time and time again until, finally, in March 1965, the RAF accepted that new inner-wing pylons (designed primarily to carry Martel missiles) would also be strong enough to carry up to four 1,000lb HE bombs each, with a further bomb on each outer wing pylon. The maximum load of HE would therefore be 10,000lb (4,535kg) externally and 6,000lb (2,720kg) internally.

The effects of high speed and associated heating on external stores meant that the supersonic dash capability at low level would only be available if suitable stores were carried. Strengthened bomb tail units and sleeker nosecones would be necessary; so-called 'low-drag' bombs. In the early stages of the project there had been considerable study into the creation of new bombs that could withstand high-speed carriage,

with internal reinforcements to permit the fuzing mechanism to survive a high-speed impact. This was necessary if there was to be a delayed detonation to allow the aircraft to escape the blast radius during a low-level lay-down attack. However, with the Air Staff's edict that no new weapons could be developed specifically for the TSR2, these studies did not directly result in any new

bombs. At a late stage the TSR2's weapons menu was rewritten to include 1,000lb HE retarded bombs to AST.1194 (with integral parachutes for retarded delivery; a much more practical idea than a bomb designed to survive high-speed impact on a hard target), and also a bomblet dispenser to AST.1197 (this became the BL755 cluster bomb).

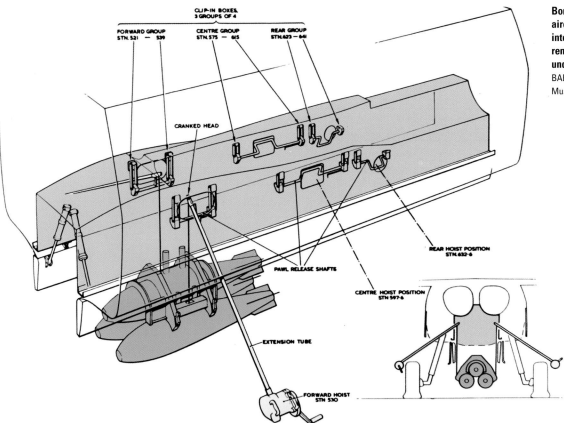

CLIP-IN BOXES
3 GROUPS OF 4

FORWARD GROUP
STN. 521 — 539

CENTRE GROUP
STN. 575 — 615

REAR GROUP
STN. 623 — 641

CRANKED HEAD

PAWL RELEASE SHAFTS

REAR HOIST POSITION
STN. 632-6

CENTRE HOIST POSITION
STN. 597-6

EXTENSION TUBE

FORWARD HOIST
STN 530

Bombs were winched into the aircraft using hoists inserted into the weapons bay through removable panels in the main undercarriage bay walls. BAE Systems via Brooklands Museum

An underwing pylon with an integral sway brace shoulder, designed for smaller stores such as bombs or rocket or countermeasures pods. A post-cancellation engineering report criticized this pylon design for poor flutter characteristics, so production pylons may well have had a different layout. BAE Systems via Warton Heritage Group

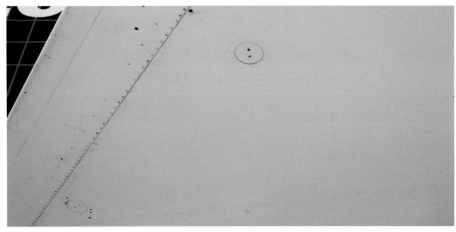

The two circular panels denote the location of the pylon pick-up points under XR220's wing. Damien Burke

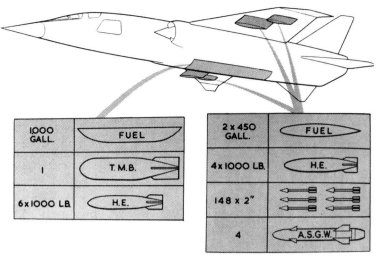

LEFT: **A low-drag 1,000lb HE bomb carried underwing. The inner pylon includes large sway braces to cope with the carriage of larger stores, particularly 450gal drop tanks. Outer pylons could carry a single 1,000lb HE bomb, and plans were afoot for larger inner pylons able to carry multiple 1,000lb HE bombs.** BAE Systems via Warton Heritage Group

ABOVE: **An illustration from an early (1960) brochure, showing Bullpups as the chosen air-to-surface guided weapons.** BAE Systems via Brooklands Museum

Missiles

The first missile linked with the TSR2 was the American AGM-12 Bullpup, then being cleared for service on the Scimitar. The Americans had developed this missile in response to the disappointing bombing accuracy they had experienced during the Korean War, and accuracy had been more important to them than hitting power. The Bullpup's weedy warhead, limited range and the need for the delivery aircraft to continue to fly towards the target during the attack soon made its carriage on the TSR2 an unattractive prospect. Later, in service with the RN, it came to be viewed by many Fleet Air Arm pilots as little more than a marvellously entertaining firework for peacetime practice use, and a liability in combat conditions. The RAF reached a similar conclusion, and by January 1962 had cancelled any plans to acquire Bullpup for any of their aircraft, including TSR2.

The next missile to be considered, in February 1962, was the French AS.30, a radio-guided visually-aimed HE missile flown all the way to the target by an operator tracking a bright flare on the weapon's tail until it hit the target. Powered by a solid-propellant rocket motor, the AS.30 weighed in at more than 1,100lb (500kg), of which 500lb (225kg) comprised the HE warhead. It had a range of about 7 miles (11km) and

could reach a top speed of Mach 1.5. Having looked into replacing Bullpup by AS.30, BAC Preston believed that, if the existing pylon designs drawn up for Bullpup could be retained, it would be a fairly straightforward swap, though jettison requirements would need some work because the existing jettison guns as used on Canberra pylons were

not strong enough to separate an AS.30 safely from a TSR2 at higher speeds.

In December 1962 the RAE produced a paper outlining the amount of development necessary for the TSR2 to carry the AS.30, and the results were a rude shock to BAC and the Air Staff. Instead of being a good option as a cheap interim fit, pending the

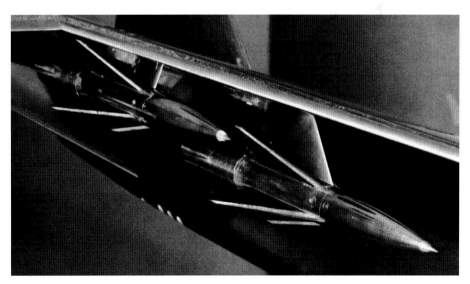

A windtunnel model with AS.30 missiles mounted on the pylons originally designed to carry Bullpups. The tactical drawbacks of both Bullpup and AS.30 were considerable for an aircraft like the TSR2, and both missiles were dropped from the project by 1963. BAE Systems via Brooklands Museum

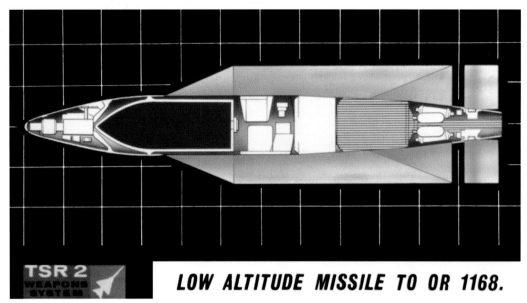

LEFT: **Bristol's Tychon stand-off missile was one contender for OR.1168, and was offered in nuclear, TV-guided HE and anti-radar versions. This is the TV-guided version. TSR2 could have carried four of these on the wing pylons, but the Tychon lost out to the Anglo-French AS.37 (also known as AJ.168 or Martel).** BAE Systems via Brooklands Museum

BELOW: **The Martel missile was selected for TSR2 use, in both TV-guided and anti-radar versions (the latter is shown here). The datalink electronics for the TV-guided version would have been installed in a weapons bay pack, rather than being carried in an external pod as on the Buccaneer.** Damien Burke

LOW ALTITUDE MISSILE TO OR 1168.

BELOW: **The conventional weapons control panel was another interchangeable role panel located at the bottom left of the navigator's instrument panel. This mockup predates the increase in maximum conventional bomb load to sixteen 1,000lb bombs, and has controls and indicators for a maximum of ten bombs, along with controls for missiles (fired singly) and rockets (fired in single, slow or fast ripple modes with any combination of pods).** BAE Systems via Warton Heritage Group

arrival of a more modern weapon, the AS.30 required considerable development effort to be expended to integrate it with the TSR2. The Air Staff then looked at AS.30 in relation to typical TSR2 mission profiles. The consensus of opinion was that AS.30 would be of marginal use against undefended targets, and a total waste of time against a target with any kind of sophisticated defence, owing to the need to follow the missile while guiding it. Moreover, AS.30 also had kinetic-heating limits that meant it could only be carried while subsonic, 450kt (520mph; 830km/h) being about the upper limit.

During the period TSR2 was being developed, the AS.30 was entering service with the RAF's Canberra interdictor squadrons. Initially it was thought some of these stocks could be used if AS.30 capability was to be incorporated within the TSR2, but the rocket motors had limited shelf lives and it was soon realized that, by the

Projected TSR2 armament loads as of March 1965. Damien Burke

TYPICAL ARMAMENT LOADS

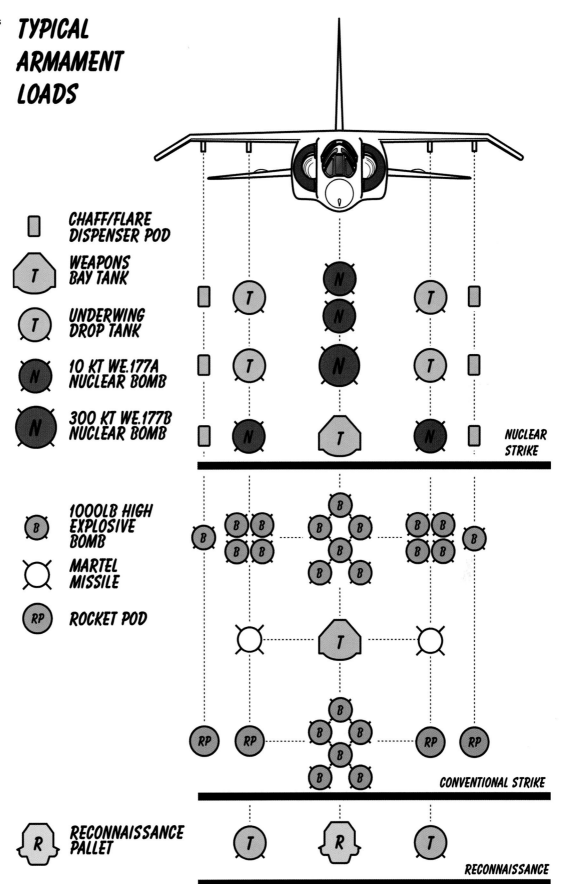

CHAFF/FLARE DISPENSER POD

WEAPONS BAY TANK

UNDERWING DROP TANK

10 KT WE.177A NUCLEAR BOMB

300 KT WE.177B NUCLEAR BOMB

NUCLEAR STRIKE

1000LB HIGH EXPLOSIVE BOMB

MARTEL MISSILE

RP ROCKET POD

CONVENTIONAL STRIKE

RECONNAISSANCE PALLET

RECONNAISSANCE

time TSR2 entered service, most if not all of the existing AS.30 stocks would also need replacing. In February 1963 the RAF decided there was little point in continuing to consider using AS.30, and that efforts should be concentrated elsewhere, particularly on the AST/OR.1168 project, and the requirement to carry AS.30 was cancelled in May 1963.

The missile developed to fulfil OR.1168 would eventually result in the Martel, the product of an Anglo-French collaboration, available in both TV-guided and anti-radar versions. Development of Martel proceeded independently of the TSR2 programme, and while the TSR2 was expected to carry at least two Martels (both TV-guided and anti-radar versions) on underwing pylons, no serious work to link the two took place before the TSR2's cancellation. A few weeks before this the Air Staff had decided to accept a suspension of the entire requirement to carry the missile on the TSR2 as a (hopefully temporary) cost-saving measure.

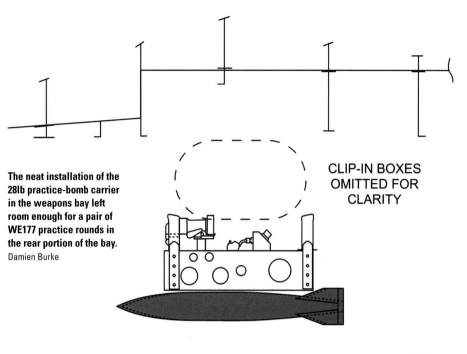

The neat installation of the 28lb practice-bomb carrier in the weapons bay left room enough for a pair of WE177 practice rounds in the rear portion of the bay.
Damien Burke

CLIP-IN BOXES OMITTED FOR CLARITY

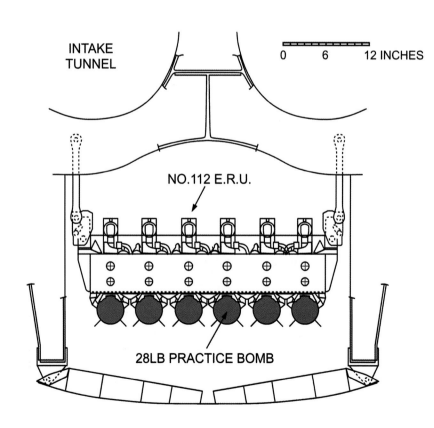

INTAKE TUNNEL

0   6   12 INCHES

NO.112 E.R.U.

28LB PRACTICE BOMB

Practice bombs

A carrier to hold six AST.1198 28lb practice bombs was developed along with a nuclear-response simulator unit, both to be held within the weapons bay. These would enable the crew to practise the complete nuclear weapons delivery process multiple times on a single training sortie. In addition, one or two practice 'shapes' could be carried that would better represent the size and weight of a genuine nuclear bomb. As well as giving more realistic aircraft response to the release, these would also have given groundcrew valuable training in the handling and loading of the real thing.

Non-conventional weapons

No serious thought seems to have been given to the carriage of more unusual weapons by the TSR2. Early information-gathering efforts in 1957, while GOR.339 was being drafted, did bring up the possibility of napalm carriage, and this was felt to be straightforward, but no evidence has come to light of any work on this having been carried out during the TSR2 programme. The RAF was impressed during 1961 by the US Navy's efforts to develop a slew of modern weapons in the 'Eye' series (so-called because they were mostly to be aimed using the Mk 1 eyeball), and a brief note summarizing these is to be found among the papers of the TSR2 Weapons Carriage & Release sub-panel. These were Hawkeye II, an anti-tank bomblet dispenser; Sadeye, an anti-personnel grenade dispenser; Weteye, a chemical weapon dispenser filled with up to 350lb (160kg) of 'nasty liquid' and finally Walleye, a free-fall HE bomb with a TV camera in the nose for automatic target homing. As all of these were designed for release at low level they had obvious attractions for TSR2 use, but no work on their use appears to have been carried out.

CHAPTER TEN

RAF Service

While TSR2 never reached squadron service, the RAF had been planning how to introduce it for some time before the project's cancellation. Consequently there is some evidence for how the TSR2 would have begun its RAF service.

Initial training

The RAF was already experiencing difficulties in introducing the Lightning into service, and the sophistication and complexity of the TSR2 was a world apart from that aircraft. The training of systems specialists, as had been required for the Lightning, was going to be necessary, and BAC put forward a plan to train RAF groundcrews at schools set up within BAC and BSEL. BAC Warton would host a Structure and Airframe Installations course; BAC Weybridge would host courses on the Nav/Attack system, AFCS, reconnaissance, communications, armament, and general instrument and electrical installations; and BSEL at Bristol would host courses on the ECU (engine installation being handled at Warton).

Courses would be laid on for both ground- and aircrews, differing levels of detail being provided and ranging from more general overviews for staff officers to more comprehensive courses for the systems specialists. Most lengthy of all the various courses would be those on the nav/attack system and AFCS, early estimates reckoning that these would take fifty-six weeks. The RAF would be expected to provide lead-in training on basic aspects.

Electronic Introduction Team

The Electronic Introduction Team (EIT) was tasked with monitoring, on behalf of the Air Ministry, the development of the TSR2's electronic systems and any problems associated with their installation in the aircraft. In this manner the RAF would have direct input to and knowledge of the design of the systems, their associated maintenance needs and test equipment. The EIT would liaise with all stakeholder units in the RAF, such as the various units within the CSDE, and was itself a sub-unit of the Radio Introduction Unit at RAF Medmenham. As a small team the EIT had no home base as such, personnel working wherever it made the most sense at various stages in the project, for example BAC Weybridge, with the intention that it would work from RAF Coningsby, Lincolnshire once the aircraft was entering RAF service.

A building was to be erected at Coningsby to house the 'Stage 3' rig (soon given the much snappier name 'TSR2 Electronics System Servicing and Servicing Development Rig' by the RAF), and the EIT was to have use of this. An additional rig was to be set up for the Ground Training School, and when it was thought that this would be co-located at Coningsby, the intention was to make the new building large enough to

The stage 3 rig at Weybridge, which enabled the various electronic systems to be connected and operated as a complete system. Similar rigs would have been acquired by the RAF for training use.
BAE Systems via Warton Heritage Group

house them both. The EIT would also have use of a complete collection of aircraft equipment broken down into discrete 'black boxes', along with both first- and second-line test equipment.

When the time was right the EIT would have been merged into the Operational Development Squadron (ODS).

Ground Training School

While initial training courses were set up by BAC and BSEL, the RAF took over as it became more experienced, and ran its own training. Initial thoughts centred on technical training taking place at the same location as flying training, but at a late stage the decision was taken to house all TSR2 technical training at RAF Hemswell in Lincolnshire because of the lack of accommodation at Coningsby. (Buildings already extant at Coningsby lacked sufficient soundproofing to be suitable for classroom duties.)

Previously placed under Care and Maintenance after a short period in use as a Thor missile base, RAF Hemswell was reactivated on 31 August 1964, the Ground Training School (GTS) for TSR2 ground personnel being established on 1 October. The first course began on 14 January 1965, and courses continued for some months after cancellation of the project, the GTS not being closed down until 8 September 1965. Hemswell was only ever to have been the location of the GTS, and would never have been home to any actual TSR2s. As well as having a Phase 3 rig as provided to the EIT, it had a variety of demonstration rigs of other TSR2 systems (hydraulics, fuel, electrical, undercarriage and so on).

Before the project's cancellation the plan was to move the GTS from Hemswell to RAF Newton at some point from 1970 to 1972. Newton already had suitable training accommodation, whereas putting this in place at Coningsby would have been a significant expense, despite the advantages of having ground crew being trained on a

type they could then see in use on the same station.

Tactical Strike Establishment

RAF Coningsby was selected as the initial home of the TSR2 at a meeting of the Air Council on 23 May 1963, with the various TSR2-related units on the station to come under the aegis of the Tactical Strike Establishment (TSE).

The existing Vulcan squadrons would move out, as supporting both TSR2s and Vulcans would be too much of a stretch for the station personnel, especially as none of them would have any significant TSR2 experience to begin with. The intention was that the Vulcans would depart and leave a clear month in which any remaining work on the station infrastructure could be finished off before the arrival of the first TSR2s. In 1963 the RAF's schedule for Coningsby was that the TSR2 flight simulator would be ready for use in July 1966,

Several visits to Boscombe Down were made by RAF crews selected for the TSR2, and various group photographs were taken. These visits continued for some months after the cancellation announcement.
via Solent Sky

RIGHT: **The TSR2 was of similar length to a Vulcan, but its much smaller wingspan and height would have enabled greater use to be made of existing hangarage.**
Damien Burke

BELOW: **The proposed ASP for RAF Coningsby. A similar ASP was eventually constructed for F-4 Phantom operations.**
Damien Burke

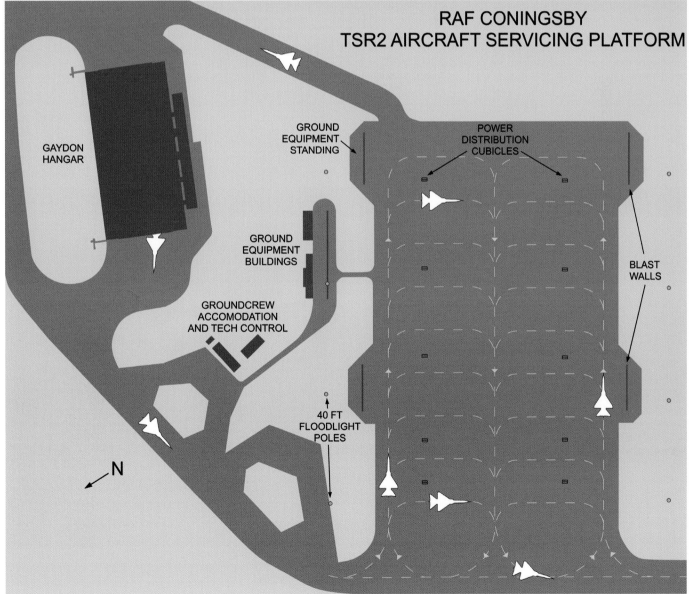

RAF CONINGSBY
TSR2 AIRCRAFT SERVICING PLATFORM

GAYDON HANGAR

GROUND EQUIPMENT STANDING

POWER DISTRIBUTION CUBICLES

GROUND EQUIPMENT BUILDINGS

GROUNDCREW ACCOMODATION AND TECH CONTROL

BLAST WALLS

40 FT FLOODLIGHT POLES

N

and the ODS would form from some time around September 1966 and carry out intensive flying trials and initial Qualified Flying Instructor conversions.

Plans were put into place to add a huge expanse of concrete, an aircraft servicing platform (ASP), between the hangars at the western edge of the station and the main runway, to avoid the wasted time and manpower involved in operating from various dispersals scattered around the airfield. Electronics, flight-simulator and support buildings were to be built to the northeast of the ASP, with taxyways linking the hangars to the ASP and the ASP to the runways. Jet-blast and noise deflectors would be positioned around the ASP as well. Land was to be requisitioned at either end of the airfield to permit the construction of barrier overrun areas at either end of the main runway, if shown to be necessary by initial flight trials.

Concerns were also raised about the security of these particularly expensive aircraft. Proposals were put forward to surround each TSR2 base with chain-link fencing to a height of 8ft (2.4m), with barbed-wire overhangs, though within the RAF it was felt it might be tricky to get Treasury approval for such an increase in security when the nuclear-armed V-force had no such protection. By December 1964 plans were well advanced for two new buildings at Coningsby, the flight-simulator and training-rig buildings, but these were then delayed pending the results of noise trials, to see what level of soundproofing would be needed. Doubts about the project's future then put any further work in abeyance.

Modern-day Coningsby shows little evidence of the planned TSR2 work. The station became home to the Phantom OCU (the Phantom being bought to replace the Hawker P.1154), and because of this would not have been available for the F-111 OCU, which was instead planned to be based at RAF Honington (which became a Buccaneer base once the TSR2/TFX/F-111 dust settled). The main ASP layout drawn up for the TSR2 OCU was modified for Phantom operations, and constructed closer to the Gaydon hangar with a narrower width (ironically, it later proved to be too small, and a disused runway was used as the base for an additional strip of ASP a short distance away). Chain-link fences do now surround most of the airfield, though they were finally put in place some time later.

Operational Development Squadron

The RAF's TSR2 Steering Committee decided in 1962 that TSR2 flying in the RAF would begin with an ODS, to be numbered 40 Squadron, formed with the first six pre-production aircraft intended for RAF service. The fifteenth and sixteenth TSR2 airframes would be the first two assigned to the ODS, delivery initially being expected in September 1966 (later this slipped to April 1967). The squadron's tasks would be to evaluate operational tactics, to set up an Operational Reliability Trial to establish reliability factors and assess equipment wastage rates, and to train prospective instructors for the first OCU course,

Slippage in the programme meant that the initial plans for the Operational Development Squadron to form with the first six pre-production aircraft would have needed bolstering by early aircrew experience on development-batch airframes at Boscombe Down or Warton. BAE Systems via Warton Heritage Group

expected to start in the second quarter of 1967 (later slipped to January of 1968).

By January 1965 things had changed. Aircraft No. 15 was now earmarked for identification friend or foe (IFF) and alternator trials, and aircraft 16 was reserved against any major contingencies in the flight-test programme, such as the loss of an aircraft in a crash. This would result in a delay of at least another six months before the first airframe became available to the ODS. A further blow was that the A&AEE stated that, in the timeframe available, it was likely that the first airframes assigned to the ODS would only be available under a limited flight clearance, with restrictions in speed, altitude and bank angle, and no clearance to use the nav/attack system. Thus training of navigator instructors would be impossible, and only limited pilot flying training would be possible (circuit training only, for example). The delay in the start of flying at the ODS would also mean that crews going through the ground training programme would be finished before aircraft were available for them to fly, so refresher flying training in another type (such as the Lightning) would become necessary.

The recommended alternative plan was to give prospective navigators a part in the development programme, flying with A&AEE pilots, and for prospective pilots to fly under the supervision of manufacturer's test pilots or A&AEE pilots, with the ODS forming at either Warton, or preferably at the A&AEE's base at Boscombe Down. In that event, formation of the ODS would consist of two phases, Phase 1 being at Boscombe and Phase 2 taking place with the move, two or three months down the line, to RAF Coningsby.

By December 1968 the unit's pre-production airframes would be replaced by six production aircraft, and the unit would then move to another base to form the core of the first strike squadron.

Operational Conversion Unit

The major TSR2 flying unit at Coningsby was to be the OCU, numbered 237 OCU (though early plans mentioned 231 OCU). The OCU would include two flying squadrons; a TSR2 squadron that would build up from production aircraft to a total of seventeen or eighteen airframes (as originally planned; by early 1965 this had been reduced to ten airframes in the face of a reduction in the TSR2 buy), and a

Hunter squadron consisting of twelve Hunter T.66 trainers (a large-bore-Avon-engined version of the T.7). There would also be ground-training and simulator squadrons within the OCU, with two flight simulators. According to early plans the unit was expected to accept its first TSR2 in June 1967, the same month in which Hunter training would begin; TSR2 training would then begin in September 1967. These dates later slipped to February and April 1968 respectively.

Each course was to consist of forty weeks of extremely demanding training, only the cream of Bomber Command's crop being eligible even to enter the first few courses. Courses would begin every six weeks. Crews entering the OCU would already have logged around 300hr in trainers including the Hunter, and would be expected to add at least 45hr of TSR2 time to their logbooks along with 76hr of simulator time by the end of their OCU course (initial plans had been for up to 70hr of TSR2 time).

Aircrew training: TSR2 dual-control trainer

From very early on in the project it was clear to the RAF that its new advanced bomber was going to benefit from a dedicated trainer variant. Such would be the expense of each airframe that the cost of losses due to inadequately experienced pilots making errors would be far higher than the cost involved in acquiring some trainer airframes. Early in 1960 BAC made its first proposals to this end, carried out some preliminary project studies and constructed a mock-up forward fuselage. The Air Staff had initially asked for a trainer version with side-by-side seating for two pilots, on which instruction and standardization checks could be carried out. These would cover both flying and operational techniques, including weapon delivery. The cost of such a major redesign of the fuselage turned out to be prohibitive, and the resulting airframe would not have been representative of the operational variant, nor would it have been capable of easy conversion to/from the operational variant. The requirement was put to one side, and a revised training plan put together to do without a dual TSR2 and rely instead on lead-in training with Hunters and extensive flight simulator use.

In September 1960 the dual TSR2 was revisited and a revised specification put together covering a tandem-seat dual-

control version that could be converted back into an operational aircraft in time of emergency. The existing tandem mock-up was modified to bring the rear cockpit floor upwards to improve the instructor's eye line. This was a much more workable plan, and Vickers estimated £12,000 would cover a complete design study.

It was not until early 1962 that BAC was invited again to submit timescales and costs involved in carrying out a full design study for a genuine TSR2 trainer variant. This it did in May, quoting a cost of £16,000 for the design study and an additional £10,000 for windtunnel models and a mock-up, but it was then not until nearly the end of the year that the Air Ministry began drafting a report on the need for the trainer, to present to the Defence Research Policy Committee (DRPC) in an effort to get it to agree and proceed further. In the meantime the RAF had even considered doing without the Lightning T.5 (and sticking with the T.4, which did not have the cockpit instrumentation for the F.3 and later variants of Lightning) in an effort to save money to put towards the dual TSR2. Luckily for a generation of Lightning pilots, the T.5 went ahead.

Months had been wasted in the interim period, which included discussion about whether asking for a trainer would expose the RAF to 'attack' from the RN, which managed to get by without dual trainer versions of most of its aircraft (including, of course, the NA.39). This led to deeper discussion of the whole training syllabus within the RAF, and how operational squadrons were established. The RN method was to 'work-up' a squadron of more-or-less fixed personnel make-up in an intense period of shore training before embarking in a carrier as an operational unit, repeating the process as necessary. The RAF, by contrast, established a squadron and then drip-fed personnel into it, each needing further training to become truly operational. Thus an RAF squadron, while nominally operational, could consist of a mix of experienced and well-trained crews and crews that were essentially non-operational owing to lack of experience and training. A similar RN squadron would either be fully operational or entirely non-operational during its work-up period. Some within the RAF even admitted the RN method could well be better; its front-line squadrons had a uniform standard of efficiency, and it had a reliable and easily predictable number of non-operational units. The RAF's front line

A January 1965 brochure illustration of the Type 595 TSR2 dual-control trainer. Trainers would have been capable of conversion to strike aircraft by RAF personnel over the course of seven days or so.
BAE Systems via Brooklands Museum

varied in efficiency, and on-squadron training often took a back seat when operational commitments interfered.

The next significant progress was not made until September 1963, when the DRPC decided to award a contract for BAC to begin its design study, though further months would be spent on the usual contract wrangling before a signed contract was with BAC. Meanwhile, a meeting was held on 24 October between some of the Air Staff and BAC to detail the RAF's current requirements for the trainer. This would be for a total of nine aircraft, seven of which would be for use by the OCU, and two for use as strike aircraft, to be converted to trainers as required. The RAF wanted the trainers to be capable of conversion back to strike aircraft within a week if necessary, and to be able to fly a small number of strike missions with the trainer canopy still in place if time constraints prevented full conversion

back to strike fit. A working party would be formed to work on a detailed specification, and costs would be kept as low as possible by earmarking one of the production aircraft as a trainer prototype, with no second airframe as an insurance backup.

The contract for the design study was finally signed in March 1964, and BAC's Weybridge division (i.e. Vickers) did the design work, designating the prospective aircraft the Type 595. Windtunnel testing was delayed by work on the VC10, and it was not until September that the Warton windtunnels were available. The Preston division of BAC also supported the study, with work on compatibility with the rear fuselage, wings and tail surfaces, plus the benefit of its experience with the Lightning and Canberra trainer variants. The finished design-study brochure, produced in January 1965, was entitled *Type 595 Pilot Trainer Aircraft* (for further details, *see* Chapter 12).

Unfortunately, the timing of the trainer brochure could not have been worse, reaching the Air Staff while they were busy considering the implications of the TSR2 being cancelled and possibly replaced by the TFX. In February the Air Staff decided that the pressing need for the trainer was not quite as pressing as the need to try and bring costs down, so they postponed any idea of going ahead with the trainer in the hope that they would be able to reintroduce the requirement when (or if) the project was on a surer footing. The RAF's Directorate of Flying Training turned out to be less than impressed with the view from this proposed trainer, declaring in March 1965 that 'the present BAC proposals for a dual TSR2 are unacceptable', and that 'they have demonstrated the incompatibility of good rear-seat vision and quick conversion to the operational role'. The minimum possible improvement that could be made to make the aircraft acceptable would be provision of a binocular periscope, but preferably this plus a larger (perhaps two-piece) canopy would really be best. To this end the directorate was prepared to accept performance limitations of a maximum indicated air speed of 450kt (520mph; 835km/h) at sea level/Mach 1.4 and ceiling of 40,000ft (12,000m). No further work on improving the design study was undertaken before the TSR2 project was cancelled.

Gnat lead-in training

The existing Gnat T.1 was not considered at all suitable as a lead-in trainer for the TSR2 force, but Folland had put forward a proposal for the Gnat T.2 in mid-1960. This was fitted with some basic navigational equipment, including a master reference gyro similar to that of the Lightning. The

RAF did not consider it a worthwhile effort, and Folland came back with a brochure on its proposed Gnat Mk 5 in September 1960. This was a more radical effort, with twin engines and a radar in the nose, somewhat larger and heavier than the 'normal' Gnat and with a higher landing speed. While slightly more suited for use as a lead-in trainer for the TSR2, it was still felt to be far inferior to existing types such as the Hunter or Lightning two-seaters and, as a new development, could have resulted in an expensive and protracted additional procurement. Accordingly the Gnat was never a serious contender as a TSR2 trainer in any of its proposed forms.

Lightning TSR2 trainer

In late 1960 English Electric began a study into creating a variant of the Lightning T.5

that could be used as a TSR2 pilot trainer. A report on this was finished in January 1961. The proposed trainer would be fitted with the TSR2's FLR, repackaged so that it would fit in the Lightning's bullet radome by relocating some parts of the radar to the forward armament bay. Significantly enlarging the bullet was not an option, as the reduction of airflow to the engines would have demanded a different engine version and loss of supersonic performance. A basic HUD would be fitted in place of the Light Fighter Sight normally fitted; for space reasons this would have to be a simpler unit than the TSR2 HUD. A simplified navigation computer, possibly with Decca Doppler, could be developed and mounted within the main equipment bay if needed, along with a radio altimeter. Standard Martin-Baker Mk 4 ejection seats would be retained, as neither the proposed Martin-Baker nor North American TSR2 seats would fit in the

The Lightning T.5 was proposed as the basis for a TSR2 trainer, with the missile pack replaced by a TSR2 navigation kit and the TSR2 FLR replacing the AI.23 radar, along with a TSR2-style HUD. BAE Systems

Details of modifications to the standard Lightning trainer that would have been required for a dedicated TSR2 Lightning lead-in pilot trainer. Damien Burke

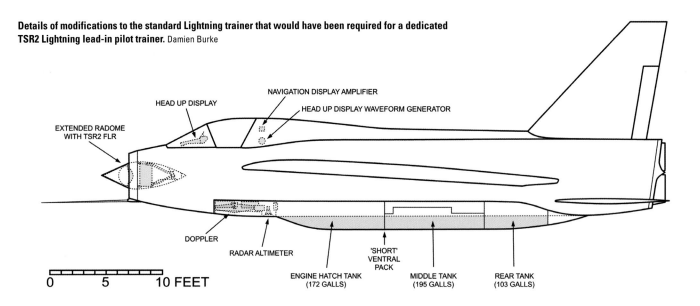

NAVIGATION DISPLAY AMPLIFIER

HEAD UP DISPLAY

HEAD UP DISPLAY WAVEFORM GENERATOR

EXTENDED RADOME WITH TSR2 FLR

DOPPLER

RADAR ALTIMETER

ENGINE HATCH TANK (172 GALLS)

'SHORT' VENTRAL PACK

MIDDLE TANK (195 GALLS)

REAR TANK (103 GALLS)

0   5   10 FEET

Lightning's cockpit. The large ventral tank already developed (but which the RAF's T.5 would not use) allowed for additional fuel.

The report ended by summarizing the proposal in lukewarm terms: 'This might prove to be a satisfactory alternative to a fully equipped special TSR-2 trainer.' The proposal languished for a long time, and when the TSR2 trainer came up for discussion again in late 1963, BAC Warton submitted the Lightning TSR2 trainer variant to BAC Weybridge for its thoughts. Henry Gardner's first question was whether they

would be damaging the prospects for an order for the TSR2 trainer by offering a cheaper alternative, but it was eventually also offered to the RAF, who, no doubt to BAC's relief, confirmed its preference for a full TSR2 trainer variant instead.

Hunter lead-in training

As mentioned above, the Air Staff had provisionally planned to use Hunter T.66s for lead-in training for the TSR2 force.

Powered by the gutsier Avon 203, this 'big-bore' Hunter two-seater had been introduced for the Indian and Jordanian air forces, and could be provided either by converting existing F.6s as they left squadron service or by upgrading Hunter T.7s. Five low-level flights in a T.66 were laid on for various RAF pilots and navigators in May 1961, flying from Dunsfold through relatively unpopulated areas of Somerset, Devon and Cornwall. They were extremely valuable in demonstrating some of the challenges inherent in high-speed low-level

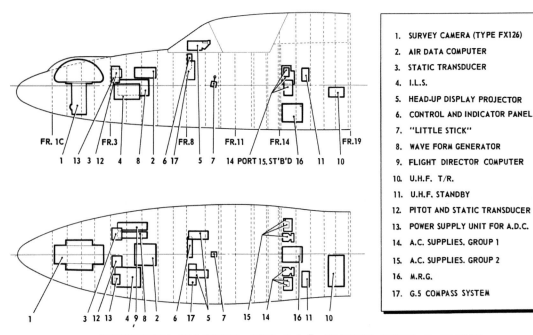

1. SURVEY CAMERA (TYPE FX126)
2. AIR DATA COMPUTER
3. STATIC TRANSDUCER
4. I.L.S.
5. HEAD-UP DISPLAY PROJECTOR
6. CONTROL AND INDICATOR PANEL
7. "LITTLE STICK"
8. WAVE FORM GENERATOR
9. FLIGHT DIRECTOR COMPUTER
10. U.H.F. T/R.
11. U.H.F. STANDBY
12. PITOT AND STATIC TRANSDUCER
13. POWER SUPPLY UNIT FOR A.D.C.
14. A.C. SUPPLIES. GROUP 1
15. A.C. SUPPLIES. GROUP 2
16. M.R.G.
17. G.5 COMPASS SYSTEM

The Hunter T.12 could well have formed the basis of a lead-in trainer for TSR2 crews, though it had not been built for this purpose and had been procured by the RAE purely for HUD and FX.126 camera trials. BAE Systems via Brooklands Museum

FR. 1C   FR.3   FR.8   FR.11   FR.14   FR.19

1 13 3 12   4   8 2 6 17   5 7   14 PORT 15. ST'B'D 16   11   10

1   3 12 13   4 9 8 2   6 17 5 7   15 14   16 11   10

EQUIPMENT DIAGRAM FOR R.A.E. HUNTER MK.12 2 SEATER

flying and navigation, and all of the RAF officers involved strongly supported the use of the Hunter as a lead-in trainer for TSR2 crews. A side-effect of these five flights was the level of public protest generated, RAF Chivenor being inundated by telephone complaints and the RAF receiving thirty letters of complaint afterwards. The implications for TSR2 low-level training in the UK were obvious, and led to further efforts to investigate the use of overseas low-level training areas.

Hawker also produced a one-off Hunter T.12 airframe, XE531, for the RAE to use as a demonstrator for a HUD and the new FX 126 camera. Based on the T.66 specification, the T.12 was a conversion of an F.6 airframe with the distance-measuring equipment, IFF, *Green Salad* UHF homer, nose radar, gunsights and recorder cameras, guns and auto-stabilization removed; upgrades of compass, attitude indicator, oxygen system, electrical supply and braking parachute; and the addition of HUD, an FX 126 survey camera (requiring a bulge on top of the nose to make room for this downward-facing camera), a master reference gyro, an air data computer and ILS (all to be linked to the HUD), and a 'little stick' side controller for the Flight Director. The RAE chose an attractive paint scheme of brilliant green with a white nose flash, spine and fin.

The T.12 also caught the RAF's eye. With work already done to modify the basic Hunter trainer airframe to carry some items of equipment destined for the TSR2, this struck the Service as a relatively cheap way to train TSR2 crews in the use of some TSR2 systems. Flight trials of the HUD in late 1963 were very successful, and the pilots considered that the aircraft could well make a suitable TSR2 lead-in trainer, though it would benefit from the addition of tactical air navigation kit and the reintroduction of the standard Hunter yaw damper, particularly for flight at high speed under turbulent conditions.

Initial plans had centred on introducing the TSR2 to RAF Germany before any UK front-line units were formed, RAF Brüggen and RAF Laarbruch being chosen as the two bases that would be used for TSR2 units. Gütersloh was considered an imprudent choice, being forward of the planned high-altitude air-defence missile zone. Geilenkirchen was planned to be a Lightning base, and Wildenrath, with its transport hub, was considered likely to be too congested in times of tension. Brüggen and Laarbruch both already had many of the facilities required; nuclear weapons storage, Quick Reaction Alert (QRA) compounds and a Mobile Field Photographic Unit. Brüggen also had a Maintenance Unit based there, which was considered to be particularly useful when introducing the TSR2. (In fact 431 MU was an equipment depot only, not a repair or servicing unit. Laarbruch's 420 MU was the repair, salvage and modification unit.) Moreover, the run-down of the Canberra force was beginning with Brüggen's 213 Squadron, then operating the Canberra B(I).6, and this would leave ample room for a new TSR2 squadron to form there. It was decided that, for the first year, all TSR2 facilities would centre on Brüggen, with Laarbruch coming on line as a TSR2 station a year later (NATO recommendations being that no more than one squadron be based on an airfield, to reduce vulnerability to surprise attack).

However, the Spotswood report on the future shape and size of the RAF, produced in early 1964, changed these plans. The major change here was to withdraw all plans for basing TSR2s in Germany. This would substantially reduce their vulnerability to surprise attack, and also ease maintenance and indirect running costs. Thus the TSR2 line-up was recommended to be changed as follows (*see* box, below).

No adjustment in total numbers was authorized despite the increase to 140 that would have been necessary. The Spotswood

report had far-reaching consequences for the make-up of the RAF. One of the first effects was the change of 40 Squadron's base, which was now to be RAF Marham in Norfolk. A second strike squadron would form within six months of 40 Squadron's establishment, also building up to twelve aircraft, and also at Marham. No specific squadron number is mentioned in surviving documentation, nor are any hints given as to the identity of this squadron. At least one flight simulator would also have been provided at Marham, possibly two.

Initial Operational Capability: reconnaissance squadron

A further eight airframes, fitted out for reconnaissance, would form a third squadron after the two strike squadrons had been established. While no specific squadron number is mentioned in surviving documentation, the Director of Air Staff Plans did write to the AOC Bomber Command on 14 April 1964, stating: '... re-equipment of the Canberra PR.7 squadron should be completed in early 1969'. This indicates that the first TSR2 reconnaissance squadron was likely to have been 13 Squadron, as this was the only Bomber Command Canberra PR.7 unit at the time.

When the plan had been to introduce the TSR2 into service in RAF Germany first, the first reconnaissance units were to have replaced Canberra squadrons there. These would probably have been 17 and 31 Squadrons.

As the TSR2 reconnaissance force was to be a low-level tactical reconnaissance force, it was felt that it would not necessarily require direct access to the Central Reconnaissance Establishment by being based at RAF Wyton, though this was an initial suggestion, and RAF Marham was favoured in later planning and confirmed several times as discussions progressed.

Initial Operational Capability: strike squadrons

The first operational TSR2 strike unit would have been 40 Squadron (previously a Canberra unit from 1953, until it merged with 50 Squadron and then disbanded in 1957), and the intention was for it to build up from its initial six ODS airframes in March 1968 (later slipped to January 1969) to a total of twelve aircraft within a year.

Location	Original		Post-Spotswood	
	Strike	*Recce*	*Strike*	*Recce*
Coningsby	17 (trainer)		18 (trainer)	
Marham	24	8	48	16
Brüggen	12	8	Nil	
Laarbruch	12	8	Nil	
Akrotiri	16	8	12	8
Tengah	10 (combined strike recce)		12	8
Reserve	15		20	
TOTAL	138		140	

Operational turnaround at a main base. Here, RAF personnel are shown winching a triple rack of 1,000lb HE bombs into the weapons bay while fuel and oxygen are replenished and a starter cart stands by. BAE Systems via Brooklands Museum

Operational use

The RAF initially intended reconnaissance squadrons to carry out no training for the strike role, and to specialize entirely in reconnaissance, a decision slightly at odds with the multi-role ability of the aircraft. By contrast, strike squadrons would be expected to carry out limited reconnaissance tasks using the permanent fit of cameras in the aircraft, in support of overall reconnaissance operations, post-strike assessment and pre-strike intelligence gathering. For the reconnaissance squadrons, choice of the reconnaissance equipment used would be dictated by the quality of imagery required, the weather and the speed with which the information was needed. For optimum imagery, day photographic coverage was best (and at night, active linescan); for getting information back to base as soon as possible, linescan with data transmission; and, when the weather was too poor for visual reconnaissance, radar reconnaissance would be used.

If nuclear conflict looked likely, the TSR2 force would be dispersed to a variety of airstrips, usually no more than two aircraft per strip. The various ground functions required to support strike or reconnaissance operations, weapons provision, photo interpreters and so on, would be dispersed to fewer locations, so any sorties flown would need to recover to this more limited subset of dispersal airstrips.

At the outset of nuclear war the TSR2 strike force would strike its pre-planned targets with whatever combination of nuclear weapons was judged appropriate to each one, and return to a base capable of rearming and refuelling the aircraft; if any still existed. Further strike operations would depend entirely on the level of devastation inflicted upon friendly forces, and could possibly involve support of army operations if poor weather precluded the use of more suitable close-air-support platforms (which would, in NATO planning, be provided by other air forces). The TSR2 reconnaissance force would have pre-planned targets within both enemy and friendly territory, the former to be reconnoitred for target acquisition purposes, and the latter to be visited after the initial nuclear exchange in order to assess the level of damage inflicted by the enemy. In a conventional conflict this latter task would be of much less importance.

Night-time operations would have been commonplace for the TSR2 force.
BAE Systems via Brooklands Museum

Under ideal conditions, the interpretation of reconnaissance information gathered by the TSR2 reconnaissance force would take the form of three phases. First of all a brief report giving essential operational information; secondly more detail, produced within hours and based on the study of film and radar prints; and thirdly very detailed information of a technical or specialist nature produced over a matter of days. In a nuclear conflict it was felt that only first-phase interpretation would be possible. No intelligence centre was likely to survive for an extended period, and a nuclear conflict could be over within days. Only a sustained conventional war would both require and allow the luxury of in-depth study of reconnaissance material.

The TSR2 strike force was not intended to take any part in a strictly conventional war in Europe. Its aircraft would sit out such a conflict in dispersed sites, only coming into use if the conflict escalated into a nuclear one. The reconnaissance force would be available for army support, but not in strike operations because of their lack of relevant training. A conventional conflict outside of NATO could, however, see use of the TSR2 strike force with conventional weapons. In this case a typical bomb load would be six 1,000lb HE bombs in the weapons bay, and would not normally rise beyond a total of ten bombs. Rearming with the same type of load was to take no more than half an hour; a change from conventional to nuclear loads no more than 75min.

While the requirement had called for the ability of the aircraft to be 'weatherproof and remain serviceable with only the minimum of routine attention for thirty days in the open', it was soon obvious that the sheer complexity of the many onboard systems would make this a challenge unlikely to be met. One possible solution was the provision of temporary hangars, and with that in mind P. Frankenstein & Sons teamed up with Handley Page to create the FHP Air-Portable Hangar, an impressive affair capable of being transported by the RAF's then-current transport types (such as the Argosy) and erected within hours at a dispersed site. This was large enough to accommodate up to three TSR2s for storage, or partly accommodate two with room enough for groundcrew to carry out basic servicing. With its fabric doors closed, the hangar was designed to be able to withstand winds of up to 75kt (85mph; 140km/h) and substantial structural loading including a hefty deposit of snow.

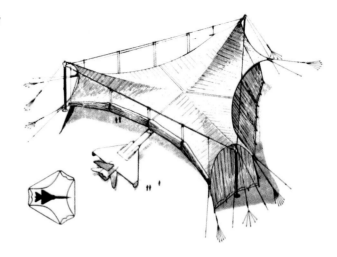

The Frankenstein/Handley Page Air-Portable Hangar would have been a near-necessity for dispersed TSR2 operations.
BAE Systems

Centralized servicing

Initially, RAF Marham was suggested as the servicing base for the TSR2 force, but when the plans for the first reconnaissance squadron changed and they were scheduled to be based at Marham, Wyton became the first choice for servicing base. Like Marham, it was large enough to handle a significant number of airframes and the various requirements in terms of new buildings and taxyways.

Other bases

Basic parameters for acceptable airfields were set out:

- Runway length of 8,000ft (2,440m) or more required for normal basing, with permanent arrester installation
- Runway length of 6,000ft (1,830m) or more for exercises, with portable arrester gear
- Runway length of 2,400ft (730m) or more for operational use when required

The primary reasoning behind such large runways for an aircraft design for STOL performance was the single-engine-failure safety case. An engine failure on take-off, in the short-take-off configuration would leave the aircraft unable to climb away, so it would be normal peacetime practice to use less take-off flap and extend the take-off run, enabling a faster climb-out and reducing the risk of a crash if an engine was to be lost at a critical moment. Similarly, at normal approach speeds and flap settings, as would be used for a short landing run, a single engine failure would result in the aircraft

failing to maintain height against the drag of the flaps, and thus a lower flap, or zero flap, setting would be required. In the case of a fully loaded aircraft this would increase landing distance to above 7,000ft (2,130m). Wet conditions, or high crosswinds causing reduced brake parachute use, could well extend the landing run to above 9,000ft (2,740m).

As well as stations already mentioned, Akrotiri in Cyprus and Tengah in Singapore were both of suitable size to cater for regular TSR2 operations, and were at one point or another earmarked as TSR2 bases. A list of possible Master Diversion Bases was also put together; these were airfields large enough to accept TSR2 diversions and situated close to normal training areas or TSR2 bases. Each would be equipped with suitable barrier or arrester gear. The list included Leuchars and Waddington.

Overseas training

Low-flying training has always involved a certain amount of nuisance to those who live under the flight paths, and the amount of noise expected to be generated by the TSR2 was thought to preclude any possibility of significant low-level training being carried out in the UK, or even in Germany, where, since the end of the War, there had been a casual disregard of the population's wishes or opinions on aircraft noise.

With the UK and Europe mostly out of the picture for low-level flying, the hunt was on for alternative parts of the world, and these boiled down to a number of possibilities including Australia, Libya and Canada. With the Australian's decision to buy the TFX, plans to use Australian ranges for

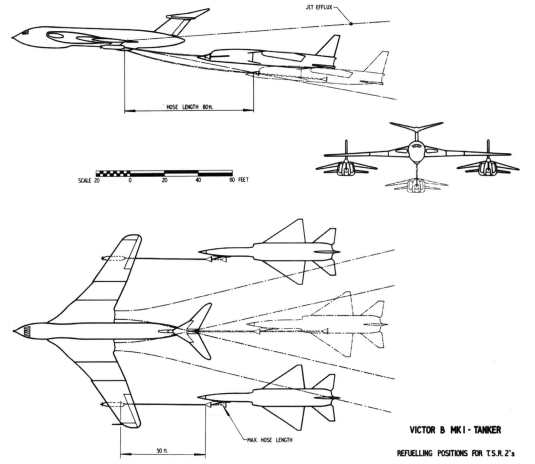

JET EFFLUX

HOSE LENGTH 80ft.

SCALE 20   0   20   40   60 FEET

50 ft.

MAX. HOSE LENGTH

VICTOR B MK I - TANKER

REFUELLING POSITIONS FOR T.S.R.2's

Compatibility with the Victor tanker force was investigated early in the project, and this diagram from Handley Page, showing refuelling positions, was drawn up even before the TSR2's final configuration was decided upon. In-flight refuelling was initially considered only in relation to ferrying operations, such as transits to overseas training areas. BAE Systems

TSR2 training evaporated also, and the political situation in Libya looked increasingly likely to preclude any reliable basing there in the future. Hal Far in Malta became the favoured choice for a base for Near East training (the actual low-level flying was to be carried in Libya or Turkey if circumstances permitted), with RAF Goose Bay in Canada the primary alternative, offering terrain similar to that of Eastern Europe. To avoid the expense of setting up bombing ranges overseas, training with practice and live weapons would be carried out on existing UK ranges.

Colour schemes

In 1963 overall white anti-flash was the colour scheme in vogue for the RAF's nuclear bomber force. The effects of nuclear weapons were still being researched, and the initial fears had been that the thermal overload from a nearby nuclear flash would critically damage vulnerable portions of an aircraft, such as parts constructed from lighter gauge metal, like ailerons. The TSR2

was expected to be no different, with some fuselage panels made of lighter-gauge metal and wing and fin trailing edges made from a honeycomb sandwich that was also more vulnerable to high temperature doses. Accordingly, BAC intended to produce the TSR2 in an overall white finish with pale red and blue markings. Pale red was reserved for warning items, such as ejection-seat warning triangles, with pale blue for everything else.

The RAF was already uncomfortable with white for its new low-level strike aircraft, suggesting in February 1963 that light grey was a slightly better option that would retain some thermal protection while making the aircraft somewhat less conspicuous, if only while parked on an airfield, or operating at medium to high altitude. However, research later in 1963 found that the whole anti-flash philosophy had been something of a waste of paint. Three threat scenarios had been envisaged, from near misses by the following weapons:

1. Attack by intercontinental ballistic missile while parked or scrambling.

2. Attack by nuclear-tipped SAM while airborne.
3. Reflected flash from the aircraft's own weapons delivered in a lay-down attack under the worst possible conditions of reflectivity (such as snow-covered ground and cloud cover).

In the first two cases it was clear that anti-flash paint was only going to help if the weapons in question had missed by quite some margin, but it had not been realized that the safe distance at which thermal overload could be dealt with by white paint was still within the significant overpressure zone created by the blast. In simple terms, the blast was either going to get you or not, and if it did not, the thermal pulse from the flash was not going to be that significant. This meant that paint with far less reflectivity, namely camouflage, could safely be applied. This led to the introduction of camouflage to the V-force bombers, and the question of camouflage for the TSR2 force was then also raised.

Discussions in mid-1964 revolved around applying a similar scheme to that for the V-

The all-white colour scheme was an anti-flash paint job applied to minimize the thermal dose received by the airframe in the event of a nearby nuclear detonation. By 1964 camouflage was in favour, and the TSR2 would not have worn the anti-flash scheme in RAF service. Damien Burke

bomber force: a topside mix of Dark Green and Medium Sea Grey, with undersides remaining anti-flash white. In the case of the underside, thermal protection against nuclear flash was still judged to be more important than any attempt to hide a low-flying aircraft from ground observers. The flash of white that would be visible to an airborne fighter pilot looking towards a turning TSR2 was not considered. (Indeed, it took until the mid-1970s for light undersides to be replaced by wraparound camouflage on other types, such as the Buccaneer.) Overall Dark Green was briefly favoured, despite being of little use to hide an aircraft parked on the ground.

The consensus of opinion by July 1964 was that existing NATO-standard documents on bomber camouflage would be suitable, and in September 1964 BAC was instructed to apply one of the NATO standard colour schemes from NATO STANAG 3085. This was scheme 1a; topsides in Dark Green and Dark Sea Grey with undersides in Silver, all colours being applied with a high-speed (semi-gloss) finish. BAC was not wildly impressed with this directive, as many of the airframe skin thicknesses had been defined by the thermal parameters they were expected to experience, including nuclear flash. A change of paint finish to darker hues would increase the thermal dose, which was of particular concern in the area of the forward fuel tank, which was integral with the outer skin of the forward fuselage. The company's initial suggestion was to apply camouflage to only two aircraft, from either the development batch or pre-production batch, to assess the paint's performance. While the RAF wanted camouflage applied immediately, and certainly no later than then tenth (first pre-production) aircraft, BAC could not oblige, as production was too far advanced.

At a meeting on 9 October the new external paint finish requirements were discussed. The undersurface colour of silver was not available in the new acrylic paints that were to be used, and it was accepted that pale grey or white might have to do instead. Some concessions had been granted to BAC to avoid the use of certain standard markings, such as yellow-and-black RESCUE arrows, on the white-painted airframes, but these concessions would not have applied to camouflaged aircraft, which would have been expected to conform to all of the RAF's standards of the time.

A preliminary camouflage scheme layout for the aircraft, which included a white underside, was drawn up by BAC in November 1964. (It was an unusual scheme that the RAF would have been unlikely to accept, owing to the high fuselage demarcation line.) As all electrical transparencies on the aircraft were manufactured in a white finish and had to be left unpainted, and many components had already been painted white, this would simplify the application of camouflage to the pre-production airframes, as fewer items would have needed to be stripped and repainted. Cancellation came before any camouflage paint was ever applied to a TSR2 airframe.

A pre-production airframe in the BAC camouflage colour scheme drawn up in November 1964. The radome, fin tip and wing panels were dielectric areas manufactured in a white finish; BAC was keen to save money by using already-manufactured items, but they would not have been acceptable to the RAF in these colours and have thus been depicted in black instead. Ronnie Olsthoorn

Ground support

Servicing and readiness vehicle and turn-round and readiness vehicle

The creation of a dedicated TSR2 servicing and readiness vehicle (SRV) was proposed by BAC in late 1960, and this was finally approved by the Air Staff in July 1961, but the MoA saw no need for it and blocked any progress. The RAF restated its requirement for it in June 1962, but a brick wall was still put up by the MoA. This became an increasingly unsatisfactory situation, as items relating to the functionality of the vehicle (such as the provision of air conditioning to keep the aircraft's electronics cool on the ground while it was being worked on) were going to be required during development-batch flying. Instead of permitting the vehicle to go ahead, the MoA placed individual contracts for these items

as the need for them became ever more urgent.

Things came to a head at the end of 1963, with the RAF insisting that the Ministry had to allow development to begin or the aircraft would be entering service without appropriate ground support. To enable the SRV to be of any use at dispersed sites it needed to be air-transportable by Argosy, and light enough (less than 17,000lb (7,700kg)) to enable an Argosy to carry it at least 750nm (860 miles; 1,380km). The SRV had to encompass the majority of support services needed by a TSR2, both at dispersed sites and at normal bases. The SRV would not provide all the services a TSR2 needed, but it was to provide LP air for air-conditioning of the cockpits and equipment bays, air for engine starting, electrical power, hydraulic power and a refuelling pump. A towing capability was also

envisaged. It had to be capable of starting both of the TSR2's engines within one minute to meet the tactical requirement (a requirement later relaxed). Use of the SRV within hangars was not felt to be practical owing to noise and space requirements, so the RAF also expected to have to duplicate most of the services provided by the SRV in separate pieces of equipment.

By April 1964 the Air Staff had completed their studies on the subject, and decided that the SRV was a step too far, and that development time and costs would be excessive. A simpler turn-round and readiness vehicle (TRRV) would be a cheaper option, deleting the engine-starting assistance (the TSR2, after all, had an onboard Cumulus AAPP for this purpose) and hydraulic supply (again, with engines running, the TSR2 could provide its own hydraulic power for testing purposes). All

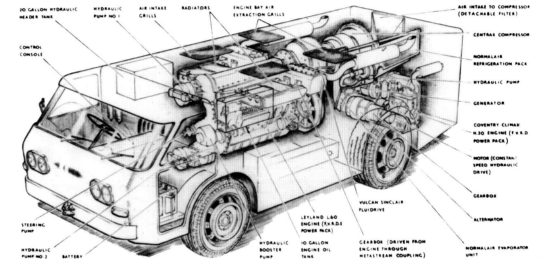

The SRV fell foul of cost cutting as the overall programme cost rose ever higher. BAE Systems via Brooklands Museum

A TSR2 at standby in the proverbial 'cabbage patch', with an SRV in attendance. BAE Systems via Brooklands Museum

of the remaining required components could be mounted on a standard 3-ton four-by-four Bedford lorry, already approved for Argosy carriage and cross-country driving. As a bonus, the various separate items could be removed from the vehicle for in-hangar use at main bases as required, so there would be no need to buy two of everything.

The final make-up of the proposed TRVV was as follows:

- Oil replenishment – redesigned 'Juniper' rig
- Air conditioning – vapour cycle unit operated by Rover APU
- Electrical services – 15/20 KVickers generator
- Liquid oxygen – 75L or 185L LOX unit redesigned to reduce weight
- High-pressure nitrogen – standard cylinder
- Hydraulic fluid replenishment – special-to-type dispenser

Space was also to be provided for containers and replenishment equipment for helium, demineralized water, lissapol detergent and defrosting fluid, plus brake-parachute drying equipment, a tyre inflation kit and a towing arm. No records of actual development of the TRRV have come to light, and it is thought that the RAF was deferring specific procurement actions on this score until nearer the time the TSR2 would have entered service.

Automatic test equipment

The expected complexity of the TSR2's electronics suite would have created maintenance and fault-diagnosis problems beyond any the RAF had already experienced. The level of expertise and knowledge required would have been far beyond the RAF's own personnel, and, even had the expertise been available, the amount of maintenance hours per flight hour would have made operating the type prohibitively expensive. One solution to assist with this was the provision of automatic test equipment (ATE), which could be plugged into the aircraft's various systems to make sure everything was working as it should, or to assist with diagnosis of problems. Discussions on this began early in the project, during 1959, but it was not added to the requirement until March 1961. Progress from that point was stiflingly slow, with no agreed specification for the equipment until

early 1963, at which point submissions were invited from various firms including BAC itself (in co-operation with Honeywell), de Havilland and Hawker Siddeley, the last-named being awarded the contract.

The ATE was to be plugged in to various test sockets provided on the aircraft (around forty of them), and could check various subsystems of the nav/attack system, either separately or as part of the overall system. These included the air data system, attitude monitor, AFCS, CCS, compass system, Doppler radar, FLR, head-down instrument display, HUD, moving map, radio altimeter and SLR. Three operators were to run the ATE, which was to be installed in a mobile trailer or vehicle suitable for air transportation. One operator would run the ATE directly, with the other two seated in the TSR2 to operate systems from the cockpits as required. Each circuit tested would have a range of acceptable outputs, and if the ATE picked up any out of the acceptable range a 'NO GO' signal would be flagged and the ATE would either stop and await operator attention, or go into an automatic

diagnosis subroutine. All readings, as well as being displayed visually, could be printed out on paper tape for maintenance records and historical defect analysis.

Hawker Siddeley's brochure for its proposed ATE described a four-wheel trolley approximately 10ft long, 5ft wide and 5ft high (3m × 1.5m × 1.5m), weighing around 3,000lb (1,400kg). Construction would be of steel, making it sufficiently robust to carry the weight of two men on top and thus double as a servicing platform, an access ladder being built into the end of the trolley. The major electronic units built into the trolley were to be mounted on telescopic runners enabling easy access for servicing or replacement, and normally covered by lockable doors. At one side of the trolley would be the control panel and display unit, along with warning lamps, with the printer and tape recorder mounted below. A remote control unit attached to the unit by a retracting cable would enable the operator to control the trolley's various test functions while some distance away, while seated in one of the TSR2's cockpits, for example.

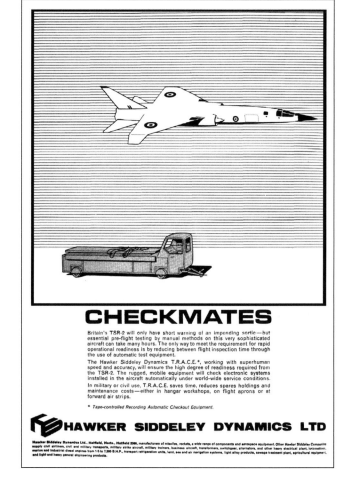

This Hawker Siddeley Dynamics advertisement of January 1965 included a sketch of their ATE vehicle, designed to be parked underneath a TSR2 and enabling ready access to the equipment bays on each side, using the vehicle itself as an access platform. via Brooklands Museum

CHAPTER ELEVEN

Cancellation

The TSR2 had been experiencing a rocky ride since before its birth, and plenty of people predicted that its cost would rise beyond those of all previous projects. An informal discussion between Vickers-Armstrongs/ English Electric personnel and the Army's Tactical Intelligence Steering Committee (TISC) in June 1959 even revealed that, at this early point, the TISC believed that the RAF had 'pulled a fast one' by getting the project pushed through with Army help on the basis of a 500nm reconnaissance sortie, when the RAF was really interested in nothing other than the 1,000nm strike sortie. Now the Army recognised that 'the TSR2 was going to be available in too small quantities and would be too expensive for battlefield surveillance or close support'. What it really wanted was a small, cheap drone for reconnaissance tasks. The Deputy Chief of the Imperial General Staff, Lieutenant-General Sir Harold Pyman, wrote in 1960: 'I do not believe we can afford to develop an aircraft as expensive as TSR2 to carry out these tasks. We must somehow find a cheaper solution', and went on to suggest the NA.39 as an alternative. The RAF pointed out that the Army wanted to spend similar sums of money on warheads for the Davy Crockett nuclear recoilless rifle (a weapon of such dubious utility and high cost that it was no surprise when cooler heads prevailed and the UK's requirement for it was cancelled in 1962, before any had entered service).

The really vehement opposition to the aircraft arose during 1960, when the first hints of its rising costs and 'outmoded' design hit the press. The two most high-profile opponents were Earl Mountbatten of Burma, Admiral of the Fleet and Chief of the Defence Staff, and Mary Goldring, a journalist working for *The Economist*. Each attacked the programme continually, one privately, the other publicly. Goldring was a particularly effective public voice against the project, as she was not only an excellent writer but also an incisive and confident broadcaster. BAC personnel would come to hate 'that vile bloody woman' for what

seemed at times to be an almost weekly onslaught on TV (on *Division*, for example) or radio broadcasts.

In September 1960 Prime Minister Harold Macmillan asked his Minister of Defence, Harold Watkinson, three questions:

1. Was a replacement needed for the Canberra?
2. Did the operational requirement – OR.339 – still stand?
3. Would it be possible to compromise by accepting an aircraft that did not meet OR.339, e.g. the NA.39?

These were put to a meeting of the Chiefs of the Defence Staff, who fought off this early threat. The answers boiled down to 'Yes', 'Yes' and 'No, absolutely not!', though behind the scenes the Chief of the Defence Staff himself (Mountbatten) and the Chief of the Imperial General Staff (Field Marshal

Sir Francis Festing) had confided to the government's Scientific Advisor, Sir Solly Zuckerman, that they were both opposed to continuing with TSR2. In fact, Mountbatten had bumped into Blackburn Aircraft's managing director, Captain Duncan Lewin, at the Farnborough Air Show, and suggested to him that the time was ripe to put NA.39 up for assessment once again. Lewin pointed out that TSR2's major differences to the NA.39 were that it had Mach 2 capability at altitude, and could operate from rough strips. However, Mach 2 at altitude was a recipe for getting yourself shot down, and TSR2 was likely to be staying subsonic at low level for most of its life, just like the NA.39, and if supersonic burst was that important, this could be added to the NA.39 relatively easily. Lewin also considered rough-strip operation unrealistic for such a technologically complex aircraft. His prediction was that TSR2 would not enter service until 1967 (a very

The Blackburn NA.39, or Buccaneer, dogged the TSR2 throughout its brief life, being pushed time and again as a suitable aircraft for the RAF. Damien Burke

good guess for the time), and that it would be better either to go with the cheaper and simpler NA.39 (or rather B.111/113, with RB.168 engines with reheat, which could carry out 90 per cent of the task), or to go all-out to make TSR2 even more advanced, and accept that this would delay the in-service date until 1970. Both of these were excellent suggestions, and both were ignored. The RAF had also quietly admitted to the fact that an aircraft of the size of the TSR2 was no longer really a viable close-air-support vehicle, and was looking at the much smaller, cheaper and less-sophisticated Hawker P.1127 as the means of fulfilling this role.

The year 1961 was fairly quiet as far as TSR2 critics were concerned, and it was not until March 1962 that rising costs and delays really began to cause trouble. An examination was made of possible economies, with little practical result, and the project rolled onwards through the summer with the MoA and the RAF increasingly frustrated by matters, but seemingly unable to do anything about it. The Cuban missile crisis in October focused minds on the reality of nuclear war, and afterwards the TSR2 was given an unexpected boost from, of all people, the Americans. Kennedy's administration had unilaterally cancelled the Skybolt missile programme, and the TSR2 was suddenly in a position to fill a limited stop-gap strategic nuclear deterrent role. The RAF was put in a stronger position than had previously been the case. While the Treasury refused to extend further funding until the project had been fully investigated (again), there was now little choice but to continue, and the RAF knew it.

In March 1963 the RAF was once again forced to take another look at possible economy measures on the project, in response to the Treasury's point-blank refusal to authorize the expenditure required to cover the eleven pre-production aircraft. Its study assigned costs to particular items of equipment or developments, and spelled out the effect of each kind of cost reduction on the aircraft's capability. This was a pretty laughable and transparent exercise in keeping the government off its back, with no intention of losing any aspect of the project. For instance, nearly £43 million could be saved if they did not bother having engines, nearly £10 million could be saved by having no means of navigating the aircraft, and so on.

A study was also begun into the possibility of buying seventy-eight fewer TSR2s and purchasing Buccaneer Mk 2s to plug the resulting gap. The attentive reader can probably guess by this point what the conclusion of this study was: the Buccaneer was no good and the idea could not be recommended. A meeting of the Chiefs of Staff on 26 March then unanimously concluded that the TSR2 should proceed as planned, and that the essential commitments in UK strategy would be harmed by the replacement of TSR2 with any alternative. With an estimated project cost of between £175 and £200 million (excluding the cost of the production aircraft at £2.3 million each), TSR2 development costs were now approaching six times the price of the original Ministry estimates (about twice that of the collected firms' estimates once a firm specification was in place).

Exasperated, the Prime Minister sent a terse memo to the Minister of Aviation on 24 April: 'Can you give me the latest position on the T.S.R.2? What will it cost? Will it ever fly?' The answers boiled down to 'around £500 million all in' and 'some time next year, but we're not entirely sure when', and cannot have reassured him. The project, however, once again escaped the axe and continued funding was reluctantly authorized.

Australia and the TFX

Confidence in the project was badly shaken later in 1963 by events in Australia. The RAAF had been interested in TSR2 since 1959, to meet its Air Staff Requirement AIR/36 (which read like a near carbon copy of OR.339), and had been kept regularly appraised of developments, with BAC delegations visiting from time to time to present the latest sales brochures. Substantial effort went into this sales drive, with almost no support from the UK government. In mid-1963 BAC was fully expecting to sell around twenty-four TSR2s to the Australians. By August, however, the RAAF had found out that, even at this late stage, the RAF was continuing to evaluate alternatives, such as the Buccaneer Mk 2, and no firm production order had been placed for the RAF. The government was urged to place a firm order to give the Australians the confidence to proceed, but initially refused to do so, and as a compromise only leaked news that an order for long-dated raw materials had been placed. While the politicians and public in Australia knew what TFX was going to look like, nobody had seen so much as a single photo of the TSR2, despite the first airframe being

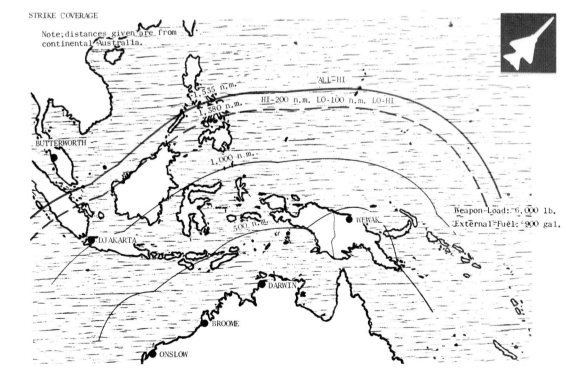

BAE Systems via
Brooklands Museum

very nearly complete. Those in BAC's publicity department could bite their tongues no longer, and begged for permission to publish, at the very least, an artist's impression so that the press and public in Australia (and, indeed, in the UK) would have some idea that the aircraft actually existed and was not just a 'paper aeroplane'. In the words of Charles Gardner, BAC's publicity manager, '... the image of TSR-2 in both the UK and the USA is a ghost-like one, in which there is a tendency to disbelieve. We want to give the ghost a bit more substance.' Incredibly, even with an export order at stake, no such permission was forthcoming from the MoA.

Meanwhile, the RAAF had been evaluating the aircraft types it could possibly buy, looking at the Phantom II, Dassault Mirage IV, Vigilante, TSR2 and TFX. None of the immediately available types could fully meet its needs, though the Vigilante came close. The TSR2 would do the job, but was several years away. The TFX was even better, and cheaper, but again lay in the future.

The RAAF's Air Marshal Sir Frederick Scherger had always preferred the TSR2, though he pointed out that his boss, Air Marshal Hancock, Australia's Chief of the Air Staff, would have the final say. On a visit to the UK Scherger had a meeting with Earl Mountbatten, who took the opportunity to press the case for the Buccaneer. After this, Scherger's preference changed, and he now

favoured the TFX over the TSR2, as did his boss. The mixed messages coming from the UK's government and the Chief of the Defence Staff had been a disaster for Australian confidence in the TSR2, and therefore its export prospects.

The final RAAF recommendation came as a surprise to many; it recommended buying the Vigilante, as it was immediately available, whereas the really capable aircraft would not be realistically available until the next decade. This was a 'cunning plan', plumping for second best (or indeed third

best), knowing full well that it would look like poor value for money to the politicians to order an aircraft that would be superseded in less than a decade. By this point TSR2 was firmly out of the running. The UK government belatedly realized the seriousness of the situation, and there was a last-minute flurry of effort to put together a good deal for the Australians, while they also finally announced a firm RAF production order. An offer was put together to sell the aircraft as part of a government-to-government deal at cost price only; BAC and

Radii of action for Australia-based TSR2s, from a brochure prepared for the RAAF in June 1963.
BAE Systems via Brooklands Museum

BSEL both agreed to waive their normal commissions on such deals, and Prime Minister Harold Macmillan put this offer forward on 3 October. There was no immediate response. The Australians were now weighing up the relative benefits of going with TFX or spending the extra and going with TSR2. The Americans offered all manner of inducements, including the loan of Boeing B-47s or F-4 Phantoms as an interim measure. Despite urging, the UK government was slow to make any similar offer. It did not help that Macmillan had been taken seriously ill (he resigned on the 18th after an emergency operation), and the Treasury also interfered, making sure that the Australians would be charged for any training required.

On 24 October 1963 the government sent a telegram offering a further 10 per cent discount on TSR2, along with participation in the trials, evaluation and development flying, and twelve Valiants at an 'insignificant' price as an interim measure until the first TSR2s were delivered in 1969. The total cost of twenty-four TSR2s would be £48 million, and refurbishment of the Valiants to RAAF standards would be an additional £2 million. It was too little and far too late. Just hours later, with the

telegram as yet undelivered, the Australians ordered the TFX instead, at a total cost of £45 million including spares and training, and with delivery of the first aircraft expected in 1967, two years before the TSR2. This was a strong blow to the TSR2's chances of survival. While an order for just twenty-four airframes would have not made a huge difference to the unit costs, and therefore the total cost to the UK, it could conceivably have led to other export orders, and made cancellation a trickier proposition when there was another customer to support. George Edwards later said that he was '... convinced that the American aircraft industry was out to slaughter the British industry and was prepared to sell below cost to achieve that'.

Four days after the Australian decision, the UK government finally allowed BAC to issue a press release describing the TSR2, with some photos of the first TSR2 in its nearly complete state. At last the UK taxpayer had some idea of what the 'ghost' looked like, and the press was able to describe it in more detail. Despite this release of information there were those within the Air Ministry who continued to block any public discussion of the aircraft. The Shadow Minister of Aviation, John

Cronin MP, visited BAC in November to seek more information on the project to back up his (generally constructive and fair) views on the project. An Air Ministry representative sat in on his meeting with George Edwards and blocked any discussion of what he considered to be sensitive aspects, many of which had already been accurately covered in the press in recent weeks. Cronin was furious, and in a letter to Minister of Aviation Julian Amery decried this policy of 'fatuous obscurantism' and summed up by saying: 'The way things are going at present your Ministry and the Air Ministry are going to have the illusion of security about the TSR2 without having the TSR2, like the smile on the face of the Cheshire Cat in Alice in Wonderland, which persisted after the Cat had disappeared.'

TSR2 reaches crisis point

Having failed to sell the aircraft to the Australians, Britain's new Prime Minister, Alec Douglas-Home, now had an expensive project on his hands and doubts that it could be afforded by the UK on its own. Writing to the Ministries of Aviation and Defence on 15 November 1963, he noted: 'I am rather troubled about this project. It seems to be turning out to be considerably more expensive than we thought ...', and added: 'Ought we to have ... a new look at the whole venture and satisfy ourselves that is is still an integral element in our defence programme?' The opposition did not miss any opportunity to have a go too, with Denis Healey, Labour's spokesman for defence matters, saying that the TSR2 affair was 'the biggest scandal in British politics since the South Sea Island Bubble'.

In January 1964, on finding out that TSR2 costs had risen once more, by a staggering £130 million, Julian Amery wrote to the Minister of Defence, Peter Thorneycroft, saying: '... I am appalled by this. Whether we cancel or go forward with the project, politically we could be faced with a scandalous situation', and 'We are now reaching a position where, to put it brutally, the British aircraft industry is destroying our military air power.' The letter went on to suggest that, unless the TSR2's cost could be reduced, the only alternative would be to buy the TFX from the Americans instead; at £2 million a unit, even allowing for wasted costs on TSR2 to date, a serious saving could be made. A 'tough line' would have

One of the first photos of XR219 finally released in late October 1963 to show that the TSR2 was more than just a paper project. Unfortunately by this time the Australian decision had already been made and any public relations value was lost. BAE Systems via Brooklands Museum

to be taken with BAC. Even the Chief of the Air Staff was appalled at the new costs: 'The situation ... is of the utmost gravity. ... we are in no doubt that the aircraft is unacceptable at this price.' The Minister of Defence was of like mind, and for the first time the government was seriously looking at buying TFX and cancelling TSR2. Air Vice-Marshal Emson, Assistant Chief of the Air Staff (OR), wrote that he had '... no confidence in the ability of the management of BAC to give us the aeroplane we want, when we want it and at the right price', and that 'The real problem is, of course, that Sir George Edwards is the only man who can make anything of the mediocrity at his disposal and he has not the time.'

In a meeting at the Ministry of Aviation, George Edwards was bluntly told that the project was now in danger of cancellation because its cost was felt to be uncontrollable. He was willing to negotiate fixed prices for the development batch and pre-production aircraft, but the prices would be likely to 'frighten rather than reassure' the Ministry. Within the Air Ministry the question was even being raised as to whether it would be worthwhile to drop the Mach 2 requirement and reduce the aircraft's top speed to around Mach 1.3. The savings in materials and engine development (in particular, the need for continuous reheat operation) could be considerable. However, this was a step too far and the idea was buried.

The Treasury, meanwhile, embargoed the approval of any additional funding for the project, even for items that would normally not need their authority, and in May the MoA finally had agreement from George Edwards that a big management shake-up was necessary at BAC. The result was that Freddie Page was put in control of the project as a whole, and this, along with introduction of Value Engineering, was expected to have a large positive effect.

By June the RAF was expecting an in-service weight of more than 103,000lb (46,750kg) and the RAF's Resident Project Officer at Weybridge, Group Captain P. Walker, was predicting (accurately) that the aircraft would not meet the specification and that rising costs were inevitably going to result in a smaller buy, with delays resulting in no serious front-line force being in existence until 1969 or even later. He ended his assessment thus: 'I ... believe ... that we ought to take one final long, hard, look at the TSR2.' Very soon the Air Staff would push the MoA to begin an in-depth review of the project. It seemed that the RAF was,

at a late stage, getting cold feet about the whole thing.

Just days before XR219 was to fly, the RAF, MoA and Treasury officials held a meeting to discuss the additional financial authority necessary to continue with the project, covering funding through to about February 1965. The Treasury, with an eye on a possible change of government in October, was still unwilling to release the full amount. It would, however, release enough to fund the project through to December, but withheld any authority for items it considered to be additions to the original requirement or changes to it.

Export customers

BAC had not just tried to sell the aircraft to Australia. Detailed brochures had also been given to the Royal New Zealand Air Force (which lost interest some time before the Australian decision) and the Royal Canadian Air Force (RCAF) (which also lost interest, in late 1963). Additionally, dossiers of unclassified material on the aircraft had been prepared for the Royal Netherlands Air Force, Indian Air Force and Iranian Air Force (which showed 'mild interest' in late 1964, including a visit to Boscombe by the Iranian Air Force's Commanding General, General Khatami). France had shown some mild interest in March 1962, suggesting that it would replace its Mirage Vs with licence-built TSR2s some time in the late 1960s. This prompted a question from the Prime Minister as to whether it was entirely 'out' to equip the French with TSR2s earlier than that, and equip the RAF with the Mirage V! Needless to say this idea went nowhere.

The only other country to express any serious interest was West Germany. In March 1961 the Germans were invited to play a part in the development of the TSR2 (limited co-operation on the P.1127 already being under way), but this came to nothing. German interest continued in the aircraft itself, however, and by 1963 they appeared highly interested in acquiring the TSR2 as a replacement for the Lockheed F-104G, an aircraft the Luftwaffe had only acquired after Lockheed bribed German politicians to buy an aircraft somewhat unsuited to German needs (and killed off any chance of the German Navy buying the NA.39 in the process). After several exchanges of information, a German delegation including their Minister of Defence, Herr Kai Uwe

von Hassel, along with several senior military officers, made a visit to BAC Weybridge in 1964 to look at the production line and systems rigs, and gather detailed information. One of the officers attending was in the Luftwaffe's Operational Requirements department, and gave the impression that the F-104G replacement was not an urgent matter (though they were actually dropping out of the sky and killing Luftwaffe pilots with alarming regularity), but that an aircraft of the TSR2/TFX type was certainly a serious option.

There was concern within the government that arming Germany with such an aircraft, when they had access to US nuclear weapons as part of NATO, would mean that a German aircraft could conceivably get as far as Moscow and attack the city with a nuclear weapon. Giving Germany this capability could damage relations with the Soviet Union. German interest then appeared to end abruptly just three months later, when General Buchs of the Joint Staff said very firmly that 'Germany had never had any interest in adopting for itself the TSR.2/TFX type of aircraft', stating that any mention they had made of it was in the terms of a multinational NATO force, not German acquisition of such an aircraft. This was a puzzling statement, and von Hassel later wrote a response in which he assured the UK government that Germany was still interested, but had no immediate need, and would therefore keep a close eye on the project as it progressed.

Ironically, BAC had also tried to interest the Americans in buying the TSR2 to satisfy the very requirement, SOR.183, that resulted in the creation of the TFX/F-111. This went as far as Boeing even agreeing to push the TSR2 as a 'cheap and happy' alternative to the development of a fully fledged variable-sweep type, and a suggestion from the Americans that the USAF would buy TSR2s while the RAF could perhaps buy North American B-70s to suit its strategic needs (a complete non-starter of an idea, given the cancellation of OR.330). However, with TSR2 unable to operate from carriers, there was no serious chance it could be acceptable to satisfy SOR.183; and even when TFX development branched into separate versions for the US Navy and USAF, TSR2 was still of no interest. This was a disappointment to Glenn Martin, which had licence-built the Canberra when the Americans bought that type in the 1950s, and was keen to do the same with the TSR2.

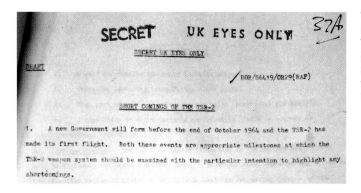

The RAF loses faith

In early October 1964, just days after XR219 had flown, the RAF's Operational Requirements unit was working on a report entitled *Short Comings of the TSR-2*. That long hard look had been taken, and the RAF did not like what it had found. The report admitted that the likelihood of open conflict in Europe was receding. However, limited war elsewhere was more likely than ever. Therefore it was felt pertinent to ask if the TSR2 still met the RAF's requirements, particularly in the conventional role. The conclusions made uncomfortable reading: 'The outstanding and all-pervading shortcoming of the TSR2 is its high cost ... has virtually no conventional strike capability at night or in bad weather ... does not have a real all-weather reconnaissance capability ... navigation system, being dependent on accurately mapped fix points, is ideally suited to northwest Europe but is unlikely to be as effective in the probable areas of limited war ... it will be useless at altitude over northwest Europe ... has no armed reconnaissance capability ... considerable shortfall in the originally specified airfield performance ... more or less tied to operations from paved runways ... fundamentally bad engine tunnel installation and accessories bays ... low reliability ... wing design seems to be too heavily biased in favour of low gust response/good crew environment ...', and so on.

The RAF had belatedly realized that its own requirements had led to an aircraft that did not do what the Service wanted, seven years down the line. Many of the criticisms in the report were hardly fair on BAC, such as the assertions that that the conventional weapons load was not heavy enough and the ferry range was insufficient, when both were in excess of the original requirement. However, weighed against what the RAF now needed, the aircraft was falling well short.

A change of government

On 15 October 1964 the General Election saw a change in the UK's government, with the Labour Party winning power by just four seats. The outgoing Conservative Chancellor of the Exchequer, Reggie Maudling, is reputed to have greeted his incoming replacement at No. 11 Downing Street, Jim Callaghan, with the words: 'Sorry to leave things in such a mess, old cock!'. The country's finances were in a parlous state, and expensive projects were surely going to be at the top of the new government's hit list. In fact the Labour Party's manifesto had included in a section on defence policy the statement that: 'Many thousands of millions have been spent on the aircraft industry, but because of lurches in strategic policy, wrong priorities, and grave errors in the choice of aircraft, we are now in a position where obsolete types have not been replaced, and for such urgently needed machines as helicopters (which could make a great contribution to the security and effectiveness of our troops in Malaysia) we are dependent on the United States.' With so many Labour MPs having been vocally anti-TSR2 and other big-ticket defence projects before the election, it was no surprise to anybody that all of the RAF's large projects soon came under the spotlight. Despite promises from local MPs in the areas most strongly associated with TSR2 production that 'Your jobs are safe under Labour', the Cabinet had other plans. By the end of the year rumours were rife that TSR2 in particular was being lined up for the chop.

In America the similarities in requirement and performance between TSR2 and TFX that had so interested Boeing in 1963 now brought the aircraft to the attention of

HAROLD WILSON TELLS TSR2 WORKERS

YOUR JOBS ARE GUARANTEED UNDER LABOUR

LABOUR WILL NOT CANCEL THE TSR2.

Amery knows he will not be Minister of Aviation after next Friday. His lie about the TSR2 is a political gambler's last desperate throw to keep his Parliamentary Seat in Preston North.
Harold Wilson himself nailed this lie in Preston last June when he said he foresaw a "long and useful life for this magnificent aircraft in a conventional role."
Who are you going to believe? A discredited Tory Minister — or your next Prime Minister?

LABOUR HAS BIG PLANS FOR THE AIRCRAFT INDUSTRY.

Only Tory muddle and stop-go policies have prevented this industry playing its proper role.
Labour's Plan calls for an industry working at full capacity. Labour will EXPAND our highly skilled aircraft engineering teams. They will be central to our export drive.
Under Labour's Plan, your skill will be at a premium and overtime (not short time) will be the likely order of the day. Labour is confident that our aircraft workers will rise to the challenge of turning-out aircraft in really large numbers for a ready sale in the developing nations of the world.

THERE IS A GREAT FUTURE FOR THE BRITISH AIRCRAFT INDUSTRY — UNDER A LABOUR GOVERNMENT

The infamous Labour Party leaflet issued in the Preston South constituency before the 1964 General Election. After the cancellation, Preston South's Labour MP, Peter Mahon, denied any responsibility for the issuing of this leaflet.

the British government. They were smitten with American know-how and attracted by the promised lower price of buying TFX instead of continuing with the home-grown but troubled and costly TSR2, and a visit was made to the USA in mid-December to discuss the possibilities. The team sent was a joint MoA and MoD one, led by the Deputy Chief of the Air Staff, Air Marshal Sir Christopher Hartley.

The Air Staff had initially reacted with some horror to the reality of losing TSR2 and having to put up with TFX, as they viewed it as inferior in many ways. In particular, its navigation-attack system was more primitive, and there was no reconnaissance capability whatsoever. Improving TFX by fitting British nav/attack and reconnaissance equipment would result in the British version of the TFX taking longer to arrive, perhaps not until 1969, and add millions to the cost, though they admitted that even then it would still be cheaper than TSR2. News of investigations into buying TFX soon got back to BAC.

In fact the Defence Council had put together a proposed package that would gut the RAF's entire line-up of new types and replace them with mostly American equipment. This included:

- Cancelling the buy of 158 TSR2s and buying 110 TFX instead
- Cancelling the buy of 182 P.1154s and buying 150 F-4s and 110 P.1127s instead
- Cancelling the buy of 62 HS.681s and buying 82 C-130s instead
- Cancelling the buy of 60 OR.357s (Shackleton replacements) and buying 38 Comets instead

The RAF was thought likely to roll over and accept all of this except for the TSR2 cancellation. The problem was that the government had no idea what the ultimate capital cost of the TSR2 buy would be; BAC had been asked for up-to-date costs in November, but had failed to respond. It was feared that, given the cost history of the project, the final figure could be in the order of £1,000 million. It had become 'quite impossible' to retain TSR2. The biggest attraction of the American equipment, beyond near-immediate availability, was that the Americans were willing to offer a big loan at a reasonable interest rate to pay for it all, spreading the cost over ten to fifteen years, something that was not possible if the government stuck with the UK

projects. The results would be a much-slimmed-down UK aviation industry, but the government already believed that there should be just one main airframe group.

Rumours of cancellation were so strong by early January 1965 that many of the contractors involved with TSR2, such as EMI and Elliott, wrote to the new Minister of Aviation, Roy Jenkins, pointing out how many jobs were at stake, along with Britain's technological prowess and hopes of future exports of advanced electronic equipment. George Edwards visited Henry Hardman at the MoA on 12 January to express his own concerns, stating that he would 'have to go and work for Arnold Hall' (Hawker Siddeley) if TSR2 was cancelled, as there would be no room for two large aviation firms with so little work to go around. Had Edwards known that the government already had both the P.1154 (supersonic VTOL close-support aircraft) and HS.681 (STOL transport) projects drawing their last breath, the meeting would doubtless have gone rather differently.

On 14 January 1965 10,000 workers from Vickers and Hawker Siddeley marched through London to Hyde Park to demonstrate against predicted job losses that would result from cancelling the TSR2 and P.1154. At the same time Roy Jenkins was contesting the proposed cancellation of the TSR2 at a meeting of the Defence Council, due to the industrial consequences. However, the Secretary of State for Defence, Denis Healey, thought there was '... no chance whatever (sic) of achieving worthwhile economies on the Defence Budget unless the TSR 2 were cancelled.' On the question of maintaining a TSR2 design team, he saw no value in this, since the next generation of aircraft was going to be vastly more expensive and beyond the ability of the UK to fund independently. On the same day, Lord Portal and George Edwards of BAC were at a meeting with the President of the Board of Trade. Asked what their preference would be if either TSR2 or Concorde had to be cancelled, both agreed that they would rather see Concorde go. That evening Mary Goldring was on TV again, on *This Week*, and asserted that the RAF did not need the TSR2 because such a sophisticated aircraft was unnecessary when we had Polaris nuclear missiles, but that the RAF needed the F-111 instead!

The next day an informal meeting was held at Chequers, with the Prime Minister dining with the Minister of Aviation and representatives from the aviation industry:

George Edwards of BAC, Arnold Hall of the Hawker Siddeley Group, R.V. Smith of BSEL, D. Pearson of Rolls-Royce and C.E. Wrangham of Shorts. The cost and future of the TSR2 was the main topic of conversation in a meeting that went on until nearly midnight. George Edwards admitted that costs were high but pointed out that the limited production run hardly helped, and said that the TSR2 had 'gone wrong' because 'it was the result of an over-sophisticated requirement laid down by the RAF which was itself under pressure to produce an all-purpose aircraft'. The only substantial suggestion for cutting costs that he could offer the government was to spread the buy over a longer period, a suggestion that was not viewed as likely to make any real difference. The PM assured the industry representatives that 'there was no intention of rushing into decisions'.

On 18 January Denis Healey wrote to the Prime Minister about 'International Co-operation in Research and Development'. The opening of this letter was revealing: 'The cancellations of the TSR.2 and the P.1154 development contracts and, to a lesser extent, of the HS.681, should release valuable technical resources'. The letter went on to discuss the attractions of buying defence equipment off the shelf, without having to pay R&D costs, which the UK could no longer afford. However, carrying out no R&D would lead to the UK losing any technological bargaining and political power. Healey suggested that the only solution was to go into co-operation with a European power, and the French, despite less-than-perfect political relations, were the most obvious candidates. Joint R&D efforts with the Americans had not gone well; they simply did not need any help, and knew it. The Americans, however, were now offering a joint R&D agreement in which British and US firms would bid for projects and the best technical submissions would win. Healey was naïve enough to believe this could work, but did not consider that it was an agreement that could proceed until '... we have reshaped our defence budget and eliminated some of our current aircraft projects'.

By 25 January the government had made up its mind to cancel the P.1154 and HS.681 projects, opting to buy the F-4 Phantom and C-130 Hercules instead. Development of Hawker's P.1127 (forerunner of the Harrier) would continue. The TSR2's fate hung by a thread, with many within the government, and the RAF, recommending cancellation of this project too. Research began into the likely effects of a cancellation upon an industry already badly hit by the loss of other projects. The most serious job losses were considered to be those that could be lost at Preston, Weybridge and Luton, totalling up to 23,000 skilled workers, or around 7 per cent of the total employed by the aviation industry. On 9 February more than 5,000 Hawker Siddeley and BAC workers marched through London to protest at the cancellation of P.1154 and HS.681, carrying a coffin symbolizing the 'murdered aircraft industry'. A debate in the House of Commons dissolved into chaos, and the government pushed through its plans with only five votes between them and defeat.

The release of already authorized funds to enable BAC to continue production build-up was quietly blocked.

Final cost-saving efforts

On 27 January BAC and the MoA had come to an agreement that BAC would try to come up with a fixed-price offer to complete the TSR2 programme, based on a reduced specification (as detailed in Chapter 4). The Air Staff had accepted surprising reductions in the aircraft's performance, and on 3 February the Air Staff met again to take a long hard look at what else could be shaved off the TSR2 programme to try to

make it more affordable, even if only in the short term. They also looked at some of the problem areas that threatened to cripple the project. The most obvious of these was computer capacity, and the upgraded Verdan D9D-1 was chosen as the lowest-cost option. Though it gave little room for any future expansion, its improved capacity compared with the D9D did at least mean that the existing (previously downgraded) nav/attack requirements could actually be met. Fuel jettison had to stay, as did the engine accessories bay redesign. Temporarily dropped to save money were the trainer version, arrester hook, AJ168 (Martel) missile carriage, rocket pods, twin-suspension HE bomb carriage, the HE lay-down attack,

A rare shot of XR219 and XR220 together in the hangar at Boscombe Down. With XR220 just weeks away from flying, desperate efforts were under way to try to cut the cost of the programme, even if it meant reducing the aircraft's capability. BAE Systems via Warton Heritage Group

The Weybridge-manufactured fuselage of XR225 arrives at Samlesbury for final assembly in March 1965. This was to be the first of the development-batch airframes to be assembled and then flown from Samlesbury to Warton. BAE Systems via Warton Heritage Group

IFF on the development batch aircraft and the Selcall and telebriefing facilities.

The CA called a meeting with the Air Staff on 12 February 1965 to discuss these further economy measures on the TSR2 programme. The Air Staff, if truth be told, were now no longer entirely supportive of keeping the TSR2, and realized they had a difficult balancing act to perform. If they agreed to further reductions in performance or equipment sufficient to make the aircraft affordable, the RAF could be lumbered with an aircraft that did not meet its requirements. The TFX, however, was becoming more attractive with each passing day.

The result was that the Air Staff rejected measures to reduce the number of development-batch aircraft (which would only lead to an extended and more-expensive flight test programme); the carrying out of nav/attack system trials in the UK instead of Australia (adverse weather was expected

to lengthen trials and wipe out any savings); plus a whole host of minor modifications, such as deleting the moving map from the pilot's cockpit. The previous administration had, in July 1964, also asked BAC what savings would result if the aircraft's top speed was reduced to Mach 1.7. These could have been substantial, as the lower temperatures alone would allow much less use of high-cost materials, a simpler intake system, much reduced engine operating temperatures and so on. The Air Staff, however, insisted on the magic Mach 2.0 figure, citing the savings as being insufficient compared with the operational disadvantages.

The requirement to transmit linescan information while airborne was, however, deleted, along with the requirement for associated ground stations. This saved £2.76 million (the Army's requirements, after all, were now the least of the RAF's worries). Possible additional savings could be had

by refurbishing three of the development-batch aircraft once trials were complete, to save building three new airframes, saving £6 million in production costs. The need for a trainer version was also reconsidered, it being suggested that up to £10.25 million could be saved by dropping it entirely. On the whole, though, even these savings would be minuscule when weighed against the cost of the entire project.

The Ministry then wrote to BAC on the 20 February to ask if the company could come up with any further changes that, while leaving 'an aircraft capable of fulfilling an effective operational role', would yield major savings in development, production, or both. By this point BAC's Value Engineering programme and preceding cost-saving suggestion scheme had been in place for months, and numerous ways of saving costs had already been examined. Many had already been incorporated, and others were still under consideration as to their merits. (It was often the case that a modification to reduce cost would increase weight, for example.) There was no magic fix that BAC had been sitting on, and no major saving to be made. BAC now felt under extreme pressure to get a second and third aircraft into the air, in the hope that a demonstration of progress in flight-testing would put the project on firmer footing, but it was not to be. Once again the delivery of flight-capable engines was delayed, by as much as six weeks, postponing any flight of a second aircraft until late March at the earliest; and to top it all a crack had been discovered in XR220's jetpipe.

Interviewed by Mary Goldring on BBC2's *Encounter* on 25 February, Roy Jenkins said of the TSR2: 'People say the whole future of the aircraft industry depends on it. I don't quite agree', and 'Manufacturing for a solely British market, at present research and development costs, is out. If you do this, you get into a TSR2 position, in which you are staggering under the weight of the development costs you are carrying for a small production line.'

More trouble with Mountbatten

At the beginning of March a second visit to the USA was made by another joint MoA/MoD team to investigate the TFX further, and particularly the proposals on the Mk 2 version. A week after the team's return, on 19 March, a report by the Joint Service Group on Requirement for TSR2/TFX Type Strike/Reconnaissance Aircraft in the RAF was delivered. The report's conclusions were as follows:

Numbers – The front line needed is the same for the TFX Mark 2 as for the TSR2. If we had the TFX Mark 1 we might in the long run need rather more, though we could not without closer analysis say exactly how many. With either mark of TFX we might be able to reduce the training provision – by three aircraft in the case of a front line of 74 – though further study would be needed to confirm this.

Training in the USA – Initial figures we have received from the Americans suggest that there would be little difference in costs, although

training in the USA would involve dollar expenditure.

Deployment – All the front-line TSR2 or TFX aircraft to be based in the United Kingdom would be provided to meet reinforcement commitments. If they were all deployed permanently overseas we could not make do with any fewer in total, and we shall have to accept financial and other disadvantages greatly outweighing the advantages.

The basic assumptions of the report were that the aircraft would not be fully assigned to NATO and none would be based in Germany (thus allowing a reduction to 110 aircraft instead of 158). By this point it was clear that the Joint Service Group had turned to the TFX as its preference. The TSR2 was described as being 'bound to be unreliable', the Buccaneer was described in similar terms, the 'relatively simple' Phantom was expected to be the most reliable (based upon manufacturer's information), and the TFX nearly as reliable as the Phantom (based entirely on manufacturer's predictions; BAC was never given such blind faith in its predictions). The TFX was expected to have dual controls, and therefore there would be no need to develop a trainer variant; in the event the F-111 never had a dual-control option.

The Chiefs of the Defence Staff all agreed to endorse the report and its basic conclusion that the RAF still needed a supersonic strike aircraft, whether it be TSR2 or TFX, and informed Healey of this on 23 March. However, Mountbatten had been on an overseas tour, leaving his deputy to deal with things in his absence. On his return he examined the report himself, and made no comment to the other staff chiefs. However, he then approached Healey himself and, plunging in a final dagger, urged him to consider once again that the RAF could have the Buccaneer, and that TSR2 (or TFX) was really not at all necessary. The Chief of the Air Staff, Air Chief Marshal Sir Charles Elworthy, was absolutely enraged, considering this '... a grave breach of Chiefs of Staff propriety, and of frankness and fair dealing. If CDS dissented from the clear agreement reached unanimously by the Chiefs of Staff Committee in properly constituted session, the very least he should have done was to give his colleagues immediate and explicit notice of this ... before he express any opinions to Ministers.'

Throughout the closing days of March the actual implications of cancelling TSR2 were looked at in some detail by the

After delays in completing its rear fuselage, XR225 was moved into the marry-up jig at the end of March 1965. Nearly-complete Lightning F.6 XR752 is on the right. Lightning production for Saudi Arabia would soon become BAC's lifeline.
BAE Systems via Warton Heritage Group

RIGHT: **Another view of XR225 being craned into the Samlesbury factory; its rear fuselage can be seen in the background, under the main undercarriage bay.** BAE Systems via Warton Heritage Group

BELOW: **XR221 practically complete, undergoing electrical and functional checks at Weybridge in March 1965.** BAE Systems via Warton Heritage Group

government. The major concern was that of the supersonic transport project, Concorde, which would be directly affected insomuch as it was to be powered by a similar engine and faced many of the same airframe heating problems as TSR2. Existing estimates at the time were of a further £10 million needing to be spent on the development of the Olympus engine for the TSR2, which, given the direct benefits to the supersonic transport's powerplant, would result in a similar figure being added to the airliner's development costs. BAC had warned that its own overheads would have to be spread over other projects if the TSR2 was to be cancelled, and this would affect costs of the BAC One-Eleven and VC10 airliners. The French made it plain that cancellation of TSR2 could seriously affect Olympus 593 development, but were brushed off. Indeed, one internal memo suggested that the losing the TSR2 would only result in a closer relationship with the French, presumably on the Anglo-French advanced-trainer project. Also, the results of cancelling P.1154 and HS.681 were now evident in terms of redundancies and unemployment, and, to the government's surprise, these were not as bad as had been forecast. It appeared that not only had Hawker Siddeley managed to retain more staff than expected, but those it had made redundant had, for the most part, been able to find alternative employment relatively easily. If a similar pattern was followed by BAC after cancellation of the TSR2, the resulting unemployment loading on the state would not be as bad as once feared.

On 26 March the American Secretary of Defense, Robert McNamara, made the following firm offer to Denis Healey:

Contingent upon your contracting by 1 October 1965 for 110 F-111A aircraft, as presently configured, with TF-30 engines and Mark I avionics, we will sell such aircraft at an average unit flyaway price equal to the average unit development and production cost of the entire F-111A program but not to exceed $5.95 million per aircraft. This is based upon delivery of the 110 aircraft between August 1967 and December 1969.

Support, ground equipment and spares costs were not included in this figure. This sealed the deal as far as the Air Staff were concerned. At those prices, for the same number of aircraft, buying F-111 would save the RAF £300 million. While TSR2 was still technically preferable on a few criteria (primarily better low-level radius

With cancellation imminent, at Samlesbury the rear fuselages of the first two pre-production aircraft, XS660 and XS661, were structurally complete and undergoing equipment installation, while XR225 was being married up to its rear fuselage, seen in the background. BAE Systems via Warton Heritage Group

of action, navigational accuracy and reconnaissance capability), that extra £300 million was a killer.

The axe falls

The events immediately leading up to the cancellation, and the manner in which it was announced, were quite unlike the treatment given to any defence project before; or since. Two cabinet meetings on 1 April decided the fate of the TSR2. The 10am meeting discussed the various options for continuing, reducing or cancelling the TSR2 project, and how the capability of the aircraft could possibly be fulfilled by other types including the Buccaneer, Phantom and TFX. The meeting ended with an agreement to reconvene later in the day. The second meeting was at 10pm, and while some of the cabinet argued that postponement of any decision should be made until a review of overseas commitments showed whether there was still a requirement for this type of aircraft, the balance of opinion was in favour of cancelling the TSR2 entirely and securing an option on the TFX. The Americans would be invited to convey

terms formally on the purchase of the TFX, along with an assurance that there was no firm commitment actually to purchase any aircraft just yet. The TSR2 project cancellation would be announced in the Chancellor's Budget Speech on 6 April.

At 2.30pm on 5 April 1965 a cabinet meeting was held to decide the arrangements for the cancellation announcement. BAC would be informed at 2.30pm on 6 April, while a public announcement would come in the form of a relevant section during the Budget Speech. The actions necessary to ensure a smooth dismantling of the project were also reviewed, and it was decided that a single month would be an unrealistically short period in which to run down the project, and that it could take up to three months. Work on the aircraft's electronic systems would be reviewed at a later date, in case they had any application on future projects, such as the Buccaneer Mk 2 or the Phantom. At 5.30pm Denis Healey signed up to the option to buy the F-111A from the USA. This had been slightly renegotiated, and now gave the UK until 1 January 1966 to make up its mind. Later in the day telegraphs were sent to each overseas embassy, warning British ambassadors that the project's cancellation would be announced the next day, with notes on the reasoning behind the cancellation and a cautionary paragraph that included the words: 'It is not a decision to cancel the British aircraft in favour of an American one', though, of course, it was precisely that.

At 2.30pm the next day – 6 April, Budget Day – the Minister of Aviation, Roy Jenkins, and junior ministers from the Department of Economic Affairs and the MoD informed representatives of BAC and BSEL that the TSR2 project was to be cancelled with immediate effect. Jenkins also instructed the CA to ground both airworthy aircraft immediately to stop any further flights from taking place. The First Secretary and the Minister of Labour informed representatives of the Trades Union Congress and the Confederation of Shipbuilding and Engineering Unions (CSEU, which, despite the name, included aerospace workers), extending the meeting until 4pm to minimize the possibility of leaks before the public announcement. During the meeting with the CSEU representatives Roy Jenkins informed them that there was a possibility of a developed British aircraft meeting future defence needs. At 3.30pm the cancellation was publicly announced in the Budget Speech made by Chancellor of the Exchequer James Callaghan. The reason given was primarily the saving of manpower for more important projects:

Altogether, about 1½ million men and women are employed in the Forces and in industry to supply them. These are important and scarce resources of manpower, needed for industrial expansion and for exports. It is against this background that the Government have had to consider the future of the TSR2 project.

The effect of this decision is to save £35 million of Government expenditure in 1965–66, after taking account of the terminal costs which may become due to be paid this year. We all admire the technical skill that has been put into this advanced aircraft. But, so far, this aircraft has cost £125 million, and the cost is mounting fast every week. It has, and would have, diverted hundreds of factories employing thousands of skilled and semi-skilled men from other work of national importance, including exports in particular. This is not a sensible use of our overstrained resources. The Government's decision will, in the next five years, release £350 million of resources of an advanced kind for more productive work.

A further statement was made by the Secretary of State for Defence, Denis Healey,

at 6.20pm, 40min earlier than promised by the Chancellor earlier in the day. It was a statement interrupted time and time again by opposition MPs, furious with the manner in which the cancellation and the further statement were being made.

The Government have been wrestling continuously with this problem ever since they took office some six months ago. It has always been obvious that the cost of continuing the TSR2 programme was likely to impose an intolerable burden on the national economy, in general, and the defence budget, in particular. But we have had to consider also the operational needs of our defence forces and the needs of the sort of aircraft industry which Britain is likely to require in the 1970s for both military, technological and commercial reasons.

We discovered when we came into office that the programme for the TSR2 planned by the previous Government would have cost about £750 million for research, development and production. An order for 150 aircraft would have meant that each one would have cost £5 million. The smaller the order the higher the cost per aircraft. For example, an order for 100 aircraft would have meant that each aircraft would have cost over £6 million, of which nearly £5 million would still remain to be spent. These were the figures which the previous Government accepted as the basis of their policy. I submit that a programme of this order was not one which, in any circumstances, could be held to represent value for money. It was not only too costly in terms of defence expenditure. It was also making far too great a demand on our country's scarce resources of highly skilled manpower.

Nevertheless, I do not believe the Government would have been justified in taking a decision to cancel the TSR2 at the time when they decided on the other changes in our military aircraft programme two months ago. We needed better information than we then possessed on the probable cost of the TSR2 and on the cost and performance of possible alternative aircraft. As the Prime Minister explained on 2 February, it was the mounting cost of the TSR2 programme on which the previous Administration had embarked which was the essential reason for the review which has been undertaken.

We now have enough further information to take a decision, and it is clear that no more significant information is likely to be obtained for some months. The House of Commons was informed earlier that we should seek a fixed price for the TSR2. In view of all the complexities of the programme, the manufacturers have not been able to offer such a price. The best arrangements that they have felt able to offer would have given

no assurance that Her Majesty's Government's ultimate financial liability would have been limited. The likely course of completing the development of the TSR2 would have been as high as, or even higher than, previous estimates. Meanwhile, every week that the programme continues it is costing the taxpayer something of the order of £1 million.

In the circumstances, we do not feel that we can justify any further delay. With deep reluctance, Her Majesty's Government have decided that they must now cancel the TSR2 programme. I hope that no one believes that this has been an easy or welcome decision, particularly at a moment when the aircraft was making good progress in its development programme. We are fully conscious of the disappointment our decision must cause to those thousands of people who have worked so long and so hard on a project which has been cancelled through no fault of theirs. The fundamental reason for the cancellation – I ask the Committee to accept this – is the stark fact that the economic implications of modern military technology rule out British development and production of this type of aircraft for a purely national market.

The quoted cost figures were exaggerated only a little from the estimates generated by BAC, BSEL and the MoA itself, but had been presented simplistically, leading to much complaint that the government lied about the costs. This was not really the case; while the only individual airframes that would cost £5 million each were the pre-production batch of eleven aircraft, and the production examples would cost £2.8 million each, it was clear that the Minister was referring to a unit cost that included R&D costs, rather than presenting these separately.

At 8pm a press conference was held for the defence correspondents of various publications. Part of the press release contained the basic summary that 'The basic facts are that TSR2 was too expensive and that it should have been stopped long ago'. Two days after the cancellation Roy Jenkins wrote to the CA to thank him and his staff at the MoA for '... the enormous amount of work which they have done during the past few months on the TSR2 and in particular on placing before the Government the mass of material which was required before a decision could be taken'. No such communication of admiration was sent to the thousands of men and women who had put so much work into the aircraft itself. BAC would be given three months to close the project down; 6 July was to be the end.

Position of individual TSR2 airframes at cancellation

Airframe	Location	Notes	Fate
XR219	BAC Warton	Grounded with various alterations, including addition of anti-spin parachute, scheduled	To Shoeburyness 14/8/66 for weapons testing, remains scrapped 1982
XR220	A&AEE Boscombe Down	Ready to fly	To Henlow 20/6/67 for RAF Museum. Preserved at Cosford
1st static test airframe	RAE Farnborough	Undergoing fuselage repair; to be fitted with wing from XS663	Largely scrapped by 1971
XR221	BAC Weybridge	Complete with engines fitted; to be transferred to Wisley on 11 April and fly in June	To Shoeburyness 12/9/65 for weapons testing
XR222	BAC Weybridge	Substantially complete; electrics awaiting testing, AAPP bay, undercarriage and fuel system needing work; first flight expected mid-December	To Cranfield 23–31/10/65 for College of Aeronautics. To Duxford 1978. Preserved at Duxford. Has wingtips from XR223
XR223	BAC Weybridge	Substantially complete; work ongoing on hydraulics, fuel system including tank leaks and flying controls	To Shoeburyness 28/9/65 for weapons testing
XR224	BAC Weybridge	Awaiting fin and tailplanes and various systems checks	Cut up 9/65 and taken to R.J. Coley's yard at Hanworth. Scrapped by 1969
XR225	Mostly at Samlesbury	Undergoing electrical installation and fuel testing, awaiting fuselage marry-up	Cut up 9/65 and taken to R.J. Coley's yard at Hanworth. Scrapped by 1969
XR226	Spread across BAC's various sites	Similar to XR225, painting scheduled for April	Cut up 9/65 and taken to R.J. Coley's yard at Hanworth. Scrapped by 1969
XR227	As above	Similar to XR225; undergoing rear and mid-fuselage marry-up	Cut up 9/65 and taken to R.J. Coley's yard at Hanworth. Scrapped by 1969
2nd static test airframe	Spread across BAC's northern sites	Similar to XR227; scheduled to be assembled at Warton by end of April	Cut up 9/65 and taken to R.J. Coley's yard at Hanworth. Scrapped by 1969
XS660	As above, but mostly at BAC Samlesbury	Similar to XR225; undergoing electrical installation, possible six-month delay owing to cockpit changes requested by test pilots	Cut up 12/65 and taken to Alcan Enfield Alloys' yard at Bradford. Scrapped by 1969
XS661	Spread across BAC's various sites	Rear fuselage at Stage 2	Rear fuselage cut up 12/65 and taken to Alcan Enfield Alloys' yard at Bradford. Scrapped by 1969. Nose to R.J. Coley, scrapped 1968
XS662	As above	Rear fuselage at Stage 2	Nose to R.J. Coley, scrapped 1968
XS663	As above	Rear fuselage at Stage 2	Cut up 9/65 and taken to R.J. Coley's yard at Hanworth. Scrapped in 1969
XS664	As above	Rear fuselage at Stage 2	Moved to Weybridge 9/65. Scrapped later
XS665	As above	Rear fuselage at Stage 2	To R.J. Coley 13/6/65. Largely scrapped by 1969
XS666	As above	Rear fuselage at Stage 2	To R.J. Coley 13/6/65. Largely scrapped by 1969
XS667	As above	Rear fuselage at Stage 2	Believed scrapped at Droylesden
XS668	As above	Rear fuselage at Stage 2	Believed scrapped at Droylesden
XS669	As above	Rear fuselage at Stage 1	Believed scrapped at Droylesden
XS670	As above	Rear fuselage at Stage 1	Believed scrapped at Droylesden
XS944	As above	Fuselage frames production begun	Scrapped on site

Attempts to keep TSR2 flying

The day after the cancellation the Director of the RAF Aircraft Department at the MoA invited BAC to examine the whole programme to consider what elements, including limited flying on the first two or three aircraft, could be shown to warrant continuation on the basis of research having direct application to current projects or future ones. A flight-test programme using XR219 and XR220 was proposed by BAC. It would cover expansion of the flight envelope to Mach 2 at altitude, and then use the aircraft's ability to fly continuously at this speed to gather data on engine handling and engine control system behaviour, experience of specialized engine instrumentation and telemetry, and data on component and bay temperatures, engine cooling systems, engine relighting and correlation between flight and ground tests of intake

gauze bias work, all in aid of the Concorde engine programme. As a further aid to Concorde development, data could be gathered on engine ejector-nozzle performance and drag, intake performance and drag, intake buzz, thrust meter development, structural temperatures, flutter and vibration, sonic boom investigation, simulation of Concorde air traffic control problems, rain erosion at high speeds, and so on. As a bonus, some of the design concepts (gust response and its effect on crew comfort) and AFCS features (stability augmentation) could be compared against theoretical work carried out to that point. The programme would consist of 160 flying hours, lasting until late summer 1966. This proposal was submitted to the Ministry by BAC on 14 April, along with a suggestion to continue static and fatigue tests on structural test specimens – airframes already completed but not airworthy.

With XR221 also complete it was tempting to try to find a use for that airframe too, and on 15 April BAC's manager at Boscombe Down roughed out a possible programme for it. Assuming a go-ahead at the beginning of May, the airframe would be completed, then broken down and transported to Warton, rebuilt, and flown at the end of September. He admitted: 'It is very difficult to find a strong technical case for carrying out this programme', but said it could be used for low-level testing of the TFR and navigation system in more realistic conditions than those in the Buccaneer and Comet used up to that point. The vulnerability of low-level aircraft to ground defences could also be an area of useful research. This proposal was submitted as an addendum to the programme covering XR219 and XR220.

By 20 April BAC was trying to assess the amount of spares it would need to keep

OPPOSITE PAGE:
The sad scene at Samlesbury one week after the cancellation announcement. Now united with its rear fuselage, XR225 is in as advanced a state of construction as it would ever get. BAE Systems via Warton Heritage Group

THIS PAGE:
The first aircraft, XR219, remained at Warton until August 1966, and had a starring role in the static display at the 1966 Families Day. This family grouping of Canberra WD937, Lightning XR755 and TSR2 was arranged and recorded for posterity. BAE Systems via Warton Heritage Group

three airframes in the air for a short flight-test programme. This was complicated by most such spares having been declared redundant and effectively held under MoA control. In addition, some stocks were still at subcontractors and, with work having stopped, MoA authority would also be necessary for work to continue with providing these spares. Some firms had not yet been paid, and would be unlikely to consider delivery without receiving what they were owed. As it appeared impossible to ensure that all of the various spares needed could be acquired in the limited time remaining before the TSR2 project was finally terminated, one suggestion was to obtain three aircraft carcasses to rob for parts as required.

The government looked at the proposal, and initially the prospect of spending another £2 million on top of the £200 million already spent to gain some concrete benefits was attractive. There were obvious benefits, not only to the Concorde programme but also possibly to the UK version of the F-111, the Anglo-French Variable-Geometry (AFVG) project, and even to a possible improved Buccaneer, as well as providing valuable flight confirmation of test-cell work at the NGTE some twelve months before the Vulcan testbed would be available for the Olympus 593. Weighed against this was the short flight-test programme already carried out, and the efforts that had been needed from all involved to manage it. It was thought that the likelihood of minor problems continually halting any new flight-test programme would be very high, and therefore costs would inevitably rise once more, perhaps to £3 million. The experience of the Bristol 188 research aircraft tended to bear out the government's fears in this respect. Moreover, the MoA did not believe that any of the proposed research work other than engine flight-testing would be of any direct benefit to Concorde.

The company's hopes for an early decision on the matter were soon dashed, as it became clear that not only were the MoA's various departments all examining the proposals, but that they had also gone to the MoD, and higher up – to the Cabinet. The government's biggest real concern was that the public would see TSR2 in the air again. They had received so much grief when they cancelled it that letting it fly again would be highly embarrassing. However, Roy Jenkins supported the proposal, as long as a fixed-cost contract could be put in place to reduce risk. The overall MoA

An AFVG windtunnel model. Following the cancellation of the P.1154, AW.681 and TSR2, this was an attempt to build a cheaper and more flexible strike aircraft in co-operation with the French. BAE Systems via Warton Heritage Group

response, despite some reservations, was also positive, but at the MoD the Assistant Chief of the Air Staff (Operational Requirements), Air Vice-Marshal Emson, opposed the idea, believing the risk to be too great. It was a final twist of the knife from the very Service that had begun the project and had, over the last six months, abandoned it in an attempt to end up with something – anything – as long as it was not a Buccaneer.

On 3 May BAC submitted an additional proposal relating to structural research on redundant TSR2 materials, covering further investigation of the static-test wing failure; crack propagation on wingtips; bird impact on leading edges, radomes and nose sections; noise fatigue on flaps, honeycomb trailing edges and tailplanes; endurance tests on bearings; pressure cycling to destruction on nose sections and fatigue tests on fins. Throughout May, while the physical dismantling of the project was beginning to be carried out, no news was received.

On 2 June the Defence and Overseas Policy Committee decided against any further test flying. On 4 June BAC found out (via the press) that it was not to be. The government had leaked a letter from Roy Jenkins to a Colonel Lancaster, explaining the decision, and later that day, in answer to a question raised in the House of Commons

on the matter, Roy Jenkins put an official end to the hopes of seeing TSR2 in the air once more:

> I have examined very carefully the possibilities of flying the TSR2 during the next few years in aid of our research programme, using the three aircraft with engines and spare parts which are now available. I have regretfully concluded, however, that the information we should be likely to derive from the flying would not justify the £2 million–£3 million which would be the minimum cost involved in maintaining and operating these complex aircraft.

Of course, BAC was bitterly disappointed, but its structural research proposal met with more luck, and in mid-June many of the components that had been earmarked to be retained in early May were now listed as required for the structural research programme.

A glimmer of hope that the aircraft could fly once more then appeared from the MoA. Freddie Page of BAC spoke to the CA, Morien Morgan, on 21 June, and was requested to keep XR219 and XR220 'oiled and greased', and told that Air Commodore Bonser, the Director of RAF Aircraft Development at the Ministry, would be spoken to to stop them from being stripped completely. However, any further flying was 'out for the present as the decision was a political one'. In fact BAC had already been keeping both airframes not only oiled and greased, but in full running order, and had been carrying out regular engine runs. Page instructed his men to draw up a programme of ground testing, including taxy trials over rough ground, as well as any A&AEE and RAE requirements. An attempt by BAC's Ollie Heath to phone Bonser the next day to discuss a much-reduced research programme, but including a limited amount of flying, did not get an encouraging reception. Bonser was out, but one of his colleagues immediately asked if the proposal was to include flying. Heath was informed that they had 'not a chance in Hell', as a decision that there should be no more flying had already been taken at Cabinet level. The reduced proposal included using XR221 for the rough-surface trials, but there was 'little point in doing odd jobs on other aircraft' and the current MoA proposal was for XR221, and XR219, to undergo 'vulnerability trials' at Shoeburyness; in other words, to be shot to bits. Incredibly, the MoA's plan was to carry out some of these trials with engines running, despite the massive headaches involved in disassembling, transporting and reassembling the airframes and getting them back into running condition.

As a result, BAC's next research proposal, submitted on the 24th, did not include flying, and nor did it include the use of XR221. The rough-surface trials were suggested as being a combined RAE/BAC task using either XR219 at Warton or XR220 at Boscombe Down. Other trials would be noise and vibration tests at various engine revolutions to vindicate design decisions on life and reliability of structures (XR220 being already instrumented for such work); further resonance tests (as considerable differences had shown up between such tests on XR220 and predicted values – XR219's gust response results had shown much less structural resonance than predicted too); work on measuring IR and radar signatures; running aircraft systems independently of engines to aid future strike and fighter aircraft development; water contamination tests on DP47 hydraulic fluid; firing of the engine fire extinguishers to test extinguishant distribution; and various rig tests in aid of future simulations. The Ministry's reaction to this was much more positive, immediate instructions being given to hand over XR220 to the A&AEE at Boscombe Down as it was, without removing all of the

test instrumentation installed in the aircraft (BAC had been about to do this to both XR219 and XR220), and the A&AEE would end up carrying out some of the suggested research. However, XR219 was still to be dismantled for transport and instrumentation that BAC wanted to retain could be removed. But BAC resisted this, and on further consideration by the Ministry was told to hold XR219 at Warton pending decisions on each individual aspect of the ground-research proposals.

The company had also drawn up another flight-research programme proposal. A much reduced programme costing less than a quarter of a million pounds, it would use either XR219 (fitted with XR220's fin, equipped for flutter clearance) or XR220 (with the addition of some performance and handling instrumentation). Whichever was chosen, the AFCS would not be fitted, so speed would be limited to Mach 1.7. Total flying would be 30hr, at around 5hr per month, to cover stability and control characteristics, engine and airframe performance and drag, and engine handling characteristics with the Olympus electronic control system (including relighting). Response to turbulence could also be checked as the opportunity arose. However, despite support from the Aeronautical Research Council, this proposal was also vetoed; the TSR2 simply could not be allowed to fly again.

There was to be just one further proposal to get TSR2 back into the air, and this came from the Central Fighter Establishment at RAF Binbrook. A paper entitled *Use of the TSR2 for Towing of Supersonic Targets*, issued by Squadron Leader Ken Hayr on 1 September 1965, recommended that a study be made of the feasibility of doing just that. It went out to the MoA, MoD, A&AEE and RAE, and suggested that, rather than using the aircraft as a target for testing air-to-ground armament, they would be better employed as supersonic target-towing vehicles for trials of *Red Top* and other British missiles, and for possible future use in conjunction with the Fighter Command Missile Practice Camp. The MoA had been looking for a suitable supersonic target system for many years without success. The French CT41 drone had showed promise but lacked performance, and now the USA had been asked to develop a suitable towed-target system. A pair of Lightnings and support staff were planning to deploy to Point Mugu in the USA, at some considerable expense, for *Red Top* trials on their weapons range,

and top target speed there would be Mach 1.4, rather than the Mach 2.0 the MoA really wanted. In comparison a TSR2 could attain Mach 1.7 and had a large weapons bay suitable for installing a reel-and-winch system for the target, of which suitable items were available off the shelf from the USA (such as the RMU-8A/TDU-9B). Flight Refuelling Limited also manufactured a similar system under licence which could fit in the TSR2 weapons bay. The paper's final conclusion was that: 'If the TSR2 were to be adapted to perform target towing duties it might well confer upon the United Kingdom the most flexible high-performance target system in the world, and instead of British missiles being tested abroad, the situation could be reversed.'

Sadly the MoD thought that the proposal would 'founder on the grounds of cost and spares', so no attempt was made to take it further.

Aftermath

Contrary to popular belief, no general order was issued calling for the immediate destruction of all evidence of the project within hours of the cancellation announcement. The pair of surviving airframes should be enough proof of that. Standard practice was to include a break clause in any major contract, which spelled out broadly what was to be done if the project was cancelled. The contractor was to be paid a fair price for all the raw materials, bought-out components, partly fabricated parts, etc., which would then be disposed of by the MoA as it saw fit, and the same applied to TSR2. For this to happen the contractor would have to list each item and its cost. The contractor could also choose to retain some items if it had a use for them, in which case it would effectively buy them back from the MoA. With a project of the scale of TSR2 this meant listing hundreds of thousands of individual items, most of which had no more than scrap value, an accounting task for which the Ministry would have to pay, and for which neither BAC nor the Ministry had any appetite. Instead, BAC agreed with the Ministry at a meeting on 12 April simply to come up with an overall figure for its outstanding costs plus an agreed amount of profit. The company would then list just the items of any residual value (such as unused raw materials, standard items of equipment that could be reused on other aircraft, etc.), all major assemblies (in case some use could be found for them, such as complete airframes for ground-training tasks) plus all jigs, tools and test equipment (of which the Ministry already had a register). A general destruction order simply could not have coexisted with this situation, and despite anecdotal evidence that jigs, parts and airframes began to be cut up within hours of the cancellation, no documentary evidence has come to light to prove that this happened, or indeed that orders were given to do this, though a wealth of evidence to the contrary does exist. (Indeed, one senior BAC officer confirmed to the author that he had never seen any such order, and, at a dinner with Denis Healey around forty years later, Healey asked him if he had any idea who had started the story.) A single newspaper report claimed that jigs were 'torn out of the concrete' by cranes at Weybridge on 9 April, but this sounds an incredibly destructive way of dismantling a jig. BAC was certainly not 'instructed immediately to scrap all the aircraft on the line' as soon as the cancellation was announced (a claim made in Charles Gardner's book *British Aircraft Corporation*, and which the continued existence of XR222 alone disproves).

On 15 April the TSR2 Project Office at Warton sent a memo to other departments, informing them that the Project Office held complete sets of minutes for the various regular meetings (progress, production, project control, and so on) that been held throughout the project, and that departmental heads could assume they had no need to retain their own copies in addition to these. A TSR2 Master File would be kept, containing every relevant document, and if any departments were destroying files, anything referring to TSR2 had to be checked to see if it was contained in the Master File, and forwarded for inclusion if necessary. This process may have given rise to the popular myth that every single TSR2 document was ordered to be destroyed, when the basic process was really one of consolidation.

As for physical parts of the project, at Weybridge the Production Manager assured Warton on 20 April, in response to an enquiry on spares holdings to back up the proposed flight-research programme, that 'no disposal instruction had yet been received'. Works Order 16A was issued there on 27 April, backdated to the 7th, and covered all costs arising from the clearing up, lifting of jigs, restoring of working areas, run-down of work and possible waiting

Wings that would never fly, XR226 in the foreground. Contrary to popular belief, there was no immediate general destruction order and many TSR2 components, wings in particular, survived beyond the end of the project. BAE Systems via Warton Heritage Group

time for staff pending reallocation to other work. Work orders 17A and 18A, issued on the same date, covered other work related to the project's draw-down. The covering memo stated: 'It will be appreciated that due to the magnitude of the task associated with the cancellation of the TSR2 project it is essential that full and proper records are maintained of the costs that will be incurred in putting the cancellation into effect'.

A TSR2 Disposals Team was formed by the Ministry to plan and execute a disposal programme, and the Ministry agreed with BAC's listing of valuable items fairly quickly and progress began on the physical disposal of items which both BAC and the Ministry agreed were worth only their scrap value, such as airframe subassemblies. These items had effectively become government property at this point, and BAC would understandably have wanted them out of the way anyway. Large components were disposed of by the simple expedient of cutting them into manageable pieces and having them carted off to scrapyards for reprocessing. The first mention of this cutting-up of parts appears on 27 April, in a memo from the TSR2 Project Office on *Cutting Up of TSR.2 Components*. The structural and material authorities on TSR2 had been

consulted on any possible dangers, and pointed out that PTFE-coated wiring gave off toxic fumes when subjected to heat, that many fuel tanks had been pressure tested using fuel, that PRC sealants gave off possibly toxic fumes when burnt, and that anything containing DP47 hydraulic fluid should also not be subjected to cutting torches. The incomplete rear fuselages of XS669 and XS670 were scrapped the next day; the more complete rear fuselage sections of XS665 to XS668 were removed from their jigs and scrapped the following week.

On 6 and 7 May a meeting was held at BAC Weybridge to discuss which parts BAC should retain for the time being, primarily in aid of possible research programmes. These included all of the wings, rear fuselages and tailplanes so far delivered to Weybridge, plus a variety of wings and associated parts (tips, apexes, flaps, etc.), rear fuselages, tailplanes and associated parts, fins, bay doors, airbrakes and so on built at Samlesbury and Preston, mainly for airframes XR225 to XR227 and XS660 to XS663. The remaining structural items could then be considered for the scrapping programme that was already under way. Throughout late May and June the

As the summer of 1965 wore on, those TSR2 components that had not had a use found for them were nearing the end of their days. By this point XR225 was dumped outside the factory at Samlesbury, awaiting the scrapman's cutting torches. BAE Systems via Warton Heritage Group

ABOVE: Throughout June XR219 was used as the backdrop for many group photographs of BAC staff. 'Ollie' Heath (TSR2 Project Manager) and Ivan Yates (Aerodynamics and control, Joint Design Team and later Chief Project Engineer) stand out as the tallest members of this particular group. BAE Systems via Warton Heritage Group

LEFT: In a quiet corner of Warton Airfield on 30 June 1965, far from the eyes of the workers, a myth is about to be born. The primarily wooden rear-fuselage mockup, along with the wooden mockups of various other items such as the wing box, are piled up in readiness for a fiery end. Note the employee sitting in the grass, cine camera at the ready. BAE Systems via Warton Heritage Group

BELOW: **Buckets of fuel having been thrown over the mockup, the TSR2's funeral pyre was soon burning fiercely. Roland Beamont later said that airframes themselves had been dragged out and burnt, with the magnesium burning 'like a holocaust'. The TSR2 had hardly any magnesium components, and there is no doubt that he was actually referring to the burning of the Warton mockup.** BAE Systems via Warton Heritage Group

BELOW: **Early September 1965, and XR226 is in the scrapping compound at Samlesbury. A particularly brave or foolhardy cutting-torch operator has already sliced through the forward fuselage, right through the main fuselage fuel tank, and has also cut off the intake area.**
BAE Systems via Warton Heritage Group

bureaucracy of closing down the project carried on, with individual tasks (design directives) being closed, mostly with no additional work authorized, though further work was permitted on the technical publications such as the maintenance manual and spares catalogue. On 20 May a meeting about reduction of staff in BAC's Lancashire facilities mentioned the jigs at Accrington, which the Ministry was insisting be retained, and asked whether it would be better to store them in a hangar at Warton or cocoon them and store them outside at Accrington. This tends to indicate that any destruction of jigs was nonexistent or extremely limited, at least to start with.

The factories at BAC Warton, Samlesbury and Weybridge were required by the MoD to host 'open days' of a sort in the early days of June, allowing members of the RAF, RAE, RRE, NGTE and so on to inspect the redundant equipment with a view to expressing an interest in acquiring any particular items. A letter of 18 June from Air Commodore Bonser, Director, RAF Aircraft Development, at the MoA to Roy Jenkins clearly stated: 'The disposal of other fuselages [than the three completed airframes], which are in varying states of completion, and of components is still under discussion ...'. Furthermore, a letter of 5 July from F.S. Wood on behalf of Air Commodore Bonser mentioned the quarantined airframe subassemblies of interest to the RAE Structures Department, which had made a request to use various structural components (wings, tailplanes, fins and fuselage assemblies) in a programme of structural research based on BAC proposals. While the extent of this programme was decided upon, all such components were protected from disposal. In particular, a large number of completed wings were preserved for research purposes.

On 24 June BAC was ordered by the MoA to take no action to remove instrumentation from XR220 as planned, but instead to hand the airframe over to the A&AEE 'as lying'. BAC Weybridge was asked to segregate sufficient spares backing to support the aircraft for 25hr-worth of engine running, along with any special-to-type tools and technical manuals. Work to remove instrumentation from XR219 could continue before dismantling it in preparation for transport elsewhere.

It was common practice at every aviation company also to scrap jigs at some point after production was terminated on any project. They are rather large and unwieldy bits of metal to keep hanging around on the offchance that they will be of use again. Occasionally this kind of disposal would happen very quickly indeed. Vickers had wasted no time in 'clearing the decks' when the Vickers V1000 airliner was cancelled, for instance. The scrapping of jigs was a very visible end to the project for the workers, and suited BAC management, because it served to concentrate the workforce's collective minds on the hard work they had ahead of them if the company was to remain a viable aircraft manufacturer, such as work on Lightning and Canberra upgrades and impending export sales of Lightnings to Saudi Arabia. Company photographers carefully documented the eventual scrapping of example airframe subassemblies, and when, in late June, the time came at Warton to clear some space in the corner of a hangar occupied by the wooden TSR2 mock-up, it was broken up and transported to a quiet corner of the airfield for a suitably dramatic (and photogenic) end. With fuel-soaked rags stuffed in and around it and a cine camera man and a couple of photographers waiting, the mock-up's remains were set alight to produce the dramatic stills and film footage that would become the core of countless stories of the heartless destruction of Britain's wonder jet. It was not 'dragged out and burned in front of the workers', as the location for

the burning was beyond the southern end of Warton's disused north-south runway, about as far from the factory as you could get while remaining within the airfield perimeter. None of the actual airframe subassemblies was burned. While some early scrapping had taken place, most of this work was not carried out until September 1965.

The MoA required a complete set of master drawings to be archived on microfiche, but decided in August/September 1965 that keeping the many thousands of paper copies of the drawings was not only unnecessary but also a security risk, and ordered these to be destroyed. (News of this was leaked to the press, and the *Sunday Mirror* published a report about a 'Funeral' for the TSR2 on 5 September 1965, to the government's embarrassment.) There were many tens of thousands of these drawings, and it took the men at Warton tasked with the disposal many months to burn them all while accounting for each one in the process. Items of zero scrap value were often simply dumped as rubbish in a handy spot. For this reason, many of the concrete and rubber formers over which skin panels were stretched can still be found piled up in rows at the former Vickers plant at Weybridge, now the site of the Brooklands Museum.

As for the situation outside BAC, many contractors only destroyed paperwork many years later to free up storage space (BSEL regretted doing so after the fact; Martin-Baker only did so in 2003, sadly not long before research for this volume began),

whereas for some companies TSR2 was such a minor part of their work that it warranted no effort in retaining documentation beyond the statutory periods demanded of accounting information. Reams of correspondence, progress reports, technical manuals, brochures and so on were kept in various locations, notably the Air Ministry and MoA, much of which can now be inspected at the National Archives at Kew or in the BAC and ancestor-company archives at Weybridge (Brooklands Museum), Warton and Farnborough (both BAE Systems). Brooklands also holds a very small sub-set of the drawings on several hundred microfiche cards, and BAE Systems Heritage at Warton has a substantial archive of drawings, though by no means a complete set (there were around 80,000 drawings in existence by the time the project was cancelled). The RAF Museum at Hendon also holds a selection of drawings. The eventual fate of the complete archive of drawings on microfiche that was ordered to be kept by the MoA is, at the time of publication, still unknown, but it is feared it may have been disposed of in the late 1970s.

Equipment associated with the TSR2 was mostly cancelled, including the navigation SLR and associated RPU and radio altimeter, the linescan datalink and the flight-refuelling beacon associated with the FLR. Development of the FLR and linescan continued pending a decision as to their suitability for use on the proposed Buccaneer Mk 2*; work on the Doppler continued as it could be useful for the maritime

Comet (the Nimrod); work on the missile warning receiver continued as it could be useful on the Phantom. Similarly, development of the reconnaissance SLR and some other reconnaissance pack contents continued, and was destined to end up in the large EMI reconnaissance pod later carried by RAF Phantoms. Work on IFF Mk 10 also continued, as it was intended for use in a variety of other types. The HF transmitter-receiver ended up being used on the Nimrod and Phantom.

Surviving airframes

In the end the only research work carried out by the remaining airframes was ground use only; XR219, XR221 and XR223 were destined to be shot to bits at the Proof & Experimental Establishment at Foulness, lingering on in ever more shattered fashion through the 1970s. The millions spent on them made them probably the most expensive 'damage to aircraft' research tools in history. The fate of XR219, the only flyer, was particularly sad. An enthusiast had written to the Air Ministry in March 1966 to see if the aircraft could be saved and form the centrepiece of a new aeronautical museum near Warton, but with no luck. By the summer of 1968 *Flight* magazine had published a photo of XR219, now at Shoeburyness. A number of letters from concerned readers, outraged by the aircraft's fate, followed, and on 30 May Roger Bacon's 'Straight and Level' column in the magazine also mentioned the aircraft being 'cynically and insultingly consigned as a ground target', though the writer thought it would not come to any harm because 'the blokes on the range won't destroy it'. This sort of negative publicity certainly ruffled feathers at the new Ministry of Technology, the MoA's successor. A letter from one G.G. Woodward at the Ministry addressed the subject and included the closing remarks that 'XR219 is filling a valuable requirement at Shoeburyness of benefit to the country's defence. The needs of posterity – and of Roger Bacon – will be catered for by the exhibition of XR220 in the RAF Museum.' This completely ignored the fact that the people at Shoeburyness were busy blowing several other TSR2s to bits, so XR219 need not have suffered the same fate. The RAF Museum, in a delightful coincidence, wrote to Mr Woodward just days later, asking if they could swap XR220 for XR219, as the latter was of much more historical interest, so he was forced to ask RAE

RIGHT: **By the mid-1970s XR219, at Shoeburyness, was a shattered hulk propped up by breeze blocks, having been subjected to a sustained series of weapons effectiveness tests.** BAE Systems via Warton Heritage Group

BELOW: **A scene of desolation and destruction at Shoeburyness just a few years later. Pieces of XR219, identifiable only by the presence of the main undercarriage tie tube and wedged-open auxiliary intakes, are scattered on the Shoeburyness dump. By 1982 this yard was cleared and the only TSR2 to have flown was finally history.** Brooklands Museum

Farnborough (for whom the Shoeburyness trials were being carried out) if this would be possible, and if not (perhaps owing to excessive damage), whether XR219 could donate parts to make XR220 complete (by this time it lacked engines, jetpipes, a wingtip and various cockpit contents).

Sadly the RAE's response was unhelpful. It could no longer be guaranteed that XR219 was entirely original. Only the fuselage was identifiable, having XR219 painted on it, and the wings, tailplanes, fin and so on could be from any airframe, as various components had arrived at Shoeburyness

ABOVE: Staff members of BAC line up in front of XR220 at Boscombe Down. The aircraft would soon be handed over to the A&AEE for various trials work, primarily noise trials in relation to the Concorde project. BAE Systems via Warton Heritage Group

RIGHT: The second aircraft, XR220, at Boscombe Down during the post-cancellation noise trials. The aircraft is tied down, with the auxiliary intake doors strutted open to enable full-power runs, and a microphone is positioned close to the jetpipes. Solent Sky collection

BELOW: At Henlow in 1974, XR220 is loaded up and ready for transport to Cosford for refurbishment and, as it turned out, permanent display. Glenn Surtees

and been used indiscriminately to assemble 'XR219'. The RAE also pointed out that the RAF Museum was 'notoriously difficult to foot the bill for their acquisitions', and it could not accept the bill for any work itself; nor would it want any delay to its ongoing weapons trials. So XR219 stayed put, and while there were some unofficial efforts to protect it from the worst that could be thrown at it, the staff on the range could not hold back the trials for long. In May 1974 the Southend Historic Aircraft Museum enquired about the possibility of acquiring XR219 or another TSR2 airframe once they were no longer useful for research. Sadly, Shoeburyness had only shattered wreckage by this time, so there was nothing suitable for a museum. The last remnants of XR219 were scrapped in 1982. Various portions of the other airframes and other incomplete TSR2s, notably complete wings (a hold-over from the mass preservation of wing sections for structural research), could still be found in the undergrowth at Shoeburyness until they were also scrapped in the 1990s.

The second aircraft, XR220, stayed at Boscombe Down and was handed over to the A&AEE on 9 July 1965 to be used for many of the ground-research trials mentioned earlier, including noise trials investigating the efficiency of detuners on the noise footprint in the surrounding area and acoustic-fatigue effects on the airframe itself. By the end of February 1966 the A&AEE had just about completed its trials work with the aircraft (or 'ground test vehicle' as the A&AEE described it) and made the first noises about disposing of the airframe. On 5 May 1966 the MoA formally revoked the airframe's certification as a military aircraft, and a week later the A&AEE wrote to the Ministry pointing out that, owing to resurfacing of its main apron, it had limited parking space available and with regards to XR220 would 'welcome early disposal instructions'.

The Ministry wrote to several interested parties, asking if they had any further use for the aircraft, including RRE Pershore, the Empire Test Pilots School, the Blind Landing Experimental Unit, RAE Bedford, RAE Farnborough, the Civil Aviation Flying Unit and various RAF departments. All answered in the negative except for the RAF's Air Historical Branch (AHB). However, it was unwilling to pay anything for the aircraft, so progress on disposal was slow. The engines were removed in October and placed in storage at the MoA's Central

Stores Depot at Sevenhampton near Swindon. While Treasury authority was gained for a transfer without charge between the A&AEE and AHB, the aircraft remained parked outdoors at Boscombe Down. It was not until February 1967 that all the required paperwork had been drawn up to allow the aircraft to be transferred. For accounting purposes the aircraft was valued at the grand sum of £1,000 (somewhat severe depreciation considering it had cost around £3 million to build).

More delays ensued, and it was not until 11 April 1967 that the new MoD authorized

the transfer of XR220 from the A&AEE to RAF Henlow (then intended to be the site of a new RAF Museum), assigned the instructional airframe serial number 7933M and allotted for 'Display' purposes. Number 71 Maintenance Unit was given the task of dismantling, transporting and re-erecting the aircraft at Henlow, and transported it there on 20 June 1967. By August 1968 the RAF Museum had surveyed XR220 to find out just which bits were missing (a long list resulted, including the previously mentioned items plus both canopies, the nose radome, ejection seats, etc.), and some of

In 2010 XR220 dominates the RAF Museum Cosford's 'Test Flight' exhibition, towering over every other aircraft in the hangar and continuing to stop visitors in their tracks forty-five years after cancellation. Damien Burke

these components were in due course sourced from Shoeburyness (in many cases there was no way to identify the donor aircraft). Further components to complete the aircraft were donated by Ferranti in 1969. In 1974 XR220 was transferred from Henlow to RAF Cosford, originally for refurbishment, but the airframe stayed on to become part of the new RAF Museum outpost at Cosford, and remains there to this day. Various other missing components have come to light over the intervening years, and as a result XR220 is now substantially complete (the major missing items being the engines) and, having never been repainted, is a particularly authentic-looking specimen. Close examination will even show signs of the repairs effected after the aircraft's accident on arrival at Boscombe Down in 1964. At the time of writing the RAF Museum at Hendon sells surplus TSR2

titanium bolts to visitors for 50p each. The original cost to the taxpayer of these bolts was more than twice that, which works out at about £17 each in 2010 prices.

The other survivor, XR222, was not entirely complete at the time of cancellation, and along with the other substantially structurally complete but unequipped airframes was expected to be doled out to various MoA, RAF or educational establishments. Most ended up being scrapped, as so few establishments were interested in taking on an airframe of no obvious use to them. However, the Principal of the College of Aeronautics at Cranfield, Professor A.J. Murphy, wrote to the MoA on 16 June 1965 to request allocation of a complete airframe plus various discrete components. The college chose to ask for XR222, which was not complete enough to be of any particular security concern (unlike XR221), and by 9

July it had been sent the good news that it could have XR222. The airframe was dismantled in October and transported by road in the last week of that month. It served its purpose as an educational tool for budding aircraft designers for the next decade, but by 1975 the college was making noises about disposing of the airframe as it did 'take up an awful lot of space'. It hung on 'for sentimental reasons' until April 1978, when Cranfield donated XR222 to the Imperial War Museum at its then-new out-station at Duxford Airfield in Cambridgeshire. As XR222 had never been completed it lacked various panels and components, and during its time at Duxford it has undergone two restorations during which it was cosmetically completed, with missing panels fabricated as necessary. The second and most most in-depth restoration (including a complete strip-down and repaint) was

Ex-BAC personnel including pilots Jimmy Dell (in white) and Don Knight (left of Jimmy) stand in front of XR222 on the occasion of its formal unveiling on 16 December 2005. Damien Burke

completed in 2005, but many internal items are still missing. Several external items are also missing, but these are really only obvious to those intimately familiar with the type. The aircraft is now displayed within the AirSpace exhibition at Duxford.

More useful work was carried out using the TSR2 forebody originally constructed for ejection-seat and air-conditioning trials with the RAE at Farnborough. After these tests it was scheduled to be used for further air-conditioning and demisting tests of the intended trainer version, both at Farnborough and back at Weybridge in the stratospheric test chamber. However, with the project cancelled the nose section stayed with the RAE and was allocated to it for further use as appropriate. Some further use was made of it for thermal and materials tests in aid of the Concorde programme (in particular, investigation of crew comfort at high speeds with associated kinetic heating), but it went on to spend most of its useful life having dead chickens fired at it from a compressed-air cannon. After some years of these birdstrike trials it ended up on the dump at Farnborough, and was eventually rescued by the Brooklands Museum at Weybridge. Returned 'home' in 1992, the nose section was cosmetically restored and at the time of writing remains on external display at the museum, a short distance from the collection's Concorde airframe.

A scattering of other components also survives in various museums. There is a wing apex from XR227 at the Newark Air Museum (ex-RAF Cranwell, where it was used to demonstrate integral fuel tank construc-

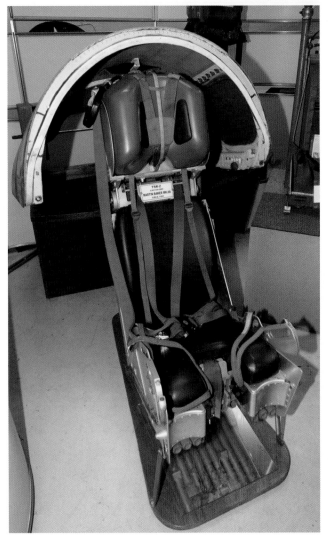

ABOVE: **Test forebody T5 was used for thermal, air-conditioning and escape-system trials during the TSR2 project, and then remained at RAE Farnborough for further thermal and bird-strike trials for years afterwards. Rescued from the Farnborough dump in 1992, it is now on display at its birthplace, Weybridge, home of the Brooklands Museum, where is seen in January 2010, undergoing even more thermal trials!** Damien Burke

LEFT: **A TSR2 ejection seat and navigator's canopy at the Midland Air Museum in February 2010.** Damien Burke

ABOVE: **TSR2 skin forming templates at the Brooklands Museum.** Damien Burke

tion), along with an engine access door from XR222; a nose undercarriage leg, rudder pedal, control column assembly, canopy and ejection seat at the Midland Air Museum (all ex-Cranfield); Olympus 320 engines at the RAF Museum Cosford, the Science Museum and the Gatwick Aviation Museum among other places; an ejection seat is also on display at the RAF Museum Cosford (in addition to those in XR220). Of the electronics, including the nav/attack system, very little remains; BAE Systems' Rochester archive holds a few items, as does the RAF Museum's stores.

Flight of the phoenix?

In late 1969 rumours abounded of XR220 being prepared for flight once more, to act as an Olympus 593 flying test bed, and a campaign was begun to try to get the then-Conservative government to resurrect the entire programme. This was somewhat ill-timed, as agreement on building MRCA as a pan-European co-operative project had just been reached. Nothing came of the campaign, though several newspapers reported the supposed plan, including a particularly detailed story in the *Daily Mail* of 27 August 1970. In this story (one can hardly call it a 'report') the paper claimed that 'A team of scientists and RAF engineers are to restore a prototype of the hedge-hopping 1,600mph bomber to flying trim. Tests are already well advanced on increasing the enormous power of the Rolls-Royce Olympus engines which powered the only TSR2 to fly', and furthermore, '... one of the completed prototypes was secretly saved by the RAF and kept in 'mothballs' at Boscombe Down. Now it has been moved by lorry to RAF Henlow, Bedfordshire, and work will begin shortly on rebuilding it piece by piece.' This was, of course, nothing more than lurid fiction based on the disposal of the aircraft to the nascent RAF Museum.

Seven years after that, a more serious attempt to revive the TSR2 was born, though 'serious' is stretching the credibility of this effort also. Christopher de Vere, through his company Interflight Ltd, began looking at reviving TSR2 in 1977. By March 1979 de Vere had written to Stephen Hastings, Conservative MP and author of *The Murder of TSR2*, asking for help on how to proceed with his grand plan to resurrect the TSR2. Hastings, to give him credit, managed to reply with an entirely calm and rational recommendation that de Vere go

away and return with further information; specifically, what roles the TSR2 could fulfil that the Tornado could not; whether there was a definite Service operational requirement for the aircraft; that the type had not been overtaken by technology and made obsolete; and that there would be good export potential. It was basically a polite brush-off, but de Vere was not put off and produced a paper entitled *The Need for TSR2 in 1979*, which talked of re-engining the aircraft with Olympus 593s and giving it square intakes so that the UK would have a means of delivering nuclear weapons to Russia in the mid-1980s, when the Royal Navy's nuclear submarines were expected to be worn out and a confrontation with Russia was 'most probable'. He also suggested that it could also carry out long-range air defence, loaded down with missiles and fuel, and could operate from island bases on long-range maritime patrol. As for being made obsolete, it could easily be fitted with up-to-date electronics, and regarding export potential, well, the Canadians needed an air-defence aircraft just like this (the cancellation of the Avro Arrow in 1959 having presumably passed de Vere by) and the US Navy could team up with the RN to form a Euro-American force to control the Indian Ocean using a maritime version based on Diego Garcia or Gan (cue several paragraphs going off at a tangent bemoaning the UK's treatment of the natives of the Maldives). Other suggested export customers were Australia, China, South Africa and Japan. De Vere said XR220 could be back in the air by the 1980 Farnborough Air Show, and new TSR2s in service by 1984. Entertaining as this all was, even better was a supporting letter sent to de Vere in August 1979 in which the author, no doubt with tongue firmly in cheek, suggested that there was '... no sound argument against putting the TSR2 into production, and getting negotiations with the US Department of Defense under way'. As the first production RAF Tornado GR.1 had rolled off the production line the month before, there was at least one sound argument against resurrecting the TSR2.

Later that month de Vere had an aircraft maintenance engineer inspect XR220 at Cosford and produce a report on its condition. This was, however, a less-than-detailed study carried out without opening a single panel; nothing more than a visual study without a single piece of internal equipment being seen. Regardless, the report predicted that twelve to eighteen months of work

would be necessary to carry out a real check of the airframe. It said that 'engine installations may be a difficult area' (masterful understatement, given the engines' history of development problems), but that overall '... the feasibility, from the engineering standpoint, of restoring the aircraft to a standard of airworthiness necessary to continue with the development of the type subsequent to the production of a new Series of aircraft, is quite valid and could well be the means of recouping a considerable amount of the vast amount of public monies already expended on the project, which currently stands as a complete loss to the British taxpayer.'

Armed with this apparent good news, de Vere then wrote to the Chief of the Defence Staff in November 1979, enclosing his proposal, entitled *TSR2 – The Choice for the 1980s*. In this paper, amidst the hyperbole and outright nonsense used to try to justify the resurrection, de Vere outlined his plan to refit XR220 with Olympus 320 engines that by now were 'benefiting from the extra years of development' (though work on the 320 had ceased in 1965); manufacture production aircraft to be fitted with the Olympus 593 as used on Concorde; mount cruise missiles on the aircraft; use it for air defence against hordes of *Backfire* and *Fencer* bombers; and control the seas from the Indian Ocean to the South Atlantic via bases such as Gan and Ascension. Exports to the USA, Australia, Canada and France were on the cards (China, South Africa and Japan having quietly disappeared from the list). There was no reason why the aircraft could not be airborne at Farnborough in September 1980 (conveniently ignoring the report produced by his own engineer), and in production for the RAF by 1984. The Chief of the Defence Staff no doubt guffawed heartily and passed de Vere's communication to the Chief of the Air Staff, who no doubt guffawed heartily and passed it to his Assistant, Air Vice Marshal Hall, for a reply. The reply was polite, and pointed out that modern requirements and financial realities made the resurrection impossible.

However, de Vere was not downhearted, and replied in December 1979 in typically verbose style, attempting to justify his plan once more and suggesting that a mere £24 million would get two prototypes in the air; thirty men could dismantle the two airframes at Cosford and Duxford, transport them to BAC's Filton plant, report on their condition and reassemble them within four months. This time the reply from the Assistant Chief of the Air Staff was shorter – and still very much in the negative. Admiral of the Fleet The Lord Hill-Norton was next on de Vere's list, and after a visit in January 1980 wrote back to him: '... I do not think your proposal is a serious runner'. Lord Home received another copy of the proposal, passing it to the Secretary for Defence, Francis Pym, who replied to Lord Home, acknowledging that they were already aware of de Vere's efforts and had been corresponding with him already, and further claiming that his paper had been 'studied carefully by my Department' but that 'It certainly could not be accommodated within the defence budget unless we were to abandon or at least disrupt key equipment projects for which the services have a real need'.

The next stop on de Vere's increasingly tiresome tour was Roland Beamont himself. Beamont humoured him and pointed out a few basic flaws (for air defence, for example, the high wing loading made turning performance inadequate) and the costs of incorporating a different engine. He then added the *coup de grace*, pointing out that the RAF was now a tactical air force, not a strategic one, and until the Air Staff and Government accepted the need for a strategic nuclear role the TSR2 was never going to be of interest. Even if it was, a 'fully developed' TSR2 would only 'possibly' be cheaper than developing an entirely new aircraft.

The next person to be hit by the campaign was Group Captain Mason at the

RAF Staff College. He too was unimpressed but, obviously appreciating a good laugh, asked de Vere to please forward on any other papers that he considered would influence his arguments. Things were not going well, and de Vere decided that the similarities of all the replies he was getting meant there was some conspiracy behind the scenes to derail his plan. Stephen Hastings MP received another verbose and rambling letter in March 1980, to which he replied with a typically restrained re-statement of the fundamental problem that the RAF had no strategic role. De Vere was not put off, and, amplifying his achievements, contacts and prospects somewhat, went back to Roland Beamont, who simply pointed out the key obstacles as he saw them: the Olympus 320 engine and undercarriage problems which still needed some work to fix them when the project was cancelled.

The whole sorry story went on, to appear as an article in *Air Pictorial* magazine in September 1981. Basically a straight copy of de Vere's long-winded justifications for the idea, this version of the story was represented as being kicked-off by the Conservative Aviation Committee asking 'a group of aviation engineers' to 'study the feasibility of rebuilding the TSR-2'. This was hardly an accurate portrayal of Stephen Hastings's initial response to de Vere's letter, and it gave rise to a myth that Margaret Thatcher's incoming government threatened to restart TSR2 as Tornado was suffering delays. Nothing could have been further from the truth.

Alternatives to TSR2

With TSR2 dead, and TFX lined up to take its place, no time was wasted in looking for alternatives that could retain some genuine UK involvement in design and production, rather than handing over all future RAF contracts to the USA. On the near horizon was the AFVG, stemming from a confused combined requirement for a TSR2-lite for the RAF and an interceptor for the French Air Force which owed more to the government's wish for European cooperation than to any real need for yet another new strike aircraft. However, it would be some years before it was a sure thing, and BAC needed to get new work going immediately.

P.28 (mod) Canberra

The first, and most desperate, attempt was a design study on improving the Canberra. A BAC board meeting within days of the TSR2 cancellation authorized another look at the clipped-wing Canberra variant, the P.28, first studied way back in 1958. The study, which had concluded that reducing the wingspan and fitting more-powerful Avon engines could result in a useful low-level bomber, was dug out of the archives, dusted off and reappraised in light of current engine developments and TSR2 experience. The result was a selection of three suggested Canberra variants encompassing ever-greater changes to the basic airframe, with the Phases 0 and 1 as simpler, cheaper options for possible overseas customers and

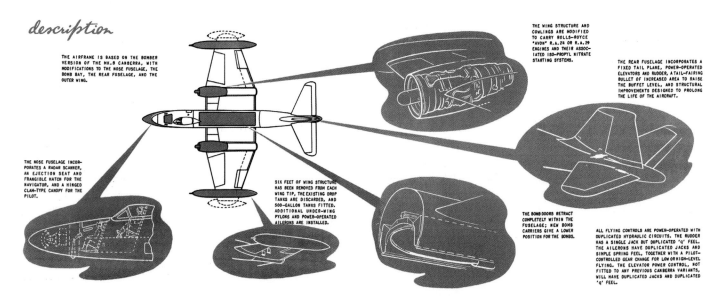

description

THE AIRFRAME IS BASED ON THE BOMBER VERSION OF THE MK.8 CANBERRA, WITH MODIFICATIONS TO THE NOSE FUSELAGE, THE BOMB BAY, THE REAR FUSELAGE, AND THE OUTER WING.

THE WING STRUCTURE AND COWLINGS ARE MODIFIED TO CARRY ROLLS-ROYCE "AVON" R.A.28 OR R.A.29 ENGINES AND THEIR ASSOCIATED ISO-PROPYL NITRATE STARTING SYSTEMS.

THE REAR FUSELAGE INCORPORATES A FIXED TAIL PLANE, POWER-OPERATED ELEVATORS AND RUDDER, A TAIL-FAIRING BULLET OF INCREASED AREA TO RAISE THE BUFFET LEVEL, AND STRUCTURAL IMPROVEMENTS DESIGNED TO PROLONG THE LIFE OF THE AIRCRAFT.

THE NOSE FUSELAGE INCORPORATES A RADAR SCANNER, AN EJECTION SEAT AND FRANGIBLE HATCH FOR THE NAVIGATOR, AND A HINGED CLAM-TYPE CANOPY FOR THE PILOT.

SIX FEET OF WING STRUCTURE HAS BEEN REMOVED FROM EACH WING TIP, THE EXISTING DROP TANKS ARE DISCARDED, AND 500-GALLON TANKS FITTED. ADDITIONAL UNDER-WING PYLONS AND POWER-OPERATED AILERONS ARE INSTALLED.

THE BOMB DOORS RETRACT COMPLETELY WITHIN THE FUSELAGE; NEW BOMB CARRIERS GIVE A LOWER POSITION FOR THE BOMBS.

ALL FLYING CONTROLS ARE POWER-OPERATED WITH DUPLICATED HYDRAULIC CIRCUITS. THE RUDDER HAS A SINGLE JACK BUT DUPLICATED 'q' FEEL. THE AILERONS HAVE DUPLICATED JACKS AND SIMPLE SPRING FEEL, TOGETHER WITH A PILOT-CONTROLLED GEAR CHANGE FOR LOW OR HIGH-LEVEL FLYING. THE ELEVATOR POWER CONTROL, NOT FITTED TO ANY PREVIOUS CANBERRA VARIANTS, WILL HAVE DUPLICATED JACKS AND DUPLICATED 'q' FEEL.

The P.28 Canberra design study proposed an upgraded Canberra, but was of no interest to the RAF. BAE Systems via Warton Heritage Group

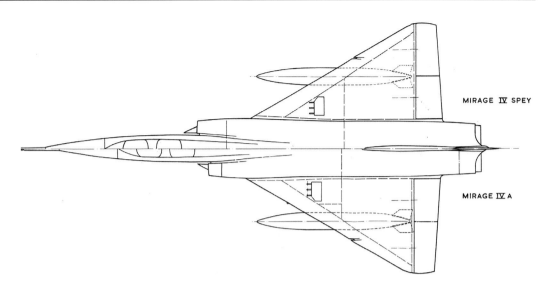

The Mirage IVA, re-engined with Speys and fitted with TSR2 reconnaissance equipment and P.1154 avionics, was an interesting co-operative proposal from BAC and Dassault, but again found little favour with the RAF. BAE Systems via Brooklands Museum

MIRAGE IV SPEY

MIRAGE IV A

the Phase 2 version for the RAF. This would basically be the B.2 airframe with the strengthened tailplane of the PR.9, a larger fin, six feet chopped off each wing, powered flying controls, Spey engines, integral tip tanks, and a nose similar to that of the PR.9 but lengthened and incorporating the TSR2's FLR. A reconnaissance pack could be fitted in the weapons bay; either the TSR2 pack (a scheme had already been drawn up for Canberra carriage of test packs during TSR2 development), or the pack then proposed for the South African Air Force but fitted with TSR2 cameras. Low-level range would be similar to that of the Buccaneer, but speed at low level would be Mach 0.75, versus 0.85 for the Buccaneer. It will come as no surprise to the reader that the RAF did not think much of this proposal when it was fully expecting to be operating the TFX and AFVG in the near future.

Spey Mirage IV

Later, in May 1965, BAC approached General Aeronautique Marcel Dassault in France to sound it out on a possible derivative of its Mirage IV. The proposal was to re-engine the type with the Spey and kit it out with various pieces of TSR2 equipment, co-operate on the build, and hopefully sell this new low-level version of the Mirage IV both to the French Air Force and Royal Air Force, and possibly others. Dassault responded with alacrity. It was, after all, teaming up with BAC on the AFVG project also, and in mid-July BAC submitted a basic proposal to the MoA.

BAC described the Spey Mirage IV as a 'straightforward development of the Mirage IV-A'; while designed as a high-level strate-gic bomber, its structure was suitable for transonic operation at low level and its fatigue life would be good enough if low-level operation was restricted to 20 per cent of its flying life. Take-off thrust would be increased from 30,000lb (13,600kg) to 41,700lb (18,900kg) by using Speys instead of the existing Atar 9K turbojets, and specific fuel consumption reduced by 30 per cent. The result would be an aircraft that could nearly match the TSR2's combat radius while carrying a somewhat higher conventional bomb load. All of the reconnaissance equipment designed for the TSR2 could be carried, and there was an agreement to develop a new nav/attack system including terrain following, comparable with that of the TSR2 (this was based on the P.1154 system, with a French Antilope FLR). An in-service date for the first sixteen aircraft of March 1970 was predicted by BAC, if an instruction to proceed was given in March 1966. Unit cost would be £2.321 million if fifty were ordered, reducing to £2.067 million each if 110 were ordered. If the French Air Force also bought some the unit cost would fall even more. Regardless, it would be a cheaper aircraft than TFX, particularly as only half of the cost would be in foreign currency.

The attractions were obvious, and an A&AEE team even visited France during September 1965 to fly one of the first production Mirage IV-As, making a total of eleven flights and logging 15hr, including flight at Mach 2.0 and transonic at low level. The verdict from the two Boscombe pilots was positive, but the RAF was luke-warm on the subject; Mirage IV with Spey did not have the airfield performance of the TFX, nor the range. By December the matter had been debated in the Commons and the government made it clear that they regarded Mirage IV with Spey as a paper project that would arrive later than TFX with inferior performance. The French were unimpressed, as they saw the UK's possible acquisition of TFX as a slap in the face and a threat to the AFVG project. If the UK was to buy TFX, the threat went, then France would pull out of AFVG.

With the UK's option to buy TFX expiring at the beginning of 1966, the government requested an extension from the Americans to give them more time to make a decision, and this was granted. In February 1966 they exercised the option and ordered fifty TFX. Mirage IV Spey was forgotten. As for the French threat to AFVG, well, they did indeed pull out, but not until July 1967, after Dassault had launched its own Mirage G variable-geometry type, pressuring the French government to order these instead of continuing with AVFG. Mirage G had no doubt benefited from some development assistance from the joint Anglo-French work on variable sweep. Outraged, BAC viewed the entire French part in AFVG as little more than an information grab on VG (this was a little unfair, given that Dassault's development of Mirage G had begun some years before). But Dassault's victory was pyrrhic. The French government delayed funding, never made a firm order, and the Mirage G programme suffered even more changed requirements and cost increases than TSR2, ending in cancellation in the mid-1970s. Similarly, TFX, suffered development problems and cost overruns and the UK government cancelled that order in January 1968, paying cancellation fees on top of the millions already spent.

A general-arrangement drawing of the AFVG. As it was the product of a political requirement rather than a military one, it was hardly surprising that the AFVG never took to the air. Damien Burke

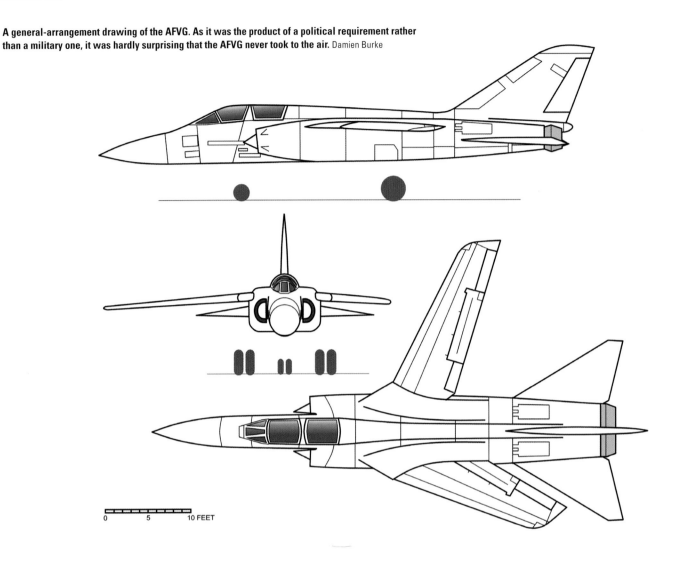

0   5   10 FEET

The AFVG did not get beyond the mockup stage (seen here in a long exposure showing the variations in wing sweep), the French pulling out in 1967 and the project continuing on as UKVG until it was cancelled entirely later in the year. Jaguar did rather better; the tail of a mockup is just about visible here. BAE Systems via Warton Heritage Group

Conclusion

The TSR2, as this book has revealed, was not quite the wonder jet of popular myth. It was certainly far more capable than the RAF had any right to expect after producing an operational requirement that included just about everything except the kitchen sink, but, as shown by the report on its short-comings and the last-minute revision of the specification, the TSR2 was some distance away from actually meeting either the original requirements or the RAF's real needs. This is not to take too much away from its likely capability as a strike aircraft. Differences of hundreds of yards in take-off roll or a few hundred miles in combat radius would not, in reality, have made it any less useful for delivering tactical nuclear weapons, and the world of fewer and changed defence commitments could not have been foreseen by the planners of 1957. As a flying machine it was by all accounts a remarkably successful design, managing to pull off a workable compromise between the ridiculous combination of 'cabbage patch' operations, high-subsonic low-level operations and high-supersonic medium- to high-altitude missions. It remained superbly controllable throughout the entire flight envelope in which it would realistically have spent most of its time, even without the sophisticated autostabilization and flight control system it was intended to use.

As with any narrative covering an engineering project, the problems have provided the interest, but many of the problems related in this book were either fixed or well understood and on their way to being resolved. The more serious issues would have been those of reliability. Electronic components of the time were a world away from the reliability and longevity that is now commonplace, and early studies on TSR2 reliability did not instil confidence. A protracted and painful introduction into RAF service could well have been the result; perhaps even as painful as the first decade of F-111 service, which was blighted by several fatal crashes.

Much of what has been written about the aircraft has naturally come from those closely involved with the project, by far the most prolific of these being Roland Beamont himself, who was always overwhelmingly positive about the quality of the aircraft and the entirely political nature of its cancellation. While the author enjoys a good polemic aimed at politicians as much as the next man, the available evidence points only to sheer cost as the reason. No government could have held out for long before either cancelling or further downgrading the specification, and TSR2 was already too expensive to survive as a downgraded weapons system. Had the project continued any longer, it could well have bled both BAC and the RAF dry, resulting in a far more disastrous ending for all concerned.

The Tornado GR.1 entered front-line service in 1982, some seventeen years after the TSR2 was cancelled, finally giving the RAF a supersonic strike aircraft, though with a top speed limited to only Mach 1.3 and a combat radius of 400nm (460 miles; 740km). It also had no significant reconnaissance capability until the introduction of the GR.1A in 1989; this version was equipped with a comprehensive IR reconnaissance suite including linescan. The further upgraded GR.4A, seen here, entered service in 2001. Damien Burke

While BAC suffered significant redundancies, it did not undergo the near-total collapse predicted before the cancellation. This was in no small part down to the hard work of everybody at BAC resulting in the export success of the Lightning and the firm manner in which George Edwards took the company forward into other projects without wasting time worrying unnecessarily about what might have been.

Ironically, the RAF ended up with the one aircraft it had never wanted, the NA.39/Buccaneer, which proved to be a superb asset. Upon its retirement in 1994, RAF pilots complained that the only real replacement for a Buccaneer was a new Buccaneer. It is perhaps the saddest part of the story that the RAF's opposition to the type meant that Blackburn was never permitted to develop its excellent aircraft fully, and exports were thus limited to a handful of sales to South Africa. Earl Mountbatten

and the RN have been painted as the villains in many discussions of the TSR2 fiasco, but the evidence of repeated RAF attempts to sabotage both the Buccaneer and the Spey engine appears to indicate that Mountbatten was really only beating the Service at its own game. It is particularly shameful that the behaviour of all three branches of the armed forces conspired to cause such damage to the nation's defence, with single-Service needs being put above all else, regardless of the consequences.

The efforts put into TSR2 were not entirely wasted. Much of the knowledge and system principles, and a few of the electronic systems, found their way into other aircraft projects, directly benefiting the Jaguar, Concorde, Phantom, Buccaneer, Tornado and others. The aviation industry learned the invaluable lesson that it is much harder for a government to cancel its way out of a contract if that contract is a multinational

one. Jaguar, Concorde and Typhoon all survived delays and cost increases that would have killed any entirely home-grown project.

The Soviet Union countered developments like TSR2 by pouring money into fighter and missile defences, and into its own advanced bombers, and, in the process, eventually reduced the standard of living of its population to unsustainable levels. In the end it was bankrupted by the cost of countering advanced NATO technology, and thus the TSR2 played its own small part in winning the Cold War without ever entering service. Thankfully, therefore, no Soviet target ever had to suffer the fate illustrated on the cover of this book, and TSR2 was never called upon to add any new names to the list of cities such as Hamburg and Hiroshima that have suffered the obscenity of a firestorm.

Sunset on Duxford's TSR2. The end of the project did not spell an end to the British aviation industry, but it was one of the last entirely home-grown military aircraft, and since 1965 the only entirely British military projects have been the first-generation Harriers, the Strikemaster, Hawk and Nimrod. Damien Burke

CHAPTER TWELVE

Unbuilt Versions

Various investigations and proposals into novel variants of the TSR2 were made both during the initial 1959/60 design progression and at later dates. Some of these are described here.

STOL

Vickers-Armstrongs's project office carried out an investigation into incorporating nose lifting engines during July/August 1959; the investigation that had so enraged Shorts when it found out about it. The idea was to reduce take-off and landing distances by adding a vertical-thrust component to enable the nose to be lifted earlier in the take-off roll than would otherwise be possible. Vickers was well aware that the idea was not new, and its own report referred to the previous English Electric/Shorts work. Vickers began by looking at adding the lift engines with the minimum of changes to the airframe, but it was clear that adding the lift engines far enough forward to be of use would unbalance the aircraft to such an extent that the wings would need to be moved forward, or considerable ballast would have to be added to the tail. Installing the lift engines nearer the c.g. would defeat the purpose almost entirely. There was little choice but to work on a more substantial redesign of the airframe. This entailed reducing the wing area from 675sq ft (62.7sq m) to 610sq ft (56.7sq m), reducing the tailplane area from 144sq ft (13.38sq m) to 124sq ft (11.5sq m), increasing the fuselage height and moving the wing up 4in (10cm) to allow extra fuel capacity (thickening the wing was another option), reducing the nose length by 2.5ft (0.76m) and moving the engines 1ft (0.3m) aft. The additional weight of the lifting engines and extra fuel was nearly all counteracted by the reduction in the aircraft's overall size, but it would still

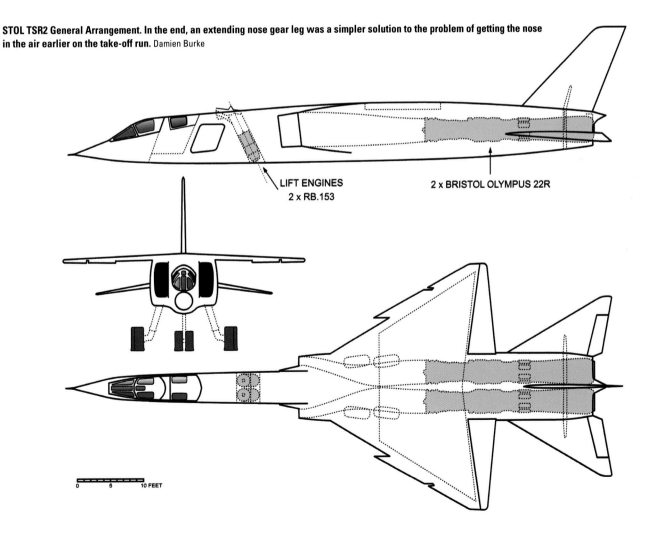

STOL TSR2 General Arrangement. In the end, an extending nose gear leg was a simpler solution to the problem of getting the nose in the air earlier on the take-off run. Damien Burke

LIFT ENGINES
2 x RB.153

2 x BRISTOL OLYMPUS 22R

0   5   10 FEET

end up being around 900lb (400kg) heavier. The lifting engines themselves would not be the RB.108s already available, but a developed version, the RB.153, which gave 4,000lb (1,800kg) of thrust, compared with the RB.108's 2,350lb (1,060kg). For the 450nm high/low sortie the improvements in airfield performance would be a take-off and landing roll 60yd (55m) shorter, unsticking at 138kt (207mph; 333km/h) instead of 149kt (171mph; 276km/h), plus a reduction in approach speed from 138kt (207mph; 333km/h) to 118kt (136mph; 218km/h). For the 1,000nm sortie the improvements were less impressive, knocking only 20yd (18m) off the take-off roll and 35yd (32m) from the landing roll, unstick speed barely changing and approach speed reduced to 123kt (141mph; 227km/h).

Drawbacks of the scheme were that increased tailplane travel would be needed to trim out the jet lift engine effects, and lack of ground clearance meant the tailplane would ideally need to be mounted higher on the fuselage, into possible interference of airflow from the mainplane. All in all, the many disadvantages of all such schemes outweighed the benefits, and the much simpler idea of the extending nose gear leg was adopted instead.

VTOL

Although VTOL had of course been discarded early on in the design process, 1961 changed things a little. Hawker's P.1127 had flown successfully, and the company was working on the P.1154, a supersonic VTOL strike fighter for the RAF and RN. There was some concern that, if it was successful, this aircraft could threaten the TSR2, as it was capable of carrying out a portion of the TSR2's role and VTOL would give it vastly more operational flexibility. In response, BAC put together a rough design for a lightweight 'baby TSR2' as part of a costing exercise. The idea was to predict costs for a small, cheap, VTOL type (the baby TSR2) and compare them with the costs for the standard TSR2 and a heavier VTOL type with variable-geometry wings.

The 'baby TSR2' was specified as being a single-seat delta-wing type, weighing around 32,700lb (14,840kg) for vertical take-off, with an overload of up to 48,000lb (20,000kg) possible for a short take-off of 1,220ft (372m). Powered by a single RB.168 with reheat and ten RB.162 lift engines, the aircraft would have a combat radius of 250nm (290 miles; 470km) at 200ft (60m) and Mach 0.92, with a weapon load of 2,000lb (900kg). Ferry range would be 1,500nm (1,725 miles; 2,775km). In terms of appearance, about the only remaining aspects of TSR2 were the nose and intake shapes. The VTOL variable-geometry type, apparently a study that was already independently under way (and for which sadly no drawings were included in the report), was to be powered by two thrust engines with provision for thrust deflection, and six lift engines carried in the forward fuselage. Throwing a variable-geometry wing into this mix seems an odd case of overkill.

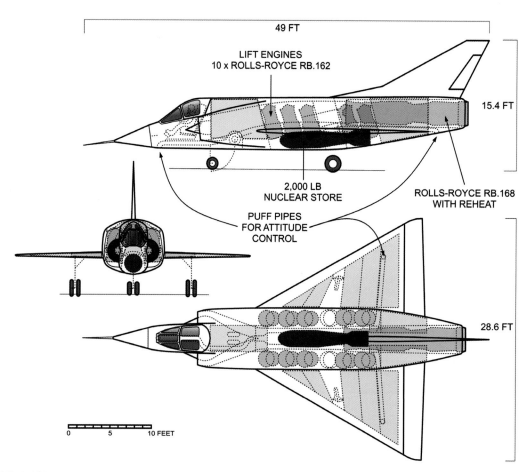

This VTOL 'Baby TSR2' was a purely paper exercise produced as a baseline for comparison of a minimally-sized VTOL type against the standard TSR2 or a VTOL and VG version. Damien Burke

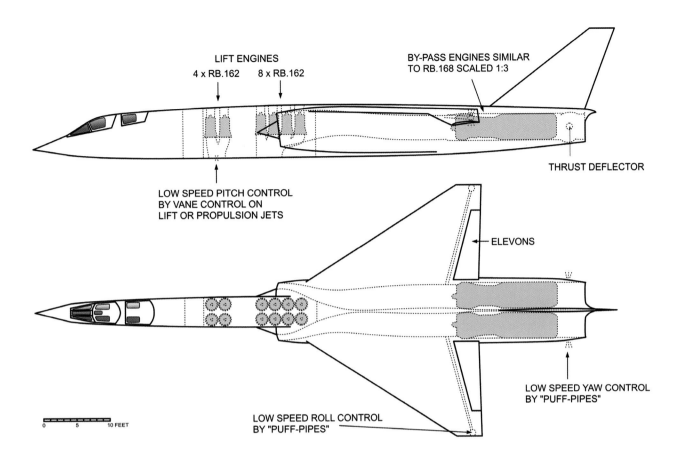

LIFT ENGINES
4 x RB.162   8 x RB.162

BY-PASS ENGINES SIMILAR TO RB.168 SCALED 1:3

THRUST DEFLECTOR

LOW SPEED PITCH CONTROL BY VANE CONTROL ON LIFT OR PROPULSION JETS

ELEVONS

LOW SPEED YAW CONTROL BY "PUFF-PIPES"

LOW SPEED ROLL CONTROL BY "PUFF-PIPES"

0   5   10 FEET

VTOL TSR2 General Arrangement. This was suggested as a 'minimal changes' solution to incorporating VTOL within the TSR2 to provide a research airframe. A tailplane was thought unnecessary as pitch control would be provided by elevons on the mainplane at high speeds, and via vectored thrust at low speeds.
Damien Burke

The basic response of BAC to the threat of a VTOL type was that at light weights, and operating over shorter ranges, the TSR2 had the capability to operate from short, rough strips and thus carry out the close-air-support role without the need for a complex VTOL system. The larger TSR2 could also carry more weapons and hit more targets than a single smaller VTOL type, and thus fewer would be needed. Of course, the TSR2 was more expensive, and, as a larger aircraft, more vulnerable to being hit by enemy fire than a smaller type. Against this was the argument that a TSR2 was less likely to be hit in the first place by virtue of its terrain-following ability. As for cost, comments on the value of the TSR2's additional capabilities (reconnaissance, all-weather attack) and the costs of supporting dispersed operations for VTOL types dotted about the countryside in forest clearings and the like left the report's readers to make up their own minds about which was better value for money, even before reaching

the meat of the report. The graphs showing break-even points for various 'efficiency factors' (the number of TSR2s you would need to replace a single VTOL type; always less than one, of course). Even the most basic VTOL type would need to be produced in thousands to 'save money', argued BAC, whereas one could simply buy a few more TSR2s and give them the close-air-support role. Needless to say, BAC's figures and common sense did not make good bedfellows, and the P.1154 programme was never seriously challenged by any prospect of more TSR2s being purchased instead.

Variable geometry

Variable geometry (also known as variable sweep or the 'swing wing'), had been a pet project of Barnes Wallis at Vickers since 1948, research being funded by the company and some contribution from the government. Wallis had put together a

brochure on a revolutionary variable-sweep bomber to be called the Swallow, and spent years trying to get it built, to no avail, as many of the additional features of the aircraft (such as abandoning conventional flying controls and controlling the aircraft via swivelling engines on the wingtips) were believed by most to be a step too far. Early Vickers work on the GOR.339 submission had looked at variable geometry and discarded it as being unnecessary. The requirement could be met by the fixed-wing designs being drawn up, and no weight or range advantages could be found. Similar opinions had shot down Wallis's own submission of a Swallow variant to GOR.339, and as a result Wallis had turned to the US-funded Mutual Weapons Development Pact in April 1958, which resulted in Wallis and his team visiting the USA in late 1958.

The USA had already carried out some development flying of experimental variable-sweep aircraft (the Bell X-5 and

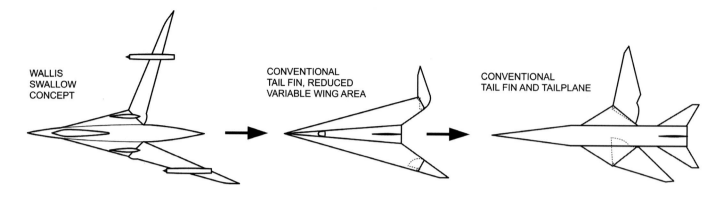

NASA Langley took the Wallis Swallow design and basically discarded much of the concept, concentrating on the separate outboard pivots to produce a more practical variable-sweep design, leading eventually to the TFX/F-111. Damien Burke

Grumman XF10F-1 Jaguar), and had found that stability and control were serious problems. Moreover, the weight and complexity of a translation mechanism to shift the wings forward and backward when sweep angle changed, to keep the wing's aerodynamic centre near the airframe's c.g., had pretty much brought variable geometry to a grinding halt there. Researchers at NASA Langley studied Wallis's Swallow with great interest, but found that it exhibited longitudinal instability at relatively low pitch angles when fully swept, and also at moderate pitch angles when unswept. The amount of control available from the pivoting engines was insufficient, and loss of an engine could lead to disastrous loss of control authority in the unswept configuration, when the deflection angle available to the engines would be insufficient to cope with the large moments introduced by the great distance between the engines on each side. Although NASA tried replacing the engines with a pivoting tail surface mounted on the wingtips, this led to even more complexity and did not substantially help stability, as the wing's longitudinal position still needed to be moved to deal with the changes in aerodynamic centre when the sweep angle was changed. Even more worrying was an apparent tendency for the aircraft to pitch up owing to interference between the variable sweep wing and the fixed forebody.

However, NASA's researchers came up with a more successful solution to the stability problem. In a drastically simplified version of the Swallow, a larger inner swept portion of the wing or fuselage forebody was fixed, a smaller outer section pivoting about a point at the leading edge of the

fixed portion. The swivelling engines were replaced by conventional engines in the fuselage and a conventional fin. No translation was needed, as the moving part of the wing was so much smaller and the resulting shift of the aerodynamic centre was of much lesser magnitude. The Americans thought it was a breakthrough, but Wallis was less than impressed by what he saw as a minor piece of tinkering with the wing and an invalidation of almost the entire remainder of the Swallow concept. But NASA's researchers could not have cared less, soon realizing that Wallis's laterally separated pair of pivots were the breakthrough they had been seeking in their own attempts to create a successful variable-geometry design. The most important part of their 'new' concept was the pair of outboard pivots, and with these the pivoting wing could equally be applied to a much more conventional fuselage layout, discarding entirely the Swallow's large forebody and the wing-mounted engines that doubled as a means of control. This also gave NASA the excuse it needed to claim that this was all its own work, and it wasted no time in providing the results of its research to the American aviation firms. Wallis did not realize it, but his attempt to gain funding from the Americans had helped to doom the GOR.339 project.

While Wallis returned to the UK disappointed with the Swallow's reception, Vickers took note of the NASA findings, backed up by its own windtunnel research, and sketched out a version of the TSR2 fitted with what was now described as the 'NASA wing'. However, with a history of years of frustrated effort behind the company in this field, it was clear that the benefits of

this kind of wing could be wiped out by development problems and weight gains, and variable geometry was put aside, to be looked at again in the future if circumstances permitted. In October 1960 the Minister of Defence, Harold Watkinson, visited Vickers and, concerned that the press would portray TSR2 as on obsolete design when the Americans were working on a tactical bomber employing variable sweep, knocked up a press release that did nothing more than draw the attention of the press to precisely that! The Ministry also asked Vickers to provide a list of its variable-sweep patents to give to the Americans, so that the Americans would have 'no difficulties' in paying for design rights if they did end up using a variable-sweep design for their new bomber.

By late 1962 the American TFX programme was well under way, and Vickers was a little surprised to find it had a variable-geometry wing, in fact the NASA wing, and that no offers of payments had been made by the Americans. It appeared to Vickers that the 1958–1959 joint research programme had been nothing less than a successful attempt by the Americans to grab a load of useful information for their own purposes. Vickers instructed its American lawyers to find out how successful it might be in pursuing a legal case against General Dynamics, but there was no support forthcoming from the UK government, and NASA's researchers had successfully applied for patents on 'their' variable-sweep wings (US patents Nos 3,087,692 and 3,053,484). After months of work Vickers eventually decided that these patents were couched in such general terms that it would be difficult to prove a direct infringement of Wallis's

Using the 'NASA wing', Vickers-Armstrongs drew up a VG version of the TSR2, but with the airframe having been designed for a challenging combination of short strips and supersonic performance already, the advantages offered by the VG wing were not thought to be worth the extra development effort. Damien Burke

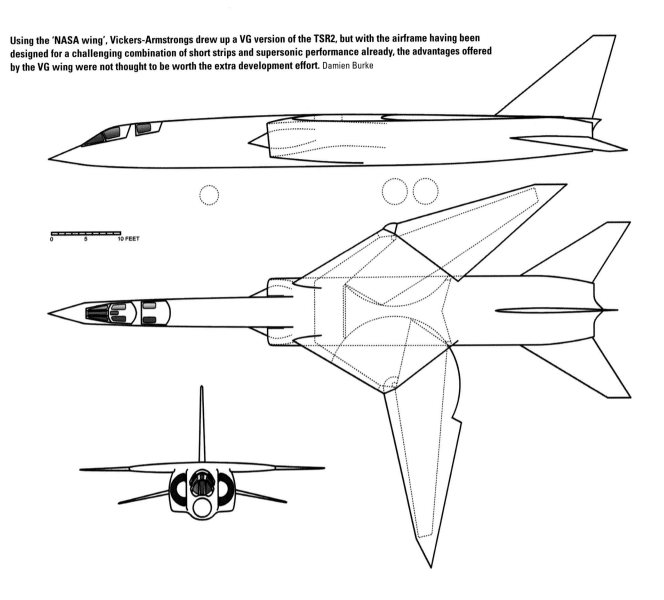

0   5   10 FEET

own patents or invalidate the patents on the basis of prior publication of relevant work, because much of it was only in print in brochures of a 'Secret' classification, which could not count as prior publication. Vickers reluctantly drew back from a legal battle, keeping a wary eye on TFX and its incarnation of variable-geometry nonetheless in case any royalties could be squeezed out of the Americans.

In late 1963 the subject of variable geometry was raised again. Since the early work on incorporating the 'NASA wing' in 1960, both OR.343 and design of the airframe had undergone various changes, and Ministry attention had now also turned to the American TFX and its variable-geometry wing. Accordingly, it was felt worthwhile to revisit variable geometry, particularly as Vickers was also still working

on the OR.346 naval requirement for a variable-geometry fighter (Types 581, 583 and 589, all of which would come to naught in the end). During January 1964 a brief study was carried out into the effect of fitting a variable-geometry wing to the TSR2, this time using the wing planform designed for the Type 583. This had a maximum sweep of 74 degrees and was calculated to incur a weight penalty of some 5,000lb (2,300kg). However, with an accompanying reduction in fuel capacity, the take-off weight was actually only going to be some 3,000lb (1,400kg) greater than that of the standard TSR2 and there would be some serious performance benefits. The take-off ground roll was reduced by 23 per cent and landing approach speed by 14 per cent; subsonic endurance was increased by 45 per cent, and range by 18 per cent. The only downer was

that supersonic range would be reduced by 8 per cent. The indications were that fitting the basic airframe with a variable-geometry wing could be a useful exercise, and could possibly be carried out as a major modification to existing airframes, as changes could be limited to fitting a redeveloped centre-fuselage area. However, the fact remained that the aircraft as already designed looked like it was going to meet the existing operational requirement, and changing things would only delay its entry into service. The conclusion was obvious. Variable geometry was a distraction, and no further efforts were made to gain support for a variable-geometry TSR2.

As for the TFX, General Dynamics, unaware that it had come very close to being taken to court by BAC, welcomed a delegation from the British company in

Another study into applying VG to the TSR2 was carried out in January 1964, this time using the wing planform drawn up for the Vickers Type 583, a naval strike fighter project. Damien Burke

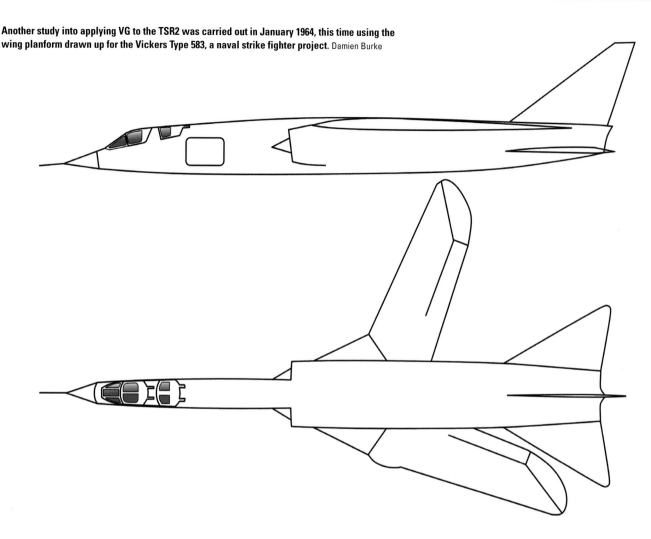

October 1964. The members had a good look at the aircraft and gleaned a lot of information about its development, and the decisions taken along the way, which was all of particular interest to BAC for future projects. The president of General Dynamics, Frank Davis, later claimed that the TFX's variable-sweep wing owed nothing to Wallis's work, and NASA published a working paper in 1966 entitled *Summary of NACA/NASA Variable-Sweep Research and Development leading to the F-111 (TFX)*, in which it was claimed that: 'Late in 1958 a research breakthrough at Langley provided the technology for designing a variable-sweep wing having satisfactory stability through a wide sweep angle range without the necessity for fore and aft translation of the wing', and that '... the variable-sweep concept [was] born at NACA/NASA (Langley) ...'. A thorough read of the paper reveals plenty of references to Vickers and the Swallow, but little hint that the Swallow was actually the research breakthrough on which all of NASA's work was based.

TSR2 in the strategic role

In May 1960 the Minister of Defence, Harold Watkinson, had expressed the opinion that 'we could give the TSR2 an increased strategic capacity by fitting it with some sort of missile'. Not only would this make the aircraft better value, but it could also interest the Americans. This kick-started a sequence of events that led to TSR2 moving away from its original purely tactical role to a wider-ranging role that would include the delivery of larger nuclear weapons at distances far removed from the original battlefield scenarios. The MoS (soon to become the Ministry of Aviation (MoA)) was tasked with advising what was possible. George Edwards at Vickers was asked for his opinion, and was, of course, keen to assist; adding a capability to keep the customer happy is not something you normally refuse. The MoA and the Air Ministry started off by outlining some possibilities to arm the aircraft with a strategic weapon.

Blue Steel was out: there was insufficient ground clearance to mount it underneath, and costly structural modifications would be needed to carry it on top of the aircraft. Performance and range would suffer badly. A pair of Skybolts could possibly be carried on top of the wings without so much aerodynamic penalty, but structural modifications and changes to the aircraft's fin would be needed, and costs would be substantial. There was also little point, as the combination would be inferior in most ways to the planned Vulcan and Skybolt combination, with low-level use of the missile leaving it unable to use its star tracker for navigation (because of likely cloud cover), and thus reducing its accuracy substantially. Development of a suitable ballistic missile to be carried in the TSR2's weapons bay, and capable of navigational autonomy over a long distance, would be a task approaching the size and cost of the TSR2 itself. A simpler propelled bomb with guidance system and 50 miles (80km) range when flown at Mach 2.5 at 200ft (60m) would be easier

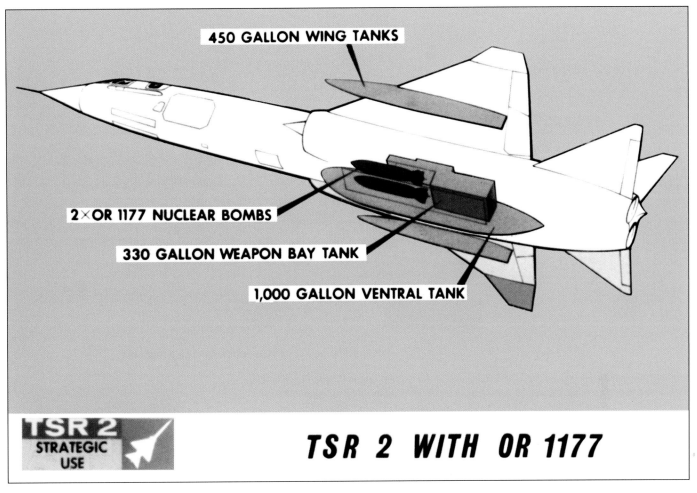

450 GALLON WING TANKS

2 × OR 1177 NUCLEAR BOMBS

330 GALLON WEAPON BAY TANK

1,000 GALLON VENTRAL TANK

TSR 2
STRATEGIC
USE

TSR 2 WITH OR 1177

The TSR2 already had some strategic capability with overload fuel and twin WE177 carriage, though vulnerability over strategic targets would have been an issue. BAE Systems via Brooklands Museum

but was still a technical challenge, and would cost somewhere between £60 million and £150 million.

In September 1960 BAC produced a report entitled *A Study of the Use of the TSR2 in the Overload Condition to Fulfil Other Roles*, covering the various possibilities as it saw them, and summed up all the suggestions it had been putting forward up to this point. The aircraft could be safely overloaded to a weight of 120,000lb (54,500kg), and this would enable a significant increase in armament and/or fuel load when it was operated from large airfields. A long-distance sortie was postulated, carrying a strategic nuclear weapon (a bomb fitted with the *Red Snow* warhead used in *Blue Steel* and, in modified form, slated for use in Skybolt) with high-level weapon delivery in which targets up to 1,800nm (2,070 miles; 3,330km) from base could be hit. If the 200nm (230 miles; 370km) entry into and exit from the immediate target area was at low level, the

combat radius would be reduced to 1,600nm (1,840 miles; 2,960km); still a respectable figure. This would require the carriage of underwing and ventral fuel tanks, all jettisoned before the attack.

English Electric was already developing a surface-to-surface nuclear missile for the Army, *Blue Water*, and the study found that this could be modified for TSR2 carriage, half-buried in the bomb bay (along with a bomb-bay fuel tank), and would have a range of 70 to 100 miles (110 to 160km), either low level all the way at Mach 1.5 or taking a more ballistic trajectory, in which case it could reach Mach 3 at 70,000ft (21,000m). An alternative was to create a new missile more suited to TSR2 carriage, using *Blue Water* components repackaged as appropriate. This would have larger wings and a pair of rocket motors side by side, giving improved lift/drag characteristics and longer range; up to 200nm (230 miles; 370km) from a low-level launch, with the

TSR2 itself able to take the missile up to 1,340nm (1,540 miles; 2,480km) from base before launch. Development, however, would probably require as much time and effort as the entire existing *Blue Water* programme.

The third missile suggestion from BAC was to carry a single-stage ballistic missile carrying a Polaris re-entry head. The largest possible such missile that could still fit in the TSR2 weapons bay would have a range of 350nm (400 miles; 640km), but this sort of distance risked unacceptable navigational inaccuracy, so it was suggested that a smaller missile with a range of 200nm would be more viable. This would weigh 5,500lb (2,500kg), have a diameter of 26in (66cm) and climb to a maximum altitude of 300,000ft (90,000m) before its trajectory took it back down towards the target. From a high-low-high sortie this could mean a total combat radius of 1,740nm (2,000 miles; 3,220km). However, if the TSR2

303

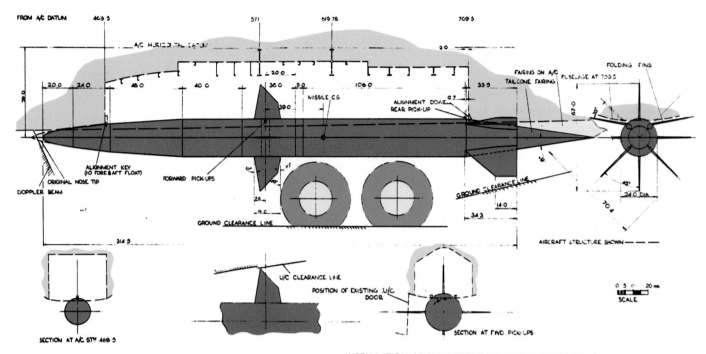

INSTALLATION OF BLUE WATER ON T.S.R. 2 AIRCRAFT

BAC's first suggestion for a more impressive strategic weapon for the TSR2 was to fit their own *Blue Water* nuclear missile to the aircraft; the missile, with minor changes, could just about be squeezed into a semi-conformal fit under the fuselage. BAE Systems via Brooklands Museum

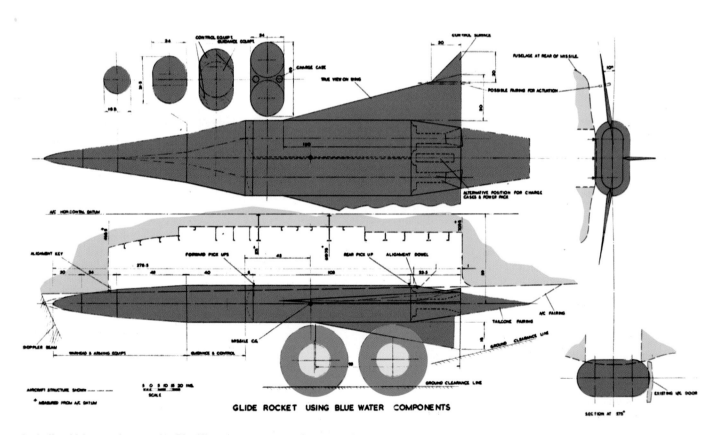

GLIDE ROCKET USING BLUE WATER COMPONENTS

A missile with improved range using *Blue Water* components was also proposed.

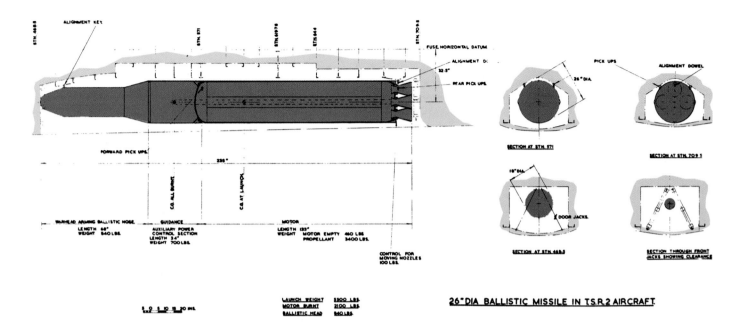

BAC's third suggestion was a dedicated ballistic missile, using a Polaris re-entry head and fitting entirely within the existing TSR2 weapons bay. BAE Systems via Brooklands Museum

stayed at altitude and launched the missile from there, the missile would gain an extra 100nm (115 miles; 185km) and the total combat radius would be a whopping 2,000nm (2,300 miles; 3,700km).

The final missile suggested was a high-speed cruise missile using a modified Bristol Aircraft BT3 ramjet engine, able to fly at Mach 2 at 200ft (60m) with onboard inertial navigation and terrain clearance. The length of any such design precluded weapons-bay or even semi-conformal carriage, but there was a possibility of under-wing carriage. However, the problems of the cost of development of such a weapon, and particularly its terrain-clearance system, 'should not be underestimated'.

BAC was unwilling to predict even basic costs or timescales, however, and the Ministry suspected it was looking at something in the region of £40 million for even the most basic of the proposals, rising to a development cost equal to the entire TSR2 project for a home-grown air-launched ballistic missile. The British Nuclear Deterrent Study Group looked at the proposals and was unimpressed. It considered every stand-off weapon suggested to be 'so unattractive on technical, financial and development time considerations that they were not worthy of further study'. The group believed that all quoted costs were too low, and all performance figures exaggerated. The planned Europe-based TSR2 strike

squadrons assigned to Supreme Allied Commander, Europe, would be capable of striking Soviet strategic targets with free-fall bombs anyway, given their long-range capability. The deterrent value was already there. To give a fuller deterrent capability the easiest thing to do would be to equip the aircraft with megaton-range weapons, delivered in a low-level lay-down attack with delayed detonation to enable the aircraft to escape. The real question was whether there was any point, when Skybolt was going to be a much more capable option, and the conclusion was that '... this course of action would not be justified so long as the Skybolt solution to the deterrent problem remained valid. On the other hand, if the Skybolt development project failed, the development of the TSR2 weapons system would represent a real insurance.'

Bolt from the blue

Everything changed in November 1962, when the Americans unilaterally cancelled the Skybolt programme, leaving Britain high and dry, with the future nuclear deterrent policy in tatters. No time was wasted by BAC in responding to this, and the company issued a series of brochures in early 1963, once more pushing the TSR2 in the strategic role. The first of these, entitled

TSR2 Strategic Weapons Systems, described the type's use in the strategic role with lay-down bombs and stand-off missiles, based on the earlier study of 1960. The aircraft was already able to carry four low-yield OR.1177 weapons, and for the strategic role this was reduced to two high-yield OR.1177s with additional fuel to extend the combat radius. With space freed in the bomb bay by the carriage of just two bombs, a 330gal (1,500L) bomb bay tank could be fitted, along with a pair of underwing drop tanks of 450gal (2,045L) each and a 1,000gal (4,545L) ventral tank. A scenario was postulated in which the aircraft could return to a base 300nm (345 miles; 555km) nearer to the target than the home base from which the strike was launched (after all, it was a fair bet that home base was ground zero for an enemy strike), which in combination with the additional fuel would give a combat radius of 1,860nm (2,140 miles; 3,440km), of which 200nm (230 miles; 370km) would be flown at low level at Mach 0.9. Sticking to low level for 1,000nm (1,500 miles; 2,400km) would reduce the combat radius to a still very respectable 1,600nm (1,840 miles; 2,960km) under the same conditions of landing somewhere other than the smoking hole in the ground from which the mission had begun. The underwing and ventral drop tanks would all have to be jettisoned immediately they were empty, or the extra drag would seriously reduce the combat

Illustration of a TSR2 firing the first of its twin *Blue Waters* from the 1963 TSR2 *Strategic Weapons Systems* brochure. BAE Systems via Brooklands Museum

radius. Even with the heaviest possible load of two OR.1177 high-yield bombs and 2,230gal (10,130L) of extra fuel, the take-off roll would still be around 1,350yd (1,235m) and required an LCN of just 44, so a large number of airfields would be suitable; over sixty within the eastern half of England, for instance. The combat radius offered would put targets such as Leningrad, Moscow, Kirov, Kazan and Volgograd (Stalingrad) within range of bases throughout England, Europe and Cyprus.

Even more attractive was the pairing of TSR2 with a stand-off missile, specifically the *Blue Water* missile which had been under development by English Electric as a ground-to-ground tactical nuclear missile for the Army until the programme was cancelled in August 1962. BAC was clearly keen to see that its work on this missile was not wasted, and suggested fitting it with a megaton-class warhead to give the TSR2

a valuable stand-off strategic capability. Unlike the 1960 proposal, this was for the carriage of two missiles, to be carried underwing on special pylons fitted at the mid-wing point and providing refrigerant to keep the missile's guidance electronics cool before release, though no underwing drop tanks could then be carried. The original Army design for *Blue Water* had included the need to fire the missile at a 50-degree angle. This would entail a loft manoeuvre for the aircraft before release, and to avoid this dangerous exposure to enemy defences BAC proposed to release the missile in level flight at 200ft (60m) instead. This would reduce its range slightly, by 4 miles (6km), but still afforded a stand-off distance of 90 miles (145km), more than sufficient to keep the aircraft out of the high-density defences around most strategic targets. While the bomb bay did not have to carry any bombs for a *Blue Water* mission, some room would

still be needed in there for an electronics pack. Even with this, however, the bomb bay fuel tank could be larger than for the OR.1177 mission, at 450gal (2,045L). Coupled with the 1,000gal (4,545L) ventral tank, this would give a combat radius of 1,580nm (1,820miles; 2,920km); not quite sufficient to hit Kirov, Kazan or Volgograd, but the aircraft would be much less vulnerable to being shot down. An alternative load, which retained the 1,860nm (2,140 miles; 3,440km) combat radius of the OR.1177 mission, was just one *Blue Water* in a semi-recessed ventral fit as per the 1960 study, retaining the normal under-wing 450gal (2,045L) drop tanks and a smaller bomb bay fuel tank of 350gal (1,590L). Another drawback was accuracy. *Blue Water* was expected to have a CEP of not more than 5,000ft (1,500m) at maximum range of both missile and aircraft. To put this in perspective, this would be like aiming the

TSR2 with *Blue Water*, in single and long-range double carriage fit. With *Blue Water* having been cancelled in 1962, there was never any serious chance of it being resurrected for TSR2 use. Damien Burke

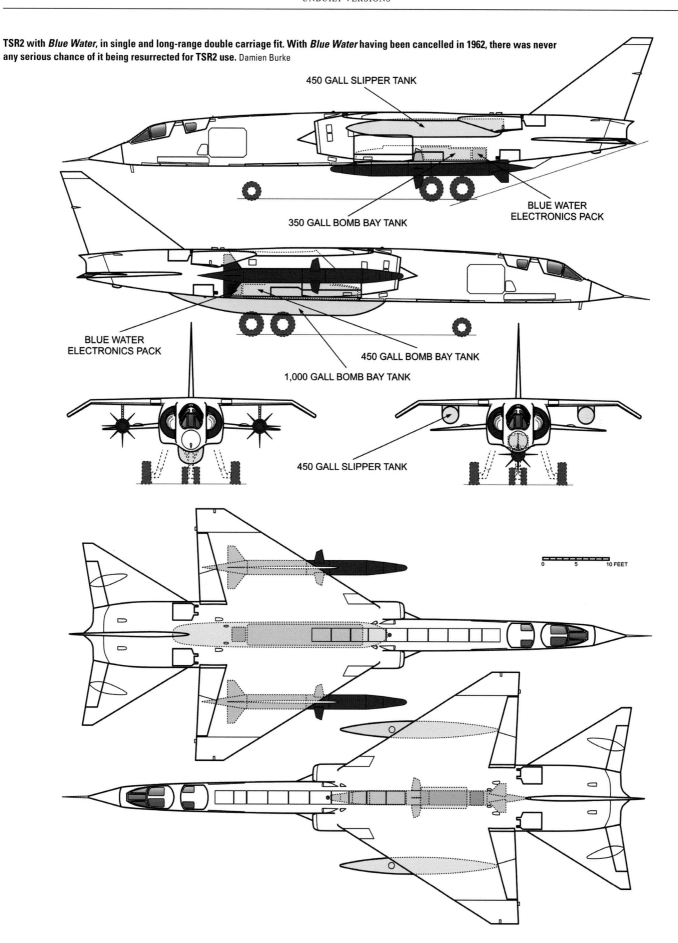

450 GALL SLIPPER TANK

BLUE WATER
ELECTRONICS PACK

350 GALL BOMB BAY TANK

BLUE WATER
ELECTRONICS PACK

450 GALL BOMB BAY TANK

1,000 GALL BOMB BAY TANK

450 GALL SLIPPER TANK

0   5   10 FEET

missile at 10 Downing Street and having it explode over Clapham Common. If that missile had a 1-megaton warhead, No. 10 could well have survived intact, which was not ideal, so *Blue Water* would have needed to have been 5 megatons or larger to guarantee sufficient destruction to include its intended target within the CEP.

At this time BAC was expecting the TSR2 to enter service in late 1965, and predicted that if it was given an immediate intention to proceed it could get the *Blue Water* fit into service by early 1967. This bold prediction was made possible only by the large amount of work that had already gone into *Blue Water* before its development was cancelled by the government. Total

development costs of £33.9 million were predicted by BAC, of which £16.6 million had already been spent. As *Blue Water* had been cancelled largely on grounds of cost, this was perhaps not the attractive bargain that BAC thought it was! The brochure ended with a few paragraphs on future developments, including mention of a ballistic missile to be carried by TSR2 with a 500nm (575-mile; 925km) stand-off range but similar accuracy to *Blue Water*, to be in service by 1970 and costing up to £40 million; and also also an 'air-supported missile controlled to fly a terrain-following course similar to that of TSR2', which presumably referred to the ramjet suggestion of 1960.

Grand Slam

BAC's final strategic brochure, entitled *TSR2 Strategic Weapon System with GRAND-SLAM*, described an alternative to the *Blue Water* fit. Grand Slam was named after the massive 22,000lb (10,000kg) HE 'earthquake bomb' used in the last two years of the Second World War. The Grand Slam missile was not quite so heavy, weighing a mere 7,500lb (3,400kg), of which only 600lb (270kg) comprised the warhead, but that warhead was 1.2 megatons, dwarfing its namesake. The brochure was coy about this megatonnage, mentioning no figures and only stating that the warhead was 'that which was to be used

TSR2 with the proposed Grand Slam missile, a sophisticated stand-off weapon complete with its own on-board suite of decoy rockets.
Damien Burke

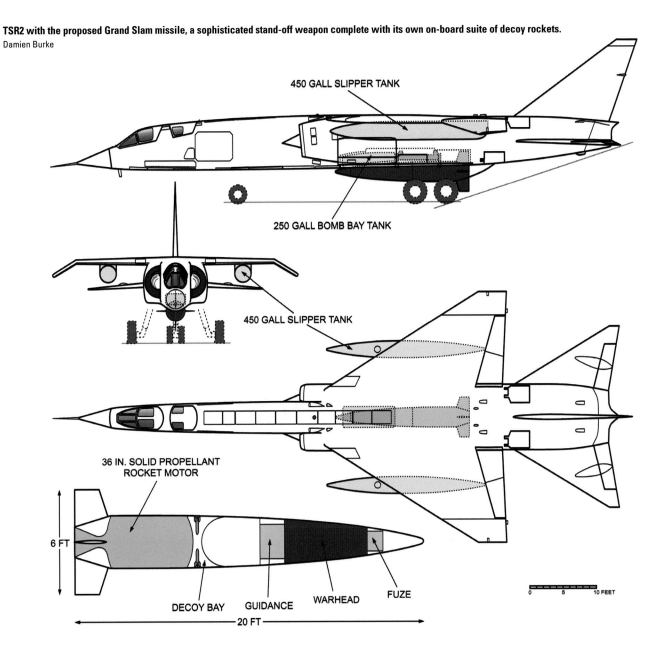

for Skybolt'. Grand Slam's major attraction compared with *Blue Water* was accuracy. Its CEP was predicted to be within 1nm (more than sufficient to reduce No. 10 to rubble even if the missile arrived on top of Buckingham Palace). Grand Slam's chances of arriving on the target without interference by anti-missile systems was also greatly enhanced by its ballistic flight profile and a comprehensive decoy fit. On release from the aircraft (at 40 degrees in a loft manoeuvre, but at 100nm (115 miles; 185km) from the target, hopefully not putting the aircraft at too great a risk) the missile's rocket motor would ignite three seconds later, powering it to a speed of 5,000ft/sec (1,500m/sec) and an altitude of 67,000ft (20,400m). The warhead stage would separate and continue onwards and upwards, firing radar-reflective decoys and reaching a maximum altitude of 170,000ft

(52,000m) (with decoys above and below), its speed reducing to Mach 2.7. On the ballistic path back to earth the speed would increase to Mach 3.5, and in less than 4min from release the warhead would explode over or on the target. The large number of decoys and the high speed of arrival would hopefully guarantee that the warhead arrived unmolested by any of the Soviet Union's anti-ballistic-missile systems.

Grand Slam's fitment on TSR2 was to be as a semi-recessed store, approximately 50 per cent buried within the bomb bay (with a 250gal (1,140L) fuel tank taking up much of the remainder of the bay). The missile's lower and side fins were detachable, and would be fitted to it once the missile itself had been loaded in the aircraft. Combat radius with bomb bay fuel, underwing drop tanks and the aforementioned 300nm shorter return trip would be 1,600nm

(1,840 miles; 2,960km), which let Kazan and Kirov off the hook, and meant Volgograd was only reachable from Cyprus. This could be increased to 1,740nm (2,000 miles, 3,220km) if a return was made to a base 600nm (690 miles; 1,110km) closer than home base – in which case, bad luck Volgograd!

Brochure 13 from BAC was entitled *TSR2 Strategic Weapon System – AIRBORNE ALERT*, and recognized that an essential part of any strategic deterrent was the second-strike capability; the ability to take revenge on the Soviet Union even if it had struck first and removed all of the TSR2 bases from the world map. The solution was the standing airborne alert, as famously practised by Strategic Air Command's Boeing B-52s and other bombers throughout the Cold War. Thus TSR2s in strategic fit would take off with maximum

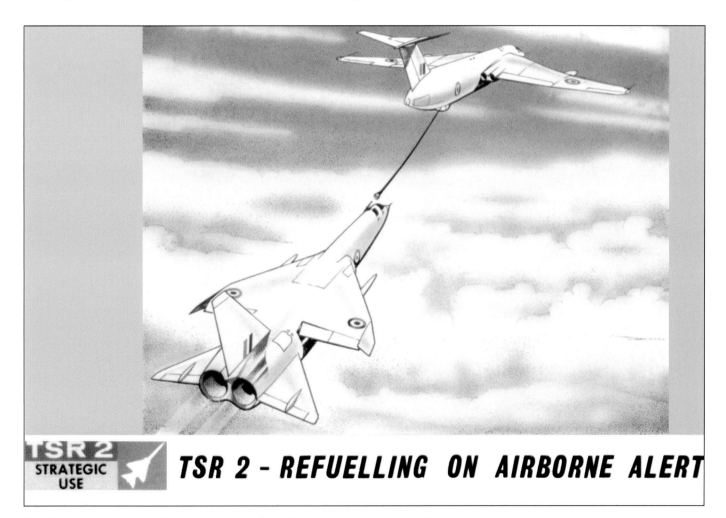

TSR 2 – REFUELLING ON AIRBORNE ALERT

The airborne alert study produced a simpler proposal involving the carriage of nuclear bombs in the weapons bay and the use of overload fuel tanks, topping up from Victor tankers whenever fuel state ran below a useful minimum. Up to ten TSR2s would be on constant airborne patrol. BAE Systems via Brooklands Museum

overload fuel and patrol over the North Sea until their fuel state was reduced to the minimum possible for a useful sortie, at which point they would refuel from Victor tankers to restore maximum fuel state. External ventral and underwing drop tanks would be retained throughout the patrol and only dropped if a live mission was begun while airborne. The length of an uneventful patrol would be limited by crew endurance, a figure of 8hr being suggested.

With full fuel on board the bomber, the Soviet Union would be the TSR2's oyster, with targets as far away as Kazan and Kirov reachable (assuming, once again, a return to somewhere other than 'RAF Radioactive Rubble'; Norway, for example). Range would be successively reduced through the patrol time until the minimum sortie level was reached, which basically boiled down to being able to hit Leningrad only. With a force of sixty TSR2s, ten would need to be airborne on patrol at all times, which would require the support of fourteen Victor tankers, of which two would need to be airborne throughout. Modifications to the airframe would be minimal. Some undercarriage strengthening and brake improvements were needed to deal with the much higher AUWs when using full overload fuel, and some space for crew rations. Optionally, a tape reader could be fitted so that the navigator could programme the Verdan computer with a preset target which would be picked from those within range

at any given fuel state (this was optional because it could be entered manually, given adequate time to do so).

One problem of the patrol idea was that if the ventral tank could not be carried (for example, if a ventrally mounted *Blue Water* or Grand Slam was carried), then more frequent refuelling would be necessary. BAC suggested the addition of a ventral tank that could completely enclose the missile while still holding 1,000gal (4,454L) of fuel. The brochure did not expand upon this, but clearly a much larger ventral tank fairing would have been necessary compared with the standard 1,000gal tank, and this would have introduced ground-clearance issues. Finally, the brochure mentioned that a standard TSR2 could also carry out the airborne alert mission, but would inevitably have reduced combat radius as, without the undercarriage modifications, it would be unable to take off safely with such a large fuel load (or land in an emergency if a large amount of fuel was still on board).

The big wing

The Aerodynamics Department at Weybridge had also been busy looking at more-extensive changes for an airborne-alert TSR2. The most obvious thing to look at was the wing, which, understandably, had been optimized entirely towards the aircraft's raison d'être, the tactical role. For

the strategic role that small and highly-loaded wing was a drawback. Increasing its size and aspect ratio could bring useful improvements to the combat radius owing to the greater room for internal fuel and higher lift, primarily of use in the economical cruise portion of the sortie. The low-level penetration portion of the sortie would suffer. Lower wing loading meant degraded gust response, and a serious reduction in crew comfort as a result.

Two new enlarged wings were considered, both retaining the existing wing's root dimensions. The span of wing 1 was increased from the basic 37.14ft (11.32m) to 44.36ft (13.52m) and its leading-edge sweep was reduced from 58.5 degrees to 53.5 degrees. Its total area was 840sq ft (78.03sq m) (compared with 703sq ft (65.3sq m) for the standard wing). On wing 2 the span was further increased to 51.80ft (15.78m), the sweep reduced to 48 degrees and the wing area increased to 980sq ft (91.04sq m). The tailplane in each case was left unchanged, as the less-concentrated downwash field from the larger wing meant that it retained its overall effectiveness, even though the tailplane size remained identical. This did have a drawback, in that the increased take-off weights meant that the tailplane's authority would be reduced, and the provision of nose gear leg-extension would almost certainly be necessary to keep the take-off roll within limits. Additionally, the tailplane's roll

The two enlarged wing planforms considered in January 1963 for a possible strategic version of the TSR2.
Damien Burke

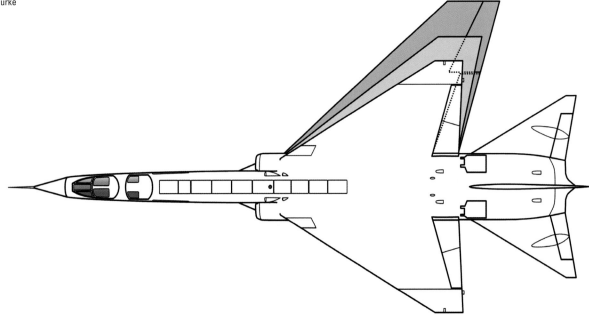

authority needed to be augmented by the fitting of conventional ailerons to the larger wing 2.

The NA.39's designers would no doubt have been delighted to hear the suggestion that penetration speed could be reduced to Mach 0.7 to deal with the issue of reduced crew comfort owing to these larger wings! In the end, though, the study on enlarging the wing of the aircraft to help with the airborne alert proposal was a dead end, BAC rightly judging that, once again, the cost/benefit case was only going to embarrass it once more, and the Airborne Alert brochure makes no mention of changing the TSR2's wing.

As the RAF's nuclear deterrent was in disarray with the loss of Skybolt, the idea of a strategic deterrent role for the TSR2 was of great interest to the Air Staff. They were continually fighting a battle against Treasury men aghast at the ever-increasing cost of TSR2, so the bonus of a strategic capability was not to be ignored. However, they could not justify any immediate expenditure on these expensive new strategic capabilities, so the V-force soldiered on for a few more years until the RN's new nuclear submarines entered service.

Trainer version

As detailed in Chapter 10, studies of a dual-control TSR2 variant began in 1960, but serious work only began in late 1964, resulting in a brochure entitled *Type 595 Pilot Trainer Aircraft* being issued in January 1965. The Type 595 retained the basic tandem seating arrangement of the normal TSR2. The rear (navigator's) cockpit would be replaced by an instructor's cockpit with full flying controls, and the existing separate cockpit canopies were to be replaced by a single clear-vision canopy. (Initial investigation had found that the standards of view through the normal canopies would be insufficient to enable the instructor to monitor the student pilot's flying safely.)

Three forms of aircraft were studied; a prototype trainer converted from one of the existing normal aircraft on the build line; aircraft built as trainers right from the outset and supplied to the RAF as pure trainers, and aircraft built and supplied for the strike role but capable of being converted into trainers by RAF personnel (and converted

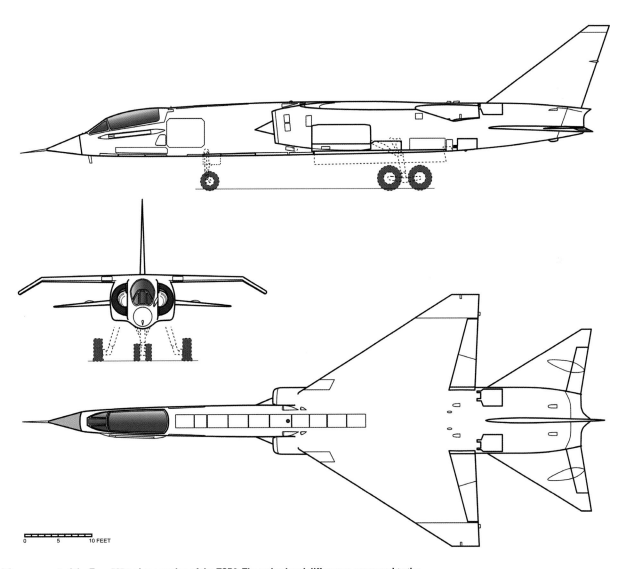

General Arrangement of the Type 595 trainer version of the TSR2. The only visual difference compared to the strike version was the one-piece canopy. Damien Burke

0   5   10 FEET

311

While visually the aircraft would change little, the packed nose section had to make room for extra flying controls, displacing some equipment and reducing the aircraft's strike capabilities accordingly. BAE Systems via Brooklands Museum

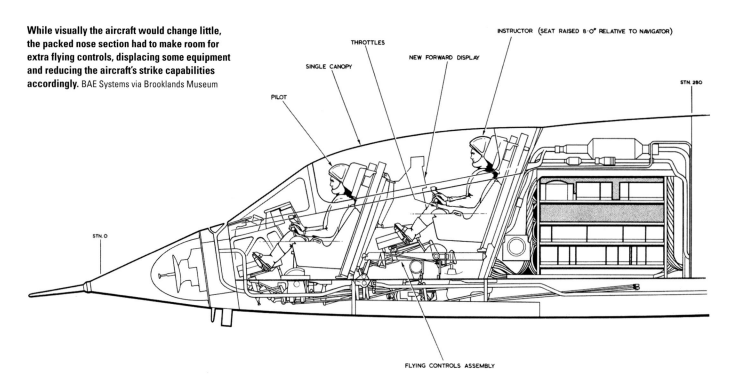

INSTRUCTOR (SEAT RAISED 8·0" RELATIVE TO NAVIGATOR)

THROTTLES

NEW FORWARD DISPLAY

SINGLE CANOPY

STN. 280

PILOT

STN. 0

FLYING CONTROLS ASSEMBLY

Construction and structural breakdown of the new forebody section for the trainer version. BAE Systems via Brooklands Museum

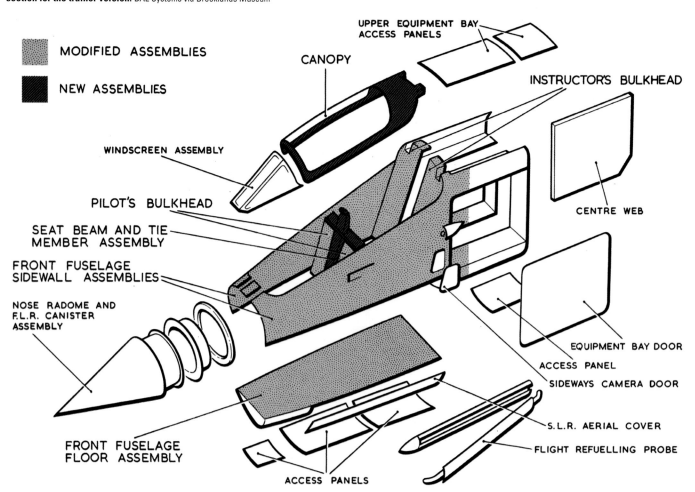

MODIFIED ASSEMBLIES

NEW ASSEMBLIES

UPPER EQUIPMENT BAY
ACCESS PANELS

CANOPY

INSTRUCTOR'S BULKHEAD

WINDSCREEN ASSEMBLY

PILOT'S BULKHEAD

SEAT BEAM AND TIE
MEMBER ASSEMBLY

FRONT FUSELAGE
SIDEWALL ASSEMBLIES

NOSE RADOME AND
F.L.R. CANISTER
ASSEMBLY

CENTRE WEB

EQUIPMENT BAY DOOR

ACCESS PANEL

SIDEWAYS CAMERA DOOR

S.L.R. AERIAL COVER

FLIGHT REFUELLING PROBE

FRONT FUSELAGE
FLOOR ASSEMBLY

ACCESS PANELS

back to the strike role as required). Conversion would have been most straightforward if the aircraft included a break joint just forward of the equipment bays, but the structure had not been designed with such a joint in mind, and considerable redesign would have been necessary. Accordingly, a plan was drawn up to limit the conversion to the areas that would actually be different on the trainer; the cockpits. Converting an existing development-batch strike aircraft to a trainer would be a lengthy job, entailing the removal of most of the rear cockpit contents, cutting off the structure between the two canopies, cutting into the floor to break into the existing flying-control looms, adding a joystick and all the various consoles and panels required in the instructor's cockpit, then repairing the cut area of the cockpit sill and introducing a new sill edge with locking mechanisms for the new canopy. The alternative, of producing aircraft that were built as trainers from an early stage in their construction, with associated interconnects and joints in areas such as the inter-canopy area, would create far less

wastage and save many months of additional work. The same parts could be used to build the third type of aircraft, strike airframes embodying the capability for conversion to trainers if circumstances dictated.

In terms of external appearance, the trainer would differ only in the area of the canopy. Windtunnel tests had shown that the new one-piece canopy had little effect on the aerodynamics other than minor flow separation at higher speeds, thus reducing the maximum attainable Mach number and slightly reducing fuel economy. The much larger area of canopy transparency would also introduce temperature limitations, further cutting down on the top speed, but this was an acceptable limitation. More significant was the loss of some items of equipment to make room for the added flying controls and rear pilots displays, etc. The most serious effect would have been on the FLR, as the items to be dropped included the groundspeed and drift indicators from the CCS, and the FLR scope normally found in the navigator's cockpit. Without these items the terrain-avoidance system

would be limited in usefulness, with a 500ft (150m) safe limit rather than 200ft (60m).

The loss of the navigator's role panel would remove the ability to aim and release weapons, though the airframe would remain capable of carrying them and they could all be jettisoned in an emergency as normal using the 'wing clearance' switch in the front cockpit. The role panel would normally supply the signals to the FLR and HUD to generate and display the aiming and release cues for conventional weapons, while the CCS provided nuclear-weapon aiming cues. The instructor would instead be given switches to simulate the pull-up signal and pilot's warning light operation, enabling the practice of release manoeuvres. The other major task of the navigator was operation of the SLR and dealing with fix points to keep the aircraft's position accurate. Without any of the navigator's panels all of this was redundant, and so a simpler navigation system using the Doppler, moving map and gyro-magnetic compass would be used instead, with a consequent loss in navigational accuracy.

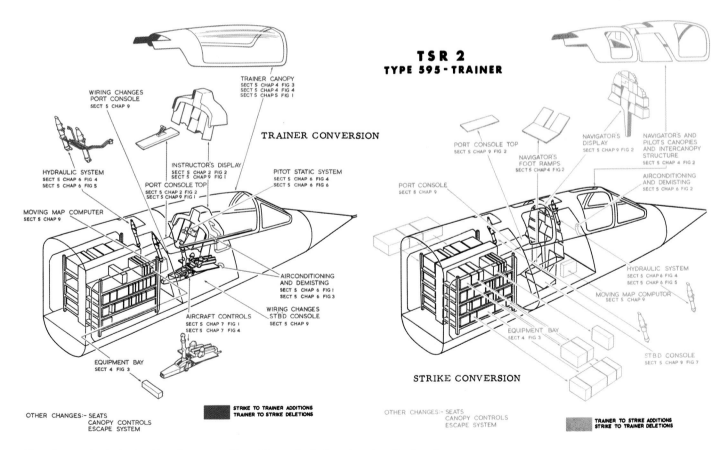

The trainer version had to be able to be converted to a strike version in time of need, and back again if need be. The design study brochure detailed the process and the various items of equipment that would be needed. BAE Systems via Brooklands Museum

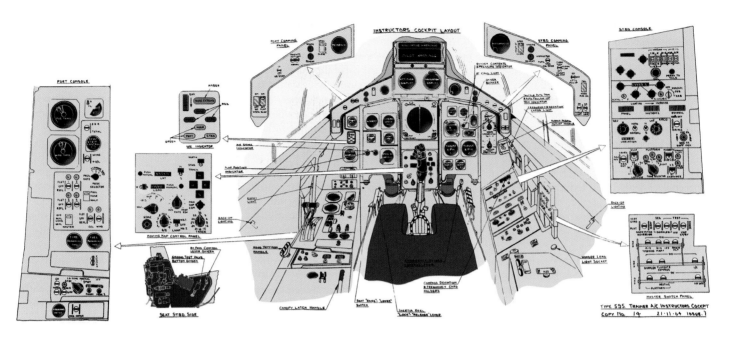

TSR2 trainer – instructor's cockpit layout. BAE Systems via Brooklands Museum

Trainer canopy separation trials with a wind tunnel model. BAE Systems via Brooklands Museum

For the anticipated length of training sorties this was again an acceptable degradation in overall performance.

The loss of weapon aiming and release capability in trainer configuration obviously made the ability to convert trainers back into strike aircraft not just useful, but practically essential if maximum value was to be had from the TSR2 fleet. Accordingly, BAC concentrated its efforts on making this conversion a straightforward task. The intention was that complete conversion kits would be built, consisting of various modules that would be pre-tested and ready for RAF personnel to use to carry out conversions as required. To facilitate rapid conversions, aircraft built as trainers (or built as strike aircraft with provision for trainer conversion) would have a large number of changes incorporated within the forebody section, such as a reinforced rear-canopy hinge, flying and engine control connections under the floor and within the side consoles, trainer canopy demisting tubes, and various minor structural changes for attaching the changed panels used in the trainer rear cockpit. All of these would be permanently fitted, with the aircraft in strike role carrying a small weight penalty of 40lb (18kg) as a result (in trainer fit, the aircraft would be 2,400lb (1,090kg) lighter than the strike version).

The entire conversion process from trainer to strike was predicted to take just under a week, and a couple of days longer for strike to trainer, assuming continuous 8hr shifts with up to twelve men working on each shift.

Cockpit arrangement

The front (pilot's) cockpit would be basically identical to that of a normal strike TSR2, but the rear (instructor pilot's) cockpit was almost entirely different from the navigator's cockpit. The existing port console, instrument panel and flooring would all be replaced. The floor, and thus the rear pilot's eye level, was raised 6in (15cm) compared with the normal navigator position, and the ejection seat would be identical to the pilot's, giving two inches of additional upward adjustment.

The existing front pilot's seat headrest was large, and would have blocked a significant amount of the instructor's forward view, so the intention was to reshape the headrest and reduce its width to improve the view for the rear pilot. Alternative headrests would be part of the conversion kit. The new forward instrument panel for the instructor was designed to mimic the front pilot's panel closely, as was the port console. The starboard console was left unchanged, with its controls slightly further from the pilot than would normally be the case owing to its lower position in relation to the new floor and seat height.

The new canopy was to be a one-piece, single-shell 'blown' canopy of ½inch-thick cross-linked acrylic (Oroglas 55), slightly bulged in comparison to the existing canopy lines, thus affording the instructor pilot more head movement and ejection seat height alteration than would otherwise be the case. No central joint or spine would be present, as there was no structural advantage in having one, though BAC did suggest it could be masked off to provide a better match of the strike aircraft's more restricted view if necessary. The rear hinge on both the new canopy and the airframe would be strengthened, but designed to match the existing rear-canopy hinge physically so that no change was necessary in this area during role conversion. An additional latching hook would be installed in the cockpit sill to give the additional locking required by the longer trainer canopy.

At its heart the escape system would be basically unchanged, though command ejection would now be available for the rear pilot. In the strike role the navigator could only eject himself, while if the pilot ejected it would trigger the navigator's seat to fire first. In trainer fit, either pilot ejecting would result in both going, the instructor's seat always firing first.

The contract for the design study had specified that six aircraft would be built as trainers initially, followed by a further two, then sixteen strike aircraft embodying the latent trainer capability. The company recommended that, at a suitable point, it would make economic sense to manufacture all strike aircraft with the latent capability, to keep a common production standard. By the end of February 1965, however, the Air Staff were busily scrabbling for cost savings on the TSR2 and the intended trainer buy was reduced from the total of twenty-four down to just eight. Then the requirement was set aside to await the final decision on whether to continue with the TSR2 at all, after some questioning of whether the trainer version was at all necessary, given the test pilots' high praise of the TSR2's handling qualities in the take-off, approach and landing configurations.

Fighter version

English Electric had originally proposed a fighter version of the P.17, the P.22 (as briefly mentioned in Chapter 2), but had been careful not to make too much fuss about it, as it went against the concept of the 1957 Defence White Paper. It had even given it the P.22 designation for security reasons; any inadvertent mention of the P.22 would not lead back to the P.17 and draw adverse comment upon that project. Later the company had come to realize that in the P.22 it had an aircraft that could compete against its own P.1, with far greater endurance and combat radius and even, supposedly, slightly better manoeuvrability. With the GOR.339 project under way and the Lightning in production for the RAF, the P.22 was quietly killed off lest it affect either project's chances. However, the basic concept was not forgotten.

A preliminary study entitled *Vickers/English Electric RB192D. Note on Performance in a Fighter Role* was then undertaken, investigating the possible use of the TSR2 as a fighter. This was undated, but was presumably carried out during 1959 or 1960. It described the use of the basic TSR2 in the interceptor role. With a Mach 2 attacker detected at 250nm (290 miles; 460km) range by ground radar, a TSR2 interceptor could be scrambled within three minutes and intercept the target using a head-on attack while it was still 70nm (80 miles; 130km) away. Alternatively, a combat air patrol at 100nm (115 miles; 185km) from base could be carried out for 3.5hr on internal fuel only with a 2,000lb (900kg) load of unspecified air-to-air missiles. With a sea level rate of climb of 65,000ft (20,000m) per minute, and an acceleration profile that would enable it to reach Mach 2 at 60,000ft (18,300m) within four minutes of take-off, it was certainly a realistic option to use the aircraft as an interceptor. No mention was made of a manoeuvring fight; given the type's high wing loading, it would not have made a very effective dogfighter.

The Tushino Air Display in Russia on 9 July 1961 led to a revival of the fighter idea. At this air show various large Russian bombers were seen carrying stand-off missiles. This was a rude shock to NATO, which hitherto had only had hints that the Soviets were developing such weapons. The supersonic *Blinder*, subsonic *Badger* and turboprop *Bear* bombers were all clearly capable of reaching the UK, and each could carry stand-off missiles, the most worrying

General Arrangement of the two proposed fighter variants of the TSR2. The original report illustrated a Firestreak missile, but captioned it as *Red Top*; the staggered weapons bay missile stowage illustrated here is a speculative interpretation based on the report's contents. Damien Burke

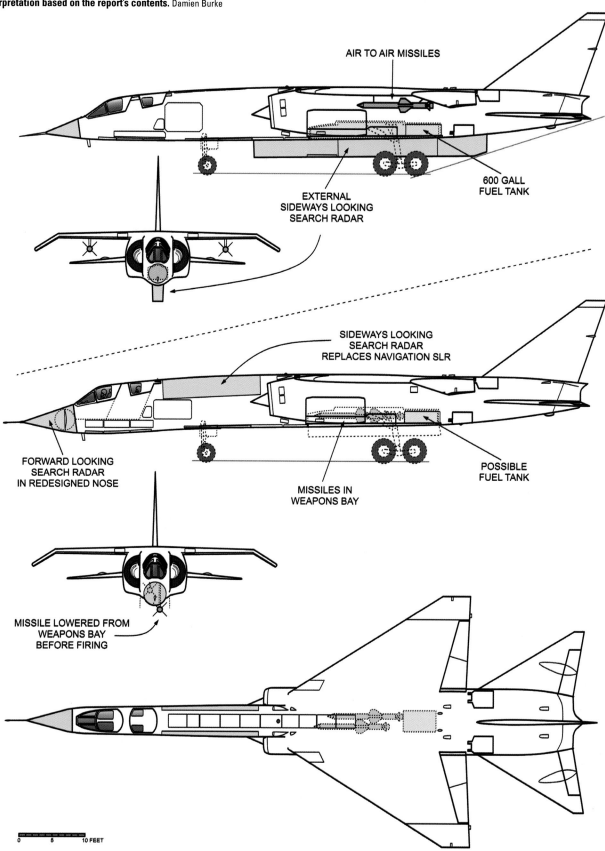

AIR TO AIR MISSILES

600 GALL
FUEL TANK

EXTERNAL
SIDEWAYS LOOKING
SEARCH RADAR

SIDEWAYS LOOKING
SEARCH RADAR
REPLACES NAVIGATION SLR

FORWARD LOOKING
SEARCH RADAR
IN REDESIGNED NOSE

MISSILES IN
WEAPONS BAY

POSSIBLE
FUEL TANK

MISSILE LOWERED FROM
WEAPONS BAY
BEFORE FIRING

0   5   10 FEET

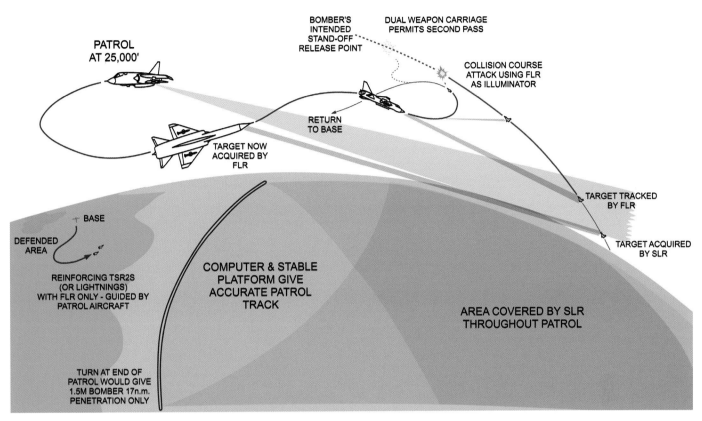

TSR2 fighter variant patrol and attack profile. The idea of an 'armed AWACS' had some attractiveness, but neither the RCAF nor the RAF saw a real need for an interceptor of this type. Damien Burke

of which was suspected of having a range of up to 600nm (690 miles; 1,110km) and a top speed of Mach 2. Lightnings would be hard-pressed to cope with the missile, and unable to deal with the bombers before they had fired their missiles and turned for home. Radar coverage over such large distances was unavailable, and airborne fighter-style radars might not have been powerful enough to pick up small missiles. English Electric believed that by far the cheapest and quickest solution to the new threat was a fighter version of the TSR.2, as it had the necessary range, volume and power for either interceptor or standing-patrol attacks. In January 1962 it produced a report on just such an aircraft.

The big difference between a standard TSR.2 and this fighter (or, rather, interceptor) version would be in the radar fit. Ferranti was proposing a promising new development combining a sideways-looking X-band aerial for search within a 250nm (290-mile; 460km) range and a forward-looking 36in (90cm)-diameter dish for target illumination. To fit all of this within the TSR.2 airframe required some changes. The larger SLR aerials would not fit in the space

for the existing navigation SLR, and even an extension in nose length would still require cheek bulges. Accordingly, the nose would be extended by 39in (99cm) and the new SLR aerials installed as a shoulder fit, high up on the fuselage between the rear cockpit and the intakes. The equipment bay would be reduced in size as a result, but the deletion of navigation SLR (Doppler being sufficient for fighter tasks) would compensate for this. Some loss in fuel volume would also take place, to the tune of about 2,500lb (1,135kg). The new FLR would require a larger radome, so the nose would be bulged downwards and outwards to permit this. Compared with the strike version, the fighter version would be around 1,250lb (570kg) heavier.

The weapons bay could carry a single missile of up to 36in (90cm) span, with a cradle to lower it into launching position, and possibly an additional fuel tank taking up any unused space. Patrols could be carried out up to 470nm (540 miles; 870km) from base (with 1.7hr endurance), enabling the fighter TSR.2 to deal with *Blinders* even before they reached their launch position. Alternatively, a patrol at 200nm (230 miles;

370km) from base would give an endurance of 2.7hr.

An alternative fit was also proposed, to avoid redesign of the nose. In this the new SLR would be installed in a large under-fuselage fairing. This would have a 6 per cent-thick aerofoil section and be 35ft (10.6m) long, with the weapons bay carrying a 600gal (2,725L) fuel tank. Missiles would need to be carried under the wings. Despite the drag of the SLR fairing and underwing missiles this version would also have slightly greater endurance because of its heavier fuel load; 2.8hr for the 200nm patrol and 1.8hr at 470nm.

As for weapons, the *Red Top* heat-seeking missile was the only available British type for dealing with high-performance targets, but with a range of less than 15nm (17 miles; 27km) it would be necessary to get uncomfortably close to the target. A radar-guided version had been studied, but nothing had so far resulted from this. BAC was also working on Sig.16, a ship-launched surface-to-air missile for the RN, which would have twice the range and radar guidance, though it would need some rearrangement to cope with supersonic carriage and launch. The

French Matra 530 was also suggested as a possible contender, though it had shorter range than *Red Top*. The normal load would be a pair of missiles underwing, assuming the external SLR fit, though up to four were possible with a reduction of around half an hour in patrol endurance.

A typical sortie would entail take-off and climb to an economical cruising height for transit to the patrol area. The patrol line would be an arc of a circle with radius of 200nm (230 miles; 370km), and would be about 70nm (80 miles; 130km) long. With the SLR having a range of 250nm (290 miles; 460km), this meant a single fighter could continuously monitor a front of 200nm and, even in the worst case of the fighter carrying out its turn at either end of the patrol line, no target could reach further than 30nm (35 miles; 55km) within the patrol area before being detected. On detection of a target the fighter would turn towards it on to an interception course, climb from the patrol height (22,000 to 28,000ft (6,700 to 8,500m), depending on fuel state) to 36,000ft (10,970m) and accelerate from patrol speed (Mach 0.9) to Mach 1.7. The climb would then continue to 50,000ft (15,200m) and the attack would begin when the target was within range of whatever missiles the fighter was carrying. Return to base would be subsonic at economical cruise settings.

The sales division of BAC was very nervous of putting forward this version. It could have had a deleterious effect on Lightning sales, and there were serious doubts that a new supersonic interceptor was politically acceptable, even though several years had passed since the 1957 Defence White Paper. This changed in February 1963, when the Canadians began to get interested in the TSR2, though it was not until July 1963 that serious work began on a preliminary brochure. This was not for domestic

consumption, but purely to be shown to the RCAF. More-effective missiles of US origin were now added to the mix, such as the Douglas MB-1 Genie, Hughes GAR-11 Nuclear Falcon, Raytheon Sparrow IIIb and Hughes GAR-9 Phoenix. A BAC delegation then visited Canada in August 1963 to discuss, primarily, the TSR2 strike aircraft, and in this discussion they learned that the RCAF still required a manned interceptor for the period 1970 to 1980, which could intercept both subsonic and supersonic targets, identify them visually from long range and even deal with high-performance supersonic types similar to Concorde. The TSR2 fighter version was mentioned, and the delegation was invited to return in October with a proposal, having been told that 'any guided missile available' should be suggested if it could meet RCAF needs.

The delegation returned to RCAF HQ in October 1963 to make a further presentation on both the strike and fighter versions of TSR2, though the sales division had already suggested that they had nothing better than an 'outside chance' of selling the TSR2 interceptor to the RCAF. Unfortunately for BAC the reception was even worse than expected, the presentation being received 'in polite – cordial – silence'. The RCAF was, it transpired, predicting a withdrawal from Europe-based NATO commitments in the near future, and saw no need whatsoever for the strike version. The fighter also provoked no obvious interest, which was surprising after the previous meeting, but perhaps not so surprising in the light of the 1959 cancellation of the Arrow.

Coincidentally, just after this, in December 1963, the RAF's OR department produced an internal paper on the subject of using TSR2 in both the interceptor and low-level, low-speed strike roles. (This was triggered by concerns that the USA's new

TFX aircraft was capable of performing more roles than the TSR2.) The OR department was obviously unaware of the details of BAC's fighter proposal, and looked at the subject anew. It correctly considered the existing FLR clearly inadequate as an AI radar, lacking power and therefore range, and having an extremely limited azimuth and elevation scan. Installation of one of the proposed AI radars for the P.1154 was suggested as a possibility, as they all had some multirole capability. The most suitable such radar, however, had a 27in (69cm) dish, compared with the 15in (38cm) dish of the TSR2's FLR, so (surprise, surprise) the nose would need to be redesigned. Both pilot and navigator would need extra displays; the pilot's radar display could possibly be via the HUD (quite how this was to be achieved was not mentioned), and the navigator's by a redesign of his existing radar plan position indicator. The navigator would also need a control stick for the AI radar. As for weapons, it appeared that the *Red Top* missile could be carried externally, though significant additional work would be needed to integrate it with the existing systems. The airframe configuration would handicap the aircraft at typical interception altitudes, as the TSR2 needed to be supersonic to stay in level flight above 38,000ft (11,600m), and at Mach 1.5 the best rate of turn would produce a 10nm (11-mile; 17km) turning circle. By the time the aircraft was at 50,000ft (15,000m) it would be struggling to remain airborne, let alone carry out an interception: 'such a beginning in the intercept role could hardly be acceptable'. It seems BAC was wise to avoid trying to get the RAF interested in a fighter version, though, ironically, the aircraft's lack of fighter capability would be used against it in some comparisons with the TFX in early 1965.

General Operational Requirement 339

The following is the text of the general operational requirement to which each firm submitted a design. Various modifications were made to it at one time or another, but this is the first issue, as issued in March 1957.

SECRET

AIR STAFF GENERAL OPERATIONAL REQUIREMENT NO. GOR.339

TACTICAL STRIKE/RECONNAISSANCE AIRCRAFT

INTRODUCTION

1. The advent of the hydrogen bomb has enormously strengthened the power of the deterrent and the likelihood of global war has decreased. It is now recognised that, provided the deterrent is maintained, the main threat to our freedom and security will come from an intensification of the cold war and an increasing danger of limited wars. Thus, our defence forces must be adequately equipped and prepared not only for global war but also for the outbreak of limited wars, in which the possible use of nuclear weapons cannot be excluded. Weapons systems in the tactical field must therefore have the best possible limited war capability as well as meeting such global war requirements as are called for by our commitments to SACEUR.

2. In a nuclear land/air battle, the ability of tactical air forces to provide timely nuclear counter bombardment and reconnaissance becomes a decisive factor in the conduct of operations. Conventional air support is also essential if the small forces at our disposal are to be capable of dealing with outbreaks of limited war, in which HE weapons only are used.

3. The vulnerability to nuclear attacks of large fixed targets in the tactical area is well appreciated and every effort will be made to achieve dispersal. Thus, the tactical strike/reconnaissance task is likely to demand a primary ability to seek out and destroy a large number of targets whose positions are not accurately known.

4. A ballistic missile offers advantages of easy dispersal and relative invulnerability but it has no capacity for attacking unknown position targets, has no reconnaissance capabilities, is unsuitable for meeting cold war requirements and is a most uneconomical means of delivering HE should this be required. The Air Staff believe that the tactical strike/reconnaissance requirements can more adequately be met by a manned aircraft weapon system.

5. The need is for a self-contained all-weather bombing system with adequate range to permit effective operations from our limited number of overseas bases or, in global war, from outside the highly vulnerable tactical area. Ideally complete independence of airfields is desirable. However, if runways must be used, the need is to keep take-off and landing requirements to the minimum to facilitate operations from existing airfields which may have been damaged, or from dispersed strips.

6. The Canberras must continue to provide our tactical strike and reconnaissance force far some time to come. It is difficult to say for how long they can be regarded as an effective tactical force but, operated strictly at low level, they may continue at best to 1965 in terms of limited war, or 1963 in global war. Thus, there is an urgent need to define an Operational Requirement for a tactical strike/reconnaissance aircraft for use in conducting the tactical offensive.

ROLES

7. The roles of the aircraft, in order of priority are:-
   (a) Delivering effectively the tactical nuclear weapon from low altitudes up to the maximum ranges obtainable and with a minimum consideration for prevailing weather conditions, by day and by night.
   (b) Meeting the tactical requirements for day medium and low-level and night low-level photographic reconnaissance.
   (c) All-weather electronic reconnaissance within the limits set by the necessity that this requirement is not to compromise performance in the primary role.
   (d) Delivering effectively by day and by night tactical nuclear weapons from medium altitudes under visual conditions or, regardless of visibility using blind bombing techniques.
   (e) Delivering effectively under visual conditions HE bomb or rocket loads as an alternative to the tactical nuclear weapon.

GENERAL DESIGN CONSIDERATIONS

8. In order to minimise the effect of enemy defences, the greatest possible portion of the flight to and from the target will be made at a mean height of 1,000 feet, or less, above the ground. This is accepted as implying an average cruising altitude of 1500ft above sea level. No defensive armament is required.

9. To increase the flexibility of the system an alternative medium-altitude capability is highly desirable. It is appreciated that requirements for low-altitude operation, long range and assisted take-off on the one hand and good medium altitude performance on the other are not readily compatible. Low-altitude capability is to be considered of primary importance and the aim must be to provide the best possible medium-altitude performance that does not compromise requirements for the low-level role.

10. Close attention is required to minimise permanent base requirements, and it is also necessary to cater for operations from dispersed sites. The increasing importance of dispersal emphasises the need to reduce the required runway dimensions to the minimum. The Air Staff wish any worthwhile, though possibly unconventional, means of improving take-off and landing performances to be thoroughly examined. If runways are used operation is to be practical from strips 3,000ft in length. A LCN not exceeding 40 is desired.

11. The aircraft is to be suitable far worldwide operation.

PERFORMANCE

Radius of Action

12. Without resort to in-flight refuelling the aircraft must be capable of attacking targets at a radius of 1,000 nautical miles from base with at least the final 200 nautical miles to and the 200 nautical miles from the target being flown at low level. A ferry range of 2,000 nautical miles is required. These figures are to be extended appropriately when in-flight refuelling is used.

Speed

13. The continuous operating speed throughout the aircraft's route through enemy early warning and defence cover is to be as high as possible. This penetration speed is to be not less than M = 0.95 at sea level. Additionally a supersonic dash capability at sea level is desirable and the Air Staff wish to be advised on the penalties incurred. It may be assumed that for half the radius of action the use of more economical cruising settings will be acceptable.

Handling

14. The aircraft must be capable of releasing a bomb in a loft manoeuvre at low level or in a dive toss attack from medium level.

15. The loft manoeuvre is an attack in which the aircraft approaches the target in level flight and commences a loop. The bomb may be released between 45° and 110° to the horizontal and the aircraft continues to loop with a roll out to escape.

16. In a dive toss attack, the aircraft approaches the target in a dive and releases the bomb whilst decreasing the angle of dive. The aircraft completes the attack by a loop and roll out to escape.

OPERATIONAL EQUIPMENT

Armament

17. The aircraft is to be capable of carrying the bomb specified in OR.1127. As an alternative secondary role, it is desirable that the aircraft should carry a normal load of 4 × 1000lb bombs and a minimum of 6 × 1000lb in an overload case.

18. The aircraft is to be capable of carrying either of the following alternative rocket loads:-
    (a) A minimum of 74 two-inch rockets.
    (b) A minimum of 12 OR.1099 rockets

Navigation

19. A self-contained navigation system is to be incorporated to provide a clear display showing actual or DR position continuously in a form that will enable the navigator to adhere closely to track and on the correct heading right up to the moment of bomb release. The system is to permit the aircraft to be flown along the chosen route to an accuracy of 1 nautical mile when operating at low altitude and 2 nautical miles when operating at medium latitude. In addition positive position fixes must be possible when using ground aids to navigation.

Bombing

20. When using the bomb to OR.1127 a bombing accuracy of 1,200ft CEP is required. The Air Staff are prepared to accept that, at low altitudes, this accuracy will be achieved only under visual conditions at any radius of action and under blind conditions up to a radius of action of about 200 nautical miles from ground radio stations. However, future developments of nuclear weapons may permit same relaxation of the required bombing accuracy. An all weather bombing capability at any radius of action is most desirable and the Air Staff wish to know the accuracy which could be expected from an adaptation of the self contained navigation system for blind bombing.

21. A HE bombing accuracy of 600ft CEP is required. Visual bomb aiming may be effected by means of either a pilot attack sight or a standard navigator operated sight. It is accepted that effective blind HE bombing will be achieved only within the ranges at which the ground based radio aid gives adequate accuracy.

Photographic Reconnaissance

22. Photographic reconnaissance is required at low and medium altitudes. The Air Staff are prepared to accept that the full photographic reconnaissance capability may be possible only as an alternative role. Nevertheless, for reasons of flexibility it should be possible easily to convert between the strike and reconnaissance roles.

23. Low altitude. The following photographic capability is required:-
    (a) Vertical photography, by day, in poor light and at night from 500ft to 5,000 feet. Lateral angular coverage to be not less than 60° and film for forward coverage at 500ft must be sufficient for at least 80 nautical miles. The scale of photography should be not less than 1:10,000.
    (b) Oblique photography by day from 200ft to 5,000 feet. Both forward facing and lateral oblique cameras are required; the camera field of view is to extend from the horizon to a 30° depression angle.

24. Medium Altitude. Vertical photography by day is required from 5,000ft to 36,000 feet. The overall lateral angular coverage of this camera system is to be not less than 30° sufficient film for forward coverage, at 36,000 feet, of at least 200 nautical miles must be carried. A scale of 1:18,000 at the maximum height is required, but if it can be shown that there are significant advantages in accepting smaller-scale photography at maximum altitude, the Air Staff are prepared to consider granting concessions.

25. General. The ground position of each photograph is to be recorded, and the record must be available for first phase interpretation. Automatic control of image movement compensation is required. Automatic control of exposure is desirable and should be provided for poor light conditions.

Radar Reconnaissance

26. An all-weather radar reconnaissance capability is desirable. Full advantage is to be taken of the possibilities of adopting the self contained navigation system to meet this requirement.

Line Scan Reconnaissance

27. The timely receipt of reconnaissance information can be of decisive importance. Line scan techniques are being developed to permit in-flight transmission of reconnaissance information and it is desirable that this equipment be fitted in the aircraft.

Flight Control System

28. An automatic control sub-system consisting of auto flight control and instrument displays is to be provided which will allow the aircraft to be flown as easily as possible throughout all operational flight conditions. The sub-system is to respond to signals, set in manually by the pilot, or received from the navigation, bombing or automatic landing system. Signals from the bombing system may include a demand for a programmed loop and roll out manoeuvre. Emphasis must be placed on reliability and safety.

Radio and Radar Sub-systems

29. The following radio and radar sub-systems are required in addition to the components of the integrated flight control system:-
    (a) Two-way pilot operated communication up to extreme range at all altitudes, with facilities for automatic transmission of position data.
    (b) Intercommunication.

(c) Attack warning system.
(d) Flight refuelling positioning system.
(e) IFF Mark 10.

CREW STATIONS

Crew Composition

30. The crew will consist of a pilot and a navigator.

Crew Comfort

31. The greatest attention is to be paid to crew comfort. It will be necessary to provide some form of gust alleviation if tolerable crew comfort is to be maintained during long periods of high speed, low altitude flight. The Air Staff wish to be advised on the type of protection possible.

32. It must be possible far the crew to carry cut all their duties without moving from their seats.

View

33. The crew must have good clear view at all times. There must be:-
(a) Adequate forward and downward view:-
(i) For the pilot to avoid obstacles and identify landmarks.
(ii) For the navigator to map read.
(b) Adequate side view for pilot and navigator to gather and co-relate information to ensure accurate track holding.
(c) A downwards view for one of the crew members, approximately equal to the area being covered by the vertical cameras.
(d) Means to enable a crew member to inspect the wings and control surfaces, to see whether condensation trials are being formed and to search the rear hemisphere for attack warning purposes.

Heating and Ventilation

34. It will be essential to provide an adequate air supply for cooling and heating. Aircrew are to be protected against heat and cold at low level in the event of failure of cabin conditioning. The Air Staff would like to make the advisory recommendations contained in AP.970, Part 2, Leaflet 105/1 mandatory for this aircraft and wish to be advised if this is not acceptable.

Pilot's Station

35. During high-speed low flying, it will be necessary for the pilot to give the greater part of his attention to obstacle clearance. Cockpit design, therefore, must ensure that instruments – in particular those required for low-level flight and combing manoeuvres – are suitably placed.
36. The best possible view is required during take-off and landing. If there is any doubt about the efficiency of the means of ensuring clear vision at all tines, direct vision is to be provided for emergency use in approach and landing.

Navigator's Station

37. Physical access between the pilot's and navigator's stations is desirable.

DE-ICING AND DEMISTING

Engine and Airframe

36. Engine and intake de-icing is essential for protracted periods of flight at low altitude. Airframe de-icing is highly desirable but the penalties of incorporating it may be unacceptably severe. The Air Staff wish to be advised on this.

FUEL SYSTEM

General

39. It is essential that the fuel system should be simple and, as far as possible, automatic in operation. The need for the pilot to distract his attention for the purpose of fuel management must be kept to a minimum.

40. The aircraft is to be designed for the use of AVTAG fuel. However, if the use of AVTUR shows considerable performance advantages it may be assumed that this fuel will be used for certain operational missions.

Flight Refuelling

41. Provision is to be made for flight refuelling at a rate of not less than 300gal per minute. It must be possible to refuel all tanks this way. It may be assumed that a modified 'V'-class bomber aircraft will act as the tanker. However, the Air Staff would like advice on the implications of the 'Buddy' system of flight refuelling. In the interests of weight saving, it is desirable that flight refuelling should be carried out through the same system as ground refuelling.

Fuel Jettisoning

42. In order to permit the pilot to reduce the aircraft's weight in emergency or so as to return to base should a mission have to be abandoned soon after take-off, a system of fuel jettison with a high flow rate is highly desirable. A study of the problem is to be made and the Air Staff informed of the penalties involved.

SAFETY AND SURVIVAL

Oxygen

43. The demand oxygen system is required. Sufficient oxygen is to be provided for the full endurance of the aircraft when operated at maximum altitude. Provision is to be made for increasing the oxygen capacity so as to allow for the use of in-flight refuelling. The system is to be based on the use of liquid oxygen for crew breathing.

Aircrew Protection

44. Means must be provided to prevent contamination of the cabin and camera compartment by radio active material or BW and CW agents, when the aircraft is on the ground ready for flight and at all altitudes. In addition, integrating or rate meters may be needed and safe positions for this equipment should be considered.

Ejection Seats

45. Two fully automatic ejection seats are required. It must be possible to use these at all heights from ground level to the maximum attainable. It is desirable that escape should be possible also at all speeds. The Air Staff wish to be advised on the possibilities of meeting this latter requirement. It is essential that action to fire the seat should also clear the ejection path.

Canopy Jettisoning and/or Escape Hatches

46. Apart from any arrangements that may be made under paragraph 45, it must be possible to jettison the canopy and/or escape hatches by simple hand operated mechanical controls to enable the crew to leave the aircraft quickly in the event of ditching or crash landing.

Armour Protection

47. The aircraft is to be designed with a view to reducing vulnerability. Wherever possible structure or equipment is to be placed so as to provide protection for the crew and important components of the aircraft. The possibility of providing some armour below and behind the crew positions is to be examined and the penalties involved made known to the Air Staff.

TARGET DATE

48. The Air Staff require this aircraft in Service in 1964 or as soon thereafter as possible.

Air Ministry, (D.O.R (A))
March 1957.

Operational Requirement 343

The following is the text of the operational requirement that TSR2 was built to satisfy. It is based on the first issue of the OR, as covered by BAC's original development contract. Compared with GOR.339, the major differences were that top speed was increased from Mach 1.7 to 2.0; low-level flight decreased to 200ft (60m) from 500ft (150m); and runway requirements were made stricter, with take-off distances halved and surface quality reduced. Several modifications were made to this requirement through the project's life span; first of all in issue 2 in May 1961, which introduced several changes, followed by five amendment lists (AL1 to AL5 from August 1961 to June 1963), each of which made small changes. All of these changes are noted in italic.

SECRET

Air Staff Requirement No. O.R.343

TACTICAL STRIKE/RECONNAISSANCE AIRCRAFT

INTRODUCTION

By 1965 a new aircraft will be required by the Royal Air Force for tactical strike and reconnaissance operations using nuclear and conventional weapons. Such an aircraft will enable the Royal Air Force to continue to provide tactical support for the Army, to make an effective contribution to the strength of SACEUR's shield forces, and our other Regional Pacts.

It is the Air Staff's primary intention to exploit to the full a combination of high speed with low altitude and thus gain all possible advantage from the difficulties which an enemy will face in producing an effective defence in these conditions, The aircraft's operational flexibility will, however, be greatly enhanced by a Mach 2 capability at medium altitude.

Importance is attached to the provision of a system which will permit effective delivery of nuclear or HE weapons from low altitude in poor visibility and at night. An alternative delivery capability from medium altitudes is also required.

Of equal importance is the provision of a comprehensive system for all-weather reconnaissance, thus giving the aircraft a major alternative role.

The flexibility of role and tactics outlined above is dependent upon a comparable ground flexibility. This can only be realised by an ability to use small airfields with rudimentary surfaces and restricted maintenance facilities.

To advance a study into the possibilities of combining likely developments in aircraft and equipment design in time to meet the required In Service date of 1965, the Air Staff issued a General Operational Requirement, GOR.339, to the MoS in March 1957. This stated in broad terms the outline of this Operational Requirement. The following Operational Requirement is based upon analysis by the Air Staff and MoS of the studies of GOR.339 made by the Aircraft Industry and the Research Establishments.

The dependence of the aircraft upon its equipment to enable it to exploit fully all weather conditions, and to deliver accurately its weapons, necessitates a Weapon System approach to the problem. By this approach all aspects of the aircraft, its weapons and associated equipment are to be designed and developed concurrently, and mutually, so that the final product is a complete and integrated air weapon. Without compatible ground equipment the capabilities of the aircraft weapon system will be nullified, and adequate attention must be paid to this aspect of the requirement.

REQUIREMENT

The Air Staff require a Tactical Strike and Reconnaissance Weapon System to the requirements which follow.

ROLES OF THE AIRCRAFT

The aircraft is to undertake the following roles:-

To obtain reconnaissance information for all tactical purposes, including target mapping at low altitudes, under all-weather conditions by day and by night using radar and/or photographic methods.

To deliver effectively tactical nuclear weapons from low altitudes at the maximum ranges obtainable, and with minimum consideration for the prevailing weather conditions, by day and by night.

To deliver effectively high explosive weapons as an alternative to the tactical nuclear weapon.

To increase the flexibility of the weapon system an alternative medium-altitude strike and reconnaissance capability is required.

GENERAL DESIGN REQUIREMENTS

The Air Staff require the aircraft design to incorporate two engines.

No defensive armament is required. In order to minimise the effect of enemy defences, primary emphasis will be given to penetration to, and escape from, the target at low altitude. The design is to provide the best possible gust response characteristics, consistent with the airfield performance specified, in order to ensure the maximum operating efficiency of the crew. Low-altitude operations may be carried out down to 200ft or less above ground level. Under blind conditions periodic ascents to 1,000ft to increase the radar fix acquisition will be acceptable if the navigation system so demands. Such ascents will not be made within 50nm of the target except as necessary during weapon delivery.

It is accepted that strike and high-grade reconnaissance will not be combined in a single sortie. However, as every opportunity must be taken at all times to obtain reconnaissance information, the aircraft will be required to carry out the maximum photographic and/or radar reconnaissance without prejudice to the strike role.

The servicing time needed for changing roles should be as short as possible and must be less than 6 hours under airfield servicing conditions. The turn round time between sorties when used in the same role is to be as short as possible.

The aircraft and its ground equipment is to be weatherproof and remain serviceable with only the minimum of routine attention for 30 days in the open. The aircraft is to be weatherproof in flight and is to be suitable for operations in any part of the world.

PERFORMANCE

Speed

Penetration to target at sea level is to be used at a speed of not less than 0.9M with an ability to make a short burst at supersonic speed provided that this can be done without affecting the design of the weapon system. An ability to attain 2.0M at the tropopause is required.

Radius of Action

Without resort to in-flight refuelling or overload fuel tanks the aircraft is to be capable of attacking targets at a radius of action of at least 1,000nm

A ferry range of at least 2,500nm in still air without overload fuel or inflight refuelling is required.

Sortie Profiles

A typical 1,000nm radius sortie profile is to comprise:

Take-off and climb economically to cruise altitude.

Cruise economically to a point approximately 650nm from base.

Accelerate to and cruise at a speed exceeding 1.7M for 100nm.

Descend at maximum speed to low altitude.

Fly 200nm at a height of 200ft or less above ground level at a speed not less than 0.9M.

Deliver a 2,000lb weapon.

Return to 200nm from the target at low altitude at a speed not less than 0.9M.

Climb to cruising altitude and return to overhead base at economic speed.

Descend to base to arrive with fuel reserves to permit 8 minutes loiter at 1,000ft above ground level plus 5% of the total internal fuel.

For a shorter tactical sortie of not less than 450nm radius of action typical flight profiles might comprise either:-

A high/low approach to the target including 100nm supersonic cruise at altitude and 200nm at low altitude at a speed not less than 0.9M.
[Issue 2: 'supersonic' replaced by not less than 1.7M]

or

A low-altitude flight all the way to and from the target at a speed not less than 0.9M. The Air Staff would like to be informed of any penalty involved in this.

The fuel load is to enable either flight profile to be accomplished with fuel reserves to permit 8 minutes loiter at 1,000ft above ground level plus 5% of the starting fuel.
[Issue 2: ceiling of continuous operation at 56,000ft added]

Runway Performance

It is the intention normally to operate the aircraft from airfields having paved runways about 2,000yd in length, when safety margins are required. However, under the threat of an attack it will be necessary to disperse to semi-prepared airstrips, or existing airfields, whose length may be less than 1,500yd and which may have surfaces which have deteriorated or are rudimentary. When such dispersed, or emergency, operations are undertaken some abatement of the margins of safety during takeoff and landing may be accepted.

To enable the maximum number of inferior airfields to be used the aircraft must require the shortest practicable ground roll. Take-off and landing procedures which will exploit to the fullest extent the capabilities of the aircraft may be adopted.

The aircraft is to be capable of operating from the widest variety of airfield surfaces which may be undulating or uneven. The lowest possible runway classification number (LCN) is required and LCN, as near to 20 as possible should be aimed at. Tyre pressures should be such that the risk of rutting the airfield surface is minimised.

It must be appreciated that it may, on occasions, be necessary to make a landing as soon as possible after take-off and the undercarriage design must permit the greatest possible landing weight.

Operations under Normal Conditions

Take-off. In conditions of still air, or in a steady crosswind of 35kt at right angles to the runway, in a temperature of ISA +30°C at sea level, the aircraft is to be capable of taking off with a ground roll of less than 1,300yd. The take-off weight is to enable the 1,000nm radius sortie to be accomplished.

Landing. In conditions similar to those in para. 25 above the aircraft is to be capable of being stopped on a wet runway with a ground roll less than 1,300yd. The landing weight is to include 2,000lb in the weapon bay plus 10% of the total internal fuel.

Operations Under Emergency or Dispersed Conditions

Take-off. The aircraft is to be capable of taking-off in a temperature of ISA +30°C at sea level with a ground roll of less than 1,000yd for the 1,000nm radius sortie, or less than 600yd ground roll for the 450nm radius sortie in ISA conditions.

Landing. The aircraft is to be capable of being stopped in a ground roll of less than 600yd on a wet surface in ISA conditions at sea level. The landing weight is to include 2,000lb in the weapon bay plus 10% of the starting fuel.

Aids to Take-off and Landing

Rocket Assisted Take-off Gear is not required. The landing performance specified is to be met without the use of ground aids such as arrester wires. A tail braking parachute may be used if necessary. It is to be expected that at some airfields safety barriers may be available.
[Issue 2 – safety barrier sentence deleted]

NAVIGATION, ARMAMENT, RECONNAISSANCE AND FLIGHT CONTROL SYSTEMS

General Requirements

The weapon system will be effective only if it is easy to operate. The best possible aircraft handling qualities are to be realised particularly below 10,000 feet.

The navigation and flight instrument displays are to be readily and simply interpreted so that accurate height, ground speed and track can be maintained at all times.

The complete weapon system is to be so designed that it gives the enemy little or no help in detecting the approach of the aircraft, and is to have the greatest possible immunity to enemy countermeasures.

Terrain Clearance and Forward Radar
[Issue 2: terrain clearance replaced by terrain following]

Terrain clearance equipment is to be provided since this will greatly enhance the flexibility of the aircraft, reduce vulnerability by permitting flight at lower altitude, and add to operating safety. The Air Staff appreciate that the problems are complex, therefore the desired performance may not be available by the introduction date of the aircraft. The design must enable the aircraft automatically to maintain a selected height down to 200ft above the ground under all-weather conditions. Additionally, the design must permit this target to be met without major modification to the airframe should an interim equipment be found necessary when the aircraft is first introduced into Service.

A display is required which indicates the nature of the commands being transmitted by the terrain clearance equipment to the Automatic Flight Control System (AFCS) and which provides director information to the pilot.

The forward radar necessary to provide terrain clearance is to include a radar ranging mode which is to be displayed to enable rocket attacks to be launched. It is highly desirable that the forward radar provides a means of direct sighting for bombing discrete targets from medium altitude. It is accepted that the forward radar will provide indication of only one mode at a time.

The forward radar must be capable of providing homing facilities to assist in the approach and landing phase. This information may be provided in conjunction with a transponder beacon on the ground similar to that required for air to air homing for flight refuelling. See paragraph 70.

Navigation System

The navigation system is to be based primarily on precise dead reckoning corrected at intervals by selected visual and/or predicted radar fixes. The accuracy of the DR equipment is to be such that the interval between radar fixes may be 100nm, and between visual fixes 50nm The system is to permit a reasonable choice of predictable radar fixes and is to work at all heights of which the aircraft is capable.
[Issue 2: visual fix interval increased to 100nm]

The navigation system is to operate without manual adjustment between latitudes 75°N and 75°S. The accuracy of the system is not to be seriously degraded over periods of up to 2 minutes during violent aircraft manoeuvres, or during a climb or a descent. At low altitude it is to permit the aircraft to be flown along a chosen route to an accuracy of 1nm.

The navigation system is to provide, when required, a permanent record of such radar information as can be of use for reconnaissance purposes, when the special reconnaissance equipment is not fitted or not working.

Armament

The Air Staff require the aircraft to carry internally the weapons referred to below and to release them from any altitude or at any speed of which it is capable. Degradation of the specified accuracies is acceptable in extreme conditions. Additionally, the design should permit the carriage, when necessary, of weapons externally, in which case the Air Staff will accept limitations imposed by the weapons themselves.

A means of attacking a target with any weapon without the aircraft climbing above its minimum approach height is desirable.

Tactical Nuclear Weapons

Provision is to be made for the internal carriage of the tactical nuclear weapon specified in OR.1127. This weapon will be employed both at low and medium altitudes in LABS and dive-toss attacks. The following accuracies are required both with the aircraft flying at 200ft and 0.9M and at 25,000ft and 1.7M.

Visual conditions 600ft. 50% CEP.

Blind (when a suitable radar fix exists within 30nm of the target) 1,200ft. 50% CEP.
[Issue 2: external carriage of two similar weapons added; AL1: internal carriage of two tactical nuclear weapons rather than one.]

1,000lb HE Bombs

Provision is to be made for the internal carriage of four or more 1,000lb HE bombs. These bombs will be employed both at low and medium altitudes in dive and dive-toss attacks. The following accuracies are required.

Visual conditions in dive attack. 100ft. 50% CEP.

Visual conditions in dive-toss attack. 200ft. 50% CEP.
[Issue 2: increased specifically to six 1,000lb bombs, and internal carriage of not less than six 25lb practice bombs added]

Rockets

Provision is to be made for the internal carriage of
24 × 3" Rockets with 60lb or alternative 24lb warheads.

or

74 × 2" Rockets.
[Issue 2: deleted, and replaced by external carriage of four 37 × 2in rocket pods.]

These rockets will be employed in shallow dive attacks in which the speed of
the aircraft will be limited by kinematics of the attack and the performance
of the weapons.

Air-to-Surface Guided Weapons

Provision is to be made for the internal carriage of two or more air-to-surface
guided weapons to Air Staff Requirement No. OR.1173, with HE warheads.
These weapons will be employed in visual attacks from low altitude. The aircraft is to provide a launching platform which will enable the ASGW to
attain its accuracy capability. The Air Staff attach the greatest importance to
accurate delivery of HE, and an accuracy of the order of 20ft 50% CEP at
20,000ft slant range when the aircraft is flying at 0.9M is required.
[Issue 2: deleted and replaced by external carriage of four similar weapons.]

Reconnaissance Systems

An all-weather reconnaissance capability using photographic and electronic equipment is required. This equipment is to provide reconnaissance for
tactical purposes and target area mapping.

Target area mapping by electronic means is required to give ground co-ordinates
for a subsequent blind attack with the accuracies quoted in paragraph 42 (b).

Photographic Reconnaissance. Photographic Reconnaissance is required at
low and medium altitudes as follows:-

By Day.

Low level Oblique Cameras. Forward facing and lateral oblique cameras of
the F.95 type are required in the basic aircraft for both strike and reconnaissance roles.
[Issue 2: forward facing camera realigned to vertical.]

Vertical Cameras. Vertical photography is required from 5,000ft up to the
ceiling of the aircraft. In order that this requirement may be based upon existing cameras or modification to existing cameras, the Air Staff accept the possibility of having alternative camera fits based upon knowledge before take-
off of the likely operating height band. Forward coverage is to be at least
150nm in all cases, and lateral coverage of 10,000ft is required from altitudes
of 20,000ft or above. Photography must be fully interpretable when taken
from any altitude up to at least 35,000ft but the Air Staff are prepared to
accept a scale of less than 1:10,000 from heights above 20,000ft provided that
the reduction in scale is compensated by improvements in resolution.

By Night. Vertical photography at heights between 500 and 1,200ft is
required. (But see also paragraph 53.)

General. Automatic control of exposure is desirable, particularly for low-
level cameras. Camera magazines must be easily and rapidly removed after a

sortie and must be capable of fitment in, and be removable from, cameras in
situ. Means must be provided to protect camera installations including radar
equipment using photographic materials against nuclear radiation when the
aircraft is on the ground ready for flight, and at all altitudes.

Line Scan Reconnaissance. Line scan reconnaissance is required capable of
acquiring by day or by night, from any altitude between 200 and 1,000 feet,
video signals which, when related to a receiving and display system on the
ground will produce a picture of sufficient clarity to disclose the presence of
a single vehicle of 3-ton truck dimensions. When flying at 1,000ft the picture coverage of the ground beneath the aircraft is to be continuous along
track, and include at least ½nm on either side of track. At heights between.
200 and 1,000 feet, the widest possible picture coverage is required within
the definition limits specified.

Direct transmission between the aircraft and a ground station of the line scan
signals, with the aircraft's DR position at 4nm intervals is required. Air Staff
Requirement No. OR.2153 specifies the ground station which will be used
in conjunction with the airborne equipment. The use of an airborne relay
located over friendly territory will be acceptable if this is necessary to achieve
the required range of at least 110nm. This communication system is to be as
free as possible from interception and interference.

The airborne transmitter, together with recording equipment capable of stor-
ing line scan signals acquired over at least 50nm of track, is to be developed
as an integral part of the line scan installation. The equipment must be capable of transmitting a picture irrespective of aircraft heading, and adjustment
of directional aerials (if such are required) is to be automatic. Adjustment of
the main equipment is also to be fully automatic and the visual head is to
operate over the widest practicable range of photographic conditions without resort to manual adjustment in the air.

Providing the performance of line scan at night is adequate, the Air Staff are
prepared to accept this as fulfilling the night PR requirement.

Radar Reconnaissance. The Army's requirement for tactical radar reconnaissance calls for the best possible resolution and is to incorporate Moving Target Indication (MTI). An all-weather capability from medium altitude (but
without MTI) is also required. A facility for instantaneous or delayed transmission of radar reconnaissance information to a ground station is highly
desirable, and a method of integrating this with the similar line scan requirement should be attempted.

Data Recording. Automatic recording of data essential for all phases of
reconnaissance interpretation is required. DR position at least is to be readily available for first phase interpretation of film or radar reconnaissance
records.

Automatic Flight Control Facilities

An automatic flight control system (AFCS) is required, which at the discretion of the pilot will provide either automatic control of the aircraft or flight
director instructions, or both, during the following manoeuvres.

Approach and landing using an instrument landing system and suitable radio
altimeter. All selections to be made by the pilot.

Maintenance of track and mean true altitude over the ground as selected by
the navigator. The pilot is to have overriding control of aircraft height. (See
paragraph (f) and (g) below.)

Bombing – selections to be made by the pilot or navigator according to the bombing system being used.

Turn on to and hold any heading selected by the pilot or navigator. It is desirable that the pilot or navigator should be able to preselect this manoeuvre at least 20 seconds before initiating it.

Turn left or right, regardless of the heading selected on the pilot's or navigator's display, at a rate determined by the deflection of the pilot's control.

Maintenance of any barometric or true height and/or Mach number as selected by the pilot.

Descend or climb at any rate of change of true height selected by the pilot. It is highly desirable that the aircraft should level out automatically at any height pre-selected by the pilot, and that director steering instructions should be provided to assist him when manually levelling out at a predetermined height.

Maintenance of flight conditions for maximum range.

The AFCS is required to operate at the lowest practicable altitude. The pilot is to have overriding authority under all circumstances. Attention should be given to means of preventing the inadvertent operation of one mode of the weapon system when any other mode is selected.

Pilot's Display

To enable the pilot to fly the aircraft manually, and to monitor its progress during automatic flight, he must be provided with a situation display of the following information in a form that is easily appreciated. This must include, on the main instrument display, an indication in flight director form, of the nature of the commands being transmitted to the controls by the autopilot.

Aerodynamic data comprising attitude, heading, speed and height. This may be displayed by a presentation based on the Instrument System OR.946.

Manoeuvring data in the form of flight director signals both on the instruments in sub-para, (a) above, and also on a collimated windscreen display which must include an artificial horizon. The director signals are to cover the following range of manoeuvres :-

Take-off.

Maintenance of track and altitude during cruise.

Climb and descent to preselected heights.

Attack.

Approach and landing.
[Issue 2: 'windscreen' replaced by 'head up' and approach and landing part deleted.]

Director and information display fed from the terrain clearance system to enable the pilot to take the best tactical path in pitch to avoid high ground or to monitor the AFCS performing the same task.
[Issue 2: changed to enabling pilot to follow ground contours.]

Standby instruments are required to meet the safety requirements in para. 61 below.

A navigation display based on the concept of OR.946 (including Instrument Landing mode), plus a topographic display giving progress along track, or base position, in addition to aircraft heading. This display should be fed from any of the navigation aids at will.
[Issue 2: topographic display replaced by moving map display.]

For rocket firing the pilot is to have suitable sighting and aiming data provided by the forward radar and flight director in the head up windscreen display.
[Issue 2: para 59 deleted, covered under HUD.]

Navigator's Display

The navigator is to be given a clear display showing continuously the aircraft's position accurately in a form that will enable him to follow closely a pre-planned track, and maintain the correct heading right up to the moment of weapon release. The display must, however, enable the navigator to regain track after unplanned departures therefrom. When D.R. position is displayed it must be possible to correct it quickly and accurately from visual or other fixes.

The still-air range remaining, under the following preselected conditions is to be displayed :-

Assuming the present conditions of flight are maintained.

Assuming that optimum range conditions of flight will be adopted as quickly as possible.
[Issue 2: replaced by flight time remaining display assuming economic cruise.]

Safety Measures

The AFCS must not accelerate the aircraft so as to incapacitate the crew, stall the aircraft or exceed its load factor.

After any single failure within the main electrical generating system the aircraft must be capable of completing its mission without loss of the use of sub-systems. After any two failures in the main electrical generating system, or after any single failure within the navigation, armament, reconnaissance or flight control subsystems, sufficient power and services must be available for the crew to be able to complete the sortie. To do this they must have the following minimum facilities :-

Sufficient control of the aircraft to allow for return from the most distant point on any sortie.

DR information to enable the aircraft to arrive sufficiently near to base to obtain air traffic control assistance by R/T. Where the nature of the failure so demands DR information should be available from an air data system with manually-set wind.

An adequate display of :-

Heading - this should be at least a stand-by directional gyro with magnetic monitoring.

Attitude.

Speed.

Height.

[Issue 2: added para – In the terrain following mode, no single failure is to endanger the aircraft. If after one failure has occurred, the terrain following facility is still being employed, no second failure is to endanger the aircraft.]

No single failure in the bomb release system must cause inadvertent release of the weapon(s), neither should a failure prevent the weapon(s) from being jettisoned if necessary.

OPERATIONAL EQUIPMENT

Counter Measure Equipment

The aircraft will carry such electronic countermeasures as may be dictated by the nature of the opposing weapon systems in the theatre concerned. These counter measures cannot be precisely specified until the feasibility of future developments has been assessed, but at least a passive warning receiver system is required, providing visual and aural warning of attack from any direction, and capable of automatic triggering of any of the countermeasures listed below. This equipment is to weigh not more than 50lb. nor exceed 1 cubic foot in volume. It is to be fitted permanently in the airframe.

Other countermeasures will be developed as part of the ECM programme and will be the subject of ORs of more general application. The extent to which they are required will depend upon the operational environment. One, or a combination of the following is to be allowed for in the design of the aircraft :-

Between 6 and 12 rocket propelled radar and infra-red decoys, which may be about 44 inches in length, 3 inches in diameter and weigh approximately 30lb each and would fly forwards and upwards from the aircraft.

24 cartridges of explosively launched very rapidly blooming Window.

One of a series of noise jammers, or a deception jammer, designed to confuse specific radar systems. Their aerial system will require, as far as possible, a view all round the aircraft and may comprise several interchangeable units.
[Issue 2: changed (b) to 'a method of launching window'.]
[AL1: deleted all of (c) noise/deception jammers.]

In order to permit the carriage of these countermeasures adequate provision of weight, space, power and cooling is to be made, which should not be less than 350lb, 8 cubic feet and 5KW. This power demand need not be covered by reserve aircraft generating capacity, and in the event of a power failure it is accepted that the countermeasures will be switched off. Carriage in the weapon-bay with the least limitation of the weapon load is acceptable. If carried in an external pod some loss of performance will be accepted. In either case the installation is to be self-contained.

Communication Equipment

The following communication equipment is required :-

Two-way voice communication with the ground up to the maximum radius of action of the aircraft at all altitudes. The equipment is to have not less than 24 channels and is to be controllable by either crew member. The necessary ground equipment is to be developed concurrently to Air Staff Requirement No. OR.2109.
[Issue 2: need for control by either crew member deleted.]

Multi-channel UHF derived from the equipment developed to Air Staff Requirement No. OR.3502. An audible channel annunciator is required.
[Issue 2: added new sub-para covering standby UHF operated from aircraft emergency electrical supply.]

Intercommunication equipment operating independently of (a) and (b) above.
[AL2: added VHF.]

Identification Equipment

Provision is to be made for the installation of IFF Mark 12.
[Issue 2: replaced by IFF Mk 10.]

Flight Refuelling Positioning Equipment

A system is required which will allow the aircraft to home on to a tanker from at least 100nm down to a minimum which will enable contact to be established in conditions of ½nm visibility. The Air Staff consider that full advantage should be taken of the possibility of adapting the forward radar to provide this facility. The 'Buddy' tanker fit is to incorporate a suitable transponder beacon.
[AL4: buddy tanker fit deleted.]

CREW STATIONS

Crew Composition

The crew will consist of a pilot and a navigator.

Crew Stations - General

The crew are to be provided as far as possible with an environment which will enable effective accomplishment of their duties during high speed low altitude flight. The maximum degree of comfort is essential and it must be possible to carry out all duties without moving from the seats.

The crew must have good view at all times. There is to be :-

For the pilot a real downward view of 18°. Limited deterioration of view in any forward direction must not reduce the real downward view below a critical value of 11°. (The real downward view is the view forward and downward measured from the horizontal over the nose with the aircraft in its approach configuration, at instrument approach speed on a 3° glide path).

Adequate sideways and forward view for the pilot and navigator to gather and correlate information to ensure accurate track holding.

A downward view for one of the crew members approximately equal to the area being covered by the vertical cameras.
[Issue 2: sub-para (c) replaced by: In the reconnaissance role the forward and downward view for the navigator is to be sufficient for tracking and operation of the vertical cameras.]

Heating and Ventilation

It is essential to provide an adequate air supply for cooling and heating. The crew are to be protected against heat and cold at low altitude in the event of failure of the cabin conditioning. It is essential that adequate means are provided to ensure proper ventilation and cooling of the crew space while the aircraft is on the ground with engines stopped, and when taxying.

The mean cabin air temperature is to be automatically controlled throughout flight between reasonable limits of any value selected by the crew between +15°C and +35°C. The aim should be to achieve limits of the order of ± 2°C. Under the conditions chosen by the crew, the temperature at the hottest and coldest points of the crew station should be as constant as possible and ideally should not differ by more than 5°C.

Pressurisation

A cabin pressurisation system is required. The system is to have a single differential pressure only of 5lb per square inch.

The rate of change of pressure should be kept to the minimum during descent. If possible this rate should not exceed 1lb. per square inch per minute for normal descent. For tactical descents it is acceptable to fly at low altitude with negative differential pressure in order to obtain a reasonably low rate of change of pressure.

ANTI-ICING/MISTING

Windscreen and Transparencies

Good view is essential at all times with no optical distortion where sighting of armament is involved. Means are to be provided, to be effective throughout the full sortie, to prevent the windscreen or transparencies, including camera windows, from icing or misting up, or becoming obscured by precipitation or insects. The rain removal system should be capable of clearing an area sufficient to give an adequate view for approach and landing in heavy rain, and to see straight ahead in cruising flight in moderate rain. The system is to be effective against dust, dirt and insects during taxying and take-off. A blast air/aerodynamic system is required.

Engine

An ice warning detector is required. Adequate engine and intake anti-icing is required for half the duration of the aircraft.

FUEL SYSTEM

General

It is essential that the fuel system should be simple and, so far as possible, automatic in operation. The pilot must not be distracted by having to pay attention to fuel management.

The aircraft is to operate with AVTAG, AVTUR or AVCAT fuel without the need for engine adjustments. The aircraft performance is to be based on the use of AVTAG. The Air Staff wish to be informed of the penalties in performance or design imposed by AVTAG.
[Issue 2: performance to be based on AVTUR.]

Refuelling

Provision is to be made for flight refuelling at a rate of not less than 300gal/minute. It is to be possible to refuel all tanks in this way. It is desirable that flight refuelling should be carried out through the same system as ground refuelling. Ground refuelling is normally to be by a pressure fuelling system but the alternative of open line refuelling is required.
[Issue 2: open line refuelling deleted.]

It is to be possible to flight refuel from a 'V' Class tanker aircraft. Additionally a 'Buddy' type refuelling capability is required. The system must be designed to permit easy conversion of the basic aircraft to the tanker role and vice versa. Conversion under squadron servicing conditions is not to exceed 6 hours. The off loading capability of the 'Buddy' tanker, compatible with its own requirements, is to be not less than 300gal per minute.
[AL4: buddy refuelling deleted.]

Fuel Monitoring System

A fuel flow-meter is required, and space provision is to be made for the installation of a combined range, endurance and fuel remaining computer. Air Staff Requirement No. OR.998 defines this system.
[Issue 2: replaced by: Manually operated controls which override the automatic system are to be provided to permit corrective action to be taken. An accurate indication, at all times, showing usable fuel remaining is required.]

Fuel Jettison System

In order to permit the pilot to reduce the aircraft's weight in an emergency, or should a mission have to be abandoned, a system of fuel jettisoning with a high flow rate is required. It is to be impossible to jettison more than 80% of the total internal capacity. Switching off is to be automatic or at the discretion of the pilot. If it is possible to carry out an emergency landing at the maximum take-off weight less 1000lbs. of fuel, and without any external stores, then fuel jettison is not required. Under these conditions it may be assumed that when landing on the runway stipulated in para. 28 above, a safety barrier will be available.

SAFETY AND SURVIVAL

Oxygen

A demand oxygen system using liquid oxygen is required. Sufficient oxygen is to be provided for the full endurance of the aircraft when operated at the worst altitude for oxygen consumption, and allowing for the use of one in-flight refuelling. If sufficient advantages accrue it will be acceptable for the entire oxygen system for each crew member to be incorporated in the ejection seat.

Ejection Seats

Two fully automatic ejection seats are required. It must be possible to use the seats at all heights from ground level to 50,000ft and at speeds up to 750kt EAS or Mach 2. Single-action release is to clear the ejection path and fire the seat. The achievement of escape at the higher speeds should not prejudice escape at the lower speeds.
[Issue 2: increased to 56,000ft.]

Canopy Jettisoning and/or Escape Hatches

Apart from any arrangements that may be made under para. 87 it is to be possible to jettison the canopy and/or escape hatches by a simple hand operated control to enable the crew to leave the aircraft quickly in the event of ditching or crash landing.

Protection Against Bird Strikes

The windscreen is to be capable of withstanding the impact of a 3lb. bird when the aircraft is flying at 750kts EAS. As far as practicable, consideration should also be given to protecting the air intakes and engines against damage due to bird strikes.

Access

Suitable access is to be provided which will enable the crew to enter and leave the aircraft without assistance or special ground equipment.

Aircrew Flying Clothing

Since the aircraft is to be designed primarily for operation at low altitude, with only a medium-altitude capability as an alternative, it is intended that the crew shall wear the least possible special clothing. However, adequate protection from the effects of ejection at high indicated airspeeds must be provided by the clothing if it is not provided by the design of the seat.

It is intended that the crew shall wear :-

Air ventilated suit.

Lightweight overalls.

Anti-G trousers.

Protective helmet.

P-type mask or a suitable development thereof.
[Issue 2: added new sub-para (f) covering a partial pressure jerkin for use above 50,000ft only.]

A combined connector (OR.928) is to be provided at each crew station.

OTHER FEATURES

Night Flying Equipment

Full night flying equipment is required. Cockpit lighting is to be based on the use of integrally lit instruments, plastic plate illumination for consoles, and red floods for standby systems. Landing lights, taxy lamps and flashing 3-intensity navigation and collision warning lights are required.
[Issue 2: flashing 3-intensity navigation and collision warning lights changed to standard steady navigation lights and flashing anti-collision warning lights.]

Blackout

It is to be possible to blackout the navigator's station so as to prevent light from entering the pilot's station or showing externally, and to exclude atomic flash from the navigator's compartment. Suitable atomic flash screens controllable by the pilot are to be available at the pilot's station.

Sunblinds

Adjustable sunblinds are to be fitted to the cockpit transparencies.

Anti-Dazzle Lighting

Anti-dazzle white lighting is required.

Protection Against Effects of Nuclear Weapons

The airframe is to be designed so as to withstand to the maximum extent practicable the effects of thermal flash and shock pressures. The airframe should be capable of withstanding a thermal flux of 100 calories per square centimetre. The Air Staff wish to be advised of the penalties of meeting this figure.

Radar Echoing Area

The radar echoing area of the aircraft is to be kept to a minimum, especially in the head on aspect. Features with bad echoing characteristics are to be avoided as far as possible by attention to detail design. Suitable radio absorbent materials are to be used when necessary and practicable.

Fatigue Life

The best possible fatigue life is required. A fatigue load meter is required. On the basis of the sortie profile defined in paragraph 19 the minimum acceptable fatigue life is 3,000 hours based on fatigue meter readings. It is to be assumed that half of the aircraft's flying will be done in tropical climates.

Explosion Suppression

Continuous internal fuel tank protection is required.
[AL3: gas purging of fuel tanks deleted.]

Engine Starting

A self-contained engine starting system is required. Consideration will be given to any novel means of self-starting which may alleviate weight or structural problems.

Engine Control

Means should be provided automatically to ensure that the engine limitations are not exceeded under any conditions within the flight envelope of the aircraft.

Thrust Measurement

An accurate means of measuring thrust is required for each engine.

Weapon Bay Air Conditioning

The aircraft weapon bay should be provided with air conditioning for the tactical nuclear weapon compatible with the arrangements for air conditioning the store on the ground during the 30-day standby period. The temperature range for the bomb is +18°C to +28°C.

Infra-red Suppression

Infra-red emission is to be reduced to the minimum practicable without impairing performance.

Brake Parachute

Release mechanisms should not incorporate an armament release unit.

Warning Systems

The standard warning system is required. Aural warning of an emergency should be considered, specifically far warning that structural temperature limitations are being reached.

Cockpit Colour Scheme

A grey colour scheme is required.

TRAINING

(a) Flight Training. There will be a requirement for facilities for pilot training on the type. Attention should be given, in the design of the basic aircraft, to means of making a conversion trainer as easy as possible.

(b) Flight Simulator. A full crew simulator is required at least six months before introduction of the aircraft into Service, It is to be developed concurrently with the weapon system and will form the subject of a separate Air Staff Requirement.

(c) Other Synthetic Training Aids. Synthetic aids for crew training, and where applicable systems servicing training, are to be provided six months before the introduction of the weapon system into Service.

SERVICING

The aircraft and its equipment are to be so designed and constructed as to reduce to a minimum the need for servicing or inspection, other than the replacement of consumable stores, over any period of 100 flying hours or four months elapsed time, whichever is the shorter. As an aid to servicing as much as possible of the aircraft's equipment is to be installed on the package principle.

It must be possible to change major components in the field. Replacement of those items which are more likely to sustain damage, e.g. wheels, must be quick and simple.

Servicing of the aircraft, including exchange of components is, so far as practicable, to be possible without removing or disturbing parts of another system. It is to be possible to service the aircraft for flight without removing the weapons.

In pursuance of the Weapon System concept all ground servicing equipment which has special application to this aircraft is to be designed and developed concurrently with the aircraft. Special attention is to be given to making this equipment air transportable.

TARGET DATE

The Air Staff require a CA Release for this weapon system which will enable a squadron to be fully equipped by 31st December, 1965.

Air Ministry, (D.O.R.(A))
8th May, 1959
8th May, 1959

Flight Reference Cards

Some idea of the relatively simple nature of the first two aircraft can be gleaned from the normal and emergency drills on the crew's Flight Reference Cards (FRCs), reproduced below:

BRITISH AIRCRAFT CORPORATION
(PRESTON DIVISION)

T.S.R. 2

(XR220)

FLIGHT REFERENCE CARDS (1)

PILOT'S
NORMAL OPERATING DRILLS

ISSUE 1, APRIL 1965

Issued by - Technical Publications Dept.,
WARTON AERODROME, LANCS.

COCKPIT CHECKS

BEFORE ENTERING

Emergency oxygen	1,800lb/in^2 maximum
Seat safety pins	Inserted in seat gun, chute withdrawal guillotine, firing handle, canopy jettison handle:
	Removed from head restraint guillotine, drogue gun and barostat. Check linkages.

AFTER ENTERING

Rocket pack	Sear pin removed
C.W.P.	Unmuted; press to test; cancel attention-getters
AFCS channel switches	FIN and TAILN off (up); cover raised
AUD. WN switch	NORM/guarded
Rapid start panel	All ganged switches ON (up); FLIGHT/MOTOR OVER to MOTOR OVER
100% OXY/AIRMIX switch	AIRMIX
Strap in	
Radio switch 4	I/C NORM. Check with navigator. Call for oxygen. Check OXY and NAV. OK warnings out
Mask/jerkin	Press to test
Stand-by regulator	Check functioning; return to main regulator
Emergency oxygen control	Fully home
Trim indicators	Main trim switches for live circuit and normal functioning
	Standby trim for normal functioning
ROLL/YAW GEARING switch and indicator	Test individual switch pairs for travel over full range; set at 0.

LEFT-TO-RIGHT CHECK

Port console :-	
Instrumentation Switches	As Flight Briefing Schedule
CONE switches	MANUAL; Cones at 17 °
	(DO NOT MOVE CONES ON GROUND)
Throttles	COCK OFF
Fuel contents	Agree with navigator
Fueldraulic PUMP switch	NORM
C.G. datum switch	(inoperative)
Manual transfer switch	off (central)
Autobalance master switch	Select GAUGE and FLOW in turn, for each check CROSSFEED cock OPEN; select off (central), check cock SHUT.
Emergency throttle switches	Normal/guarded.
C.G. meter	Same indication for G and FL; agree with navigator. Leave at G.
Port coaming panel :-	
NOSE LEG EXTEND switch	Normal (central) / guarded
	(EXTEND inoperative).
FLAP BLOW switch	ON / guarded
PARACHUTE JETTISON switch	NORMAL
P'CHUTE DOOR indicator	Black (shut)
Parachute AUTO/MANUAL switch	(Inoperative)
Parachute MAX/REEFED switch	MAX
OPEN / guarded	OPEN / guarded

Port instrument panel :-	
C.S.I.	Scale zeros coinciding
Stand-by ASI	Needle 12 o'clock approx.
Flap BLOW gauge	0 °
Flap position indicator	0 °
Stand-by horizon	Power failure flag clear; Check erecting
Air-brake indicator	Fully in
AIL. GEAR indicator	5
Autothrottle indicator	(Inoperative)
Autotrim indicator	(Inoperative)
V.S.I.	Zero
Stand-by altimeter	Set QFE, check zero
Brake accumulator pressure	2,000lb/in² min.
	Parking brake on
	Line pressures (with navigator)
Head-down display :-	
Attitude indicator	Failure flag clear; Director ring off display
Navigation display	Select FG, check warning flag clear: check DG flag appears when navigator selects DG (IP is inoperative). Depress ILS TEST button and check ILS bars move to ¾ full up and right deflection
TACAN :-	ON; Select channel and DIST. BRG.
	MASTER SWITCH : ON
Starboard instrument panel :-	
Auxiliary intakes	(inoperative)
Altimeter	Power failure flag clear; set QFE, check zero
Airframe temperature gauge	-
Cabin altimeter	-
Oxygen contents	7/8 +
Oxygen pressure	60 – 110lb/in2
Oxygen flow indicator	Operating
Thrust/RPM meters	Power failure flags clear
	RPM selected (THRUST inoperative).
Turbine temperature gauges	Power failure flags clear
Nozzle position indicators	SHUT
Starboard coaming panel :-	
L.P. COCK switch	OPEN/guarded
Head-up display switches	SPEED, ALT and DIR on, check appearance, then as required
Vr scale	Set Vr for take-off if required
Brilliance	Adjust
Accelerometer	Reset
Radio Panel :-	
ILS	As required
Radio (left-to-right)	
Switch 1	VHF/UHF T/R
Switch 2	Off
Switch 3	Select EMER, nav. checks I/C.P. (C.W.P.).
return to off (central)	
Switch 4	Select ST/BY, check stand-by I/C; leave at I/C NORM.
Switch 5	Off
I/C call lights	Check with navigator
UHF channel	As required
Aerial switch	As required
Starboard console panel :-	
GEN CONTROL switches	OFF
E/GEN switch	normal / guarded
CAB. S/O VALVE switch	SHUT
CAB DEPRESS switch	NORM / guarded
CAB. AIR ISOL switch	Off (central)
ANTI-ICE switches	OFF
Navigation light switch	Off (central)
Temperature controller	AUTO / as required
Lighting switch dimmers	As required
WINDMILL RELIGHT switches	Normal / guarded
EMERG. GEN switch	HYD. 2 / guarded
HIGH INTENS. switch	OFF
W/S WASH switch	OFF
W/S DISP switch	OFF (right back)
ROLL/YAW switch	NORM / guarded
U/C EXTREME EMERG. switch	NORM / guarded
FUEL JETT. switch	Off / guarded
	Jettison cock SHUT
ANTI-G STOP VALVE	(Inoperative)
AVS	(Inoperative)
RAM AIR VALVE	CLOSE
Control column :-	
Nosewheel steering	Disengaged
Port rear console :-	
HEAD-UP DISPLAY switch	Select TEST, check
	Horizon level

	Director central
	Range circle: second half only
	Height: 800ft
	Speed: 160kt
	Vr marker: 160kt
	Return to NORM
AIR DATA TEST switch	Select 1, Record
	Main altimeter reading
	Ram air temp. reading
	RAM T. warning on
	Select 2, Record
	Main altimeter reading
	RAM T. warning out
	Return to NORM, check main altimeter returns to zero +- 50 feet.
FIRE TEST switch (Navigator)	For each position, check fire warning, check/cancel attention-getter
	1 – No. 1 ENG
	2 – No. 1 RHT
	3 – No. 1 ENG
	4 – No. 2 ENG
	5 – No. 2 RHT
	6 – No. 2 ENG
Return to OFF	
C.W.P.	Check warnings :-
Red :- OIL 1 & 2, CONT 1 & 2, CANPY.	
Amber :- GEN 1 & 2, SERV 1 & 2, CAV 1 & 2, PUMP 1, 2, 3, 4, FIN	

Remove remaining escape system safety pins (4)

STARTING / FAIL TO START

STARTING

Confirm or set :-

Cockpit checks	Complete
Palouste trolley	Connected and started
	Start No. 1 engine first

STARTING DRILL :-

	(Max permissible temperature at any time 550°C)
Throttle	'Start' mark
	Ground running doors open (crew chief)
FLIGHT/MOTOR OVER switch	FLIGHT
Start/relight button	Press firmly for 5 seconds (Check ignition interference on I/C)
Throttle to IDLE as temperature stabilizes, falls slightly.	
Temperature again rises, then falls as RPM rises.	
	Call '30% RPM' to ground crew
	'Air valve closed' from crew chief.

NO HANDLING TILL STEADY AT IDLING

IDLING CHECK :-

RPM	60% approx.
Turbine temperature	400°C maximum
Warnings remaining	Red: OIL 2, CONT 2, CANPY
	Amber: GEN.1, SERV. 2, CAV. 2, GEN. 2, PUMP 2, PUMP 4.
Both GEN CONTROL switches	RESET and normal / guarded.
GEN 1 light out	
TRU TEST switch	Hold at 1 till amber
	DC warning lights; release, check instrumentation master warning light on,
	reselect tape and trace if necessary

If THROT warnings light, select EMERG throttle for 3 seconds; return to normal and check warnings out.

Starting No. 2 engine :-

Fueldraulic PUMP switch	X-OVER
No. 1 engine	70% RPM

Carry out STARTING DRILL for No. 2 engine.

With both engines at IDLE :-
Air conditioning (Hampson) trolley disconnected.

External electrics	Disconnected
Both RPM	Approx 60%
Both turbine temperature	400°C maximum
Warnings	All out except CANPY
Undercarriage indicator	All reds out
Brake cooling fans on	(crew chief)
Controls hydraulic pressures	(crew chief)

FAILURE TO START

ENGINE DOES NOT ROTATE :-

ENGINE MASTER switch	OFF and ON again

Make one further attempt.

ENGINE ROTATES BUT FAILS TO LIGHT by 12 % RPM

Throttle	COCK OFF
Allow engine to stop completely	
ENGINE MASTER switch	OFF and ON again
FLIGHT/MOTOR OVER switch	MOTOR OVER
Start/relight button	Press for 45 seconds
FLIGHT/MOTOR OVER switch	FLIGHT
Throttle	At 'start' mark

Carry out STARTING DRILL once more.

AFTER-STARTING / PRE TAKE-OFF

AFTER-STARTING CHECKS :-

Hydraulic pressures :-	
Brake accumulators	4,000 +/- 200lb/in2
Systems (navigator)	4,000 +/- 200lb/in2
Air brakes	Check operation, leave fully in
D.C. throttle control	Select EMERG for each engine
(Throttles at red marks)	Check THROT warning and response on d.c. throttle switch
	Return to normal
Fueldraulic PUMP switch	NORM
CABIN S/O VALVE	NORM
GEN. CONTROL 1 switch	Select OFF, check GEN 1 warning, select RESET and return to centre, check warning out.
GEN. CONTROL 2 switch	Check GEN 2 warnings as above
W/S DISP switch	½ to disperse accumulated water then as required.
AFCS :-	FIN and TAILN switches on (down), cover closed. All modes disengaged.
AFCS Confidence testing: (all off at even positions)	
1) (resetting)	13) TNR.CD, TAILN., FIN
3) TRN.CD, TAILN.	15) TNR.CD, TAILN., FIN
5) TRN.CD, TAILN.	17) TNR.CD, TAILN., FIN
7) TRN.CD, TAILN.	19) TNR.CD, FIN
9) TRN.CD, TAILN.	21) TNR.CD, FIN
11) TRN.CD, TAILN.	23) TNR.CD, FIN

FLAP BLOWING CHECK :-

No. 1 Engine	No. 2 Engine	FLAP BLOW	Flaps	BLOW gauge
			0°	0°
MAX.	MAX.	ON	20°	20° double band
DRY	DRY			35° double band
		OFF	35°	0°
IDLE		ON		35° single band
MAX. DRY	IDLE			

Set for take-off :-	Flaps 20°
	FLAP BLOW ON
NOZZLE OV/RIDE switches	Select MAX DRY at 90% RPM.
	Check nozzles close: return to NORMAL

TAKE-OFF CHECKS :-

TRIM	YAW : 0
	ROLL : 0
	PITCH : 1 divn. nose-up
	ROLL/YAW : 0
AIR BRAKES	Fully in
FUEL	CROSSFEED cock SHUT
	Manual transfer off
	With navigator:
	Contents
	CG (at G and FL); leave at G.
INSTRUMENTS	Attitude indicator erected
	Stand-by horizon erected
	Nav. display FG
	Check with navigator
OXYGEN	Contents
	Pressure
	Flow
	Check with navigator
HOOD	Closed and locked
	Shoot bolts home
	Selector OPEN
	Check with navigator
HARNESS	Tight and locked
	Check with navigator
HYDRAULICS	Flying controls check
	Brake accumulator pressures
	Systems pressures with navigator
WARNINGS	All out

TAKE-OFF :-
MAX. DRY power, brakes holding on a dry surface
Nozzles at 'max dry' marks
Stabilized limits (NORMAL DOUBLE DATUM) :-
No. 1 engine 99.5% / 775°C
No. 2 engine 100% / 774°C
Release brakes and apply MAX. REHT.
Check nozzles open

Temperatures and RPM still within limits

CHECKS AFTER TAKE-OFF :-
Nosewheel steering   Disengage
Undercarriage   Select UP before 240knots
                                            Lights out by 315kt
Flaps   Select 0°
                                            0° by 300kt
DOUBLE DATUM switches   INTERMEDIATE
Cancel reheat

DESCENT AND APPROACH :-
DESCENT PROCEDURES (Throttles at IDLE)
Normal descent (airbrakes OUT)   0.9M / 350knots
Slow descent (airbrakes IN)   0.9M / 320knots
Single engine descents identical

CIRCUIT

APPROACH SETTINGS (FLAP BLOW ON)

	U/C	Flap	A/Brake	RPM	Speed
Level	Up	20°	In	85%	250-220
Level	Down	35°	In	90.5%	220-180
Glide Path	Down	35°	Out	95%	180 minimum

LANDING AND OVERSHOOTING
CHECKS BEFORE LANDING :-
DOUBLE DATUM switches   NORMAL
FLAP BLOW   ON
Flaps   20° below 250knots
Undercarriage   DOWN below 240knots : 3 greens
Flaps   35° below 225knots
Blowing gauge   In 20° double band (approx.)
Fuel   Contents
Harness   Tight and locked
                                            Check with navigator
Brakes   Accumulator pressure
                                            4000 +/- 200lb/in2
                                            Apply brakes:
                                            4 line pressures 1,750lb/in2 max.
                                            Release brakes, pressures zero
Nosewheel steering   Disengaged
Parachute   MAX.
Trim   ROLL/YAW : 0 (or optimum)

APPROACH AND TOUCHDOWN
Speeds   Approach 180knots
                                            Touchdown 170knots

After touchdown :-
Throttles   IDLE
Aerodynamic braking down to 155knots
Nosewheel   Lower, engage steering
Parachute   PULL ONCE to stream at 150knots
Brakes   As required
CABIN S/O VALVE   SHUT
RAM AIR VALVE   OPEN before unlocking canopy.

TWO-ENGINE OVERSHOOT
MAX DRY power, air brakes IN, maintain configuration, accelerate to 220knots and climb into circuit.

BRITISH AIRCRAFT CORPORATION
(PRESTON DIVISION)

T.S.R. 2

(XR219)

FLIGHT REFERENCE CARDS (2)

NAVIGATOR'S
NORMAL OPERATING DRILLS

ISSUE 1, AUGUST 1964
INCORPORATING AMENDMENT LIST 2, AUGUST 1964

Issued by - Technical Publications Dept.,
WARTON AERODROME, LANCS.

COCKPIT CHECKS

PRELIMINARIES (ground power on and air supplies connected).
BEFORE ENTERING AIRCRAFT

Emergency oxygen pressure	1,800psi min.
Safety pins	Inserted in seat gun, 'chute withdrawal guillotine, firing handle, canopy jettison handle. Removed from head restraint guillotine.

AFTER ENTERING AIRCRAFT

Centralized warning panel	OXY, PL OX, ADC, and possibly BAL, warnings on. Check other filaments.
Inertial platform control unit :	
LATITUDE control	Local latitude
N LAT-S LAT switch	N LAT
Alignment switch	STANDBY
	(Proceed with alignment – separate stages or ALIGN 2 and FLIGHT – at intervals, when 'stage complete' lamps light during following checks)
Rapid start panel	All ganged switches ON, ADC warning out
Auto variation control unit:	
DEV control	As required
AUTO-MANUAL switch	MANUAL, set variation
N-S switch	N
LAT control	Local latitude, then synchronize compass on MAG.
Safety pins	Check removed from rocket pack sear and both canopy external jettison breeches.
Strap in, connect P.E.C.	OXY warning out (PL OX out when pilot connects)
Services selector switch No. 4	I/C NORM
Instrumentation switch panel	Check time base and ident. readouts zeroed in both compartments
Instrumentation master switch	Check with pilot that switch is on
(Pilot's compartment)	

INTERNAL CHECKS
PORT CONSOLE

FUEL CONTENTS SAMPLING switch	NORMAL
Ess. a.c. busbar frequency meter	398 +/- 8 c.p.s.
Fuel panel :-	
Refuel/defuel MASTER switch	OFF
Refuel level switch	FULL
RESET and trim unit	Auto and press. BAL warning out
Tank switches	FLGT
Fuel contents	Check TOTAL and 2 & 4, + O/L and WING (BAL warning at 2 & 4). Compare with pilot's readings. Set TOTAL and O/L
Mode selector	PRES RATE
FLIGHT TIME REMAINING	418 minutes
FUEL REMAINING	Equals total of gauges
c.g. meter	Check agreement of G and F positions. Set F then check with pilot's G position
A.F.C.S. 'frig' box	Check INITIATE switch OFF – guarded – and lamp out
Brake pressure gauges	Check parking brake pressure 1 and 2 FWD-1750psi max, min.

FORWARD PANEL – PORT

Instrumentation switch panel :	
ENG and AFCS power lamps	On
Engineering tape recorder	START, recording lamp on
Crash recorder	Check running
Downward sight	ON. Function and set aft view
B.S.E. RECORDER	Check HT neon on. Select according to Flight Test Schedule.
Oxygen contents	Sufficient for flight
Oxygen pressure	70 – 85psi
Oxygen flow indicator	Operating
Intercomm CALL lamp	Press. Pilot confirms function by pressing his CALL lamp

PORT INDICATOR UNIT

V.S.I.	Zero
Altimeter	Monitor during A.D.C. test Power failure flag clear, set 1013.2 mbs
Combined speed indicator	Monitor during A.D.C. test
All pointers zero	

STARBOARD INDICATOR UNIT
Artificial horizon
Compass and heading indicator

Power failure flag clear, check erecting then fast erect
Power failure flag clear. Check DG position with pilot, set MAG.

FORWARD PANEL – STARBOARD
Tacan

Check channel with pilot and compare direct range and bearing. Set offset computer as required by pilot

Engine instrumentation panel :
No. 1 and 2 H.P. turb. air temp.
No. 1 and 2 Rear bearing temp.
No. 1 and 2 Oil inlet temp.
No. 1 and 2 Rear bearing diff. press.
No. 1 and 2 Flowmeters
No. 1 and 2 Nozzle positions

Warning lamps out. Press to test
Warning lamps out. Press to test
'
Zero
Zero
Closed

STARBOARD CONSOLE
U.H.F. - I/C control unit (H.F. not fitted):
Switch No. 1
Switches No. 2, 3 and 5
Switch No. 4
Switch No. 3

UHF T/R
Off. Pilots transmit and received heard in headphones
Check STBY, return to NORM
EMER (3 min warm up). I/C N warning

PANEL, INSTRMTS, and GENERAL lighting
100% OXY/AIRMIX switch
A.D.C. mix switch
Anti-g stop-cock lever
Anti-g control valve
A.V.S. temperature control
A.V.S. flow control
UHF ST/BY switch
H.F. (if fitted)
SEAT
Mask / jerkin

As required
As required
ADC MIX
On (forward)
Set H or L, press TEST button
Inoperative
Inoperative
Hold at TEST, check emer. UHF Switch No. 3 to R + G
Check radio, and aerial change-over

Mask – check by pressing inboard button
Jerkin – check by lifting guard and pressing both buttons

Regulator change-over lever
Emergency oxygen control

Select stand-by regulator, check for at least 18 sec., no OXY warning. Return to main regulator
Fully home

BEFORE STARTING
Confirm cockpit checks complete

AFTER-STARTING CHECKS

No. 2 engine ground idle:
No. 2 H.P. turb. air temp.
No. 2 Rear Bearing temp.
No. 2 Oil inlet temp.
No. 2 Flowmeter
No. 2 Nozzle position
No. 2 Rear bearing diff. press.

Warning lamps out, Indicators functioning
Warning lamps out, Indicators functioning
Indicators functioning
Indicators functioning
Closed
For ground use only

No. 1 engine ground idle:
As per No. 2 engine
Fuel panel:
FLIGHT TIME REMAINING
FUEL REMAINING
Ess. a.c. busbar frequency meter
Brake pressure gauges
I.P. alignment switch
A.V.C.U.
C.W.P.
Canopy

Canopy jettison handle
Seat

Indicator functioning
Indicator functioning
398 +/- 8 c.p.s.
Pressures 1 and 2 PORT, 1 and 2 STBD, between   - 1750psi
To FLIGHT when alignment complete
Set variation to zero, resynchronize
All warnings out. Press to test.
Select CLOSE, pull closed; push down latching handle, check mechanical indicators LOCKED and
selector moves to OPEN
Remove pin and stow
Remove pins and stow

BEFORE TAKE-OFF CHECKS

Fuel
Instrumentation switch panel
Altimeter
Artificial horizon
Compass and heading indicator
Tacan
Oxygen
Canopy
Harness
C.W.P.

Check contents
Switch according to Flight Test Schedule
Set QNH, 'drome ht. +/- 20ft.
Erected
Check against runway hdg.
Check BRG and DIST readout
Contents/press., 100% OXY/AIRMIX as required. Flow indicator operating.
Check LOCKED
Tight and locked
All warnings out

TAKE-OFF CHECKS

(engines at max dry)
Brake pressures
No. 1 and 2 H.P. turb. air temp.
No. 1 and 2 Rear bearing temp.
No. 1 and 2 Oil inlet temp.
No. 1 and 2 Flowmeters
No. 1 and 2 Nozzle positions

1,750psi max.
Warning lamp out. Temps within Flight Clearance Note limits
Warning lamp out. Temps within Flight Clearance Note limits
Temps within Flight Clearance Note limits
Check functioning
Open to max. dry position

Brakes released. Reheat on :

No. 1 and 2 Nozzle positions	Fully open

BEFORE LANDING CHECKS

Undercarriage	Check down through downward sight
Fuel	Check contents and c.g. position
Brake pressure	1,750psi max.
Harness	Tight and locked

AFTER LANDING CHECKS

Brake temperatures	Check
Brake pressures	1,750psi max.

SHUT-DOWN CHECKS

(ground power on)	
Instrumentation master switch	Leave on
Engineering tape recorder	Leave running
B.S.E. RECORDER	All switches off
Crash recorder	Check off
Tank switches	All OFF
Downward sight	AZIMUTH control pushed in, switch OFF
Rapid start panel	All switches off
I.P. alignment switch	STANDBY (aircraft must not be moved for at least 20 min.)
Canopy jettison handle	Safety pin fitted
Seat	Safe for parking
Cockpit lighting	Off

BRITISH AIRCRAFT CORPORATION
(PRESTON DIVISION)

T.S.R. 2

(XR219 & 220)

FLIGHT REFERENCE CARDS (3)

EMERGENCY DRILLS

(1) AIRCRAFT ENGINE AND AFCS FAILURES

ISSUE 2, JUNE 1964
INCORPORATING AMENDMENT LIST 6, APRIL 1965

Issued by - Technical Publications Dept.,
WARTON AERODROME, LANCS.

BARRIER ENGAGEMENT

Call for barrier
Throttles COCK OFF
Nosewheel on ground
Steer by differential braking (n/w steering lost)
Enter between verticals, centre if possible
Steady braking throughout
Parking brake on at rest
Lox cock shut (navigator)

Note :- N/w steering may be regained by selecting U/C EMERG.

FIRE DRILLS; ABANDONING
PREPARE TO ABANDON THE AIRCRAFT IF ANY FIRE
WARNING PERSISTS 3 MINUTES AFTER TAKING ACTION

ENG FIRE WARNING	
Throttle	COCK OFF
L.P. COCK	CLOSED
Speed	Reduce if possible
Extinguisher	Operate

Return to base, using SINGLE ENGINE RECOVERY
Note: No further extinguishant is available.

REHEAT FIRE WARNING	
Throttle	IDLE
Extinguisher	Operate

Return to base, avoiding use of reheat
Note: Extinguishant still available on other side

EJECTION

Recommended speed	250knots
Maximum speed	500knots
Full auto sequence	above 300knots
Individual (navigator first)	below 300knots
Canopies first	below 75knots

Straight and level or climbing
Above 42,000ft. DEPRESS for 30 seconds if possible

FAILURE OF AUTO-SEPARATION :-
Press button and lift EMERGENCY HARNESS RELEASE handle to full extent; roll out of seat, pull 'chute D-ring

Note :-
EMERGENCY oxygen not available when separated from seat

TAKE-OFF ENGINE FAILURES

1. At or below V stop :-

Throttles	IDLE
Parachute	Pull ONCE to stream
Brakes	Apply fully
Barrier	Call to raise

2. Above V stop :-
No immediate action
Accelerate to 220knots, climb into circuit

Dead engine	COCK OFF

Approach as in SINGLE ENGINE RECOVERY

Strain gauge warning :-

Leave for up to 20 seconds, then see IN-FLIGHT ENGINE FAILURES (9)

IN-FLIGHT ENGINE FAILURES

1. Mechanical defect, Nozzle runaway open, OIL warning :-

Throttle	COCK OFF
L.P. COCK	CLOSE

Use SINGLE-ENGINE RECOVERY

2. Nozzle runaway closed :-
Throttle back to dry range. No further use of reheat.

3. THROT warning, No throttle response, RPM fluctuating :-
DO NOT MOVE THROTTLE LEVER (TCU failure)

Emergency throttle switch	EMERG
NOZZLE OV/RIDE switch	MAX.DRY

Check RPM and temperature within limits

TO CANCEL REHEAT :-
Reduce to approx 95% RPM (*NOT below*) on d.c. throttle
Throttle lever back to dry range
Reheat cannot be reselected

NOTE:-
(a) No automatic P3, top temperature or acceleration control or RPM governing on d.c. throttle. Handle engine with care and monitor frequently, especially when climbing or decelerating.
(b) If THROT warning appeared suddenly, or together with GEN warning, make one attempt only to regain normal control, after stabilizing engine.

4. P3 warning
Throttle back to clear

5. Nozzle area fluctuating :-
Cancel reheat if in use
If unsuccessful, select MAX DRY.
If still unsuccessful, select EMERG throttle.

6. AUX. DR warning :-
Reduce speed to below 300knots
Return to base

7. *REHEAT* extinguishes or fails to light :-
Cancel selection
Attempt re-selection after 8 seconds minimum
If no light-up within 3 seconds, cancel

8. TCV warning :-
Throttle: IDLE
(a) *IF WARNING GOES OUT :-* (failed open)
 Engine may be used for cruise if warning stays out
Expect reappearance of warning when reducing IAS
Shut down for approach and landing.
(b) *IF WARNING REMAINS :-* (failed closed)
Switch OFF associated generator <u>unless</u> other has failed; wait 5 seconds and RESET

Leave throttle at IDLE until TCV warning goes out

9. Strain gauge warning (NOT 220)
Return to base at min. RPM on both engines
 Navigator cancel and reset warning

RELIGHTING

FLAMEOUT :-
IMMEDIATE RELIGHT :-
Throttle   Slam to IDLE
Fueldraulic PUMP switch   X-OVER
Start / relight   Press and hold

IF NO RELIGHT WITHIN 15 SECONDS :-
Throttle   COCK OFF
NORMAL RELIGHT after 1 minute.

NORMAL RELIGHT :-
Speed   Above 250kt
                                                            Below 350kt / 0.9M
Height   Below 35,000 feet
Throttle   COCK OFF
WINDMILL RELIGHT switch   Aft (assist) below 18% RPM
Fwd. (guarded) above 18% RPM
Fueldraulic PUMP switch   X-OVER
Start / relight   Press and hold
Throttle   Slowly to IDLE in about 10 seconds

NO RELIGHT WITHIN 15 SEC. OF REACHING IDLE
                OR
TURBINE TEMPERATURE EXCEEDS 550°C
Throttle   COCK OFF
Try again after 1 minute.

CONSISTENT FAILURE TO RELIGHT :-
Suspect throttle runaway closed (no THROT warning)
Relight on d.c. throttle (below).

DOUBLE FLAMEOUT :-
Throttles   Slam to IDLE
IMMEDIATE RELIGHT on both engines; if neither lights,
Speed   Above 250knots
Commence fast descent to 35,000ft.
Restrict flying controls operation to a minimum
NORMAL RELIGHT on one engine only, at or below 35,000ft. When one engine is running, relight the other.

RELIGHT ON D.C. THROTTLE :-
EMERG switch   EMERG (THROT warning)
Throttle   COCK OFF
D.C. throttle switch   'close' for 30 seconds
NOZZLE OV/RIDE switch   MAX. DRY
WINDMILL RELIGHT switch   Aft (assist) below 18% RPM
                                                            Fwd. (guarded) above 18% RPM
Fueldraulic PUMP switch   X-OVER
Start / relight   Press and hold
Throttle   To red mark
D.C. throttle switch   'open' slowly (i.e. not continuously)

IF NO RELIGHT WITHIN 20 SECONDS
(of start of D.C. throttle opening)
OR TURBINE TEMPERATURE EXCEEDS 550°C
Throttle   COCK OFF
D.C. throttle switch   'close' for 30 seconds
Try again after 1 minute

AFTER RELIGHT :-
Fueldraulic PUMP switch   NORM (220 ONLY)
<u>Ensure</u> WINDMILL RELIGHT switches forward / guarded

SINGLE-ENGINE RECOVERY

Note :- Gearbox X-OVER is limited to 8 minutes with the LP COCK CLOSED. (No limit with cock OPEN)
1. *IMMEDIATELY :-*
GEARBOX drive   DIS
GEN. CONTROL switch   OFF
EM. GEN switch   To remaining HYD system
Warnings   OIL, CONT, SERV. GEN on
                          (Stay at fueldraulic PUMP   X-OVER regardless)
Autobalance master switch   GAUGE
                                                            Check CROSSFEED cock OPEN
c.g. meters   Both at G.

2. *RECOVERY*
Cruise at 330kt (subject to M limitation)
Specific range increases with altitude and M.

Maintain c.g. position by MAN. TRANS as necessary
Navigator eliminates resulting BAL warnings with AUTO reset.

3. *DOWNWIND, BEFORE UNDERCARRIAGE SELECTION :-*
GEARBOX drive   X-OVER
Warnings   CONT, SERV out

4. *APPROACH (NORMAL DOUBLE DATUM)*
Remaining engine   Reheat
Flaps   20°
Air brakes   IN
Approach at 190kt; touchdown 180knots

5. *APPROACH ON D.C. THROTTLE*
Remaining engine   Maximum dry thrust
Flaps   20°
Air brakes   IN
Undercarriage   Delay DOWN until long finals
Speeds   230kt downwind, 210kt reducing to 200 on approach; 190kt touchdown.

6. *AFTER SECOND* **GEN** *WARNING*
No possible action
Emergency generator only remains
Cancel reheat before any hydraulic selection
No simultaneous hydraulic selections
Proceed as for 3 : (Normal U/C DOWN operative).

7. *AFTER SECOND* **CONT** *WARNING :-*
GEARBOX DRIVE   X-OVER
Warnings   CONT, SERV out

8. *AFTER SECOND* **SERV** *WARNING :-*
EM. GEN switch   Dead engine HYD system
           (GEARBOX drive to X-OVER if second GEN warning appears).
ROLL / YAW   GEARING: 0
Reduce speed   Pitch and yaw feel lost
To select air brakes or flaps :-
GEARBOX DRIVE   X-OVER, make selection and return to DIS
To select undercarriage :-
GEARBOX DRIVE   X-OVER
U/C selector   DOWN (1 or 2 greens)
U/C EMERG   EMERG.
and if SERV. 2 warning remains :-
ROLL / YAW   EMERG at end of downwind leg, wings level; Expect roll to Port
(Only if 8° aileron required)

AFCS FAILURES

FIN warning :-
FIN channel off (up); return to base

TAILN warning :-
TAILN channel off (up); return to base

TRN. CD warning :-
No action; no serious fault possible

BRITISH AIRCRAFT CORPORATION
(PRESTON DIVISION)

T.S.R. 2

(XR219)

FLIGHT REFERENCE CARDS (3)

EMERGENCY DRILLS

(2) SYSTEMS FAILURES

ISSUE 2, JUNE 1964
INCORPORATING AMENDMENT LIST 6, APRIL 1965

Issued by - Technical Publications Dept.,
WARTON AERODROME, LANCS.

OXYGEN FAILURE

OXY warning :-
Select stand-by regulator
1. IF warning goes out, check contents adequate and pressure above 50lb/in2, and confirm gauge readings with other crew member.
2. IF warning stays on :-
Pull 'green apple'
Descend to cabin altitude 10,000ft or below.
Note :- Oxygen 'blinker' inoperative on stand-by regulator.

PL. OX or NAV. OX warning :-
        Warn other crew member to proceed as above.

Flow indicator failure :-
        Without OXY warning : remain on main regulator.
        With OXY warning : Select stand-by regulator, proceed as in OXY warning (1) as above.

Low contents and/or pressure below 60lb/in2 :
        Confirm gauge readings with other crew member.
    If readings agree :-
        Anticipate OXY warning and when received proceed as in OXY warning (2) above.

TAILERON FLAP, FLAP OR FLAP BLOW FAILURE

T.FLAP warning
    NOTE: be prepared for roll resulting from pitch input in asymmetric case.

    With flaps UP :-
        Taileron flap unlocked; stick force/g halved
        Reduce speed to and maintain below 300knots
        Use small stick movements only
        Return to base
        Check warning out when flaps are lowered

    With flaps DOWN :-
        Taileron flap still locked : flare capability reduced
        Maintain c.g. as far aft as possible within aircraft limits
        Make flatter approach at normal speeds : be prepared for large stick movements at flare. (Normal approach likely to be tailplane control-limited).

FLAP FAILURE
    Make flatter approach, with reduced flare
    Speeds :-

Max. obtainable flap	Approach	Touchdown
0°	200	190
20°	190	180

BLOW FAILURE
        (indicator shows 0° with flaps down)
    Use 20° flap only
    Make flatter approach, with reduced flare
    Approach at 190knots, touchdown 180knots

HYDRAULIC FAILURES

Note :- In all cases, confirm warning by checking system pressure at navigator's gauges. If gauge reads more than 3,000lb/in2 assume false.

Single SERV warning :-
    On take-off :-
            Do not raise undercarriage
            Carry out circuit and landing

    In flight :-
            Select U/C DOWN to obtain 1 or 2 greens
                    U/C EMERG to complete lowering

        Services lost and further actions :-

No. 1 : Aft brakes (accumulator braking down to 2000lb/in2)
No. 2 : Fwd. brakes (accumulator braking down to 2000lb/in2)
      Nosewheel steering (stand-by from accumulator – use with restraint)
      EMERG. GEN : HYD 1 immediately
      ROLL / YAW : GEARING to 0 immediately
          EMERG last action on downwind leg, wings level; prepare to correct up to 40° bank.

Double SERV warning :-
    Q feel, flaps, air brakes lost
    Reduce speed to 300knots maximum
    Use small stick movements only
    If U/C is down, aircraft may be landed. Delay brake application to minimum speed to conserve fluid. Select U/C EMERG to give standby steering.

Single CONT warning :-
    Reduce speed to, and maintain below 300kt if possible
    Return to base
    Carry out a normal approach and landing

Double CONT warning :-
    Accumulators only remain (20 seconds approx.)
    Prepare to abandon aircraft

AIR SYSTEM FAILURES

CABIN warning (pressurization failure) :-
    Mask toggle down
    Inform navigator
    Descend to 30,000ft or below
    Return to base
    Use RAM AIR if necessary for ventilation

AIR warning :-
    Single warning :-
        No action
        Stay subsonic

    Double warning :-
        No action unless pressure fluctuation in cabin becomes severe, when :-
            CABIN S/O VALVE   SHUT
            Proceed as for CABIN warning
    Maintain RPM above 75% (to keep generators on line)

Overheating / overcooling :-
    Temperature controller in MANUAL sector
    Hold at COOL/WARM for 10-15 seconds

    IF successful :-
        Leave at MANUAL

    IF unsuccessful :-
        Select CABIN S/O VALVE to SHUT
        Proceed as for CABIN warning above

Smoke in cockpit :-
    Mask toggle   down
    Airmix switch   100% OXY

    IF smoke is from cabin air inlets :-
        CAB AIR ISOL switch 1
    Wait approximately 30 seconds

    IF smoke clears, leave No.1 engine isolated.
        IF smoke persists;
        CAB AIR ISOL switch 2
    Wait approximately 30 seconds

    IF smoke clears, leave No.2 engine isolated
    IF smoke still persists,
    CABIN S/O VALVE   SHUT
    Proceed as for CABIN warning above

    IF smoke is from elsewhere in cockpit :-
        Attempt to locate source
        Switch off if possible

UNDERCARRIAGE EMERGENCIES

1: UP SELECTION :-
    a.   Any leg fails to lock up :-
        Reselect down, using normal system.
    b.   Any door fails to close :- LEAVE MAIN SELECTOR 'UP'
        Reselect down using U/C EMERG.
2: DOWN SELECTION :-
    a.   3 greens not obtained :-
        Navigator inspect U/C
        Appears normally down :-
            Select U/C EMERG to give green or confirm electrical fault
            Safe to land

Leg up or partly down :-
        Following actions in given order until successful
        (i.e., green <u>or</u> leg appears normally down)
(1) Reselect normally several times
(2) Leave at DOWN; select U/C EMERG.
(3) Leave U/C EMERG; select U/C UP
(4) Select U/C DOWN; leave U/C EMERG
(5) Select U/C EXTREME EMERGENCY
 (no use with leg partly down).
Do not attempt to land with any leg fully or partly retracted.
    b.   3 greens with 1 or more reds.
Navigator: inspect undercarriage
(a) Undercarriage door(s) not closed :-
Safe to land
Directional stability decreased
(b) Bogie not de-rotated :-
Try to de-rotate with U/C EMERG
 then U/C EXTREME EMERGENCY (if necessary)
Safe to land if ankle lock is free (bogie beam clear of leg).

3. AMBER EXTEND INDICATION :-
    Select EMERG. SHORT
        (NOSE LEG EXTEND switch)

FUEL EMERGENCIES

CAV warning :-
    Throttle back to clear
        (No action if one engine failed)

PUMP warnings :-
    (a) Single warnings
     Double warnings (1 & 3) (1 & 4) (2 & 3) (2 & 4)
219 : Fueldraulic PUMP switch NORM   } return
220 : No action; watch for CAV warnings } to base
    (b) PUMP (1 & 2) or (3 & 4) or any three :-
        Increase to 85% + RPM on both engines
        Fueldraulic PUMP switch   X-OVER
        IF state (a) is achieved :-
        Recover normally, maintaining RPM above 85%
        IF unsuccessful :-
        Descend to low altitude
        Fly to CAV warnings
        IF affected engine cannot sustain IDLE and engine is required :-
        Autobalance master switch: GAUGE
                (CROSSFEED cock OPEN)
        Prepare for serious changes in pitch stability due to c.g. shift
        Land as quickly as possible, using the minimum possible amount of fuel

BAL warning :-
    (unless cause is known, e.g. manual transfer).
    <u>Check</u> for CG out of limits :-
        If both CG meters agree out of limits, restore balance with MAN. TRANS and AUTO reset.
        If CG meters disagree or show no out-of-limits :-
    <u>Check</u> gauging system, for any unusual movement or position of contents gauge pointer(s).
        If fault revealed :-
            Pilot set CG meter to F.
            Recover, maintaining CG within limits.
        If no fault is evident :-
    <u>Check</u> flowmeter system, for FUEL REMAINING indicator not reducing or not showing combined total of gauges
        If fault revealed :-
            Navigator set CG meter to G.
        If no fault revealed :-
            Assume spurious warning.

ELECTRICAL EMERGENCIES

1. Single GEN warning :-
    Engine 80% RPM approx.
    GEN. CONTROL switch: RESET and back to normal
    If unsuccessful : No further action
        No services lost
2. Amber DC warning :-
    No action
    No services lost

3. Double DC warning :-
    No possible action
    Accept loss of MAIN DC supplies

4. Single or double GEN and both DC warnings :-
    Engines 80% RPM approx.
    Both GEN. CONTROL: RESET and back to normal
    If successful (lights out) :-
    E/GEN switch: RESET and back to normal
    If unsuccessful :-
    Accept loss of MAIN AC and MAIN DC supplies.

5. Double GEN warning (no DC warnings) :-
    Total power loss
    E/GEN switch : EMERG
    If successful (DC warnings on) :-
    Proceed as in 4.
    If unsuccessful :-
    Both GEN. CONTROL : RESET and back to normal
    If successful (one or both GEN warnings out) :-
        No further action
        Recover to base
    If unsuccessful :-
        BATTERY only remains
        Select: DC throttles, Stand-by UHF
        Aircraft may be flown but not landed

ELECTRICAL SERVICES DISTRIBUTION

MAIN AC & MAIN DC :
Air data computer
Main UHF & I/C

MAIN DC :
Normal air-brake control
U/C emergency down
Air system :-
AUTO temperature control
CAB. AIR ISOL switch
CWP test

BATTERY :
Fire protection
Stand-by UHF & I/C
Generator controls
DC throttles
H.P. & L.P. cocks
Engine start control
Fuel contents
(navigator only – with MASTER switch to REFUEL)
U/C extreme emergency (port)

ESSENTIAL AC :
Vertical gyro (head-down attitude)
Main throttle control
RPM gauges
Turbine temperature gauges
Fuel gauging system
Stand-by trim actuators
Flux-gate compassl
Oxygen pressure / contents
Cabin shut-off valve
Parachute de-reefing
Navigator's stand-by horizon
Seat adjustment
Navigation lights

MAIN AC :
Fuel flowmeter system
Main trim actuators
TACAN
Pilot's stand-by horizon
Navigator's downward sight
Screen and canopy demist
Pitot-static probe heating
Rain dispersal
Brake cooling
Parachute jettison

ESSENTIAL DC :
Flap, air-brake, trim positions
Stand-by air-brake control
Flap blowing selector
U/C main selector
U/C position indicator
Nosewheel steering selector
U/C extreme emergency (stbd.)
Air system :-
MANUAL temperature control
Cabin depressurization
Reheat selector relays
Fuel :

Manual transfer
Fueldraulic X-OVER
Oxygen regulators
Parachute stream
Most CWP warnings
CWP mute / cance
Anti-collision lights

**XR219's pristine white finish soon became a grubby mix of new and old panels as flight testing progressed.
Sadly the aircraft was not preserved and met its end at the Proof & Experimental Establishment at Shoeburyness,
shot to pieces and finally scrapped.** Ronnie Olsthoorn

Now preserved at the RAF Museum at Cosford, XR220 was to be primarily used for flutter and vibration testing of both the airframe and external stores. Camera fairings were scabbed onto the intake sides to enable visual monitoring of pylon and store flutter. Ronnie Olsthoorn

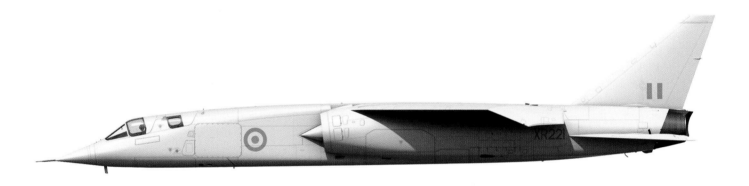

The first TSR2 with AFCS installed was scheduled to be used for nav/attack system trials. However, XR221 never flew and met its end at Shoeburyness along with most other TSR2 airframes. Ronnie Olsthoorn

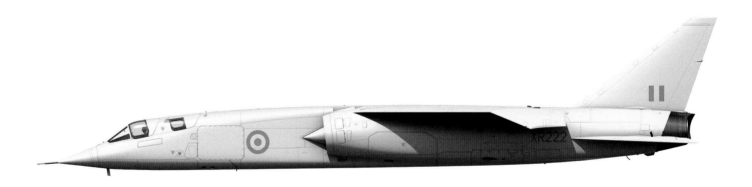

Now preserved at the Imperial War Museum at Duxford, XR222 was scheduled to carry out AFCS and terrain following radar trials. Ronnie Olsthoorn

347

Index